Network Analysis & Synthesis

Network Analysis & Synthesis

Editor:

Gerard Ian Prudhomme

ArclerPress

www.arclerpress.com

Network Analysis & Synthesis

Editor: Gerard Ian Prudhomme

708 3rd Avenue, 6th Floor
New York
NY 10017
United States of America
www.arclerpress.com

ISBN: 978-1-68094-453-2

Library of Congress Control Number: 2016951146

About the Editor

Gerard Ian Prudhomme

Gerard I. Prudhomme has a graduate degree (M.S.) for Computer Science from University College London (UCL). He has also worked as a software programmer and tech writer for different Fortune 500 companies, and studied at UCL, Harvard, and Oxford.

Contents

List of Contributors

Yousef Ali Al-Gumaei
Department of Electrical Engineering, Faculty of Engineering, University of Malaya, Kuala Lumpur, Malaysia,

Kamarul Ariffin Noordin
Department of Electrical Engineering, Faculty of Engineering, University of Malaya, Kuala Lumpur, Malaysia,

Ahmed Wasif Reza
Department of Electrical Engineering, Faculty of Engineering, University of Malaya, Kuala Lumpur, Malaysia,

Kaharudin Dimyati
Department of Electrical and Electronics Engineering, Faculty of Engineering, National Defence University of Malaysia, Kuala Lumpur, Malaysia

Harish S. Bhat
Applied Mathematics Unit, University of California Merced, Merced, California, United States of America

Garnet J. Vaz
Applied Mathematics Unit, University of California Merced, Merced, California, United States of America

Mahendra Piraveenan
Centre for Complex Systems Research, Faculty of Engineering and IT, The University of Sydney, New South Wales, Australia,

Mikhail Prokopenko
CSIRO Information and Communications Technology Centre, Epping, New South Wales, Australia,
School of Physics, The University of Sydney, New South Wales, Australia

Liaquat Hossain
Centre for Complex Systems Research, Faculty of Engineering and IT, The University of Sydney, New South Wales, Australia,

Jie Duan
Communication and Information Engineering, Chongqing University of Posts and Telecommunications (CQUPT), Chongqing, China,

Xiong Wang
Communication and Information Engineering, University of Electronic Science and Technology of China (UESTC), Chengdu, China

Shizhong Xu
Communication and Information Engineering, University of Electronic Science and Technology of China (UESTC), Chengdu, China

Yuanni Liu
Communication and Information Engineering, Chongqing University of Posts and Telecommunications (CQUPT), Chongqing, China,

Chuan Xu
Communication and Information Engineering, Chongqing University of Posts and Telecommunications (CQUPT), Chongqing, China,

Guofeng Zhao
Communication and Information Engineering, Chongqing University of Posts and Telecommunications (CQUPT), Chongqing, China,

Lizhi Xing
Department of Business Administration, School of Economics and Management, Beijing University of Technology, Beijing, China,

Qing Ye
Department of Finance, School of Economics and Management, Beijing University of Technology, Beijing, China

Jun Guan
Department of Business Administration, School of Economics and Management, Beijing University of Technology, Beijing, China,

Kai Yuan
Reliability Evaluation of Power Systems Group, School of Electrical Engineering, Wuhan University, Hubei, China,

Jian Liu
Distribution Network Risk Evaluation and Reliability and Life-Cycle Cost Research Unit, School of Electrical Engineering, Wuhan University, Hubei, China,

Kaipei Liu
Distribution Network Power Quality Problem Group, School of Electrical Engineering, Wuhan University, Hubei, China,

Tianyuan Tan
Distribution Network Risk Evaluation and Reliability Research Team, School of Electrical Engineering, Wuhan University, Hubei, China

Nicky Zachariou
Department of Physics, Blackett Laboratory, Imperial College London, Prince Consort Road, South Kensington Campus, London SW7 2AZ, United Kingdom,
Centre for Complexity Science, Electrical & Electronic Engineering Building, Imperial College London, South Kensington Campus, London SW7 2AZ, United Kingdom,

Paul Expert
Department of Physics, Blackett Laboratory, Imperial College London, Prince Consort Road, South Kensington Campus, London SW7 2AZ, United Kingdom,
Centre for Complexity Science, Electrical & Electronic Engineering Building, Imperial College London, South Kensington Campus, London SW7 2AZ, United Kingdom,
Centre for Neuroimaging Sciences, Institute of Psychiatry, Psychology and Neuroscience, De Crespigny Park, King's College London, London SE5 8AF, United Kingdom,

Misako Takayasu
Department of Computational Intelligence and Systems Science, Interdisciplinary Graduate School of Science and Engineering, Tokyo Institute of Technology, 4259 Nagatsuta-cho, Midori-ku, Yokohama 226-8502, Japan

Kim Christensen
Department of Physics, Blackett Laboratory, Imperial College London, Prince Consort Road, South Kensington Campus, London SW7 2AZ, United Kingdom,
Centre for Complexity Science, Electrical & Electronic Engineering Building, Imperial College London, South Kensington Campus, London SW7 2AZ, United Kingdom,

Nikita Vladimirov
IBM T. J. Watson Research Center, Yorktown Heights, New York, United States of America

Roger D. Traub
IBM T. J. Watson Research Center, Yorktown Heights, New York, United States of America

Yuhai Tu
IBM T. J. Watson Research Center, Yorktown Heights, New York, United States of America

Tiaza Bem
Institute of Biocybernetics and Biomedical Engineering, Polish Academy of Sciences, Warsaw, Poland,

Pierre Meyrand
Centre de Neuroscience Inte´gratives et Cognitives, Universite´ Bordeaux 1 and CNRS, UMR 5228, Talence, France,

Pascal Branchereau
Centre de Neuroscience Inte´gratives et Cognitives, Universite´ Bordeaux 1 and CNRS, UMR 5228, Talence, France,

John Hallam
Maersk Mc-Kinney Moller Institute, University of Southern Denmark, Odense, Denmark

Alessandro Chessa
IMT Institute for Advanced Studies, Lucca, Italy

Irene Crimaldi
IMT Institute for Advanced Studies, Lucca, Italy

Massimo Riccaboni
IMT Institute for Advanced Studies, Lucca, Italy

Luca Trapin
IMT Institute for Advanced Studies, Lucca, Italy

Tianyuan Tan
School of Electrical Engineering, Wuhan University, Wuhan, Hubei, China

Shuan Dong
Department of Electrical and Computer Engineering, University of British Columbia, Vancouver, BC, Canada

Yingwei Huang
Department of Electrical and Computer Engineering, University of British Columbia, Vancouver, BC, Canada

Jian Liu
School of Electrical Engineering, Wuhan University, Wuhan, Hubei, China

Jian Le
[1]School of Electrical Engineering, Wuhan University, Wuhan, Hubei, China,

Kaipei Liu
School of Electrical Engineering, Wuhan University, Wuhan, Hubei, China,
Ali M. Humada
Faculty of Electrical & Electronics Engineering, University Malaysia Pahang, Pekan, Malaysia,
Electricity Production Directorate of Salahaldeen, Ministry of Electricity, 34007, Baiji, Iraq,

Mojgan Hojabri
Faculty of Electrical & Electronics Engineering, University Malaysia Pahang, Pekan, Malaysia,

Mohd Herwan Bin Sulaiman
Faculty of Electrical & Electronics Engineering, University Malaysia Pahang, Pekan, Malaysia,

Hussein M. Hamada
Faculty of Civil Engineering & Earth Resources, Universiti Malaysia Pahang, 26300, Gambang, Malaysia

Mushtaq N. Ahmed[1]
Faculty of Electrical & Electronics Engineering, University Malaysia Pahang, Pekan, Malaysia,

Shibing Wang
Faculty of Electronic Information and Electrical Engineering, Dalian University of Technology, Dalian, 116024, China,
School of Computer and Information Engineering, Fuyang Normal University, Fuyang, 236041, China

Xingyuan Wang
Faculty of Electronic Information and Electrical Engineering, Dalian University of Technology, Dalian, 116024, China,

Bo Han
Faculty of Electronic Information and Electrical Engineering, Dalian University of Technology, Dalian, 116024, China,
School of Computer and Information Engineering, Fuyang Normal University, Fuyang, 236041, China

Jianming Zhou
School of Information and Electronics, Beijing Institute of Technology, Beijing, 100081, China,

Qiuyuan Lu
School of Information and Electronics, Beijing Institute of Technology, Beijing, 100081, China,

Fan Liu
School of Information and Electronics, Beijing Institute of Technology, Beijing, 100081, China,

Yinqiao Li
Institute of Telecommunication Satellite, CAST, Beijing, 100094, China

Kühnlenz F
University of Oulu, Department of Communications Engineering, Oulu, FI-90014, Finland.

Nardelli PH
University of Oulu, Department of Communications Engineering, Oulu, FI-90014, Finland.

Dryden MD
Department of Chemistry, University of Toronto, Toronto, ON, Canada.

Wheeler AR
Department of Chemistry, University of Toronto, Toronto, ON, Canada; Institute for Biomaterials and Biomedical Engineering, University of Toronto, Toronto, ON, Canada; Donnelly Centre for Cellular and Biomolecular Research, 160 College Street, Toronto, ON, Canada.

Fakir Sharif Hossain
Department of Electrical and Electronic Engineering, International Islamic University Chittagong, Chittagong, Bangladesh

Md. Liakot Ali
Institute of Information and Communication Technology, Bangladesh University of Engineering and technology, Dhaka, Bangladesh
University of Kent, United Kingdom

Zhu-Xing Liang
18-4-102 Shuixiehuadu, Zhufengdajie, Shijiazhuang, Hebei, 050035, China

Yi Liang
University of California San Diego, UNITED STATES

Jianming Zhou
School of Information and Electronics, Beijing Institute of Technology, Beijing, 100081, China.

Xiao Yang
School of Information and Electronics, Beijing Institute of Technology, Beijing, 100081, China.

Qiuyuan Lu
School of Information and Electronics, Beijing Institute of Technology, Beijing, 100081, China.

Fan Liu
School of Information and Electronics, Beijing Institute of Technology, Beijing, 100081, China.

Hao Z
School of Technology, Beijing Forestry University, Beijing, China.

Wang G
School of Technology, Beijing Forestry University, Beijing, China.

Li W
School of Technology, Beijing Forestry University, Beijing, China.

Zhang J
School of Technology, Beijing Forestry University, Beijing, China.

Kan J
School of Technology, Beijing Forestry University, Beijing, China.

Yandong Xiao
Science and Technology on Information Systems Engineering Laboratory, National University of Defense Technology, Changsha, Hunan, China

Songyang Lao
Science and Technology on Information Systems Engineering Laboratory, National University of Defense Technology, Changsha, Hunan, China

Lvlin Hou
Science and Technology on Information Systems Engineering Laboratory, National University of Defense Technology, Changsha, Hunan, China

Michael Small
School of Mathematics and Statistics, The University of Western Australia, Crawley, WA, Australia

Liang Bai
Science and Technology on Information Systems Engineering Laboratory, National University of Defense Technology, Changsha, Hunan, China

Preface

Network Analysis for electric powered circuits are the distinct valuable strategies linked to currents, power, emfs, as well as resistance voltages in these kinds of circuits. By examining circuits, the specialist decides the different voltages that will exist within the system. In electronic technology, Network Theory is the learning of the way to rectify circuit difficulties. Samples of using this method are : Thevenin's theorem, Delta/Star as well as Star/Delta transformation, as well as Norton's theorem, and so forth.

There are a few basic ways to perform network analysis. One way uses impedance and is assessed in ohms as well as characterized by the symbol "Z." The technological description of an ohm is the volume of resistance that can control 1V of potential to a flow of one ampere. The technological description of a volt is the electromotive force required to drive one ampere of existing current through the resistance of one ohm. Current (that could be assessed in amperes) is the pace of a stream of electric current. Voltage is the drive that pushes the existing current by means of electronic circuits. These are the essential factors that handle each and every electronic circuit all over the planet. Consequently, a circuit which has 12A running through it, will have thrice as many electrons as a circuit which has 4A. You will discover there are a handful of theorems which can be applied to determine the solutions of electronic systems by simplifying the system on its own, or perhaps they could be utilized to determine their analytic solution conveniently. The first chapter covers energy-efficient power control. Chapter 2 reviews nonlinear electrical oscillator networks and the implications of Fourier analysis. Chapter 3 gives an overview of the significance of a node in a sophisticated system. Chapter 4 outlines Network Analysis for an Information-Centric Network. Chapter 5 shows industrial areas with complicated network systems from the point of view of econophysics. Chapter 6 looks at assessments of electrical energy supply systems. Chapter 7 reviews generalised sandpile dynamics. Chapter 8 shows the functionality of random (Erdös-Rényi) networks. Chapter 9 scrutinizes swapping between in-phase (IP) together with anti-phase (AP) action forms. Chapter 10 recognizes groupings of "positional equivalent" players. Chapter 11 gives an overview of active resonance dampers. Chapter 12 analyzes photovoltaic systems. Chapter 13 considers generalized synchronization. Chapter 14 peruses ultra-wideband (UWB) radar networks. Chapter 15 suggests a straightforward strategy to grasp the intricacy of multilayer structures. Chapter 16 views electroanalytical strategies that must have the accurate management of the possibilities in an electrochemical cell. Chapter 17 probes the performance of the Advanced Encryption Standard (AES). Chapter 18 deals with frozen-in field lines subject matter as well as realizes that, in the research of the frozen-in field lines approach, capacitive together with inductive reactance have actually been overlooked. Chapter 19 offers an overview of a high-performance monocycle picosecond pulse engine. Chapter 20 evaluates the fact that the current between a upright tree as well as the encompassing dirt is widely seen as a revolutionary alternative energy resource. Chapter 21 studies how edge direction may vastly improve the structural controllability of sophisticated systems.

Editor
Gerard Ian Prudhomme
Hawaii, US

CHAPTER 1

A NOVEL UTILITY FUNCTION FOR ENERGY-EFFICIENT POWER CONTROL GAME IN COGNITIVE RADIO NETWORKS

Yousef Ali Al-Gumaei[1] , Kamarul Ariffin Noordin[1] , Ahmed Wasif Reza[1], Kaharudin Dimyati[2]

[1]Department of Electrical Engineering, Faculty of Engineering, University of Malaya, Kuala Lumpur, Malaysia,

[2]Department of Electrical and Electronics Engineering, Faculty of Engineering, National Defence University of Malaysia, Kuala Lumpur, Malaysia

ABSTRACT

Spectrum scarcity is a major challenge in wireless communications systems requiring efficient usage and utilization. Cognitive radio network (CRN) is found as a promising technique to solve this problem of spectrum scarcity. It allows licensed and unlicensed users to share the same licensed spectrum band. Interference resulting from cognitive radios (CRs) has undesirable effects on quality of service (QoS) of both licensed and unlicensed systems where it causes degradation in received signal-to-noise ratio (SIR) of users. Power control is one of the most important techniques that can be used to mitigate interference and guarantee QoS in both systems. In this paper, we develop a new approach of a distributed power control for CRN based on utility and pricing. QoS of CR user is presented as a utility function via pricing and a distributed power control as a non-cooperative game in which users maximize their net utility (utility-price). We define the price as a real function of transmit power to increase pricing charge of the farthest CR users. We prove that the power control game proposed in this study has Nash Equilibrium as well as it is unique. The obtained results show that the proposed power control algorithm based on a new utility function has a significant reduction in transmit power consumption and high improvement in speed of convergence.

INTRODUCTION

Growth of wireless communication users and services in recent years causes scarcity in radio spectrum resources. Spectrum measurements indicate that more than 70% of licensed spectrum is underutilized in some locations and times while on the other hand, unlicensed spectrum has been growing dramatically [1].

Citation: Al-Gumaei YA, Noordin KA, Reza AW, Dimyati K. A Novel Utility Function for Energy-Efficient Power Control Game in Cognitive Radio Networks. Georgantzis N, ed. PLoS ONE. 2015;10(8):e0135137. doi:10.1371/journal.pone.0135137.

Cognitive radio (CR) is an empowering technique that has an ability to solve the spectrum scarcity and improve spectrum efficiency. CR can observe the wireless environment, learn the usage pattern of spectrum frequency, and adjust to changing the wireless environment conditions. The effective process to utilize the spectrum is by allowing CRs to access the unused parts of licensed spectrums (spectrum holes) that resulted because of the absence of licensed users. Spectrum sharing between licensed users, and CRs led to an efficient utilization of spectrum, but the presence of CRs causes an increase in interference. Increasing interference causes degradation in quality of service (QoS) of licensed (primary) system that owns the rights over these bands. Therefore, Federal Communications Commission (FCC) proposed an interference temperature metric referred to as "interference temperature" limit in order to limit CR interference and protect primary and CR systems [2].

To mitigate interference produced from CRs during spectrum sharing, an efficient power control algorithm is necessary in CR devices. In addition, power control is essential to maintain the required signal-to-interference-ratio (SIR), and extend battery life of CR devices. The concept of economic and game theory has been used in recent years as an alternative approach to power control problem in wireless data networks, in which service preference was dependent on utility function. The challenge in game theory approach is the formulation of a utility function that it has a physical meaning and the game outcome is not trivial [3]. There are various and different ways to design a power control algorithm based on utility and price functions. Some researchers proposed utility as a difference between utility and pricing functions, and users seek to maximize this utility in a selfish manner. In this case, the utility function should be quasi-concave and an optimal point is selected to be somewhere within the practical parameter range, such as minimum and maximum power, and it depends on other users' behavior [3]. The special case of this type of utility function is energy efficiency, in which the utility has a physical meaning of the number of successfully received information bits per joule of energy cost. All users adjust their transmit power to achieve the required SIR that is not defined directly inside the utility function, but depends on the supposed efficiency function.

On the other hand, some other researchers proposed the utility (cost) function as a difference between price and utility functions, and users seek to minimize this cost function in a selfish manner. In this case, the cost function should be quasi-convex and the optimal point (minimum point) is selected to be somewhere within the practical parameter. In the cost function approach, all users try to achieve the required SIR (target SIR $\gamma_i \cong \Gamma_i$) defined directly in the cost function. The differences between the two approaches can be summarized, as shown in Table 1. In the following, we review the most important works on power control based on different utility and cost functions and innovative pricing techniques used for system improvement.

Table 1: Differences between utility and cost function based power control.

	Power control based on Utility function	Power control based on Cost function
Definition	Difference between utility and price (Utility-Price)	Difference between utility and price (Price-Utility)
Users goal	Maximize their own utility	Minimize their own cost
Function shape	Quasi-concave (maxima)	Quasi-convex (minima)
Final SIR	The SIR achieved depends on efficiency function that is defined in utility function	The SIR achieved is equal to the target that is declared in cost function
Others	Similarly to optimization theory	Similarly to control theory

In [4][5], authors introduced the utility function that reflects user's preference regarding to SIR and transmitter power. The utility function in [6] has been defined as the number of information bits received successfully per joule of energy expended, and authors introduced linear pricing combined with the utility function to obtain Pareto improvement to improve system performance. On the other hand, the power control problem has been studied in [7] using game theory based on cost function, in which each user tried to minimize its own cost to achieve the target SIR. The cost function in [7] has been defined as a weighted sum of power and square of SIR error.

The main goal of power control algorithms in cognitive radio network (CRN) context is to maximize spectrum utilization by allowing many CRs to share licensed users. During the existence of CRs (spectrum sharing), all CRs terminals should be working under the interference temperature limit to protect the QoS of primary system as well as the CR system. To achieve this goal, some researchers focus on the development of power control algorithms in the low priority unlicensed network (CRN) and neglect the interaction of high priority network (primary system). In this case, the development of the power control algorithm is similar to those applied in wireless data networks without any effect on the structure of CRN.

Authors in [8] proposed another power control game based on cost function where the target of transmit power has been included as the target SIR. The cost function in [8] is defined as a weighted sum of logarithm of SIR error and logarithm of power error. The algorithm has many advantages, such as fast convergence, better anti-noise, and capacity. Also, the author [9] proposed a non-cooperative power control algorithm based on a cost function similar to [8] by using the square root function instead of logarithm function to speed up their proposed algorithm. Authors in [10] proposed power control game in CRNs based on the cost function and they used two SIR thresholds in order to adjust the interference factor of power and improve the fairness. In our previous work [11], we proposed a new SIR-based sigmoid power control game in CRNs based on the cost function. The cost function was defined as a weighted sum of square of SIR error and a sigmoid weighting factor of power, which resulted on a considerable saving on, transmit power compared to well-known algorithms. More detailed explanations for the concept of game theory and its application in CRNs can be found in [12]. In [13], the authors introduced a certain degree of hierarchy in the non-cooperative power control game to improve individual energy efficiency of all users. The pricing issue of uplink power control game has been studied in [14], in which CRs adjust their transmission power levels to maximize their own utilities; conversely, primary service will charge them on their transmitted power level to enhance its own income. Authors in [15] considered a non-cooperative power control game for maximum energy efficiency with a fairness constraint on the maximum received power of CRs, in which the results indicate that CRs have a beneficial impact on the whole network throughput. Channel and power allocation have been proposed and evaluated in [16] using game theory based on local information, which analyzes the problem under the interference model. The no-regret learning algorithm has been also used in [16] to overcome the convergence limitations of local game and perform joint channel and power allocation.

Utility function via pricing has been also considered in recent years to solve the problem of power control in CRNs. Authors in [17] introduced a concept of target SIR to modify the utility function and also Shuffled Frog Leaping Algorithm (SFLA) to improve the accuracy of the solution. In [18], the power control game has been improved based on the outage probability of primary user in a spectrum-underlay CRN. In addition, authors in [18] designed an efficient swarm intelligent algorithm to improve the convergence speed and improve the energy-efficiency. A payment-based power control scheme based on the non-cooperative power control game has been considered in [19], in which the distance of CRs and the value of SIR were used as a reference for punishment price setting.

In this paper, we proposed a novel utility function that consists of a weighted exponential of the ratio of target SIR and the desired signal, and the pricing function that comprises a power function of CR's transmitting power. Important features of the proposed power control scheme are: (i) it can preserve the required QoS of all CRs efficiently with insignificant reduction in SIR, (ii) the algorithm can be practically implemented in a distributive manner without requiring additional information, (iii) a significant reduction, and better power allocation to all CRs, and (iv) fast convergence to the Nash Equilibrium. The novelty of the proposed power control scheme is the new sigmoid exponential efficiency function and the power function that applies to the pricing part. The choice of the proposed utility and pricing functions is key to enable each CR to choose its transmitting power efficiently. It guides closest CRs to the base station to achieve their QoS requirement with low cost, whereas it guides farthest CRs from the base station to achieve their QoS requirement with high cost to mitigate the interference. Furthermore, we proved the existence and Nash Equilibrium of the power control game and the conditions of the selected pricing factors. Furthermore, we explained the difference between the linear and power functions to the pricing function, and the effect of weighting factor to the utility function and transmit power. On the other hand, the proposed efficient non-cooperative power control algorithm (EF-NPGP) can be practically implemented in a distributive manner without requiring additional information.

The rest of this paper is as follows. Section 2 describes the system model of CR, the non-cooperative power control game based on the utility function and the EF-NPGP algorithm. Section 3 presents the numerical results and discussion. The limitation of this study and future works are discussed in Section 4. The conclusion is presented in Section 5.

MATERIALS AND METHODS

System Model

In this paper, we consider a single cell CRN with one cognitive base station (CBS) and one primary access point (PAP) as shown in Fig 1, and focus on uplink power control case. There are N CRs sharing the same licensed spectrum with a single primary user and they employ code division multiple access (CDMA) technique to utilize the available spectrum in their own communications. It is assumed that CRs are stationary and distributed inside the coverage area of the cell. We denote p_i to the transmit power of ith cognitive user and h_i to the channel link gain (path gain) between the ith cognitive user and CBS.

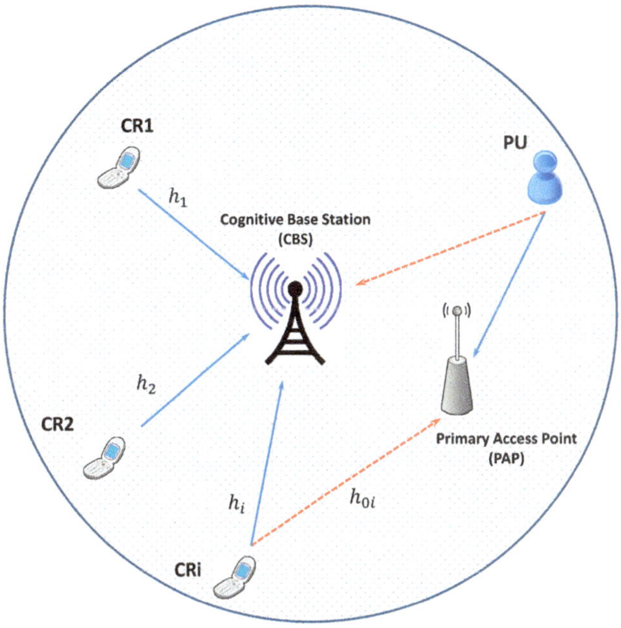

Figure 1: System model of cognitive radio network.

A general formula for SIR in the single cell cognitive radio CDMA system of ith CR can be expressed as

$$\gamma_i(p_i) = \frac{G\,p_i h_i}{\sum_{j\neq i}^{N} p_j h_j + \sigma_i^2} \geq \Gamma_i \quad ,i = 1,2,\ldots,n \tag{1}$$

where G denotes the processing gain of the spread spectrum system, Γ_i is the threshold SIR, and σ_i^2 is the power of the Gaussian noise. The sum of interference, including noise in the denominator of Eq (1) can be denoted as $I_i(\mathbf{p}_{-i})$, hence Eq (1) can be rewritten as a function of user transmit power and the transmit power of other users as:

$$\gamma_i(p_i, \mathbf{p}_{-i}) = \frac{G\,p_i h_i}{I_i(\mathbf{p}_{-i})} = \frac{G\,p_i h_i}{\sum_{j\neq i}^{N} p_j h_j + \sigma_i^2} \tag{2}$$

The subscript $-i$ indicates the interference that depends on the power of all users except the ith user.

In this model, the primary system objective is to maximize its own revenue (profit) by allowing many CRs to share its own spectrum. The revenue maximizing is restricted by the limited performance degradation of primary users or the interference temperature limit [3].

The total interference power made by CRs should be less than a given threshold that is called interference temperature limit and this constraint can be expressed as

$$\sum_{i=1}^{N} p_i h_{0i} \leq I_{TL} \quad (3)$$

where h_{0i} is the channel gain from the transmitter of cognitive radio i to the access point of the primary system, and I_{TL} is the interference temperature limit.

Non-cooperative power control game with pricing

In recent years, the concepts of microeconomics and game theory have been used to define users QoS in terms of utility (cost) function instead of SIR [3]. In general, the power control game model consists of three elements (i) mobile users (or CRs) that represent the players or decision makers of the game, (ii) power strategy which represents the game strategy or action space, and (iii) utility function (preference of users). Each user in the network seeks to maximize its own utility in a selfish manner. The non-cooperative power control (NPG) game model can be expressed as

$$\Phi = [N, \{P_i\}, \{U_i(.)\}] \quad (4)$$

where $N = \{1,2,\ldots, n\}$ is the index set of players (CRs), Pi=[0,Pmaxi] represents the transmission power strategy set of user i, and Pmaxi is the maximum transmission power of user i. The utility function of user i is referred to as $U_i(.)$, in which each user in the network seeks to maximize its own utility in a selfish manner. To reduce power consumed by CRs, achieve the required SIR, and mitigate interference in CRN; the payoff function (utility function) of the power control game in Eq (4) should consider the following properties as in [20]:

- The utility is a function of CR's transmit power and SIR. The SIR of CR is a function of CR's transmit power and the transmit power of other users.
- When CR user increases its power level, this will increase its own SIR, but will decrease the SIR of other CRs.
- For a fixed SIR, the CR prefers the lower power level to higher ones to extend battery life and reduce interference.
- For a fixed power, the CR prefers higher SIR to lower SIR in order to obtain a good channel condition.

In CRN, similar to any wireless network, each CR transmits its information over the air using multiple access system. Since air is a common medium for all the signals, each CR's signal acts as interference to other user's signal. This interference plus fading, multipath and background noise cause signal distortion as its traveling from the source to destination. The denominator of the SIR in Eq (1) represents all these impediments of the signal. In addition, CR users are battery-based devices, so the transmitter power is another important commodity for them. Therefore, SIR and transmit power are the most important parameters that will be used to formulate the expression, which determines user satisfaction using the network [21].

Information sent from transmitters to receivers in wireless data and CRNs are in the form of frames (or packets) of length M bits, containing L < M information bits at a data rate of R bits/sec. Assuming that all errors in the received signal can be detected by the system and the incorrect data can be re-transmitted. Then, the achieved throughput T can be defined as

$$T = R f(\gamma) \quad (5)$$

where $f(\gamma)$ is the efficiency function of transmission. The efficiency function $f(\gamma)$ should depend on SIR achieved over the channel, and its value varies from zero to one (i.e., $f(\gamma) \in [0,1]$). Further, if the user's $i$transmitted power is p_i, then the utility function of user i can be expressed as the number of information bits received successfully per joule of energy consumed as [22]

$$U_i(p_i, \mathbf{p}_{-i}) = \frac{LRf(\gamma_i)}{M\,p_i} \quad (6)$$

The Nash Equilibrium resulting from non-cooperative power control is inefficient because it ignores the cost (harm) it imposes on other terminals by the interference it generates. Therefore, the concept of pricing has been used to encourage the users to use the network resource more efficiently. The general expression of non-cooperative power control game with pricing (NPGP) can be written as

$$\Phi^C = [N, \{P_i\}, \{U_i^C(.)\}] \quad (7)$$

where UCi(.) is the utility function via pricing that can be defined as

$$U_i^C(p_i, \mathbf{p}_{-i}) = U_i(p_i, \mathbf{p}_{-i}) - C_i(p_i, \mathbf{p}_{-i}) \quad (8)$$

Several works considered the problem of power control by introducing dissimilar utility and pricing functions. In [6], the authors proposed the utility function as

$$\text{NPGP}: U_i^C(p_i, \mathbf{p}_{-i}) = \frac{LR}{M\,p_i}(1 - e^{-\gamma_i/2})^M - C_1 p_i \quad (9)$$

where C_1 is the positive pricing factor. Based on Eq (9), authors in [17] used the same utility function in [6], and they introduced a new pricing function where the non-cooperative power control game (NPG) was established using the modified Shuffled Frog Leaping Algorithm (MSFLA) as follows

$$\text{NPG} - \text{MSFLA}: U_i^C(p_i, \mathbf{p}_{-i}) = \frac{LR}{M\,p_i}(1 - e^{-\gamma_i/2})^M - C_2 e^{p_i} - C_3(\gamma_i - \Gamma_i) \quad (10)$$

where C_2 and C_3 are positive pricing factors. The efficiency function that has been used in [6] and [17], is the same, which is related to the non-coherent frequency shift keying (FSK) modulation scheme. The efficiency function is expressed as

$$f_1(\gamma_i) = (1 - e^{-\gamma_i/2})^M \quad (11)$$

In [18], the authors proposed a utility function depending on the sigmoid function, and they introduced a new designed pricing function as defined where the non-cooperative power game with pricing (NPGP) was established using the efficient swarm intelligent algorithm (ESIA) as

$$\text{NPGP} - \text{ESIA} : U_i^C(p_i, \mathbf{p}_{-i}) = \frac{LR}{M\,p_i}\frac{1-e^{-\gamma_i}}{1+e^{\Gamma_i-\gamma_i}} - \alpha\, e^{\beta((\gamma_i/\Gamma_i)-1)}\frac{p_i}{p^{th}} \quad (12)$$

where α and β are the positive pricing factors, p^{th} is the average interference power which can be obtained by taking the mean value of $p_i^{th} : p^{th} = (p_1^{th} + p_2^{th} + \ldots + p_i^{th})/N$, and the sigmoid efficiency function is expressed as

$$f_2(\gamma_i) = \frac{1-e^{-\gamma_i}}{1+e^{\Gamma_i-\gamma_i}} \quad (13)$$

The fair power control game in [19] proposed the utility function based on the simplified sigmoid function used in [18], and they introduced a new non-linear pricing function where the non-cooperative power game with pricing (NPGP) was established using a sliding model, called (R-NPGP) as

$$\text{R} - \text{NPGP} : U_i^C(p_i, \mathbf{p}_{-i}) = \frac{LR}{M\,p_i}\frac{1}{1+e^{\Gamma_i-\gamma_i}} - \mu\,\lambda_i\frac{p_i}{p^{th}} \quad (14)$$

where μ is a positive pricing factor and λ_i is another pricing factor that varies for different CRs based on their generated conditions, and the efficiency function is expressed as

$$f_3(\gamma_i) = \frac{1}{1+e^{\Gamma_i-\gamma_i}} \quad (15)$$

Proposed Game Model

In this subsection, we propose a novel utility function based on a new sigmoid efficiency function and a power function of user's transmit power pricing function. We introduce a sigmoid efficiency function as the exponential ratio of target SIR and the desired signal as

$$f_4(\gamma_i) = \exp\left(-\left(\frac{a\,\Gamma_i}{\gamma_i}\right)^b\right) \quad (16)$$

where a and b are non-negative weighting factors. The efficiency function in Eq (16) is a sigmoidal function with $f(\infty) = 1$, and $f(0) = 0$ to ensure $U_i = 0$ when $p_i = 0$. Moreover, the efficiency function $f_4(\gamma_i)$ with data rate R represents the throughput of the system. The comparison of the above efficiency functions is shown in Fig 2. According to Eq (6), the utility function of the ith CR can be written as

$$U_i = \frac{LR}{M\,p_i}\exp\left(-\left(\frac{a\,\Gamma_i}{\gamma_i}\right)^b\right)\frac{\text{bits}}{\text{joule}} \quad (17)$$

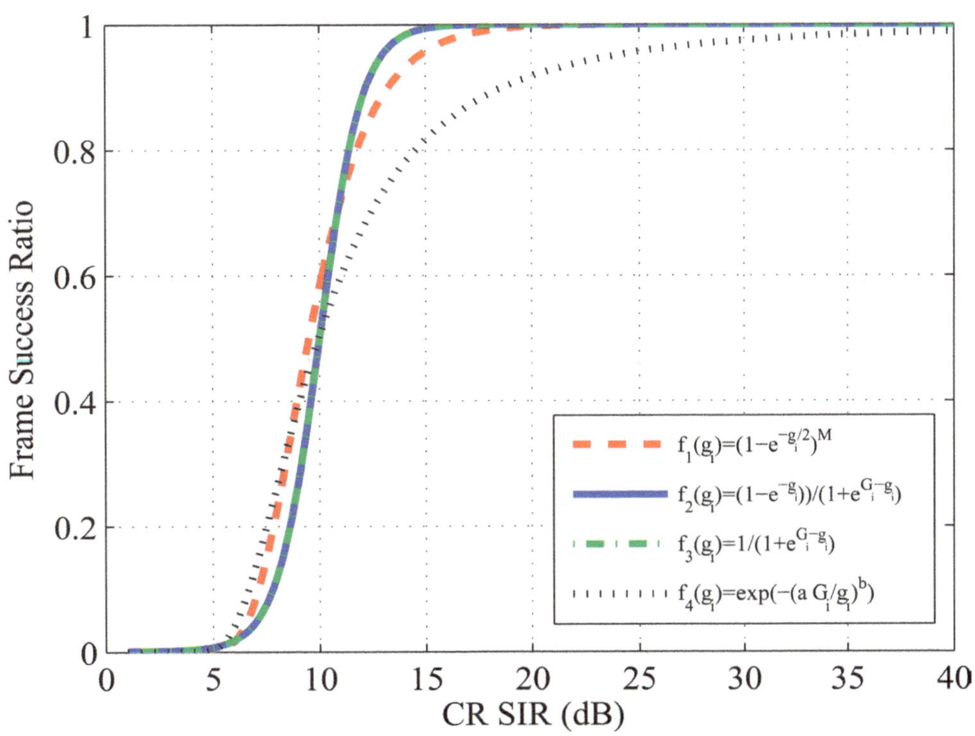

Figure 2: Efficiency function comparison $\Gamma i = 10$, $a = 0.8$, $b = 3$, $M = 80$.

The utility function in Eq (17) represents the tradeoff between the throughput and battery life and it is particularly appropriate for applications where saving power is more important than achieving a high throughput, such as green cognitive radio [23]. Assuming that the value of target SIR is fixed at the cognitive radio system, the proposed utility function can be tuned using the weighting factor a. The user's optimal transmit power will be changed depending on the maxima of utility function. Fig 3 shows the curves of our proposed utility function with respect to transmit power in different values of a. It is shown that the utility increases and the transmitting power decreases by decreasing the value of the parameter a, but this will decrease the target of SIR of the system. The factor a can be broadcast by the primary system to the cognitive networks to adjust the target SIR depending on the amount of interference. The primary system sends a lower value of a when the amount of interference approximately reaches the interference temperature limit.

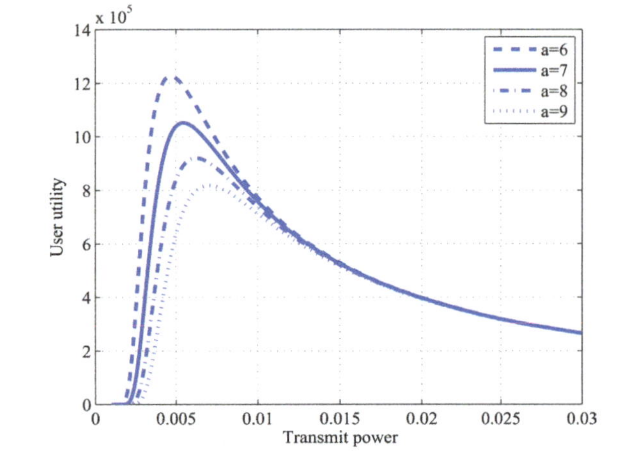

Figure 3: User's utility function as a function of transmit power for fixed interference and different value of weighting factor ***a***.

Further, we introduce a new design of the pricing function to improve the system performance by encouraging CRs to use system resources efficiently. The contribution in our design is to apply a high cost to the users that use high power, such as the farthest users from the base station. Therefore, we introduce a power function of the transmit power instead of traditional linear pricing. Fig 4 shows an example of the difference between the linear and power pricing techniques. We assumed that user transmit power varies between the minimum and maximum power strategy space [0, 2], and price functions computed numerically. It is shown that the power function pricing is lower than the linear function pricing for CRs who use low transmit power (closer users), whereas a high pricing cost will be applied to the CRs who use high transmit power (farthest users).

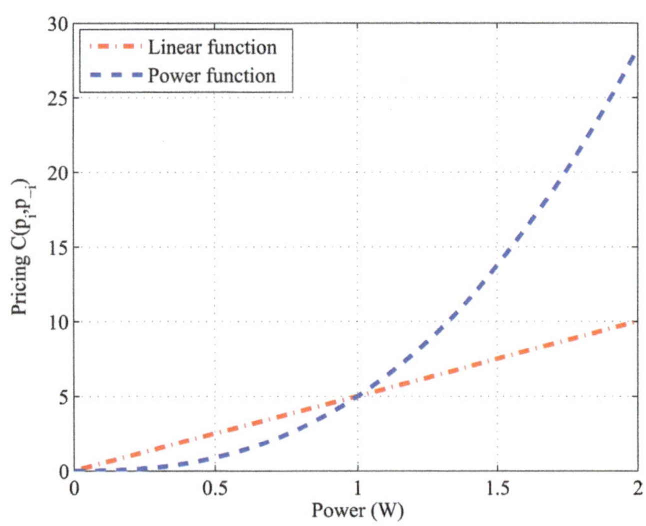

Figure 4: Linear and power function pricing comparison.

Thus, the proposed pricing function is expressed as

$$C_i(p_i, \mathbf{p}_{-i}) = c\, p_i^{\alpha} \tag{18}$$

where c and α are the pricing factors. Thus, the utility function with pricing can be expressed as

$$U_i^C(p_i, \mathbf{p}_{-i}) = \frac{L\,R}{M\,p_i}\exp\left(-\left(\frac{a\,\Gamma_i}{\gamma_i}\right)^b\right) - c\,p_i^{\alpha} \tag{19}$$

Therefore, the proposed energy efficient non-cooperative power control in the game with pricing (EF-NPGP) is expressed as

$$\text{EF}-\text{NPGP}:\ \max_{p_i \in P_i} U_i^C(p_i, \mathbf{p}_{-i}) = \frac{L\,R}{M\,p_i}\exp\left(-\left(\frac{a\,\Gamma_i}{\gamma_i}\right)^b\right) - c\,p_i^{\alpha} \tag{20}$$

The advantage of this pricing function is its ability to guide CRs to an efficient Nash Equilibrium point. This is done by increasing the cost of the farthest users who use high transmit power in their communication. Moreover, the pricing function reduced the cost applied to the nearest CRs who use low transmit power in their communication. Each CR seeks to maximize its own profit (utility-price) by adjusting its transmit power in a distributed manner. The expected Nash Equilibrium result from the power control game is the balanced power of all CRs that no single CR can increase the benefit by changing its own transmits power. To derive an algorithm of non-cooperative power control game, we adopt a power control algorithm in which each CR will maximize its net utility $U_i^C(p_i, \mathbf{p}_{-i})$. For power optimization, the maximization can be achieved at a point for which the partial derivative of $U_i^C(p_i, \mathbf{p}_{-i})$ with respect to power p_i is equal to zero. For simple analysis, we get

$$\frac{\partial U_i^C}{\partial p_i} = \frac{L\,R}{M\,p_i^2}\left(\gamma_i \frac{\partial f_4(\gamma_i)}{\partial \gamma_i} - f_4(\gamma_i)\right) - \alpha\, c\, p_i^{\alpha-1} \tag{21}$$

Existence of Nash Equilibrium

In non-cooperative power control game, the ith CR maximizes its utility by choosing a proper strategy from the strategy set $P_i = [0, p_i^{\max}]$.

A Nash Equilibrium exists in non-cooperative power control game, if for all i = 1,2,.., n meet the following two conditions [24]:

1. The action set P_i is non-empty, convex, and compact subset of some Euclidean R^N.
2. The utility function $U_i^C(p_i, \mathbf{p}_{-i})$ is continuous in **p** and $(\partial^2 U_i^C / \partial p_i \partial p_j) \geq 0\ \forall j \neq i \in N$.

The transmit power space strategy for each CR in our game is defined by the minimum and maximum powers, and the value of powers is between these values. Therefore, the first condition of action set P_i is satisfied.

To show that the CR utility function is quasi-concave in p_i, the second derivative of $U_i^C(p_i, \mathbf{p}_{-i})$ is obtained with respect to p_i.

$$\frac{\partial U_i^C}{\partial p_i} = \frac{L\,R}{M\,p_i^2}\left(\gamma_i \frac{\partial f_4(\gamma_i)}{\partial \gamma_i} - f_4(\gamma_i)\right) - \alpha\, c\, p_i^{\alpha-1} \tag{22}$$

$$\begin{aligned}\frac{\partial^2 U_i^C}{\partial p_i \partial p_j} &= \frac{L\,R}{M\,p_i^2}\left(\frac{\partial \gamma_i}{\partial p_j}\frac{\partial f_4(\gamma_i)}{\partial \gamma_i} + \gamma_i \frac{\partial \gamma_i}{\partial p_j}\frac{\partial^2 f_4(\gamma_i)}{\partial \gamma_i^2} - \frac{\partial \gamma_i}{\partial p_j}\frac{\partial f_4(\gamma_i)}{\partial \gamma_i}\right) \\ &= \frac{L\,R}{M\,p_i^2}\left(\gamma_i \frac{\partial \gamma_i}{\partial p_j}\frac{\partial^2 f_4(\gamma_i)}{\partial \gamma_i^2}\right)\end{aligned} \tag{23}$$

Because the first-order derivative of γ_i with respect to p_j is $(\partial\gamma_i/\partial p_j) = -(Gh_ih_jp_i/\sum_{i\neq i} h_jp_j + \sigma^2) < 0,$ so we need the second-order derivative of our efficiency function with respect to γ_i be $\partial^2 f_4(\gamma_i)/\partial\gamma_i^2 \le 0.$

$$\frac{\partial f_4(\gamma_i)}{\partial\gamma_i} = \frac{\partial e^{\left(-\left(\frac{a\Gamma_i}{\gamma_i}\right)^b\right)}}{\partial\gamma_i}$$

$$= \frac{b\left(-\left(\frac{a\Gamma_i}{\gamma_i}\right)^b\right)e^{\left(-\left(\frac{a\Gamma_i}{\gamma_i}\right)^b\right)}}{\gamma_i} \tag{24}$$

$$\frac{\partial^2 f_4(\gamma_i)}{\partial\gamma_i^2} = -\frac{be^{\left(-\left(\frac{a\Gamma_i}{\gamma_i}\right)^b\right)}\left(b\left(\frac{a\Gamma_i}{\gamma_i}\right)^b + \left(\frac{a\Gamma_i}{\gamma_i}\right)^b - b\left(\frac{a\Gamma_i}{\gamma_i}\right)^{2b}\right)}{\gamma_i^2} \tag{25}$$

Because be

$\left(-\left(\frac{a\Gamma_i}{\gamma_i}\right)^b\right)/\gamma_i > 0$, in order to $\partial^2 f_4(\gamma_i)/\partial\gamma_i^2 \le 0$

$$\left(b\left(\frac{a\Gamma_i}{\gamma_i}\right)^b + \left(\frac{a\Gamma_i}{\gamma_i}\right)^b - b\left(\frac{a\Gamma_i}{\gamma_i}\right)^{2b}\right) \ge 0$$

$$\Rightarrow b+1 \ge b\left(\frac{a\Gamma_i}{\gamma_i}\right)^b$$

$$\frac{(b+1)^{1/b}}{ab} \ge \frac{\Gamma_i}{\gamma_i} \tag{26}$$

According to Eq (26) and by selecting the pricing factors carefully, the second condition has been satisfied. Hence, the proposed power control game has a unique Nash Equilibrium solution.

EF-NPGP Algorithm

We suppose that each CR i updates its transmit power at time instances $T_i = \{t_{i1}, t_{i2}, \ldots,\}$ where $t_{ik} < t_{i(k+1)}$ and by considering the proposed EF-NPGP as given in Eq (20), generate a sequence of powers as follows

i. Initialize transmit power vector $p = [p_1^0, p_2^0, p_3^0, \ldots \;\; .. \;\; , p_N^0]$ randomly at time t_0

ii. For all i ∈ N, at time instant t_k

   a. Update $\gamma_i(t_k)$ using Eq (1)

   b. Given $p_i(t_{k-1})$, compute ri(tk)= $\arg\max_{p_i \in P_i} U_i^C(p_i, \mathbf{p}_{-i}(t_{k-1}))$

   c. Assign the transmit power as $p_i(t_k) = \min(r_i(t_k), p_i^{\max})$

iii. If $\|p(t_k) - p(t_{k-1})\| \le \varepsilon$, stop iteration and declare Nash Equilibrium as $p(t_k)$. Else, k = k + 1 and go to Step II.

where $r_i(t_k)$ represents the set of best transmit powers for ith CR at time instant k. The flow chart of the proposed EF-NPGP algorithm is shown in Fig 5.

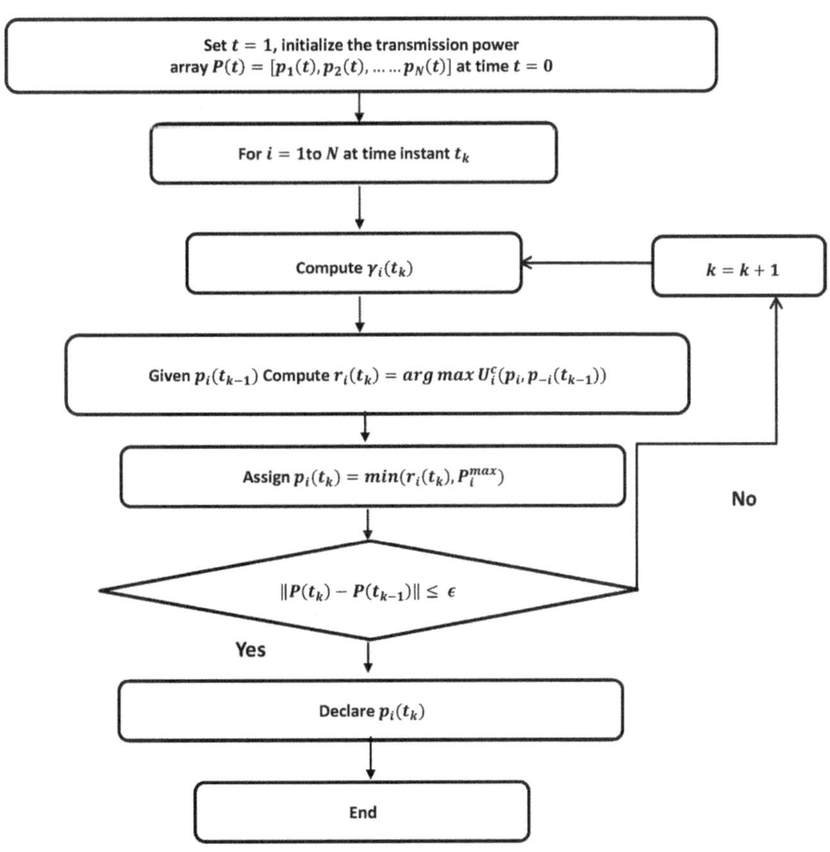

Figure 5: Flowchart illustrating the EF-NPGP algorithm.

Numerical Results and Discussion

In this section, we compare the performance of our proposed power control game algorithm with NPG_MSFLIA [17], NPG-ESIA [18], and R-NPGP [19]. The utility functions that have been used in the comparison are explained in Eqs (10), (12), and (14). We applied the same numerical computation to obtain the Nash Equilibrium solution of utility functions in order to present the advantages of our proposed utility function. The constant system parameters used in the simulation are listed in Table 2.

Table 2: **System parameters**

Parameter	Value
Total number of bits per frame, M	80
Number of information bits of each frame, L	64
Spread spectrum processing gain, G	100
Data rate, R	10 kbps
AWGN power at receiver, σ^2	5e-15 Watts
Maximum power constraint, p_i^{max}	2 Watts
Target SIR, Γ_i	10
Weighting factors a,b,c, and α	0.88, 3, 1e4, 2.5

We have considered a simple system model based on a single-cell cognitive radio CDMA system with a fixed packet size and no coding for forward error correction. For the general efficiency function defined in Eq (11), the equilibrium SIR is found by solving the formula $f'(\gamma)\gamma - f(\gamma) = 0$ that guarantee maximum utility of $\gamma^* = 12.4$. The value of γ^* is the real target SIR that all CRs achieve to maximize their own utility function. For the cognitive radio CDMA system, the feasibility condition for γ^* is giving by the following bound on the number of users [25]:

$$N \leq 1 + (G/\gamma^*) = 9.05 \text{ CR terminals} \tag{27}$$

According to (27), we assume that there are not more than 9 CRs in the system and their distance from the base station d = [368m, 490m, 580m, 630m, 720m, 810m, 950m, 1070m, 1140m].

In this paper, we use a simple propagation model in which all the path gains are deterministic functions, with path loss exponent β, of the distance between the cognitive radio i and CBS

$$h_i = \frac{K}{r_i^{\beta}} \tag{28}$$

where r_i is the distance between the ith user and base station, β is the path loss exponent, which is supposed to be 4 that is usually between 2 and 6, and $K = 0.097$ is a constant. This value of $K = 0.097$ is selected to establish a transmit power of 2 W for a CR terminal operating at 1140 meters from CBC in the system with 9 CRs, and all operating with γ^*. In this simulation, all cognitive users start with initial power $p_i^{(0)} = 2.22 \times 10^{-16}$ W for all algorithms and $\varepsilon = 10^{-5}$. In this simulation, the weighting and pricing factors have been tuned until all algorithms achieve the same average value of SIR.

Fig 6 explains the results of SIR at Nash Equilibrium that are achieved by CR according to the distance between each CR and base station. All CR users maintain their SIR above the target value ($\Gamma_i = 10$) and SIR value is decreased by increasing the distance for all algorithms. The comparison of SIR for all algorithms shows that our proposed algorithm EF-NPGP is more efficient, especially for the first 7 users, where the values of SIRs are the highest comparing with other algorithms. The farthest CRs consume the highest powers and they represent the origin of interference, therefore our proposed algorithm applied a higher cost to the farthest users. Fig 7 shows the curves of transmit power in Watts with the distance between the CR and the base station for all algorithms where the transmit power increases gradually by increasing the distance of the user. It can be seen that the transmit power curve of the proposed EF-NPGP is the lowest comparing to NPG-MSFLIA, NPGP-ESIA, and R-NPGP.

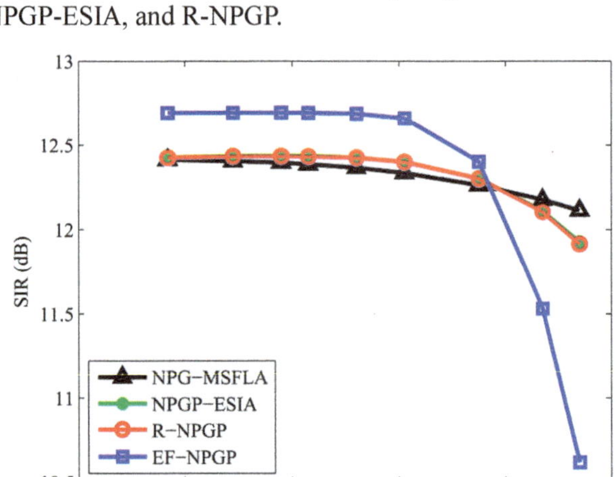

Figure 6: Comparison curves of each CR's SIR for all algorithms.

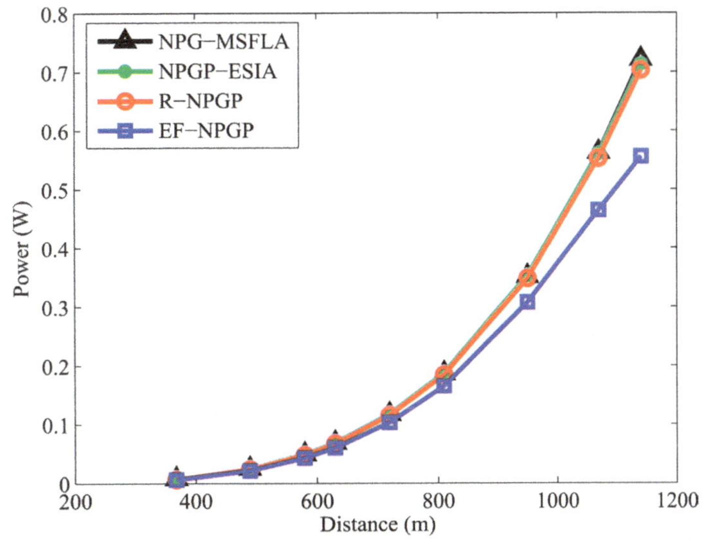

Figure 7: Comparison curves of each CR's transmit power for all algorithms.

Table 3 shows the SIR of CR users at the end of the network algorithm simulation. This table shows that the EF-NPGP with our proposed price function achieve the highest value of SIR. The SIR of the last two CR users is smaller due to applied higher cost. Therefore, it can reach a better equilibrium point by restricting the minimum required SIR for terminals with bad channel conditions.

Table 3: **Final SIR of CR users**

CR user #	Final SIR of NPG_MSFLIA [17]	Final SIR of NPG-ESIA [18]	Final SIR of R-NPGP [19]	Final SIR of Proposed EF-NPGP
1	12.41	12.42	12.42	12.69
2	12.4	12.43	12.43	12.69
3	12.4	12.43	12.43	12.69
4	12.39	12.43	12.43	12.69
5	12.37	12.42	12.42	12.68
6	12.33	12.4	12.4	12.66
7	12.26	12.3	12.3	12.4
8	12.18	12.1	12.1	11.53
9	12.11	11.92	11.91	10.61

Next, we test the average power and average SIR for all algorithms to determine the convergence speed of algorithms and the reduction of average power. In this test, the horizontal axis represents the iteration time that needs to obtain the Nash Equilibrium and the vertical axis represents the average SIR and average power. It is shown in Fig 8 that all algorithms approximately achieve the same value of average SIR without any significant differences, but the speeds of convergence are not equal. It is found that our proposed EF-NPGP algorithm can obtain the Nash Equilibrium with only 133 iterations while it needs 333, 360, and 323 for NPG-MSFLA, NPGP-ESIA and R-NPGP, respectively. On the other hand, Fig 9 shows the comparison curves of average transmit power obtained by all algorithms. It can be seen from Fig 9 that the average power consumption of the proposed EF-NPGP algorithm has a significant reduction comparing with other algorithms. The result obtained from Fig 9 indicates that the amount of interference measured at the primary system from the proposed EF-NPGP is the lowest comparing with other algorithms. This feature of the proposed EF-NPGP algorithm makes it the best for maximizing the spectrum sharing and QoS guarantees in both systems. The speed convergence of all algorithms can be seen clearly in Fig 9, in which it founds that our proposed EF-NPGP is the fastest comparing with other algorithms. In Table 4, we explained the average power in Watt, and the number of process iterations of all algorithms.

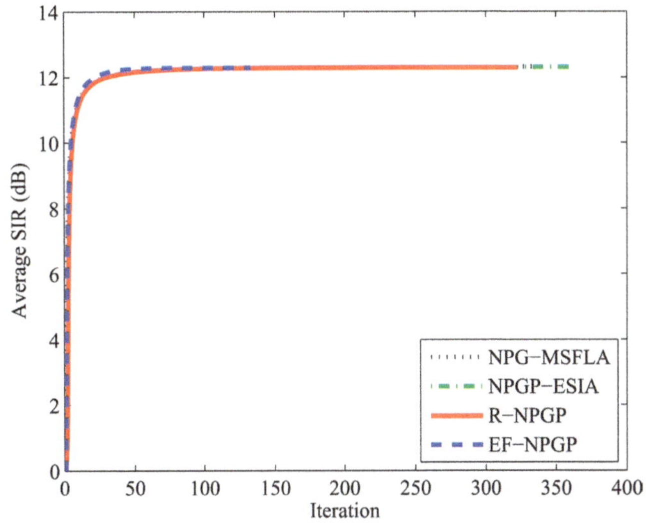

Figure 8: Comparison curves of average SIR for all algorithms with number of iterations.

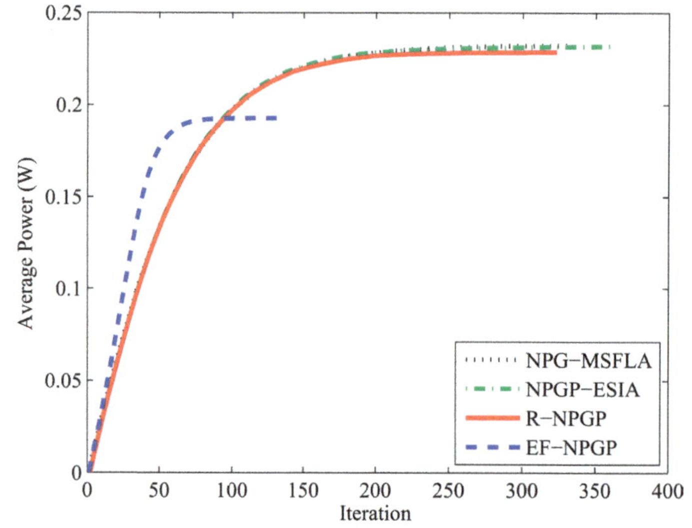

Figure 9: Comparison curves of average power for all algorithms with number of iterations.

Table 4: Values of average power and number of iterations of algorithms

Algorithm	Average Power (W)	Number of iterations
NPG-MSFLA	0.2321	333
NPGP-ESIA	0.2319	360
R-NPGP	0.2287	323
EF-NPGP	0.1926	133

The impact of noise to all algorithms is shown in Fig 10. We test the algorithm using the same parameters that applied to the previous test. We range the value of noise from 3×10^{-17} W to 10^{-14} W. As shown in Fig 10, the average power increases with the increase of noise because the power is proportional to noise, while the average SIRs decreased with the increase of noise because SIR is inversely proportional to noise as in Eq (1). The proposed EF-NPGP algorithm provides significant savings of power in high noise case, in which ($p_{EF-NPGP} = 0.2078$ W), and ($p = 0.3127$ W) for all other algorithms. On the other hand, the reduction in average SIR is insignificant compared to other algorithms.

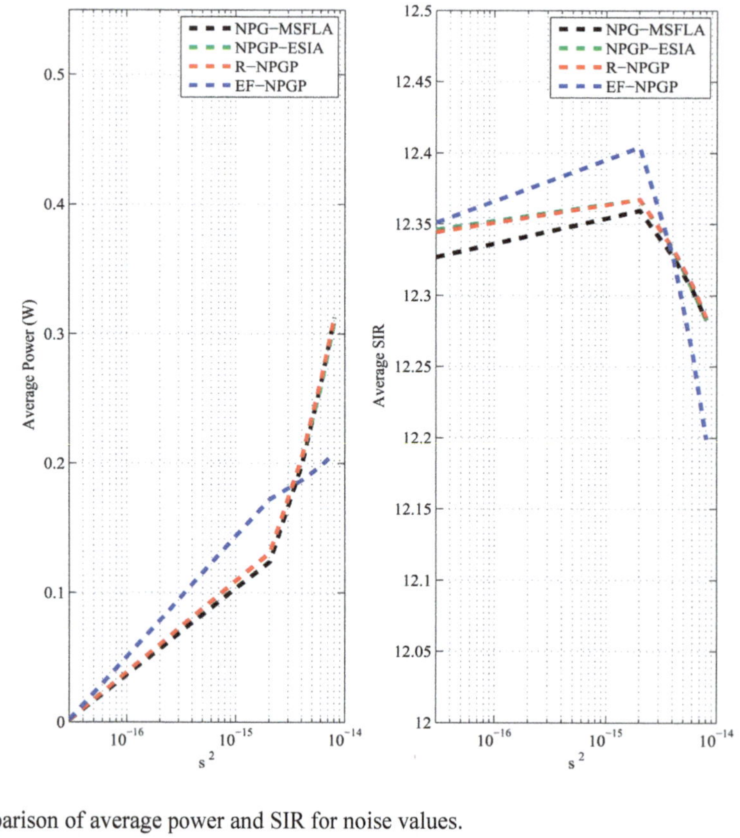

Figure 10: Performance comparison of average power and SIR for noise values.

LIMITATIONS AND FUTURE WORKS

The main objective of this work is to reallocate the transmit power among CRs to maintain the required QoS of CRs to obtain a significant decrease in power consumption and mitigate the aggregate interference. Under no pricing, all above utilities are maximized at the same value of SIR, which can be obtained by solving the following formula

$$f'(\gamma)\,\gamma = f(\gamma) \quad (29)$$

The value of SIR is determined according to the design of the efficiency function that depends on the system characteristic. As the pricing function is applied and the value of pricing factor is increased, CRs attain lower SIR, lower power, and higher utilities. Due to the pricing, SIRs are no longer equal at the equilibrium for all CRs. In actual fact, a user closer to the base station achieves higher SIR than a user farther away. The reduction of CR's SIR, the increase of CR's utilities, and the algorithm speed of convergence are depending on the selected values of pricing factors c and α. In future works, we will consider an addition algorithm to select the best values of pricing factors c_{BEST} and α_{BEST} that can be applied to the network (base station) side to get more significant improvement.

CONCLUSION

We have presented a non-cooperative power control algorithm in cognitive radio networks. The QoS of a CR user refers to an efficient utility function via pricing. By introducing the new utility and price functions, an efficient non-cooperative power control game has been produced and the existence and uniqueness of Nash Equilibrium is proved. Numerical results indicate that the non-cooperative power control algorithm proposed in this paper has better power saving and faster convergence compared to recently available works in the literature. In addition, most of closer CR users in our proposed algorithm can meet higher SIR than the users in other algorithms. The higher pricing only applied to the farthest users that represent a higher source of undesirable interference. The proposed scheme offers an improved performance, in which the CRN can now share extra licensed band under the interference temperature limits. The significant reduction in the transmit power of the proposed power control algorithm gives the highest preference to apply it in cognitive radio sensor networks and green cognitive radio networks. As future work, it is suggested to study the proposed algorithm with the higher load system and with the existence of primary users.

ACKNOWLEDGMENTS

The authors would like to thank the anonymous reviewers for their valuable suggestions and comments on the manuscript. The authors would also like to thank Dr. Mohammed Nasser for checking English text in our manuscript.

REFERENCES

1. Marcus M, Burtle J, Franca B, Lahjouji A, McNeil N. Federal Communications Commission Spectrum Policy Task Force. Report of the Unlicensed Devices and Experimental Licenses Working Group. 2002.
2. Haykin S. Cognitive radio: brain-empowered wireless communications. IEEE Journal on Selected Areas in Communications. 2005;23(2):201–220.
3. Hossain E, Niyato D, Han Z. Dynamic spectrum access and management in cognitive radio networks Cambridge University Press; 2009.
4. Ji H, Huang C-Y. Non-cooperative uplink power control in cellular radio systems. Wireless Networks. Springer-Verlag New York, Inc.; 1998;4(3):233–240.
5. Xiao M, Shroff NB, Chong EK. Utility-based power control in cellular wireless systems. Twentieth Annual Joint Conference of the IEEE Computer and Communications Societies Proceedings. 2001. p. 412–421.
6. Saraydar CU, Mandayam NB, Goodman DJ. Efficient power control via pricing in wireless data networks. IEEE Transactions on Communications. 2002;50(2):291–303.
7. Koskie S, Gajic Z. A Nash game algorithm for SIR-based power control in 3G wireless CDMA networks. IEEE/ACM Transactions on Networking (TON). 2005;13(5):1017–1026.
8. Li F, Tan X, Wang L. A new game algorithm for power control in cognitive radio networks. IEEE Transactions on Vehicular Technology. 2011;60(9):4384–4391.
9. Junhui Z, Tao Y, Yi G, Jiao W, Lei F. Power control algorithm of cognitive radio based on non-cooperative game theory. Communications, China. 2013;10(11):143–154.
10. Lu K, Zhang L, Yang J. An efficient SIR-first adaptive power control method in cognitive radio network. IEEE of Global High Tech Congress on Electronics (GHTCE). 2012. p. 91–94.
11. Al-Gumaei YA, Noordin KA, Reza AW, Dimyati K. A New SIR-Based Sigmoid Power Control Game in Cognitive Radio Networks. PloS one. Public Library of Science; 2014;9(10):e109077 doi:10.1371/journal.pone.0109077
12. Wang B, Wu Y, Liu K. Game theory for cognitive radio networks: An overview. Computer networks. Elsevier; 2010;54(14):2537–2561.
13. Lasaulce S, Hayel Y, El Azouzi R, Debbah M. Introducing hierarchy in energy games. IEEE Transactions on Wireless Communications. 2009;8(7):3833–3843.
14. Yu H, Gao L, Li Z, Wang X, Hossain E. Pricing for uplink power control in cognitive radio networks.IEEE Transactions on Vehicular Technology. 2010;59(4):1769–1778.
15. Buzzi S, Saturnino D. A game-theoretic approach to energy-efficient power control and receiver design in cognitive CDMA wireless networks. IEEE Journal of Selected Topics in Signal Processing,. 2011;5(1):137–150.
16. Gállego JR, Canales M, Ortin J. Distributed resource allocation in cognitive radio networks with a game learning approach to improve aggregate system capacity. Ad Hoc Networks. Elsevier; 2012;10(6):1076–1089.
17. Zhang X, Zhang Y, Shi Y, Zhao L, Zou C. Power control algorithm in cognitive radio system based on modified Shuffled Frog Leaping Algorithm. AEU-International

Journal of Electronics and Communications. Elsevier; 2012;66(6):448–454.

18. Kuo Y, Yang J, Chen J. Efficient swarm intelligent algorithm for power control game in cognitive radio networks. IET Communications. 2013;7(11): 1089–1098.

19. Xie X, Yang H, Vasilakos AV, He L. Fair power control using game theory with pricing scheme in cognitive radio networks. Journal of Communications and Networks. 2014;16(2):183–192.

20. MacKenzie AB, DaSilva LA. Game theory for wireless engineers. Synthesis Lectures on Communications. Morgan \& Claypool Publishers; 2006;1(1):1–86.

21. Shah V, Mandayam NB, Goodman D. Power control for wireless data based on utility and pricing. The Ninth IEEE International Symposium on Personal, Indoor and Mobile Radio Communications. 1998. p. 1427–1432.

22. Goodman D, Mandayam N. Power control for wireless data. IEEE Personal Communications. 2000;7(2):48–54.

23. Meshkati F, Chiang M, Poor HV, Schwartz SC. A game-theoretic approach to energy-efficient power control in multicarrier CDMA systems. IEEE Journal on Selected Areas in Communications. 2006;24(6):1115–1129.

24. Topkis DM. Supermodularity and complementarity Princeton university press; 1998.

25. Yates RD. A framework for uplink power control in cellular radio systems. IEEE Journal on Selected Areas in Communications. 1995;13(7):1341–1347.

CHAPTER 2

FREQUENCY RESPONSE AND GAP TUNING FOR NONLINEAR ELECTRICAL OSCILLATOR NETWORKS

Harish S. Bhat, Garnet J. Vaz

Applied Mathematics Unit, University of California Merced, Merced, California, United States of America

ABSTRACT

We study nonlinear electrical oscillator networks, the smallest example of which consists of a voltage-dependent capacitor, an inductor, and a resistor driven by a pure tone source. By allowing the network topology to be that of any connected graph, such circuits generalize spatially discrete nonlinear transmission lines/lattices that have proven useful in high frequency analog devices. For such networks, we develop two algorithms to compute the steady-state response when a subset of nodes are driven at the same fixed frequency. The algorithms we devise are orders of magnitude more accurate and efficient than stepping towards the steady-state using a standard numerical integrator. We seek to enhance a given network's nonlinear behavior by altering the eigenvalues of the graph Laplacian, i.e., the resonances of the linearized system. We develop a Newton-type method that solves for the network inductances such that the graph Laplacian achieves a desired set of eigenvalues; this method enables one to move the eigenvalues while keeping the network topology fixed. Running numerical experiments using three different random graph models, we show that shrinking the gap between the graph Laplacian's first two eigenvalues dramatically improves a network's ability to (i) transfer energy to higher harmonics, and (ii) generate large-amplitude signals. Our results shed light on the relationship between a network's structure, encoded by the graph Laplacian, and its function, defined in this case by the presence of strongly nonlinear effects in the frequency response.

INTRODUCTION

Networks of nonlinear electrical oscillators have found recent application in several microwave frequency analog devices [1]–[6]. The fundamental unit in these networks is a nonlinear oscillator wired as in Figure 1; this oscillator consists of one inductor, one voltage-dependent capacitor, one source, and one sink (a resistor). While many nonlinear oscillatory circuits have been studied for their chaotic behavior, the particular oscillator in Figure 1 does not exhibit sensitive dependence on initial conditions in the regime of operation that we consider. Instead, assuming the source is of the form $A\cos(\omega t+\phi)$, the oscillator reaches a steady-state consisting of a sum of harmonics with fundamental frequency ω [7].

Citation: Bhat HS, Vaz GJ. Frequency Response and Gap Tuning for Nonlinear Electrical Oscillator Networks. Gomez-Gardenes J, ed. PLoS ONE. 2013;8(11):e78009. doi:10.1371/journal.pone.0078009.

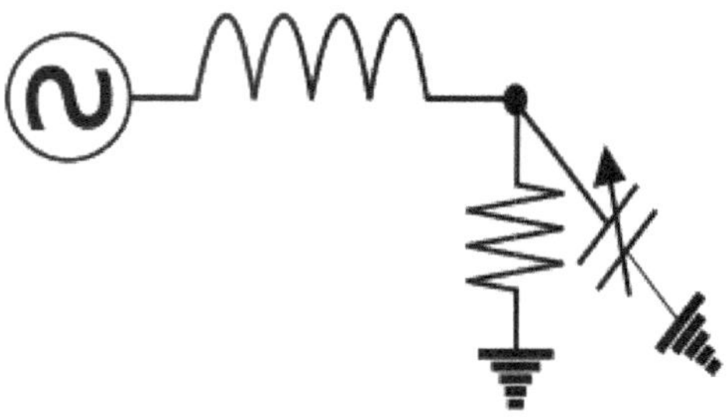

Figure 1: Schematic of a single nonlinear oscillator.

When networks of these oscillators have been studied, the network topology has either been a one-dimensional linear chain, in which case the circuit is called a nonlinear transmission line [8]–[13]—see Figure 2, or a two-dimensional rectangular lattice [14]–[18]—see Figure 3. Even if each individual block in the chain/lattice is weakly nonlinear, the overall circuit can exhibit strongly nonlinear behavior. It is this property that is exploited for microwave device applications, enabling low-frequency, low-power inputs to be transformed into high-frequency, high-power outputs.

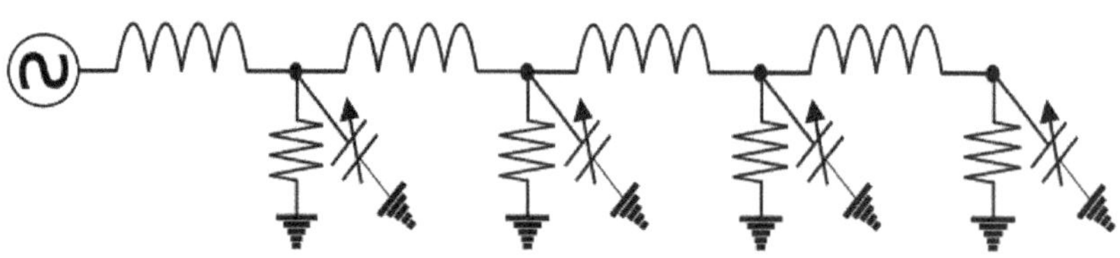

Figure 2: An example of a nonlinear transmission line.

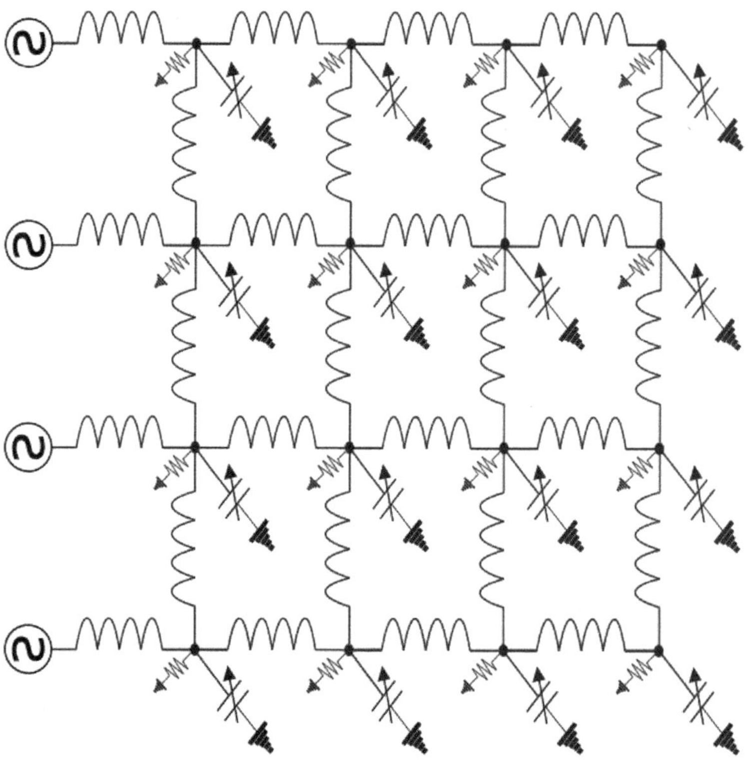

Figure 3: An example of a nonlinear lattice.

The first objective of this work is to develop numerical algorithms to compute the frequency response of a nonlinear electrical network with topology given by an arbitrary connected graph. Here we are motivated by the successful application of computational techniques in the design of the high-frequency analog devices referenced above. As we show, to compute steady-state solutions with comparable accuracy, both the perturbative and iterative algorithms developed in this paper require orders of magnitude less computational time than standard numerical integration. While the perturbative algorithm generalizes derivations given in prior work [7], [18], the iterative algorithm has not been previously applied to nonlinear electrical networks. Both new algorithms show exponential convergence in the number of iterations, and for a test problem on a network with $N=400$ nodes, less than 20 iterations are required to achieve machine precision errors.

The second objective of this work is to relate structural properties of the network to the dynamics of the nonlinear oscillator system. The derivation of the perturbative algorithm indicates that nonlinearity in the electrical network manifests itself through energy transfer from the fundamental forcing frequency to higher harmonics. This helps us understand why properties such as amplitude boosting [7], [18] and frequency upconversion [1], observed in nonlinear electrical networks with regular lattice topologies, can be expected when the topology is that of a random, disordered network. Additionally, we observe that an inductance-weighted graph Laplacian matrix features prominently in both algorithms for computing the steady-state solution. This graph Laplacian matrix encodes the structure of the network, and its eigenvalues are the squares of the resonant frequencies for the undamped, linear version of the circuit. Driving the damped, linearized circuit at one of these resonances results in large amplitude outputs. It is reasonable to hypothesize that the locations of these resonances play a large role in the dynamics of the nonlinear network.

This motivates the following question: how do the eigenvalues of the graph Laplacian influence the nonlinear network›s properties of frequency upconversion and amplitude boosting? While it is possible to alter the spectrum of the graph Laplacian by changing the node-edge relationships in the graph, we can also change its spectrum by keeping the topology fixed and manipulating the network›s inductances. We formulate and solve the inverse problem of finding the inductances such that the graph Laplacian achieves a prescribed spectrum. The solution proceeds via a Newton-type algorithm that takes the desired spectrum as input and iteratively alters the inductances until a convergence criterion is met.

For three types of random graphs, we find that the Newton-type method effectively finds circuit inductances that close the gap between the first two eigenvalues of the graph Laplacian. We conduct a series of numerical experiments to examine the effect of closing this eigenvalue gap on a given circuit›s ability (i) to transfer energy from the fundamental driving frequency to higher harmonics, and (ii) to generate high-amplitude output signals. The results indicate that the two metrics (i-ii) can be improved dramatically by closing the gap between the graph Laplacian›s first two eigenvalues. Table 1 shows results we obtained for graphs with $N = 175$ nodes. Though this a small portion of the results we describe later, this table already illustrates the effect of gap tuning on network performance. Note that each *pre* and *post* circuit have the same graph topology, differing only in their edge inductances.

Table 1: Portion of results for graphs with $N = 175$ **nodes**

	% of energy in higher harmonics		Maximum magnitude voltage	
	Pre	Post	Pre	Post
Barabási-Albert (BA)	0.410	4.063	0.01548	0.31684
Watts-Strogatz (WS)	1.006	8.701	0.03399	0.51157
Erdös-Rényi (ER)	0.033	7.534	0.002956	0.78902

Note that we have made available open-source Python implementations of all algorithms described in this work. The Python code, together with R code used for plotting, has been posted on a public repository. This enables the reader to reproduce all results in this paper. Instructions on how to download this code is given below.

Connections to Other Systems

We can make several connections between the problem studied in this paper and other problems of interest:

- ***Random Elastic Networks***: Using a mechanical analogy between inductorscapacitors and massessprings, the nonlinear electronic network can be transformed into a mathematically equivalent network of masses and anharmonic springs [19, Appendix I]. Such random elastic networks have been of recent interest as models of amorphous solids [20]–[22]. For such networks, quartic spring potential energies have been considered [23]. Nonlinear random elastic networks have also been used to model molecular machines; in this context, tuning the gap between the first two eigenvalues of the linearized system enables the construction of networks with properties similar to those of real proteins [24]. Despite this activity, algorithms for computing and manipulating the frequency response of nonlinear elastic networks have not been developed. Our work addresses this issue directly.
- ***Nonlinear electromagnetic media***: The circuit we analyze, for particular values of the circuit parameters, arises naturally as a finite volume discretization of Maxwell's equations for TE/TM modes in a nonlinear medium [25], [26]. The arbitrary connected graph topology of the circuit corresponds to a finite volume discretization on an arbitrary unstructured mesh. The algorithms developed here can be used to compute and optimize the frequency response of nonlinear electromagnetic media.
- ***Coupled phase oscillator networks***: There has been intense interest in nonlinear phase oscillator networks, primarily due to the ability of such networks to model biophysical systems featuring synchronization. Though synchronization is not of primary interest in our system, we may still draw parallels. The effect of network topology on the properties of coupled phase oscillators has been studied extensively [27]–[30]. Manipulating eigenvalues of the Laplacian matrix enables one to enhance a network's synchronization properties [31]. More recently, several authors have developed algorithms for optimizing the synchronization of phase oscillator networks [32]–[37]. The questions considered in this subset of the coupled phase oscillator literature are related to the issues addressed in the present work.

METHODS

Problem Formulation

Let $H(N,e)$ be a connected, simple graph with N nodes and e edges. Each edge corresponds to an inductor that physically connects two nodes. Each node corresponds to a capacitor and resistor, wired in parallel, that physically connect the node to a common ground. Let $f \leq N$ be the number of nodes that are driven by prescribed sources. Since the voltage at the prescribed source is known, we do not model it using a node. The connection between the source and the node that it drives is modeled by a half-edge, also known as a dangling edge since one end is connected to a driven node and the other end does not connect to any node. We let $H(N,e,f)$ denote the graph together with the f half-edges.

The capacitance and conductance (inverse resistance) at node j are C_j and G_j, respectively. We let $V_j(t)$ denote the voltage from node j to ground at time t. The inductance of edge k is L_k, while the current through edge k at time t is $I_k(t)$. The exact dimensions for each component of H, along with the currents and voltages, are tabulated in Table 2.

Table 2: Summary of the notation used in the paper

Notation	Significance	Size
C	Capacitance at node	$N \times 1$
L	Inductance of edge	$(e+f) \times 1$
G	Conductance at node	$N \times 1$
V	Voltage at node	$N \times 1$
I	Current through edge	$(e+f) \times 1$
W	Input forcing	$N \times 1$
B	Signed incidence matrix	$N \times (e+f)$

In order to write down Kirchhoff's laws, we must choose an orientation of the edges. The orientation of an edge records the direction of positive current flow through the edge. If we solve the problem with opposite orientations, the only difference we will notice is that the currents will pick up a factor of -1. Consequently, the orientation we choose does not affect the solution in any material way. In what follows, we will choose a random orientation of the edges.

In Figure 4 we show an example graph corresponding to H(6,9,2). The edges are oriented randomly. The inputs are connected at nodes 1 and 6 through two inductors. These input nodes correspond to half-edges in H. On the right we view node 3 in detail. Each of the two edges connected to this node correspond

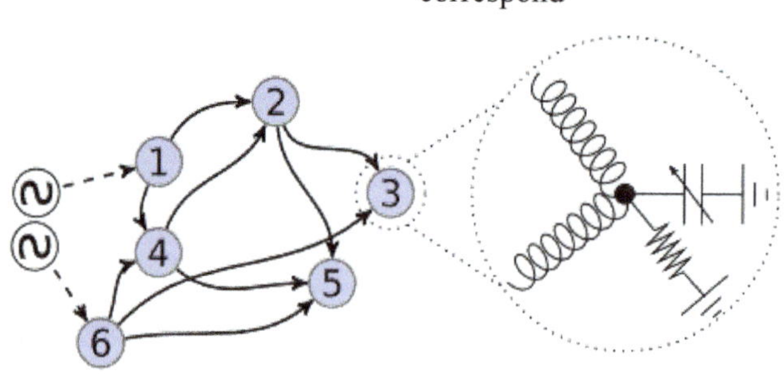

Figure 4: An example of a nonlinear electrical network.

To arrange Kirchhoff's laws compactly, we use the $N \times (e+f)$ incidence matrix of $H(N,e,f)$, denoted by B. Let j be an edge connecting the nodes i' and i. If j is oriented such that positive current starts at node i' and flows to node i, we write $j=(i',i)$. If j is a half-edge attached to node i, we write $j=(\varnothing,i)$, leaving the first slot empty and orienting the half-edge so it always points toward the forced node. The entries of the incidence matrix B are

$$B_{i,j} = \begin{cases} 1 & \text{if } j=(i',i) \text{ for some node } i' \text{ or } i'=\varnothing \\ -1 & \text{if } j=(i,i') \text{ for some node } i' \\ 0 & \text{otherwise.} \end{cases}$$

This paper will only consider single frequency time-harmonic forcing of the form $ae^{i\omega t}+\bar{a}e^{-i\omega t}$ where $a\in\mathbb{C}^N$. Let P be an $N\times(e+f)$ matrix with entries $P_{i,j}=1$ if node i is connected to an input edge j and 0 otherwise. Using the projection matrix P we define the forcing

$$W(t) = P^{\mathrm{T}}(ae^{i\omega t} + \bar{a}e^{-i\omega t}). \quad (1)$$

Using the notation summarized in Table 2, Kirchhoff's laws for the nonlinear circuit on the graph $H(N,e,f)$ can now be written compactly as

$$L\frac{\mathrm{d}I}{\mathrm{d}t} = -B^{\mathrm{T}}V + W \quad (2)$$

$$C\frac{\mathrm{d}V}{\mathrm{d}t} = BI - GV. \quad (3)$$

Here $L(\mathrm{d}I/\mathrm{d}t)$, $C(\mathrm{d}V/\mathrm{d}t)$, and GV are examples of component-wise multiplication of vectors. For $a,b\in\mathbb{C}^m$, we define $c=ab\in\mathbb{C}^m$ by $c_j=a_jb_j$ for $1\leq j\leq m$. Note that in this case, we can also write $c=diag(a)b$. Here $diag(a)$ is the $m\times m$ matrix that contains the vector a along its diagonal ($[diag(a)]_{ii}=a_i$) and is zero elsewhere.

The formulation (2–3) generalizes previous formulations [25], [38] in which the capacitors were constant and the systems considered were linear.

By differentiating (3) and inserting it into (2), we obtain a second-order system for the voltages:

$$\frac{d}{dt}\left[C\frac{dV}{dt}\right]+G\frac{dV}{dt}+\Delta V=V_{in}. \tag{4}$$

Here

$$V_{in}(t)=B[diag(L)]^{-1}W(t) \tag{5}$$

$$\Delta=B[diag(L)]^{-1}B^{T}. \tag{6}$$

Note that Δ is the weighted Laplacian for the network with edge weights given by reciprocal inductance.

We assume that the capacitance at node i depends on the voltage at node i:

$$C_i(V_i)=C^0(1-\epsilon V_i), \tag{7}$$

where $C^0 \in \mathbb{R}$ is a constant. Note that this choice of capacitance function means that (4) features a quadratic nonlinearity.

We can then formulate the *frequency response problem* for the nonlinear electrical network: given the amplitude vector a and frequency ω for the forcing function (1), determine the steady-state solution $V(t)$ of (4).

Perturbative Algorithm

We first solve the frequency response problem using a perturbative expansion in powers of ε. We use dots to denote differentiation with respect to time. Substituting the capacitance function (7) in (4) and rearranging, we obtain

$$C^0\ddot{V}+G\dot{V}+\Delta V=V_{in}+\frac{\varepsilon C^0}{2}\frac{d^2}{dt^2}[V^2]. \tag{8}$$

We expand

$$V(t)=V_0(t)+\varepsilon V_1(t)+\varepsilon^2V_2(t)+\cdots \tag{9}$$

Inserting (9) into (8), we obtain equations for each order of ε. At zeroth order, we obtain

$$C^0\ddot{V}_0+G\dot{V}_0+\Delta V_0=V_{in}. \tag{10}$$

For $k\geq 1$, the k-th order equation is

$$C^0\ddot{V}_k+G\dot{V}_k+\Delta V_k=C^0\frac{d}{dt}\left[\sum_{m=0}^{k-1}V_{k-1-m}\dot{V}_m\right]. \tag{11}$$

We now solve (10–11). Let us introduce the Fourier transform in time,

$$\hat{\psi}(\alpha)=\int_{-\infty}^{\infty}e^{-i\alpha t}\psi(t)\,dt, \tag{12}$$

with inverse Fourier transform

$$\psi(t)=\frac{1}{2\pi}\int_{-\infty}^{\infty}e^{i\alpha t}\hat{\psi}(\alpha)\,d\alpha. \tag{13}$$

Note that with these definitions,

$$\hat{\dot{\psi}}(\alpha)=i\alpha\hat{\psi}(\alpha).$$

This implies that the Fourier transforms of both sides of (10–11) can be summarized by writing

$$\mathcal{L}(\alpha)\hat{V}_k(\alpha)=\begin{cases}\hat{V}_{in} & k=0\\ -(\alpha^2/2)C^0\hat{\phi}_k(\alpha) & k\geq 1,\end{cases} \tag{14}$$

where $\mathcal{L}(\alpha)$ is the linear operator

$$\mathcal{L}(\alpha)=-\alpha^2\mathrm{diag}(C^0)+i\alpha\,\mathrm{diag}(G)+\Delta, \tag{15}$$

and

$$\phi_k(t)=\sum_{m=0}^{k-1}V_{k-1-m}V_m. \tag{16}$$

By (5) and (1), we see that

$$\hat{V}_{in}=2\pi B[\mathrm{diag}(L)]^{-1}P^{T}(a\delta(\alpha-\omega)+\overline{a}\delta(\alpha+\omega)), \tag{17}$$

where δ is the Dirac delta. Then the $k=0$ branch of (14) yields

$$\hat{V}_0(\alpha)=2\pi[a_{0,1}(\alpha)\delta(\alpha-\omega)+a_{0,-1}(\alpha)\delta(\alpha+\omega)] \tag{18a}$$

$$a_{0,1}(\alpha)=[\mathcal{L}(\alpha)]^{-1}B[\mathrm{diag}(L)]^{-1}P^{T}a \tag{18b}$$

$$a_{0,-1}(\alpha)=[\mathcal{L}(\alpha)]^{-1}B[\mathrm{diag}(L)]^{-1}P^{T}\overline{a}. \tag{18c}$$

Using the inverse Fourier transform, we have

$$V_0(t)=a_{0,1}(\omega)e^{i\omega t}+a_{0,-1}(-\omega)e^{-i\omega t}$$
$$=a_{0,1}(\omega)e^{i\omega t}+\text{c.c.},$$

where "c.c." stands for the complex conjugate of the previous terms. Here we have used the property that $\mathcal{L}(-\alpha)=\overline{\mathcal{L}(\alpha)}$.

Once we have computed $V_0(t)$, we can insert it into (16) to compute $\phi_1(t)$. We will find that $\phi_1(t)$ is a linear combination of $e^{-2i\omega t}$, $e^{0i\omega t}$, and $e^{2i\omega t}$. Using this fact in the $k=1$ branch of (14), we can solve for $\hat{V}_1(\alpha)$ and then apply the inverse Fourier transform to compute $V_1(t)$. We will find that $V_1(t)$ contains the same modes as $\phi_1(t)$.

The above shows how we get the perturbative solution algorithm started. Now let us move to the more general case where we seek $V_k(t)$ for any $k\geq 1$. Assume that we have already computed $V_j(t)$ for $0\leq j\leq k-1$, and that the solution takes the following form:

$$V_{2m}(t)=\sum_{\ell=0}^{m}a_{2m,2\ell+1}e^{(2\ell+1)i\omega t}+\text{c.c.} \tag{19a}$$

$$V_{2m+1}(t)=\sum_{\ell=0}^{m+1}a_{2m+1,2\ell}e^{(2\ell)i\omega t}+\text{c.c.} \tag{19b}$$

In words, V_{2m} contains odd modes $1,3,\ldots,2m+1$, and V_{2m+1} contains even modes $0,2,\ldots,2m+2$. Here we assume that $0\leq 2m<2m+1\leq k-1$, and that the $a_{i,j}\in\mathbb{C}^N$ coefficients are known.

In order to solve for $V_k(t)$, we use the $k\geq 1$ branch of (14), which requires us to compute (16). We have two cases, when k is odd and when k is even. In both cases, it is a simple (if tedious) algebraic exercise to show that $\phi_k(t)$ yields:

- when k is odd, a sum of even Fourier modes $-(k+1),\ldots,-2,0,2,\ldots,(k+1)$, and
- when k is even, a sum of odd Fourier modes $-(k+1),\ldots,-3,-1,1,3,\ldots,(k+1)$.

In both cases, it is clear that using (14) to solve for $\hat{V}_k(\alpha)$ results in a sum of Dirac delta›s. Applying the inverse Fourier transform yields $V_k(t)$, which will be a sum of Fourier modes. One can check that $V_k(t)$ will have precisely the form (19a) or (19b) depending on whether k is even or odd, respectively.

The algorithm is then clear. Starting with (19), we apply component-wise multiplication to particular pairs of the $a_{i,j}$ vectors in order to compute the coefficients of the Fourier modes of $\phi_k(t)$ defined in (16). Next, we combine the step of solving for $\hat{V}_k(\alpha)$ using the $k \geq 1$ branch of (14) together with the step of computing the inverse Fourier transform. After component-wise multiplication of the Fourier coefficients of ϕ_k by $-(\alpha^2/2)C^0$, we multiply each coefficient on the left by $[\mathcal{L}(\alpha)]^{-1}$ with α set to match the frequency of the corresponding Fourier mode. Dividing these coefficients by 2π yields the Fourier coefficients of $V_k(t)$, as desired.

While we have presented the algorithm in an intuitive way, the statements made above can be made rigorous, and a convergence theory for the perturbative expansion (9) can be established. This is the subject of ongoing work.

There are a few brief remarks to make about the algorithm presented above:

- As described above, we consider only those networks that contain resistance at all nodes, i.e., $G_i > 0$for all nodes i. Such an assumption is not only physically realistic; it also guarantees that for all $\alpha \in \mathbb{R}$, the matrix $\mathcal{L}(\alpha)$ is invertible. The invertibility for the $\alpha = 0$ case is a consequence of Corollary 1 proved below.
- In this work, we are interested in the weakly nonlinear regime where $\varepsilon\|a\|$ is sufficiently small such that the perturbative method converges. As the nondimensional constant $\varepsilon\|a\|$ is increased beyond the breakdown point of the perturbative method, direct numerical solutions of the equations of motion reveal subharmonic oscillations, and eventually, chaotic oscillations.
- The fact that the Fourier transform yields the steady-state solution has been explained in our earlier work [7]. By fixing an arbitrary set of initial conditions and using the Laplace transform to derive the full solution, one can show that after the decay of transients, the part of the solution that remains is precisely what we obtain using the Fourier transform. This also explains why it was not necessary for us to specify initial conditions for (4) in our derivation above—the initial conditions only influence the decaying transient part of the solution.

Iterative Algorithm

The perturbative method developed above shows us that the solution $V(t)$ is a sum of harmonics where the fundamental frequency is given by the input frequency ω. This implies that the steady-state solution $V(t)$ is periodic with period $T = 2\pi/\omega$. This observation leads us to ask whether it is possible to directly solve for the Fourier coefficients of $V(t)$ without first expanding in powers of ϵ. In this section, we develop a fixed point iteration scheme that accomplishes this task.

First, we integrate both sides of (8) from $t = 0$ to $t = T$ to derive

$$\Delta \int_0^T V(t)\mathrm{d}t = 0. \tag{20}$$

We show below that as long as the network contains at least one half-edge, Δ is invertible. Hence (20) implies

$$\int_0^T V(t)\mathrm{d}t = 0. \tag{21}$$

This means there is no zero/DC mode present in $V(t)$, motivating the Fourier series expansion

$$V(t) = \sum_{k=1}^{\infty} \alpha_k e^{ik\omega t} + \text{c.c.} \tag{22}$$

In order to compute the solution, we truncate at $k = M$, leading to an approximation $\underline{V} \approx V$:

$$\underline{V}(t) = \sum_{k=1}^{M} \alpha_k e^{ik\omega t} + \text{c.c.} \tag{23}$$

Using orthogonality we derive

$$\alpha_k = \frac{1}{T}\int_0^T e^{-ik\omega t}\underline{V}(t)\mathrm{d}t.$$

Using the T-periodicity of V and integration by parts, we have

$$\frac{1}{T}\int_0^T e^{-ik\omega t}\dot{\underline{V}}(t)\mathrm{d}t = ik\omega\alpha_k.$$

To simplify notation, we combine (1) and (5) and write $V_{\text{in}} = we^{i\omega t} + \text{c.c.}$ where

$$w = B[\text{diag}(L)]^{-1}P^{\mathrm{T}}a. \tag{24}$$

Now let $\delta_{m,n}$ denote the Kronecker delta function which equals 1 if $m = n$, and 0 otherwise. We multiply both sides of (8) by $e^{-ik\omega t}$, integrate from $t = 0$ to $t = T$, and finally divide by T to obtain

$$\mathcal{L}(k\omega)\alpha_k = w\delta_{k,1} + \overline{w}\delta_{k,-1} + \frac{\varepsilon C^0 (ik\omega)^2}{2}\widetilde{\underline{V^2}}_k, \tag{25}$$

where $\mathcal{L}$ was defined in (15) and

$$\widetilde{\underline{V^2}}_k = \frac{1}{T}\int_0^T e^{-ik\omega t}\underline{V}^2\mathrm{d}t. \tag{26}$$

Because the form of the nonlinearity is simple, we can insert (23) into (26) and derive

$$\widetilde{\underline{V^2}}_k = \sum_{\ell=-M}^{M} \alpha_\ell \alpha_{k-\ell}, \tag{27}$$

with the understanding that $\alpha_0 = 0$, $\alpha_{-j} = \overline{\alpha_j}$ for $j > 0$, and $\alpha_j = 0$ for $|j| > M$. We insert (27) into (25) and obtain

$$\mathcal{L}(k\omega)\alpha_k = w\delta_{k,1} + \overline{w}\delta_{k,-1} - \frac{\varepsilon C^0 k^2\omega^2}{2}\sum_{\ell=-M}^{M}\alpha_\ell\alpha_{k-\ell}.$$

We convert this into an iterative scheme in a natural way. Let $\alpha_k^{(j)}$ denote the j-th iterate, and assume that α_k terms appearing on the left-hand side are at iteration $j+1$, while those appearing on the right-hand side are at iteration j. Let $\mathbf{A}^{(j)}$ denote the $N \times M$ complex matrix whose k-th column is $\alpha_k^{(j)}$. Then the scheme is

$$\mathbf{A}^{(j+1)} = F^M(\mathbf{A}^{(j)}) \tag{28}$$

where the k-th column of the matrix $F^M(\mathbf{A}^{(j)})$ is

$$F_k^M(\mathbf{A}^{(j)}) = [\mathcal{L}(k\omega)]^{-1}\left(w\delta_{k,1} - \frac{\varepsilon C^0 k^2\omega^2}{2}\sum_{\ell=-M}^{M}\alpha_\ell^{(j)}\alpha_{k-\ell}^{(j)}\right). \tag{29}$$

Here we assume $1 \leq k \leq M$, which is also why we have deleted the second Kronecker delta from the right-hand side.

Starting at $\mathbf{A}^{(0)}$, we iterate forward using (28), stopping the computation when $\|F(\mathbf{A}^{(j)}) - \mathbf{A}^{(j)}\|$ is below a specified tolerance. Note that in our implementation of F, we precompute and store the LU factorization for the M matrices $\{\mathcal{L}(k\omega)\}_{k=1}^{M}$, since this part of the computation of the right-hand side of (29) does not change from one iteration to the next.

Again, we have derived the algorithm but have not proven its convergence. Instead, we will demonstrate empirically that the algorithm converges using several numerical tests.

Inverse Problem

In this section, we consider the inverse problem of finding a set of inductances such that Δ, the Laplacian defined by (6), achieves a desired spectrum. Before describing an algorithm to solve this inverse problem, we review basic spectral properties of Δ.

Lemma 1. *Assume all inductances are positive. Then Δ as defined in (6) is symmetric positive semidefinite, and all its eigenvalues must be nonnegative.*

Proof. Let $[\mathrm{diag}(L)]^{-1/2}$ be the diagonal matrix whose (i,i)-th element on the diagonal is $L_i^{-1/2}$, for $1 \leq i \leq e$. Since $L_i > 0$, the matrix $\Delta^{1/2} = B[\mathrm{diag}(L)]^{-1/2}$ is real. Then $\Delta = \Delta^{1/2}(\Delta^{1/2})^{\mathrm{T}}$, and for any $v \in \mathbb{R}^N$, we have $v^{\mathrm{T}}\Delta v = \left[(\Delta^{1/2})^{\mathrm{T}} v\right]^{\mathrm{T}} (\Delta^{1/2})^{\mathrm{T}} v \geq 0$.

Let $\{\lambda_i\}_{i=1}^N$ denote the spectrum of Δ, with eigenvalues arranged in nondecreasing order: $\lambda_1 \leq \lambda_2 \leq \cdots \leq \lambda_N$. The above argument shows that $\lambda_1 \geq 0$. We can be more precise about this: if there are no half-edges, then $\lambda_1 = 0$, while the presence of at least one half-edge causes $\lambda_1 > 0$.

Lemma 2. *Let $\mathcal{H} = H(N,e)$ be a connected graph with N nodes, e edges, and zero half-edges. For a particular orientation of the graph, let B denote the signed incidence matrix. Then $\mathrm{rank}(B) = N - 1$.*

Proof. Let r be any integer from 1 to $N-1$. Consider any subset S of r vertices of the graph. Take the sum of the rows of the incidence matrix corresponding to the elements of S. This sum cannot be zero; if it were, there would be no path connecting S to the complement S^c and the resulting graph would not be connected. Hence the sum of these rows must contain a nonzero entry. As the same would be true if we considered linear combinations of the rows corresponding to S, we conclude that any subset of at most $N-1$ rows must be linearly independent. At the same time, if we take the sum of all the rows we get a zero row, because each column contains precisely one $+1$ and one -1.

Lemma 3. *Let $\mathcal{H}' = H(N,e,f)$ be a connected graph with N nodes, e edges, and $f > 0$ half-edges. For a particular orientation of the graph, let B' denote the signed incidence matrix. Then $\mathrm{rank}(B') = N$.*

Proof. Without loss of generality, we can assume that the $N \times (e+f)$ incidence matrix B' is organized such that the first e columns correspond to full edges, while columns $e+1, \ldots, e+f$ correspond to half-edges. Now choose any j such that $1 \leq j \leq f$, and examine column $e+j$ of B. Let k be the unique row in which this column contains ± 1. Since row k of B is the only row that contains an entry in column $e+j$, row k is linearly independent from the other $N-1$ rows of B. By Lemma 2, the submatrix of B consisting of all rows other than row k has rank $N-1$. Including row k increases the rank by one, yielding a rank N matrix.

Lemma 4. *For a connected graph $\mathcal{H}' = H(N,e,f)$ with N nodes, e edges, and $f > 0$ half-edges, let Δ be the edge-weighted graph Laplacian defined in (6). Assume all inductances are positive. Then $\mathrm{rank}(\Delta) = N$.*

Proof. The $(e+f) \times (e+f)$ diagonal matrix $[\mathrm{diag}(L)]^{-1}$ has rank $e+f > N$. Let B be the signed incidence matrix for a particular orientation of $\mathcal{H}'$. By Lemma 3, $\mathrm{rank}(B) = N$, implying $\mathrm{rank}(B[\mathrm{diag}(L)]^{-1/2}) = N$, which implies $\mathrm{rank}(\Delta) = \mathrm{rank}\left[(B[\mathrm{diag}(L)]^{-1/2})(B[\mathrm{diag}(L)]^{-1/2})^{\mathrm{T}}\right] = N$.

Corollary 1. *Let $\mathcal{H}'$, Δ and the inductances satisfy the hypotheses of Lemma 4. Then Δ is symmetric positive definite and all eigenvalues of Δ are positive, i.e., $0 < \lambda_1 \leq \lambda_2 \leq \cdots \leq \lambda_N$.*

Proof. Combine Lemmas 1 and 4.

We now describe an algorithm that quantifies how we must change the vector of inductances L in order to make Δ have a desired set of eigenvalues. In what follows, we assume we work with a system that satisfies the hypotheses of Corollary 1.

For $n \leq N$, let $\lambda^* = (\lambda_1^*, \ldots, \lambda_n^*)^{\mathrm{T}}$ denote a vector of desired eigenvalues satisfying

$0 < \lambda_1^* \leq \lambda_2^* \leq \cdots \leq \lambda_n^*$.

We treat the vector of inductances L as a variable, and let $\lambda(L)$ denote the sorted vector of eigenvalues of the graph Laplacian Δ defined in (6). Since Δ is symmetric, it possesses an orthonormal basis of eigenvectors. We assume that $v_j(L)$ is the normalized eigenvector corresponding to $\lambda_j(L)$.

Now let $\mathcal{F} : \mathbb{R}^{e+f} \to \mathbb{R}^n$ be the function

$$\mathcal{F}(L) = \begin{bmatrix} \lambda_1(L) \\ \lambda_2(L) \\ \vdots \\ \lambda_n(L) \end{bmatrix} - \begin{bmatrix} \lambda_1^* \\ \lambda_2^* \\ \vdots \\ \lambda_n^* \end{bmatrix}. \tag{30}$$

We now apply a version of Newton's method to find a zero of this function. To use Newton's method we will need to compute the Jacobian $J(\mathcal{F}(L))$. Let primes denote differentiation with respect to L_k. To form the Jacobian we need to find

$$\lambda_j' := \frac{\partial}{\partial L_k} \lambda_j(L).$$

We proceed by implicit differentiation, starting from the eigenvector equation

$$\Delta v_j(L) = B[\mathrm{diag}(L)]^{-1} B^{\mathrm{T}} v_j(L) = \lambda_j(L) v_j(L).$$

Differentiating both sides with respect to L_k, and omitting the dependence on L, we obtain

$$B([\mathrm{diag}(L)]^{-1})' B^{\mathrm{T}} v_j + B[\mathrm{diag}(L)]^{-1} B^{\mathrm{T}} v_j' = \lambda_j' v_j + \lambda_j v_j'. \tag{31}$$

Since Δ is symmetric,

$$v_j^{\mathrm{T}} B[\mathrm{diag}(L)]^{-1} B^{\mathrm{T}} = (B[\mathrm{diag}(L)]^{-1} B^{\mathrm{T}} v_j)^{\mathrm{T}} = (\lambda_j v_j)^{\mathrm{T}} = v_j^{\mathrm{T}} \lambda_j. \tag{32}$$

Multiplying (34) on the left by v_j^{T} and using (35) together with $(v_j)^{\mathrm{T}} v_j = 1$, we obtain

$$v_j^{\mathrm{T}} B([\mathrm{diag}(L)]^{-1})' B^{\mathrm{T}} v_j = \lambda_j', \tag{33}$$

where

$$([\mathrm{diag}(L)]^{-1})' := \frac{\partial}{\partial L_k}([\mathrm{diag}(L)]^{-1}) = \left[0, 0, \cdots, -\frac{1}{L_k^2}, \cdots, 0\right]^{\mathrm{T}}.$$

Using λ_j^i we can compute the entries of the Jacobian matrix and the corresponding Newton›s method with pseudoinverse becomes

$$L^{(i+1)} = L^{(i)} - [J(\mathcal{F}(L))]^{\dagger}\mathcal{F}(L) \quad (34)$$

where $\dagger$ denotes the Moore-Penrose pseudoinverse.

Using (34) as shown might produce inductances such that the ratio of the largest to smallest inductance is too large. In order to avoid these large variations, we constrain $\epsilon^{-1} \leq L_i \leq \epsilon$. We incorporate these constraints using an active set approach, replacing $\mathcal{F}$ by the function $\mathcal{G}^i : \mathbb{R}^{e+f+m} \to \mathbb{R}^{n+m}$, where i denotes the iteration number and m denotes the number of constraints violated by $L^{(i)}$. Let $\mathcal{Q}^{\pm}$ denote the functions

$$\mathcal{Q}^{+}(x) = \begin{cases} \frac{1}{2}x^2 & x>0 \\ 0 & x \leq 0, \end{cases} \quad \text{and} \quad \mathcal{Q}^{-}(x) = \begin{cases} 0 & x \geq 0 \\ \frac{1}{2}x^2 & x<0. \end{cases} \quad (35)$$

For every constraint p violated from below, we set $\mathcal{G}_p^i(L) = \mathcal{Q}^{-}(L_p - \epsilon^{-1})$. For every constraint q violated from above, we set $\mathcal{G}_q^i(L) = \mathcal{Q}^{+}(L_q - \epsilon)$. Since the $\mathcal{Q}^{\pm}$ functions are continuously differentiable, it is easy to compute the Jacobian $J(\mathcal{G}^i(L))$ and then apply the algorithm

$$L^{(i+1)} = L^{(i)} - \left[J(\mathcal{G}^i(L))\right]^{\dagger}(\mathcal{G}^i(L)).$$

(36)

Algorithm (36) can be used to alter all the eigenvalues of the system if $n = N$ and $\lambda^* \in \mathbb{R}^N$. Alternatively, one can set $n = 2$ and only request the two smallest eigenvalues to be changed to λ_1^* and λ_2^*, respectively.

In the next section we show that altering the lowest eigenvalue λ_1 is enough to cause higher energy transfer to the higher modes. To show, we will use (39) to change λ_1 to some desired value, keeping λ_2 constant. We note that since we do not constrain $\lambda_3, \cdots, \lambda_N$, they can change as a result of altering L, but $\lambda_2 \leq \lambda_j$ for $j \in \{3, \cdots, N\}$ will be maintained.

For all applications of this inverse problem algorithm described in the next section, we use (36) with the initial conditions $L^{(0)} = [1, 1, \ldots, 1]^{\mathrm{T}}$ and the constraint violation parameter $\epsilon = 10^3$.

Gap Tuning: Methodology

How does the steady-state voltage in the nonlinear circuit change as a function of the gap between the first two eigenvalues of the graph Laplacian Δ? In this section, we address this question by combining the perturbative/iterative algorithms with the inverse problem algorithm. We describe numerical experiments designed to test the effect of closing the graph Laplacian's first eigenvalue gap on the circuit's ability to (a) transfer more energy to higher harmonics, and (b) generate higher-amplitude output signals.

We conduct our numerical experiments on three types of random graphs, all generated using the NetworkX package [39]:

- Barabási-Albert (BA), a preferential attachment model with one parameter, m, the number of edges to draw between each new node and existing nodes [40]. We set $m = 3$ in our experiments.
- Watts-Strogatz (WS), a small world model with two parameters, k, the number of nearest neighbor nodes to which each node is initially connected, and p, the probability of rewiring each edge [41]. In our experiments, we set $k = 5$ and $p = 0.3$.
- Erdös-Rényi (ER), a classical model in which edges are drawn independently with uniform probability p [42]. In our experiments, we set $p = 0.25$.

When we produce realizations of any of these graphs, we accept only those graphs that are connected. Suppose we have used one of these three models to generate a connected, random graph with N nodes. To make this a concrete circuit problem, we set $C_i^0 = 1$ for all nodes i, and $L_j = 1$ for all edges j. We fix the nonlinearity parameter $\epsilon = 0.5$. We select $N/10$ nodes uniformly at random, and attach half-edges to these nodes with inductance $L_j = 1$. For each node i, we set the conductance $G_i = 0.15$ for the BA and WS graphs, and $G_i = 0.5$ for the ER graphs. This selection will be explained in more detail below.

With these parameters set, we have enough information to compute the graph Laplacian Δ defined by (6). As we did before, let $\lambda_1, \ldots, \lambda_N$ denote the eigenvalues of Δ sorted in increasing order. We set the forcing frequency $\omega = \sqrt{\lambda_2}$. Since this value is a resonant frequency of the linear, undamped system we expect it lies close to a resonance for the nonlinear, damped system. The type of forcing we consider is $A \sin \omega t$, a special case of (1) with $a = A/(2i)$.

With this setup, we use both the perturbative method and the iterative method to compute the steady-state solution $V(t)$. For the perturbative method, we solve up to order 9, and for the iterative method, we solve using 20 modes. This means that the iterative scheme captures ten modes—11ω through 20ω—that are not captured by the perturbative scheme. We compare the two solutions as a check for whether the number of modes we have considered is sufficient. In all tests, we find that there is no significant difference between the solutions, implying that the first 10 harmonics—ω through 10ω—are sufficient to resolve the solution.

Since $\epsilon = 0.5$, the capacitance model (7) is valid only for $V_i < 2$. For all computed solutions, we check that the maximum voltage across all nodes in one cycle satisfies this constraint.

One quantity of interest in our simulations is the amount of energy in the higher harmonics. Let Ψ be an $N \times M$ complex matrix such that the j-th column of Ψ contains the Fourier coefficients of the $+j\omega$ mode over all N nodes. Here j goes from 1 to M, the maximum mode to which the solution is computed. We then define

$$\kappa_{\text{pre}} = \frac{1}{N} \sum_{n=1}^{N} \frac{\left\| (\Psi_{n2}, \Psi_{n3}, \ldots, \Psi_{nM})^{\mathrm{T}} \right\|_2}{\left\| (\Psi_{n1}, \Psi_{n2}, \ldots, \Psi_{nM})^{\mathrm{T}} \right\|_2}, \quad (37)$$

the fraction of energy in modes $+2\omega$ and higher, averaged over all nodes. We also compute

$$\mathrm{V}_{\text{pre}} = \max_{1 \leq i \leq N} \max_{0 \leq t \leq T} |V_i(t)|, \quad (38)$$

the maximum magnitude voltage produced anywhere in the circuit during one period. For both κ and V, the subscript "pre" denotes that these quantities have been computed before we change L to manipulate the eigenvalues of Δ.

Having computed κ_{pre}, we now study how this fraction changes when we reduce the gap between the first two eigenvalues of Δ. For a fixed $\delta \in (0,1)$, we set $\lambda_1^* = \delta\lambda_2$ and $\lambda_2^* = \lambda_2$, and then apply the inverse problem algorithm.

Using (36), we solve for a vector of inductances L^* such

that the first two eigenvalues of Δ are given by λ_1^* and λ_2^*. When we iterate forward using (36), if we find that $\|\mathcal{G}^i(L)\|_2 \geq 10^{-12}$ after 200 iterations, we generate a new random graph and restart the experiment.

We recompute the graph Laplacian Δ using the new vector inductances L^*, and again apply the perturbative and iterative algorithms to solve for the steady-state solution $V(t)$. Using this solution, we compute the energy in the higher harmonics using the right-hand side of (37), now labeling this average fraction as κ_{post}. We also compute the right-hand side of (38) and label this quantity as V_{post}.

Let us now describe how we choose the particular values of the conductance G_i and the eigenvalue fraction δ. In Table 3, we tabulate $\lambda_2 - \lambda_1$, the gap between the second and first eigenvalue for each of the three types of random graphs described above. The eigenvalue gaps we present are averaged over 200 simulations for each of four graph sizes: $N \in \{25, 75, 125, 175\}$.

Table 3: Eigenvalue gaps for random graphs

	$N=25$	$N=75$	$N=125$	$N=175$
Barabási-Albert (BA)	0.6408	0.3561	0.3155	0.2850
Watts-Strogatz (WS)	1.4180	1.3255	1.2970	1.2758
Erdös-Rényi (ER)	1.5469	8.6936	17.7061	26.5297

We observe that the eigenvalue gaps for the BA and WS graphs do not change appreciably as a function of N, while for ER graphs, the gaps grow quickly as a function of N. Our choice of δ is guided by these results. For BA and WS graphs, we choose $\delta \in [0.5, 0.99]$. For ER graphs, we choose $\delta \in [0.25, 0.75]$.

When we solve for the steady-state voltages on these three types of graphs, we also notice a difference. For ER graphs, the maximum voltage grows quickly as a function of N, while for BA and WS graphs, the same phenomenon does not occur. To counteract the large growth of maximum voltages for large graph sizes, we set the conductance G_i to the larger value of 0.5 for ER graphs, causing more energy to dissipate through resistors. For BA and WS graphs, we set G_i to 0.15.

RESULTS AND DISCUSSION

Comparison of Steady-State Algorithms

In this section, we compare steady-state solutions computed by numerical integration against the solutions computed using the perturbative and iterative methods derived earlier.

For the tests described in this section, the domain is a 20×20 square lattice with $N=400$ nodes. Nodes along the left and bottom boundaries of the lattice are driven by input forcing. The input provided is $0.03 \sin(\omega t)$ with $\omega = 1$. For the capacitance model (7), we set $C^0 = 1$ and $\epsilon = 0.5$. For each edge j, we set $L_j = 1$. The conductance G_i is set to 0.01 at all points except for the top-right corner, where it is set to 1.0.

To compare the results of the perturbative and iterative methods against the numerical integrator, we will need to obtain the steady-state solution using the numerical integrator. To do this, we start at $t=0$ and numerically integrate the first-order system (2–3) forward in time for 1500 cycles. The ODE solver uses the Dormand-Prince (*dopri5*) method with relative and absolute tolerances equal to 10^{-10} and 10^{-12}, respectively. For the parameters given above, this number of cycles is sufficient so that, from one cycle to the next, the change in the solution is on the order of the relative tolerance of the numerical integrator. Hence we take the solution over the last cycle to be the steady-state solution.

As a preliminary check, we directly compare the three steady-state solutions. We treat the solution obtained from numerical time integration as a reference solution $z^{\text{ref}}(t)$. Let $z^{(i)}(t)$ denote either the perturbative or iterative solution after i iterations—for the perturbative method, the iteration count is defined as the largest mode number present in the solution. Let T be the period of the steady-state solution, and for an integer $\tau > 0$, consider the equispaced discretization of the interval $[0, T]$ given by $\{t_k = kT/\tau\}_{k=1}^{k=\tau}$. For each iteration i, we evaluate both the the perturbative/iterative and reference solution on this equispaced grid with $\tau = 64$ points, and we compute the error

$$E(i) = \left[\frac{1}{\tau}\sum_{j=1}^{N}\sum_{k=1}^{\tau}\left(z_j^{(i)}(t_k) - z_j^{\text{ref}}(t_k)\right)^2\right]^{1/2}. \tag{39}$$

In Figure 5 we have plotted $\log_{10} E(i)$ as a function of the iteration i. While both methods initially tend towards the reference solution, we see from Figure 5 that the error does not drop below 10^{-9}. In the following subsections, we provide evidence that the reference solution is less accurate than the solutions computed using the perturbative/iterative methods. This explains why the error in Figure 5 does not go to zero, i.e., why the perturbative/iterative methods will not converge to the solution produced by time integration.

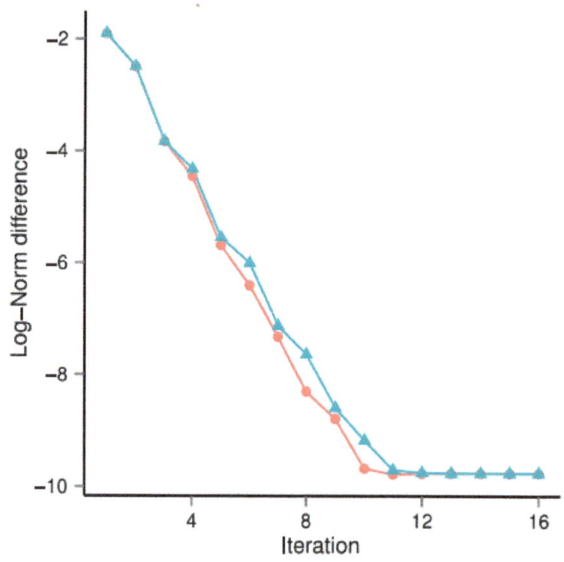

Figure 5: Error between perturbative/iterative solutions and reference solution.

Our first tests concern the Fourier coefficients of the computed solutions. In what follows, we use $\mathbf{A}$ to denote the vector of Fourier series coefficients associated with a steady-state solution computed using any of the three methods discussed above.

Fixed Point Error

Suppose that $V(t)$ is an exact T-periodic steady-state solution of (4). If we were to expand this solution in a Fourier series as in (22), the resulting (infinite) coefficient vector $\mathbf{A}$ would satisfy $\mathbf{A}=F_k^{\infty}(\mathbf{A})$ for all k, with F as in (29).

In both the perturbative and iterative methods, what we seek is a finite-mode truncation of the exact solution. For the iterative method we fix $M=20$ so that the highest mode has frequency 20ω. In the perturbative method we solve, we solve up to order 19, which implies that the highest mode in the solution has frequency 20ω.

Combining the ideas of the last two paragraphs, it is natural to use

$$\mathcal{E}_M(\mathbf{A}) = \max_{1\le k\le M} \|\alpha_k - F_k^M(\mathbf{A})\|_\infty \tag{40}$$

as an error metric for the M-mode truncation of the exact solution. In Table 4, we record (40) for solutions computed using the perturbative, iterative, and numerical integration methods. Note that the iterative and perturbative methods directly provide us with the Fourier coefficients necessary for this calculation. We compute the Fourier coefficients of the numerical integrator's solution using the FFT. Table 4 shows that the perturbative and iterative solutions are about five orders of magnitude closer to being fixed points of F_k^M than the solution obtained from numerical integration.

Table 4: Comparison of the three solutions using the fixed point error metric (40)

Scheme	$\max_{1\le k\le M}\|\alpha_k - F_k^M(\mathbf{A})\|_\infty$
Numerical	2.035×10^{-11}
Perturbative	3.4321×10^{-16}
Iterative	2.7144×10^{-16}

For the perturbative and iterative methods, let us examine how the fixed point error (40) decreases as a function of iteration count. In Figure 6, we plot $\log\mathcal{E}_M(\mathbf{A}^{(i)})$ versus the iteration number i. Here $\mathbf{A}^{(i)}$ is the vector of Fourier coefficients for the solution computed after only i iterations. The plot shows that, for both the perturbative and iterative methods, approximately 10 iterations are required to match the fixed point error of the solution computed using time integration. The error of this latter solution, taken from Table 4, is represented on Figure 6 by a horizontal black line.

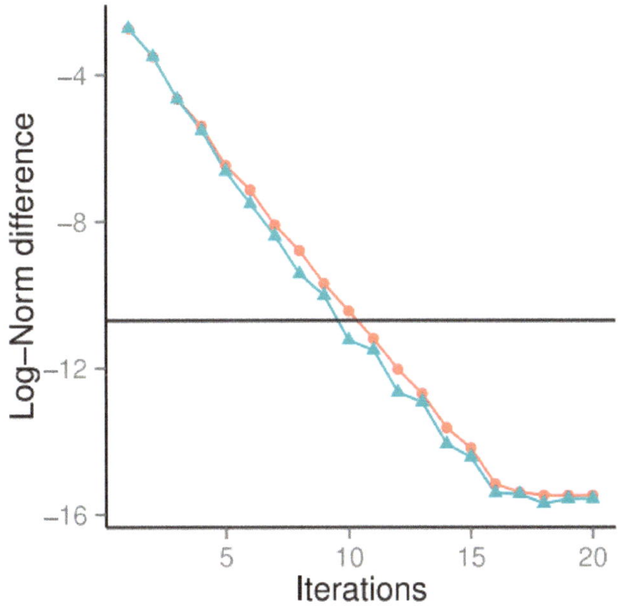

Figure 6: Log of the fixed point error (40) of the perturbative/iterative solutions after i iterations.

Figure 6 also shows that the perturbative and iterative methods converge exponentially in the number of iterations. From iteration 1 until iteration 16, fitting lines of best fit to the perturbative and iterative error curves results in slopes of -2.1407 and -2.2326, respectively. For both methods, this can be approximated by writing $\mathcal{E}_M(\mathbf{A}^{(i)})\sim e^{-2i}$. After 16 iterations, the error has approached machine epsilon, and both curves level off before reaching the final values shown in Table 4.

Decay Rate

Suppose we write the first-order system (2–3) in the form $\dot{\mathbf{z}}=\mathbf{F}(\mathbf{z},t)$, with $\mathbf{z}=(I,V)^{\mathrm{T}}$. Then on the open set $\mathcal{D}=\{I\in\mathbb{R}^{e+f}, V\in\mathbb{R}^{N}, t\in\mathbb{R} \mid |V_i|<\epsilon^{-1}, 1\leq i\leq N\}$, the vector field $\mathbf{F}:\mathcal{D}\rightarrow\mathbb{R}^{e+f+N}$ is C^∞, i.e., $\mathbf{F}$ is j times continuously differentiable for any integer $j\geq 1$. By the standard existence/uniqueness theorem for ordinary differential equations, it follows that wherever the solution $\mathbf{z}(t)=(I(t),V(t))^{\mathrm{T}}$ exists, it must also be C^∞ in t.

The above observation enables us to test the decay of the Fourier coefficients of all three solutions. For if the steady-state solution $V(t)$ is C^∞ in t, then the Fourier series coefficients of V must satisfy the following decay property:

For all $\ell\geq 1$, there exists C_ℓ such that $\|\alpha_k\|\leq C_\ell k^{-\ell}$. (41)

To examine the decay of the Fourier coefficients for the three computed solutions, we plot $\log\|\alpha_k\|$ versus k in Figure 7. For the perturbative and iterative solutions, the curves on the plot coincide and are nearly linear with slope -2.8004. This implies that $\|\alpha_k\|\sim e^{-2.8k}$, which is sufficient to satisfy the theoretical decay rate given by (41).

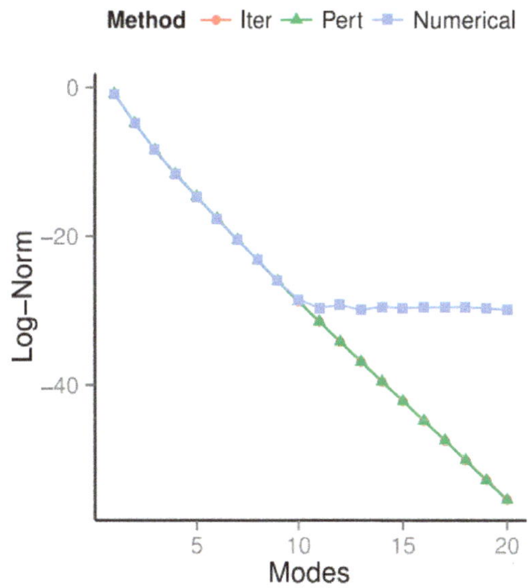

Figure 7: **Decay of Fourier coefficients.**

The Fourier coefficients obtained from the numerical integrator's solution, on the other hand, do not decay at all beyond mode 10. This violates the theoretical decay rate (41) even for $\ell=1$.

Energy Conservation

Next we test the energy conservation properties of the three computed solutions. We proceed to derive an energy balance equation. Because our capacitors are voltage-dependent, the charge Q and voltage V are related via $\mathrm{d}Q=C(V)\mathrm{d}V$, which implies

$$\frac{\mathrm{d}Q}{\mathrm{d}t}=C(V)\frac{\mathrm{d}V}{\mathrm{d}t}.$$

Using this in (3) together with (2), we obtain

$$I^{\mathrm{T}}L\frac{\mathrm{d}I}{\mathrm{d}t}+V^{\mathrm{T}}\frac{\mathrm{d}Q}{\mathrm{d}t}=I^{\mathrm{T}}W-V^{\mathrm{T}}GV. \tag{42}$$

Let $\mathbf{M}(t)$ be the total energy stored in the magnetic fields of all inductors at time t. Then

$$\frac{\mathrm{d}\mathbf{M}}{\mathrm{d}t}:=\frac{\mathrm{d}}{\mathrm{d}t}\left[\frac{1}{2}\sum_{i=1}^{e+f}L_iI_i^2\right]=\sum_{i=1}^{e+f}I_iL_i\frac{\mathrm{d}I_i}{\mathrm{d}t}=I^{\mathrm{T}}L\frac{\mathrm{d}I}{\mathrm{d}t},$$

the first term on the left-hand side of (42). Let $\mathbf{E}(t)$ be the total energy stored in the electric fields of all capacitors at time t. Then

$$\frac{\mathrm{d}\mathbf{E}}{\mathrm{d}t}:=\frac{\mathrm{d}}{\mathrm{d}t}\left[\sum_{i=1}^{N}\int_0^{Q_i(t)}V_i(q)\mathrm{d}q\right]=\sum_{i=1}^{N}V_i\frac{\mathrm{d}Q_i}{\mathrm{d}t}=V^{\mathrm{T}}\frac{\mathrm{d}Q}{\mathrm{d}t},$$

the second term on the left hand side of (42). Hence (42) reads:

$$\frac{\mathrm{d}}{\mathrm{d}t}(\mathbf{M}(t)+\mathbf{E}(t))=I^{\mathrm{T}}W-V^{\mathrm{T}}GV. \tag{43}$$

If the system has reached a T-periodic steady state, then $I(t)$, $V(t)$, $\mathbf{M}(t)$, and $\mathbf{E}(t)$ will all be T-periodic. Therefore, integrating (43) in t from $t=0$ to $t=T$, we find that the left-hand side vanishes. The remaining terms yield the following energy balance equation:

$$\int_0^T I^{\mathrm{T}} W \mathrm{d}t = \int_0^T V^{\mathrm{T}} G V \mathrm{d}t. \tag{44}$$

The left-hand side is the energy pumped into the system over one cycle, while the right-hand side denotes the energy dissipated through resistors, again over one cycle.

Table 5 shows the absolute difference between the left- and right-hand sides of (44), computed for each of the three methods. We find that for the perturbative and iterative methods' energy balance errors are below machine epsilon. The numerical integrator yields an error approximately five orders of magnitude larger than that of the two other methods.

Table 5: Comparison of the three solutions' preservation of the energy balance (44)

Scheme	$\left\|\int_0^T I^{\mathrm{T}} W \mathrm{d}t - \int_0^T V^{\mathrm{T}} G V \mathrm{d}t\right\|$
Numerical	5.7841×10^{-12}
Perturbative	2.1684×10^{-18}
Iterative	1.2576×10^{-18}

Computational Time

The results presented thus far indicate that whether we measure error using the fixed point error (40) or the violation of the energy balance (44), the solution obtained via numerical integration has errors that are approximately five orders of magnitude larger than that of the perturbative/iterative methods. The actual values of the errors committed by the numerical integrator in Tables 4 and and5,5, as well as the final error values for the curves in Figure 5, are close to the numerical integration relative and absolute tolerances of 10^{-10} and 10^{-12} , respectively. We hypothesize that, if computational time were not an issue, we could run the numerical integrator with smaller tolerances and obtain steady-state solutions that more closely match, in the same error metrics described above, the perturbative and iterative solutions.

As we now proceed to show, computational time is a major issue for the time integration method. In Table 6, we record the time required to compute steady-state solutions using the three methods. We see from the Time I column that to achieve the error of $\approx 2 \times 10^{-11}$ in Table 4, the numerical integrator requires over 483 seconds. We know from Figure 6 that the perturbative/iterative methods require 10 iterations to achieve approximately the same error as the time integrator; the remaining entries in the Time I column show that both the perturbative and iterative algorithms compute such a solution hundreds of times faster than the time integrator.

Table 6: **Timing results for three frequency response algorithms**

Scheme	Time I (to achieve comparable error)	Time II (to achieve $O(10^{-16})$ error)
Numerical	483.2126 s	N/A
Perturbative	1.71024 s	7.29115 s
Iterative	0.68374 s	0.89012 s

For the numerical method, Time I records the time required to integrate forward by 1500 cycles and obtain a solution with fixed point error $\approx 2 \times 10^{-11}$ as in Table 4. For the perturbative/iterative methods, Time I records the time required to compute 10 iterations, resulting in a fixed point error comparable to that of the numerical method—see the crossing of the curves with the black horizontal line in Figure 6. For the perturbative/iterative methods, we also record under Time II the time required to achieve the $O(10^{-16})$ errors as in Table 4. All times are averaged over 10 runs.

The Time II column in Table 6 records how long it takes the perturbative/iterative algorithms to achieve the errors recorded in Table 4. Observe that even if we run the perturbative/iterative algorithms all the way to full convergence, they are much faster than time integration. In this case, the time integrator is 542 (respectively, 66) times slower than the iterative (respectively, perturbative) algorithm.

Note that the perturbative and iterative algorithms were implemented in Python using the Numpy/Scipy packages. The *dopri5* implementation used for numerical time integration is the implementation provided by the scipy.integrate.ode module. All times reported are average times across 10 runs on the same machine.

Gap Tuning

For each $N \in \{25, 75, 125, 175\}$, and for each of 10 values δ chosen in an equispaced fashion from the intervals given above, we compute 100 runs of the complete procedure described above—see Gap Tuning: Methodology. For each such run, we compute pre/post values of $\mathcal{K}$ and V for three values of the input forcing amplitude, which we take to be the same at all input nodes k: $A_k \in \{0.001, 0.005, 0.01\}$. These results for $\mathcal{K}$ and V, averaged over the 100 runs, are plotted in Figures 8,9, and 10.

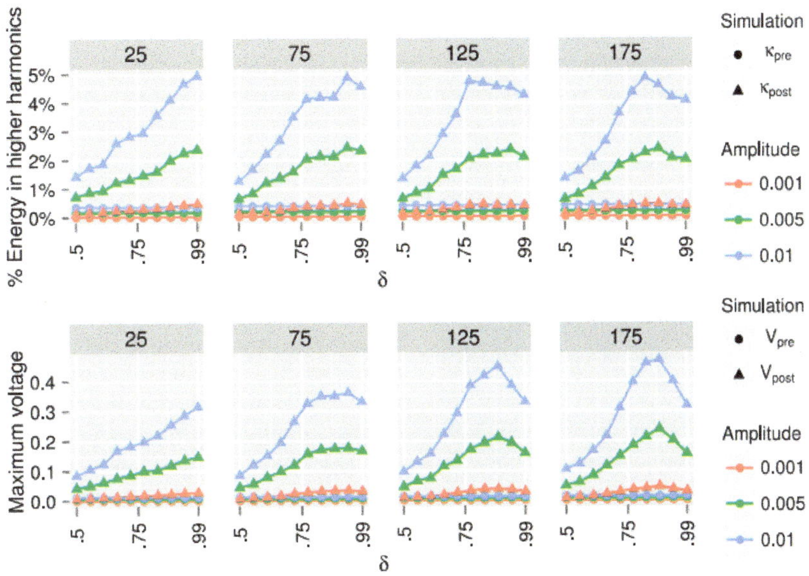

Figure 8: Barabási-Albert random graph results.

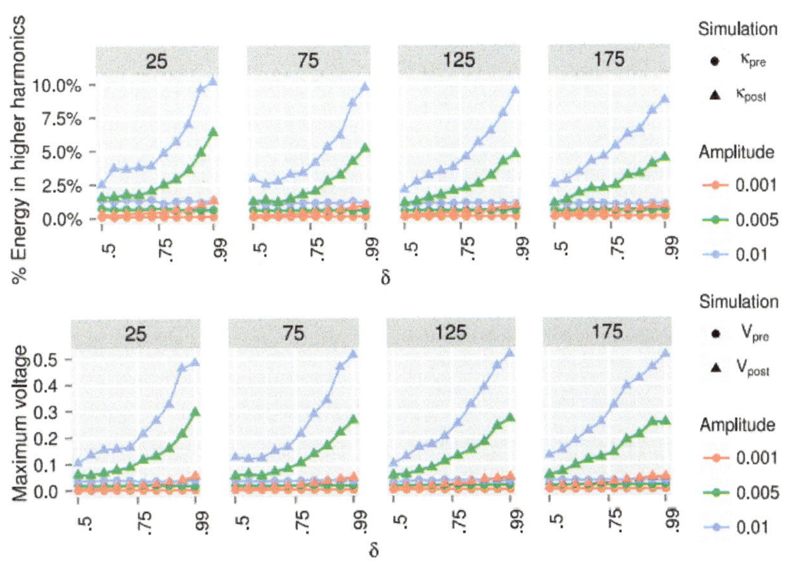

Figure 9: Watts-Strogatz random graph results.

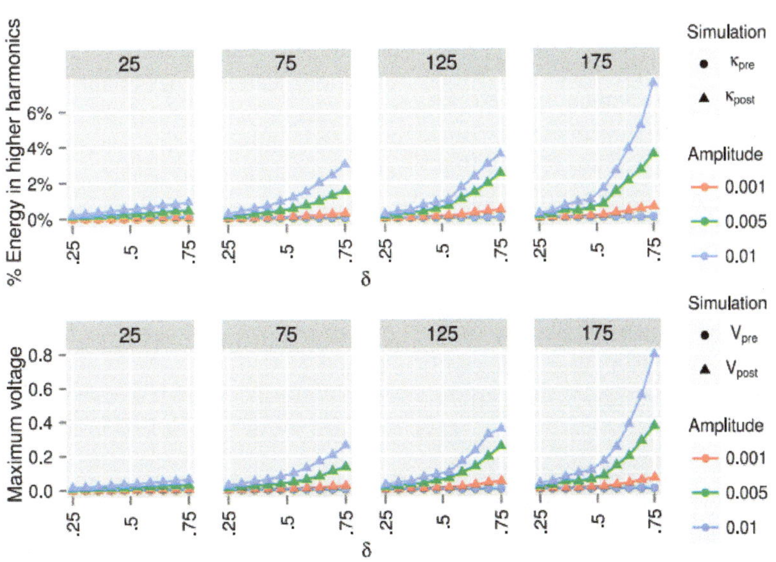

Figure 10: Erdös-Rényi random graph results.

Figure 8 shows the results for Barabási-Albert (BA) graphs. By shrinking the gap between the first two eigenvalues, the percentage of energy transferred to higher harmonics (37) can be increased by approximately one order of magnitude, for all graph sizes, while the maximum magnitude voltage (38) can be increased by a factor of 6 to 20, depending on the graph size. Note that for larger graphs, choosing $\delta = 1$, i.e., forcing the first two eigenvalues to coincide, does not yield optimal energy transfer to higher harmonics.

The results in Figure 9 for Watts-Strogatz (WS) graphs are similar to those for BA graphs. We again find that by shrinking the gap between the first two eigenvalues, the energy transferred to higher harmonics (37) can be increased. However, the values of κ_{post} for Watts-Strogatz graphs are about twice as large as the values of κ_{post} for Barabási-Albert graphs in Figure 8. For all graph sizes, tuning the eigenvalue gap can increase the percentage of energy transferred to higher harmonics by a factor of up to 8, while the maximum magnitude voltage can be increased by approximately one order of magnitude.

In Figure 10, we present the results for Erdös-Rényi graphs. The results again support the finding that by shrinking the gap between the first two eigenvalues, the circuit can transfer more energy to higher harmonics and boost the peak magnitude of output signals. Specifically, we see that the energy transferred to higher harmonics (37) can be increased to $\kappa_{post} \in [1,8]\%$, and the maximum voltage (38) can be increased to $\mathrm{v}_{post} \in [0.1, 0.8]$.

The results for Erdös-Rényi graphs are much more strongly dependent on the number of nodes N than the results shown in Figures 8 or 9. Note that the peak voltages for the $N = 175$ graphs with forcing amplitude 0.01 are the largest voltages for any graphs considered in this paper. We can increase the peak voltages for smaller graphs by choosing a smaller value of the conductance than $G_i = 0.5$ (for all nodes i), the value used to compute the results in Figure 10.

For all three types of graphs, both *pre* and *post* values of κ and v increase as a function of the input forcing amplitude.

Code

All code necessary to reproduce the above results have been posted as a public repository on GitHub, accessible at the following URL: https://github.com/GarnetVaz/Nonlinear-electrical-oscillators

We use Python together with the numpy, scipy, matplotlib, and networkx modules for all numerical computing. The code that generates Figures 8,9, and10 is set to utilize 10 processors using the open-source multiprocessing module. For plotting, we use R together with the ggplot2, plyr, and reshape packages. All languages, packages and modules used are open source.

Assuming all packages and modules have been correctly installed, one can reproduce all results by running the Python codes numerical_comparison.py and graphmulti.py. The latter code may require several hours to run. The Python codes will generate figures using R; the R codes we provide need not be run independently.

Further details on how to run the codes, including the specific versions of required packages and modules, are given in the README.md file at the URL given above.

The code that we provide can easily be modified to run simulations not described here. For example, one can compare the perturbative/iterative algorithms against numerical integration using graphs other than the 20×20 grid graph used above. One can also explore gap tuning results for random graphs with different parameters than the ones we have chosen.

CONCLUSION

For nonlinear electrical circuits on arbitrary connected graphs, we have developed two numerical methods to compute the steady-state voltage. Using both absolute metrics and relative comparisons with a solution obtained via direct numerical integration, we validated the new algorithms. The results show that for the same error tolerance, both the perturbative and iterative methods are orders of magnitude faster than the solution obtained by time stepping. Moreover, these methods are able to capture the behavior in high Fourier modes and converge to machine precision in a fixed point error metric.

In future work, we plan to apply the steady-state algorithms developed above to solve Maxwell's equations in nonlinear electromagnetic media [26]. This application makes use of the correspondence between the nonlinear electrical network and a finite volume discretization of Maxwell's equations on an unstructured mesh.

In order to enhance the nonlinearity-driven features of these circuits, we developed a Newton-like algorithm that alters the eigenvalues of a network's graph Laplacian. The algorithm leaves the topology of the network untouched, changing only the inductances, i.e., the edge weights. By applying the Newton-like algorithm to three types of random graphs, we showed that reducing the gap between the graph Laplacian's first two eigenvalues leads to enhanced nonlinear behavior. Comparing pre- and post-optimized circuits, it is evident that optimizing the eigenvalue gap significantly increases (i) energy transfer from the fundamental driving frequency to higher harmonics, and (ii) the maximum magnitude output voltage.

In both the perturbative and iterative algorithm, the only way in which the network's structure influences its frequency response is through the graph Laplacian matrix. In our experiments, we have tuned this graph Laplacian's first eigenvalue gap by holding the topology of the graph constant and altering the edge weights, i.e., inductances. What if we had instead tuned the gap by holding the edge weights constant and altering the topology of the graph? This would amount to altering the incidence matrix B instead of the inductance vector L. So long as both types of alterations result in the same graph Laplacian Δ, our results indicate that the nonlinear electrical network's functionality should be enhanced significantly. This, of course, leads to the question of whether it is possible to algorithmically alter the network topology to achieve a particular graph Laplacian matrix, an interesting avenue for further work.

ACKNOWLEDGMENTS

The authors thank the UC Merced Open Access Fund Pilot for covering this article's open access publication costs.

REFERENCES

1. Lilis GN, Park J, Lee WE, Li G, Bhat HS, et al. (2010) Harmonic generation using nonlinear LC lattices.IEEE Transactions on Microwave Theory and

Techniques 58: 1713–1723

2. Momeni O, Afshari E (2011) A broadband mm-wave and terahertz traveling-wave frequency multiplier on CMOS. IEEE Journal of Solid-State Circuits 46: 2966–2976
3. Lee W, Adnan M, Momeni O, Afshari E (2012) A nonlinear lattice for high-amplitude picosecond pulse generation in CMOS. IEEE Transactions on Microwave Theory and Techniques 60: 370–380
4. Lee W, Afshari E (2012) A CMOS noise-squeezing amplifier. IEEE Transactions on Microwave Theory and Techniques 60: 329–339
5. Han R, Afshari E (2013) A 260GHz broadband source with 1.1mWcontinuous-wave radiated power and EIRP of 15.7dBm in 65nm CMOS. In: Solid-State Circuits Conference Digest of Technical Papers (ISSCC), 2013 IEEE International. pp. 138–139.
6. Han R, Afshari E (2013) A high-power broadband passive terahertz frequency doubler in CMOS. IEEE Transactions on Microwave Theory and Techniques 61: 1150–1160
7. Bhat HS, LeeW, Lilis GN, Afshari E (2010) Steady-state perturbative theory for nonlinear circuits. Journal of Physics A: Mathematical and Theoretical 43: 205101
8. Landauer R (1960) Shock waves in nonlinear transmission lines and their effect on parametric amplification. IBM Journal of Research and Development 4: 391–401
9. Landauer R (1960) Parametric amplification along nonlinear transmission lines. Journal of Applied Physics 31: 479–484
10. Hirota R, Suzuki K (1970) Studies on lattice solitons by using electrical networks. Journal of the Physical Society of Japan 28: 1366–1367
11. Case M, Kamegawa M, Yu R, Rodwell MJW, Franklin J (1991) Impulse compression using soliton effects in a monolithic GaAs circuit. Applied Physics Letters 58: 173–175
12. Case M, Carman E, Yu R, Rodwell MJW, Kamegawa M (1992) Picosecond duration, large amplitude impulse generation using electrical soliton effects. Applied Physics Letters 60: 3019–3021
13. Afshari E, Hajimiri A (2005) Nonlinear transmission lines for pulse shaping in silicon. IEEE Journal of Solid-State Circuits 40: 744–752
14. Ostrovskii LA, Papko VV, Stepanyants YA (1980) Solitons and nonlinear resonance in two-dimensional lattices. Zhurnal Eksperimental'noi i Teoreticheskoi Fiziki 78: 831–841
15. Stepanyants YA (1981) Experimental investigation of cylindrically diverging solitons in an electric lattice. Wave Motion 3: 335–341
16. Stepanyants YA (1983) Experimental study of "Cerenkov" radiation from solitons in twodimensional LC-lattices. Radiophysics and Quantum Electronics 26: 601–607
17. Afshari E, Bhat HS, Hajimiri A, Marsden JE (2005) Extremely wideband signal shaping using one- and two-dimensional nonuniform nonlinear transmission lines. Journal of Applied Physics 99: 054901
18. Bhat HS, Afshari E (2008) Nonlinear constructive interference in electrical lattices. Physical Review E77: 066602
19. Bhat HS, Osting B (2009) The zone boundary mode in periodic nonlinear electrical lattices. Physica D238: 1216–1228
20. Wyart M, Liang H, Kabla A, Mahadevan L (2008) Elasticity of floppy and stiff random networks. Physical Review Letters 101: 215501.
21. Monthus C, Garel T (2011) Random elastic networks: a strong disorder renormalization approach.Journal of Physics A: Mathematical and Theoretical 44: 085001
22. Tighe BP (2012) Dynamic critical response in damped random spring networks. Physical Review Letters109: 168303.
23. DiDonna B, Lubensky T (2005) Nonaffine correlations in random elastic media. Physical Review E 72: 066619
24. Togashi Y, Mikhailov AS (2007) Nonlinear relaxation dynamics in elastic networks and design principles of molecular machines. Proceedings of the National Academy of Sciences 104: 8697–8702[PMC free article]
25. Bhat HS, Osting B (2011) Kirchhoff›s laws as a finite volume method for the planar Maxwell equations.IEEE Transactions on Antennas and Propagation 59: 3772–3779
26. Bhat HS, Vaz GJ (2013) Finite volume method for planar Maxwell equations in nonlinear media. In preparation.
27. Boccaletti S, Latora V, Moreno Y, Chavez M, Hwang DU (2006) Complex networks: Structure and dynamics. Physics Reports 424: 175–308
28. Kori H, Mikhailov A (2006) Strong effects of network architecture in the entrainment of coupled oscillator systems. Physical Review E 74: 066115
29. Park K, Huang L, Lai YC (2007) Desynchronization waves in small-world networks. Physical Review E75: 026211
30. Arenas A, Díaz-Guilera A, Kurths J, Moreno Y, Zhou C (2008) Synchronization in complex networks.Physics Reports 469: 93–153
31. Jalili M, Rad A, Hasler M (2008) Enhancing synchronizability of weighted dynamical networks using betweenness centrality. Physical Review E 78: 016105
32. Donetti L, Hurtado PI, Muñoz MA (2005) Entangled networks, synchronization, and optimal network topology. Physical Review Letters 95: 188701.
33. Brede M (2008) Locals vs. global synchronization in networks of non-identical Kuramoto oscillators.The European Physical Journal B 62: 87–94
34. Brede M (2008) Construction principles for highly synchronizable sparse directed networks. Physics Letters A 372: 5305–5308
35. Dadashi M, Barjasteh I, Jalili M (2010) Rewiring dynamical networks with prescribed degree distribution for enhancing synchronizability. Chaos 20: 043119–043119-6
36. Kelly D, Gottwald GA (2011) On the topology of

synchrony optimized networks of a Kuramoto-model with non-identical oscillators. Chaos 21: 025110.

37. Yanagita T, Mikhailov AS (2012) Design of oscillator networks with enhanced synchronization tolerance against noise. Physical Review E 85: 056206

38. Bhat HS, Osting B (2011) 2-D Inductor-capacitor lattice synthesis. IEEE Transactions on Computer-Aided Design of Integrated Circuits and Systems 30: 1483–1492

39. Hagberg AA, Schult DA, Swart PJ (2008) Exploring network structure, dynamics, and function using NetworkX. In: Proceedings of the 7th Python in Science Conference (SciPy2008). Pasadena, CA USA, pp. 11–15.

40. Barabási AL, Albert R (1999) Emergence of scaling in random networks. Science 286: 509–512

41. Watts DJ, Strogatz SH (1998) Collective dynamics of small-world networks. Nature 393: 440–442

42. Erdős P, Rényi A (1960) On the evolution of random graphs. Magyar Tud Akad Mat Kutató Int Közl 5: 17–61

CHAPTER 3

PERCOLATION CENTRALITY: QUANTIFYING GRAPH-THEORETIC IMPACT OF NODES DURING PERCOLATION IN NETWORKS

Mahendra Piraveenan[1], Mikhail Prokopenko[2,3], Liaquat Hossain[1]

[1]Centre for Complex Systems Research, Faculty of Engineering and IT, The University of Sydney, New South Wales, Australia,

[2]CSIRO Information and Communications Technology Centre, Epping, New South Wales, Australia,

[3]School of Physics, The University of Sydney, New South Wales, Australia

ABSTRACT

A number of centrality measures are available to determine the relative importance of a node in a complex network, and betweenness is prominent among them. However, the existing centrality measures are not adequate in network percolation scenarios (such as during infection transmission in a social network of individuals, spreading of computer viruses on computer networks, or transmission of disease over a network of towns) because they do not account for the changing percolation states of individual nodes. We propose a new measure, percolation centrality, that quantifies relative impact of nodes based on their topological connectivity, as well as their percolation states. The measure can be extended to include random walk based definitions, and its computational complexity is shown to be of the same order as that of betweenness centrality. We demonstrate the usage of percolation centrality by applying it to a canonical network as well as simulated and real world scale-free and random networks.

INTRODUCTION

Networks are ubiquitous in today's world. Communication networks such as world wide web, telephone networks and mobile phone networks are changing the way we live and we interact with other people. Social networks built on top of these, such as Facebook and Twitter, are redefining ways of keeping in touch. Vast airline and rail networks have given us access to the remotest parts of the world and reduced travel times by orders of magnitude. Our survival depends on the functioning of a number of biological and ecological networks. The energy needed for our domestic and industrial use is supplied by electric power networks. Indeed, the interest and awareness about networks are not only a trend in scientific research but also a social and cultural phenomenon of this age [1]–[5].

Percolation of a 'contagion' occurs in complex networks in a number of scenarios. For example, viral or bacterial infection can spread over social networks of people, known as contact networks. The spread of disease can also be considered at a higher level of abstraction, by contemplating a network of towns or population centres, connected by road, rail or air links. Computer viruses can spread over computer networks. Rumours or news about business offers and deals can also spread via social networks of people. In all of these scenarios, a 'contagion' spreads over the links of a complex network, altering the 'states' of the nodes as it spreads, either

Citation: Piraveenan M, Prokopenko M, Hossain L. Percolation Centrality: Quantifying Graph-Theoretic Impact of Nodes during Percolation in Networks. Holme P, ed. PLoS ONE. 2013;8(1):e53095. doi:10.1371/journal.pone.0053095.

recoverably or otherwise. For example, in an epidemiological scenario, individuals go from 'susceptible' to 'infected' state as the infection spreads. The states the individual nodes can take in the above examples could be binary (such as received/not received a piece of news), discrete (susceptible/infected/recovered), or even continuous (such as the proportion of infected people in a town), as the contagion spreads. The common feature in all these scenarios is that the spread of contagion results in the change of node states in networks.

Indeed, in the epidemiological domain, a few studies have successfully modelled epidemic spread as a specific example of percolation in networks [6]–[11]. The percolation theory is attractive because it provides connections to several well-known results from statistical physics, in terms of percolation thresholds, phase transitions, long-range connectivity, and critical phenomena in general. For instance, Newman and Watts [6]suggested using a site percolation model for disease spreading in which some fraction of the population is considered susceptible to the disease, and an initial outbreak can spread only as far as the limits of the connected cluster of susceptible individuals in which it first strikes. An epidemic can occur if the system is at or above its *percolation (epidemic) threshold* where the size of the *largest (giant) cluster* becomes comparable with the size of the entire population. Similarly, Moore and Newman [12] used a general model with two simple epidemiological parameters: (i) *susceptibility*, the probability that an individual exposed to a disease will contract it, and (ii) *transmissibility*, the probability that contact between an infected individual and a healthy but susceptible one will result in the latter contracting the disease. They pointed out that if the distribution of occupied sites or bonds is random, then the problem of when an epidemic takes place becomes equivalent to a standard percolation problem on the graph: what fraction of sites or bonds must be occupied before a "giant component" of connected sites forms whose size scales extensively with the total number of sites [12]. It has been noted [13] that the percolation of disease through a network depends on both the level of contagion and the structure of the contact network. Similarly, in other contexts such as virus spreading in a computer network or information spreading in a social network, it could be deduced that percolation is determined by both network topology and amount of the contagion spreading.

In any context, if we need to stop the contagion from spreading further, we need to supply nodes with certain resources. For example, during a disease outbreak affecting a network of towns, medical staff, medicine and other resources need to be rushed to each town to stop the infection from spreading to other towns as well as to treat people in that town. Generally, there are limited resources (vaccines, drugs, medical staff, transport, etc.) to respond in time. Therefore, choices for early intervention in the affected network need to be precise. However, 'nodes' that are individually at the highest risk are not necessarily those which will contribute most to the contagion transmission. Hence, there is a need to identify nodes that are 'central' in terms of their impact on the spread. Moreover, we need to interpret the node's impact both in terms of their topological connectivity and their current infected (percolated) state. Intuitively, an infected node makes a higher impact than a non-infected one even if their topological connectivity is identical. Furthermore, different levels of risks, susceptibility, etc. can bring about non-binary node states making the assessment of the impact even less trivial.

We may formulate the scenarios described above into a general problem: In a given complex network, to what extent the individual percolated (or partially percolated) nodes impact on the percolation process at any given time? A measure quantifying this extent needs to not only account for topological connectivity but consider the node's percolation state (including partial percolation). The existing centrality measures are not adequate for this purpose because they do not account for changing percolation states of individual nodes, and are static. Therefore a suitable centrality measure which also takes into account the percolation states of nodes is needed, which should be general enough to be applicable in all the contexts described above.

In this paper, we introduce a new centrality measure, *percolation centrality*, capturing relative impact of nodes during (possibly partial) percolation. The proposed measure subsumes betweenness centrality by explicitly accounting for percolated nodes on relevant shortest paths. When all nodes are in the percolated state this measure is shown to be equivalent to betweenness centrality. We also briefly analyze the computational complexity of percolation centrality showing that it is of the same order as that of betweenness centrality. Furthermore, we succinctly discuss possible extensions to random walk based definitions of this measure. We employ *generic scale-free networks* to analyze percolation centrality, since it has been shown that a great number of real world networks, including contact networks, social networks of people in general, transport networks, and large scale computer networks (including Internet), tend to be scale-free [1], [2],[14]–[21]. We also analyze random networks for comparison. We employ a simulation approach to illustrate how the measure of percolation centrality could be used as a tool in intervention strategies, by comparing it to betweenness centrality and shortest distance from percolated nodes. Finally we present our observations and conclusions.

ANALYSIS

Review of Centrality and Network Evolution Measures

A host of centrality measures have been proposed to analyze complex networks, especially in the domain of social network analysis. The simplest of these perhaps is the degree centrality, sometimes just called degree, of a node. A node's degree is simply the number of links it has with other nodes in the network, and therefore gives some indication about how important that node is to the network.

A family of betweenness measures have been proposed [22]–[28] to measure a node's importance as a conduit of information flow in a network. The first and perhaps most well known measure of these is the classical betweenness centrality measure proposed by [22]. Betweenness Centrality measures the fraction of shortest paths that pass through a given node, averaged over all pairs of node in a network. It is formally defined, for a directed graph, as

$$BC(v)=\frac{1}{(N-1)(N-2)}\sum_{s\neq v\neq t}\frac{\sigma_{s,t}(v)}{\sigma_{s,t}} \quad (1)$$

where $\sigma_{s,t}$ is the number of shortest paths between source node s and target node t, while $\sigma_{s,t}(v)$ is the number of shortest paths between source node s and target node t that pass through node v.

Closeness Centrality [23], [29] is a measure of how close a network is, on average, to the rest of the nodes in terms of shortest paths. It essentially measures the average geodesic distance between a given node and all other nodes in the network. It is defined as

$$CC(v)=\frac{1}{\sum_{i\neq v} d_g(v,i)} \quad (2)$$

where $d_g(v,i)$ is the shortest path (geodesic) distance between nodes v and i. Note that the average is 'inverted' so that the node which is 'closest' to all other nodes will have the highest measure of closeness centrality.

The Eigen vector centrality measure [30] is based on the assumption that a node's centrality is influenced by the centrality scores of its neighbours - that the centrality score of a node is proportional to the sum of the centrality scores of the neighbours. As such, it is defined iteratively. If the centrality scores of nodes are given by the matrix X and the adjacency matrix of the network is A, then we can define x iteratively as

$$\mathbf{x}\propto\mathbf{Ax} \quad (3)$$

i.e

$$\lambda\mathbf{x}=\mathbf{Ax} \quad (4)$$

The centrality scores are obtained by solving this matrix equation. It can be shown that, while there can be many values for λ, only the largest value will result in positive scores for all nodes [31].

The classical betweenness centrality measure assumes that information flow is through the shortest paths in a network. This is, in many instances, not a realistic assumption [24], [26], [27]. For example, in a transport network, the traffic will likely go through alternative paths if the shortest path is traffic-jammed. Rumours or infections in social networks are likely to follow random paths. A number of centrality measures based on betweenness address this. The flow centrality measure [22] measures the proportion of the 'flow' that goes through a given node, when maximum flow is 'pumped through' a pair of nodes. A random walk based betweenness measure proposed by Newman [26] considers a network to be like an electric circuit with unit resistance at any link, and measures the 'current' that goes through a node when unit current passes through a pair of nodes (In fact, the random walk based betweenness is not formally defined in this way. However, as mentioned in [26], it is the easiest way to intuitively understand this betweenness measure.).

There are a number of other centrality measures based on random walks as well, such as those described in[32], [33]. There is also the information centrality measure [27] based on closeness centrality, which measures the harmonic mean length of paths ending at a vertex v. The power centrality [26], [33] of a node $v$is the number of times a random walk is expected to pass through the node v, averaged over all possible starting points of the random walk. The random-walk centrality introduced by [32] measures the average speed with which, a randomly walking message from a node reaches the target node v, averaged over all source nodes.

A number of weighted betweenness measures, such as [28], where weights are given to links, have also been proposed recently. Klemm et al. [34] introduced another measure, *dynamical influence*, to assess the role of an individual in collective dynamics within a system of interacting elements. Dynamical influence quantifies the extent to which an initial condition of a specific node affects its final state, given the system dynamics. The new measure was applied in an epidemiological scenario, and was shown to be a good predictor of spreading efficiency in a social network (spreading efficiency measures the expected fraction of nodes reached by an epidemic outbreak initiated with a specific infected node). Dynamical influence, however, estimates the influence of a node on a potential spread before the contagion begins — it is a measure of inherent dynamics of which the system is potentially capable. It is not, however, a time-dependent measure of actual dynamics which is affected by current state of a node.

Another method to efficiently approximate the number of infections resulting from a given initially infected node in a network of susceptible individuals is described by Bauer and Lizier [35]. While this method directly considers the spreading process and provides an estimation of actual numbers of infections, it is also aimed at estimating the impact of the initial infected node on the infection spreading, rather than a time-dependent impact of any other node on the percolation in the network.

There are a number of measures that do characterise individual nodes at every step of network evolution. For example, a prominent approach to modelling cascading failures is based on a study of Goh et al. [36] and Crucitti et al. [37]. The model proposed by the latter group, Crucitti-Latora-Marchiori (CLM) model, has also been extended [38]–[40] to studies of cascading failures in power grids. In these studies, a power grid is represented as a weighted graph, and each node is characterised by a load (e.g., electrical load) which varies over time and has a fixed limited capacity. The load is defined as the number of most efficient paths (e.g., from generators to distribution substations) that pass through that node. Original CLM model considered paths between all node pairs, and the load was equivalent to weighted betweenness centrality. Consequently, the more shortest paths pass through a node, the higher is its load. A cascading failure scenario is triggered by a (random) failure of a single node, affecting its neighbours as well as relevant shortest paths, and therefore redistributing the load. When capacity of any affected node is exceeded by its new load, the overloaded node also fails, and the cascade of failures may continue. In short, the node's load is a time-dependent property. It is important to point out that overloaded nodes are not removed from the network (apart from the very first point of failure) — instead, the efficiencies of links connecting to each overloaded node are reduced in proportion to the overload. This in turn changes weighted shortest paths. That is, the changes in loads (i.e., their weighted betweenness centralities) are brought about by recalculation of shortest paths. In other words, the changes are topologically-driven, rather than being reflections of new states of nodes which remain connected in the same way.

In addition, a particular probabilistic routing scheme may be assumed instead of shortest path routing or Newman's random walk routing. This notion is generalized in another study that discussed Routing Betweenness Centrality [41]. In these variants betweenness centrality calculations assume that traffic flows over shortest paths, but use a different routing mechanism. These variants are time-independent: e.g., routing betweenness centrality of a node does not change over time, and hence does not characterise an impact that a percolated/infected node has on the network.

Further classification of measures was carried out by Borgatti and Everett [42]. In particular, their review distinguished between radial and medial measures. For example, measures that assess walks that emanate from or terminate with a given node are called radial, while the measures which are based on the number of walks that pass through a given node are called medial measures.

Percolation Centrality

As described in the previous section, a slew of centrality measures exist to determine the 'importance' of a single node in a complex network. However, these measures quantify the importance of a node in purely topological terms, and the value of the node does not depend on the 'state' of the node in any way. It remains constant regardless of network dynamics. This is true even for the weighted betweenness measures [28]. However, a node may very well be centrally located in terms of betweenness centrality or another centrality measure, but may not be 'centrally' located in the context of a network in which there is percolation. With this in mind, we propose percolation centrality (PC), which specifically measures the importance of nodes in terms of aiding the percolation through the network.

Let us denote the percolation state of node i at time t by x_i^t. When the temporal context is clear we shall simply use x_i. Specifically, $x_i^t=0$ indicates a non-percolated state at time t, $x_i^t=1$ indicates a fully percolated state at time t, while a partially percolated state corresponds to $0<x_i^t<1$ (e.g., in a network of townships, this would be the percentage of people infected in that town). The higher the value x_i, the higher is the degree of percolation of node i. In this study, we do not discuss how precisely the node states are assessed or assigned, since that is context-dependent, and assume that a mechanism for quantifying the levels of partial percolation exists. Rather we focus on determining, at any time, how important is the node to the overall process of percolation.

We define percolation centrality for a given node, at a given time, as the proportion of 'percolated paths' that go through that node. A 'percolated path' is a shortest path between a pair of nodes, where the source node is percolated (e.g., infected). The target node can be percolated or non-percolated, or in a partially percolated state. As an extension, we will later consider the case where the target node has to be specifically non-percolated (e.g., non-infected). Formally, percolation centrality of node v at time t is:

$$PC^t(v)=\frac{1}{(N-2)}\sum_{s\neq v\neq r}\frac{\sigma_{s,r}(v)}{\sigma_{s,r}}\frac{x_s^t}{[\sum x_i^t]-x_v^t} \tag{5}$$

where $\sigma_{s,r}$ and $\sigma_{s,r}(v)$ are defined as usual.

Let us examine the fraction

$$w_{s,v}^t=\frac{x_s^t}{[\sum x_i^t]-x_v^t} \tag{6}$$

in more detail, as it captures the relative contribution (weight) of each percolated path originated in the source node s to the percolation centrality $PC^t(v)$.

The percolation state associated with a source determines how much importance is given to the potential percolation paths that originate from it. The sum in the denominator is the total extent of percolation in the network, ranging from zero when there are no percolated nodes, to N when all nodes are fully percolated. The state of node v is subtracted from the total to ensure the proper normalisation (Since each percolated node can have $(N-1)$ targets, we need to normalize the weights of these nodes so that they will add up to $N-1$, and the average path has a weight of unity.):

$$\sum_{s\neq v} w_{s,v}^t=1 \tag{7}$$

The node v itself can be either counted or not counted as a source/target node in the definition of betweenness centrality [26] and consequently, in the definition of percolation centrality. We have adopted the convention of not counting v as a source or target node.

Obviously, if $x_s^t=0$ the contribution $w_{s,v}^t$ is zero, and the source s is not contributing to PC. In particular, when there are no percolated nodes, the percolation centrality is trivially zero. The first percolated node, however, will affect the PC of multiple nodes, resulting in the average PC of these nodes being significantly higher than the average betweenness of these nodes. In fact, it is possible to show that if only one node s is infected (or partially percolated to the extent $\mu\leq 1$) then for any other node v

$$w_{s,v}^t=\frac{x_s^t}{[\sum x_i^t]-x_v^t}=1 \tag{8}$$

and hence

$$PC^t(v)=\frac{1}{(N-2)}\sum_{s\neq v\neq r}\frac{\sigma_{s,r}(v)}{\sigma_{s,r}} \tag{9}$$

This in turn means that if we iterate over all possible *single* nodes s infected to the same level μ (that is, consider all possible contagion sources one by one), and then average over all these scenarios, we obtain the average percolation centrality of the node v in the face of all $(N-1)$ possible contagion origins:

$$\langle PC^t(v)\rangle=\frac{1}{(N-1)(N-2)}\sum_{s\neq v\neq r}\frac{\sigma_{s,r}(v)}{\sigma_{s,r}}=BC(v). \tag{10}$$

That is, percolation centrality averaged over all possible single contagion sources reduces to betweenness centrality.

Finally, if all nodes are fully percolated (or partially percolated to the same extent $\mu \le 1$) and $x_s^t = \mu$ for all possible sources as well as the node v itself, the contribution $w_{s,v}^t = \frac{1}{N-1}$ is constant at that time, resulting in

$$PC^t(v) = \frac{1}{(N-1)(N-2)} \sum_{s \neq v \neq r} \frac{\sigma_{s,r}(v)}{\sigma_{s,r}} = BC(v) \tag{11}$$

In this case all shortest paths become percolated paths, since all nodes are potential 'sources' of percolation. It is evident then that during the process of percolation, the PC is significantly different from betweenness at $T = 1$ for nodes near the infection, and converges to $BC(v)$ over time. It may be conjectured that on average (across the nodes) such a convergence will undergo a sharp transition, resembling a phase transition expected during network percolation. That is, when the size of the giant percolated cluster becomes comparable with the size of the entire population, the average PC becomes comparable with average BC.

We would like to note that the matrix of weights $W_{s,v}$ is easily obtainable, at any time, as

$$\mathbf{W} = \mathbf{x}^{\mathbf{T}}\mathbf{y} \tag{12}$$

where $\mathbf{x} = [x_1, x_2, \ldots, x_N]$, and elements of the N-dimensional vector $\mathbf{y}$ are defined as

$$y_i = \frac{1}{[\sum_{k=1}^{N} x_k] - x_i} \tag{13}$$

In other words, the rows of $\mathbf{W}$ correspond to the source nodes, and the columns correspond to the nodes for which the percolation centrality is being calculated.

We attached weights to the percolation paths depending on the percolation levels assigned to the *source*nodes, based on the premise that the higher the percolation level of a source node is, the more important are the paths that originate from that node. Nodes which lie on shortest paths originating from highly-percolated nodes are therefore potentially more important to the percolation. One may then ask whether the percolation level of target nodes need to be accounted for. Does the percolation level of a target node also determine the importance of shortest paths leading to it? This depends on the context of the application. For example, in the case of spread of infection, over social networks of people or networks of towns, one may argue that if the source node and target node have equal levels of percolation (infection), then the paths connecting them are insignificant. Indeed, in some contexts, a path is meaningful as a potential path of percolation (infection) spread only if the source node is at a higher level compared to the target node.

With this in mind, we may extend our definition of percolation centrality to include target node weights. In this case, we have to calculate path weights as a difference of source node weights and target node weights, and we set the path weight to zero if this difference is negative. Therefore, there will be $(N-1)(N-2)$ pairs of nodes, and the total weights of paths between all nodes have to sum up to $(N-1)(N-2)$ so that the average path weight will be unity. Thus our definition for percolation centrality, at time t, taking into account both source and target node weights, becomes

$$PC^t(v) = \sum_{s \neq v \neq r} \frac{\sigma_{s,r}(v)}{\sigma_{s,r}} w_{v,s,r}^t \tag{14}$$

where the weights are given by

$$w_{v,s,r}^t = \frac{R[x_s^t - x_r^t]}{\sum_{s \neq v \neq r} R[x_s^t - x_r^t]} \tag{15}$$

using the Ramp function R, defined as $R(x) = x$ for positive x and $R(x) = 0$ for negative x. The scaling factor $(N-2)$ has disappeared (compared to equation (5)) because it has been absorbed into the weights.

Further analysis of PC in this study is based on the weights of source node states alone. Source-target weight based percolation centrality will be discussed in a follow-up paper.

Let us note here that, while a number of weighted betweenness centrality measures already exist, such as[28], the measure we propose here is subtly different. We do not compute importance of paths based on weights of links, but based on *states* of nodes. As such, our measure is dynamic, whereas the existing weighted centrality measures are static. Even though links in our context could be interpreted as having weights, these weights are inherited from node states of source and target, do not depend on the intermediate nodes, and will change with time.

Revisiting some of the measures briefly reviewed in previous section, we note the following differences. Dynamical influence [34] assesses the influence of a node on a potential spread before the percolation begins. Hence it is not a time-dependent measure of actual dynamics, unlike the proposed percolation centrality which is affected by current states of a node.

The family of CLM models introduced time-dependence. However, the changes in the weighted betweenness centralities of nodes (their loads) occur because shortest paths are recalculated at each step due to new link efficiencies (edge weights). As pointed out in previous section, these changes do not account for dynamics of new nodes' states: betweenness centrality changes because shortest paths are different. On the contrary, percolation centrality changes because the nodes' states are updated while the shortest paths remain the same.

It is interesting to point out at this stage that percolation centrality is a hybrid measure in terms of Borgatti and Everett classification [42]: it is a medial measure because it utilises shortest paths, following betweenness centrality, and it is also a radial measure because it assesses the state of the sources (and targets).

Finally, one may argue that percolation centrality is a routing betweenness centrality variant in which time-dependence is added via percolating states of (infected) nodes, rather than updating efficiencies of links.

In addition, the proposed measure accounts for partial percolation (a node state may take any value between, say 0 and 1), and can be applied with an immunization focus: which nodes need to be immunized first, rather than with the focus on the spreading efficiency: what is the average outbreak size if the contagion originates at a specific node.

Let us also define 'Hop distance' while we discuss percolation centrality. Hop distance of a node v regarding node state x, $D_{hop}(v,x)$, is simply the shortest distance from a given node v to any node with a particular state x. For example, if we have binary node states, hop distance of any node regarding state '1' is the smallest number of hops needed from that node before we can find a node with state '1'. If the considered node itself has state '1', then its hop distance is zero. Therefore, in a scenario where contagion spreads, the immediate neighbours of the percolated nodes will have smaller hop distances with respect to the percolation state. We will use hop distance $D_{hop}(v,x)$ as a simple contrasting measure to percolation centrality in our simulations.

Percolation Centrality Based On Random Walks

As mentioned above, it is not always likely that contagion will spread along shortest paths in networks. Indeed, pathological infection is more likely to spread randomly, where a person who is a 'contact' to an infected person is vulnerable to infection with a certain probability. Therefore, following the definition of betweenness centrality based on random walks [26], percolation centrality can also be defined in terms of random walks:

$$PC^t(v) = \frac{1}{(N-2)} \sum_{s \neq v \neq r} i_{s,r}(v) w^t_{v,s} \tag{16}$$

where $w^t_{v,s}$ are the normalised weights (equation 6), and $i_{s,r}(v)$ is the 'current' that flows through node v when the unit current is pumped between nodes s and r and all links are considered to have unit resistance. Note that the 'current' through node v is to be calculated only to determine the fraction of shortest paths between nodes s and r that, on average, pass through node v, and as such this calculation will not affect the way the weight matrix is calculated (Alternatively, we can interpret the weights as the conductance of each link, and define percolation centrality then as simply the proportion of current between nodes s and r that passes through v.). Similarly, percolation centrality based on source and target weights, following equation 14, may be defined as

$$PC^t(v) = \sum_{s \neq v \neq r} i_{s,r}(v) w^t_{v,s,r} \tag{17}$$

where $w^t_{v,s,r}$ are the normalised weights (equation 15). We shall leave a detailed study of random walk based definitions of percolation centrality to future work.

Implementation and Computational Complexity

The 'straightforward' implementation of a betweenness centrality algorithm would run in $O(N^3)$ time [25],[26]. We implemented our percolation centrality measure as shown in equation 5 by modifying Brandes' fast algorithm for BC [25], which runs in $O(NM)$ time. It can be shown that the extra calculations do not result in an order of magnitude increase in time complexity, and the algorithm still runs in worst case time $O(NM)$. However, the definition of percolation centrality including target nodes (14) cannot be calculated in $O(NM)$time. Brandes' algorithm achieves $O(NM)$ efficiency by iteratively counting the shortest paths from a given source node, and does not keep track of the targets. Therefore, calculating the percolation centrality with target nodes (equation 14) takes $O(N^3)$ worst case time.

An example with a simple model network

Let us now consider a simple example to illustrate the calculation of percolation centrality. Let us assume this is a network where partial percolation states are possible. Consider the Fig. 1 (a) where a simple network of eight nodes is shown, with percolation states ranging from 0.1 to 0.5 for each node. The same topology is repeated in Fig. 1 (b), with different percolation states. By inspection we could see that in Fig. 1 (a), the nodes at the right side, i.e the nodes v_7 and v_8, have the highest (partial) percolation state values, whereas in Fig. 1 (b), it is the nodes at the left side, i.e the nodes v_1, v_2 and v_3 which have the highest percolation state values.

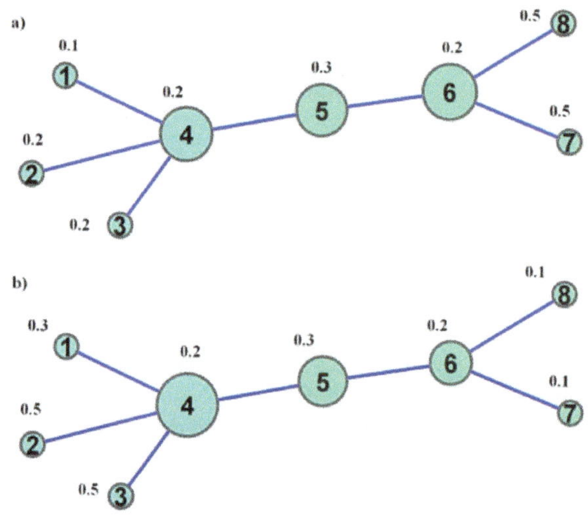

Figure 1: A simple network with $N = 8$.

Now consider nodes v_4 and v_6. Both of these nodes are centrally located in terms of network 'traffic' and would have high betweenness centrality. If we calculated their percolation centrality based on Fig. 1 (a) (the calculation, which can be done manually but quite tedious, is left to the reader), we will see that node v_4 has the percolation centrality of RC(4)=0:625 and v6 has the percolation centrality of RC(6)=0:667. Even though their percolation centrality is also influenced by their topological placement, node v6 has slightly higher percolation centrality by virtue of being close to the nodes with higher values for percolation states (nodes v_7 and v_8). Whereas if we consider Fig. 1 (b), we will find that v4 has the percolation centrality of RC(4)=0:825 and v6 has the percolation centrality of RC(6)=0:4. Here, while the topology remains the same, node v_4 has much higher percolation centrality because it is now closer to the nodes with higher percolation state values (nodes v_1, v_2 and v_3). This example demonstrates that percolation

This example demonstrates that percolation centrality of nodes in a fixed topology can vary significantly based on the percolated states of nodes in the network, and therefore the percolation centrality measure is quite dynamic unlike the centrality measures we have reviewed earlier.

RESULTS AND DISCUSSION

Simulation of Contagion Spread Using a Simple Real World Network

We will use scale-free networks with hundreds of nodes to validate and exemplify the concepts presented so far, since, as mentioned earlier, most real world networks are scale-free networks. However, let us first look at a smaller real world network (with N=39) where tracking individual nodes as the contagion spread is possible and illustrative (The topology of the network we utilize is taken from the largest component of the Gonorrhoea outbreak study in Alberta, Canada [43], however we will use it here as a generic sample network, since our focus is not on developing centrality measures for epidemiology as such. It is rather on developing a generic centrality measure for contagion spread.). The network is shown in Fig. 2. We analysed percolation centrality of nodes in this network, by simulating the contagion spread for T=20 time steps.

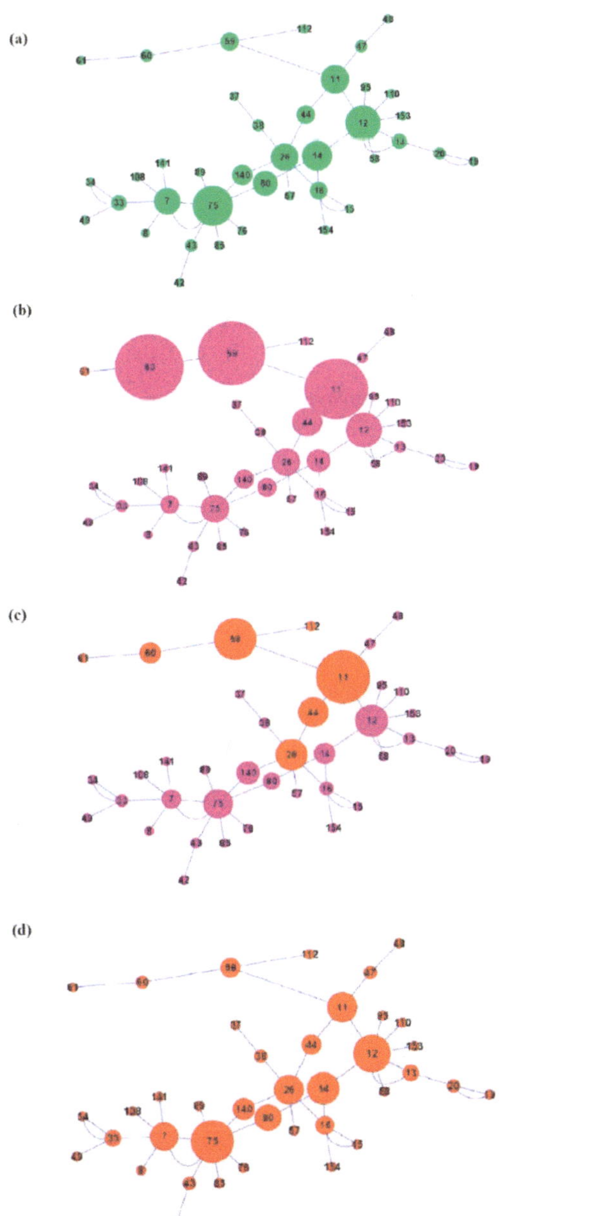

Figure 2: Betweenness and percolation centrality profiles of the Alberta model network with N=39, with node sizes matching the centrality values.

Since our aim is to demonstrate the utility of percolation centrality as a resource allocation tool, we will use a generic and simple contagion spread model. More specific spread models exist and can be used depending on the context of the application (For e.g., see [44] for an infection spread model in epidemiological scenarios). In our simulations, the contagion begins with a particular peripheral node.

For example, Let us consider a specific simulation, in which a peripheral node v_{61} (the node at the top left hand side of the network in Fig. 2) is first to be fully percolated, $x^1(v_{61})=1.0$, and all other nodes are not percolated, $x^1(v_{i\neq 61})=0.0$, at time step 1. At each time step, the nodes are further percolated with a transmission probability $p=0.2$ and no node becomes percolated without a direct contact with a percolated node (contagion spreads through links only). As the simulation progresses, the states of the percolated nodes are updated to $x^t(v)=1.0$. The number of nodes infected at each time step is shown in Fig. 3. We also trace how PC differs from BC at each time step, by considering the ratio of the averages between the measures for every node with non-zero betweenness. The ratio of averages over all N such nodes, $\frac{\sum_v PC(v)}{\sum_v BC(v)}$, is also shown in Fig. 3 (N divides both the numerator and denominator and thus cancels out.).

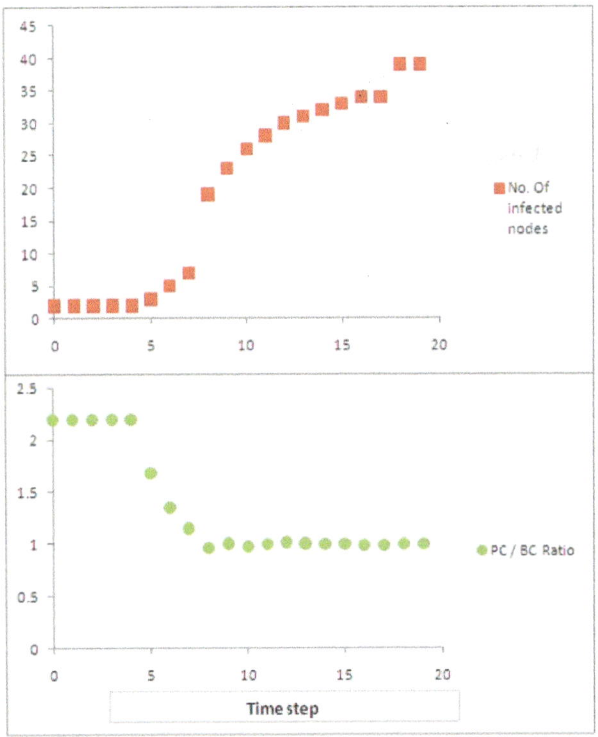

Figure 3: **The number of percolated nodes, as well as the ratio of average PC and BC values, over time, for the Alberta model network.**

We could see from Fig. 3 that at the beginning, T=1, the PC of nodes, on average, is significantly different from BC. As the contagion progresses, around time T=7, there is a sharp increase in the number of nodes fully percolated (establishing that this point corresponds to the well-known percolation phase transition is beyond the scope here). After this increase, the PC of nodes, on average, converges to the BC values. At the end of simulation, T=20, the PC of nodes, on average, are very similar to their BC counterparts. This is further illustrated in Fig. 2, where we show the network with the node sizes corresponding to their centrality values (In the figure, the nodes with zero percolation/betweenness centrality are assigned a minimal size.). We observe that at T=1, nodes v_{59} and v_{60} have the highest PC. Indeed, these nodes lie directly at the path of the potential spread of contagion, and therefore are critical for the contagion spread. The next highest node is node v_{11}, which has high overall BC, and is close enough to the percolated node. Node v_{75} is not so large, since, while being centrally located, it is far from the percolated area.

At T=7, the contagion is about to 'break through' and the number of fully percolated nodes is going to rapidly increase. There are seven fully percolated nodes, highlighted in red. Here we could see that node v_{60} has lost its importance, and node v11 has the highest PC, due to its topological prominence as well as the percolation state of its neighbours. The PC values of the nodes are still significantly different from the respective BC values. Finally, at T=20, the contagion has spread to all nodes in the largest component, and nodes v_{12} and v_{75} have the highest PC values. Indeed, the percolation centrality profile across the nodes at this stage is identical to the betweenness centrality profile of the network. Since all the nodes are fully percolated, the importance of nodes is measured based purely on topology, just like in betweenness centrality. Note that the size of nodes v_{59} and v_{60} has reduced now, since they are on the periphery and no longer exclusively close to the contagion.

We may observe a number of interesting facts even in this arguably simple example. Firstly, percolation centrality is the most relevant when the spread of contagion is at its infancy, and remains very relevant until the number of percolated nodes goes through a sharp transition. Secondly, percolation centrality is not directly correlated to the distance of a node from its closest percolated neighbour: nodes which are centrally located (such as node v_{75} at time T=7) may have higher PC, even though they are further from the contagion than some other nodes. Crucially, at the early and critical stages of the contagion spread, the percolation centrality is not directly correlated to betweenness centrality either. Thirdly, when the network is mostly percolated, the percolation centrality profile across the nodes starts to closely resemble the network's betweenness centrality profile. Therefore, it is clear that the percolation centrality measure conveys information that is most relevant to a targeted early intervention. Consequently, in order to prevent the spread of contagion, one should target precisely the non-percolated nodes that have the highest percolation centrality. In the next section, we will study percolation centrality as a resource allocation tool while using larger scale-free networks as examples.

Simulation experiments using scale-free and random networks

Scale-free networks are those networks that display similar topological features irrespective of scale. Such networks are described by power law degree distributions, formally specified as

$$p_k = Ak^{-\gamma}U(k/k_{max}) \tag{18}$$

where U is a step function specifying a cut off at $k=k_{max}$. The degree distribution of scale-free networks can be specified by a number of parameters, including maximum degree k_{max}, scale-free exponent γ, and the proportion of out-lier nodes A. Most real world networks are scale-free networks, including technical, biological and social networks [1], [16], [45]–[49]. scale-free networks have been commonly used as model networks for infectious dynamics modelling [44], to represent road and air traffic networks [50] and to represent large scale computer networks, including Internet [1], [14], [51], [52]. Therefore, scale-free networks can be used as a justifiable model to simulate contagion spread scenarios.

We used a number of scale-free networks for our studies, where the network size was up to 5000 nodes. Let us consider a typical network with the number of nodes $N=5000$, the number of links $M=15000$, and $\gamma=2.128$. We will again use the generic spread model described above to simulate contagion spread. The contagion will start from a randomly selected node (either hub or peripheral), and this node is the first to be fully percolated, and all other nodes are not percolated, at time step 1. At each time step, the nodes are further percolated with a transmission probability $p=0.2$ and no node becomes percolated without a direct contact with a percolated node (contagion spreads through links only). As the simulation progresses, the states of the percolated nodes are updated to $x^t(v)=1.0$.

The average number of nodes percolated vs timesteps is shown in Fig. 4 (averaged over 50 simulation runs). The ratio of averages, $\frac{\sum_v PC(v)}{\sum_v BC(v)}$, is also shown in the same figure. It could be seen that on average, the percolation 'breaks through' between timesteps $T=9$ and $T=14$, where there is a phase transition in the number of percolated nodes, as well as the ratio of averaged centrality measures. Once this phase transition is achieved, the ratio $\frac{\sum_v PC(v)}{\sum_v BC(v)}$ becomes close to unity. However, until the network is saturated with percolated nodes, the ratio $\frac{\sum_v PC(v)}{\sum_v BC(v)}$ is higher than unity, meaning there is high diversity between percolation centrality and betweenness centrality. We confirmed this by analysing individual PC/BC ratio profiles. For example, Fig. 5 shows these ratios (A network of size $N=500$ was used in this instance for clarity of figure.) against node IDs for a typical simulation run at time $T=10$ where we can see that, for some individual nodes, the PC/BC ratio can be as high as 3.5, indicating significant variation between percolation and betweenness centralities at the critical part of contagion spread.

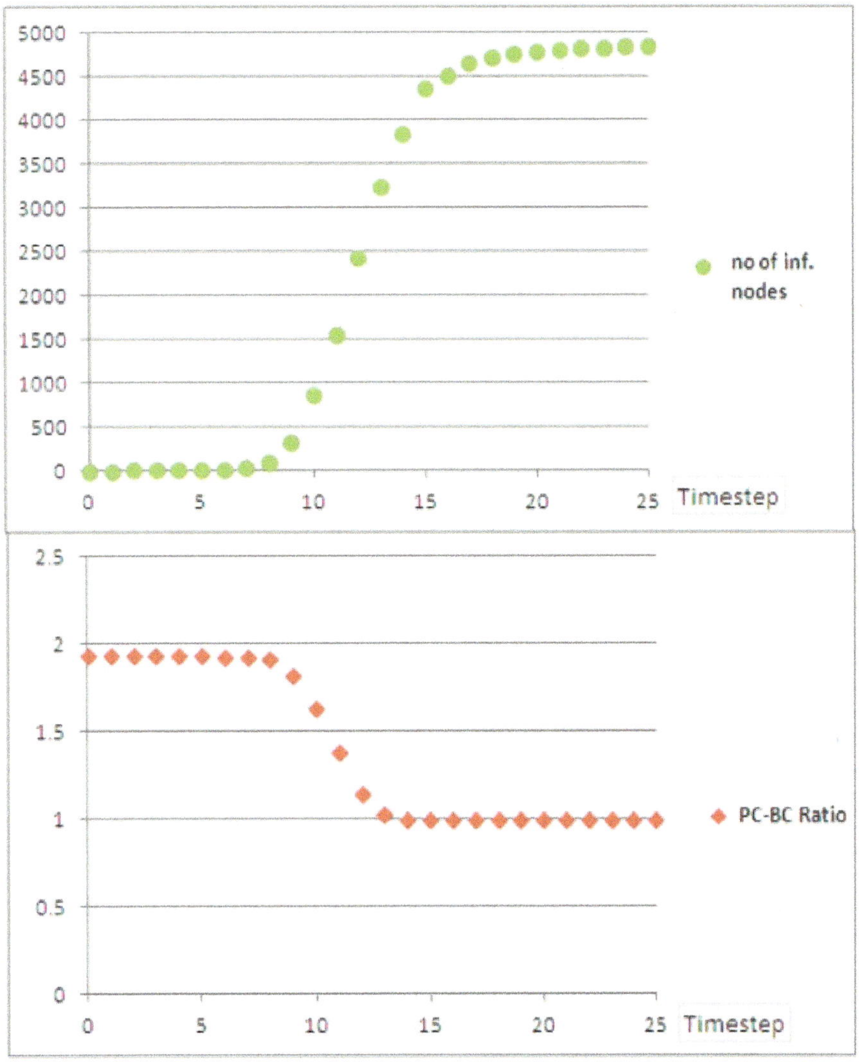

Figure 4: The number of fully percolated nodes, and the ratio of average PC and BC values over time, for a scale-free network with $N = 5000$.

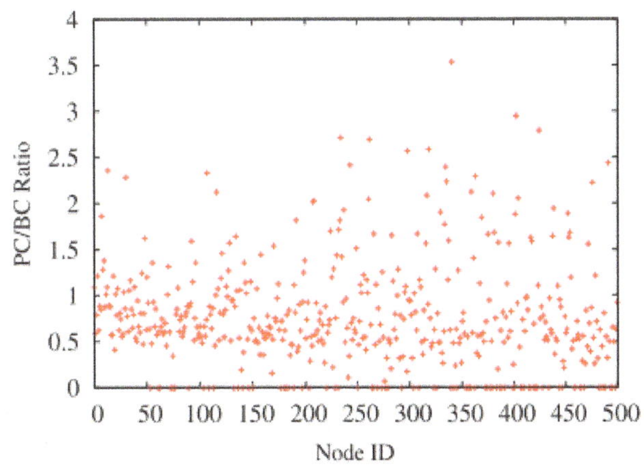

Figure 5: A typical run of the simulation, at timestep $T = 10$, for a scale-free network with $N = 500$.

To demonstrate how percolation centrality could be utilized in real world as a resource allocation tool, we simulated 'immunizing' a certain percentage of nodes after a certain number of timesteps. The contagion could not spread through a node after it had been immunized. The nodes to be immunized were chosen based on one of the three following quantities:

1. Percolation centrality
2. Betweenness centrality
3. Hop distance

We immunized nodes after a certain percentage of nodes (α) became fully percolated, and a certain percentage of nodes (β) were 'immunized' at this timestep. The nodes to be immunized were selected by calculating a centrality measure (one of the three measures above) for all nodes, and ranking nodes top to bottom based on their values. The top β percentage of nodes were then 'immunized' (their node-states made permanently zero). Then we measured the number of timesteps it took, after intervention, for the network to be 'saturated' by percolation. Since due to topological effects it is possible that the network will never be completely 'infected', we took the network to be saturated by percolation if the number of fully percolated nodes passed a certain threshold. In the experiments described below, this saturation threshold is $T_s = 350$nodes (Even so, at some instances, the immunization may be so effective that the network may never reach this threshold. For practical purposes, therefore, we aborted such simulations thirty timesteps after immunization.).

Our simulation results are summarised in Appendix: Tables 1 and .2. The rows correspond to the percentage of nodes percolated before the intervention was made (α), whereas the columns correspond to the percentage of nodes which were immunized (β). The number of timesteps it took, averaged over a number of simulations, for the network to be saturated by percolation is presented in the cells of each table. Each row has three sub-rows, corresponding to the centrality measure used for intervention: percolation centrality, betweenness centrality, and hop distance, in that order. For example, the entry of 5.8 at the top left cell means that after two percent of the nodes were fully percolated, the top one percent nodes, selected by ranking nodes based on percolation centrality, were 'immunized', and despite this immunization, the percolation saturated the network in 5.8 timesteps on average. Similarly, the entry of 12.2 at the bottom right cell means that after twenty five percent of the nodes were fully percolated, the top twenty percent nodes, selected by ranking nodes based on hop distance, were 'immunized', and despite this immunization, the percolation saturated the network in 12.2 timesteps on average.

Table 1: A comparison between the average timesteps taken for saturation of percolation when the intervention is PC based, BC based or hop distance based. the network used was a scale-free network with $N = 500$.

α(rows) β(columns)	1	2	3	4	5	6	7	8	9	10	11	12	15	20
2	5.8	6.0	6.2	7.8	10.2	10.4	11.8	15.4	15.2	17.8	22.2	24.6	27.8	30.0
	4.6	5.6	5.8	7.0	8.2	9.0	10.2	11.2	13.4	13.6	18.2	21.4	26.4	28.6
	6.4	6.8	7.2	10.2	14.4	18.8	22.4	25.2	28.6	28.4	30.0	30.0	30.0	30.0
3	4.6	5.8	7.0	8.8	9.6	10.6	11.0	13.4	14.2	18.8	22.6	24.2	28.4	29.2
	4.8	5.2	6.0	7.2	7.8	8.4	8.6	10.2	11.4	16.4	18.2	22.4	26.6	26.4
	6.2	6.4	9.2	10.8	13.0	15.6	17.6	18.8	24.4	27.6	29.2	30.0	30.0	30.0
4	4.2	6.0	6.6	7.8	9.0	10.8	11.2	13.4	15.0	16.8	19.6	24.0	27.2	29.2
	4.4	5.6	5.4	6.8	7.8	8.6	8.4	10.2	11.8	12.8	17.6	21.4	26.0	26.8
	4.0	5.6	6.2	8.0	8.4	11.0	10.4	14.2	14.4	18.8	22.4	27.8	30.0	30.0
5	4.8	5.0	5.8	7.0	8.6	9.4	10.0	11.2	13.2	14.8	18.6	20.2	28.6	28.8
	4.2	5.2	5.6	6.4	6.6	7.4	7.6	9.2	12.4	13.0	17.4	18.0	27.4	25.4
	3.8	4.2	5.4	7.2	7.8	10.2	10.4	11.0	12.2	15.2	15.8	22.6	25.4	29.6
6	3.8	4.8	6.2	7.4	8.6	9.2	10.2	11.8	14.4	16.0	19.2	25.6	27.4	28.2
	4.0	4.4	5.8	5.8	7.0	6.6	8.8	10.2	10.6	12.4	15.4	17.0	26.2	27.4
	3.6	4.2	6.0	6.6	7.8	9.4	10.6	11.2	14.8	15.2	17.2	20.2	28.2	28.4
7	4.0	5.8	6.4	5.2	8.8	9.4	10.2	12.6	15.0	14.8	17.6	22.2	26.8	27.4
	4.4	5.2	5.6	5.4	6.2	7.8	8.2	9.6	9.4	13.2	13.4	19.2	25.6	27.0
	3.4	3.6	5.4	5.2	7.6	8.8	10.0	13.2	14.2	15.0	16.6	18.6	23.2	27.8
8	3.6	4.4	5.4	6.4	7.8	9.2	10.6	11.8	12.0	16.6	18.4	23.8	28.0	28.2
	4.0	4.8	5.2	5.6	7.0	7.2	8.6	10.4	10.4	14.2	14.4	20.2	27.2	25.4
	3.2	4.0	5.2	6.0	7.2	8.6	9.4	10.4	11.6	13.2	14.4	18.2	20.2	28.4
9	3.4	4.8	5.2	7.8	10.4	9.4	11.6	13.4	14.0	15.6	18.8	20.6	27.4	27.2
	4.2	4.6	5.6	6.6	6.4	7.8	8.2	9.2	9.6	13.0	15.2	19.0	26.2	25.8
	2.4	2.8	5.0	4.4	4.2	8.4	9.2	8.8	13.0	11.0	13.4	16.8	21.8	27.4
10	3.2	3.8	4.2	5.6	7.2	7.8	7.8	9.0	10.2	13.2	16.6	16.4	26.2	26.4
	4.2	4.4	4.6	5.4	6.4	5.6	7.4	8.0	9.8	12.0	13.2	15.0	26.0	26.2
	2.2	2.8	3.2	4.0	4.8	5.0	4.8	7.2	8.4	10.2	11.0	12.2	13.2	18.4
11	3.0	4.0	5.0	6.4	8.8	8.4	10.2	11.8	12.0	15.6	14.8	18.2	26.4	26.6
	4.0	4.8	5.4	6.0	6.8	7.8	8.2	10.2	10.4	13.2	13.0	12.0	26.2	26.0
	1.8	2.0	1.8	3.4	5.6	6.4	5.8	9.8	8.4	9.8	11.8	10.4	13.4	15.2
12	2.8	3.0	4.0	4.4	5.6	5.4	7.8	8.0	9.8	10.2	11.4	13.4	25.3	26.2
	3.0	3.6	4.2	4.6	5.0	5.6	6.0	6.4	7.2	9.0	10.4	12.4	23.2	26.0
	1.6	2.2	1.6	1.4	4.2	2.8	2.8	4.2	3.6	8.2	9.6	10.6	12.0	15.6
15	2.6	2.8	3.0	4.2	3.8	5.2	6.0	6.8	7.8	8.8	11.2	12.0	18.2	20.0
	3.2	3.2	3.4	4.6	4.4	5.6	6.4	7.0	8.2	9.2	12.4	13.4	25.4	26.6
	1.4	1.6	1.6	2.8	3.0	4.2	3.8	5.8	6.0	8.0	9.2	8.8	14.2	13.8
20	2.2	2.0	3.2	3.8	4.2	4.8	5.6	5.8	6.6	7.6	9.0	11.2	14.4	17.2
	3.0	3.2	3.6	4.4	4.6	5.6	6.6	7.4	7.4	9.0	10.2	12.2	17.4	23.6
	1.2	1.6	1.4	1.4	2.0	3.8	3.2	3.8	4.0	6.2	5.8	8.0	10.6	14.4
25	1.6	1.8	2.2	2.8	3.2	2.8	4.4	6.6	6.6	7.2	7.8	9.6	13.4	16.8
	2.2	2.4	3.0	3.2	3.4	4.6	5.4	7.2	7.6	8.2	8.0	10.4	22.6	23.2
	1.4	1.2	1.2	1.2	1.6	2.0	2.6	3.8	3.4	3.6	3.2	4.4	5.8	12.2

Table 1 in this appendix summarises several thousand simulation experiments with scale-free networks and the obtained results. The rows correspond to the percentage of nodes percolated before the intervention was made (α), whereas the columns correspond to the percentage of nodes which were immunized (β). The number of timesteps it took, averaged over five simulations each, for the network to be saturated by percolation is presented in the cells of the table. Each row has three sub-rows, corresponding to the measures used for intervention: percolation centrality, betweenness centrality, and hop distance, in that order. All in all, the table presents the results of $14 \times 14 \times 3 \times 5 = 2940$ simulation experiments (14 values of α and β, 3 ways to measure centrality, repeated 5 times).

Table 2: A comparison between the average timesteps taken for saturation of percolation when the intervention is PC based, BC based or hop distance based. the network used was a random network with $N = 500$.

α(rows)/β(columns)	1	2	3	4	5	6	7	8	9	10	11	12	15	20
2	4.42	4.64	4.12	4.34	4.42	4.64	4.56	4.32	4.78	4.12	5.12	6.24	5.82	7.24
	3.02	3.30	3.36	3.42	3.78	3.98	4.00	4.12	4.04	4.08	4.96	5.04	5.24	6.08
	5.64	5.84	5.92	5.96	6.04	6,32	6.86	6.78	6.96	7.02	6.98	7.34	9.22	10.36
3	4.32	4.64	4.84	5.26	4.48	5.24	4.48	5.62	6.24	7.18	6.28	6.84	7.22	7.04
	3.42	3.72	3.56	3.92	3.90	4.44	4.46	4.88	5.22	5.68	6.00	6.42	6.78	6.66
	4.28	4.92	4.82	5.50	4.36	5.38	5.58	5.92	6.36	8.42	8.00	6.76	8.48	10.22
4	4.16	4.22	4.82	5.04	4.84	4.26	4.44	4.58	5.02	5.04	5.18	5.26	5.54	5.98
	3.86	3.98	4.12	4.04	4.22	4.12	4.08	4.22	4.48	4.78	4.88	5.02	5.24	5.30
	4.10	4.04	4.36	4.80	4.82	4.22	4.08	4.34	4.56	5.28	5.16	6.34	5.22	7.88
5	4.04	4.22	4.18	4.32	4.44	4.56	4.66	4.68	4.62	4.76	4.80	4.82	4.98	4.86
	4.14	4.18	4.24	4.28	4.36	4.40	4.48	4.52	4.58	4.66	4.70	4.78	4.84	4.86
	3.88	4.14	4.04	4.22	4.34	4.26	4.58	4.60	4.60	4.72	4.94	4.78	4.80	4.84
6	3.8	3.92	4.10	4.08	4.24	4.72	4.46	4.52	4.78	4.80	4.82	4.86	4.90	4.94
	3.74	3.96	4.04	4.06	4.18	4.38	4.44	4.50	4.62	4.74	4.78	4.82	4.86	4.90
	3.76	3.84	3.98	3.96	4.06	4.14	4.44	4.32	4.52	4.60	4.76	4.72	4.86	5.88
7	3.68	3.74	3.80	3.84	4.20	4.14	4.32	4.36	4.56	4.60	4.72	4.68	4.78	4.80
	3.60	3.76	3.78	3.80	3.92	4.04	4.20	4.28	4.44	4.56	4.54	4.66	4.74	4.78
	3.24	3.32	3.38	3.40	3.62	3.58	3.88	3.78	3.96	4.04	4.08	4.22	4.18	4.34
8	3.24	3.64	3.68	3.70	3.72	3.88	3.92	3.98	4.22	4.42	4.34	4.48	4.56	4.60
	3.44	3.56	3.70	3.68	3.70	3.92	3.90	3.94	4.12	4.28	4.32	4.44	4.50	4.54
	3.04	2.98	3.06	3.12	3.24	3.46	3.48	3.58	3.66	3.70	3.84	3.92	4.02	4.06
9	3.26	3.28	3.34	3.46	3.42	3.56	3.88	3.78	4.18	4.28	4.34	4.46	4.50	4.52
	3.28	3.34	3.38	3.44	3.48	3.52	3.68	3.74	3.86	3.96	4.26	4.48	4.42	4.48
	2.68	2.74	2.86	2.74	3.02	3.00	3.06	3.18	3.08	3.24	3.38	3.40	3.64	3.88
10	3.2	3.18	3.24	3.46	3.50	3.66	3.68	3.72	3.88	4.06	4.18	4.22	4.36	4.40
	3.12	3.20	3.22	3.48	3.46	3.58	3.64	3.76	3.80	3.92	4.20	4.18	4.26	4.34
	2.44	2.46	2.58	2.64	2.72	2.80	2.66	2.96	3.12	3.16	3.42	3.34	3.58	3.48
11	2.92	3.10	3.12	3.28	3.42	3.46	3.58	3.66	3.70	3.82	3.92	3.96	4.02	4.22
	2.98	3.14	3.16	3.24	3.48	3.42	3.60	3.62	3.68	3.70	3.88	3.90	3.96	4.34
	2.22	2.32	2.34	2.48	2.50	2.68	2.64	2.62	2.78	2.80	2.92	2.94	3.06	3.16
12	2.60	2.66	2.78	3.02	3.08	3.12	3.24	3.44	3.48	3.56	3.60	3.64	3.88	3.86
	2.56	2.70	2.82	2.94	3.12	3.08	3.16	3.52	3.46	3.54	3.58	3.60	3.72	3.84
	2.02	2.04	2.18	2.26	2.38	2.34	2.44	2.54	2.62	2.78	2.86	2.90	2.94	2.96
15	2.26	2.40	2.52	2.68	2.76	2.84	2.90	2.98	3.04	3.08	3.14	3.16	3.24	3.32
	2.36	2.44	2.56	2.74	2.74	2.78	2.92	2.96	3.08	3.06	3.24	3.10	3.18	3.30
	1.86	1.80	1.88	1.98	2.04	2.22	2.12	2.34	2.94	2.46	2.58	2.60	2.12	2.64
20	2.02	2.14	2.08	2.16	2.18	2.34	2.26	2.66	2.64	2.76	2.80	2.90	2.96	2.94
	2.06	2.18	2.20	2.24	2.28	2.22	2.36	2.70	2.66	2.80	2.78	2.92	2.94	2.90
	1.46	1.48	1.50	1.68	1.54	1.76	1.84	1.92	1.96	2.08	2.10	2.34	2.24	2.40
25	1.80	1.84	1.86	1.90	1.92	1.90	1.94	1.92	2.02	1.98	2.12	2.24	2.30	2.38
	1.84	1.88	1.90	1.94	1.96	1.98	1.92	2.00	2.06	2.08	2.18	2.30	2.44	2.48
	1.40	1.34	1.64	1.58	1.70	1.86	1.84	1.90	1.96	1.98	2.04	2.00	2.12	2.14

Table 2 summarises several thousand simulation experiments with random networks and the obtained results. In this case, given random nature of the experimental networks, we repeated the experiment for each combination of α, β, and a centrality measure 50 times. The rows denote the percentage of nodes percolated before intervention was made (parameter α), whereas the columns denote the percentage of nodes which were 'immunized' against the spread (parameter β). The first, second, and third sub-rows denote timesteps related to PC based, BC based and hop distance based intervention respectively.

We investigated two topologies: scale-free networks and Erdös-Renyi random networks. Erdös-Renyi random networks were chosen for our experiments to contrast them with scale-free networks, and to reflect common real-world topologies which are not scale-free, e.g. non-scale-free networks of towns and motorways [53], [54]. The results for scale-free networks are presented in Table 1 and Figure 6, while Table 2 and Figure 7 summarise experiments with Erdös-Renyi random networks.

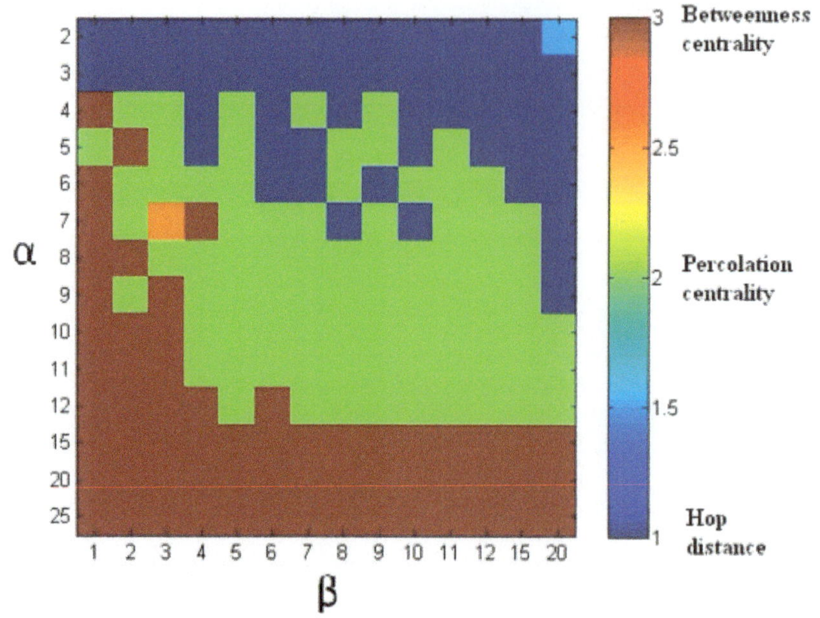

Figure 6: Scale-free network: the ranges of α and β for which the various centrality measures show the best performance.

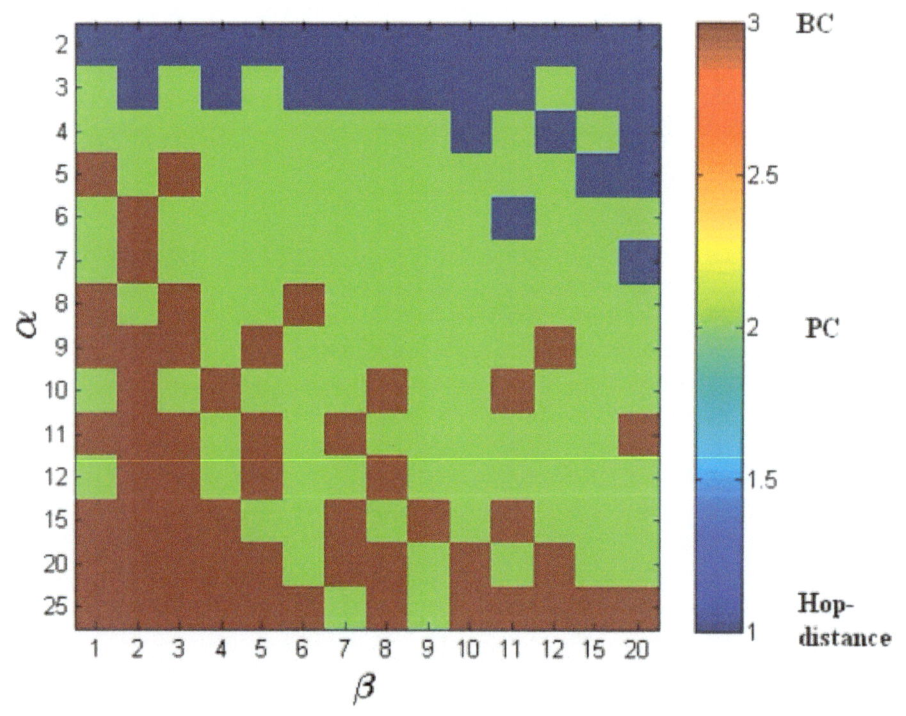

Figure 7: Random network: the ranges of α and β for which the various centrality measures show the best performance.

Figure 6 shows the matrix of α and β values used in our simulation. For a given α and β, the colour of the matrix

corresponds to the measure which returned the best performance. For example, if α=2 and β=1, we could see from Table 1 that percolation centrality based intervention resulted in an average 5.8 timesteps before the network was saturated. Similarly, betweenness centrality based intervention resulted in an average 4.6 timesteps, and hop distance based intervention resulted in an average 6.4 timesteps. Therefore, hop distance was the intervention method which delayed the saturation of percolation furthest, and the corresponding cell in the matrix is shown in blue to indicate this. A green cell shows that percolation centrality was the most useful measure, and a red cell shows that betweenness centrality was the most useful measure. Intermediate colours show there is a tie (same highest average time was obtained for more than one centrality measure).

It could be seen from Table 1 (Appendix) and Fig. 6 that, there are certain circumstances in which percolation centrality becomes a useful resource allocation tool, resulting in longer times for the network to get completely percolated. Particularly, if $\frac{\alpha}{\beta}$ ratio is high (this means either α is high or β is low, and it is easier for the contagion to spread further), then betweenness centrality is the most effective tool for resource allocation. This makes intuitive sense because if we are too late to intervene (high α) or have too few resources (low β), protecting the 'core' of the network from contagion will be our best strategy.

On the other hand, if $\frac{\alpha}{\beta}$ ratio is low (this means either α is low or β is high, and it is hard for the contagion to spread further), then hop distance becomes the most effective tool for resource allocation. Again this is not surprising, since if we have sufficient resources (high β) and sufficient time (low α), we can ring-vaccinate all the nodes around percolated nodes.

It is when the ratio $\frac{\alpha}{\beta}$ is in the medium ranges, that percolation centrality becomes the best resource allocation tool. Indeed, it can be seen that in the 'critical' middle realms of both α and β, in which the percolation is often realistically detected, percolation centrality based intervention has the longest saturation times, and thus the highest chance of slowing down the percolation process. This is the case for 41% of the cells in Fig. 6, for the range of α and β that we have selected. While this percentage is subject to the selection of α and β, the general pattern is clear. As such, the measure of percolation centrality of nodes can be effectively used as a resource allocation tool.

It can be easily seen that our conclusions hold for ER random topology as well: Figure 7 and Table 2 show that for the middle range of ratio $\frac{\alpha}{\beta}$ allocating the resources according to the percolation centrality is again the most effective way to delay percolation.

CONCLUSIONS

We introduced a new centrality measure (percolation centrality) to analyze the importance of nodes during percolation in networks. We demonstrated that when a network is fully percolated (that is, all nodes have the same state), our measure reduces to betweenness centrality. However, when only some nodes are (partially or fully) percolated, betweenness and other existing centrality measures can be ineffective in identifying the relative impact of nodes on further percolation (e.g., on the spread of infection). On the contrary, percolation centrality becomes a useful measure precisely in these scenarios when an early intervention is warranted. Percolation centrality in its basic form can be calculated in $O(NM)$ time, thus including no significant increase in time complexity from standard betweenness centrality. We stress that percolation centrality is introduced here as a generic measure applicable in the context of *any* contagion spread, ranging from computer virus proliferation to information spread in social networks. We also note that, unlike weighted betweenness measures, percolation centrality is dynamic and has relatively low computational complexity. We have also analytically derived some simple relationships between percolation centrality and betweenness centrality for extreme cases. Firstly, percolation centrality averaged over all possible single contagion sources was shown to reduce to betweenness centrality. Secondly, it was shown that if all nodes are infected (or partially percolated to the same extent), then percolation centrality also reduces to betweenness centrality.

We used a simple network of 39 nodes obtained from a contact network study to demonstrate how percolation centrality could be utilised. We simulated a contagion spread, and used percolation centrality to identify critical nodes. Since most contact networks could be modelled as scale-free networks, we also utilized scale-free networks to demonstrate the measurement of percolation centrality, and compared this with results from ER random topologies.

We demonstrated that percolation centrality can be used as a resource allocation tool. Particularly, using simulated scale-free and random networks, we showed that allocating resources according to the percolation-centrality based ranking is most effective when the stage of percolation and the amount of resources available are at a medium level. It was shown that when the percolation process is at its infancy, hop-distance based measures, such as ring vaccination, are most effective to contain the percolation. If the percolation process has affected the node states of a majority of nodes, then betweenness centrality based ranking is most effective. Similarly, if we have extremely limited resources to 'immunize' nodes to percolation, betweenness centrality based choices are most effective, and on the other hand, if we have considerable resources, hop distance based choices are most effective. Percolation centrality based ranking becomes an effective tool at the critical stage where the percolation is just about to break through, and we have a considerable but limited amount of resources to immunize nodes against the spread.

Percolation centrality lends itself to the many extensions to which betweenness centrality has been subjected in the past. For example, a definition of percolation centrality based on random walks can be proposed, where the 'walking agents' could be given weights based on source node states. Furthermore, percolation centrality could be analyzed for both source and target node states. As such, the concept has great potential for further research.

REFERENCES

1. Dorogovtsev SN, Mendes JFF (2003) Evolution of Networks: From Biological Nets to the Internet and WWW. Oxford: Oxford University Press.
2. Albert R, Barabási AL (2002) Statistical mechanics of complex networks. Reviews of Modern Physics 74: 47–97
3. Kepes F, editor (2007) Biological Networks. Singapore: World Scientific.
4. Piraveenan M, Polani D, Prokopenko M (2007) Emergence of genetic coding: an information-theoretic model. Advances in Artificial Life 42–52
5. Alon U (2007) Introduction to Systems Biology: Design Principles of Biological Circuits. London: Chapman and Hall.
6. Newman MEJ, Watts DJ (1999) Scaling and percolation in the small-world network model. Physical Review E 60: 7332–7342
7. Newman MEJ (2002) Spread of epidemic disease on networks. Phys Rev E 66: 016128
8. Meyers LA, Pourbohloul B, Newman MEJ, Skowronski DM, Brunham RC (2005) Network theory and sars: Predicting outbreak diversity. Journal of Theoretical Biology 232: 71–81

9. Meyers LA, Newman MEJ, Pourbohloul B (2006) Predicting epidemics on directed contact networks.Journal of Theoretical Biology 240: 400–418
10. Meyers LA, Newman MEJ, Martin M, Schrag S (2003) Applying network theory to epidemics: Control measures for mycoplasma pneumoniae outbreaks. Emerging Infectious Diseases 92: 204. [PMC free article]
11. Sander LM, Warren CP (2002) Percolation on heterogeneous networks as a model for epidemics. Mathematical Biosciences 180: 293–305
12. Moore C, Newman MEJ (2000) Epidemics and percolation in small-world networks. Physical Review E61: 5678–5682
13. Meyers LA (2006) Contact network epidemiology: Bond percolation applied to infectious disease prediction and control. Bulletin of The American Mathematical Society 44: 63–87
14. Solé RV, Valverde S (2004) Information theory of complex networks: on evolution and architectural constraints. In: Ben-Naim E, Frauenfelder H, Toroczkai Z, editors. Complex Networks, Volume 650 of Lecture Notes in Physics. Berlin: Springer.
15. Solé RV, Cancho RF, Montoya JM, Valverde S (2002) Selection, tinkering and emergence in complex networks —crossing the land of tinkering. Complexity 8: 20–33
16. Park J, Newman MEJ (2004) Statistical mechanics of networks. Physical Review E 70: 066117+
17. Piraveenan M, Prokopenko M, Zomaya AY (2008) Local assortativeness in scale-free networks.Europhysics Letters 84: 28002
18. Piraveenan M, Prokopenko M, Zomaya AY (2009) Assortativeness and information in scale-free networks. European Physical Journal B 67: 291–300
19. Piraveenan M, Prokopenko M, Zomaya AY (2009) Assortativity and growth of Internet. European Physical Journal B 70: 275–285
20. Piraveenan M, Prokopenko M, Zomaya AY (2010) Local assortativeness in scale-free networks — addendum. Europhysics Letters 89: 49901
21. Piraveenan M, Prokopenko M, Zomaya AY (2012) Assortative mixing in directed biological networks.IEEE Transactions on computational biology and bioinformatics 9: 66–78
22. Freeman LC (1977) A set of measures of centrality based on betweenness. Sociometry 40: 35–41
23. Freeman LC (1979) Centrality in social networks: Conceptual clarification. Social Networks 1: 215–239
24. Freeman LC (1991) Centrality in valued graphs: A measure of betweenness based on network flow.Social Networks 13: 141–154
25. Brandes U (2001) A faster algorithm for betweenness centrality. Journal of Mathematical Sociology 25: 163–177Available: http://kops.ub.uni-konstanz.de/bitstream/handle/urn:nbn:de:bsz:352-opus-71888/algorithm.pdf?sequence=1 Accessed 2012 Dec 26.
26. Newman MEJ (2005) A measure of betweenness centrality based on random walks. Social Networks 27: 39–54
27. Stephenson K, Zelen M (1989) Rethinking centrality: Methods and examples. Social Networks 11: 1–37
28. Wang H, Hernandez JM, Van Mieghem P (2008) Betweenness centrality in a weighted network. Physical Review E (Statistical, Nonlinear, and Soft Matter Physics) 77.
29. Sabidussi G (1966) The centrality index of a graph. Psychometrika 31: 581–603
30. Bonacich P (2001) Eigenvector-like measures of centrality for asymmetric relations. Social Networks 23: 191–201
31. Newman MEJ (2008) The mathematics of networks. In: Durlauf SN, Blume LE, editors. The New Palgrave Dictionary of Economics. Basingstoke, UK: Palgrave Macmillan.
32. Noh JD, Rieger H (2004) Random walks on complex networks. Physical Review Letters 92: 118701.
33. Bonacich P (1987) Power and centrality: A family of measures. American Journal of Sociology 92: 1170–1182
34. Klemm K, Serrano MA, Eguluz VM, Miguel MS (2012) A measure of individual role in collective dynamics. Scientific Reports 2 [PMC free article]
35. Bauer F, Lizier JT (2012) Identifying influential spreaders and efficiently estimating infection numbers in epidemic models: A walk counting approach. EPL (Europhysics Letters) 99: 68007
36. Goh KI, Kahng B, Kim D (2001) Universal behavior of load distribution in scale-free networks. Phys Rev Lett 87: 278701.
37. Crucitti P, Latora V, Marchiori M (2004) Model for cascading failures in complex networks. Phys Rev E69: 045104
38. Kinney R, Crucitti P, Albert R, Latora V (2005) Modeling cascading failures in the North American power grid. The European Physical Journal B 46: 101–107
39. Lizier JT, Cornforth DJ, Prokopenko M (2009) The information dynamics of cascading failures in energy networks. In: Proceedings of European Conference on Complex Systems, Coventry, UK. p. 54.
40. Cupac V, Lizier JT, Prokopenko M (2012) Comparing dynamics of cascading failures between network-centric and power flow models. International Journal of Electrical Power and Energy Systems In press.
41. Dolev S, Elovici Y, Puzis R (2010) Routing betweenness centrality. J ACM 57: 25:1–25:27
42. Borgatti S, Everett M (2006) A Graph-theoretic perspective on centrality. Social Networks 28: 466–484
43. De P, Singh AE, Wong T, Yacoub W, Jolly AM (2004) Sexual network analysis of a gonorrhoea outbreak. Sexually Transmitted Infections 280–285 [PMC free article]
44. Ferrari MJ, Bansal S, Meyers LA, Bjørnstad ON (2006) Network frailty and the geometry of herd immunity. Proceedings Biological sciences/The Royal

Society 273: 2743–2748 [PMC free article]

45. Barabási AL (2009) Scale-free networks: A decade and beyond. Science 325: 412–413

46. Barabási AL, Albert R, Jeong H (2000) Scale-free characteristics of random networks: The topology of the world-wide web. Physica A 281: 69–77

47. Barabási AL, Bonabeau E (2003) Scale-free networks. Scientific American 288: 50–59

48. Cavagna A, Cimarelli A, Giardina I, Parisi G, Santagati R, et al. . (2009). Scale-free correlations in bird flocks. Available: http://arxiv.org/abs/0911.4393 Accessed 2012 Dec 26.

49. Mitchell M (2006) Complex systems: Network thinking. Artificial Intelligence 170: 1194–1212

50. Guimera R, Sales-Pardo M, Amaral LA (2007) Classes of complex networks defined by role-to-role connectivity profiles. Nature Physics 3: 63–69 [PMC free article]

51. Zhou S, Mondragón RJ (2004) The rich-club phenomenon in the internet topology. IEEE Communications Letters 8: 180–182

52. Zhou S, Mondragón RJ (2003) Towards modelling the internet topology—the interactive growth model. Physical Review E 67: 026126

53. Adamatzky A, Akl SG, Alonso-Sanz R, van Dessel W, Ibrahim Z, et al. (2012) Are motorways rational from slime mould›s point of view? International Journal of Parallel, Emergent and Distributed SystemsAvailable: http://arxiv.org/abs/1203.2851 Accessed 2012 Dec 26.

54. Adamatzky A, Prokopenko M (2012) Slime mould evaluation of australian motorways. International Journal of Parallel, Emergent and Distributed Systems 27: 275–295

CHAPTER 4

CACHE SCHEME BASED ON PRE-FETCH OPERATION IN ICN

Jie Duan[1], Xiong Wang[2], Shizhong Xu[2], Yuanni Liu[1], Chuan Xu[1], Guofeng Zhao[1]

[1]Communication and Information Engineering, Chongqing University of Posts and Telecommunications (CQUPT), Chongqing, China,

[2]Communication and Information Engineering, University of Electronic Science and Technology of China (UESTC), Chengdu, China

ABSTRACT

Many recent researches focus on ICN (Information-Centric Network), in which named content becomes the first citizen instead of end-host. In ICN, Named content can be further divided into many small sized chunks, and chunk-based communication has merits over content-based communication. The universal in-network cache is one of the fundamental infrastructures for ICN. In this work, a chunk-level cache mechanism based on pre-fetch operation is proposed. The main idea is that, routers with cache store should pre-fetch and cache the next chunks which may be accessed in the near future according to received requests and cache policy for reducing the users' perceived latency. Two pre-fetch driven modes are present to answer when and how to pre-fetch. The LRU (Least Recently Used) is employed for the cache replacement. Simulation results show that the average user perceived latency and hops can be decreased by employed this cache mechanism based on pre-fetch operation. Furthermore, we also demonstrate that the results are influenced by many factors, such as the cache capacity, Zipf parameters and pre-fetch window size.

INTRODUCTION

Recently, most of the network applications and services only care about content distribution and retrieval, while the current Internet still relies on the host-to-host communication model. Several researchers devote to Information-Centric Network (ICN) [1–6] in recent years, which is a significant potential approach to resolve such mismatching problem mentioned above. The voice transformed in MANET [7, 8] is one type of the contents. The content objects in ICN are routed by content names, not by host locators (IP address). Named contents become the first citizen in the ICN architecture instead of end-host, which gives the opportunity to identify content objects as they travel from source to destination. In turn, given that named content objects are transferred instead of unidentifiable data containers, i.e., IP packets, these objects can be cached in the network and served to subsequent users with the similar interest.

All ICN architectures proposed share three commonalities [9, 10]. The first one is the publish/subscribe (pub/sub) paradigm. A content provider publishes a content object, while a client subscribes to the content file through describing the corresponding interest. This temporal and spatial decoupling between information generation and interest indication is a

Citation: Duan J, Wang X, Xu S, Liu Y, Xu C, Zhao G. Cache Scheme Based on Pre-Fetch Operation in ICN. Choo K-KR, ed. PLoS ONE. 2016;11(6):e0158260. doi:10.1371/journal.pone.0158260.

desirable feature for future internet. Secondly, the information oriented security model is adopted. Because content objects are signed by the original content provider, the authenticity of content can be easily verified by network elements or consumers. The web application protection techniques in [11–14] can be seen as the typical ICN information oriented security models. The third commonality is the universal in-network cache, which is the main researching concern of this paper. content in ICN can be further divided into many small-sized chunks. Chunk-based communication has merits over content-based communication, for example, user can get a content file from many different sources by the means of chunks, and fine-granularity cache scheme should be designed.

Caching and pre-fetching operation are well-known strategies deployed in application layer for improving the performance of current network. The caching scheme is composed by two key parts: i) Cache decision, which decides on whether an object should or not to be stored; and ii) Replacement policy, which is used to select the replacing objects in cache for the newly replied objects. Compared to the traditional application-layer content distribution system, the network-layer cache platform of ICN has its own prosperities: 1) Universal cache with small capacities. Almost all routers in the network can be configured with small capacity and high-speed memory technology. 2) Interaction relationship between cache configuration and network traffic. The router cache policy or capacity impacts the upward traffic through cache hit rate. Meanwhile, the downward traffic can affect the arriving rate of the cache router to further result in the cache policy or capacity deployment. 3) Provides a unified platform of network layer content caching for various flows. 4) ICN content acquisition mode provides new cache management method. In-network cache policy for ICN has attracted more attentions in last few years [15–23]. Ioannis Psaras et al. [15] determine the caching probability of a content object in each node on the path. Progressive caching [16] sequentially pushes the content to be cached closer to the edge node based on content popularity. The main idea of chunk-level cache scheme WAVE [17] is suggested that routers should dynamically adjust their cache windows for content on the basis of the content popularity, and should recommend the number of chunks to be cached at the downstream node. ABC (Age-Based Cooperation) [18] sets an age for each cached item, which should be evicted from the cache only when the age is expired. Aifang Xu et al. [19] propose use tracking store (TS) to assist caching objects. Jos´e Quevedo et al. [20] use a freshness value to design the cache policy under wireless sensor network. Pending time history is carried in interest for help to compute the better caching set for each router in [21]. Wang, W. et al. [22] exploits the correlation between content popularity and network topology information for ICN caching. ILP is used for programming the caching of the complex dynamic streaming in [23]. The different methods for the above mentioned works were proposed to improve the network performance. However, none of them has involved in pre-fetch operation to further fast the content retrieval.

By the same token, the essence of pre-fetching algorithm relies on its operation, how to pre-fetch, and the pre-fetched objects. Comparing to cache policy, pre-fetch operation is likely a strategy to hide retrieval network latency for the user rather than to reduce it. Pre-fetch operation has been studied in web service last twenty years ago [24–26]. One main drawback in Web pre-fetch system is over-prefetch, that is, when space (cache) on a server is allowed, all the referencing webs should be pre-fetched and cached to be requested. Nevertheless, many pre-fetched objects may not be issued by clients, which waste storage capacity and overlong the total network latency. Path-based pre-fetching and caching are integrated in file system [24]. The result has shown that aggressive pre-fetching is harmful to latency reduction. To offset such defects, most web pre-fetch operations concentrate on the high accuracy prediction model of pre-fetch probability (referencing objects), which include temporal locality, data mining, or more complicated mathematic models. Padmanabhan and Mogul [25] have investigated the tradeoff between network load incremental and performance gain of web pre-fetching based on renewing of dependency graph. Cao et al. [26] have studied an integrated caching and pre-fetch model on a file system from a theoretical viewpoint. The differences between in-network caching for ICN and the web caching have been listed before. Because of the characteristics of universal caching and chunk-based communication in ICN, routers could pre-fetch the following chunks for a given content, avoiding complex predication algorithm in web pre-fetch operation. The shortcoming of over-prefetch should be ignored for the LRU cache replacement in our work. Even though the number of chunks pre-fetched is large enough, the network latency is also shorter than that without pre-fetch operation. The pre-fetching operation for ICN has been studied in [27–29]. The pre-fetching is mentioned in [27] to improve the retransmission and congestion control mechanisms in ICN. But no details or following works are given about the pre-fetch operation. Authors in [28] focus on prefetching content chunks for individual mobile devices, by predicting the next network location the device is moving to, and at what time, and examine how best to partition the storage at the AP. Obviously, the pre-fetching operation here is just activated by APs, and the main contribution is about the predicting of the device's mobility and the user pattern. [29] harnesses multiple caches in ICN to pre-fetch video stream during peak congestion. Architecture for pre-fetching for video streams is presented, which combines network monitoring with ICN semantics to populate a cache ahead of the need of the video client. Our argument is that all the cache routing should determine the pre-fetch operation, and the focus is how and when to pre-fetch. Moreover, our goal is to reduce the latency experienced by clients by considering cache policy based on pre-fetch operation.

In this paper, the idea of pre-fetching and caching can be perfectly applied into in-network ICN caching together. Cache router can activate the pre-fetch operation, and pre-fetched objects should also be stored on ICN cache routers. Therefore, our main contribution is trying to answer how to design an efficient cache scheme based on pre-fetch operation to reduce latency, and measure the effect of pre-fetch windows for improving performance.

PRELIMINARY KNOWLEDGE

Our cache scheme based on pre-fetch operation can be applied onto any of chunk-level ICN architecture. In order to facilitate the presentation, the CCN (content centric network) [3] is taken as an example. The term "data" and "chunk" can be interchangeable in remain part of this paper, unless specifically stated.

In CCN, named contents are published at nodes (providers). Each router in CCN contains two main data structures (as shown in Fig 1): FIB (Forwarding Information Base) and PIT (Pending Interest Table). Routing strategies are employed to form the FIB, which directs the corresponding requests (called interests in CCN) for named contents towards the correct providers. Forwarded interests should leave bread crumbs in PIT for sending the returned data down to request generators. Some of the routers with cache function known as cache router in CCN should hold a CacheStore (CS, buffer memory) to store the very objects based on their cache scheme.

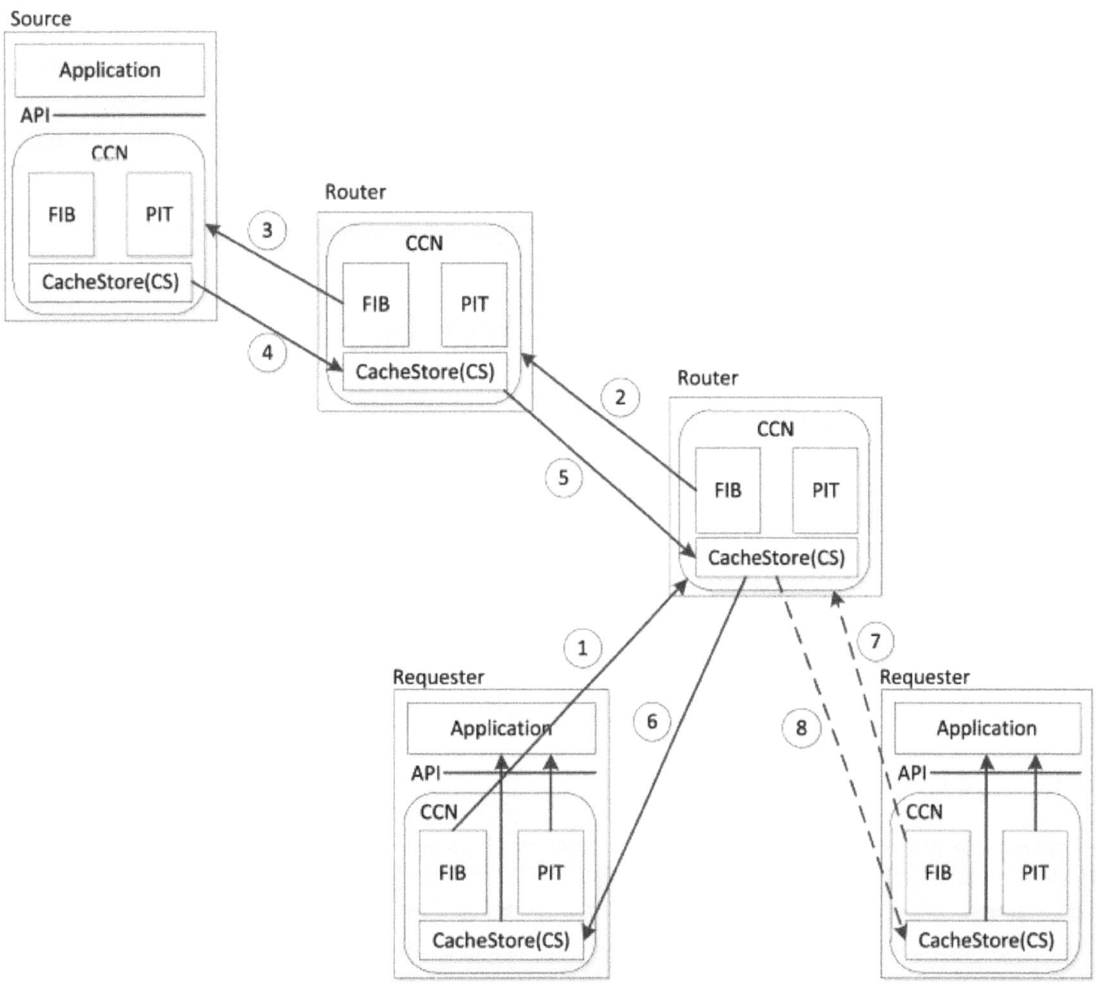

Figure 1: CCN overview.

When an interest packet arrives on an interface, the cache router first checks its local CS. If the requested data exists in the CS, the router should send it back directly through this interface, and the interest should be discarded, as illustrated by step 7–8. Otherwise, it reviews whether such an interest is already in the PIT, if so, it updates the interface in PIT to assure the correctly reply of chunk. Otherwise, router forwards the request upstream toward content source based on FIB, meanwhile, leaves a bread crumb in PIT (step 1–3). The content source of an object is not only including the content provider, but also the routers caching the object.

The process of relaying replied chunk is relatively simple, since data is only routed through the chain of PIT entries back to the original requester(s) (step 4–6). Whenever a router receives a chunk, it should decide whether to cache or not based on its own caching policy.

The request process is assumed to be the so-called "independent reference model": the probability of arriving request for a given object only depends on the object's popularity but not on the sequence of requests that came before. The popularity of content object follows generalized *Zipf* law, which have been illustrated in many realistic traffic flows [5]: the request rate $q(n)$ for the n_{th} most popular object is proportional to $1/n$ for some *Zipf* parameter (denoted by *Zipf*(*a*)). Equivalently, we also assume content requests occur at the instants of independent Poisson processes, and cache router implements LRU replacement policy.

CACHE SCHEME BASED ON PREFETCHING OPERATION

A content object can be further divided into many fine-granularity chunks with chunk-level communication model in ICN. An end user should send out the interests for all chunks of a content object to the provider, if he wants to get the whole content object. An interest is corresponding to a chunk, not for a content object.

Problem Illustration

As mentioned in section 2, by-path caching is one of the main components in CCN. The interest is forwarded by the routers following the FIB, while leaving a bread crumb in the PIT, which directs the data reply. Once a cache router receives a data, it should decide whether cache or not according to the cache policy.

The stop-and-wait request mode is assumed to be applied in CCN: end user should issue the next chunk immediately only after receiving the reply of the requested chunk. If an end user fetches a content object from the provider passing through three cache routers, and none of the cache routers has cached any chunks of such content object, the hop number for successfully achieving a chunk is accounted for 8. If the average propagation delay of each link for transmitting a chunk is d, the propagation delay experienced by the user to get a chunk should be $8d$. The propagation delay is the main factor of user perceived delay to ignore the processing and transmission time while d is large enough. If the chunk number of the content object is Nc, the total propagation delay the user experienced will be $8*Nc*d$.

For some latency-sensitive flow, such as VoD, it is intolerable for a user to wait for a long time to get the following chunks or the whole object. The bad quality of service will lead to the loss of users, which would decrease profit of network provider.

Obviously, in CCN, all the cache action is activated by the data, which is derived from the user requests in essence. In other words, only after the chunk has been asked by the users not long ago, the chunk should be stored in the cache. Should the follow-up chunks retrieval be fasted to reduce the total latency experience by user? Should the routers prepare for the chunks which will be requested in the near future? The main goal of the cache scheme based on pre-fetch operation proposed is to decrease user perceived latency. The details of the cache scheme based on pre-fetch operation are given in the following.

Pre-fetch Operation

A cache scheme should decide what to be cached and the replacement policy. Both fetched and pre-fetched chunks are considered to be cached in cache scheme based pre-fetch operation, and LRU replacement policy is used in our scheme.

The pre-fetch operation as the core function of our cache scheme should answer what to be pre-fetched and how to pre-fetch. We argue that, the probability for the downstream node (or end user) to request the following few chunks in the same content of the requested chunk deems to be rather higher than to request the other chunks far away or from other contents. Then pre-fetching the following chunks of the same content omits complex pre-fetch prediction, which is the main work in web pre-fetch or recommendation system recently. The number of pre-fetch chunks is labelled as pre-fetch window W, which is the main factor affecting the latency reduction.

In the following, we focus on how to pre-fetch. As the assumption mentioned in WAVE [17], the original servers as well as cache routers can recommend its downstream cache routers to store the chunks. We also assume the pre-fetch operation can be advised by the upstream nodes. For more efficient prefetching and caching, we need some collaboration among cache routers. In this paper, a cache router suggests the pre-fetching operation to its downstream cache routers by marking the chunk when it forwards the chunk. For this, the pre-fetch flag bit is needed in the chunk (e.g., in the Data packet header in CCN). If a cache router receives a chunk with the non-zero pre-fetch flag, the router is suggested by the upstream node with the pre-fetching operation. A cache router generates the pre-fetch operation only when meets any of the following pre-fetch-driven-modes.

- cache-driven mode: A downstream request is hit in its local cache
- data-driven mode: It receives the replied data requested by the downstream nodes (not generated by itself), and the pre-fetch flag in the header is 1.

Note that, the request mentioned in both modes should be received from the neighbour nodes, not issued by its own pre-fetch operation, which avoids the endless self-driving pre-fetch operation.

The cache-driven mode endows each cache router to decide the pre-fetch operation by itself, while the data-driven mode enable the upward nodes to recommend whether the pre-fetch operation should occur at the downstream cache router or not through setting the pre-fetch flag in the chunk packet header, which is the collaborative pre-fetch idea. The pre-fetch flag can be decided by many factors, such as the content popularity, hops to the nearest source (cache or provider), and the priority, etc. However, how to set the pre-fetch flag is beyond the scope of this paper. The pre-fetch flag here is just decided by the hop to the nearest content source.

Fig 2 gives an example of request process for cache scheme based on pre-fetch operation with pre-fetch window $W = 1$ (denoted $W(1)$), while it omits the reply process under the assumption of stop-and-wait request mode. The provider owns the whole chunks of the requested content, depicted by the numeric boxes below. No chunks for the requested content have been cached on the cache routers before. All links have the same communication delay. The pre-fetch flag here is decided only by the hop number to the nearest content source in the header. If the hop equals to 1, the pre-fetch flag is set to be 1. Otherwise, the pre-fetch flag remains 0. The dotted arrows with different colours are used to express the three classes of interests respectively: user interest, data-driven pre-fetch interest, cache-driven pre-fetch interest. The first number on the dotted arrow is the sequence number of event generated; the second one represents the requested chunk number of the content object. The numeric boxes below each cache router are the pre-fetched chunks which should be cached. For simplifying the description, we use interest[i] to represent the request for the i_{th} chunk, data[i] to denote the reply of interest[i], and (a,b) to show the event on dotted arrow.

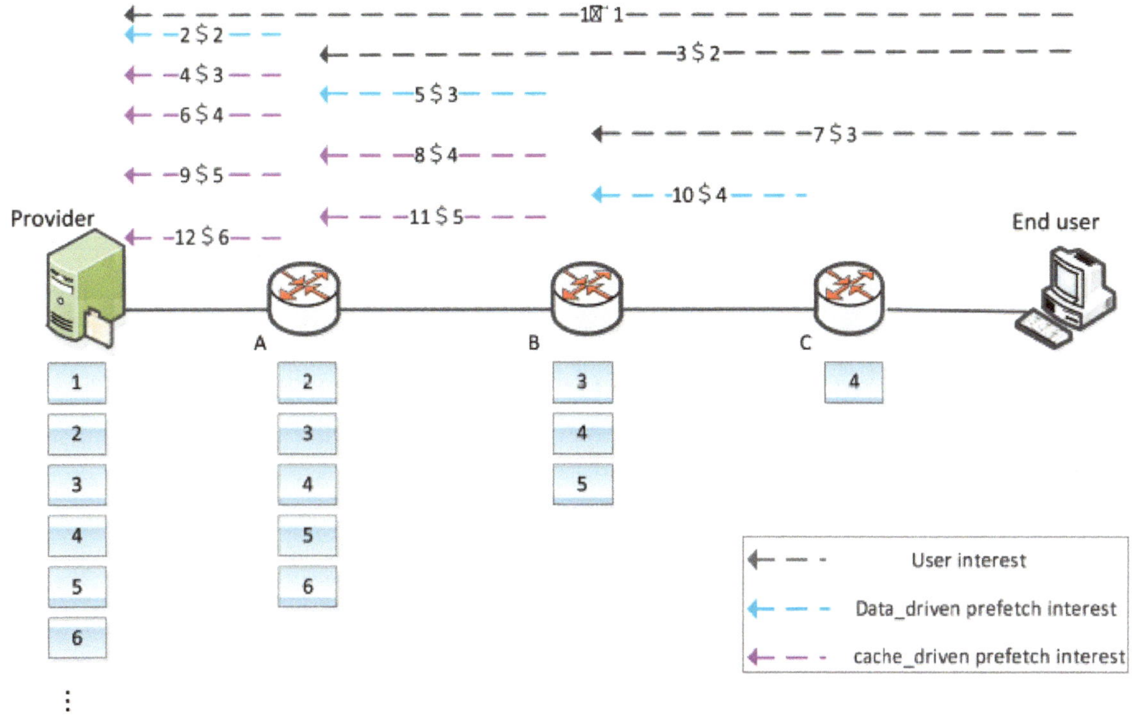

Figure 2: Example of pre-fetch operation.

The request process of cache scheme based on pre-fetch operation is given as below.

Step 1: The end user firstly sends out the user request interest[1], which should be forwarded towards the provider based on the CCN communication process (as shown in (1, 1))

Step 2: After received the data[1] (which is omitted in Fig 2 and should occur between (1,1) and (2,2)), router A should cache and forward data[1] downwards according to standard CCN replying process. Meanwhile, because the pre-fetch flag in the header is 1 (hop is 1), router A generates and sends out interest[2] to the provider for pre-fetching the 2_{nd} chunk based on data-driven mode, as shown in (2,2). Because of the LRU cache replacement, router A should cache the data[2] after received it, which is the first chunk in numeric boxes below router A. But data[2] should not be forwarded downstream without arriving interest.

Step 3: Interest[2] originated from end user (3,2) should be hit in local CS of router A because of its previous pre-fetch operation, which enables router A to pre-fetch the next chunk according to cache-driven mode, the interest[3] of event (4,3). Data[2] will be forwarded back to requestor by router A.

Step 4: The reply of data[2] allows router B to generate data-driven pre-fetch interest[3] (see event(5,3)), since the hop between router B to the nearest source of data[2] (router A) is 1, that is, the pre-fetch flag is 1. Then such interest[3] should be hit on router A for step 3. Router A should issue cache-driven pre-fetch interest[4] upstream to provider (6,4).

Step 5: User request interest[3] (7,3) can be hit on router B for event (5,3), which drives the cache-driven pre-fetch interest[4] of router B (see (8,4)). Finally in turn to cache-driven pre-fetch interest[5] of router A (9,5).

Step 6: Similarly, the reply of data[3] enable router C to pre-fetch data[4] (10,4). Cache-driven pre-fetch interest[5] (11,5) and [6] (12,6) are sequentially activated on router B and A.

After step 6, user could gain the following chunks directly on router C. At the same time, the following user interest[i] could trigger a cache-driven pre-fetch interest[i+1], [i+2] and [i+3] on router C, B and A, respectively.

Comparing to the previous average hop *8* and the total hop *8Nc*, the hops in cache scheme based on pre-fetch operation are shrinking to be (12+2 *Nc*)/ *Nc* and (12+2 *Nc*). When *Nc* is much larger than 3, the average hop reduced is 6.

The above pre-fetch process is also applicable for other pre-fetch window *W*. Then the number of pre-fetch router sent out is set to be *W*, when router performs pre-fetch operation.

Qualitative Analysis

In this section, we first give the mathematical model for network delay comparison between CCN architectures with pre-fetching and without pre-fetching. And the result of average latency comparison is given to show the validity of the pre-fetching based caching scheme in CCN.

Let *N* be the number of total content objects. Each object is composed by *K* chunks. The request rate of contents follows *Zipf* distribution. Therefore, the requested probability for n_{th} most popular content $p(n)$ is given as $p(n) = A / n^{\alpha}$, where $A = \sum_{n\in[1,N]} 1/n^{\alpha}$. α is the *Zipf* parameter. It is reasonable to apply the independent reference model at each router, because its request process results from the superposition of many independent overflow processes, each of that contributes a small fraction of overall request. In this configuration, the occupancy states of cache routers can reasonably be assumed to be statistically independent.

The total request rate on a router is the sum of rates requested by neighbouring nodes and generated by itself. If the total request content rate on a node is q, the request rate for content n should be $q(n) = q \times p(n)$. The request rate for each chunk in content n is also $q(n)$, for the chunks of the same content object with the same request rates. Given the delivery of content from server to user should traverse routers R_M, R_{M-1}, …, R_1; and the delay for each hop is T_{hop}.

We firstly give the quality analysis on standard CCN architecture without pre-fetching. Because all of the chunks belonging to the same content are assumed to have the same request rate, the hit ratios for all chunks in a router i are the same. For chunk k of content n, the hit ratio on router i is $P_i(n, k)$. For any chunks m of content n, the hit ratio satisfied that $P_i(n, k) = P_i(n, m) = P_i(n)$. On the path from server to a user with M routers, all requested chunks can be attained from server, that is, $P_{M+1}(n) = 1$.

With LRU, we use an approximation proposed by Che et al. [5] to estimate the cache hit ratio. If the cache capacity is C, the hit ratio $P_i(n, k)$ for chunk k of content n with request rate $q(n)$ can be written as $P_i(n, k) = 1 - e^{-T_C} \times q(n)$, for some parameter T_C. The capacity should hold all cached object, that is, $C = \sum_{n \in [1,N]} K(1 - e^{-T_C \times q(n)})$.

To model the delay for the chunk k of content n in CCN, it is known that only the missing requests should be forwarded upward. That is, the request k reaches on a router i only when the interest is missed in all of the downstream routers. Let $AP_i(n, k)$ to be the arrival probability of request k reaches on a router i, which can be expressed as

$$AP_i(n,k) = \prod_{j<i} (1 - p_j(n,k)) \tag{1}$$

$T_{CCN}(n, k)$ is the delay for retrieval of the chunk k in content n, which can be described as the sum of all situations that the interest k is hit on each router. Because of the all the chunks in the same content get the same hit ratio on a router. So the average delay for the chunks in content $n T_{CCN}(n)$ is also $T_{CCN}(n, k)$. That is,

$$T_{CCN}(n) = T_{CCN}(n,k) = \sum_{i \in [1, M+1]} 2iT_{hop} \times p_i(n,k) \times AP_i(n,k) \tag{2}$$

The term $2iT_{hop}$ is the round-trip-time between router i and the user. The average delay for user to get any chunk of any content should be expressed as

$$T_{CCN}\_avg = \sum_{n \in [1,N]} p(n) \times T_{CCN}(n) \tag{3}$$

Then the network latency for cache scheme based on pre-fetching is derived. Because of the pre-fetching operation, the request rate on each router is different from the one without pre-fetching, which further causes the change of the hit ratio on routers, and finally leads to the delay variation.

$W(1)$ as an example is analysed here to show the effect of the cache scheme based on pre-fetch. The other pre-fetch windows can be deduced in the same way. The online cache is functionally supposed to be composed by common cache and pre-fetching cache under the pre-fetching operation. The pre-fetched without requested downstream chunks should be stored in pre-fetching cache. The pre-fetch operation is enabled after the hit rate of common cache has been stabilized. The chunks in pre-fetching cache should be hold for a time to ensure the arrival of request downstream. The chunk should be shifted to common cache, if the chunk is requested by downstream node. The overdue of pre-fetched chunk means that the chunk should not be requested by downstream node obviously, so the chunk should be deleted from pre-fetching cache when the stored time exceeds for a limit. Although the functions of common cache and pre-fetching cache are different, they share the same buffer memory with almost the same eviction time in LRU.

For chunk k of content n, the hit rate on router R_i's common cache is $P_i^{com}(n,k)$. It is reasonable assumed that the hit rates for a given chunk on all routers' common cache are almost the same. That is, $P_i^{com}(n,k) = P_j^{com}(n,k) \ (\forall i \neq j)$, for router R_i is different from R_j. With LRU approximation mentioned before, the hit ratio of common cache can be estimated. If the common cache capacity is C, the hit rate $P_i^{com}(n,k)$ for chunk k of content n with popularity $q(n)$ can be written as $P_i^{com}(n,k) = 1 - e^{-T_C \times q(n)}$, for some parameter T_C. The capacity should hold all cached objects, that is, $C = \sum_{n \in [1,N]} K(1 - e^{-T_C \times q(n)})$. The hit rate of all chunks on server is 1, that is, $P_{M+1}^{com}(n,k) = 1$. Let $P_i^{pre}(n,k)$. to be the possibility for router R_i to pre-fetch chunk k of content n, which can also be seemed as the pre-fetch hit rate. If chunk k has been pre-fetched by router R_i before the downstream requesting, the interest should be hit. The pre-fetch operation should not occurred on server, therefore, $P_{M+1}^{pre}(n,k) = 0$.

If the total hit rate on router R_i is $H_i(n, k)$ ($i \in [1, M + 1]$), that is,

$$H_i(n,k) = P_i^{com}(n,k) + P_i^{pre}(n,k) \tag{4}$$

The hit rate of pre-fetch cache $P_i^{pre}(n,k)$ is calculated in the following section. Router R_i ($i \in [1, M]$) pre-fetches chunk k only when the following prerequisites are met: a) At first, chunk k has not been stored in common cache. The possibility is calculated as $(1 - P_i^{com}(n,k))$; b) secondly, one of the driven modes is satisfied. The downstream request for chunk k-1 must arrive and hit at router R_i in cache-driven mode; while in data-driven mode, the downstream request for chunk k-1 must arrive and be hit at router R_i+1, when the pre-fetch flag is determined by the hop in the header. For router R_i, the downstream request is the pre-fetch request generated by downstream routers, or the user request. Hence,

$$P_i^{pre}(n,k) = (1 - P_i^{com}(n,k))[(\sum_{0<j<i} P_j^{pre}(n,k-1)hit_{j,i}(n,k-1) + P_i(n,k-1)) + (\sum_{0<j<i+1} P_j^{pre}(n,k-1)hit_{j,i+1}(n,k-1) + P_{i+1}(n,k-1))] \tag{5}$$

In expression (5), $\sum_{0<j<i} P_j^{pre}(n,k-1)hit_{j,i}(n,k-1) + P_i(n,k-1)$ and $\sum_{0<j<i+1} P_j^{pre}(n,k-1)hit_{j,i+1}(n,k-1) + P_{i+1}(n,k-1)$ are the probabilities for downstream request k-1 arriving and being hit at router R_i and R_i+1, respectively. If a pre-fetch request k is generated by router R_i, the conditional probability for the

request k arrives and hits on upstream router R_j is $hit_{i,j}(n, k)$. Where,

$$hit_{i,j}(n,k) = H_i(n,k)\prod_{i<t<j}(1 - H_j(n,k)) \tag{6}$$

The delay expectation $T(n,k)$ for user to get the chunk k of content n should be

$$T(n,k) = \sum_{i\in[1,M+1]} T_i(n,k) \tag{7}$$

Where, $T_i(n, k)$ is the delay expected for user to get chunk k from router i. Let $P_i(n, k)$ and $D_i(n, k)$ to be the probability and delay experienced respectively, when user sends out the request k be hit at router R_i. Then

$$\begin{aligned} T_i(n,k) &= \prod_{j<i}(1 - H_j(n,k)) \times [P_i^{com}(n,k) \times D_i^{com}(n,k) + P_i^{pre}(n,k) \times D_i^{pre}(n,k)] \\ &= \prod_{j<i}(1 - H_j(n,k)) \times [P_i^{com}(n,k) + P_i^{pre}(n,k)] \times [\frac{P_i^{com}(n,k)}{P_i^{com}(n,k) + P_i^{pre}(n,k)} \times D_i^{com}(n,k) + \frac{P_i^{pre}(n,k)}{P_i^{com}(n,k) + P_i^{pre}(n,k)} \times D_i^{pre}(n,k)] \\ &= P_i(n,k) \times D_i(n,k) \end{aligned} \tag{8}$$

If the content k request by user is hit on the common cache of R_i, the delay is represented by Dcomi(n,k); otherwise, if the request is hit at the pre-fetch cache of R_i, the delay is Dprei(n,k). Then

$$P_i(n,k) = H_i(n,k)\prod_{j<i}(1 - H_j(n,k)) \tag{9}$$

$$D_i(n,k) = \frac{P_i^{com}(n,k)}{H_i(n,k)} \times D_i^{com}(n,k) + \frac{P_i^{pre}(n,k)}{H_i(n,k)} \times D_i^{pre}(n,k) \tag{10}$$

We calculate the delay expectation for user to get the chunk k from router R_i in the following.

It is more complex for solving $D_i(n, k)$. Because when user request k arrives at router R_i, it can be hit on the common cache. Similarly, it can be stored on the pre-fetch cache; or it has been pre-fetched but has not got the replied chunk by R_i. If the pre-fetch request generated by R_i is hit by a upstream router R_j, it also can be hit by common cache or pre-fetch operation of R_j, which is the repeat of the previous procedure. Obviously, it is too difficult to get the accurate value of $D_i(n, k)$. However, we can always find the nearest source node $S(i \le S \le M + 1)$ of chunk k from R_i. The source node is the node storing the chunk k in its common caches. Therefore, we turn to get the worst-case delay. That is, if the user request is hit by pre-fetch operation of R_i, the routers between R_i and S are assumed without pre-fetch operation. Under this situation, let $Wait_{i,S}(n, k)$ be the waiting time after request arriving at R_i.

If S is R_i, that is, user request is hit at the common cache of router R_i, $Wait_{i,S}(n, k) = 0$. If $S>i$, R_i is the nearest pre-fetching node from user. The generation time of pre-fetch request k almost is the same as the replied time of chunk k-1 on R_i. Hence, $Wait_{i,S}(n, k) = \max\{0, (S - i) - (i - 1)\} = \max\{0, S - 2i + 1\}$. Combining the above two situations, the waiting time on R_i can be expressed as

$$Wait_{i,S}(n, k) = \max\{0, (S - i) - (i - 1)\} = \max\{0, S - 2i + 1\} \tag{11}$$

The probability for the upstream router R_j of R_i acting as S is $PS_{i,j}(n, k)$, then

$$PS_{i,j}(k) = \begin{cases} P_i(n,k)/H_i(n,k), & if\ i = j \\ P_i^{pre}(n,k)/H_i(n,k) \times hit_{i,j}^{com}(n,k), & else \end{cases} \tag{12}$$

Therefore,

$$D_i(n,k) = \sum_{j\in[i,M+1]} PS_{i,j}(k) \times 2T_{hop} \times [(i+1) + wait_{i,j}(n,k)] \tag{13}$$

Substituting the expression (9)-(13) into (8), the $T_i(n,k)$ should be

$$T_i(n,k) = \prod_{j<i}(1 - H_j(n,k)) \times [P_i^{com}(n,k) + P_i^{pre}(n,k)] \times [\sum_j PS_{i,j}(n,k) \times 2T_{hop} \times [(i+1) + wait_{i,j}(n,k)]] \tag{14}$$

Then, the delay $T(n,k)$ for user getting chunk k of content n should be attained after substituting (14) into (7).

The average delay for getting any chunk of content n is

$$T\_avg(n) = \sum_{k\in[1,K]} T(n,k)/K \tag{15}$$

Thus, the average delay for user to get any chunk of any content should be

$$Delay\_avg = \sum_{n\in[1,N]} p(n) \times T\_avg(n) \tag{16}$$

To show the validity of our method, the parameters are given in the following. The content number N is 10000, and the chunk number K is 10. The number of cache routers M is 3. The cache capacities deployed on cache routers are all set from 100 to 1000. And the request rates originated from users on all routers are set as 50. The *Zipf* parameter is 0.8. Table 1 gives the results compared between the standard CCN with LRU and the cache scheme based on pre-fetch. T_{hop} is 10 ms. Table 1 gives the results compared between the standard CCN with LRU and the cache scheme based on pre-fetch. Obviously, under different cache deployment, the average delay under pre-fetching *Delay_avg* is always smaller than T_{CCN}_avg without pre-fetching.

Table 1: The other results compared with the delay without pre-fetch operation will be given in the following section through the simulation.

Average latency comparison	Cache capacity		
	100	500	1000
T_{CCN}_*avg*(ms)	72	58	47
Delay_avg(ms)	48	33	29

PERFORMANCE EVALUATIONS

The performance is shown in both the results of analysis and simulation. According to the former qualitative analysis, the efficiency of cache scheme based on pre-fetch operation can be demonstrated. While the performance evaluation is further conducted by simulation in three aspects: i) the average latency; ii) the average hops; iii) the hit rate. The simulation results will be influenced by cache capacity, ***Zipf*** distribution parameters and pre-fetch window size *W*.

Simulation Scenarios

Binary trees with 15 nodes are deployed, as shown in Fig 3. The leaves behave as clients which connected by end users who should generate the requests. The root node is the only content provider. The other intermediate nodes are cache routers with the same cache capacity, which can trigger the pre-fetch operations. The cache routers are named as level_down and level_up routers, respectively, according to the location in the topology. The uplinks refer to the links between root to level_up cache routers, while the links between level_up and level_down cache routers are named as downlink. All the links are set to be with infinite bandwidth and the same propagation delay, which set to be 100ms. As a rule of thumb, the shortest path routing is used in the experiment.

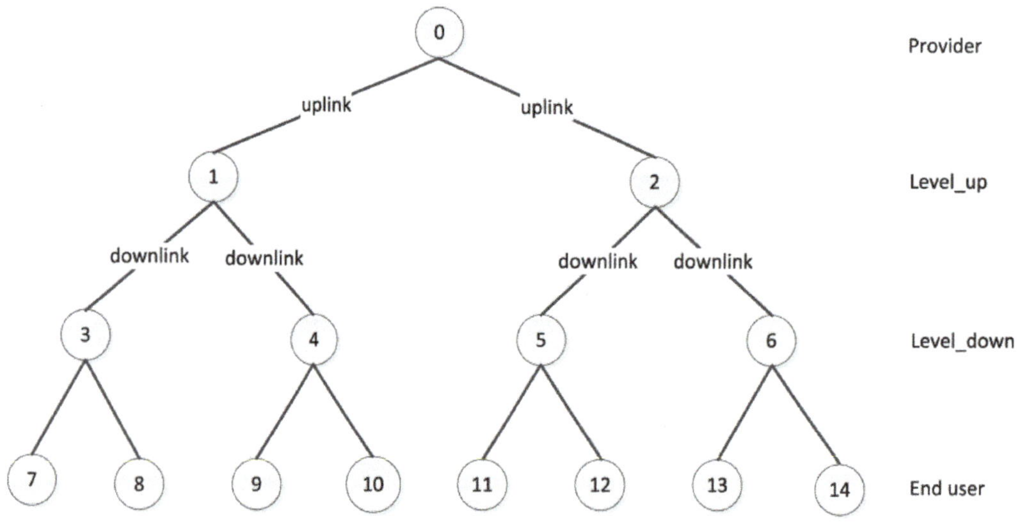

Figure 3: Simulation topology.

We study the cache scheme based on pre-fetch operation under an open source software ccnSim [30], chunk-level simulator of CCN. We assume end user should sequentially request for whole chunks of a content object. Stop-and-wait (no-overlap) request manner is employed. The content number and the average chunk number per content are set to be 10^6 and 10, respectively, which are in accordance with Youtube-like internet catalogues [27]. And all the chunks have the same size. The unit of cache capacity is chunk. The requests of the content-level are generated followed by a Poisson process. The request rate (lamda) of each client is 500/s. Two main factors, i.e., cache size and ***Zipf*** parameter , are adjustable in the experiments. At first, cache size is varied uniformly from 100 to 10^6 chunks for all cache routers. Secondly, we vary the Zipf parameter with 0.8, 1.2 and 1.6. The pre-fetch window is set to be 1, and then varies from 2 to 8 with an increment of 2.

We repeat simulations over 20 times for each combination of cache size and ***Zipf*** parameter for each pre-fetch window. Each simulation is ended by either the convergence of hit rate for all cache routers, or simulation time is over 2 hours after cache stuffed.

We should consider three performance metrics:

1. Hit rate. Hit rate is often used to measure the caching performance. In our experiments, we study the hit rates of different cache level influenced by pre-fetching operation.
2. Average latency perceived by users. Our main goal of cache scheme based on pre-fetch operation is to reducing user-perceived delay. The average latency is composed by the transmission delay, propagation delay and processing delay. Because the transmission delay and processing delay are too trivial to be ignored comparing to propagation delay in our simulation, here we only care about the propagation delay.

3. Average hops. As we demonstrated in section 3, the pre-fetch flag is decided by the hops carried by the header. So the average hop is another important metric for cache scheme based on pre-fetch operation.

Performance Results

To illustrate the effectiveness of cache scheme based on pre-fetch operation, we firstly compare the results without and with pre-fetch operations (pre-fetch windows is 1, W(1)). Fig 4 gives the hit rate comparison with different *Zipf* parameters and different cache sizes, deduced by qualitative analysis. The hit rate of level_down and level_up are presented in Fig 4(A) and 4(B), respectively. The "num" in line mark "num_n/p" represents the *Zipf* parameters, while the "n/p" represent without or with pre-fetch operation. The hit rates show three main trends: ① the hit rate with pre-fetching is significant higher in both cache levels under different *Zipf* parameters; ② no matter with pre-fetch operation or not, the hit rate rises with the incremental of *Zipf* parameter and ③ cache size in both level_up and level_down. When *Zipf* parameter is 1.2, the gap between pre-fetch and noprefetch is larger than the other situations in Fig 4(A). When the cache capacity is smaller than $5*10^3$, the level_up hit rate for *Zipf*(1.2) and *Zipf*(0.8) is almost overlapping in Fig 4(B). Meanwhile, when cache size is closer to thc 0.1 of total chunk number, both level_up hit rate for*Zipf*(1.2) and *Zipf*(0.8) are slightly higher than *Zipf*(1.6).

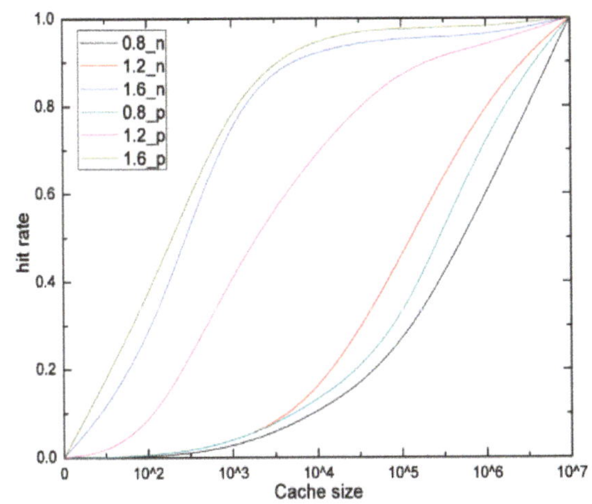

(A)

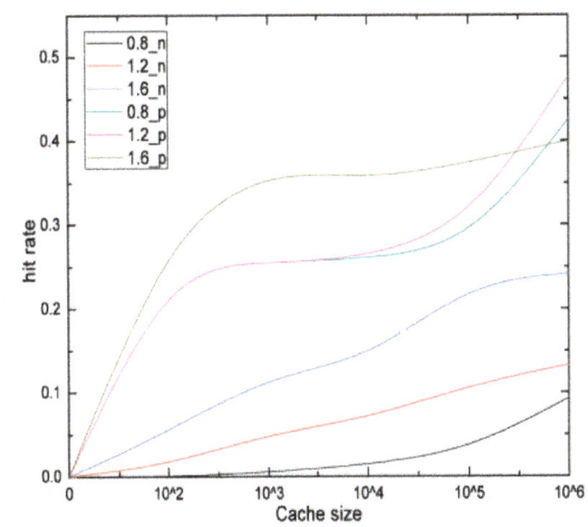

(B)

Figure 4: Comparison of hit rate between un-prefetch and W(1) (a) hit rate of level_down. (b) hit rate of level_up.

Fig 5 and 6 show the results of cache based on pre-fetching operation in terms of user perceived average delay and hops under increasing of cache capacity and *Zipf* parameter. Firstly, it is can be concluded that both the average delay and hops with pre-fetch operation are always lower than that without pre-fetch operation, which demonstrates that pre-fetch operation can effectively decrease the average delay and hops and conforms to our mathematical analysis in section 3.3. After normalized the propagation delay of each link, the average delay shows the same declining trend with hops. However, the average delay with pre-fetch operation is always smaller than average hops, as shown in Figs 5 and 6. Because when a cache router received pre-fetched data after downstream interest for a chunk, the hops in header should not to be reset, while the delay is significantly reduced.

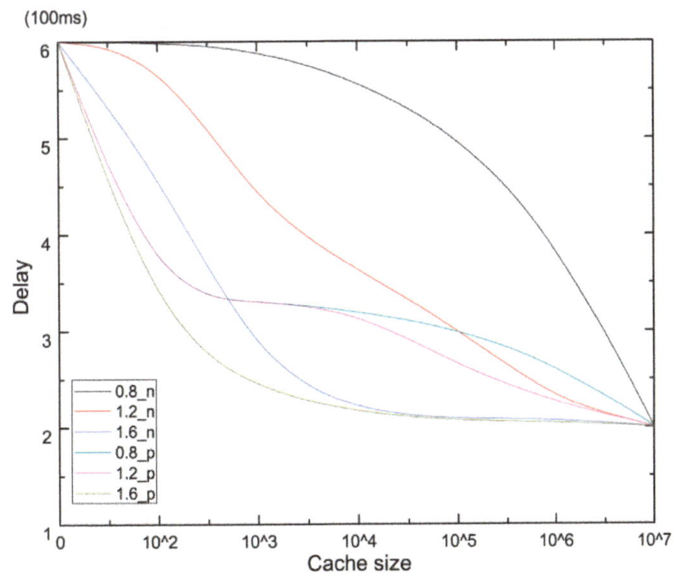

Figure 5: Average delay perceived by end user.

The max differences between pre-fetch and no-prefetch are about 300 ms, 250 ms, 100 ms, with the cache capacity is near 5000,1000,500 for *Zipf*(0.8), *Zipf*(1.2) and *Zipf*(1.6) respectively, which keeps accordance with reality that caching capacity is usually much smaller than the overall chunk population. So the pre-fetch operation is an effective method to improve the performance for end user.

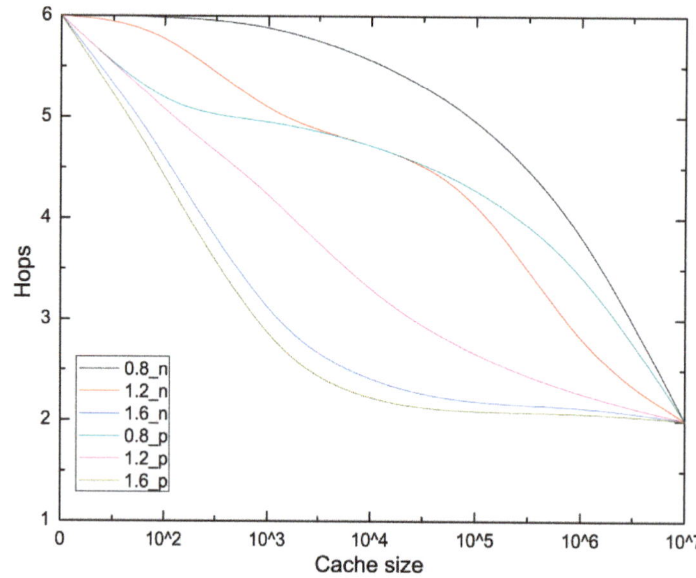

Figure 6: Average hops.

We plot the corresponding bandwidth requirement versus cache capacity for different *Zipf* parameters in Fig 7. The"uplink/downlink_n/p" means the uplink or downlink bandwidth requirement without or with pre-fetching. It can be seen that, with cache size increasing, the bandwidth needed is reduced for all *Zipf*parameters. The pre-fetch operation shouldn't raise the bandwidth requirement for *Zipf*(0.8) as described in Fig 7(A). However, the bandwidths needed of uplink and downlink under pre-fetching are both much larger for *Zipf*(1.2) and *Zipf*(1.6), as shown in Fig 7(B) and 7(C). When *Zipf* parameter is 1.2, the bandwidth required of pre-fetch operation is always over twice more than without pre-fetching. Especially, when cache size is about 10^4, the bandwidth demanded of pre-fetching is almost four times larger than without pre-fetching. However, the gap between pre-fetching and no-prefetching is narrowing with the incremental of cache capacity with *Zipf*(1.6).

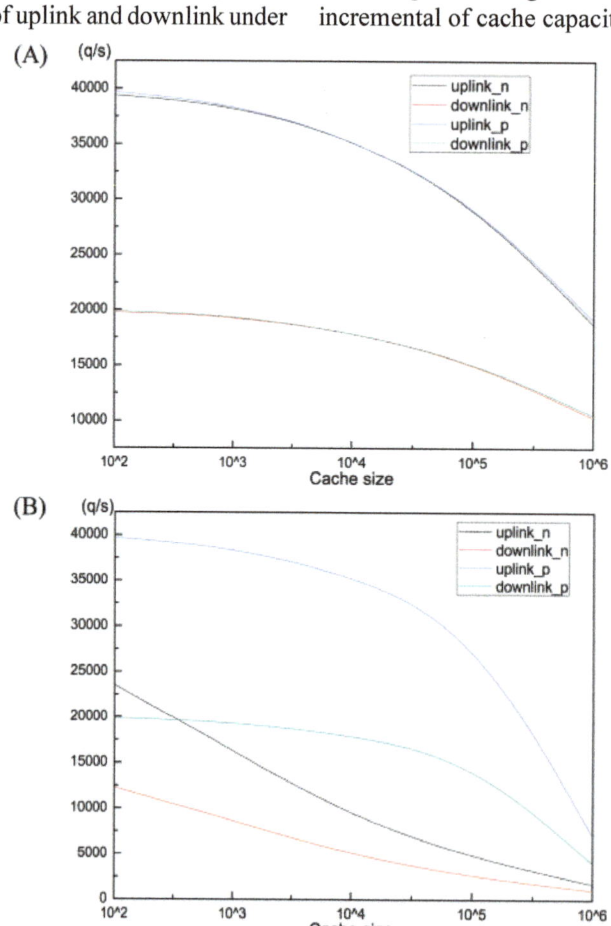

(C)

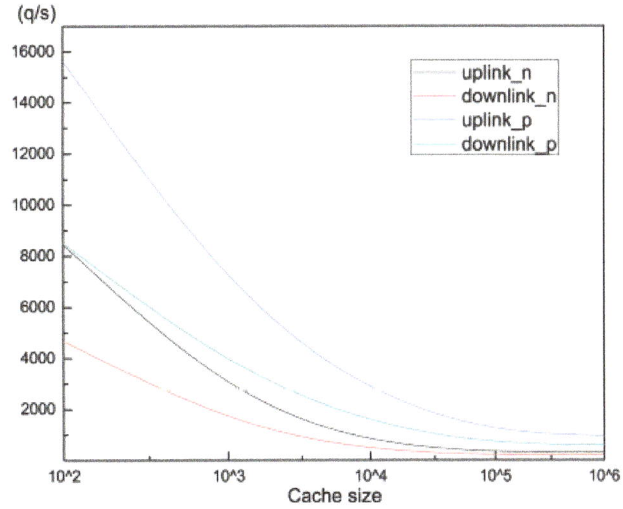

Figure 7: Bandwidth (a) *Zipf*(0.8). (b) *Zipf*(1.2). (c) *Zipf*(1.6).

Finally, we consider average delay for different *W*. Because the distinctions among delays for some *W* are too trivial to be noticed, we adopt the diversity of average delay to show the influence of W, as shown in Fig 8. Div(n1, n2) is the average delay for W(n1) minus that of W(n2), where n1 and n2 are the pre-fetch window size. The average delay for W(2) is always lower than W(1) for both *Zipf*(0.8) and *Zipf*(1.2). Meanwhile, when the cache size smaller than 5000, the delay for W(2) is also smaller than any other pre-fetch windows. The maximum difference is about 2 in *Zipf*(0.8) (in Fig 8A)), but 0.1 in *Zipf*(1.2) (in Fig 8B)).W(2) is the optimal pre-fetch window for minimal average delay, which conforms with the conclusion of [27] that enlarging pre-fetch window may worse the performance (average delay).

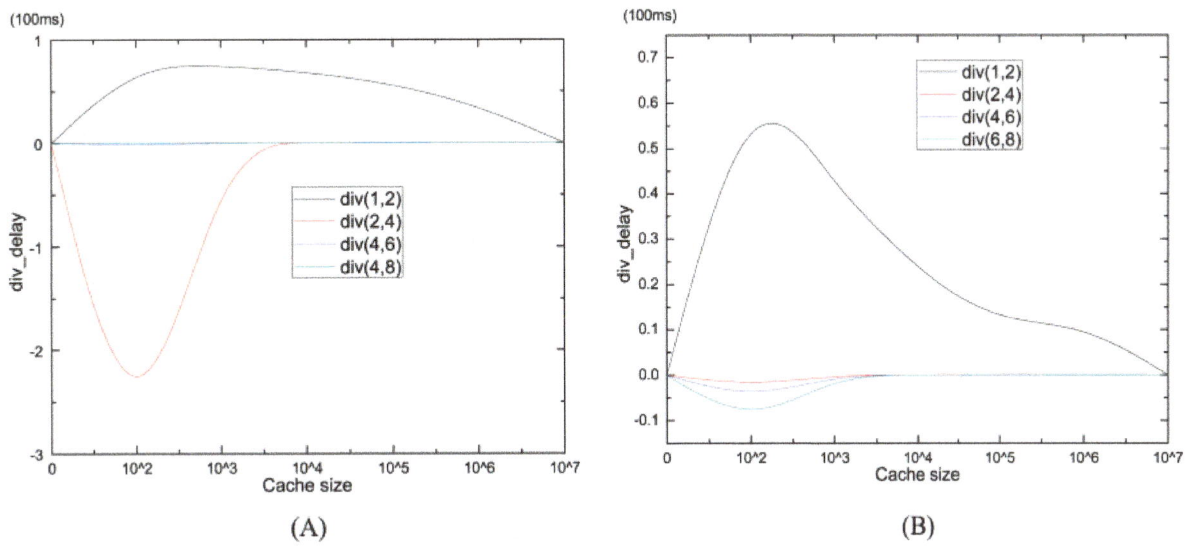

Figure 8: The delay diversity for different pre-fetch windows.

CONCLUSION

The cache scheme based on pre-fetch operation of ICN is proposed in this paper. The following chunks of the request content object should be pre-fetched to short the latency user experienced. Two pre-fetch driven modes, cache-driven and data-driven modes, are suggested. When meets one of the driven modes, router should perform pre-fetch operation. Mathematical model is formulated to qualitatively analyse the network latency for both standard CCN without and with pre-fetching operation. The calculation results demonstrate that the pre-fetch operation can reduce the average latency passed for any chunk. In the performance evaluation, simulation results illustrate cache scheme based on pre-fetch operation should always be efficient in reducing the user perceived latency and average hops. The *Zipf* parameter and cache capacity have impacts on the performance of cache scheme based on pre-fetch operation. Meanwhile, the pre-fetch window size will also affect the network latency. Our near future work will research the dynamically adjustment of pre-fetch windows for better performance, and collaborative pre-fetch scheme based on pre-fetch flag decision.

REFERENCES

1. Koponen T, Chawla M, Chun B, Ermolinskiy A, Kim KH, Shenker S, et al. A Data-Oriented (and Beyond) Network Architecture. In proceedings of 2007 conference on Applications, technologies, architectures, and protocols for computer communications. New York, NY, USA, 2007; 37(4): 181–192.
2. Jacobson V, Smetters DK, Thornton JD, Plass MF, Briggs NH, Braynard RL. Networking Named Content. In proceedings of CoNEXT '09 the 5th international conference on Emerging networking experiments and technologies. New York, NY, USA, 2009; 1–12.
3. D2.3–Architecture Definition, Component Descriptions, and Requirements. 2011. Available:http://www.psirp.org/files/Deliverables/FP7-INFSO-ICT-216173-PSIRP-D2.3_ArchitectureDefinition.pdf, 2011.
4. Ahlgren B, D'Ambrosio M, Dannewitz C, Eriksson A, Golić J, Grönvall B, et al. Second NetInf Architecture Description, 2010, available online: http://www.4ward-project.eu/, 2010
5. Detti A, Melazzi NB, Salsano S, Pomposini M. CONET: A Content Centric Inter-Networking Architecture. In proceedings of ACM SIGCOMM Workshop on Information-Centric Networking (ICN-2011). New York, NY, USA, 2011; 50–55.
6. Raychaudhuri D, Nagaraja K, Venkataramani A. MobilityFirst: a robust and trustworthy mobility-centric architecture for the future internet. ACM SIGCOMM Mobile Computing and Communications Review. July 2012; 44(3): 2–13.
7. Aburumman A, Choo K-KR. A Domain-Based Multi-cluster SIP Solution for Mobile Ad Hoc Network. In Proceedings of 10th International Conference on Security and Privacy in Communication Networks (SecureComm 2014), Beijing China, 2014; 153: 267–281.
8. Aburumman A, Seo WJ, Islam R, Khan MK, Choo K-KR. A Secure Cross-Domain SIP Solution for Mobile Ad Hoc Network using Dynamic Clustering. In Proceedings of 11th International Conference on Security and Privacy in Communication Networks (SecureComm 2015). Dallas, TX, USA. 2015; 164 649–664.
9. Choi J, Han J, Cho E, Kwon T, Choi Y. A Survey on Content-Oriented Networking for Efficient Content Delivery. IEEE communication magazine. March 2011; 49:121–127.
10. Ghodsi A, Koponen T, Raghavan B, Shenker S, Singla A, Wilcox J. Information-centric Networking: Seeing the forest for the trees. In proceedings of ACM Workshop on Hot Topics in Networks (HotNets-X), New York, NY, USA, November 2011: 1–6.
11. Osanaiye O, Choo K-KR, Dlodlo M. Distributed Denial of Service (DDoS) Resilience in Cloud: Review and Conceptual Cloud DDoS Mitigation Framework. Journal of Network and Computer Applications. 2016;67: 147–165
12. Prokhorenko V, Choo K-KR, Ashman H. Context-oriented Web Application Protection Model. Applied Mathematics and Computation. 2016; 286: 59–78.
13. Prokhorenko V, Choo K-KR, Ashman H. Web Application Protection Techniques: A Taxonomy. Journal of Network and Computer Applications. 2016; 60: 95–112.
14. Prokhorenko V, Choo K-KR, Ashman H. Intent-based Extensible Real-time PHP Supervision Framework. IEEE Transactions on Information Forensics and Security. 2016; 99: 1–11.
15. Psaras I, Chai WK, Pavlou G. Probabilistic In-Network Caching for Information-Centric Networks. In proceedings of the second edition of the ICN workshop on Information-centric networking. New York, NY, USA, 2012; 55–60.
16. Wang JM, Bensaou B. Progressive Caching in CCN. In proceedings of 2012 IEEE Global Communications Conference (GLOBECOM). Anaheim, CA, 2012; 2727–2732.
17. Cho K, Lee M, Park K, Kwon TT, Choi Y, Pack S. WAVE: Popularity-based and Collaborative In-network Caching for Content-Oriented Networks. In proceedings of IEEE INFOCOM Workshops on Emerging Design Choices in Name-Oriented Networking. Orlando, Florida, USA, 2012; 316–321.
18. Ming Z, Xu M, Wang D. Age-based Cooperative Caching in Information-Centric Networks. In proceedings of IEEE INFOCOM 2012 Workshop on Emerging Design Choices in Name-Oriented Networking. Orlando, Florida, USA, 2012: 1–8.
19. Xu A, Tan X, Tian Y. Design and Evaluation of a Utility-based Caching Mechanism for Information-centric Networks. In proceedings of IEEE ICC Next Generation Networking Symposium. LONDON, UK, 2015; 5535–5540.
20. Jose Quevedo, Corujo D, Aguiar R. Consumer Driven Information Freshness Approach for Content Centric Networking. In proceedings of 2014 IEEE INFOCOM Workshop on Name-Oriented Mobility. Toronto, ON, Canada, 2014; 482–487.
21. Suksomboon K, Fukushima M, Hayashi M, Ji Y. Pending-Interest-Driven Cache Orchestration through network function virtualization. In proceedings of Globecom 2014. Austin, TX, 2014;1867–1872.
22. Wang W, Sun Y, Guo Y, Kaafar D, Jin J, Li J, et al. CRCache: Exploiting the Correlation between Content Popularity and Network Topology Information for ICN Caching. In proceedings of IEEE ICC 2014. Sydney, Australia, 2014; 3197–3202.
23. Li W, Oteafy SMA, Hassanein HS. Dynamic Adaptive Streaming over Popularity-driven Caching in Information-Centric Networks. In proceedings of IEEE ICC 2015 Next Generation networking Symposium. London, UK, 2015: 5747–5752.
24. Zhang H. Impoving performance on WWW using path-based predictive caching and pefetching, Master Thesis, Simon Fraser University, Canada, 2001.
25. Venkata NP, Mogul JC. Using Predictive Prefetching to Improve World Wide Web Latency. ACM SIGCOMM Computer Communication Review. New York, NY, USA. 1996; 26(3): 22–36.

26. Cao P, Felten EW, Kariin A, Li K. A Study of Integrated Prefetching and Caching Strategies. In proceedings of the Joint int. Conf. on Measurement& Modeling of Computer Systems (SIGMETRICS). New York, NY, USA, May 1995; 23(1): 188–197.

27. Salsano S, Detti A, Cancellieri M, Pomposini M, Belfari-Melazzi N. Transport-Layer Issues in Information Centric Networks. In proceedings of ACM SIGCOMM workshop on ICN. Helsinki, Finland, 2012; 19–24.

28. Zhang F, Xu C, Zhang Y, Ramakrishnan KK. EdgeBuffer: Caching and prefetching content at the edge in the MobilityFirst future Internet architecture. In Proceedings of 2015 IEEE 16th International Symposium on World of Wireless, Mobile and Multimedia Networks (WoWMoM). Boston, MA, 2015; 1–9.

29. Yuy Y-T, Bronzino F, Fan R, Westphal C, Gerla M. Congestion-Aware Edge Caching for Adaptive Video Streaming in Information-Centric Networks. In proceedings of 12th Annual IEEE Consumer Communications and Networking Conference (CCNC). Las Vegas, NV, 2015; 588–596.

30. ccnSim. Available: http://perso.telecom-paristech.fr/~drossi/index.php?n=Software.ccnSim.

CHAPTER 5

SPREADING EFFECT IN INDUSTRIAL COMPLEX NETWORK BASED ON REVISED STRUCTURAL HOLES THEORY

Lizhi Xing[1], Qing Ye[2] , Jun Guan[1]

[1]Department of Business Administration, School of Economics and Management, Beijing University of Technology, Beijing, China,

[2]Department of Finance, School of Economics and Management, Beijing University of Technology, Beijing, China

ABSTRACT

This paper analyzed the spreading effect of industrial sectors with complex network model under perspective of econophysics. Input-output analysis, as an important research tool, focuses more on static analysis. However, the fundamental aim of industry analysis is to figure out how interaction between different industries makes impacts on economic development, which turns out to be a dynamic process. Thus, industrial complex network based on input-output tables from WIOD is proposed to be a bridge connecting accurate static quantitative analysis and comparable dynamic one. With application of revised structural holes theory, flow betweenness and random walk centrality were respectively chosen to evaluate industrial sectors' long-term and short-term spreading effect process in this paper. It shows that industries with higher flow betweenness or random walk centrality would bring about more intensive industrial spreading effect to the industrial chains they stands in, because value stream transmission of industrial sectors depends on how many products or services it can get from the other ones, and they are regarded as brokers with bigger information superiority and more intermediate interests.

INTRODUCTION

In last two decades, statistic physics has been wildly adopted in researching on the dynamic and statistic properties embedded in various economic behaviors and data of the global economic infrastructures [1]. The application of methodologies like stochastic dynamics, self-similarity, scale theory etc. has incurred a new interdiscipline subject—econophysics [2]. Under this circumstance, complex network with abundant utilization of statistic physics can be judged as a branch of econophysics in relevant financial and industrial researches.

As results, a large number of theoretical and empirical researches on industrial economics based on complex network have been accomplished in areas of industrial development, structure, association, organization and policy. Chmiel, et al. establishes networks of companies and branches in Poland through bipartite graph theory [3]. Similarly, Inoue, et al investigate a Japan's patent network focusing on its spatial characteristics based on the same theory [4]. Chang, et al. show that the degree distribution of nodes in a projected sub-network follows the drift power-law in general cooperation as well as in competition networks [5]. Liu, et al. propose

Citation: Xing L, Ye Q, Guan J. Spreading Effect in Industrial Complex Network Based on Revised Structural Holes Theory. Braunstein LA, ed. PLoS ONE. 2016;11(5):e0156270. doi:10.1371/journal.pone.0156270.

to study the development of China's high-tech park using complex network, and constructed the network of China's top 100 electronic and IT companies as the basic model [6]. Hou, et al. extend their research fields from monopoly market to macro-reality market to build competitive complex network model targeting logistics enterprises [7]. Li, et al. establish a global nuclear power plant network based on priority queuing network model and simulated its numerical characteristics to reflect its evolution [8]. Yao, et al. model the directed weighted competitive pressure network and made a simulation analysis on the rivalry spread effect over it [9]. Upper analyze the mechanisms of contagion in banking and financial networks [10]. Hu, et al. calculate economic distance matrices based on annual GDP of nine economic sectors from 1995–2010 in 31 Chinese provinces and autonomous regions, and built spatial economic networks through threshold and minimal spanning tree [11]. All above, scholars create various complex network models to describe inter-organization competition and cooperation analyzing differed economic phenomena. The most common method in existing researches on industrial complex networks is the introduction of unweighted and undirected network models similar to the simple physical ones, with less to be known or much to be neglected on the mechanism of informational, material and capital flows between economic entities manifested in their interdependencies.

From an empirical perspective, a handful of studies have characterized the structure of input-output (later referred to as IO) networks to better understand the topology of inter-industry dependencies and their repercussions on the industrial economics. For instance, Blöchl, et al. adopt STAN database at OECD to establish 37 countries' IO networks and derive two measures for weighted and directed network, which are, random walk centrality to reveal the most immediately affected nodes by a shock based on Freeman's closeness centrality, and counting betweenness to identify the most accumulatively affected nodes based on Newman' random walk betweenness [12]. Kagawa, et al. propose an optimal combinatorial method to find industries with large CO_2 emissions through industrial relations based on IO table, depicting environmentally important industrial clusters in Japanese automobile supply chain [13]. McNerney, et al. study the structure of inter-industry relationships using networks of capital flows between industries in 20 national economies, and found these networks vary around a typical structure characterized by a Weibull link weight distribution [14]. Martha, et al. investigate how economic shocks propagate and amplify through the IO network connecting industrial sectors in developed economies [15].

With the development of IO database, related researches are not only based on independent national systems but also on multi-regional even global systems, and most of them adopted World Input-Output Database (WIOD) as the data source. For instance, Ando measures the importance of industrial sectors under the impact of American gross output in the global IO model [16]. Cerina, et al. analyze the subgraph structure and dynamics attributions of global network with community detection techniques, pinpointing the key industries and economic entities with PageRank centrality and community coreness [17]. Grazzini and Spelta set up the cost effect index to testify the robustness of global IO network and the interdependency of intermediate inputs in production [18].

The present researches mainly mine the IO data from different aspects as an econophysics context implied in the form of networks, but restricte to static analyzing endogenous variables ignoring the process of fining and refining of variables to maintain equilibrium, let alone providing measurements and advises on optimal control of the evolution tendency of industrial structures.

METHODS

Impacts of Structural Holes

Structural holes theory is developed by Ronald Stuart Burt and applied in Social Network Analysis [19]. This theory spans the fields of sociology, economics, and computer science. Burt introduced this concept in attempt to explain the origin of differences in social capital, and found positional advantage or disadvantage of individuals result from how they are embedded in neighborhoods. For instance, individuals located on important transmission paths serve as brokers receiving non-redundant information from their contacts. In this way, they are granted with information superiority and possess advantages on top of gaining intermediate interests by connecting the other nodes.

There are two sorts of indices to measure structural holes, which are Burt's structural holes index and Freeman's between centrality. The former is mainly applied to evaluate redundancy in ego networks, while the latter is used to calculate important degree of all the nodes. For the whole network, if a node is on many geodesic paths, it actually plays an important intermediate role, usually measured by betweenness. Measured with centrality, if one node enjoys the maximum proximity closeness in a network, implying the minimum summation of geodesic distance, it occupies an important intermediate location.

For this reason, this theory is here introduced to explain the function of industrial sectors in economic circulation, because there exists complex economic independence in the process of industrial division and cooperation.

Revised Structural Holes Theory

In Burt's classic theory, holes come forth in social structures because weak ties exist in relationships between groups on the connections of opportunities, capital, and information. In addition, these holes could also reinforce competitive advantages to the individuals on this relation. As shown in Fig 1(a), *AC* is referred as a structural hole, for there is no (or very weak) direct tie between *A* and *C* in the triangle network. If *A*, *B* and *C* are in the state of resources competition, *B* is to incur information superiority and controlling advantage as an intermediate bridge, for the existence of structural hole between *A* and *C*.

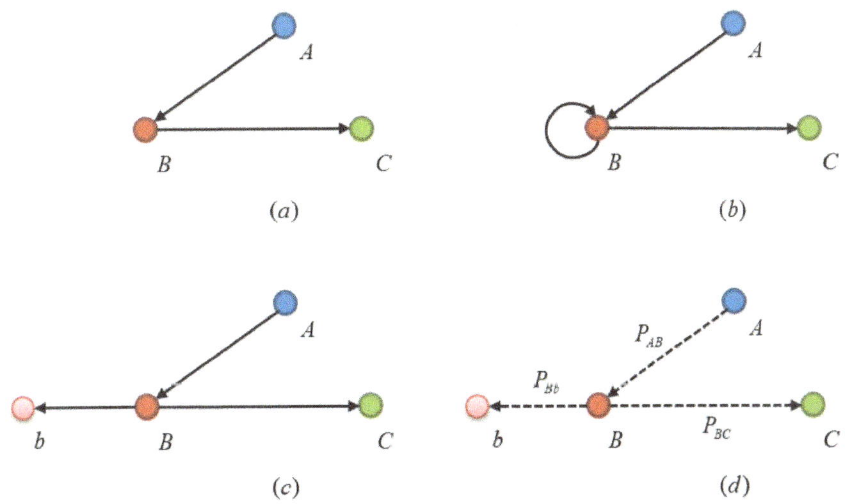

Figure 1: Structural Holes and Its Extension in Complex Social Network Analysis.

However, there is limitation of its application on complex networks due to its ignorance of weights, directions, dynamics and self-loops, which sabotages its ability on depicting infrastructures of economic systems composed of industrial sectors and the quantitative relationships in between.

If *B* has a self-loop, as shown in Fig 1(b), it is assumed that there is a shadow node *b*, hence self-loop can be replaced by a virtual edge *Bb*, as shown in Fig 1(c). Obviously, shadow nodes will only locate at the tail ends of the network, worth no consideration of their out-degree or out-strength. In view of network flow, they can be regarded as sink nodes for merely receiving from the original ones without any flow outwards.

So the index on between centrality should be modified when applied to study the dynamics of information transmission on networks with the theory of structural holes. The practical value stream transmission in present industrial networks is a Markov process in time-discrete state, taking considerations on not only the direction of value stream, say *B* should have the provision of inflow and outflow of information simultaneously with probabilities of each transmission set respectively, for instance with *P*(*A*, *B*) and *P*(*B*, *C*) referring to the probabilities of existence of information transmission from *A* to *B* and *B* to *C*, but also the worn-out and consumption of output of the industrial sector itself, for instance, the industrial sector should first meet its own needs for products and services with the probability as *P*(*B*,*b*).

Features of Value Stream in Economic System

Black argues that the fundamental cause of business cycle is the economic impact and its aftermath, which could be defined as the impacts of exogenous variables on the endogenous ones in industrial sectors. Specifically, he categorizes market prices, advances in technology, profit distribution, government policies and final demand as the exogenous variables, and the material and capital flows between different sectors as the endogenous ones [20].

The economic impacts on national economic system constituted by industrial sectors flow along the direction of intermediate inputs, and all of them converge into value stream just like network. The target sectors, in the form of sink nodes on the network, are those whose final demands have been satisfied by the additional input flows at the end of this stochastic process of economic impact. Assuming that for some external reasons, such as government policies, additional productivity in automotive industry becomes an impact or disturbance to the entire economic system, which is to be absorbed by other industries. The abundancy of extra production, on the one hand, is randomly distributed among other sectors, which could be traced from the IO table, and on the other hand, will bring about extra profits in the forms of extra manufacturing funds, labor remuneration and non-direct business taxes for the automotive industry. In this way, the external impacts aroused by automotive industry will be transformed into inputs into other industries. Then, this impact can be shown as domino effects stirring additional economic flows in the economic system, until it finally reaches a new stage of stability with all the impacts and disturbance totally absorbed by other industries.

Advantage of Input-output Table Date

Beyond all question, IO table as a quantitative technique of economic analysis represents the interdependencies between different branches of a national economy or different regional economies perfectly. Its property of being in the form of checkboard enables it to reflect the movements of products or services within the whole economic system from both production consumption to distributive utilization, which are actually the formation and distribution of values respectively. The dual identities of each industrial sector on the network as the producer and consumer at the same time, demand it not only to produce and distribute providing inputs for the other industrial sectors but also to consume inputs from other sectors to accomplish its own fabrication. This is indeed the inner identity proposed by Karl Marx. The industrial sectors in the IO table could be regarded as nodes while inter-industry value stream contributes to weighted and directed edges in the construction of network models.

Even more important, consideration should be paid on what kinds of impacts value stream bring to each industrial sector in the economic system over different temporal span. On the one hand, IO table depicts the annual inter-industry independence in a nation or region, which reflects the accumulative or long-term effect of value stream. On the other hand, any disturbance as the exogenous variables in the form of supply shocks on one of the economic industrial sector in a stable network will force it make rapid impacts on the neighboring sectors along the existing industrial structure, which reflects the instantaneous or short-term effect of value stream.

MODELS

Underlying Database

In consideration of both availability and authority, IO table is definitely the priority-first data format to establish mathematics model. For instance, it can show flows of final and intermediate goods and services defined according to industry outputs. In addition, it is provided as matrix, which can be directly or with minor modification adopted as complex network's adjacency matrix, establishing a sort of weighted and directed network.

There are four inter-country IO tables available: World Input-Output Database (WIOD), Structural Analysis Database (STAN), Global Trade Analysis Program (GTAP) and Asian International Input-Output (AIO). WIOD was chosen as underlying database in this paper.

This is because WIOD provides time-series of world IO tables for 40 independent countries, covering the period from 1995 to 2011. These tables have been constructed in a clear conceptual framework on the basis of officially published IO tables in conjunction with national accounts and international trade statistics [21]. Since publication, it has proved very useful in analyses of global chain trade [22], domestic value-added content of gross exports [23], effects of trade policies [24], offshoring on labor demand [25] and numerous policy-oriented studies [26,27]. It is foreseeable that there will be more applications of WIOD in multiple research fields.

Furthermore, there are three kinds of data type in WIOD, which are World Input-Output Tables (WIOT), Regional Input-Output Tables (RIOT) and National Input-Output Tables (NIOT), and all of them are value-type IO data. In this paper, NIOTs of China were chosen, which provide IO tables of China in current prices expressed in millions of dollars and covers 35 industrial sectors from 1995 to 2011, to establish industrial complex networks and analyze development trends of Chinese macro industrial structure during recent two decades.

Industrial Complex Network

In order to establish an industrial complex network, an industrial sector within a region was considered as a node, and the inter-industry IO relationship as a tie, whose weight represented the sale and purchase relationships between producers and consumers. Thus, we created a graph $G = (V, E, W)$ containing n nodes, that here represent all industrial sectors within a nation or region, denoted by node set V. Pairs of nodes were linked by ties reflecting their interdependencies, constituting an asymmetric tie set E. However, in valued graphs, set E can actually be replaced by weight set W, which was extracted from the quadrant I of the basic matrix of the IO table in this paper. Taking into account that the properties of nodes must be consistent, the total output and input had been ignored temporarily, such as end-use and value-added, but intermediate inputs should be emphasized reflecting inter-industry relevance. Finally, this kind of model was named as **Industrial Shock Transmission Networks**, denoted by **ISTN**, since its purpose was to reflect how value stream and economic shock transfer in national or regional industrial system [28]. For instance, topological structure of ISTN-CHN-2011 is shown in Fig 2.

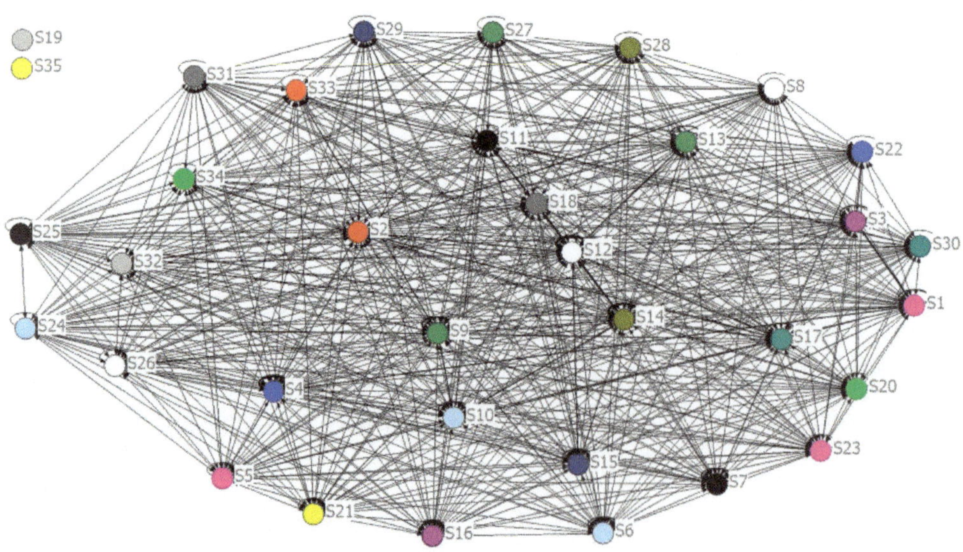

Figure 2: ISTN-CHN-2011 with Self-Loops.

From Fig 2 we can see that self-loops are allowed to exist in ISTN. In other words, e_{ii} or w_{ii} is likely to be non-zero. When exogenous variables change, value stream first affects its own before its diffusion according to the strength of the connection between the nodes. If many sectors consume a lot of its own products, there would be many self-loops with heavy weights in the network. For the sake of simplicity, self-loops are usually deleted in industrial complex networks. However, input of a sector on its own is close to or even more than half of its total output according to input-output table. For instance, China›s *"Electrical and Optical Equipment"*sector's proportion of investment on its own is more than 44.30% in 2011. So, self-loops are very important and non-ignorable. When calculating certain characteristics of network, for easy comprehension, self-loops were replaced by shadow nodes in this paper, denoted by small letter *s* as shown in Fig 3.

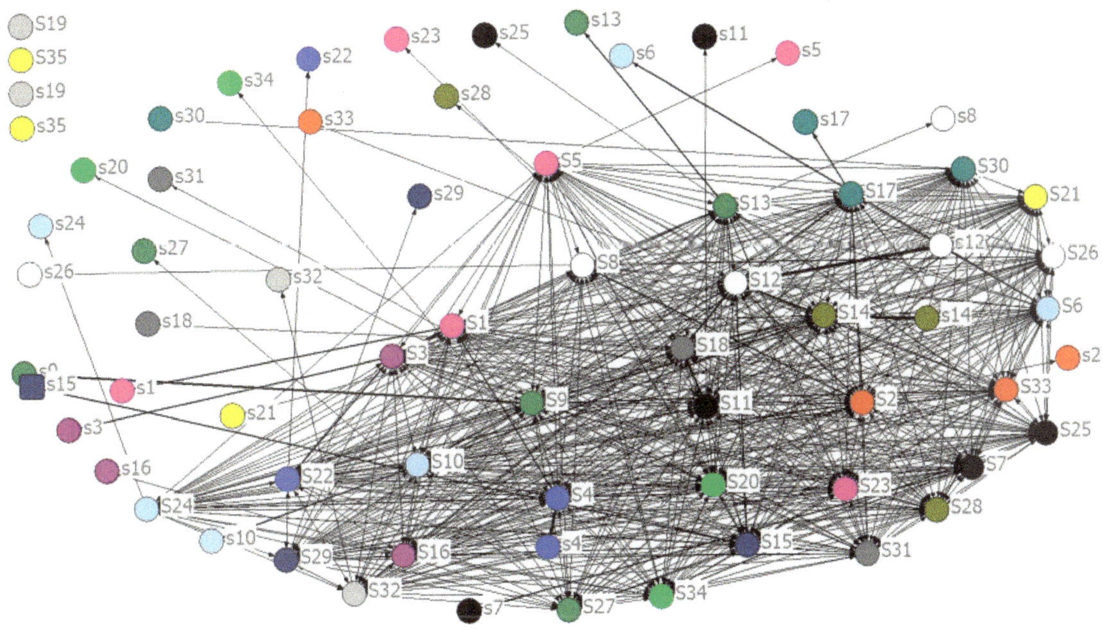

Figure 3: ISTN-CHN-2011 with Shadow Nodes.

If some nodes' in-degree (denoted by k^{in}) or out-degree (denoted by k_i^{out}) are equal to zero, such as *S19*, *S35* in Fig 2 or *S19*, *S35*, *s19*, *s35* in Fig 3, it means they are isolate from the whole network and need to be removed when calculating characteristics.

In order to evaluate nodes' contribution to transmit value stream, we applied betweenness and centrality in ISTN models. However, this kind of networks based on IO tables are different from general complex networks, because industrial sectors are almost completely connected, value stream spreads all over the industrial system, and self-consumption takes a great proportion of total out-put as mentioned above.

Thus, new betweenness and centrality measurement suitable for weighted and directed network should be introduced, then we could use them to study impacts of structural holes in context of network flow and random walk. Finally, Flow Betweenness proposed by Freeman and Random Walk Centrality proposed by Blöchl were chosen to evaluate industrial sectors' long-term and short-term spreading effect respectively.

Flow Betweenness

Freeman proposes Flow Betweenness, denoted by C_F, to develop measures of centrality into weighted and directed network analysis. It is based on Fulkerson's min-cut, max-flow theorem, which means the maximum flow from node i to j is exactly equal to the minimum cut capacity, that is, the smallest capacity of any of the $i-j$ cut set [29]. Let m_{jk} be the maximum flow from a source node i to another sink node k and $m_{jk}(i)$ be the maximum flow from j to k that passes through node i. Then the degree to which the maximum flow between all unordered pairs of nodes depends on i, where $j < k$ and $i \neq j \neq k$. The formula is:

$$C_F(i) = \sum_{j<k}\sum m_{jk}(i) \tag{1}$$

As the basis of C_F, Ford and Fulkerson defined network flow is constrained by two additional conditions, one is the flow out of source node must be equal to the flow into sink node, another is the flow out of each intermediate node on any direct path linking adjacent nodes must be equal to the flow into relative sink one [30]. But, given these condition, ISTN models meet neither of them. The reason is, ISTN models don't belong to closed network model because many raw materials, semi-finish products, finish products or various service not only transact in one national domestic economic system, but also parts of them export to other countries. In other words, gross output used by domestic industries is less than total use in consideration of regional integration of the world economy. Besides, industries consume parts of output made out by themselves, so the total input is neither equal to the total output of themselves.

Thus, when calculating normalized C_F by Ucinet 6.560, the result was beyond the limit of Ford and Fulkerson's assumption. Moreover, the function of self-loops was transferred onto shadow nodes in order to cover more flow in network as possible, although C_F of new nodes located in the tail end of all paths was certainly zero.

Random Walk Centrality

As one of basic dynamic process, the random walk is closely related with network research in many ways, especially, the nature of the network structure. Three indices are generally involved in studying random walk on networks. The first one is First Passage Time, denoted by FPT. After a source node released a walk signal, it will move to other adjacent nodes with equal probability or following certain transmission probability, thus the expected time to reach a pre-set sink node for the first time is FPT until repeating this process to arrive at it. According to FPT, the other two indices can be calculated. One is Mean First Passage Time, denoted by MFPT, which is equal to the arithmetic mean of all nodes in the network. Another is Mean Absorption Time, denoted by MAT, which is obtained by the average of FPT from each other nodes to a fixed sink node [31].

In view of progress of social network in recent years, Freeman›s close centrality has been widely applied, generally denoted by C_C. However, it restricts analyses on dense networks and nearly takes self-loops into account. Therefore, Blöchl introduced Random Walk Centrality, denoted by C_{RC}, to describe how products and services flow within economic system.

As we know, the basic form of IO table is material-type, but the widely used is value-type. WIOT taken as modelling data belongs to the latter type, so inter-industry relationships are depicted by the flow of value stream. Borgatti proposes that money exchange process can be modelled as a Markov process, and the limiting probabilities for the nodes are proportional to degree [32]. But, in ISTN models, the similar process is more complex and need to be fully described by weights on edges. In other words, the transmission probability matrix of random walk, denoted by $M(i,j)$, is subject to the impact of the importance of node j. In this paper, we defined M as follows:

$$M = S_{diag}^{-1} W \tag{2}$$

Where W is weight set or so-called weighted adjacency matrix, and S_{diag} is diagonal matrix consisting of nodes' out-strengths s_i^{out}, that is $S_{diag}(i,i) = s_i^{out}$. For unweighted networks,S_{diag} can be instead of diagonal matrix K_{diag} directly [33]. Transmission probability matrix Mdescribes possibilities when value stream transmits among product sectors by selecting next adjacent node as a path to continue, in the process of Absorption Random Walk, referred**ARW**. Hence $E(s, t)$ is used to stand for MFPT, which is the expected number of steps when a random walk starts at source node s needs to reach sink node t for the first time. The formula is:

$$E(s,t) = \sum_{r=1}^{\infty} r\Pi_{s\to t}(r) \tag{3}$$

Where $\Pi_{s\to t}(r)$ is the probability taking r steps from s to t. When $s = t$, $\Pi_{s\to t}(r) = 0$ and $E(t, t) = 0$. Even in undirected networks, $E(s, t)$ is also asymmetric. This property reflects the fact that it is much more probable to pass by central intermediate nodes of a network than other ways.

According to the Random Walk Theory, when the random walk will no longer leave t after arriving at it, so before next transfer, it is supposed to modify the transmission matrix M by deleting its t row and column in order to form M_{-t}.

In unweighted networks, paths between any different nodes are more likely to pass by central intermediate nodes with higher C_C values than surrounding ones with lower C_C values. Similarly, a weighted network such as ISTN based on the IO relationship, faster economic supply shocks tend to reach sensitive product sectors with higher C_{RC} values. Therefore, Blöchl defines random walk centrality as the inverse of the average MFPT by referring to Freeman's closeness centrality. The formula is:

$$C_{RC}(i) = \frac{N}{\sum_{j=1}^{N} E(i,j)} \tag{4}$$

From Eq (4), it is clear that shorter MFPT taken to reach i, then higher its C_{RC} value will be. In addition, from this index's derivation and calculation, it incorporates self-loops because they slow down the traffic between other nodes [34].

RESULTS

Rank of Flow Betweenness

According to assumption and formula about C_F, each industrial sector's flow betweenness in ISTN-CHN models was calculated. For simplicity, its time-varying candlestick is shown in Fig 4.

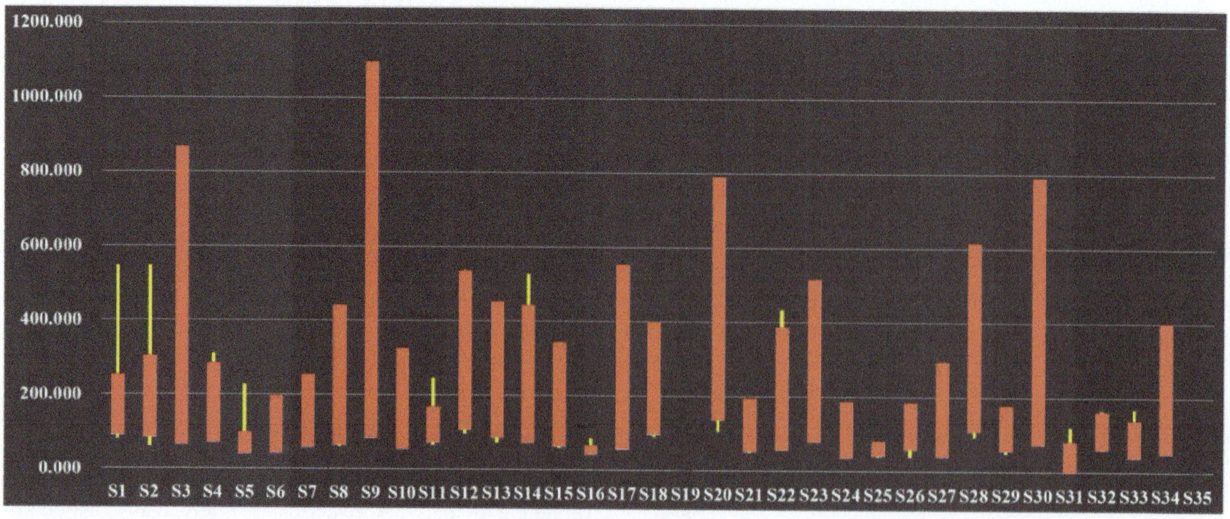

Figure 4: Candlestick of Flow Betweenness in ISTN-CHN from 1995 to 2011.

When making candlestick, four columns of results were calculated, with initial value in 1995 and final value in 2011, maximum and minimum value during 1995 to 2011. Red cylinders represent initial value is smaller than final value, in which under-cutting is initial value and upper-cutting is final value. On the contrary, green cylinders represent initial value is bigger than final value, in which under-cutting is final value and upper-cutting is initial value. Besides, the upper end of yellow fine lines is maximum value during 1995 to 2011, and low end means minimum.

From Fig 4, it is obviously that C_F of each Chinese industrial sector has risen from 1995 to 2011, which means value stream transmitted by these sectors keeps continuous growth with annual increase of Chinese GDP. But, sectors' growth degrees and variation trends are differential, for instance, some of them rise significantly or slightly, some rise first then decline, or alternatively. After all, evolution mechanism of industrial structure needs to be discovered out of these changes. Then, we carried out analyses about C_F in perspective of triple divisions of industrial sectors.

Results of C_F from 1995 to 2011 have shown that long-term spreading effect of *"Agriculture,Hunting, Forestry and Fishing"* (represented by node *S1*) in primary industries obviously subjects to time-varying fluctuation law. But, as downstream industry, C_F of *"Food, Beverages and Tobacco"* (represented by node *S3*) keeps grow all the time, and one of reasons may be that Chinese import ratio of agricultural products increases year by year, which makes it the biggest importing country for agricultural products in the world. Thus, no matter how domestic upstream supply side fluctuates, inputs from abroad keep downstream demand side steady increase. However, although ensuring domestic grain supply safety is crucial, the Chinese authorities must be aware of the potential industrial risk and implement industrial policies on promoting agricultural modernization, adjusting product price and protecting cultivated land resource. Besides, this phenomen occurs to *"Mining and Quarrying"* (*S2*), which means the rapid growth of Chinese manufacturing industries relies on imported minerals.

In ISTN-CHN models, nodes from *S4* to *S18* represent industrial sectors in secondary industries, in which distinct forward and direct relationships exist among certain adjacent sectors, in other words they respectively locate on upstream and downstream segments in industrial value chain. For instance, *"Coke, Refined Petroleum and Nuclear Fuel"* (*S8*) provides chemicals and raw materials to *"Chemicals and Chemical Products"*, *"Rubber and Plastics"*, and *"Other Non-Metallic Mineral"* (*S9*, *S10* and *S11*), and *"Basic Metals and Fabricated Metal"*(*S12*) provides various modern manufacturing industries with intermediate products. However, some phenomena are found in their variation trends of C_F. On the one hand, C_F growth range of node *S8* is very large, in the meanwhile, nodes *S9* and *S10* supposed to be pulled up are lower than *S8*, for which reasons may be downstream sectors do not get motive power from upstream sectors effectively and upstream sectors' production technique and process needs improving. On the other hand, C_F growth range of node *S11* is far from nodes *S13*, *S14* and*S15*, representing *"Machinery, Nec"*, *"Electrical and Optical Equipment"* and *"Transport Equipment"*, for which reasons may be downstream sectors' urgent demand to intermediate products can't be satisfied by domestic supply, so they need a great deal of import from other countries. Besides, C_F growth range of node *S12* matches to its downstream sectors, but Chinese steelworks cannot produce many standards of special steel and its products. In sum, Chinese industrial structure is still in process of heavy industrialization, and capital-intensive industries, such as coal, steel and oil, are on key developmental stage, so China as a large-scale manufacturing country needs science and technology to transform into powerful manufacturing country.

Tertiary industries' connotation is much more complex, so in this paper we adopted Singlemann's classification to distinguish their types, which include circulation services, producer servives, social services and personal services [35]. In circulation services, C_F growth range of *"Wholesale Trade and Commission Trade, Except of Motor Vehicles and Motorcycles"* and *"Inland Transport"* (*S20* and *S23*) are very large, which means they make great contribution to the development of economic society. In addition, *"Financial Intermediation and Renting of M&Eq"* and *"Other Business Activities"* (*S28* and *S30*) have the highest correlation with economic development level, and continuous increase of their C_F indicates they transmit more and more value stream for other sectors and facilitate Chinese industrialization.

Rank of Random Walk Centrality

According to assumption and formula on C_{RC}, each industrial sector's random walk centrality in ISTN-CHN models was calculated, and the results are in S2 File in details too. Its time-varying candlestick is shown in Fig 5.

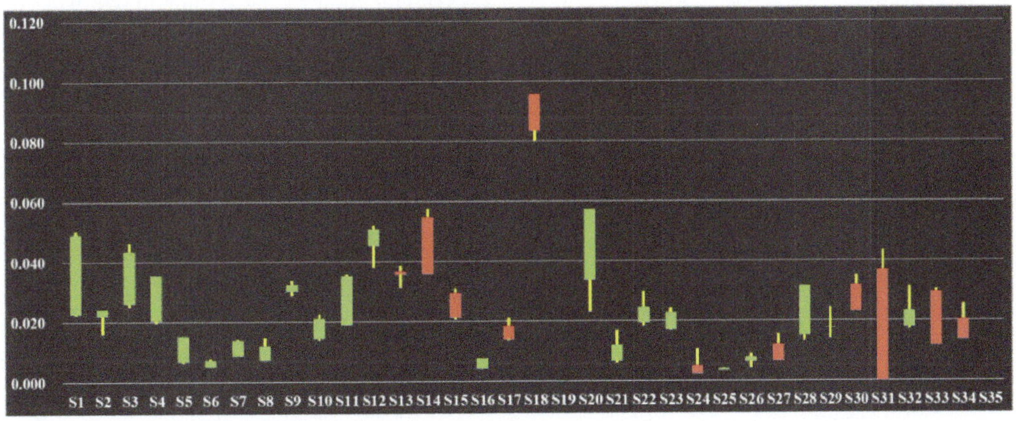

Figure 5: Candlestick of Random Walk Centrality in ISTN-CHN from 1995 to 2011.

C_{RC} measures short-term industrial spreading effect, and it depends on industrial structure. Thus, its quantitative value can be compared among different years, which means variation trends of industrial structure can be discovered by timing analysis. From Fig 5, C_{RC} of some Chinese industrial sectors rises and some declines from 1995 to 2011, and most of them are associated with varying degrees of fluctuation. Then, sectoral analyses are also carried out.

In ISTN-CHN models, C_{RC} of *"Agriculture, Hunting, Forestry and Fishing"* in primary sectors and its downstream *"Food, Beverages and Tobacco"* declines very distinctly after 1997. When we adopted NIOT to establish ISTN-CHN models, we pay more attention on domestic industrial structure of China without consideration of imported products. As the rapid growth of import ratio of agricultural goods, Chinese own agriculture has lost its crucial place in industrial value chain. In the meanwhile, capital flows to sectors with higher rate of return on investment. Thus, primary sectors' transmission function has been weakened due to both import price shock and financial capital transfer.

C_{RC} of four sectors in secondary industries has large growth, including "*Electrical and Optical Equipment*", "*Transport Equipment*", "*Electricity, Gas and Water Supply*" and "*Construction*"(*S14*, *S15*, *S17* and *S18*). The former two belong to typical modern manufacturing industries and their status enhancement in industrial system benefits from higher participation in vertical specialization. The latter two are closely bound up with Chinese urbanization, especially construction, its production value share of GDP is getting higher with deepening impact on industrial structure, for which Chinese authorities should be alert for all kinds of consequent economic and social issues, such as subprime lending crisis and over-capacity.

As production and life pattern changing, traditional services sectors' impact gradually decline for secular trend. According to variation trends of C_{RC}, most of circulation services sectors' short-term function of transmitting value stream go down, which indicates Chinese tertiary industries hit a bottleneck in process of transformation from labor intensive ones to capital intensive and technology intensive ones.

Robustness Analysis

In ISTN models, industrial sectors locate at many value chains simultaneously, thus some of them play role of redundancy in the transmission process of value stream, which contribute a lot to the robustness of network structure. In order to prove sectors with higher C_F or C_{RC} are more important to economic system, we designed two sets of comparative experiment.

Firstly, we defined the connectedness of ISTN models, which represents the measurement of flow efficiency of value stream. In general network studies, Distance between v_i and v_j is equal to the minimum number of edges connecting them, and we call a path whose length is equal to distance the Shortest Path, denoted by d_{ij}. If there is no such path between v_i and v_j, it means $d_{ij} = \infty$. As to unweighted networks, we can calculate the Average Path Length (denoted by APL) of the whole network by Floyd algorithm, which depicts the degree of separation of nodes. But, as to weighted networks, especially when the similarity of nodes is proportional to their edge weight, it is infeasible to describe the feature of value stream flowing in economic system via APL. Thus, we must revise the classic Floyd algorithm, and make the new one capable of searching the path with the rapidest transfer and the lowest distortion of information, and we named it the Strongest Relevance Path Length, denoted by SRPL. The new iterative algorithm is:

$$\tilde{d}_{ij}^{(k)} = \max_{i,j,k\in\{1,2,\ldots,N\}} \left\{ \tilde{d}_{ij}^{(k-1)}, \frac{\tilde{d}_{ik}^{(k-1)} \tilde{d}_{kj}^{(k-1)}}{\tilde{d}_{ik}^{(k-1)} + \tilde{d}_{kj}^{(k-1)}} \right\} \quad \textbf{(5)}$$

Where, $\tilde{d}_{ij}^{(k)}$ is SRPL between v_i and v_j, actually representing an industrial value chain on which each edge is the tightest and path is the shortest. According to Eq (5), we can get SRPLs between any two of nodes, and they form a new matrix $\tilde{D}^{(N)}$:

$$\tilde{D}^{(N)} = \begin{bmatrix} \tilde{d}_{11}^{(N)} & \cdots & \tilde{d}_{1N}^{(N)} \\ \tilde{d}_{21}^{(N)} & \cdots & \tilde{d}_{2N}^{(N)} \\ \vdots & & \vdots \\ \tilde{d}_{N1}^{(N)} & \cdots & \tilde{d}_{NN}^{(N)} \end{bmatrix} \quad \textbf{(6)}$$

On the basis of $\tilde{D}^{(N)}$, we chose the average of its elements to measure the flow efficiency of value stream in ISTN models, and named it Average Strongest Relevance Degree, denoted by ASRD.

Secondly, we took ISTN-CHN-2011 for example and removed a part of nodes to observe what happens to ASRD of this model. In details, we intentionally removed specific nodes from those with higher C_F or C_{RC} to lower ones in one set of experiment, then we made random removal of nodes in another set of experiment as reference. After implementing intentional and random failure for both C_F or C_{RC}, results are shown in Figs 6 and 7.

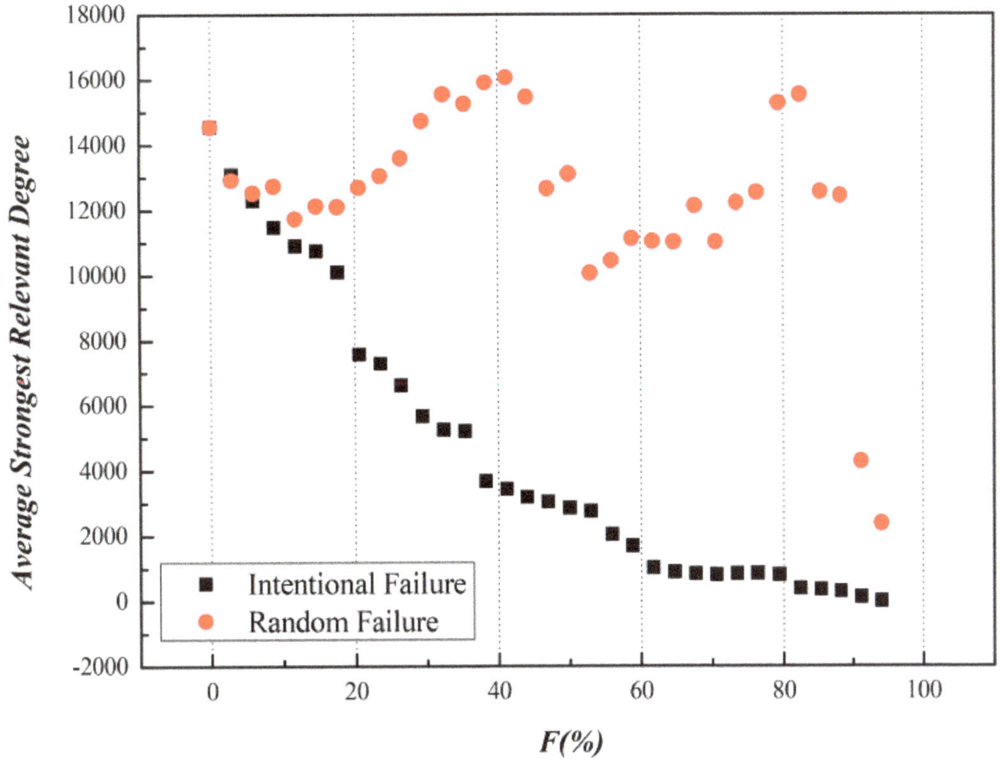

Figure 6: Impacts on ASRD Caused by Intentional Failure according to the Rank of Flow Betweenness in ISTN-CHN-2011.

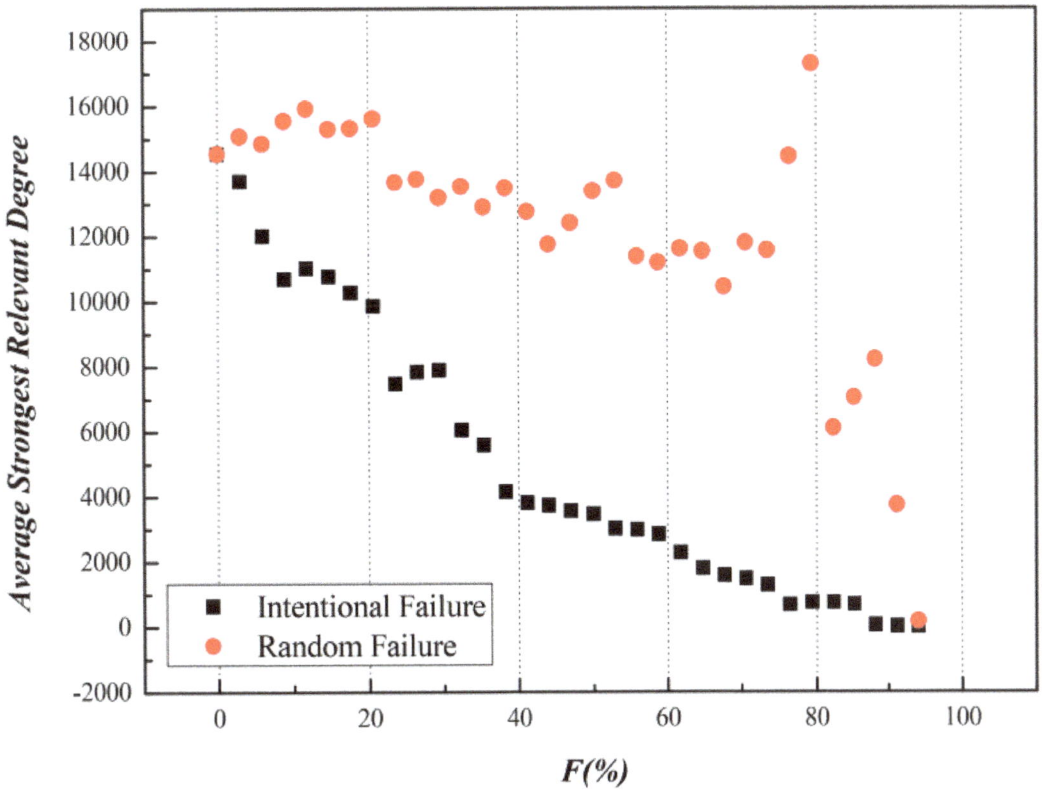

Figure 7: Impacts on ASRD Caused by Intentional Attack according to the Rank of Random Walk Centrality in ISTN-CHN-2011.

Finally, we can clearly see flow efficiency of value stream reduces by 50% when the ratio of nodes intentionally removed just reaches 20%, in the meanwhile, reference sets are far from this level of damage. Thus, on matter nodes with higher C_F or C_{RC}, they play a leading role in transmission of value stream.

Regression Analysis

In order to carry out comparative analysis, a simple linear regression between C_F or C_{RC} was done, as shown in Fig 8, and data in details.

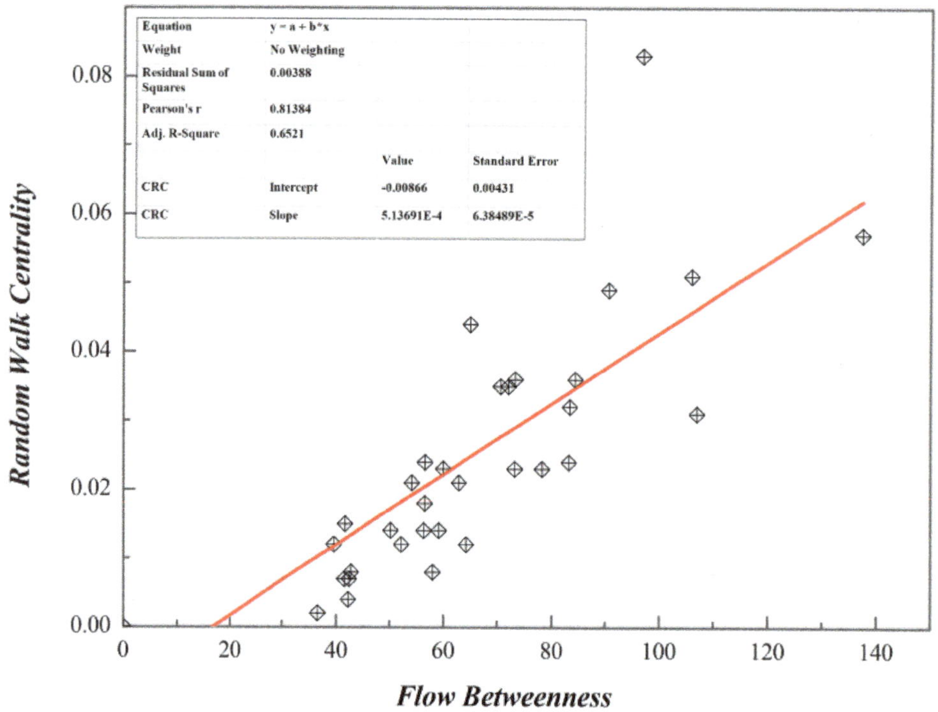

Figure 8: Regression Analysis on Flow Betweenness and Random Walk Centrality in ISTN-CHN-2011.

The results shows that and C_F or C_{RC} have a moderate linear correlation, which means that both of them have the same trend of increasing and decreasing, Adjusted R-squared is 0.65, so the relationship is reasonable.

According to fitting results, C_F or C_{RC} represent different spreading effect because of time-lag, which means there is a time process when certain industrial sector's changes lead to other ones'. In other words, temporal span makes impacts on value stream transmission, in details,C_F can be treated as accumulative effect and C_{RC} as instantaneous effect as we already described in the above. However, C_F or C_{RC} are both restricted by relatively fixed industrial structure, so they are somewhat relevant to some extent. Thus, regression analysis needed to be implemented, and data required.

Total Intermediate Consumption (denoted by *TIC*) and Total Output (denoted by *TO*) are applied, in order to conduct multiple regression with C_F. *TIC* is an accounting flow which consists of the total monetary value of goods and services consumed or used up as inputs in production by enterprises, including raw materials, services and various other operating expenses. *TO* is an economic concept used to measure total economic activity in the production of new goods and services in an accounting period. Therefore, these two indices respectively describe one sector's capital in-flow and out-flow within economic system, and the regression results will indicate which flow determines long-term industrial spreading effect.

Firstly, Hausman test was adopted, and the results show that the cross-section random effect should be rejected under the 1% confidence level. After panel data fixed effect model, Durbin-Watson stat is 1.82, (1.58<D.W. = 1.82<2.42), which shows the null hypothesis should be accepted, the disturbance term does not exist a first-order positive autocorrelation, and the higher R-squared means the goodness-of-fit of model is stronger. Then, stepwise regression was carried out, finding that *TO* has negative affect, so the final panel data fixed effect model can be expressed as follows:

$$C_{Ft} = \underset{(0.0000)}{56.25708} + \underset{(0.0000)}{0.260025C_{Ft-1}} + \underset{(0.0000)}{0.000312TIC} \tag{7}$$

All of the coefficients are significant at 1% confidence level. Eq (7) displays that C_F has positive correlation with its first-order lag, which means every 1 unit of last year will make 0.260025 impact on this year, and *TIC* also has positive affect, which contribute 0.00312 toC_{Ft} over the same period.

Similarly, Induction Coefficient (denoted by *ISD*), and Influence Coefficient (denoted by*IPD*) were also introduced for multiple regression with C_{RC}. *ISD* means in the national economy, when all industries are adding a unit of final use, thereby subjects to the needs of an industry level sensors. *IPD* refers to a national increase of one unit of end-use industries, the right of the national economy resulting from the production needs of industry, affects the degree of correlation coefficient. According to their definition, they respectively evaluate one sector's sensitivity and extraversion to industrial structure, and the regression results will show which index determines the function of short-term industrial spreading effect.

After the same estimation process, the fixed effect panel data model was used again, and *IPD*has negative affect, so the final panel data fixed effect model can be expressed as follows:

$$C_{RCt} = -0.0000519 + 0.862493C_{RCt-1} + 0.003041ISD$$
$$(0.9589) \quad (0.0000) \quad (0.0044)$$

(8)

Durbin-Watson stat is 1.76, according to D.W. Test table (1.58<D.W. = 1.76<2.42), which means that the null hypothesis should be accepted, the disturbance term does not exist a first-order positive autocorrelation. Also the higher R-squared means the goodness-of-fit of model is very strong. Eq (8) displays that C_{RC} has positive correlation with its first-order lag, which means every 1 unit of last year will have 0.862493 impact on this year.

In sum, exogenous and endogenous variables jointly influence industrial structure and make it change slowly over time, Thus, C_F and C_{RC} are relevant with their last annual status. In addition, industrial spreading effect is decided by capital in-flow and its sensitivity, not out-flow or extraversion. So, both long-term and short-term value stream transmission depend on how many products and services sectors can get. If they could get enough stuff in economic system, represented by huge intermediate consumption, they are to be regarded as brokers with bigger information superiority and more intermediate interests according to structural holes theory, which means their position and function are more important in the economic system than the others.

CONCLUSIONS

Industry analyses are concentrating more on dynamic swarm than static individual. IO analysis, as an important research tool, focuses more on static analysis. However, the fundamental aim of industry analyses are to figure out how interaction between different industries makes impacts on economic development, which turns out to be a dynamic process. So, in this paper, ISTN models were established based on IO tables as one bridge connecting accurate static quantitative analysis and comparable dynamic one.

Based on revised structural holes theory, it is obvious that industries with bigger flow betweenness or random walk centrality would bring about more intensive industrial spreading effect to the industrial chains they stands in. If they suffered from intentional failure, the connectedness of ISTN models will decline rapidly. And according to results of multiple regression, value stream transmission of industrial sectors depends on how many products and services sectors they can get from the others, and these sectors are regarded as brokers with bigger information superiority and more intermediate interests.

But, results from this paper are not enough for forecasting evolutionary trends of industrial structure. In that, past years' IO data were adopted to depict variation trends of two kinds of betweenness and centrality as well as explain dynamic mechanics of industrial effect spreading over different temporal span. However, it is necessary to accurately estimate industrial development in consideration of multiple exogenous variables' effect, and there will be big difference when different exogenous variables act on different industrial sectors. Thus, in following studies, important exogenous variables will be chosen for analogue simulation, evolutionary trends of industrial structure will be forecasted according to industrial environmental changes by scenario analysis, such as link prediction, and industrial policy to specific sectors are supposed to be proposed for promoting its scientific development.

ACKNOWLEDGMENTS

Authors thank Dr. Xianlei Dong for insightful discussions. All authors acknowledge support from the Beijing Postdoctoral Science Foundation (Grant No. 2015ZZ-42) and Beijing Municipal Commission of Education (Grant No. 14JDJGB039).

REFERENCES

1. Fan Y, Li MH, Chen JW, Gao L, Di ZR, Wu JS. Network of econophysicists: a weighted network to investigate the development of econophysics. International Journal of Modern Physics B, 2012,18(18):2505–2511.
2. Stanley, Eugene H. An introduction to econophysics. Cambridge University Press, 2000.
3. Chmiel AM, Sienkiewicz J, Suchecki K, Holyst JA. Networks of companies and branches in Poland. Physica A Statistical Mechanics & Its Applications, 2007, 383(1):134–138.
4. Inoue H, Souma W, Tamada S. Analysis of cooperative research and development networks on Japanese patents. Journal of Informetrics, 2010, 4(1):89–96.
5. Chang H, Su BB, Zhou YP, He DR. Assortativity and act degree distribution of some collaboration networks. Physica A Statistical Mechanics & Its Applications, 2007, 383(2):687–702.
6. Liu Q, Fang JQ, Li Y. Several Features of China Top-100 Electronic Information Technology Enterprise Network. Journal of Guangxi Normal University, 2008.
7. Hou R, Yang JM, Yao CZ. Research on Logistics Industry Competitive Relationship Model Based on Complex Networks. Chinese Journal of Management, 2010, 7(3):406–411.
8. Li Y, Fang JQ, Liu Q. Global Nuclear Plant Network and Its Characteristics. Atomic Energy Science & Technology, 2010, 44(9):1139–1144.
9. Yao CZ, Yang JM, Zhuang D. Rivalry Spread Effect Based on Industrial Complex Network. Chinese Journal of Management, 2011, 8(2):254–264.
10. Upper C. Simulation methods to assess the danger of contagion in interbank markets. Journal of Financial Stability, 2011, 7(3):111–125.
11. Hu S, Yang HL, Cai BL, Yang CX. Research on spatial economic structure for different economic sectors from a perspective of a complex network. Physica A Statistical Mechanics & Its Applications, 2013,392(17):3682–3697.
12. Blöchl F, Theis FJ, Vega- Redondo F, Fisher EO'N. Vertex centralities in input-output networks reveal the structure of modern economies. Physical Review E Statistical Nonlinear & Soft Matter Physics, 2011,83(4):1451–1463. [PubMed]
13. Kagawa S, Okamoto S, Suh S, Kondo Y, Nansai K. Finding environmentally important industry clusters: Multiway cut approach using nonnegative matrix

factorization. Social Networks, 2013, 35(3):423–438.

14. Mcnerney J, Fath BD, Silverberg G. Network structure of inter-industry flows. Physica A Statistical Mechanics & Its Applications, 2013, 392(24):6427–6441.
15. Contreras MGA, Giorgio F. Propagation of Economic Shocks in Input-Output Networks: A Cross-Country Analysis. Lem Papers, 2014, 90(6):062812–062812. [PubMed]
16. Ando S. Measuring US sectoral shocks in the world input—output network. Economics Letters, 2014,125(2):204–207.
17. Cerina F, Zhu Z, Chessa A, Riccaboni M. World Input-Output Network. PLOS ONE, 2015, 10(7): e0134025 doi: 10.1371/journal.pone.0134025 [PMC free article] [PubMed]
18. Grazzini J, Spelta A. An empirical analysis of the global input-output network and its evolution. DISCE—Working Papers del Dipartimento di Economia e Finanza, 2015.
19. Burt RS. Structural holes: the social structure of competition. Harvard University Press, 1992.
20. Black F. Business Cycles and Equilibrium. Journal of Finance, 2009.
21. Timmer MP, Dietzenbacher E, Los B, Stehrer R, De Vries GJ. An Illustrated User Guide to the World Input—Output Database: the Case of Global Automotive Production. Review of International Economics, 2015, 23(3):575–605.
22. Baldwin R, Lopez-Gonzalez J. Supply-chain Trade: A Portrait of Global Patterns and Several Testable Hypotheses. World Economy, 2013, NBER Working Papers.
23. Koopman R, Wang Z, Wei SJ. Estimating domestic content in exports when processing trade is pervasive. Journal of Development Economics, 2012, 99(99):178–189.
24. Ottaviano GIP, Pessoa JP, Sampson T, Van R. Brexit or Fixit? The Trade and Welfare Effects of Leaving the European Union. Cep Policy Analysis Papers, 2014.
25. Foster-Mcgregor N, Stehrer R, Vries GJD. Offshoring and the Skill Structure of Labour Demand.Review of World Economics/weltwirtschaftliches Archiv, 2012, 149(4):631–662.
26. European Commission, DG Enterprise and Industry, European Competitiveness Report 2012: Reaping the Benefits of Globalization, Brussels: EC, 2013.
27. Satio M, Ruta M, Turunen J. Trade Interconnectedness: The World with Global Value Chains. IMF Policy Paper, Washington, DC, 2013.
28. Xing LZ. Study on Industrial Structure Based on Complex Social Networks. Science Press, 2013.
29. Freeman LC, Borgatti SP, White DR. Centrality in Valued Graphs: A Measure of Betweenness Based on Network Flow. Social Networks, 1991, 13(2):141–154.
30. Ford LR, Fulkerson DR. Flows in Networks Mathematics of Computation. NJ: Princeton University Press, 1962.
31. Motwani R, Raghavan P. Randomized algorithms. Cambridge University Press, 1995.
32. Borgatti SP. Centrality and network flow. Social Network, 2005, 27(1):55–71.
33. Newman MEJ. A measure of betweenness centrality based on random walks. Social Network, 2005,27(1):39–84.
34. Bi Q, Fang JQ. Network science and statistical physics. Beijing: Peking University Press, 2011.
35. Singelmann J. From agriculture to services; the transformation of industrial employment. Sage Library of Social Research, 1978.

CHAPTER 6

A SCALABLE DISTRIBUTION NETWORK RISK EVALUATION FRAMEWORK VIA SYMBOLIC DYNAMICS

Kai Yuan[1], Jian Liu[2], Kaipei Liu[3], Tianyuan Tan[4]

[1]Reliability Evaluation of Power Systems Group, School of Electrical Engineering, Wuhan University, Hubei, China,

[2]Distribution Network Risk Evaluation and Reliability and Life-Cycle Cost Research Unit, School of Electrical Engineering, Wuhan University, Hubei, China,

[3]Distribution Network Power Quality Problem Group, School of Electrical Engineering, Wuhan University, Hubei, China,

[4]Distribution Network Risk Evaluation and Reliability Research Team, School of Electrical Engineering, Wuhan University, Hubei, China

ABSTRACT

Background

Evaluations of electric power distribution network risks must address the problems of incomplete information and changing dynamics. A risk evaluation framework should be adaptable to a specific situation and an evolving understanding of risk.

Methods

This study investigates the use of symbolic dynamics to abstract raw data. After introducing symbolic dynamics operators, Kolmogorov-Sinai entropy and Kullback-Leibler relative entropy are used to quantitatively evaluate relationships between risk sub-factors and main factors. For layered risk indicators, where the factors are categorized into four main factors – device, structure, load and special operation a merging algorithm using operators to calculate the risk factors is discussed. Finally, an example from the Sanya Power Company is given to demonstrate the feasibility of the proposed method.

Conclusion

Distribution networks are exposed and can be affected by many things. The topology and the operating mode of a distribution network are dynamic, so the faults and their consequences are probabilistic.

INTRODUCTION

Electric power distribution networks are receiving greater attention both from administrators and end users in China as new construction of rural networks and smart grids proceeds.

Citation: Yuan K, Liu J, Liu K, Tan T. A Scalable Distribution Network Risk Evaluation Framework via Symbolic Dynamics. Aegerter CM, ed. PLoS ONE. 2015;10(3):e0112940. doi:10.1371/journal.pone.0112940.

A distribution network consists of a large number and variety of devices, which are prone to external disruptions. These networks are complex systems, and it is impossible to collect all of the required information for all possible states.

Risk analysis can evaluate both the likelihood of faults occurring and the consequences, which is the traditional concept of reliability used in China. For distribution networks, the probability of faults is related to reliability, which has been the traditional focus of management in power companies. The consequences of faults, however, are usually measured in terms of power loss, which is insufficient.

Risk management has long been a topic of interest both inside and outside the power industry. Several researchers have focused on distribution network investment. Under brink attempted to relate component failures and repair times to power losses [1].Sand and others attempted to improve maintenance and reinvestment decisions through Bayesian networks by correlating certain variable indicators such as adverse weather with risk [2–4]. Janjicat tempted to decouple risk factors and state transitions based on decision tree diagrams and then adjust maintenance schedules [5].Risk-based management has been used in many aspects of power system planning [6–9].

Because a distribution network is a large-scale system, the availability of power is influenced by component reliability, the network structure, maintenance, the operating condition, the environment and other factors. Risk analysis based on component failures or system failures cannot include all of the factors affecting distribution network risk. For example, a transformer failure may be the result of poor quality manufacturing, a lightning strike, poor maintenance, prolonged overloaded operation or other reasons. Risk analysis based on the failure time would miss these details, which would be very important for risk reduction decisions.

Consequences in risk analysis cannot be simply measured or converted to failure times because this would not reflect all of the loss characteristics. For example, a one-hour power outage would not have the same consequences for a five-star hotel as for a remote village. The expected remedies would also be different, which would result in different investment decisions.

To describe distribution network risk, one-dimensional time series data, which usually fluctuate over time, should be collected from multiple sources. Processing the data using probability theory can reveal the uncertain characteristics of risk[10],e.g., for load forecasting[11]. Xiao developed probabilistic indices and attempted to control for low voltage and overload using a multi-objective approach[12].Feng processed data with a random fuzzy model and evaluated the operation risk[13]. Other researchers have used radial basis function neural networks, hybrid methods, equivalent reliability networks and other methods to simplify the analysis[14–16], but external influences were not included.

For systems with incomplete information, it is logical to consider semi-empirical methods[17]. However, as technology improves and requirements emerge, data may be added, updated or deleted from the system, so a scalable framework for risk analysis is critical.

Symbolic dynamics can be used to analyze one-dimensional time series data, and this method is widely used in anomaly detection and pattern recognition [18–19]. In this study, symbolic dynamics are used to abstract information contained in raw data, and entropy theory is used to analyze risk factor relationships.

MATERIALS AND METHODS

Risk and Symbolic Dynamics

Distribution networks are operated in the open, and they are at risk from a great many factors that are difficult to enumerate. A risk description framework should be adaptable to the current management strategy, the evolution of technology and an understanding of risk for the distribution network.

To describe risk in a distribution network, data of various types such as continuous load data or discrete user-level data should be collected. Current approaches tend to use fuzzy set theory to abstract or categorize data, but the coarse nature of fuzzy sets precludes further processing at a finer granularity.

Quantitatively, risk is defined as:

$$Risk = Possibility \times Loss \tag{1}$$

Where *Possibility* is the likelihood of the occurrence of a particular fault and *Loss* is the consequence of that fault occurring. Currently, consequences in distribution network risk analysis are mostly measured by power loss, which is inadequate. As an example, a power loss would have different effects, both in economic and social terms, in a five-star hotel and in a rural village. Additionally, a consequence in a distribution network is not static because the topology and the operating mode can change.

For a discrete time series, any set of disjoint regions $\beta = \{C_i\}_1^m$ that covers the state space$S$ is called a partition[20]; that is,

$$\beta = \{C_i\}_1^m; C_i \cap C_j = \varphi for i \neq j; \bigcup_{i=1}^{m} C_i = S \tag{2}$$

If a unique symbol $m \in \Omega$, where Ω is a symbol set defined as $\{S0,S1,S2,\ldots,Sm\text{-}1\}$, is assigned to a specific partition, then the representation of the time series data would be

$$L_X(L,i) = \sum_{p=1}^{L} m^{L-P} S(p+i) \tag{3}$$

where i is the starting index of the symbolic in the symbol set Ω and m is the length of the symbol sequence. Similar to fuzzy sets, this symbolic representation can abstract the information, but this representation permits more flexibility and uncertainty than fuzzy sets. It is assumed that the dynamical system is stationary on the fast time scale and that any nonstationarity is observable only on the slow time scale. In symbolic dynamics, the *slow time scale* is typically defined as being at least two orders of magnitude larger than the *fast time scale*.

For convenience, we define five levels to describe the risk in the distribution network, *very high*, *high*, *medium*, *low*, and *very low*, which can be represented by a symbol set $\Omega = \{A,B,C,\ldots,O\}$.

Risk Description Framework

We propose a risk description framework that includes device, structure, load and special operation factors, as Fig. 1 illustrates.

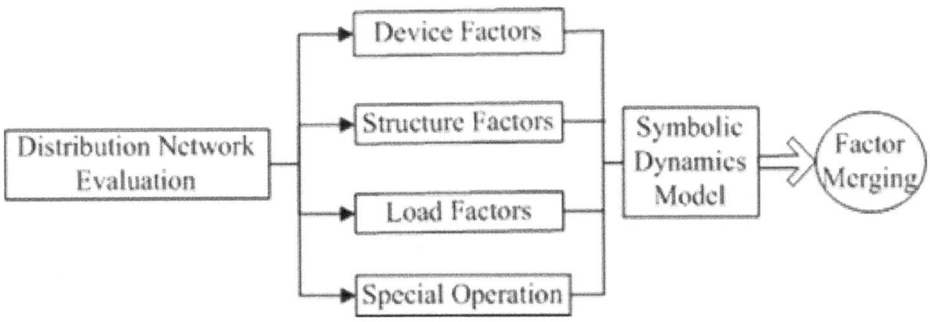

Figure 1: Risk description framework.

All risk indicators should be calculated independently according to the voltage level. For convenience, it is logical to organize the factors in a layered structure. Theoretically, the more data that are collected, the more accurate the evaluation of risk will be. Because the types of data may vary with location and time, the factor merging algorithm should be robust and flexible. As an example, the organization for the device indicators is given in Fig. 2.

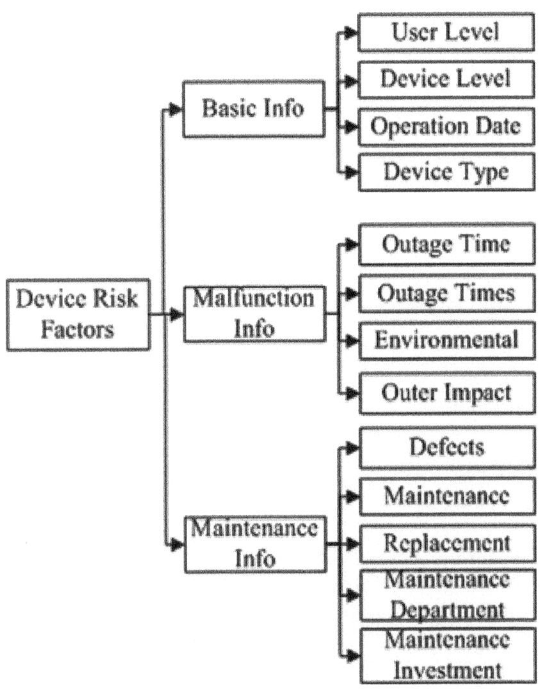

Figure 2: Example of a layered framework for device factors.

The risk factors may also have sub-factors such as environmental effects, but these will not be discussed here. As China covers vast area, it is hard to adopt uniform risk factors framework. Practically, Risk indices selection and categorization is first carried out by national standards. Then, supplementary indices are integrated into the framework according to local data collection ability and management requirement.

Raw Risk Data Processing

Risk, as defined previously, is a relative value, so a baseline should be chosen for evaluation. For a distribution network risk evaluation, a day with fine weather, a light load, and no defects or malfunctions should be chosen as the baseline. The risk factors can be mapped linearly based on the baseline extreme values. A mapping process is described in the following.

1. ***Possibility Data Processing*:** For the device factor layers shown in Fig. 2, we calculate the relative level factor for a line or a substation as

$$D_{LevelFactor} = \frac{\sum_{l=1}^{k} Device(l) \times Device_{Level}}{Device_{Count}} \quad (4)$$

Where $Device_{Count}$ and $Device_{Level}$ are self-explanatory and *Device(l)* is the device number at a specific level. After the baseline factor is calculated, a mapping from the raw data to a symbolic sequence can be defined as follows:

$$Ind_R = \begin{cases} \dfrac{Ind_{Cur} - Ind_{Min}}{(Ind_{Max} - Ind_{Min})} \times 100, Ind_{Cur} \leq Ind_{Max} \\ 100 \qquad\qquad\qquad\qquad , Ind_{Cur} > Ind_{Max} \end{cases} \qquad \textbf{(5)}$$

$$P_{Idx} = \begin{cases} \left[\dfrac{Ind_R}{20} + 1\right] \times 3, x - \left[\dfrac{Ind_R}{20}\right] \times 20 < 12 \\ \left[\dfrac{Ind_R}{20} + 1\right] \times 3 + 1, 12 \leq x - \left[\dfrac{Ind_R}{20}\right] \times 20 < 18 \\ \left[\dfrac{Ind_R}{20} + 1\right] \times 3 + 2, 18 \leq x - \left[\dfrac{Ind_R}{20}\right] \times 20 < 20 \end{cases} \qquad \textbf{(6)}$$

Where Ind_{Max} and Ind_{Min} are the maximum and minimum values of the baseline calculations, respectively, and P_{Idx} is the first symbol index in the symbol set. We chose three symbols to describe the risk probability and consequence. Other symbols are consecutive symbols after P_{Idx} indicates. The symbols indicate weights W_s of 60%, 30% and 10%, respectively. The first and second symbol weights are approximation of golden number, and the rest is allocated to the third symbol weight.

2. ***Consequence Data Processing***: The risk factors can have either direct or indirect connections to a malfunction. For factors with a direct connection such as a device failure, the mapping is defined as follows:

$$Con_R = Min\left\{100, \frac{MTTR_{Idn}}{MTTR_{Avg}} \times Level^2 \times 100\right\} \qquad (7)$$

$$C_{Idx} = \begin{cases} \left[\dfrac{Con_R}{20} + 1\right] \times 3, x - \left[\dfrac{Con_R}{20}\right] \times 20 < 12 \\ \left[\dfrac{Con_R}{20} + 1\right] \times 3 + 1, 12 \leq x - \left[\dfrac{Con_R}{20}\right] \times 20 < 18 \\ \left[\dfrac{Con_R}{20} + 1\right] \times 3 + 2, 18 \leq x - \left[\dfrac{Con_R}{20}\right] \times 20 < 20 \end{cases} \qquad (8)$$

Where C_{Idx} is similar to P_{Idx}, $MTTR_{Idn}$ and $MTTR_{Avg}$ represent the affected factor recovery time and the total line or substation recovery time expressed in terms of *MTTR* (Mean Time To Repair), and *Level* in equation (7) indicates the relative importance of the line or substation.

From equation (7), we observe that the line or substation level has a strong influence on the risk consequence.

For indirect connection factors, we convert the raw data in a relative manner. For example, the maintenance department risk consequence Con_R for a distribution line can be calculated as

$$Con_R = Min\left\{100, \frac{MTTR_{IdnMngAvg}}{MTTR_{AvgAll}} \times Level^2 \times 100\right\} \qquad \textbf{(9)}$$

Where $MTTR_{IdnMngAvg}$ is the average *MTTR* under a specific management staff and $MTTR_{AvgAll}$ is the average *MTTR* of all of the lines. The average *MTTR* is calculated from the line *MTTR* and the line length. For example, $MTTR_{IdnMngAvg}$ is calculated using equation (10)

$$MTTR_{IdnMngAvg} = \frac{MTTR_{Mng}}{Line_{MngLength}} \qquad \textbf{(10)}$$

Where $MTTR_{Avg}$ includes all of the MTTRs under a specific management staff and $Line_{MngLength}$ is the corresponding line length.

Phase-Space Reconstruction

Once the factors in the risk description have been decided, the phase-space dimension and structure are determined. It is possible to recreate the entire trajectory of the system from measurements. Based on equation (6) and the symbol sequence representation, the sequence of state vectors is represented as:

$$\bar{S}_0 = \begin{bmatrix} Ind_0(t) \\ Ind_1(t) \\ \cdots \\ Ind_{m-1}(t) \end{bmatrix}, \ldots, \bar{S}_i = \begin{bmatrix} Ind_0(t + i\Delta t) \\ Ind_1(t + i\Delta t) \\ \cdots \\ Ind_{m-1}(t + i\Delta t) \end{bmatrix} \qquad \textbf{(11)}$$

where $\{Ind_k\}$ is the sequence of the state vectors generated from the raw risk data processing and $\in N$ is a time interval in the phase-space trajectory of the system determined by the observation rate. To reflect the layered structure of the risk factors, the factors are grouped according to their place in the risk description framework, such as in Fig. 2.

Symbolic Dynamics Operators

The processing of the raw data and the phase-space reconstruction were discussed in the previous section. The symbolic dynamics operators are presented in this section to establish a foundation for factor merging.

definition 1: Sequence Index Operator ***Idx***

The sequence index operator is defined as

$$t = Idx(L_X(3)) \qquad \textbf{(12)}$$

where t is the index of the first symbol in the symbol set Ω for a given symbol sequence. The risk probability and consequence are represented by a symbol sequence of 3, $L_X(3)$.

definition 2: Shift Operator →

The shift operator is defined as

$$L_{X1}(3) = L_X(3) \rightarrow g \qquad \textbf{(13)}$$

where g is an integer indicating the amount of shift in the symbol set Ω where positive means a shift to the right and negative means a shift to the left. The shift operation cannot cross the border of the symbol set. If the shift operation reaches the symbol set border, the last symbol should be repeated. For example, if the first index is 14 or 15 and the symbol set is {A, B, …, O}, the result of the shift operator would be $L_X(3)$ = {NOO} or $L_X(3)$ = {OOO}.

definition 3: Addition Operator ⊕ The addition operator is defined as

$$Idx(L_{X1}(3) \oplus L_{X2}(3)) = \left[\sum_{l=1}^{3} \begin{matrix} (Idx(L_{X1}(3,l) \times W_s(X1,l) \\ +Idx(L_{X2}(3,l) \times W_s(X2,l)) \end{matrix}\right] \qquad \textbf{(14)}$$

where[] is the Gaussian function and $Ws(X1,l)$ and $Ws(X2,l)$ are symbol weights as described in Section II Raw Risk Data Processing. Add operator would get the first symbol index of the result symbol sequence.

definition 4: Multiplication Operator ⊗

The multiplication operator is defined as

$$Idx(L_{X1}(3) \otimes L_{X2}(3)) = \left[\sum_{l=1}^{3} \begin{matrix} (Idx(L_{X1}(3,l) \times W_s(X1,l) \\ \times Idx(L_{X2}(3,l) \times W_s(X2,l)) \end{matrix}\right] \qquad \textbf{(15)}$$

definition 5: Ratio Operator **Θ**

The ratio operator is defined as

$$Idx(L_X(3)\Theta x) = x \times [\sum_{l=1}^{3}(Idx(L_X(3,l) \times W_s(l))] \quad \textbf{(16)}$$

where x is a positive rational number.

As explained in definition 1, the operations in definitions 2–5 cannot exceed the symbol boundaries.

RESULTS

As mentioned previously, raw risk factor data may vary with location and time. Therefore, it is critical to build a scalable framework. The framework in Fig. 2 is a scalable framework that enables users to add or remove factors as necessary. In this section, the system symbolic description and operators discussed in the previous sections are used to establish an algorithm for distribution network risk evaluation that is scalable.

Risk Factor Correlation

In a layered risk evaluation framework, risk sub-factors contribute to higher-layer risk factors. Because sub-factors may have different effects on the main factor, it is important to measure the relationship between the sub-factors and the main factor. A statistical method is used with the assumption that the more information is available, the more accurate the evaluation of risk will be. Therefore, we calculate the correlations of risk factors, as illustrated Fig. 3 and as described in the following.

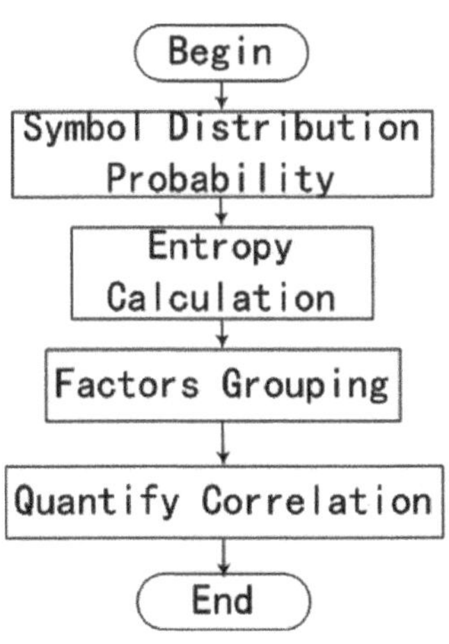

Figure 3: Risk factor correlation flowchart.

1. ***Symbol Distribution Calculation***: Based on the state vector $\{Ind_k\}$ in equation (11), a symbol j in symbol set Ω has the distribution probability

$$p_i(j) = \frac{\sum_{l=1}^{k} W_s(l)}{k \times W_s(Max)} \quad \textbf{(17)}$$

where k is the time index of the state vector, if symbol j exists, over which the symbol weights are accumulated and $W_s(Max)$ is the maximum symbol weight, say 60%.

Then, for a specific risk factor, the symbol distribution probability is calculated. For the main risk factor, the overall symbol distribution probability can be calculated as

$$P_i = \frac{\sum_{d=1}^{r}\sum_{l=1}^{k} W_s(d,l)}{k \times r \times W_s(Max)} \quad \textbf{(18)}$$

where r is the number of main risk factors, $W_s(d,l)$ is the corresponding dth sub-factor symbol weight.

2. ***Entropy Calculation***: After the symbol distribution probability has been calculated for the risk sub-factors, likeness for the sub-factors can be analyzed, which is useful for grouping them.

We use Kolmogorov-Sinai entropy, which is defined in equation (19), to measure the randomness of the risk factors, and we use the Kullback-Leibler distance in equation (20) to quantify the likeness of the risk factors.

$$H_j(c) = \sum_{c\in\Omega} p_j(c)\log_2 p_j(c) \quad \textbf{(19)}$$

$$D(p_j \parallel p_r) = \sum_{c\in\Omega} \log_2\left(\frac{p_j(c)}{p_r(c)}\right) \quad \textbf{(20)}$$

3. ***Factor Grouping***: It should be noted that the randomness of the symbol distributions affects the accuracy of the Kullback-Leibler distance. Therefore, we define a refined measurement as

$$I_{i,j} = \frac{D(p_j \parallel p_r)}{H_i \times H_r} \quad \textbf{(21)}$$

This measurement was chosen such that, even if the Kullback-Leibler distance is small, a high degree of randomness in the Kolmogorov-Sinai entropy reduces the possibility of two risk factors belonging to the same group, and vice versa. The group threshold is set at 2 to allow the largest possible grouping of similar sub-factors. For a specific main risk factor, its n sub-factors are grouped into f categories of risk subsets.

The goal is to correlate sub-factors to main factors through the symbol distribution probabilities, but if certain types of data are more abundant than others, the information in the less-abundant data may be obscured. Grouping data into categories not only reduces the dimension of the space, which further simplifies the process, it can reveal information that would otherwise be lost.

4. ***Quantification of Correlations***: This step attempts to relate the f categories of risk subsets to the main risk factor. We will describe the process using an example.

Without loss of generality, assume that a category $f1\in f$ has $m1$ sub-factors. We could then construct the time series of $f1$ as in equation (11); for example, $S_{f1}(t) = [Ind_0(t),\ldots,Ind_{m(1)-1}(t)]^T$. For each state vector in the time series, an average operation is defined as

$$Idx(S_{AvgX}(t,3)) = [\sum_{l=0}^{m_{(1)}-1} Ind_l(t)\Theta\frac{1}{m_{(1)}}] \quad \textbf{(22)}$$

In this manner, the state vector phase-space is reduced from m to f. From equations (17)–(21), we can calculate the distance between the f categories and the distribution of all the indicators as

$$I_i = \frac{D(p_j \parallel P)}{H_i \times P} \tag{23}$$

This is the quantitative distance between the sub-factor set and the main risk factor. The quantitative correlation coefficient is defined as

$$\epsilon_i = \frac{I_i^2 \times m_{(i)}}{\sum_{t=1}^{n} I_t^2 \times m_{(t)}} \tag{24}$$

This equation indicates that both the Kullback-Leibler distance and the number of factors in a sub-factor set contribute to the correlation coefficient and that the Kullback-Leibler distance has more influence.

Risk Factor Merging

Merging of risk factors simplifies the calculation of main risk factors from sub-factors. Merging is defined as

$$Idx(L_{MotherX}(t,3)) = [(\sum_{l=0}^{n} Ind_l(t)\Theta\epsilon_l)\Theta\frac{1}{n}] \tag{25}$$

where n is the number of sub-factor groups.

Event Risk Calculation

Prior to this step, the risk is calculated from the failure probability and the consequence independently.

For a specific component, line or substation, we can calculate the overall risk as

$$Idx(L_{Risk}(3)) = L_{Probability}(3) \otimes L_{Consequence}(3) \tag{26}$$

However, this definition, which was derived from equation (1), is mainly a statistical result. The variable nature of risk is not included. Therefore, an improvement is desired.

Using the shift operator in definition 2 on the phase-space in equation (11), we can obtain another time series vector for some value of g. Referring to the factor grouping and factor merging methods, we can define a fluctuation parameter as

$$P_f = [(\sum_{l=0}^{f} \|g(l,t)\| \times \epsilon_l)\Theta\frac{1}{f}] \tag{27}$$

To merge the four major types of risk factors, we define the merge operation given by equation (28),

$$Risk_{Line} =^{LineLine} (Struct_{Ind}\Theta Ind_{Society}) \otimes \{((Device_{Ind} \otimes Load_{Ind})\Theta Ind_{Weather}) \oplus Tech_{Ind}\} \tag{28}$$

where $Device_{Ind}$, $Struct_{Ind}$, $Tech_{Ind}$ and $Load_{Ind}$ are the device, structure, special operation and load factors, respectively, and $Ind_{Society}$ and $Ind_{Weather}$ are social and weather effect parameters, respectively, selected in accordance with the norms of that locality.

The final overall risk is defined as

$$Idx(L_{Risk}(3)) = (L_{Probability}(3) \otimes L_{Consequence}(3))\Theta P_f \tag{29}$$

This equation shows that greater diversity in the sub-factors results in greater risk of the event.

Algorithm Discussion

Risk is a relative concept based on probability theory. In distribution networks, if remedial measures and schedule planswere included in the risk evaluation, the failures and the losses would all have probabilistic characteristics. The proposed method is built on symbolic dynamics, and the result is intuitive, which is helpful in management. The following discussion further explains the concepts and the implementation of the method.

1. ***Information Abstraction***: A distribution network is a complex dynamic system that involves many types and large volumes of data. Therefore, information abstraction is very important.

Because risk is a relative concept, a linear demarcation of baseline data for basic risk standards as described in equations (5) and (6) is feasible, but this approach is not accurate. Furthermore, because the probabilistic nature of risk leads to vagueness in its evaluation, symbolic dynamics are used to incorporate language vagueness in the risk description.

Compared with fuzzy set abstraction, which expresses a variable using a definite category, symbolic dynamics use a symbol sequence to describe a variable, which enables further information processing.

Because all raw data are mapped into the symbol set, further uniform processing can be achieved. This relative processing technique conforms to the risk concept. The method of merging risk factors using symbolic dynamics operators offers a new way to compute risk factor relationships.

2. ***Probability-based Analysis***: Risk is a probability-based concept. For layered risk factors, sub-factors can affect risk factors in higher layers. Under these assumptions, the symbol distributions are calculated to reflect the failure and consequence probabilities. The Kullback-Leibler distance is used to measure the relationships between the sub-factors and the main risk factors and can be used as coefficients to adjust for variable randomness.

3. ***Scalability***: The data may vary with location or time, and they may have different numbers of sources. Thus, the risk framework should scale according to the data sources and should not allow data from more sources that is greater in volume to mask information conveyed by data from fewer sources.

Equation (22) provides the mean value to describe a risk factor category, and equation (25)merges risk factor categories. Regardless of the number of sub-factors in a risk category or the number of categories, this method provides a uniform risk value. Therefore, the risk can be calculated for the same description framework regardless of the number of data sources, which permits scalability.

4. ***Complexity Analysis***: Table 1 gives the approximate computational complexity estimates for the various steps in the algorithm, assuming the basic dimension of description state vector is m, as in equation (11).

Table 1: Computational Complexities of Algorithm Steps.

Step	Complexity
Symbol Distribution	$O(m^2)$
Entropy Calculation	$O(m)$
Factors Grouping	$O(m^2)$
Quantify Correlation	$O(m^2)$
Factors Merging	$O(m)$
Event Risk Calculation	$O(m)$

5. ***Algorithm Acceleration*:** The most time-consuming processes are the symbol distribution, the factor grouping and the factor merging. Because these operations are based on historical data, they can be performed at system initialization and then updated periodically. In this manner, each step can be reduced to $O(m)$complexity, which is very desirable.
6. ***Multiple Granularity Management*:** Because the risk factors are layered, grouped and calculated, the risk failure and consequence distributions can be calculated and the correlations between risk factors can be tracked. Therefore, management of risk factors with differing granularities can be implemented. From the risk failure and consequence distributions, proper countermeasures may be taken. From the correlations between risk factors, counter measures can be prioritized.

DISCUSSION

The Sanya Power Company supplies power to Sanya, a popular tourism site in China. The company controls three 220kV substations, twelve 110kV substations, seven 220kV lines, twenty-four 110kV lines and one hundred and eighty-one 10kV lines. Sanya is a tropical island, so its distribution network is prone to disruptions from weather and other environmental factors. Therefore, risk management is very important for improving reliability.

Fig. 4 shows the high-voltage distribution network in Sanya. Certain substations or lines that are not under the SPC's administration are included to simplify the calculations.

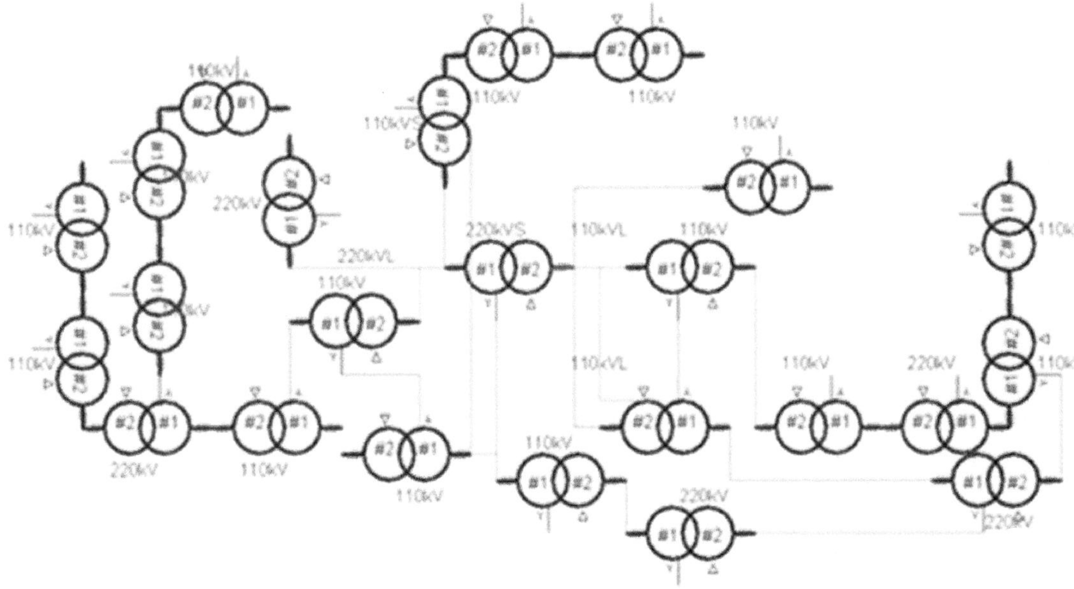

Figure 4: High-voltage distribution network.

The risk was given five levels, as shown in Table 2.

Table 2: Risk Level

Risk Level	Symbol
Very High(V)	A
High(IV)	D
Medium(III)	G
Low(II)	J
Very Low(I)	M

In our research, following data were collected:

1. Distribution network topology
2. Device accounting
3. Power flow data
4. Deficiencies and malfunctions from 2006 to 2013
5. Device-level and user-level data
6. Distribution network operation reports

Various loads, weather conditions and community activities may affect the overall risk, asequation (28) indicates. However, risk is a relative value. In our evaluation for 2013, the baseline was set at the minimum overall load day in 2009. We will list three line analysis results in this section, namely Yali II, Yali I and Yatian, which are high-risk transmission lines. The results for the substations are omitted for brevity.

In this example, the maximum overall load day and a typical rainy day in 2013were selected. The baseline, the maximum overall load day and the rainy day in 2013were evaluated using the parameters given in Table 3.

Table 3: Evaluation Parameters

Evaluation Number	IndWeather	IndSociety
1	1.0	1.0
2	1.0	1.0
3	2.0	1.4

The sub-factor correlation coefficients obtained from equations (22) to (24)are listed in Table 4.

Table 4: Line Device Indicator Correlation Coefficients

Correlation	Yali II	Yali I	Yatian
User Level	4.2	4.1	3.1
Device Level	2	1	1
Operation Date	1.0	1.3	1.5
Device Type	1.0	1.5	1.2
Outage Time	0.8	1.1	1.1
Environmental	1.8	1.9	2.2
Outer Impact	1	1.3	1.2
Defects	1.2	5.9	4.3
Maintenance	1.2	1.7	1.5
Replacement	1.1	1.5	1.3
Maintenance Department	4.2	4.6	4.3
Maintenance Investment	1.2	2.3	2.5

From Table 4, we conclude the following:

1. The user level and the maintenance are highly correlated with the overall risk.
2. Because Yali II is a relatively new line, defect management for that line has less of an effect than it does with the older lines, Yali I and Yatian.

The structure indicator varied insignificantly in our three evaluation examples. Fig. 5 and Fig. 6give the symbol distributions for a 110kV line structure failure and consequence, respectively.Table 5 lists the corresponding symbol distribution probabilities.

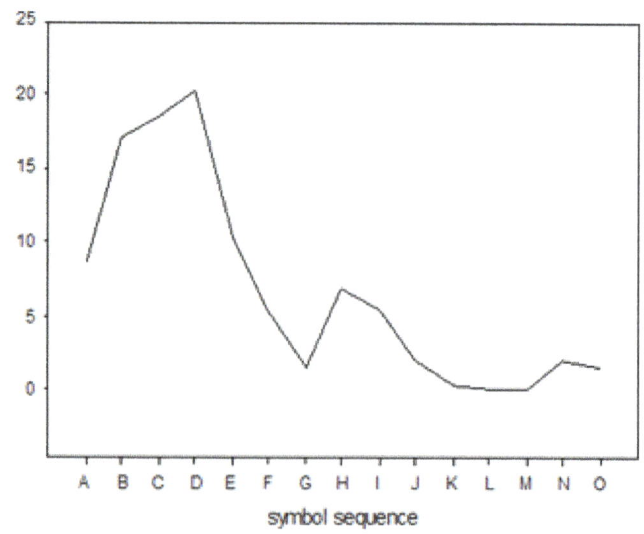

Figure 5: Device failure probability symbol distribution.

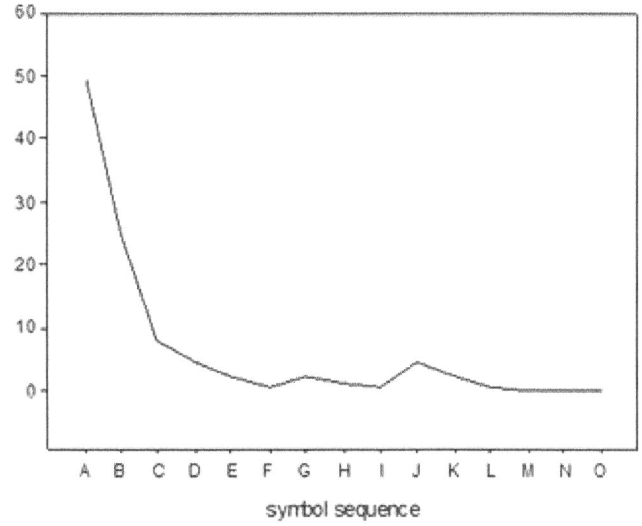

Figure 6: Device consequence probability symbol distribution.

Table 5: Symbol Distributions (%).

Symbol	Failure Symbol Distribution	Consequence Symbol Distribution
A	8.57	49.28
B	17.14	24.64
C	18.57	8.21
D	20.35	4.31
E	10.36	2.14
F	5.35	0.71
G	1.43	2.14
H	6.79	1.07
I	5.37	0.36
J	2.14	4.29
K	0.36	2.14
L	0	0.71
M	0	0
N	2.14	0
O	1.43	0

The overall device risk indicators calculated from equations (25) and (26) are listed in Table 6.

Table 6: Line Device Risk

Line	Line Risk Factor Value/Symbol		
	Evaluation 1	Evaluation 2	Evaluation 3
Yali I	1.52/BCD	1.58/BCD	2.12/CDE
Yali II	1.87/BCD	1.92/BCD	2.42/CDE
Yatian	1.87/BCD	2.01/CDE	2.15/CDE

As can be observed from Table 6, the 110kV line is relatively reliable. A comparison with a high-risk 10kV line is given in Table 7.

Table 7: 10kV Line Device Risk

Line	Line Risk Factor Value/Symbol		
	Evaluation 1	Evaluation 2	Evaluation 3
DongHaibin II	5.36/HIJ	7.35/KLM	7.35/KLM
Xijin	4.37/GHI	5.68/IJK	5.68/IJK
Dadonghai II	6.16/IJK	8.16/LMN	8.16/LMN

The overall risk values are listed in Table 8. To compare high-voltage risk characteristics, we give the risk analysis results for several10kV lines in Table 9.

Table 8: Transmission Line Overall Risk

Line Name/ Evaluation Number		Risk					
		Structure	Device	Operation	Load	Result	Risk Level
Yali I	1	23.5	1.52	1.5	1.38	84.66	IV
	2	23.5	1.58	1.5	1.46	89.64	IV
	3	23.5	2.12	1.5	1.33	234.86	V
Yali II	1	23.5	1.87	1.0	1.14	73.67	III
	2	23.5	1.92	1.0	1.24	79.34	III
	3	23.5	2.10	1.0	1.09	182.83	V
Yatian	1	14.2	1.87	1.3	1.09	44.97	II
	2	14.2	2.01	1.3	1.08	49.34	II
	3	14.2	2.15	1.3	0.85	98.68	IV

Table 9: 10kV Line Overall Risk

Line Name/Evaluation Number		Risk					
		Structure	Device	Operation	Load	Result	Risk Level
Tianhai	1	6.91	5.36	3.20	7	281.37	V
	2	8.06	7.35	3.20	12	731.68	V
	3	7.85	7.35	3.20	8	1327.59	V
Gang	1	10	4.37	7.07	3	201.8	V
	2	11.65	5.68	7.08	11	801.37	V
	3	12.38	5.68	7.08	6	1304.06	V
FengH	1	9.84	6.16	3.55	3	216.77	V
	2	13.48	8.16	3.55	6	707.83	V
	3	9.39	8.16	3.55	7	1548.47	V

Although algorithm in this paper has little constraints on data availability. As precision for symbolic dynamics data based abstraction and entropy based correlation evaluation, lack of data would have great impact on the rationality of the result. The more data available, the more precise the result is.

Although the categorization would also influence the final result, data categorization can be carried out under national or provincial system monitor, maintenance guidance, which would leads to uniform categorization in a relatively large area.

CONCLUSIONS

Distribution networks are exposed, and their operation can be disrupted for many reasons. Because the topology and the operating mode of a distribution network are dynamic, failures and their consequence are probabilistic in nature. This study investigated a risk evaluation method based on symbolic dynamics. Because of the relative nature of risk, symbolic dynamics is used to abstract the information contained in raw data. To accommodate a layered framework for risk factors, symbolic dynamics operators were discussed. To analyze the relationships between risk factors in a layered structure, quantitative correlation values were obtained using the Kullback-Leibler distance and Kolmogorov-Sinai entropy in the symbol distribution analysis. A method for merging risk factors using the symbolic dynamics operators that enables the management of risks with multiple granularities was discussed. Finally, the method was demonstrated using an example from the Sanya distribution network.

REFERENCES

1. Underbrink A, Mannheim (2006) Risk Analysis in Distribution and Transmission Networks. IEEE Trans. Power Delivery 8(3): 1–4.
2. Sand K, Catrinu MD, Kjølle GH, Bonnoit S, Aupied J, et al. (2008) Applications of Bayesian Networks in Distribution System Risk Management. In Proc. the 10th International Conf. on Probabilistic Methods Applied to Power Systems: 1–8.
3. Ming N, McCalley JD, Vijay V, Tayyib T (2003) On-line risk based security assessment. IEEE Trans. Power System 18(1): 258–265.
4. Li WY, Zhou JQ, Xie KG, Xiong XF (2008) Power System Risk Assessment Using a Hybrid Method of Fuzzy Set and Monte Carlo Simulation. IEEE Trans. Power System 23(2): 336–343.
5. Janjic AD, Popovic DS (2007) Selective Maintenance Schedule of Distribution Networks Based on Risk Management Approach. IEEE Trans. Power System 22(2): 597–604.
6. Cabeza AZ, Ridao MA, Alvarado I, Camacho EF (2008) Applying Risk Management to Combined Heat and Power Plants. IEEE Trans. Power System 23(3): 938–945.
7. Zhang J, Pu J, McCalley JD, Stern H, Gallus W (2002) A Bayesian Approach for Short-Term Transmission Line Thermal Overload Risk Assessment. IEEE Trans. Power Delivery 17(3): 770–778.

8. Li WY, Lu JP (2005) Risk Evaluation of Combinative Transmission Network and Substation Configurations and its Application in Substation Planning. IEEE Trans. Power System 20(2): 1144–1150.

9. Street A, Barroso LA, Flach B, Pereira MV, Granville S (2009) Risk Constrained Portfolio Selection of Renewable Sources in Hydrothermal Electricity Markets. IEEE Trans. Power System 24(3): 136–1144.

10. Billinton R, Pan ZM (2004) Historic Performance-Based Distribution System Risk Assessment. IEEE Trans. Power Delivery 19(4): 1759–1765.

11. Douglas AP, Breipahl AM, Lee FN, Adapa R (1998) Risk Due to Load Forecast Uncertainty in Short Term Power System Planning. IEEE Trans. Power System 13(4): 1493–1499.

12. Xiao F, McCalley JD (2009) Power System Risk Assessment and Control in a Multiobjective Framework. IEEE Trans. Power Delivery 24(1): 78–85.

13. Feng YQ, Wu WC, Zhang BM, Li YW (2008) Power System Operation Risk Assessment Using Credibility Theory. IEEE Trans. Power System 23(3): 1309–1318.

14. Kaigui W, Shao W, Anbang Z, jiaqi Z (2000) The Study on Reliability Assessment of Electrical Power Systems Using RBF Neural Network. Proceedings of the CSEE 20(6): 9–12.

15. Guocheng W, Zhen R, Risheng W, Yisi H (2004) Hybrid Method for the Reliability Evaluation of the Complex Distribution System. Proceedings of the CSEE 24(9): 92–98.

16. Guocheng W, Zhen R, Xiang T, Yisi H (2003) Study on Model of Reliability-Network-Equivalent of Distribution System Reliability Evaluation. Proceedings of the CSEE 23(5): 48–52.

17. Friedlander D, Chattopadhyay I, Ray A, Phoha S, Jacobson N (2003) Anomaly prediction in mechanical systems using symbolic dynamics. In Proc. American Control Conf. 6: 4590–4595.

18. Jin X, Guo Y, Sarkar S, Ray A, Edwards RM (2011) Anomaly Detection in Nuclear Power Plants via Symbolic Dynamic Filtering. IEEE Trans. Nulcl. Sci. 58(1): 277–288.

19. Caminal P, Vallverdú M, Giraldo B, Benito S, Vazquez G, et al. (2006) Optimized Symbolic Dynamics Approach for the Analysis of the Respiratory Pattern. IEEE Trans. On Biomedical Engineering 52(11): 1832–1839.

20. Stojanovski T, Kocarev L, Harris R (1997) Applications of Symbolic Dynamics in Chaos Synchronization. IEEE Trans. On Circuit Syst. I 44(10): 1013–1018.

CHAPTER 7

GENERALISED SANDPILE DYNAMICS ON ARTIFICIAL AND REAL-WORLD DIRECTED NETWORKS

Nicky Zachariou[1,2], Paul Expert[1,2,3], Misako Takayasu[4] , Kim Christensen[1,2]

[1]Department of Physics, Blackett Laboratory, Imperial College London, Prince Consort Road, South Kensington Campus, London SW7 2AZ, United Kingdom,

[2]Centre for Complexity Science, Electrical & Electronic Engineering Building, Imperial College London, South Kensington Campus, London SW7 2AZ, United Kingdom,

[3]Centre for Neuroimaging Sciences, Institute of Psychiatry, Psychology and Neuroscience, De Crespigny Park, King's College London, London SE5 8AF, United Kingdom,

[4]Department of Computational Intelligence and Systems Science, Interdisciplinary Graduate School of Science and Engineering, Tokyo Institute of Technology, 4259 Nagatsuta-cho, Midori-ku, Yokohama 226-8502, Japan

ABSTRACT

The main finding of this paper is a novel avalanche-size exponent τ 1.87 when the generalised sandpile dynamics evolves on the real-world Japanese inter-firm network. The topology of this network is non-layered and directed, displaying the typical bow tie structure found in real-world directed networks, with cycles and triangles. We show that one can move from a strictly layered regular lattice to a more fluid structure of the inter-firm network in a few simple steps. Relaxing the regular lattice structure by introducing an interlayer distribution for the interactions, forces the scaling exponent of the avalanche-size probability density function τ out of the two-dimensional directed sandpile universality class $\tau = 4/3$, into the mean field universality class $\tau = 3/2$. Numerical investigation shows that these two classes are the only that exist on the directed sandpile, regardless of the underlying topology, as long as it is strictly layered. Randomly adding a small proportion of links connecting non adjacent layers in an otherwise layered network takes the system out of the mean field regime to produce non-trivial avalanche-size probability density function. Although these do not display proper scaling, they closely reproduce the behaviour observed on the Japanese inter-firm network.

INTRODUCTION

A long standing problem in macroeconomic theory is explaining the large fluctuations in aggregate economic activity that result from many small, independent shocks to individual sectors. Economists are particularly interested in understanding the observed instability that a constant demand can have to the economic aggregate, since this is very costly to inventory management and scheduling at the production level [1]. Understanding the mechanisms hidden behind the behaviour of the economy as a whole, which lead to these large scale fluctuations, is not easy. Naturally, one would expect that the demand and production in different parts of the economy would be independent and hence independent shocks to different sectors would cancel in the aggregate leading to Gaussian distributed fluctuations. Unfortunately, this is not the case, which leads to the speculation that there are significant non linear and strongly localised interactions between the seemingly independent sections of the economy. A paradigm that has been proposed to explain the fluctuations on all scales caused by small independent shocks is self-organised criticality [1, 2].

Citation: Zachariou N, Expert P, Takayasu M, Christensen K. Generalised Sandpile Dynamics on Artificial and Real-World Directed Networks. Shi Y, ed. PLoS ONE. 2015;10(11):e0142685. doi:10.1371/journal.pone.0142685.

Consider a pile of sand. Dropping constantly one grain of sand at the time on top of this pile, will eventually trigger an avalanche, where some grains will topple down the slope. The size of the avalanche is defined as the number of grains involved in the toppling and interestingly, after a transient period, the avalanche-size probability density function (pdf) can be scale invariant [3]. Behaviour such as this is not only observed in the aggregate economic activity [1], but also in nature [4, 5], from lung inflation [6] and coevolution of species [7] to earthquakes [8, 9] and rainfall [10]. Self-organised criticality, a term coined by Bak, Tang, and Wiesenfeld (BTW) refers to systems with many degrees of freedom that spontaneously reach a dynamically critical state when slowly driven [3]. Once the critical state is reached, the self-organised critical system relaxes by a burst of activity. The avalanche sizes y display finite-size scaling (FSS), that is, follow a power-law pdf, $P(y;L) = y^{-\tau}\mathcal{G}(y/L^D)$ for $y \gg 1$ and $L \gg 1$, where the critical exponents τ and D are the so-called avalanche-size exponent and the avalanche dimension, respectively, and $\mathcal{G}$ is a universal scaling function [11, 12]. This property of self-organised critical systems is induced by the long-range spatial and temporal correlations that exist, via short range interactions only, when the system has naturally evolved into the critical state. The directed sandpile model is a special case of the BTW model, where relaxation follows a directional rule [13], in the sense that there is a flow of motion which cannot be reversed. The dynamics is still critical, with scale invariant avalanche-size pdf obeying finite-size scaling. Dhar and Ramaswamy have shown analytically that such a directed sandpile model on a two-dimensional lattice has a power-law avalanche-size pdf with scaling exponents $\tau = 4/3$ [13] that yields $D = 3/2$ [11].

Bak, Chen, Scheinkman and Woodford [2] showed that the classical two-dimensional directed sandpile dynamics can be used as a model for intersectoral trade and in their attempt to investigate the fluctuations in the production they recovered the same scaling exponents $\tau = 4/3$ and $D = 3/2$. We adapted the dynamics of [2, 13] to cover for different number of producers and consumers and run the dynamics on less rigid topologies.

The most realistic topology one can use for this task is the production-consumption network between firms in a real economy, such as the Japanese inter-firm network. The Japanese inter-firm data set, is a snap shot of the entire production network of all active firms in Japan, for the year 2005, where firms are represented as nodes with directed edges showing the flow of orders (or money) from the customer node to the supplier node. In comparison with the regular lattice, this network is not rigid and has a scale-free distribution both in the in- and out-degrees. It is also a very shallow network with short average path length and has many triangles, cycles and motifs [14]. On the Japanese network, we find an avalanche-size exponent of approximately $\tau = 1.87$. Although the system is still critical and reproduces qualitatively the behaviour observed by economists on aggregate production, this a novel avalanche-size exponent found which has not been observed before.

With the recent advance of complex networks theory, the behaviour of the BTW on non-lattice substrate have been investigated. In a series of papers, Goh et al. [15–18] have investigated the BTW model on scale-free undirected networks. Using a branching process approach, they found two regimes for the avalanche-size exponent τ as a function of the degree exponent γ of scale-free networks: $\tau = \gamma/(\gamma - 1)$ for $2 < \gamma < 3$ with logarithmic corrections for $\gamma = 3$ and the classical mean field avalanche-size exponent $\tau = 3/2$ which is recovered for $\gamma > 3$. The branching process is an inherent mean-field approach, as the cascading processes are uncorrelated, thus it is interesting to see that highly heterogenous networks, even treated with a mean-field approach yields an avalanche-size exponent different from the mean-field one. The behaviour of the BTW model has also been studied on undirected [19] and directed [20] small world network generated starting from a regular lattice with bidirectional links. While the system is in the mean-field universality class for all values of the rewiring probability p in the directed case, there is a cross-over from the BTW universality class when $p = 0$ to the mean-field universality class when $p > 0$ in the undirected case. Even though there have been studies of the sandpile model on complex networks, the case of directed sandpile has yet to be investigated. If one is to understand where this new avalanche-size exponent of $\tau = 1.87$ comes from, then one must break down the transition of the directed sandpile from the layered lattice, whose behaviour is very well known and documented, to the directed sandpile on a real world network of the economy. So how are these networks different and what are the ingredients needed to go from one to the other?

Firstly, we must account for the distribution of the in- and out-degrees. Thus, we keep the strictly layered structure of the lattice but we introduce an interlayer degree distribution, such as a Gaussian or the more realistic truncated scale-free distribution. The moment we introduce any interlayer heterogeneity, we observe scale invariant avalanche-size pdfs obeying FSS with the mean field scaling exponents. Clearly, this modification is not enough.

Secondly, we must account for the shallowness of the network and introduce some cycles, triangles and motifs. To do so, we relax the strictly layered constraint by allowing a small proportion of long range connections across layers both in the direction of flow and opposite to it. This last perturbation is very similar in nature to the perturbation that Watts and Strogatz used in their seminal paper to modify a regular lattice and turn it into a small-world network [21]. Now, the avalanche-size pdfs show fat tails with an avalanche-size exponent close to the one observed in the Japanese interfirm network. However, with the introduction of random long-range connections, the number of layers L is no longer the characteristic scale of the system; it is therefore not possible to perform FSS of the avalanche-size pdfs. The long range connections bring the system out of the mean field behaviour and produce non-trivial avalanche behaviour which can closely reproduce the one observed using the Japanese inter-firm network. We believe that we have identified perturbations to a strictly layered sandpile model that produces a non-trivial avalanche-size pdf consistent to what is observed on a real-world Japanese inter-firm network.

METHODS

Model Definition

Bak, Chen, Scheinkman and Woodford [2] showed that the classical two-dimensional directed sandpile dynamics can be recast in the language of intersectoral trade in their attempt to investigate the fluctuations in the production. They assumed that the economy has the form of a cylindrical lattice with L layers, where each productive unit is connected to two suppliers and two consumers directly in the layer below and above it, respectively. During production, two units of output are created by utilising two units of input taken equally from each supplier. To optimise the costs of keeping inventory, each unit can hold a maximum of one unit of new product. They independently shock the first layer of the economy and monitor the aggregate production at that period. Production occurs when an order from a customer cannot be fulfilled exclusively by utilising products from the suppliers inventory [1, 2]. The distribution of the aggregate production follows exactly the behaviour of the avalanches in the directed sandpile model described above, with the avalanche-size scaling exponents $\tau = 4/3$ and $D = 3/2$. This simple model was successful in qualitatively recreating the desired behaviour observed in the macro-economy; however, it has many drawbacks, the biggest of all being the very rigid and unrealistic layered topology used with a constant number of suppliers and customers per unit [1].

We now adapt the dynamics introduced by Bak, Chen, Scheinkman and Woodford [2] in a directed two-dimensional lattice, with co-ordination number K = 2, to a general lattice structure. Consider an economy made of N productive units arranged in L number of layers on a lattice with periodic boundary conditions connecting the left edge to the right edge. The width of the economy is defined as the circumference C of the lattice, where C = N/L.

We identify each productive unit by its coordinates in this 2-dimensional system, which are denoted by (i, j). Each productive unit has a set of suppliers (below) to buy its supplies from and a set of customers (above) to sell its products to. In the layered economy this is denoted by an unweighted directed link (n, n′) going from each supplier node n(i, j) to each customer node n′(i′, j′). Thus, the set of customers of node n(i, j) is defined as $N_{i,j} = \{n'(i', j') | n'(i', j')$ is a customer of $n(i, j)\}$.

The underlying network of the economy can be drawn by accumulating all the links, where the in- and out-degrees of each node, $k_{i,j}^{in}$ and $k_{i,j}^{out}$, are defined as the number of customers and suppliers, respectively, each company n(i, j) has. In such a system, the top layer can be thought of as the final goods producers, the bottom layer as providers of primary inputs (raw materials) and anything in between as the intermediate goods producers. Fig 1 is an illustration of a subset of such a network.

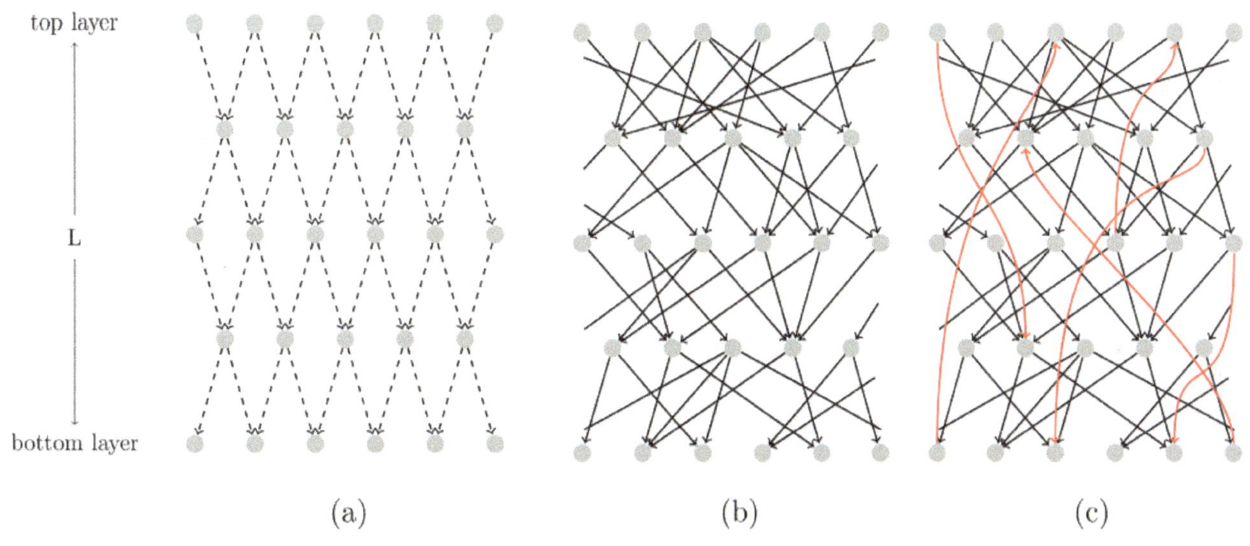

Figure 1: Diagram illustrating the different topologies on a subset of the network.

(a) Dashed black lines: two-dimensional directed lattice with coordination number K = 2. (b) Black solid lines: layered network with a randomised degree distribution (e.g. Gaussian or Scale-free) with randomly chosen neighbours in the adjacent layer below. (c) Black solid lines and red solid lines: networks created by adding links connecting non adjacent layers (red) in both directions to the layered network with randomised degree distribution (black).

At each time-step a production unit may be activated and asked to sell to its customers. In this case, the variables of interest for company n(i, j) are $x_{i,j}(t)$: the state of the inventory at time t, $y_{i,j}(t)$: the quantity of goods produced at time t and $s_{i,j}(t)$: the number of goods sold at time t. When asked to sell, the productive unit will check its inventory to see if there is enough to sell without having to produce. If this is the case, then $y_{i,j}(t) = 0$, otherwise it produces enough to cover for all its customers, $y_{i,j}(t) = k_{i,j}^{in}$. Based on these genaralised dynamics, the variables of interest can take the following values, which are dependent on the in- and out-degrees of each individual company node: $x_{i,j}(t) \in \{0, \ldots, k_{i,j}^{in} - 1\}$ for the inventory size; $y_{i,j}(t) \in \{0, k_{i,j}^{in}\}$ for the production and $s_{i,j}(t) \in \{0, \ldots, k_{i,j}^{in}\}$ for the sales. We also impose that $k_{i,j}^{in}, k_{i,j}^{out} \geq 2$ to avoid dissipation.

Production is induced when a customer's order cannot be fulfilled exclusively by utilising products from the inventories of its suppliers. The inventory of each activated production unit is updated from its previous state by adding the number of units it produced at that time-step and subtracting the number of units it sold. Hence, the equations that govern the inventory dynamics can be cast in the following general form:

$$x_{i,j}(t+1) = x_{i,j}(t) + y_{i,j}(t) - s_{i,j}(t), \tag{1}$$

where the orders received by each unit are accumulated over all its active customers at that time-step

$$s_{i,j}(t) = \sum_{n'(i',j')\in N_{ij}} \frac{y_{i',j'}(t)}{k^{in}_{i',j'}}. \tag{2}$$

Thus, an avalanche is defined as the total size of production, y(t), and is denoted by the sum of the productions over all n = 1, …, N nodes in the system.

$$y(t) = \sum_{n=1}^{N} y_{i,j}(t). \tag{3}$$

Only activated nodes will give a contribution at each time step. It is worth noting that irrespective of the amount of production of a certain node, it will give its customer one unit of raw materials. Reversely, regardless of how much raw materials a customer needs it can ask for one unit only from each of its suppliers.

Theoretical Framework

Even though a given avalanche size cannot be predicted unless one has complete knowledge of the whole system, the statistics of avalanche-size pdfs follow well-defined laws [11]. Assume that the avalanche-size pdf obeys simple FSS, that is,

$$P(y;L) = ay^{-\tau}\mathcal{G}(y/L^D) \quad \text{for } y \gg 1, L \gg 1, \tag{4}$$

where τ and D are universal avalanche-size scaling exponents, $\mathcal{G}$ a universal scaling function and a a non-universal dimensionful parameter independent of lattice size L. If data for different system sizes L are consistent with the FSS ansatz in Eq (4), then we can perform a data collapse because simple manipulation of Eq (4) yields

$$y^\tau P(y;L) = a\mathcal{G}(y/L^D). \tag{5}$$

Hence, by plotting the transformed probability density function, $y^\tau P(y;L)$ versus the rescaled observable y/L^D, all the data collapses onto the curve for the scaling function $\mathcal{G}$.

We can estimate the avalanche-size scaling exponents using moment analysis. Assuming that Eq (4) is valid for all y, and approximating the sum with an integral, we find that the kth moment

$$\langle y^k \rangle = \sum_{y=1}^{\infty} y^k P(y;L) \propto \int_1^{\infty} y^{k-\tau}\mathcal{G}(y/L^D)\,dy \propto L^{D(1+k-\tau)}, \tag{6}$$

for $L \gg 1$, $k \geq \tau - 1$. Plotting the directly measured kth moments $\langle y^k \rangle$ versus system size L in a double-logarithmic plot yields a straight line with slope $D(1 + k - \tau)$ for $L \gg 1$. Plotting the estimated slopes $D(1 + k - \tau)$ versus k yields a straight line with slope D intersecting the k-axis at $k^* = \tau - 1$, that is, $\tau = 1 + k^*$. We will use the moment scaling analysis to estimate Dand τ and then check whether the estimated avalanche-size scaling exponents produce a data collapse according to Eq (5). Due to conservation we expect the first moment $\langle y \rangle \propto L^{D(2-\tau)} \propto L$, that is $D(2 - \tau) = 1$.

RESULTS

In the simulations presented below we used the Japanese inter-firm network ($N \approx 10^6$) as given to us, and/or used three lattice sizes L = 200, 400, 600, but kept the width of the system constant, C = 2000 where appropriate ($N = 4{\cdot}10^5$, $8{\cdot}10^5$, $1.2{\cdot}10^6$). We let the simulations run for a transient period to eliminate initialisation bias and bring the system into a steady state. The transient period we used for the inter-firm network was 10^6 events, for the regular lattices the transient was 5×10^5 avalanches and for the other networks the transient was 10^6avalanches. More data was needed as the randomness in the structure of the network makes it slower to reach stationarity. Then, we started recording the avalanches for an additional 10^7events on the inter-firm network and 10^6 for all others. For the non-regular networks, we repeated the experiment on 5 different realisations of the networks and then averaged over all 5 experiments. The inventory of the first layer was kept empty to ensure that each event was non-zero.

To analyse the results we obtained from the simulations we calculated the kth moment directly. For the visualisation of the avalanche size pdfs, we used a logarithmic data binning method. We divide the horizontal axis into bins labelled j = 0, 1, …, where the jth bin covers the interval $[a^j, a^{j+1}[\ = \{r \in \mathbb{R} \mid a^j \leq r < a^{j+1}\}$. With $a > 1$, the bins are exponentially increasing in length. We let y^j_{min} and y^j_{max} denote the minimum and maximum integer avalanche sizes in bin j, and then count the number of avalanches that fall in bin j, with interval$[y^j_{min}, y^j_{max}]$. We then plot P(y; L) against the geometric mean, $y^j = \sqrt{y^j_{max} y^j_{min}}$ of the avalanche sizes in bin j as defined below:

$$P(y^j;L) = \frac{No.\ of\ avalanches\ in\ bin\ j}{N\Delta y^j} \tag{7}$$

where $\Delta y^j = y^j_{max} - y^j_{min} + 1$ is the number of integers in the interval $[y^j_{min}, y^j_{max}]$ and N the number of avalanches. The logarithmic binning we use, with a = 1.1 allows us to extract information on P(y) which would have been impossible to see in the noisy tail of our pdf graphs [12].

In the remainder of this section, we present the simulation results organised as follows: in Sec. A we show the behaviour of the generalised BTW dynamics when run on the Japanese inter-firm network; in Sec. B we show the results from the regular lattice and recover the theoretical results obtained in [13] to check our numerical framework; in Sec. C we relax the in- and out-degree distributions constraint but keep the strictly layered nature of the lattice and finally in Sec. D we relax the layeredness constraint.

Japanese Inter-Firm Network

The generalised BTW sandpile dynamics, can be used to model the production network of a country; it is analogous to our simple view of production, but without the rigidity of the strictly layered system. Instead there is a web of production with directed links imposing a direction of flow which is not strictly layered.

The Japanese inter-firm data set, which was collected by Tokyo Shoko Research Ltd. (TSR) and provided by Research Institute of Economy, Trade and Industry (RIETI), is a snap shot for the year 2005 of the entire production network of all active firms in Japan. It represents the firms of Japan as nodes joined with directed links showing the money flow from the customer node to the supplier node. With the analogy between the directed sandpile and the inter-firm trade we made, it is pertinent to study how such a simple model behaves on the production network of an entire country.

In this network there are around 1 million nodes and 4 million links. Previous analysis of the structure of the network has shown that the in- and out- degrees distributions are scale-free with exponents $\gamma = 2.35$ and $\gamma = 2.26$, respectively. Moreover, the average path length in the network is 5.62 and the maximal distance is 21 making it a very shallow network. The network has a bow-tie structure, in the sense that there is a distinct in-component where 31% of nodes have $k_{i,j}^{in} = 0$, a strongly connected component comprised of 53% of the nodes and a strict out-component formed by the remaining nodes with $k_{i,j}^{out} = 0$ [14]. We will treat the in-component as the top layer and interpret it as the final retailers where all propagation begins, the out-component as the bottom layer formed of primary producers where final orders are placed and observe how avalanches of production fluctuate within the strongly connected component. The constraints on the inventory, production and sales of each firm remain the same and are defined by the in-degree of each firm.

The avalanche-size pdf, which is shown in Fig 2 (solid black line), display a broad distribution that is consistent with a power-law decay over three orders of magnitude, with an estimated avalanche-size exponent $\tau = 1.87$. This clearly different from the two universality classes characterised by avalanches size exponents $\tau = 4/3$ and $\tau = 3/2$ (grey dashed lines).

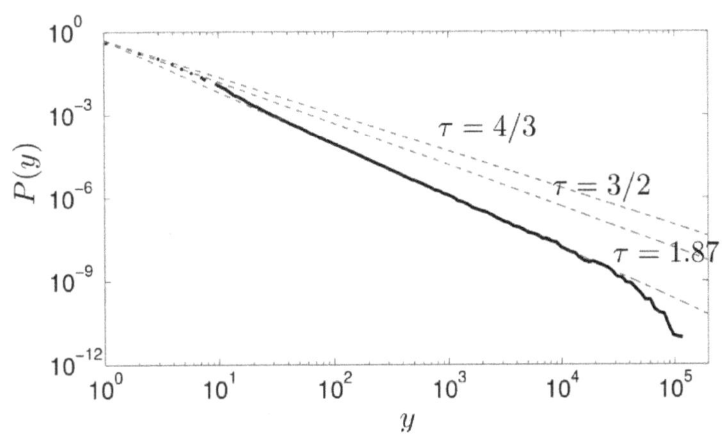

Figure 2: The avalanche-size pdf P(y) versus the avalanche size y obtained using the inter-firm Japanese network (solid black line). The grey dashed lines are guides to the eyes for the different universality classes' avalanche-size exponents.

Regular Lattice

First, we reproduce the result of Bak et al. [2] on the regular lattice with fixed coordination number K = 2. We then go one step further by increasing the coordination number and observe the change this has on the avalanches produced. In this extension of the original model, we have that $k_{i,j}^{in} = k_{i,j}^{out} = K$, where $K \in \mathbb{N}^+$ and $K \geq 2$. Following the dynamical rules as prescribed in the Model definition section, we have the following constraints on the range of inventory $x_{i,j}(t) \in \{0, \ldots, K-1\}$, production $y_{i,j}(t) \in \{0, K\}$ and sales $s_{i,j}(t) \in \{0, \ldots, K\}$ for all nodes in the system. All exponents are consistent with the universality class of the two-dimensional directed sandpile model. The results are displayed in Fig 3(a) and the associated scaling exponents estimated using the moment analysis method are reported in Table 1. For each system, both scaling exponents are within error bars of the universality class of the two-dimensional directed sandpile model. The pdfs display the characteristic "bump" in their tails. This is a typical finite-size effect and is due to the fact that the number of avalanches that reach the last row is not only avalanches of that size but also all the other avalanches that would have carried on.

The large figures show the data collapse obtained by plotting the transformed avalanche-size pdf $y^{\tau_P}(y; L)$ vs. the rescaled avalanche size y/L^D using the estimates of the avalanche-size scaling exponents τ and D obtained from moment scaling analysis, see Tables 1, 2, 3 and 4. For all figures, including insets, the line style indicates the system size, dashed-dotted: L = 100; dotted line: L = 200; dashed line: L = 400; solid line: L = 600 (a) Regular lattice; grey: K = 2, red: K = 4, blue: K = 6, black: K = 8, L = 200, 400, 600 (b) Gaussian out-degree distribution; red: $\sigma = 0$, blue: $\sigma = 1$, black: $\sigma = 2$, L = 200, 400, 600 (c) Truncated scale-free out-degree distribution; red: $\gamma = 2.5$, blue: = 3.0, black: = 3.5, L = 200, 400, 600 (d) Truncated scale-free in- and out-degree distribution; red: $\gamma = 2.5$, L = 100, 200, 400, black: $\gamma = 3.5$, L = 200, 400, 600.

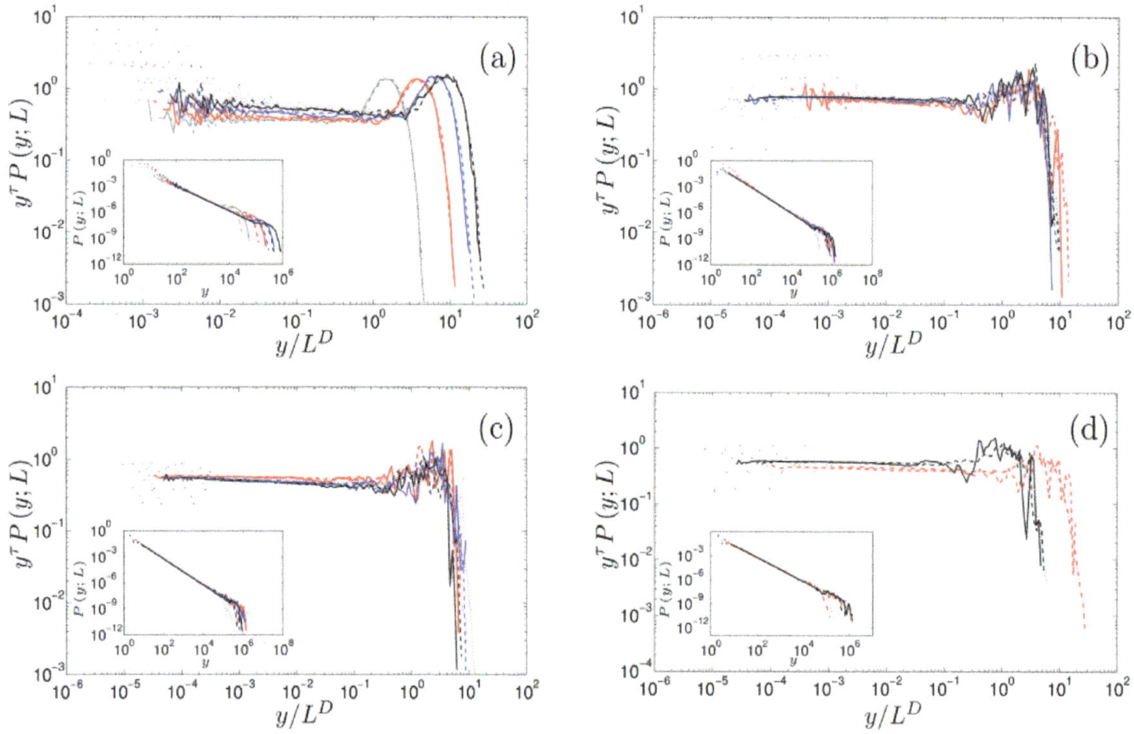

Figure 3: For all panels, the inset displays the avalanche-size pdf P (y; L) vs. the avalanche size y.

Table 1: The avalanche-size exponent, ***τ***, and the avalanche-dimension, D, for regular lattice structures with coordination numbers, K = 2, 4, 6, 8 and circumference C, see Fig 3(a) for the data collapse

K	C	τ	D	D(2 − τ)
2	2000	1.33(5)	1.47(10)	0.98
4	2000	1.35(5)	1.55(10)	1.00
6	2000	1.37(5)	1.60(10)	1.00
8	2000	1.39(5)	1.63(10)	1.00
8	4000	1.37(5)	1.61(10)	1.00

The scaling relation D(2 − τ) = 1 is fulfilled and, within error bars, both scaling exponents (apart from K = 8 and C = 2000) are consistent with the universality class of the two-dimensional directed sandpile model τ = 4/3 and D = 3/2. The numerical result for K = 8, C = 2000 and 4000 suggests that the apparent drift is due to finite size effects.

http://dx.doi.org/10.1371/journal.pone.0142685.t001

We observe that τ and D seem to increase slightly as the coordination number K increases for the rigid networks (see Table 1). Comparing numerical results for K = 8 and C = 2000, 4000 suggests that the apparent drift is due to finite-size effects. Hence, we deduce that the model on a regular lattice falls within the classical universality class of τ = 4/3 and D = 3/2 for all K.

Layered Lattice with Inter-Layer Distribution of Interactions

A natural generalisation from the regular networks described above is to maintain the strictly layered structure of the lattice, but introduce heterogeneity in the in- and out-degree distributions of the production units, also referred to as nodes. The constraints on the range of the dynamical variables follow the rules as described in Model definition section, which are now node-dependent. With these in place we can proceed with our investigation into the different inter-layer distributions.

In the first setting, the out-degree of a node is drawn from a Gaussian distribution $k_{ij}^{out} \sim \mathcal{N}(\mu, \sigma^2)$ and its neighbours chosen at random from the layer below it avoiding multiple links between nodes. We rejected out-degrees smaller than 2. The central limit theorem ensures that the in-degree distribution will asymptotically follow the same Gaussian distribution as the out-degree. We have set the mean to μ = 4 and used three values for the standard deviation σ = 0, 1, 2. Note that when σ = 0, we obtain a rewired version of the regular lattice with K = 4. The results are displayed in Fig 3(b) and the associated scaling exponents estimated using the moment analysis are reported in Table 2. For each system, both scaling exponents are within error bars of the universality class of the mean-field model.

Table 2: The avalanche-size exponent, τ, and the avalanche-dimension, D, for networks with nodes' out-degrees drawn from a Gausssian distribution with a fixed mean coordination number $\mu = 4$, and standard deviations $\sigma = 0, 1, 2$.

σ	τ	D	$D(2-\tau)$
0	1.45(5)	1.8(2)	1.00
1	1.47(5)	1.9(2)	1.00
2	1.48(5)	1.9(2)	1.00

Note that the case of $\sigma = 0$ is just a randomly rewired version of the regular lattice with coordination number K = 4, see Fig 3(b) for the data collapse. Within error bars, both scaling exponents are consistent with the mean-field model $\tau = 3/2$ and D = 2.

In the second case, we draw the out-degree of each node from a scale-free distribution $k_{i,j}^{out} \propto K^{-\gamma}$ for $\gamma = 2.5, 3.0, 3.5$ and truncated at $\max(k^{out}) = 20$. Links are then placed randomly between nodes in adjacent layers, avoiding multiple links between nodes. As in the previous case, the central limit theorem yields that the in-degree distribution is Gaussian. The results are displayed in Fig 3(c) and the associated scaling exponents estimated using the moment analysis are reported in Table 3. For each system, both scaling exponents are within error bars of the universality class of the mean-field model.

Table 3: The avalanche-size exponent, τ, and the avalanche-dimension, D, for networks with nodes' out-degrees drawn from a truncated scale free distribution with exponent $\gamma = 2.5, 3.0, 3.5$, see Fig 3(c) for the data collapse.

The central limit theorem ensures the distribution of in-degrees is Gaussian. Within error bars, both scaling exponents are consistent with the mean-field model $\tau = 3/2$ and D = 2.

γ	τ	D	$D(2-\tau)$
2.5	1.48(5)	1.9(2)	1.00
3.0	1.47(5)	1.9(2)	1.00
3.5	1.46(5)	1.9(2)	1.00

In the last setting, the out-degrees of the nodes were drawn from a scale-free distribution $k_{i,j}^{out} \propto K^{-\gamma}$ for $\gamma = 2.5, 3.5$ and truncated at $\max(k^{out}) = 20$. The in-degrees of the layer below were then drawn at random from the realised distribution of the layer above. The stubs are then matched avoiding multiple connections between nodes. The results are displayed in Fig 3(d) and the associated scaling exponents estimated using the moment analysis are reported in Table 4. For each system, both scaling exponents are within error bars of the mean-field model exponents.

Table 4: The avalanche-size exponent, τ, and the avalanche-dimension, D, for networks with nodes' in- and out-degrees were both drawn from a truncated scale free distribution with exponents $\gamma = 2.5, 3.5$, see Fig 3(d) for the data collapse.

Within error bars, both scaling exponents are consistent with the mean field-model $\tau = 3/2$ and D = 2.

γ	τ	D	$D(2-\tau)$
2.5	1.50(5)	2.0(2)	1.01
3.5	1.48(5)	1.9(2)	1.00

Notice that for a degree distribution exponent of $\gamma = 2.5$ the branching process approach predicts an avalanche-size exponent $\tau = 5/3$ [15] which differs from the exponent $\tau = 3/2$ we find.

Long Range Connections across Layers

We have seen that any perturbation of the underlying network topology, which keeps the layered structure, puts the system into the mean field exponent $\tau = 3/2$. The fact that the Japanese inter-firm network does not have a unique direction of flow in the strongly connected component, as it is not strictly layered, might be what gives rise to the avalanche-size exponent $\tau = 1.87$. Indeed, the characteristic small average path length (5.62) of the Japanese inter-firm network is a direct consequence of the lack of unique direction of flow and the non strictly layered structure.

We proceed with this hypothesis and introduce a small proportion of long range interactions in an otherwise layered network, both in the direction of the flow and opposite to it. This modification mimics the shallowness of the Japanese inter-firm network by reducing the path length of the lattice and also creates cycles in the system. As in the case of the Japanese inter-firm network, the first layer plays the role of the in-component and the last layer the role of out-component. Unlike the Japanese inter-firm network, we do not impose having a strongly connected component in the middle.

We implement long range connections on the third type of networks described in the previous section, as they have scale-free degree distribution for both the in- and out-degree, like the Japanese inter-firm network. Each node has a probability p_{lr} to have one of its link connected to another random node in the network, with the only constraint that it is not in an adjacent layer. We ran simulations with $p_{lr} \in [0.05, 0.10, 0.25, 0.50, 0.75]$. This simple modification brings the system out of the mean field and produces a non-trivial avalanche behaviour. As shown in Fig 4, the case $p_{lr} = 0.25$ reproduces approximately the avalanche-size pdf found in the Japanese inter-firm network. For this particular network, the long range connections have reduced the average path length from 114 to 12, bringing it to the same order of magnitude as the Japanese inter-firm network which is 5.62. We want to point out that the real network did not evolve to its current structure from a layered structure, but rather evolved as a scale-free network that possess a bow-tie like structure with a strongly connected component. In a shallow strictly layered network, large avalanches are impossible. However, the introduction of long-range connections in such networks is an essential structural characteristic that allows the existence of large avalanches and hence a non-trivial avalanche-size pdf.

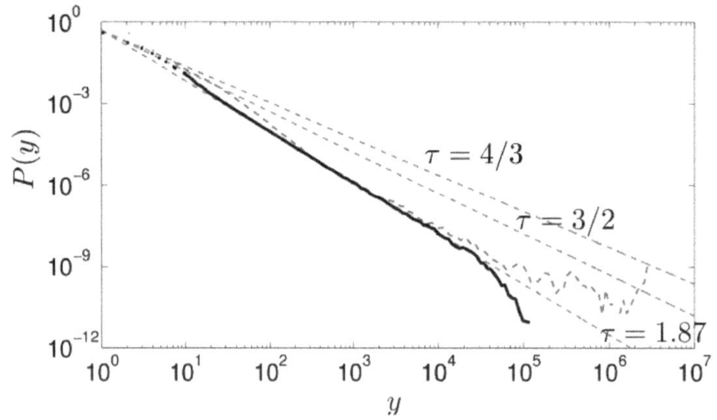

Figure 4: The avalanche-size pdf P(y) versus the avalanche-size y obtained using the inter-firm Japanese network (solid black line).

With 25% of long range connections across layers in an otherwise layered network with nodes in- and out- degree drawn from a truncated scale-free distribution with exponent $\gamma = 2.5$ and system size L = 400 (dashed red line). The grey dashed lines are guides to the eyes for the different universality classes' avalanche-size exponents.

DISCUSSION

Characterisation of complex networks and measurements of them is still a developing field [22] that is relevant for a variety of research areas such as neuroscience [23, 24], finance [14] and computational chemistry [25–27] to mention a few.

Several conclusions and leads for future research can be drawn from our results. Many different universality classes exist for sandpile models depending on the dynamics considered, like the stochastic Manna model [28], whose universality classes have been studied in detail on directed lattices [29–32]. However, when considering the generalised deterministic BTW dynamics on strictly layered and directed lattices, and despite exploring the effect of in- and out-degree distribution in strictly layered networks, we only observe two universality classes: the classical two-dimensional directed sandpile model with $\tau = 4/3$ and $D = 3/2$ and the mean field universality class with $\tau = 3/2$ and $D = 2$ [13].

The intuition behind the existence of only two universality classes is that the highly constrained structure of strictly layered and regular lattices creates correlations in the activity, but these correlations are destroyed as soon as any rewiring is introduced that disturbs the rigid lattice structure, such as having the having the nodes connected in a random fashion between layers. For example, in the regular lattice where K = 4 we clearly observe the classical two-dimensional directed sandpile model class (see Table 1) but in the case where the out-degree of a node is drawn from a Gaussian distribution $k_{i,j}^{out} \sim \mathcal{N}(4, 0)$ we clearly observe mean field behaviour (see Table 2). Since the latter example can be considered as a rewired version of the former, where nodes still have 4 neighbours but are connected randomly within the layers, we deduce that the transition between the two classes seems to be abrupt. For strictly layered lattice, we observed mean-field behaviour with Gaussian-Gaussian, Gaussian-Scale free and Scale free-Scale free in- and out- degree distributions.

However, when moving to a complex non-layered directed network, a new avalanche behaviour emerges with a non-trivial avalanche-size exponent of $\tau = 1.87$. The avalanche-size exponent is steeper than both the two-dimensional directed sandpile model and the mean-field: $1.87 > 3/2 > 4/3$. It is indeed rare to observe an avalanche-size exponent greater than the mean-field avalanche-size exponent $\tau = 3/2$ in sandpile models [11].

We have shown that by simply adding a small proportion of random long-range links, and so destroying the strict layer structure of the system but without the constraint of having a strongly connected component, one can produce non-trivial avalanche-sizes pdf. Although these probability density functions are qualitatively close to the result obtained with the Japanese inter-firm network, no scaling is present, implying that other structural constraints need to be imposed. We cannot perform FSS because the structural heterogeneity induced by the presence of long-range links makes the effective system size (that would enter into FSS) not well defined.

We believe that these facts taken together may point towards the existence of new universality class for the directed sandpile model and that long-range links are an essential component. It would be of great scientific interest to determine whether such a new universality class indeed exists as the underlying structure giving rise to this behaviour is found in human engineered networks. We must also identify the finer structural properties that allow for SOC to appear, since the large events might be detrimental to the system. In the case of the economy, it is highly desirable if one could mitigate or even prevent these emerging large fluctuations in the production-consumption network.

ACKNOWLEDGMENTS

All numerical simulations on artificial networks have been performed on the Imperial College High Performance Computing Service,http://www.imperial.ac.uk/ict/services/teachingandresearchservices/highperformancecomputing.

REFERENCES

1. Scheinkman JA, Woodford M. Self-organized criticality and economic fluctuations. The American Economic Review. 1994:417–21.
2. Bak P, Chen K, Scheinkman J, Woodford M. Aggregate fluctuations from independent sectoral shocks: self-organized criticality in a model of production and inventory dynamics. Ricerche Economiche. 1993;47(1):3–30. doi: 10.1016/0035-5054(93)90023-V
3. Bak P, Tang C, Wiesenfeld K. Self-organized criticality: An explanation of the 1/f noise. Physical review letters. 1987;59(4):381 doi: 10.1103/PhysRevLett.59.381
4. Jensen HJ. Self-organized criticality: emergent complex behavior in physical and biological systems: Cambridge university press; 1998.
5. Bak P. How Nature Works: The Science of Self Organized Criticality Springer Verlag. New York; 1996.
6. Suki B, Barabasi A-L, Hantos Z, Peták F, Stanley HE. Avalanches and power-law behaviour in lung inflation. Nature. 1994;368(6472):615–8. doi: 10.1038/368615a0
7. Bak P, Sneppen K. Punctuated equilibrium and criticality in a simple model of evolution. Physical review letters. 1993;71(24):4083 doi: 10.1103/PhysRevLett.71.4083
8. Bak P, Tang C. Earthquakes as a self-organized critical phenomenon. Journal of Geophysical Research: Solid Earth (1978–2012). 1989;94(B11):15635–7. doi: 10.1029/JB094iB11p15635
9. Bak P, Christensen K, Danon L, Scanlon T. Unified scaling law for earthquakes. Physical Review Letters. 2002;88(17):178501 doi: 10.1103/PhysRevLett.88.178501
10. Peters O, Hertlein C, Christensen K. A complexity view of rainfall. Physical review letters. 2001;88(1):018701 doi: 10.1103/PhysRevLett.88.018701
11. Pruessner G. Self-organised criticality: theory, models and characterisation: Cambridge University Press; 2012.
12. Christensen K, Moloney NR. Complexity and criticality: Imperial College Press; 2005.
13. Dhar D, Ramaswamy R. Exactly solved model of self-organized critical phenomena. Physical Review Letters. 1989;63(16):1659 doi: 10.1103/PhysRevLett.63.1659
14. Ohnishi T, Takayasu H, Takayasu M. Hubs and authorities on Japanese inter-firm network: Characterization of nodes in very large directed networks. Progress of Theoretical Physics Supplement. 2009;179:157–66. doi: 10.1143/PTPS.179.157
15. Goh K-I, Lee D S, Kahng B, Kim D. Sandpile on scale-free networks. Physical review letters. 2003;91(14):148701 doi: 10.1103/PhysRevLett.91.148701
16. Lee D, Goh K, Kahng B, Kim D. Branching process approach to avalanche dynamics on complex networks. JOURNAL-KOREAN PHYSICAL SOCIETY. 2004;44(1):633–7.
17. Lee D-S, Goh K-I, Kahng B, Kim D. Sandpile avalanche dynamics on scale-free networks. Physica A: Statistical Mechanics and its Applications. 2004;338(1):84–91. doi: 10.1016/j.physa.2004.02.028
18. Goh K-I, Lee D-S, Kahng B, Kim D. Cascading toppling dynamics on scale-free networks. Physica A: Statistical Mechanics and its Applications. 2005;346(1):93–103. doi: 10.1016/j.physa.2004.08.054
19. De Arcangelis L, Herrmann H. Self-organized criticality on small world networks. Physica A: Statistical Mechanics and its Applications. 2002;308(1):545–9. doi: 10.1016/S0378-4371(02)00549-6
20. Pan G-J, Zhang D-M, Yin Y-P, He M-H. Sandpile on directed small-world networks. Physica A: Statistical Mechanics and its Applications. 2007;383(2):435–42. doi: 10.1016/j.physa.2007.04.113
21. Watts DJ, Strogatz SH. Collective dynamics of 'small-world'networks. nature. 1998;393(6684):440–2.
22. Costa LdF, Rodrigues FA, Travieso G, Villas Boas PR. Characterization of complex networks: A survey of measurements. Advances in Physics. 2007;56(1):167–242. doi: 10.1080/00018730601170527
23. Lord L-D, Allen P, Expert P, Howes O, Broome M, Lambiotte R, et al. Functional brain networks before the onset of psychosis: a prospective fMRI study with graph theoretical analysis. NeuroImage: Clinical. 2012;1(1):91–8. doi: 10.1016/j.nicl.2012.09.008
24. Pandit AS, Expert P, Lambiotte R, Bonnelle V, Leech R, Turkheimer FE, et al. Traumatic brain injury impairs small-world topology. Neurology. 2013;80(20):1826–33. doi: 10.1212/WNL.0b013e3182929f38
25. Kraus V, Dehmer M, Schutte M. On sphere-regular graphs and the extremality of information-theoretic network measures. MATCH Commun Math Comput Chem. 2013;70(3):885–900.
26. Cao S, Dehmer M, Shi Y. Extremality of degree-based graph entropies. Information Sciences. 2014;278:22–33. doi: 10.1016/j.ins.2014.03.133
27. Dehmer M, Grabner M. The discrimination power of molecular identification numbers revisited.MATCH

Commun Math Com put Chem. 2013;69(3):785–94.

28. Manna S, Chakrabarti A, Cafiero R. Critical states in a dissipative sandpile model. Physical Review E. 1999;60(5):R5005 doi: 10.1103/PhysRevE.60.R5005

29. Pastor-Satorras R, Vespignani A. Universality classes in directed sandpile models. Journal of Physics A: Mathematical and General. 2000;33(3):L33 doi: 10.1088/0305-4470/33/3/101

30. Pastor-Satorras R, Vespignani A. Critical behavior and conservation in directed sandpiles. Physical Review E. 2000;62(5):6195 doi: 10.1103/PhysRevE.62.6195

31. Kloster M, Maslov S, Tang C. Exact solution of a stochastic directed sandpile model. Physical Review E. 2001;63(2):026111 doi: 10.1103/PhysRevE.63.026111

32. Paczuski M, Bassler KE. Theoretical results for sandpile models of self-organized criticality with multiple topplings. Physical Review E. 2000;62(4):5347 doi: 10.1103/PhysRevE.62.5347

CHAPTER 8

WAVE SPEED IN EXCITABLE RANDOM NETWORKS WITH SPATIALLY CONSTRAINED CONNECTIONS

Nikita Vladimirov, Roger D. Traub and Yuhai Tu

IBM T. J. Watson Research Center, Yorktown Heights, New York, United States of America

ABSTRACT

Very fast oscillations (VFO) in neocortex are widely observed before epileptic seizures, and there is growing evidence that they are caused by networks of pyramidal neurons connected by gap junctions between their axons. We are motivated by the spatio-temporal waves of activity recorded using electrocorticography (ECoG), and study the speed of activity propagation through a network of neurons axonally coupled by gap junctions. We simulate wave propagation by excitable cellular automata (CA) on random (Erdös-Rényi) networks of special type, with spatially constrained connections. From the cellular automaton model, we derive a mean field theory to predict wave propagation. The governing equation resolved by the Fisher-Kolmogorov PDE fails to describe wave speed. A new (hyperbolic) PDE is suggested, which provides adequate wave speed $v(\langle k \rangle)$ that saturates with network degree $\langle k \rangle$, in agreement with intuitive expectations and CA simulations. We further show that the *maximum*length of connection is a much better predictor of the wave speed than the *mean* length. When tested in networks with various degree distributions, wave speeds are found to strongly depend on the ratio of network moments $\langle k^2 \rangle / \langle k \rangle$ rather than on mean degree $\langle k \rangle$, which is explained by general network theory. The wave speeds are strikingly similar in a diverse set of networks, including regular, Poisson, exponential and power law distributions, supporting our theory for various network topologies. Our results suggest practical predictions for networks of electrically coupled neurons, and our mean field method can be readily applied for a wide class of similar problems, such as spread of epidemics through spatial networks.

INTRODUCTION

Different types of networks are found across many scales, from metabolic networks in a single cell, to neural networks in brain, up to social and technological global networks. The theory of networks receives increasing attention since the pioneering works that formulated random graphs [1], and the recently discovered ubiquity of small-world networks [2] and scale-free networks [3]. Reviews on general theory of networks can be found in [4]–[6]. A comprehensive up-to-date review of spatial networks is given in [7].

Since its first formulation [1], the Erdös-Rényi (ER) graph became a cornerstone of network theory. An ER graph G_{NM} consists of N nodes and M links (edges), and each link

Citation: Vladimirov N, Traub RD, Tu Y. Wave Speed in Excitable Random Networks with Spatially Constrained Connections. Perc M, ed. PLoS ONE. 2011;6(6):e20536. doi:10.1371/journal.pone.0020536.

connects two nodes which are selected randomly. In a sufficiently large network, the number of links emanating from a node (*degree*) is a random variable with Poisson distribution $P(k)=\langle k\rangle^k e^{-\langle k\rangle}/k!$, where $\langle k\rangle$ is the network mean degree, $\langle k\rangle=2M/N$. Despite its advantages, the ER graph is not suitable for studying *spatial* phenomena because it is spatially homogeneous. However, in most real-world networks the connections are spatial and variable in length. Also, the maximum length of connection is usually limited by the available resources or other natural restrictions. To address this problem, spatial generalizations of the ER graph were suggested. For example, two nodes can be connected only if the distance between them is below threshold r_c [8]. This model was used to simulate spatio-temporal activity in networks of electrically coupled neurons [9]. Another example is the Waxman model, in which the probability that two nodes are connected is a decreasing function of distance between the nodes [10]. The latter model was used to simulate the Internet [11].

In many networks the nodes are excitable, meaning that active state can arise and propagate from one node to another if they are connected. In this way, action potentials propagate through neural networks, computer viruses spread in the Internet, and diseases are transmitted through transport networks. If the nodes are excitable, dynamical states propagate through a network both temporally and spatially, leading to waves and more complex patterns.

A case study in our work is the emergence of spatiotemporal patterns with very fast oscillations (VFO, $>$ 80 Hz) measured by electrocorticography [9], recorded in neocortex of patients prior to epileptic seizures (Figure 1A). There is growing experimental and theoretical evidence that VFO are caused by electrically coupled pyramidal neurons which are connected by gap junctions, thus providing direct excitation from one to another, which does not require synaptic transmission [9], [12], [13].

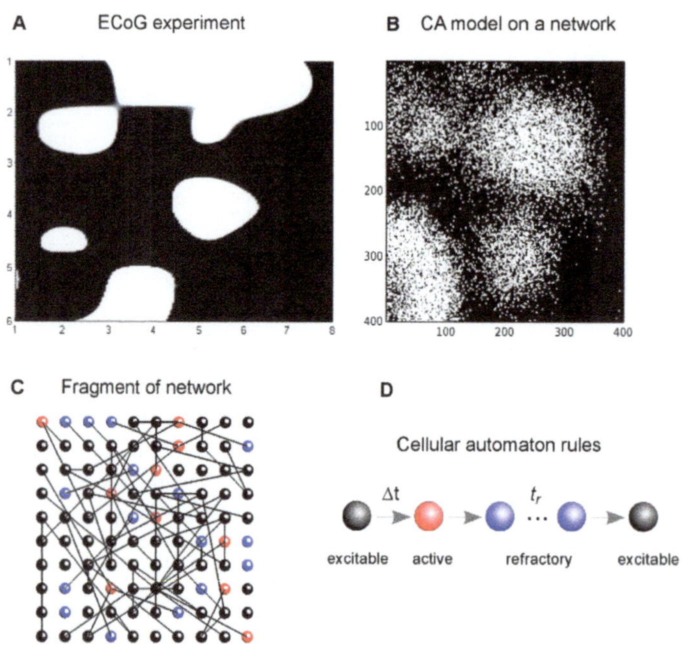

Figure 1: Neural network activity in experiments and in the cellular automaton model.

A. A snapshot of electrocorticographic (ECoG) data of brain activity, measured by 8×6 subdural array of electrodes. Data is interpolated between nodes, white areas correspond to high activity. B. A snapshot of activity from a cellular automaton model in an 400×400 network. The network is subject to noisy input from spontaneously activating cells (rate 1.25×10^{-5}). Active cells are white, refractory and excitable are black (simplified color code). C. Snapshot of activity in a 10×10 sub-network with detailed color code: red for active, blue for refractory, black for excitable nodes. Lines show links between nodes. D. Rules of the CA model: excitable node (black) may become active (red), if activated by a neighbor. After being activated, the node becomes refractory (blue) for a period of time t_r, after which it becomes excitable again. Data in A is a courtesy of Miles Whittington, recorded in Patient B of [29].

Nodes in such a network are dynamical excitable units. Although their intrinsic behavior can be complex and require detailed multi-compartment model of each neuron [14]–[16], understanding of the neural network spatiotemporal oscillations requires highly reduced models, such as cellular automata which capture three main states (resting, firing, refractory) with a minimal set of parameters [13]. The system can be described by a *network* version of Greenberg-Hastings cellular automaton (GHCA), a discrete model of an excitable medium [17]. Variations of GHCA have been used in many studies, including collective oscillations of pyramidal cells in the hippocampus [8], [13], [18], sensory networks [19], [20], and the evolution of HIV infection [21].

In the network version of GHCA that we use, cellular interactions can be distant rather than next-neighbor [8]. The cells are connected into Erdös-Rényi random graph with spatially constrained connections (hereafter SCC), so the distance between connected nodes is not greater than connectivity radius r_c. Under random spontaneous activation of some of the resting cells, large networks demonstrate oscillatory dynamics with complex spatio-temporal activity driven by many interacting waves. Traub and coauthors [9] have recently demonstrated these patterns to be strikingly similar to those observed in ECoG recordings (Figure 1B). In the model, the complex patterns of activity arise when multiple waves are born from spontaneously activated cells and they grow and coalesce in time and space.

A single active node may generate an expanding circular wave of excitation, if the mean network connectivity is high enough. The wave maintains its shape and travels with constant speed, which is an important characteristic of system's excitability and depends on network topology. Knowledge of wave speed in excitable networks allows prediction of how fast the active state (neuronal activity, viral infection) propagates and invades the rest of the network. Although simulations can be done in each particular case, it is important to have a basic mean field theory (MFT) to understand and predict the network dynamics without simulations.

In this paper we derive an MFT to predict wave speed in a random (Erdös-Rényi type) network with spatially constrained connections (SCC), for given connectivity radius r_c and mean degree$\langle k\rangle$. The results are generalized to Erdös-Rényi type networks with various radii distributions, and further to non-Erdös-Rényi networks with various degree distributions, suggesting universality of our mean field theory.

RESULTS

The System

In the following section we describe the system and its dynamic properties, along with simulations that demonstrate its typical behavior.

2D Network

We study a 2D network of excitable cells (nodes), which are are set on a uniform $N_x \times N_y$grid, with unit space between adjacent nodes (Figure 1C). Connections (links) are bidirectional, i.e. activity can be transmitted in both directions. Links can be long but limited by r_c: within a circle of radius r_c (network with round 'footprint') or within a square with side r_c (network with square 'footprint') [8]. Generally, the connectivity radius r_c is much larger than 1, but much smaller than array dimensions $N_x(N_y)$. The number of links per node (*degree*) follows the Poisson distribution $P(k) = \langle k\rangle^k e^{-\langle k\rangle}/k!$, whereas the distribution of link lengths is uniform in $(1,\dots,r_c)$, unless stated otherwise.

Quasi-1D Network

To treat the system analytically, we reduce it to a quasi one-dimensional network: the length of links is limited only along X but may be unlimited in the Y coordinate. In other words, it is a 2D network which has an interval footprint ($|x - x_0| \le r_c$). A quasi-1D network provides the same wave speed along X as the 2D network with square footprint (with same r_c), which is also consistent with 2D network with round footprint (simulations not shown).

Cellular automaton model.

A node in excitable state (E) becomes firing (F) if one or more of its connected neighbors in the network are firing. After one time step Δt the firing node becomes refractory $(R_1,\dots,R_{t_r})$for a relatively long period t_r, after which it becomes excitable again. Thus each node rests in (E) or undergoes a sequence of states $(E,F,R_1,\dots,R_{t_r},E)$ if activated by a neighbor (Figure 1D). Initially all nodes are in excitable state, except a small number of firing nodes that initiate the wave. Node states are updated simultaneously at each time step.

Initiation of wave in a small 2D network is shown in Figure 2 (first four time steps). Although directions of links are random, activity propagates outwards from the initial point because it is followed by refractory state, prohibiting backward propagation. Propagation of waves in large 2D networks is shown in Figure 3A–C. Waves in networks with round and square footprint do not differ qualitatively (not shown), because neighbors of each node are chosen as random lattice points from round or square neighborhood (respectively), which differ only in relatively small corner areas.

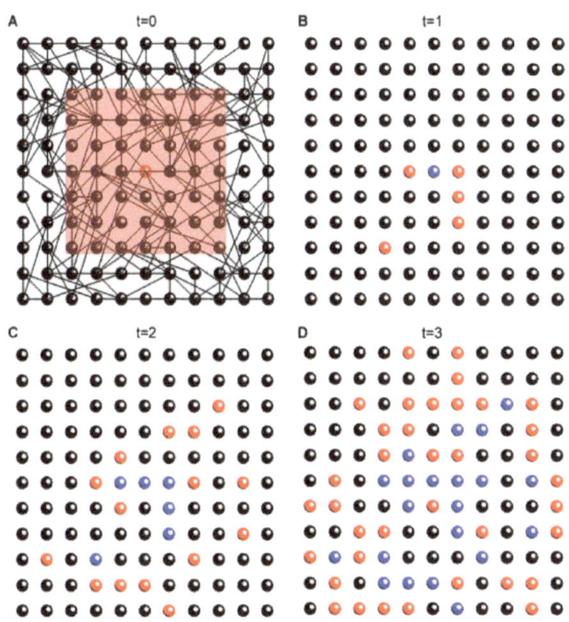

Figure 2: Initiation of wave in a CA model on a random network.

The first 4 time steps of wave initiation are shown for an 11×11 network. A. t=0; B. t=1; C. t=2; D. t=3. Colorcode: red for active, blue for refractory, black for excitable cells. Lines show links between cells, red square shows the connectivity footprint of the central cell (shown only in A). Parameters: $\langle k\rangle$=4, $r_c = 3$ (small for demonstration purposes).

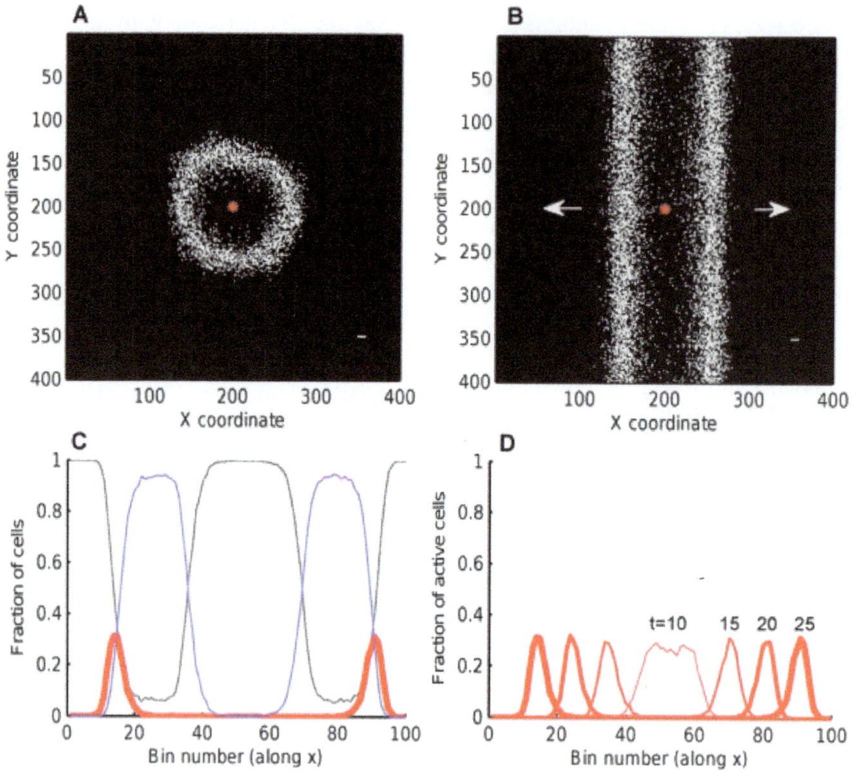

Figure 3: Traveling waves of activity in random networks.

Traveling waves emerging in the CA model on random networks with A. square, B. quasi-1D connectivity footprint. The cell which initiates the wave is shown by a red asterisk. Active cells are white, refractory and excitable cells are black. Directions of wave propagation are shown by arrows. C. A snapshot of wave ($t=25$) with spatial profiles of all three states: grey for excitable, bold red for active, light blue for refractory cell density. In the center, the wake of excitable cells (grey) grows by recovering from the refractory state (blue). D. Profiles of the active state at four time steps, showing two traveling waves emerged from a single active cell. Once formed, the speed and width of a wave remain constant. Profiles were calculated by averaging active cell counts over 100 bins along X. Parameters $\langle k\rangle=3, t_r=10, r_c=10$ (r_c is shown in the bottom right corners in A,B).

http://dx.doi.org/10.1371/journal.pone.0020536.g003

In the rest of the paper, we work with quasi-1D networks, because they allow transparent mean field analysis, and yet behave almost identically to 2D networks, with the only difference that wave fronts are linear rather than circular (Figure 3B vs. A). Next, we start from simpler case where all links have maximum length ($r=r_c$), and then analyse the case where links are distributed randomly ($0<r\leq r_c$).

Mean Field Theory

Links of Maximum Length

In order to treat the system analytically, we assume that the network is regular (all nodes have same degree k), and all links have same length ($r=r_c$). Later we will show that these crude assumptions provide a good approximation for more general cases.

We assume that each excitable cell can become firing by one (and only one) of its neighbors that is firing, which is true for wave front where firing cells are rare. Each firing cell is surrounded by excitable cells, and may produce at maximum $(k-1)$ firing neighbors. One of k links is missing because it points to a cell from which firing has come. In other words, if a cell is excitable (probability E), it can be activated by one of its neighbors (probability $\langle F\rangle$, spatial average of F). Otherwise, if a cell is already firing (F) and there are excitable neighbors (prob. $\langle E\rangle$), it produces $(k-1)$ firing cells. These relations can be written as

$$F(x,t+\Delta t)=E(x,t)\langle F\rangle+(k-1)F(x,t)\langle E\rangle \quad (1)$$

where F and E are the probabilities of a cell to be in firing or excitable state, respectively, $\langle F\rangle$ and $\langle E\rangle$ are spatially averaged F and E in the neighborhood of x. This equation holds only for wave front, where firing cells are scarce, excitable cells are abundant, and there are no refractory cells yet.

With the notion that most cells are excitable ($F\approx 0, E=1-F\approx 1$), the E-terms become unitary (linearized equation). In the quasi-1D system, $\langle F\rangle=\frac{1}{2}(F(x-r,t)+F(x+r,t))$, and the equation simplifies to

$$F(x,t+\Delta t)=\frac{1}{2}(F(x-r,t)+F(x+r,t))+(k-1)F(x,t) \quad (2)$$

Taylor's expansion in x at the right hand side gives

$$F(t+\Delta t)=(F+\frac{r^2}{2}F_{xx})+(k-1)F \quad (3)$$

Taylor's expansion in t at the left hand side gives

$$F+\Delta tF_t+\frac{1}{2}\Delta t^2F_{tt}=(F+\frac{r^2}{2}F_{xx})+(k-1)F \quad (4)$$

Parabolic (Fisher-Kolmogorov) Equation

Taking into account only the first time derivative, we arrive at a linearized version of Fisher-Kolmogorov equation

$$F_t = DF_{xx} + \frac{k-1}{\Delta t}F \qquad (5)$$

where $D=\frac{r^2}{2\Delta t}$ is a diffusion coefficient [22], $\frac{k-1}{\Delta t}$ is the growth rate, and the second-order extinction term is omitted for wave speed analysis. The well-known [23] formula for Fisher-Kolmogorov wave speed $v_{FK}=2\sqrt{D(k-1)/\Delta t}=\frac{r_c}{\Delta t}\sqrt{2(k-1)}$ gives infinite growth of speed with mean degree k (Figure 4, upper line). Taking high-order terms into account in the right hand side of the PDE does not alter the principal behavior of wave speed (simulations not shown), demonstrating that parabolic PDEs are not suitable for wave speed prediction.

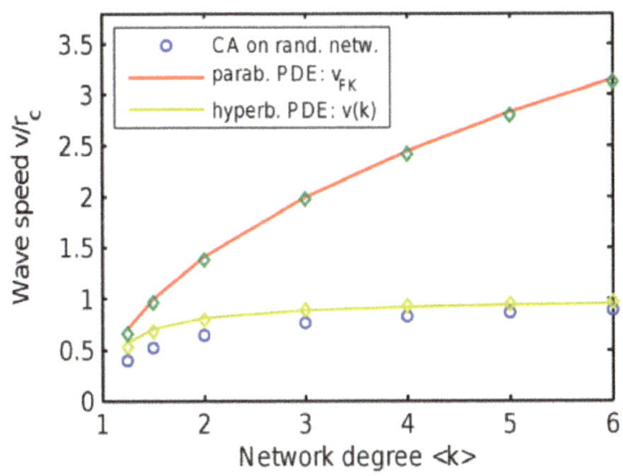

Figure 4: Wave speed predicted by the parabolic and hyperbolic PDEs compared to simulations of CA on random networks.

The parabolic (Fisher-Kolmogorov) PDE gives wave speed v_{FK} that indefinitely grows with network degree (red line and diamonds). In contrast, the suggested hyperbolic PDE (given in text) provides a reaso`nable wave speed $v(k)$ (given in text, shown by green line and diamonds). The $v(k)$ grows moderately and saturates to the maximum possible speed $(r_c/\Delta t)$, in agreement with CA simulations (blue circles) and intuitive expectations. The solid lines show analytic formulae, the diamonds show simulations of corresponding full PDE systems.

Hyperbolic Equation

Keeping both first and second time derivatives in the left part of Eqn. 4, we obtain a hyperbolic equation for firing node density

$$F_t + \frac{\Delta t}{2}F_{tt} = DF_{xx} + \frac{(k-1)}{\Delta t}F \qquad (6)$$

Wave speed can be found by marginal stability analysis [24]. Substituting variable $z=x-vt$, we obtain the equation $(D-\frac{\Delta t}{2}v^2)F''+vF'+\frac{(k-1)}{\Delta t}F=0$. Solution in the form $F=e^{-\lambda z}$ yields a characteristic equation $(D-\frac{\Delta t}{2}v^2)\lambda^2-v\lambda+\frac{(k-1)}{\Delta t}=0$. The roots of the characteristic equation must be real, which gives the minimum wave speed

$$v(k)=2\sqrt{\frac{D(k-1)}{\Delta t(1+2(k-1))}}=\frac{r_c}{\Delta t}\sqrt{\frac{2(k-1)}{1+2(k-1)}} \qquad (7)$$

We put the time step $\Delta t=1$ as in the CA model, and $k=\langle k\rangle$. This wave speed demonstrates qualitative agreement with the CA model on an ER SCC network (Figure 4, lower line). Most importantly, $v(k)$ gradually saturates to the maximum possible speed $v(k)\to r_c$ for high $k\gg 1$, in agreement with CA simulations and intuitive expectations.

The wave speed $v(k)$ is shown in more detail in Figure 5 (upper solid line). One can see that $v(k)$ falls near to CA simulations on networks where all links have maximum length r_c (Figure 5, triangles), as expected. Surprisingly, $v(k)$ also approximates well the CA simulations on networks where links have random length $0<r\le r_c$ (Figure 5, circles), which is our primary model. This phenomenon is explained in the next section.

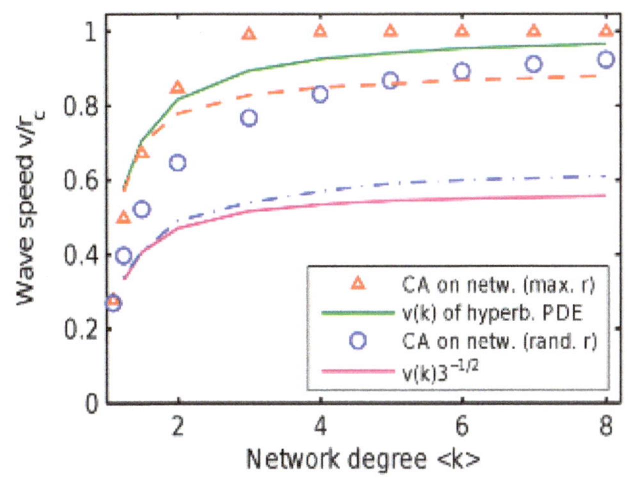

Figure 5: Wave speed derived from the hyperbolic PDE compared to CA simulations.

The wave speed $v(k)$ (red line, high) is derived assuming all links have maximum length. CA simulations are shown in two variants, with maximum-length links (red triangles) and generic random-length links (blue circles). The naive speed scaling $v(k)/\sqrt{3}$ (blue line, low) is derived assuming that link lengths are uniformly distributed. This discrepancy is explained in Results, showing that maximum-length link is a better predictor of wave speed. The dashed lines show the high-order analysis, proving that the hyperbolic PDEs capture the wave behavior sufficiently well, and derivatives of order above 2 are not necessary.

MFT for Links with Random Length

The case where links have random length $0<r\le r_c$ is derived similarly to the maximum-length case shown above. Recall that the spatial scale between nodes is unity, $r_c\gg 1$ and $r=1\ldots r_c$. Let all lengths be equally probable, $P(r)=1/r_c$. All nodes have degree k, so the fraction of nodes with at least one link of length r is $kP(r)=\frac{k}{r_c}$. The evolution of firing nodes density in time is given by

$$\frac{k}{r_c}F(x,t+\Delta t)=E(x,t)\frac{k}{2r_c}(F(x-r,t)+F(x+r,t))$$
$$+(k-1)\frac{k}{r_c}F(x,t) \quad \textbf{(8)}$$

Integration over $0<r\leq r_c$ and omitting $E\sim 1$ gives

$$F(t+\Delta t)=\frac{1}{2r_c}\int_{-r_c}^{r_c}F(x+r)dr+(k-1)F \quad \textbf{(9)}$$

Taylor's expansion up to second derivative of the function under the integral gives the equation

$$F(t+\Delta t)=(F+\frac{r_c^2}{6}F_{xx})+(k-1)F \quad \textbf{(10)}$$

The latter equation is equivalent to Eqn. 3, with the only difference being a reduced radius ($r=\frac{r_c}{\sqrt{3}}$). Therefore, the wave speed for the random-length links would be simply scaled by $\sqrt{3}$ relatively to $v(k)$: $v_{rand}(k)=\frac{v(k)}{\sqrt{3}}\approx 0.58v(k)$.

However, this naive scaling based on uniform radii distribution underestimates the wave speed of CA roughly by a factor of two (Figure 5, lower solid line, compare to circles). This happens because cells in the wave *front* have actually non-uniform distribution of links from which they have received their activation (Figure 6A). The distribution is strongly biased towards the longest links. A wave front generates a new wave front at the next time step by sending activity through the longest links out of available k. To support this notion, we generated sets of k i.i.d. discrete random variables r uniformly distributed in $(1,\ldots,r_c)$ and computed their mean maxima $\langle max(r_1,\ldots,r_k)\rangle$ as a plausible estimate of wave speed, that is a contribution of activity propagation from each single node to a global propagation of wave per unit time. As one can see in Figure 6B (broken line), the mean maxima of k random radii gives a good measure of CA wave speed (circles), especially for high k. These numerical calculations are supported by analytic formula for the expected mean of maxima (black solid line), $\langle max(r_1,\ldots,r_k)\rangle=r_c2^{-1/k}$, derived for a uniform continuous distribution $r\in(0,r_c)$. This formula gives a very good prediction of CA wave speed at high k, demonstrating that the wave propagation is indeed mainly determined by the mean maximum of k radii, which converges in the limit $(k\to\infty)$ to the maximum possible radius r_c. In other words, it is not the average, but rather the *maximum* link length that determines the wave speed in a random network with random radii distribution.

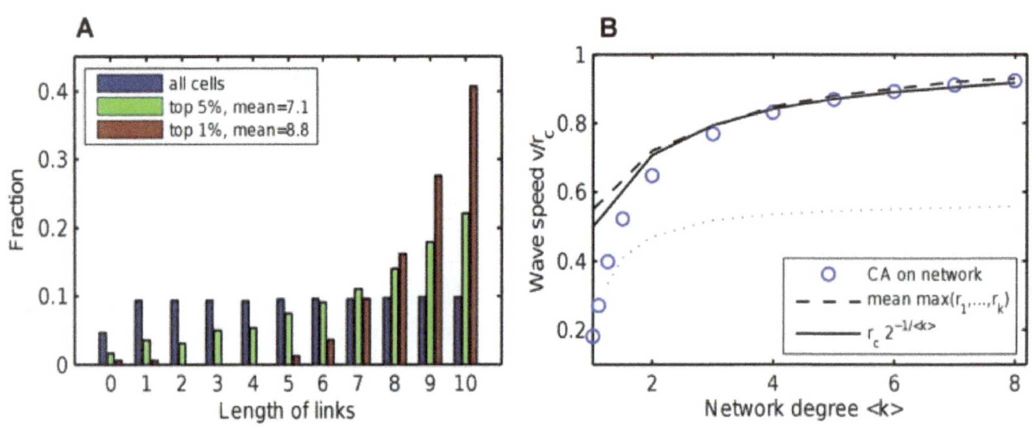

Figure 6: Role of maximum link lengths in wave propagation.

- The distribution of link lengths between the cells at the wave front, and the cells which triggered their firing. The front cells (top 1 or 5 %) were selected by their positions in a wave. The mean distances are given in the legend, parameters $r_c=10$, $\langle k\rangle=3$. B. Estimate of the wave speed by numerical estimate of mean maxima of k i.i.d radii taken from uniform distribution $r\in(1,\ldots,r_c)$ (broken line). The formula $r_c2^{-1/k}$ is the expected value of the mean maxima (solid line). The CA simulations of wave speed are shown by circles. As seen, the mean maxima give a good wave speed estimate, in contrast to naive scaling $v(k)/\sqrt{3}$ derived earlier from the PDE (dotted line).

Role of Link Length Distribution

To study the effects of other possible radii distributions, we simulated networks with five distributions (Figure 7A): the uniform radii distribution, the fixed-value distribution ($r\equiv r_c$), a bell-shaped and two exponential distributions (increasing and decreasing, respectively). The speeds of wave propagation in resulting random networks are qualitatively similar and always significantly higher than the average value of the corresponding distribution (Figure 7B). Broken lines in Figure 7B are mean maxima of k radii generated from each distribution, which served as a good estimate of wave speed in four out of five distributions. Note that the distribution for which our maximum link hypothesis works the least is the one with an exponentially small probability of reaching the maximum link length r_c (see the purple line in Figure 7A).

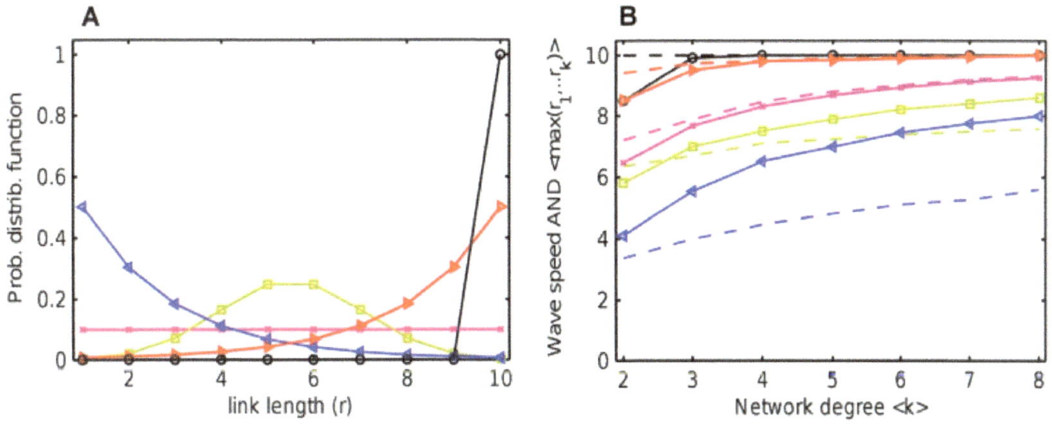

Figure 7: Effect of link lengths (radii) distribution on wave speed.

A. The radii distributions between nodes in the random networks: black o - fixed value, cyan x - uniform, red (blue) triangles - exponentially increasing (decreasing), green squares - bell-shaped distribution (see Methods for detailed formulae). B. Wave speeds in the networks with corresponding radii distributions (markers are consistent with panel A). Broken lines are computed mean maxima out of $\langle k \rangle$ radii samples from each distribution, used as a plausible estimates of the true wave speeds (solid lines). Networks are Erdös-Rényi SCC, so the degree distribution (links per node) is Poissonian.

Although we can not provide an analytic estimate of the effective radius in each distribution, these simulations support the notion that wave speed is predominantly determined by the maximum rather than average radius, with maximum taken out of $\langle k \rangle$ radius realizations.

High-Order Analysis

The use of Taylor's approximation in the PDE derivation could potentially bring unwanted errors because Δt and r are in fact not small. We use a high-order analysis to estimate wave speed in exact terms, by looking for a traveling wave solution in the form $F(x,t)=e^{-\lambda(x-vt)}$ without using Taylor's expansion. See Methods and Algorithms for details. Figure 5 shows that wave speed v^* (upper dashed line) obtained by this method is close to $v(k)$ obtained from a hyperbolic PDE (upper solid line). This confirms that considering derivatives of order above 2 (in time and space) will not affect the wave speed qualitatively. Therefore, the hyperbolic PDE is both necessary and sufficient for qualitative wave speed prediction.

Role of Degree Distribution

The variation of node degrees depends on degree distribution of a network and strongly affects the wave speed. To ultimately simplify the network and add the variance in stages, we simulated the CA model on spatial networks the following degree distributions:

- regular network (each node has same degree k),
  $\{k-1,k,k+1\}$ distribution: a node's degree is chosen randomly from $\{k-1,k,k+1\}, k \geq 2$,
- Poisson distribution (ER graph), $P(k)=\langle k \rangle^k e^{-\langle k \rangle}/k!$
- exponential distribution $P(k)=e^{-k/\lambda}, \lambda=0.75\ldots5$,
- power-law distribution with exponential cutoff $P(k)=Ck^{-\tau}e^{-k/\lambda}$ and parameters:
  1. $\tau=2, \lambda=2\ldots100;$
  2. $\tau=2.5, \lambda=3\ldots800.$

In all networks, the lengths of links between nodes were uniformly distributed in $(0<r\leq r_c)$. As one can see in Figure 8A, the wave speed profiles vary widely when plotted against network mean degree $\langle k \rangle$. However, they merge into nearly the same shape when plotted against $\langle k^2 \rangle / \langle k \rangle$ (Figure 8B, inset). The key role of $\langle k^2 \rangle / \langle k \rangle$ ratio is evident from general network theory. For a randomly chosen link, the degree of a node on its end follows the nearest-neighbor distribution $P_{nn}(k)=\frac{k}{\langle k \rangle}P(k)$, where $P(k)$ is the original network degree distribution [6]. The mean degree of a *connected* node $\langle k \rangle_{nn}$ is therefore different from a randomly picked node: $\langle k \rangle_{nn}=\sum kP_{nn}(k)=\frac{\langle k^2 \rangle}{\langle k \rangle}$, so our ratio is merely the nearest-neighbor mean degree. In other words, when activation travels from one node to another, the degree of a node in the end of a link follows the nearest-neighbor distribution $P_{nn}(k)$, which has a mean of $\langle k \rangle_{nn}=\frac{\langle k^2 \rangle}{\langle k \rangle}$ and gives the actual branching ratio of the activation in the new node.

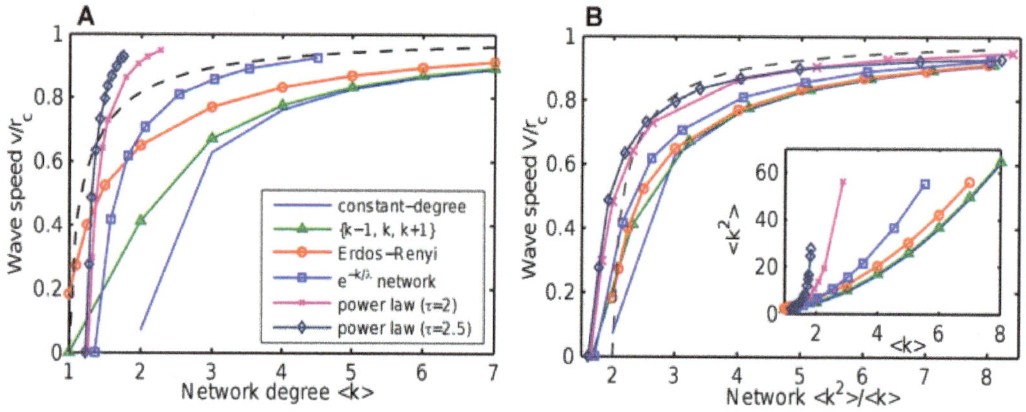

Figure 8: Wave speeds in networks with different degree distributions.

Wave speeds in networks of six different degree distributions (explained in legend) are plotted A. against mean degree $\langle k \rangle$; B. against ratio of network moments $\langle k^2 \rangle / \langle k \rangle$. Note the convergence of wave speeds in B. The mean field formulae are shown in both panels by broken lines (Eqn. 7 in A; Eqn. 11 in B). *Inset.* The $\langle k^2 \rangle$ versus $\langle k \rangle$ in the simulated networks. Line markers are consistent with legend in panel A. Errorbars are smaller than symbols, due to simulations on many networks of large size (1000×1000).

For an ER graph, $\langle k \rangle_{nn} = \langle k \rangle + 1$. Substitution of $\langle k \rangle = \langle k \rangle_{nn} - 1$ into wave speed (7) gives us a more general formula for fitting wave speeds

$$v(\langle k \rangle_{nn}) = r_c \sqrt{\frac{2(\langle k \rangle_{nn} - 2)}{1 + 2(\langle k \rangle_{nn} - 2)}} \qquad (11)$$

where $\langle k \rangle_{nn} = \frac{\langle k^2 \rangle}{\langle k \rangle}$ as before. As shown in (Figure 8, inset), this formula gives a good estimate of wave speeds in a variety of network degree distributions.

DISCUSSION

In summary, we have analysed behavior of excitable random networks with spatially constrained connections (SCC), and derived a mean field theory of the activity propagation. We conclude that the hyperbolic PDE

$$F_t + \frac{\Delta t}{2} F_{tt} = D F_{xx} + \frac{(k-1)}{\Delta t} F \qquad (12)$$

is necessary and sufficient to capture the wave speed in random (uncorrelated) networks with spatially constrained connections.

The wave speed is mainly determined by the longest possible connection between the firing node and a node it can activate, so the mean maximum of $\langle k \rangle$ random radii $\langle max(r_1, \ldots, r_k) \rangle$ serves as a good predictor of wave speed in Erdös-Rényi SCC networks with various radii distributions.

We have derived formula (7) for wave speed $v(\langle k \rangle)$, which agrees with simulated behavior of CA on Erdös-Rényi SCC networks. Simulations of CA on networks with other (non-Poisson) degree distributions suggest a more general formula (11) for wave speed, which depends on $\langle k \rangle_{nn} = \frac{\langle k^2 \rangle}{\langle k \rangle}$, the nearest-neighbor mean degree. So, our mean field theory extends to networks with various degree distributions, provided that $\frac{\langle k^2 \rangle}{\langle k \rangle}$ is used as a more universal measure of network's average branching, rather than simple $\langle k \rangle$, which is explained by general network theory.

The original [8], [9], [13] cellular automaton model of very fast brain oscillations assumed that pyramidal neurons are connected via gap junctions into an Erdös-Rényi SCC network. Our results show that wave speed (hence network excitability) will scale with radius r_c and degree $\langle k \rangle_{nn}$ the same way even if the network topology is different. This has experimental implications: accounting for the wave speed does not require reconstruction of full gap junction network topology. Rather, determining the mean $\langle k \rangle$ and variance $(\sigma^2 = \langle k^2 \rangle - \langle k \rangle^2)$ of the gap junctions per cell, and the maximum inter-neuronal distance (r_c) for coupled cells should suffice. Also, our simulations show that wave speed is primarily driven by the longest of $\langle k \rangle$ connections emanating from an average node. Therefore knowledge of the longest axoaxonal connections is more important than recovering their full range.

Our present knowledge of wave speed will facilitate a detailed analysis of waves interaction and coalescence, which generate complex oscillatory dynamics in large networks shown in [9].

In general perspective, the fact that wave speed depends on $\frac{\langle k^2 \rangle}{\langle k \rangle}$ shows that variation in node degree plays an important role in wave propagation. High variation of node degrees provides high wave speed, presumably due to presence of highly-connected nodes (hubs).

The hyperbolic PDE (12) should not be confused with similar-looking telegrapher's equation, because the $(k-1)$ term in Eqn 12 is positive and gives a self-sustaining wave in time, in contrast to the decaying solution of telegrapher's equation.

The special type of networks we study (with spatially constrained connections) should not be confused with small-world networks. The limited length of link is crucial for spatial phenomena, whereas in conventional small-world networks the "short-cuts" are unlimited in length. This makes wave speed infinite and destroys spatial coherence, but improves temporal coherence[25], [26]. However, small-world networks might be constructed with spatially constrained shortcuts, which could be an interesting system for analysis.

The CA model we use is similar to epidemiological SIRS

model (susceptible-infected-recovery-susceptible). Therefore, our theory may help predict spatial spread of epidemics in large networks. For example, it may be applied to predict spatial spread of SIR type malware through a sufficiently large network of WiFi routers [27], where the length of connections is limited by the router's range.

We studied networks with degree distributions that cover a broad spectrum of possible $\langle k^2\rangle$versus $\langle k\rangle$ combinations (Figure 8B, inset), suggesting that our MFT holds for uncorrelated networks of arbitrary degree distribution (with spatially constrained connections). The degree distributions studied here appear in real-world networks, such as the neuronal network of *C. elegans*, the power grid network, acquaintance networks and the WWW (see [4] and references therein). Our MFT apply to these and other networks, provided there is a metric to measure connection length, and connections are limited by some constant r_c.

METHODS

Cellular Automaton Model

A node in excitable state (E) becomes firing (F) if one or more of its neighbours are (F). After one time step Δt the firing (F) node becomes refractory $(R_1,\dots,R_{t_r})$ for a relatively long period t_r, after which it becomes excitable (E) again. Thus each node rests in (E) or undergoes a sequence of states $(E,F,R_1,\dots,R_{t_r},E)$ if activated by a neighbor. The formal rules of CA are as follows

1. excitable (E) $\rightarrow$ firing (F) if any neighbor is (F)
2. F $\rightarrow$ refractory (R_1)
3. $R_i \rightarrow R_{(i+1)}$
4. $R_{t_r} \rightarrow E$

The states of all nodes are updated simultaneously every time step. Initially all nodes are in excitable (E) state, except a small number of firing nodes that initiate the wave.

Network with spatially constrained connections

The network consists of excitable nodes, which are are set on a uniform $N_x \times N_y$ grid, with unit space between adjacent nodes. The network with defined degree distribution $P(k)$ and connectivity radius r_c is constructed by a procedure similar to that for spatially homogeneous networks [28]. Initially, each node is assigned to a random number of 'stubs' k, which is picked from distribution $P(k)$. Next, the program picks nodes from a randomized (shuffled) list of all nodes. The list of nodes must be randomized to avoid artificial correlations imposed by node order. For each picked node with nonzero number of stubs, the program randomly picks one of its neighbor within distance r_c. If the neighbor has nonzero number of stubs, too, both nodes are linked. Their numbers of stubs are decremented by -1, and their numbers of links are incremented by +1. The procedure is repeated until all stubs of the chosen node become links. To avoid infinitely long search in a situation when all neighbors are already linked and they have no more free stubs, the search of potential neighbors is stopped after 10^4 unsuccessful attempts. The procedure is repeated for each node. The 2D network differs from the quasi-1D network only by the way that the connectivity distance is measured. In 2D network, connectivity of node (x_0,y_0) is $((x-x_0)^2+(y-y_0)^2)^{1/2} \le r_c$ (round 'footprint') or $|x-x_0| \le r_c, |y-y_0| \le r_c$ (square 'footprint'). In quasi one-dimensional network, $|x-x_0| \le r_c$ (interval footprint). In most simulations $r_c = 10$, if not specified otherwise.

Single networks of size up to 400×400 were simulated in Matlab. Large-scale simulations of multiple (64 to 128) networks of size 1000×1000 with $r_c = 20$ (used in Figure 8) were carried out in C/C++ MPI program on an IBM Blue Gene supercomputer.

High-Order Analysis

The use of Taylor's approximation in space and time could potentially bring unwanted errors because Δt and r are in fact not small. Here we estimate wave speed in exact terms by looking for a traveling wave solution in the form $F(x,t) = e^{-\lambda(x-vt)}$ without using Taylor's expansion, thus taking all high-order terms into account. Both cases of links with maximum and random length are analyzed below.

Maximum Length

Substitution of $F(x,t) = e^{-\lambda(x-vt)}$ into Eqn. 2 gives

$$e^{\lambda v \Delta t} = \frac{1}{2}(e^{-\lambda r} + e^{\lambda r}) + (k-1) \qquad (13)$$

For convenience, we will change to new variables $\lambda_r = \lambda r$ and $v^* = \frac{v\Delta t}{r}$. The equation then reads $e^{\lambda_r v^*} = \frac{1}{2}(e^{-\lambda_r} + e^{\lambda_r}) + (k-1)$ and can be solved numerically for marginal stability analysis.

In order to find the minimal wave speed, we need to find v^* such that the function in the left part $f_1(\lambda_r) = e^{\lambda_r v^*}$ has a unique common point with the function in the right part $f_2(\lambda_r) = \frac{1}{2}(e^{-\lambda_r} + e^{\lambda_r}) + (k-1)$, for given k. This happens when $f_1 = f_2$ and $f_1' = f_2'$(plots touch each other). Parameter v^* is the minimal wave speed, normalized to the radius r.Figure 5 shows that v^* (upper dashed line) obtained by this method is close to $v(k)$ obtained from a hyperbolic PDE (upper solid line), so considering derivatives of order above 2 (in time and space) will not affect the wave speed qualitatively. Therefore, the hyperbolic PDE is both necessary and sufficient for qualitative wave speed prediction.

Random Length

This case is analyzed in a similar way. Eqn. 2 linearized around the unstable steady state reads: $F(t+\Delta t) = \frac{1}{2r_c}\int_{-r_c}^{r_c} F(x+r)dr + (k-1)F$. Substitution of $F(x,t) = e^{-\lambda(x-vt)}$and changing to v^* and λ_r gives

$$e^{\lambda_r v^*} = \frac{1}{2\lambda_r}(e^{-\lambda_r} - e^{\lambda_r}) + (k-1) \qquad (14)$$

This equation is solved numerically in the same way as in the maximum-length case. As one can see in Figure 5, the obtained minimal wave speed v^* (lower dashed line) is close to $v(k)$obtained in hyperbolic PDE (lower solid line). However, as shown in Results, the MFT for maximum link length provides better approximation of CA simulations, so this case is shown here only for completeness of analysis.

Radii Distributions

We studied five different radii distributions: uniform in $1\ldots10$, fixed-value (always 10), bell-shaped $f(x=k+1)=C_9^k 0.5^n$ with binomial coefficients $C_9^k, k=0..9$, and two exponentially shaped distributions $f_1(x)\sim\lambda e^{\lambda x}, f_2(x)\sim\lambda e^{-\lambda(r_c-x)}, x\in(0,r_c]$, both normalized to compensate the cutoff of exponential tails.

Numerical integration of PDE System

Analytic formulas for wave speeds are supported by numerical integration of corresponding PDE systems. In the hyperbolic case, the closed nonlinear system reads

$$\begin{cases} F_t+\frac{\Delta t}{2}F_{tt}=DF_{xx}+(k-1)F(1-F-R) \\ R_t=F-\frac{1}{t_r}R \end{cases} \quad \mathbf{(15)}$$

By the normalization $F+R+E=1$ the equation for E is not necessary. Parameters are $\Delta t=1, r=1, D=\frac{r^2}{2\Delta t}, t_r=15$. This system was replaced by a system of three parabolic PDEs (by introducing $G=F_t$), which was solved by a method of lines in Matlab, with parameters $dx=0.1$, $dt=0.002$, mesh size 200×200, and explicit Euler scheme. Initial conditions were $F=R=0$ in all points except the center line where $F=1$.

Simulations of traveling waves in the Fisher-Kolmogorov equation were carried out similarly, with the first equation changed to $F_t=DF_{xx}+(k-1)F(1-F-R)$.

Both systems demonstrate the effect of wave coalescence – two waves cancel each other at the areas where they meet, while their outer borders merge into one big circular wave. The main difference between the two PDE systems is the speed of wave, which grows infinitely with k in the Fisher-Kolmogorov system, but saturates to unity for the hyperbolic PDE system, as discussed in the Results.

ACKNOWLEDGMENTS

We thank Nancy Kopell for stimulating discussions.

REFERENCES

1. Erdős P, Rényi A. On random graphs. I. Publ Math Debrecen. 1959;6:290–297.
2. Watts D, Strogatz S. Collective dynamics of small-world networks. Nature. 1998;393:440–442.
3. Barabási AL, Albert R. Emergence of scaling in random networks. Science. 1999;286:509–512.
4. Strogatz S. Exploring complex networks. Nature. 2001;410:268–276.
5. Boccaletti S, Latora V, Moreno Y, Chavez M, Hwang DU. Complex networks: Structure and dynamics.Physics Reports. 2006;424:175–308.
6. Dorogovtsev SN, Goltsev AV, Mendes JFF. Critical phenomena in complex networks. Rev Mod Phys.2008;80:1275–1335.
7. Barthelemy M. Spatial networks. Physics Reports. 2011;499:1–101.
8. Lewis TJ, Rinzel J. Self-organized synchronous oscillations in a network of excitable cells coupled by gap junctions. Network: Computation in Neural Systems. 2000;11:299–320.
9. Traub R, Duncan R, Russell A, Baldeweg T, Tu Y, et al. Spatiotemporal patterns of electrocorticographic very fast oscillations (>80 Hz) consistent with a network model based on electrical coupling between principal neurons. Epilepsia. 2010;51:1587–1597.
10. Waxman B. Routing of multipoint connections. IEEE Journal on Selected Areas in Communications.1988;6:1617–1622.
11. Zegura E, Calvert K, Bhattacharjee S. How to model an internetwork. Proceedings of IEEE Infocom. 1996;volume 2:594–602.
12. Traub R, Whittington M. Oxford University Press; 2010. Cortical oscillations in health and disease.
13. Traub RD, Schmitz D, Jefferys JGR, Draguhn A. High-frequency population oscillations are predicted to occur in hippocampal pyramidal neuronal networks interconnected by axoaxonal gap junctions. Neuroscience. 1999;92:407–426.
14. Traub R, Contreras D, Cunningham M, Murray H, LeBeau F, et al. Single-column thalamocortical network model exhibiting gamma oscillations, sleep spindles, and epileptogenic bursts. Journal of Neurophysiology. 2005;93:2194.
15. Roopun AK, Middleton SJ, Cunningham MO, LeBeau FEN, Bibbig A, et al. A beta2-frequency (20–30 Hz) oscillation in nonsynaptic networks of somatosensory cortex. Proc Natl Acad Sci U S A.2006;103:15646–15650.
16. Traub R, Middleton S, Knoepfel T, Whittington M. Model of very fast (>75 Hz) network oscillations generated by electrical coupling between the proximal axons of cerebellar Purkinje cells. European Journal of Neuroscience. 2008;28:1603–1616.
17. Greenberg JM, Hastings SP. Spatial patterns for discrete models of diffusion in excitable media. SIAM J Appl Math. 1978;34:515–523.
18. Munro E, Boergers C. Mechanisms of very fast oscillations in networks of axons coupled by gap junctions. Journal of Computational Neuroscience. 2010;28:539–555.
19. Kinouchi O, Copelli M. Optimal dynamical range of excitable networks at criticality. Nature Physics.2006;2:348–351.
20. Furtado L, Copelli M. Response of electrically coupled spiking neurons: a cellular automaton approach.Phys Rev E. 2006;73:11907.
21. Zorzenon dos Santos R, Coutinho S. Dynamics of HIV infection: A cellular automata approach. Phys Rev Lett. 2001;87:168102.
22. Berg HC. Princeton University Press; 1993. Random Walks in Biology.
23. Murray JD. Springer; 2003. Mathematical Biology II.
24. Aronson DG, Weinberger HF. Multidimensional nonlinear diffusion arising in population genetics. Adv Math. 1978;30:33–76.
25. Perc M. Effects of small-world connectivity on noise-induced temporal and spatial order in neural media. Chaos, Solitons & Fractals. 2007;31:280–291.

26. Sun X, Perc M, Lu Q, Kurths J. Spatial coherence resonance on diffusive and small-world networks of Hodgkin–Huxley neurons. Chaos: An Interdisciplinary Journal of Nonlinear Science. 2008;18:023102.

27. Hu H, Myers S, Colizza V, Vespignani A. WiFi networks and malware epidemiology. Proc Natl Acad Sci U S A. 2009;106:1318.

28. Newman MEJ, Strogatz SH, Watts DJ. Random graphs with arbitrary degree distributions and their applications. Phys Rev E. 2001;64:026118.

29. Roopun A, Traub R, Baldeweg T, Cunningham M, Whittaker R, et al. Detecting seizure origin using basic, multiscale population dynamic measures: Preliminary findings. Epilepsy and Behavior. 2009;14:39–46.

CHAPTER 9

MULTI-STABILITY AND PATTERN-SELECTION IN OSCILLATORY NETWORKS WITH FAST INHIBITION AND ELECTRICAL SYNAPSES

Tiaza Bem[1], Pierre Meyrand[2] , Pascal Branchereau[2] , John Hallam[3]

[1]Institute of Biocybernetics and Biomedical Engineering, Polish Academy of Sciences, Warsaw, Poland,

[2]Centre de Neuroscience Inte´gratives et Cognitives, Universite´ Bordeaux 1 and CNRS, UMR 5228, Talence, France,

[3]Maersk Mc-Kinney Moller Institute, University of Southern Denmark, Odense, Denmark

ABSTRACT

A model or hybrid network consisting of oscillatory cells interconnected by inhibitory and electrical synapses may express different stable activity patterns without any change of network topology or parameters, and switching between the patterns can be induced by specific transient signals. However, little is known of properties of such signals. In the present study, we employ numerical simulations of neural networks of different size composed of relaxation oscillators, to investigate switching between in-phase (IP) and anti-phase (AP) activity patterns. We show that the time windows of susceptibility to switching between the patterns are similar in 2-, 4- and 6-cell fully-connected networks. Moreover, in a network (N = 4, 6) expressing a given AP pattern, a stimulus with a given profile consisting of depolarizing and hyperpolarizing signals sent to different subpopulations of cells can evoke switching to another AP pattern. Interestingly, the resulting pattern encodes the profile of the switching stimulus. These results can be extended to different network architectures. Indeed, relaxation oscillators are not only models of cellular pacemakers, bursting or spiking, but are also analogous to firing-rate models of neural activity. We show that rules of switching similar to those found for relaxation oscillators apply to oscillating circuits of excitatory cells interconnected by electrical synapses and cross-inhibition. Our results suggest that incoming information, arriving in a proper time window, may be stored in an oscillatory network in the form of a specific spatio-temporal activity pattern which is expressed until new pertinent information arrives.

INTRODUCTION

Multi-stability of a dynamic system consists of the ability to express, for a given set of parameters, multiple stable states and to switch between these states in response to some external transient input. A few decades ago, the discovery of bi-stable cell properties (plateau activity) transformed understanding of the operation of the neural cell (see review[1]) as well as neural network operation[2]–[5]. More recently, studies in computational processes in non-oscillatory networks gave rise to the concept of a binary memory switch, where transient inputs can turn a plateau like activity on or off in a sub-set of cells within the network[6]–[12]. In the present study, we are interested in multi-stability of oscillatory networks generating rhythmic output. Bi-stability of in-phase (IP) and anti-phase (AP) solutions was first found in a half-center network model

Citation: Bem T, Meyrand P, Branchereau P, Hallam J. Multi-Stability and Pattern-Selection in Oscillatory Networks with Fast Inhibition and Electrical Synapses. Sporns O, ed. PLoS ONE. 2008;3(11):e3830. doi:10.1371/journal.pone.0003830.

consisting of two inhibitory neurons with slow synaptic kinetics[13]. Such bi-stability does not necessarily require slow synaptic transmission and, indeed, it was also found when fast synaptic inhibition was combined with electrical coupling in similar network models[14]–[16]. Bi-stable behavior of a 2-cell inhibitory network has also been confirmed in dynamic clamp experiments on hybrid networks consisting of biological neurons of different intrinsic properties[15],[17].

Instantaneous reconfiguration of activity patterns by brief signals is potentially important for network operations, but the conditions and robustness of switching in a multi-stable oscillatory network still remain unknown. Here we analyze switching between patterns in a model network comprising relaxation oscillators interconnected by fast inhibitory synapses and electrical coupling. A relaxation oscillator is a model of a cellular pacemaker, commonly used to describe the slow envelope of membrane potential oscillation in bursting neurons (for example[18]). Also, in a short duty cycle regime (i.e. if a cell exerts synaptic action over a short part of the cycle), it is applicable to spiking neurons, in which an intrinsic regenerative mechanism is fast compared to recovery variable time scale[16]. Interestingly, moreover, relaxation oscillators are formally analogous to firing-rate models of excitatory neural network activity with slow negative feedback, like synaptic depression or cellular adaptation. Such population firing-rate models are used to study the bursting activity of populations of neurons which by themselves do not have pacemaker properties, as for example CPG networks in the developing spinal cord[19]. Moreover, if reciprocally interconnected via inhibitory subpopulations such network models serve for study of neural competition in such phenomena like binocular rivalry, perceptual bistability[20]–[22]or perceptual decision making[23].

In this paper we are interested in switching between in phase (IP) and anti-phase (AP) states in fully-connected homogenous networks of 2, 4 and 6 relaxation oscillators of short duty cycle. Our goal was to understand how switching rules, i.e. polarity, intensity and phase of stimulus producing a given switch, found for a 2-cell network can be generalized to a larger network. Although due to symmetry of the system one might expect that switching between IP and AP behavior will occur within the same window of the oscillatory cycle independently on the network size it was not clear whether the intensity of such switching stimuli remained the same. Indeed, increasing the size of a fully-connected network requires scaling of coupling parameters such that if total conductance of a single cell is kept constant synaptic coupling between any two cells decreases. This in turn may affect the basin of attraction of the IP or AP pattern and therefore efficacy of a switching stimulus of a given intensity.

Moreover, networks of larger size can generate several distinct AP patterns which is not the case in a 2-cell network. Here, our goal was to test whether properties of stimuli producing switching between AP patterns can be encoded in the resulting pattern of activity. This would not only provide a mechanism for storing signals incoming to the network in the form of a given activity pattern, as in models of working memory and line attractors, but also, since switching should occur only in specific time windows of the oscillatory cycle, offers an additional dimension of encoding.

Finally, a large inhibitory network in addition to IP and AP behaviors may express a multiplicity of other stable states, some of which may co-exist with IP and AP behaviors in some parameter domaines. If so, in addition to a transition between IP and AP switching from IP (or AP) to other states would be possible. Therefore, in order to explore and eliminate this possibility, we examined how the occurrence of multi-stable patterns depends on network size and determined an invariant parameter space for exclusive co-existence of the IP and AP states.

We first find a domain of coupling parameters in which only IP and AP patterns coexist independent of the network size. Thereafter we compare properties of stimuli producing switching between the patterns in networks of different sizes, for the same set of coupling parameters. We show that increasing the number of cells does not alter the properties of switching stimuli. Moreover, in the 4 or 6 cell network switching between different AP patterns was possible, the resultant AP pattern being completely determined by the profile of the switching stimulus, i.e. by the distribution of depolarizing and hyperpolarizing signals among cells. Finally we demonstrate that a firing-rate model network consisting of two oscillatory populations of excitatory cells interconnected by cross-inhibition and electrical coupling expresses switching between patterns according to rules similar to those found for two relaxation oscillators.

RESULTS

Bi-stability of a 2-cell inhibitory network is a robust phenomenon. It has been demonstrated in modeling studies either for the slow inhibitory synapses alone[13]or for fast inhibition combined with electrical coupling[14]–[16]and, moreover, can easily be found in hybrid networks in which biological cells from snail ganglion[15]or cortical slices[17] are interconnected by a dynamic clamp system. In order to illustrate bistability of a 2-cell network we use model cells (relaxation oscillators) interconnected by fast inhibition and electrical synapses. In the model, IP (Fig. 1A, synchronous spikes are indicated by black dots above recordings) or AP (Fig. 1B) behavior is expressed for the same set of network parameters and switching between the two patterns can occur spontaneously if noise of sufficient amplitude is introduced to the network (Fig. 1C). As mentioned above, bistable behavior of a 2-cell model network has been already described[16]. We re-calculate here the occurrence of patterns in such a network (Fig. 2C1) in order to compare it with the behavior of larger networks (Fig. 2C2–3). In the 2-cell network, three types of activity pattern can be expressed depending on coupling strength: IP, AP and almost-in-phase (AIP). In contrast to IP and AP patterns which are symmetrical (cells' trajectories in the phase plane are identical), the AIP pattern is not symmetrical (trajectories of the cells differ) and consists in two cells' active phases expressed with the phase shift $\Phi<0.5$ (see[16]). Note that the AIP pattern is expressed if oscillations underlying spiking are in a relaxation regime (the recovery variable time constant is large comparing to the membrane time constant); otherwise, instead of AIP, the AP pattern is present, as in a network consisting of reciprocally inhibitory integrate-and-fire cell models. The occurrence of the three patterns as a function of the inhibitory and electrical synaptic strength is shown inFigure 2C1. For inhibition alone, only the asymmetrical pattern is stable (see oblique line area,Fig. 2C1). Increasing electrical coupling produces a transition from this pattern to the symmetrical AP pattern (phase shift Φ=0.5) (see horizontal dashed line area,Fig. 2C1). Further increase of the electrical coupling leads to the appearance of the IP pattern (see vertical line area,Fig. 2C1), which coexists with AP in some parameter domain (underlined surfaceFig. 2C1).

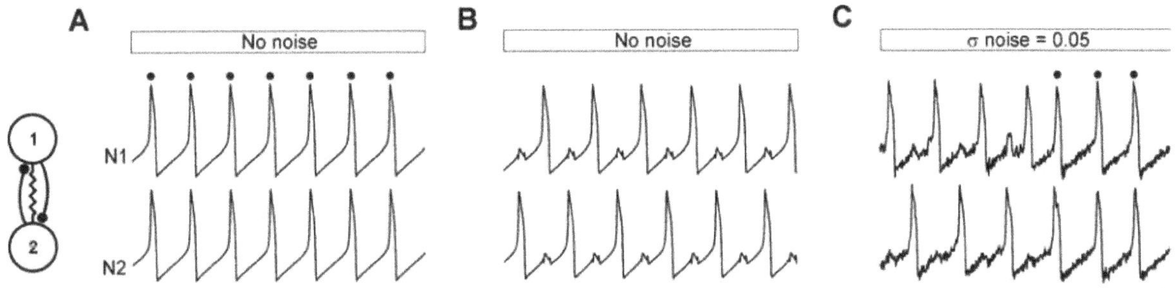

Figure 1: Bi-stability in model 2-cell networks.

Networks consist of two cells interconnected by electrical synapses (resistor symbol in network diagram) and instantaneous reciprocal inhibitory synapses (solid lines with dots in network diagram). A. Model network consisting of relaxation oscillators expresses in-phase (IP) (A), or anti-phase (AP) (B) activity patterns for the same set of synaptic parameters. Introducing stochastic current input to both cells produces spontaneous transition between AP and IP (see black dots) patterns (C). Abbreviations: N relaxation oscillator model neuron. Parameters:g^{syn}=0.032,g^{el}=0.18, σ_noise=0.05 (C).

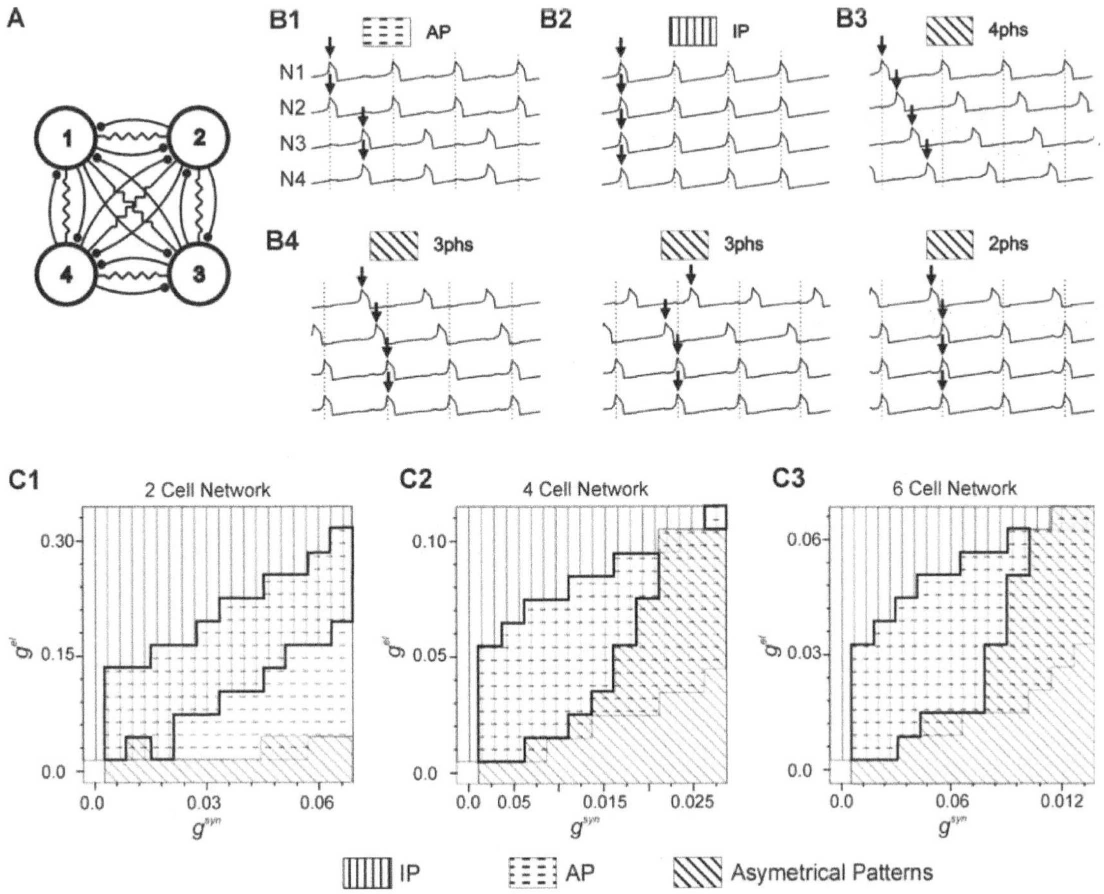

Figure 2: Multiple stable activity patterns in 2-, 4- and 6-cell network.

A. Wiring diagram of 4-cell oscillatory network with full synaptic connections. B. Examples of various oscillatory behaviors expressed by the 4-cell network. Two symmetrical patterns: AP (B1) and IP (B2) are characterized by identical trajectory of all network members. Asymmetrical patterns characterized by different cell trajectories consist of 4 phase (4 phs, B3) or 3 and 2 phase behavior (3 phs, 2 phs respectively, B4). Notice the synergic group of 2 or 3 cells in B4. C. Occurrence of activity patterns as a function of synaptic strength in 2- (C1), 4- (C2) and 6-cell (C3) network. Parameters:g^{syn}=0.014 (B),g^{el}=0.06 (B1–B2), 0.01 (B3–B4), σ_noise=0.005, independent identically distributed Gaussian for each 0.2 unit integration step in B and C.

The next larger network with a similar symmetry to the 2-cell network is a 4-cell network fully connected by inhibitory and electrical synapses (Fig. 2A). For this (and the larger) network we used intrinsic cell parameters identical to the 2-cell model network but scaled the synaptic conductance to maintain constant the total synaptic conductance of a single model cell. In other words, assuming network size equal N, a total electrical or inhibitory coupling between a given cell and the remaining N-1 cells was made independent of N.

With increasing network size, the number of stable patterns expressed increases. Indeed, in the 4-cell network, 4 stable asymmetrical and 2 symmetrical patterns were found in the presence of a relatively large amplitude noise input to the network (Fig. 2B). Like the 2-cell network, the 4-cell network expressed symmetrical AP (Fig. 2B1), and IP behavior (Fig. 2B2). Among asymmetrical patterns we found a 4 phase pattern in which all 4 cells fire at different phases within the cycle (Fig. 2B3), and 3 and 2 phase patterns in which synchronous firing occurs in groups of 2 or 3 cells (Fig. 2B4). Interestingly, the emergence of patterns seems to follow the same principle as in the 2-cell network (compareFig 2C1 and C2). Indeed, with dominating inhibitory coupling, only asymmetrical patterns were expressed (see oblique line area,Fig. 2C2) whereas introducing electrical coupling led first to the appearance of AP and then IP behaviors (horizontal dashed and vertical line areas, respectively,Fig. 2C2) until, for a sufficiently strong electrical coupling, only the IP pattern remains. Importantly, the IP and AP patterns coexist in a similar subspace of coupling parameters as in the 2-cell network (compare underlined surfaces,Fig. 2C1 and C2). Finally, increasing the number of cells in the network to 6 did not change the qualitative distribution of pattern occurrence in the two dimensional parameter space (compareFig. 2C1, C2 and 2C3).

In the next section we will investigate transitions between these patterns. As illustrated inFigure 3, such transitions may occur spontaneously due to stochastic inputs. Indeed, with a low level of noise, the 4-cell network expresses either AP (Fig. 3A1) or IP (Fig. 3A2) patterns which persist an arbitrarily long time, while increasing the noise amplitude provokes spontaneous switching within a short time interval (Fig. 3A3).

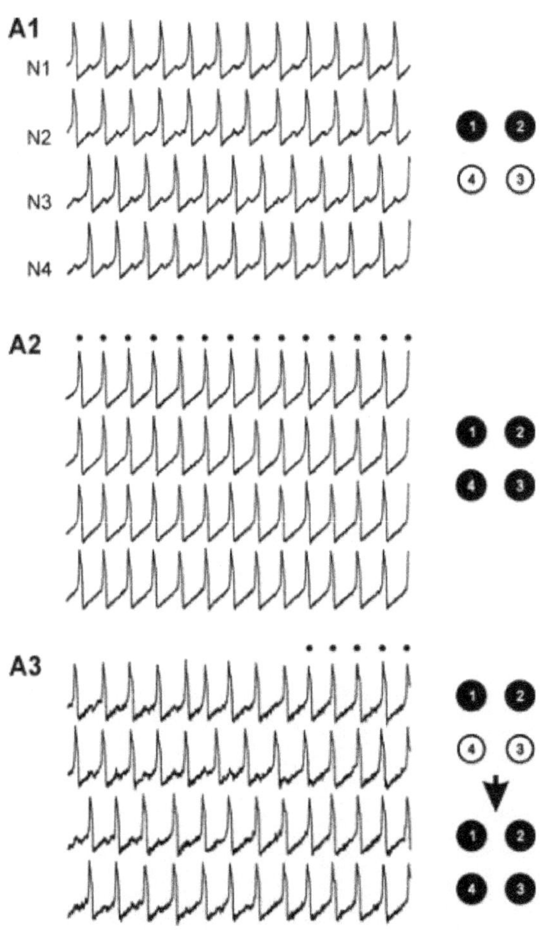

Figure 3: Bi-stability in 4-cell fully-connected model network.

For a given parameter set the network either is divided into 2 groups of synergic cells (N1,2 in black and N3,4 in white) oscillating in AP (A1) or expresses synchronous activity (A2) where all the spikes occur simultaneously from N1 to N4 (see dots and scheme where all the cells are black). Spontaneous switching between these two modes of activity occurs due to the stochastic input signal (A3) (see transition from upper network scheme to bottom one). Notice increase of noise amplitude in A3 compared to A1 and A2. Parameters:g^{syn}=0.014,g^{el}=0.06, σ_noise=0.025 (A1, A2), 0.05 (A3).

We will now consider non-spontaneous switching evoked by extrinsic stimuli. Since the network is oscillating, one may expect that the impact of a given stimulus will be phase-dependent. Therefore, we study not only the effect of polarity and intensity of a stimulus but also its efficacy depending on the time of delivery within the cycle. This is tested with respect to three types of switching: from IP to AP (Fig. 4A), from AP to IP (Fig. 4B) and between different AP patterns (Fig. 4C). In all these cases, initial and resultant states of the network are illustrated in diagrams showing clusters of synchronous cells (group of cells either black or white). For example, a switch from IP to AP is illustrated as a transition between four black cells to two black and two white cells (right panel,Fig. 4A). Here the stimulus profile is described as "0 0 – –" indicating that cell N1 and N2 do not receive any input whereas a transient hyperpolarizing input is delivered to cells N3 and N4. An identical stimulus profile evokes a reverse switch between AP to IP (Fig. 4B).

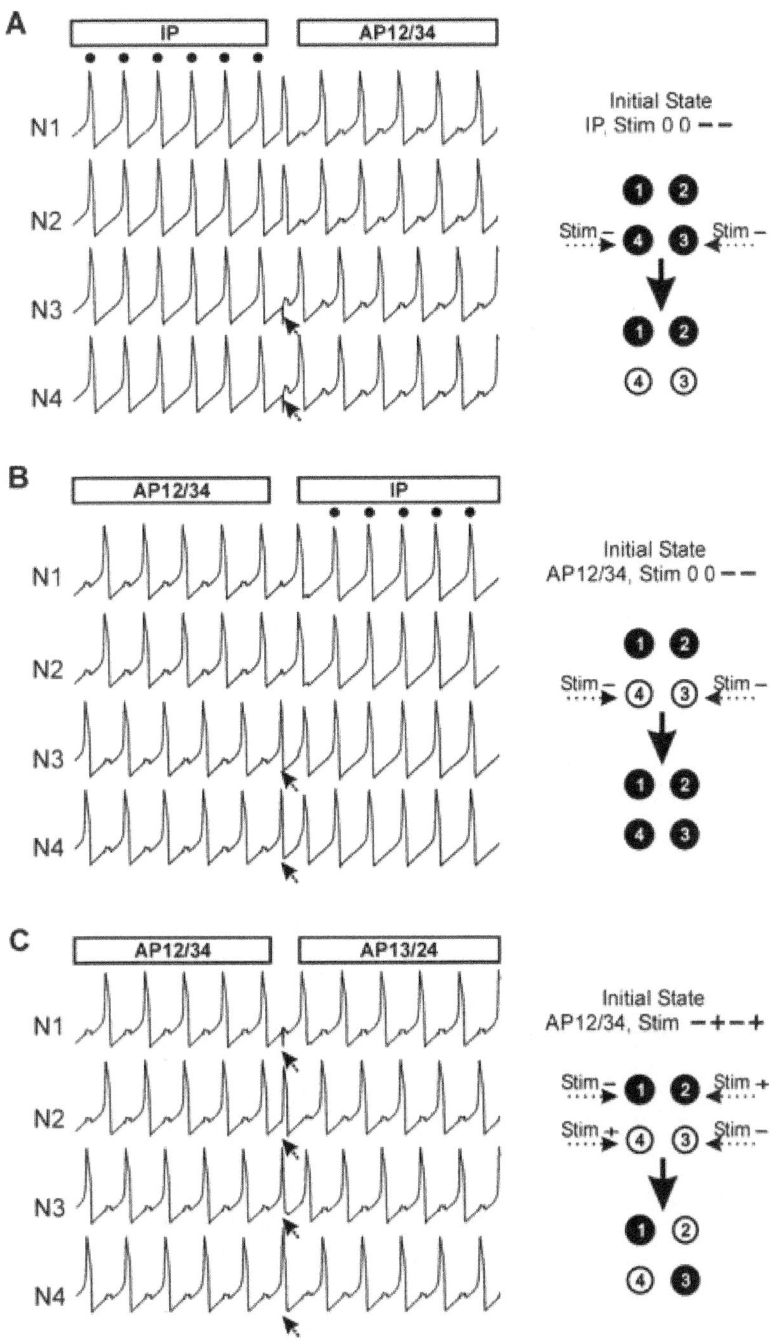

Figure 4: Transition between two stable states may be evoked by different types of stimuli.

A. Delivery of transient hyperpolarizing stimuli to N3 and N4 (see arrows) during ongoing IP activity produces a sudden transition to AP behavior in which cells N3 and N4 oscillate out of phase with cells N1 and N2. This transition is schematically represented on the right panel. The profile of stimulus (here Stim "0 0 – –") is encoded in a series of symbols corresponding to stimulus occurrence (0 no stimulus, + depolarizing stimulus, – hyperpolarizing stimulus) delivered to cell N1, N2, N3 and N4 respectively. B. The same type of stimulus (see right panel) during ongoing AP activity may produce the re-establishment of IP behavior. In this case the initial state is defined as AP12/34 indicating antagonistic activity of two groups of cells: N1, N2 and N3, N4, respectively. C: Stimulation of all cell members with the stimuli of mixed polarity (see right panel) may produce a transition between different AP patterns. Compare initial state AP12/34 with the resulting AP13/24 pattern. Parameters:g^{syn}=0.014,g^{el}=0.06, stimulus intensity=0.4.

Notice that the AP pattern shown infigure 4A–Bis not the only possible AP behavior of the network. Indeed, an AP state consists in a division of the network into 2 groups of synchronous cells, the groups oscillating in anti-phase. Therefore in the 4-cell network there are 3 possible such divisions: AP12/34, AP13/24 and AP14/23. Here switching from AP12/34 to AP13/24 was evoked by delivering hyperpolarizing inputs to 2 cells (N1 and N3) and depolarizing inputs to the 2 remaining cells (N2 and N4) (see stimulus profile "– + – +",Fig. 4C).

All examples illustrated inFigure 4show successful switching. As we shall see in the next sections, they occurred because stimuli were applied at the proper time within the cycle. Indeed, as shown in[15], in the 2-cell network switching from IP to AP was possible, for example, when a depolarizing stimulus was applied to one of the cells at a time halfway between two successive spikes. Here we explore this switching again by delivering depolarizing stimuli of different intensity (see scale bar, topFig 5) to one of the cells (see Stim "+ 0",Fig. 5A1) while the network is expressing IP behavior (initial state). In order to explore the phase dependence of stimulus impact, we delivered it at different moments of the cycle from phase Φ=0 to 1, corresponding to the maxima of depolarization of the consecutive spikes of cell N1 (see central insetFig. 5A1). For low intensity stimulus, the initial state of the network remains unchanged independently of the timing of stimulus delivery within the cycle (see lighter grey bar,Fig. 5A1). Increasing the intensity of stimulus provided a time window around the middle of the cycle where switching to the AP behavior occurred (Fig. 5A1). Further increase stimulus intensity did not substantially alter this window. Interestingly, the application of analogous stimuli (i. e. depolarizing stimulus to 50% of cells) for a 4-cell network (see Stim "+ + 0 0",Fig. 5A2), revealed a very similar window for switching (Fig. 5 A2).

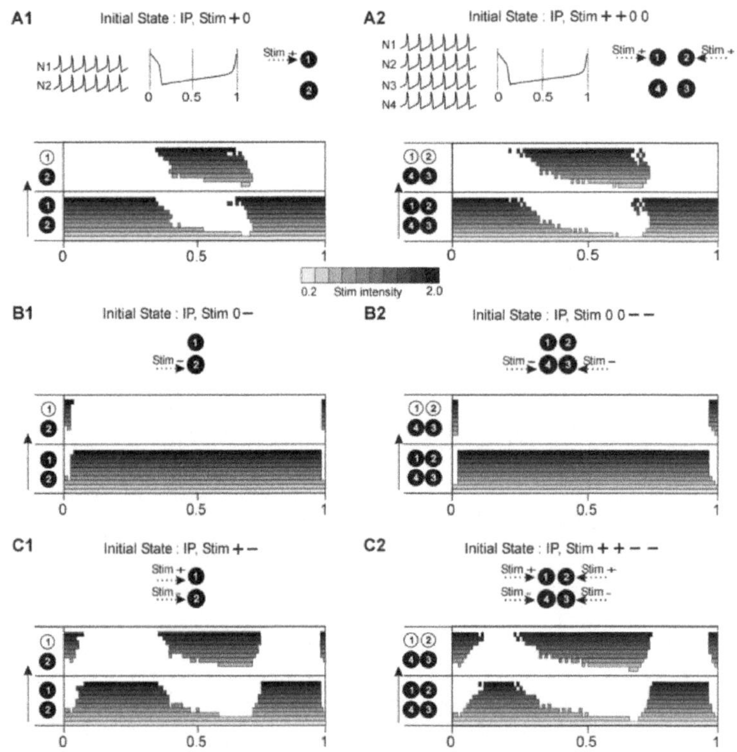

Figure 5: Time windows of susceptibility to switching from IP to AP pattern in 2- and 4-cell network.

A. Shown is ongoing in-phase activity, sketch of the oscillatory cycle and diagram of stimulus profile in the 2-cell (upper panel, A1) and 4-cell (upper panel, A2) networks. In each bottom panel switching diagrams are shown for different intensities of depolarizing stimulus, represented by different intensities of gray (see scale). The diagram is divided into the bottom part, representing the initial state, and the top part representing the resulting pattern. For each current intensity, stimuli of duration 0.3 time units are delivered in different phases of the cycle with a step of 0.2 time units (cycle period is c. 20 time units for all patterns shown). The stimulus of lowest intensity does not produce a switch in any phase of the cycle. This is indicated by a continuous horizontal bar in the bottom part of the diagram (A1, A2). Increasing the stimulus intensity results, in some phases of the cycle, in an effective stimulation which is indicated by a gray bar in the upper part of diagram. Notice a similar mid-cycle window in the 2-cell (A1) and 4-cell (A2) networks. B. With an hyperpolarizing stimulus switching is effective only during the firing phase of the stimulated cell for the 2-cell (B1) and 4-cell (B2) networks. C. Stimulus of mixed polarity (see upper panel) evokes switching both in mid-cycle and in vicinity of cells' firing phases in 2- (C1) and 4- (C2) cell networks. 2- and 4-cell network parameters are the same as infigures 1Aand2B1–B2, respectively.

By contrast to depolarizing stimuli, which offered relatively large switching windows (up to half of the cycle), hyperpolarizing stimuli distributed among 50% of cells produced switching only if delivered in a very narrow time window during firing of stimulated cells in both the 2-cell (Fig. 5 B1) and the 4-cell network (Fig. 5 B2). Finally, simultaneous application of stimuli of opposite polarities, each now delivered to 50% of cells (see stimulus profiles,Fig. 5C1 and C2), resulted in switching windows which combined the main features of the two types of switching window corresponding to the singe stimulus polarities (Fig. 5 C1, C2). Indeed, with this type of stimulus, switching from IP to AP behaviors was produced in the middle part of the cycle as well as around the spike generation phase (i.e. Φ=0 and 1). (Note that although the compound window is a qualitative sum of components it is not a simple linear combination.)

We will now consider reverse transitions, i.e., switching from the AP to the IP pattern. When the network is in AP mode it is divided into two groups of cells (see top panels inFig. 6A1–A2); this asymmetry increases the number of distinct stimulus types.

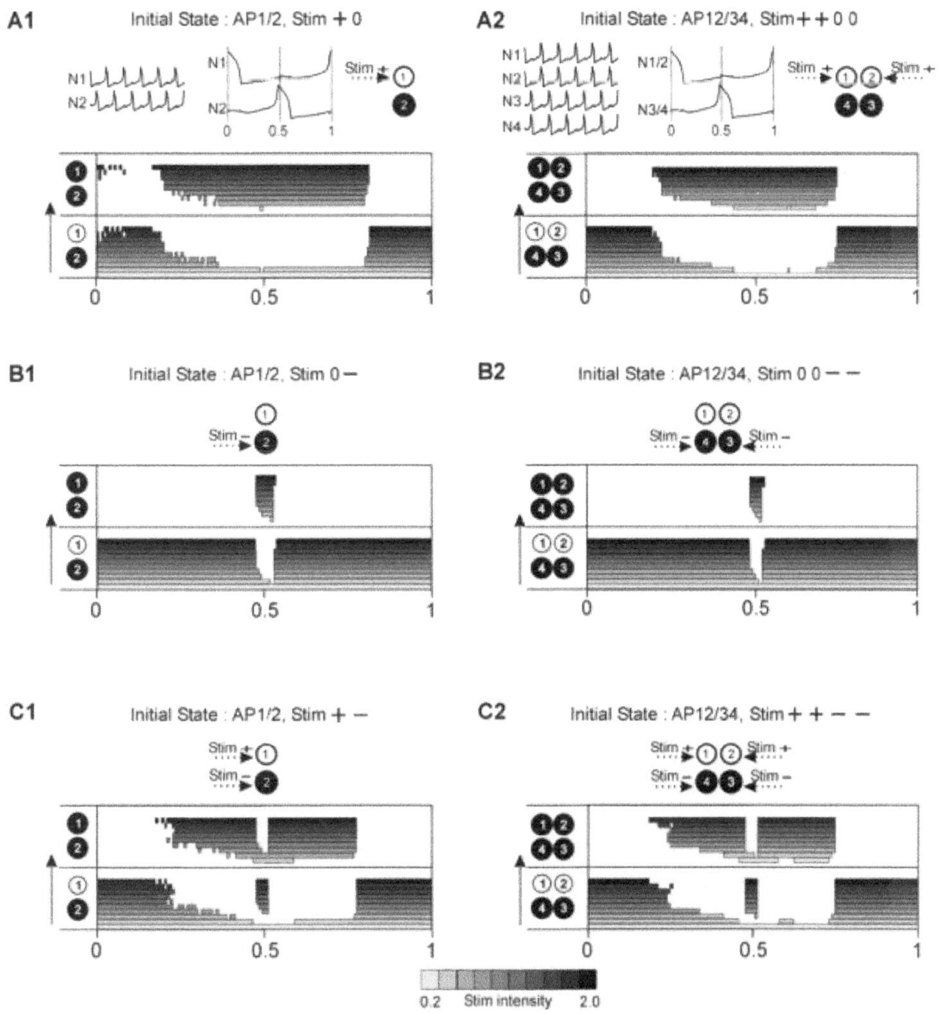

Figure 6: Time windows of susceptibility to switching from AP to IP pattern in 2- and 4-cell network using homogenous stimulus to synergic 50% of cells.

A1–2. The schematic representation in the upper panel is the same as described inFig. 5A. Depolarizing stimulus delivered to cell N1 (A1) or cells N1, N2 (A2) evokes a switch if applied in a large mid-cycle window. B1–2. Hyperpolarizing stimulus delivered to cell N2 (B1) or cells N3, N4 (B2) evokes switching only in a narrow window around Φ=0.5. C1–2. Mixed polarity stimulus delivered to all network members has a similar effect as depolarizing stimulus except around Φ=0.5 where switching fails. Network and stimulus parameters as inFig. 5.

First, if we apply a stimulus of a given polarity to just one of the two groups (see stimulus profiles inFig. 6A, B), switching windows show features similar to those which characterize transitions from IP to AP behavior. Indeed, in both 2-cell and the 4-cell model networks, positive stimuli delivered to one group of synergic cells evoked switching to the IP behaviors when applied in the middle of the cycle (Fig. 6A1, A2). Here the window for switching is wide, occupying approximately half of the cycle, similar to the analogous window for IP to AP transitions (seeFig. 5A1, A2). Furthermore, negative stimuli delivered to just one group of cells are likewise effective only when applied during spiking of the stimulated cells (Fig. 6B1, B2) as was the case for IP to AP switching (Fig. 5B1, B2). Notice however, that the window is now located at Φ=0.5 since the stimulated group is now phase shifted by 0.5 with respect to the reference cell in the initial AP behavior. Finally, when stimuli of opposite polarities were delivered to the two antagonistic groups of cells, switching to IP was still evoked in a large window located around the middle of the cycle (Fig 6 C1, C2). However, at Φ=0.5 these transitions were not possible: here, delivery of the stimuli produced simultaneous exchange of the phases of the two groups - spiking cells became silent and silent cells became spiking. This resulted in a reset of the ongoing activity (not shown) but did not change the AP pattern.

Second, stimuli of a given polarity can be delivered to cells belonging to both antagonistic groups such that only 50% of network members receive input (see stimulus profiles,Fig. 7). If depolarizing, such a stimulus is very effective and produces switching to the IP behavior independently of the phase of delivery (Fig. 7A). If hyperpolarizing, its impact is again restricted to phases when one of stimulated cells fires (Φ=0, 0.5, 1,Fig. 7B). (For a mixed stimulus of this type, see below.) It must be noted that similar features are expressed by the 2-cell network if both cells are stimulated with the same polarity (data not shown).

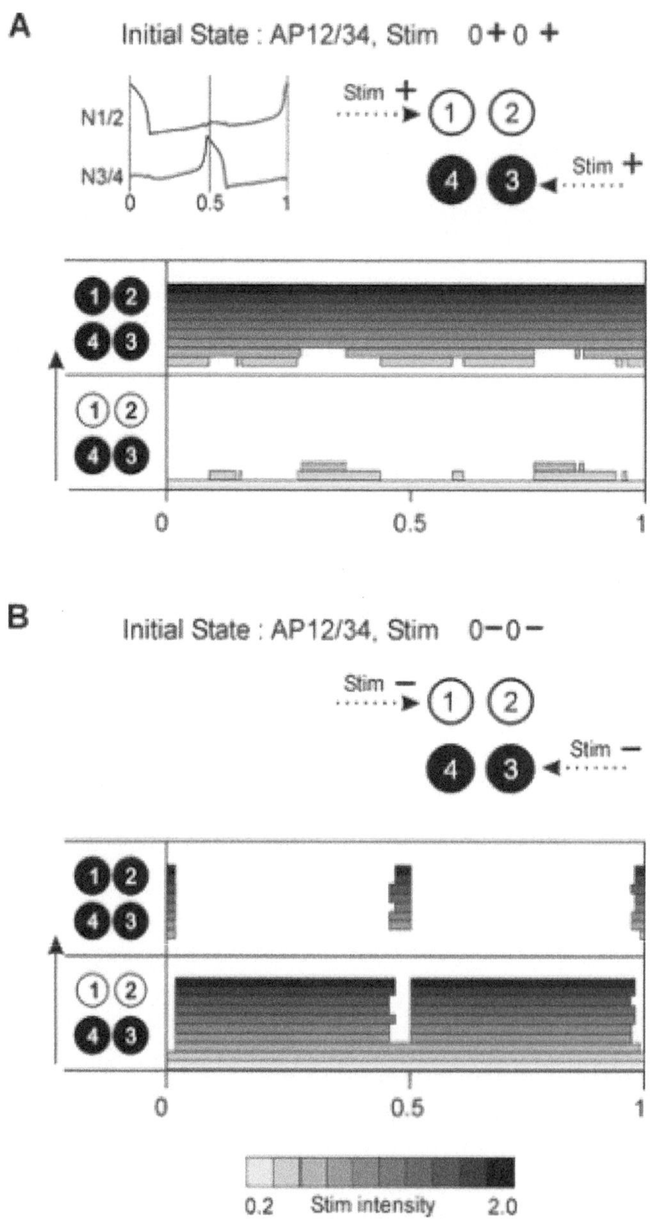

Figure 7: Time windows for AP to IP switching with homogenous stimuli delivered to 50% of cells in each synergic group.

A. Depolarizing stimulus produces switching independently of the time of its delivery. B. Hyperpolarizing stimulus is effective only if applied during firing phases. Network and stimulus parameters as inFig. 5.

Third, stimuli of opposite polarities delivered to antagonistic groups, again such that only 50% of network members receive input, (see stimulus profile,Fig. 8A) evokes switching to IP behavior when applied in a large window around middle of the cycle, except at Φ=0.5 (Fig. 8 A). At Φ=0.5 a switch into a new AP pattern occurs (from AP 12/34 to AP 13/24) because both stimulated cells, belonging to different synergic groups, exchange their memberships: at Φ=0.5 the spiking cell (N4) become silent due to hyperpolarizing stimulus whereas the silent cell (N1) generates a spike in response to depolarizing stimulus. Applying the same type of stimulus also to the remaining 50% of cells, in such a way that in each synergic group the cells received stimuli of different polarities (see stimulus profile,Fig. 8B), always produced switching to the IP pattern, except if applied during cells' spiking phases (Φ=0, 0.5, 1) (Fig. 8B) where switching to another AP pattern took place (from AP 12/34 to AP 13/24). Indeed, in each spiking phase, a pair of cells receiving stimuli of opposite polarity and belonging to different synergic groups can exchange their memberships, as described above. Notice, importantly, that the distribution of delivered stimulus is now encoded in the resulting AP pattern. Indeed, cells which receive a stimulus of the same polarity will form new synergic groups (see N1, N3 and N2, N4,Fig. 8B). This results in a new division of the network which is equivalent to a new AP behavior (AP 13/24). Finally, it must be noted that for very high stimulus intensity, another AP pattern variant may emerge instead of the expected pattern (see top panel inFig. 8B).

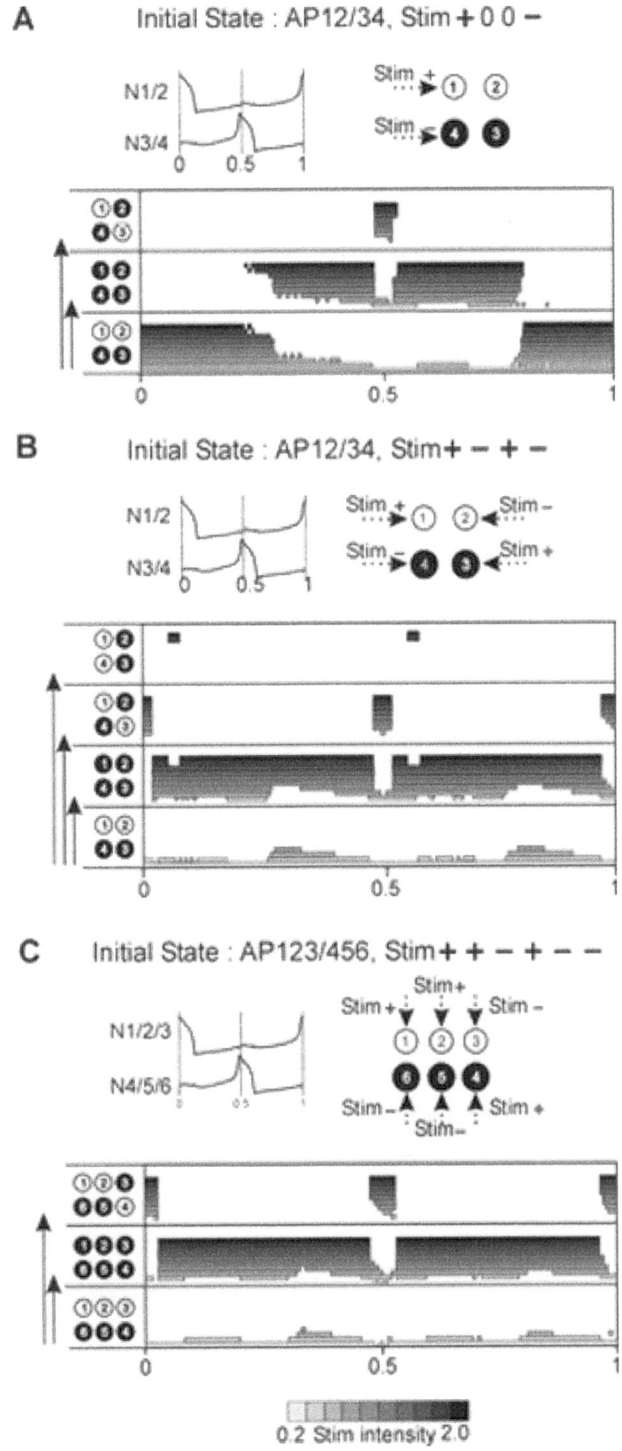

Figure 8: Mixed stimulus may produce switching between different AP behaviors in 4- and 6-cell network.

A. Stimulus of opposite polarities delivered to antagonistic cells (50% of network members) may produce either switching to IP if delivered within a large mid-cycle window except $\Phi=0.5$ or switching to another AP pattern if delivered at $\Phi=0.5$. B. Mixed stimuli applied to the whole population with opposite polarities distributed among synergic cells (see upper panel) evokes switching to IP everywhere in the cycle except if delivered close to firing phases where switches to another AP pattern occur. The new AP pattern expresses the map of activity corresponding to the stimulus profile (AP13/24). Note that stimuli of very high intensity may produce AP with activity map different from both the stimulus profile and the initial AP map (see AP14/23). C. Qualitatively similar switching is found for the 6-cell network.

Although the 4-cell network reveals some general rules of encoding the stimulus profile as resulting pattern, the network is nevertheless insufficiently general. In particular, it is never possible to switch a majority (or minority) of a synergic group with a corresponding set of cells in the other group – because groups comprise just 2 cells (and since only 1 cell can be switched it is always 50% of a group). Therefore, to generalize the above encoding rules, we used a similar approach on the 6-cell network. Here, within each group of synergic cells consisting of 3 cells, 2 cells receive stimulus of the same polarity (see stimulus profile,Fig. 8C) and therefore are supposed to remain synergic in the resulting AP pattern. Interestingly, switching indeed occurs from AP123/456 to AP124/356 so that pairs (N1, N2) and (N5, N6) which received homogenous stimuli remained synergic. By contrast cells N3 and N4 switch their memberships because the signals they receive are of opposite polarity to the signals sent to the other group members. Moreover, time windows for switching to the new AP pattern were the same as in the 4-cell network: such switching occurred only if the stimulus was delivered during the cells' spiking phases; otherwise stimulus delivery resulted in full network synchrony (Fig. 8C). It should be stressed that in the 6-cell network the distribution of the applied stimuli again determines the resulting AP pattern (N1, N2 and N4 received depolarizing stimuli and N3, N5 and N6 hyperpolarizing inputs, therefore clusters 1, 2, 4 and 3, 5, 6 are formed).

As mentioned in the Introduction, there is a formal analogy between a relaxation oscillator and a firing-rate model of excitatory neural network activity with slow negative feedback[19]. We therefore tested whether our results are applicable to a model network consisting of two excitatory populations with recurrent connectivity, in which synaptic depression played the role of a slow process underlying oscillations. Both populations were connected by electrical synapses and projected to a common inhibitory pool which provided cross inhibition (Fig. 9A, see alsoMethod). (It must be noted similar network behavior to that described below is expressed if populations E1 and E2 project to separate inhibitory pools.) As illustrated, such a model network expresses bistability of IP and AP patterns (Fig. 9B) and switching between these can be produced by transient inputs in similar time windows to those for a network consisting of relaxation oscillators (comparefigures 9C1and6A1,9D1and6B 1,9C2and5A1,9D2and5B1). This also suggests that switching in larger networks consisting of many oscillatory units will be similar independently of whether a "unit" consists of a single cell or of a population of cells.

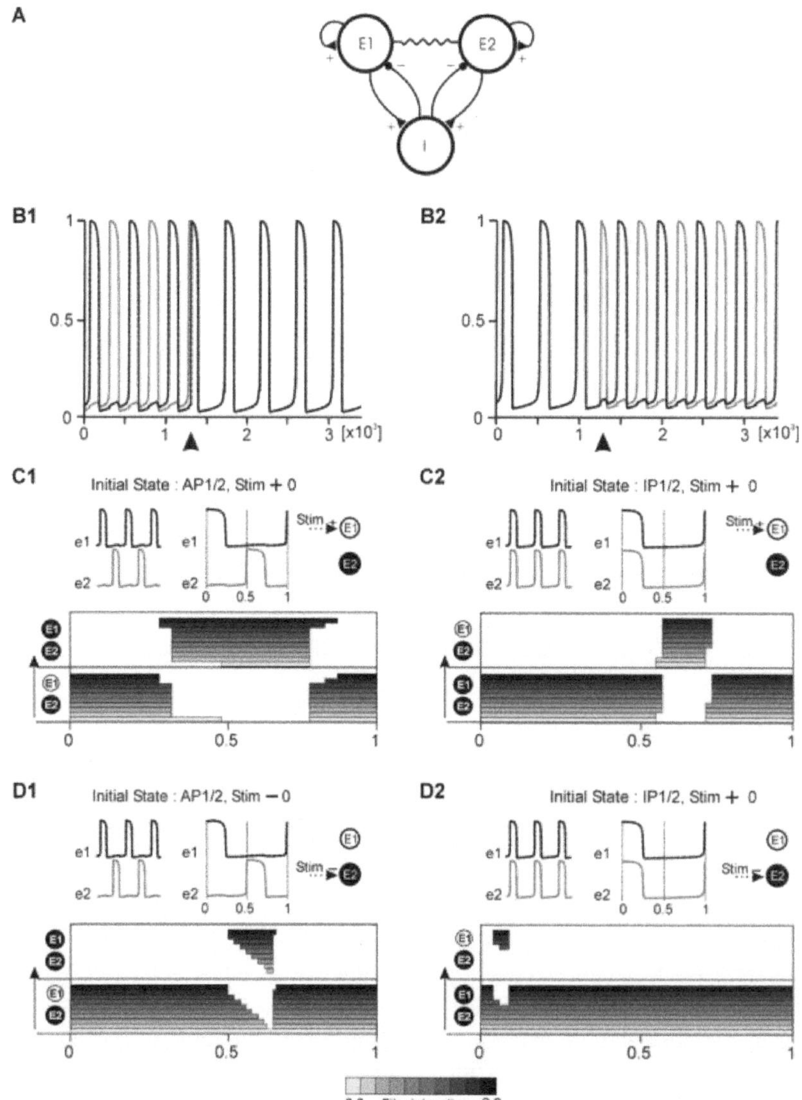

Figure 9: Bistable behavior of two excitatory populations interconnected by cross-inhibition and electrical coupling.

A. Network architecture. Excitatory and inhibitory connections are represented by triangles and filled circles, respectively whereas resistor symbol represents electrical coupling. E1, E2 represents excitatory and I inhibitory populations. B. Time course of activity e1 (black line) and e2 (gray line) in populations E1 and E2. Transient input (arrow head) produces switching from AP to IP (B1) or vive versa (B2). Positive stimuli (C1, C2) are more efficient in switching than negative, which are restricted only to active phases (D1, D2). Parameters:τ_e=1,τ_s=250,w=0.7,V=0.17,β =0.06,i_tr=0.3,g=0.075,g_s=0.025,θ=0.3ks=0.05ke= 0.05.V_{app}=0.1 (in B), 0.02–0.2 (in C and D, see bottom bar), stimulus duration=10 time units.

DISCUSSION

In the present study, we demonstrate that an oscillatory model network, consisting of more than 2 cells, fully interconnected with fast inhibitory and electrical synapses, generates a large variety of stable activity patterns, the number of which depends on the number of cells as well as on the coupling parameter domain (seeFig. 2). Moreover, for a given set of synaptic strengths, multiple stable patterns can be expressed and switching between them can be induced by a suitable transient external stimulus. In this paper, we focused on the parameter domain where only IP and different AP patterns co-exist. We generalized rules governing switching between IP and AP patterns by comparing behaviors of networks of different sizes.

It must be noted that whereas increasing the network size diminishes the strength of intra-network cell-to-cell connectivity – a condition necessary for exclusive coexistence of AP and IP patterns (seeFig. 2) – the intensity of external stimulus per cell, required for a given switch, remains the same (seeFig. 5and6). The other scaling, providing a constant cell-to-cell synaptic strength, may seem to be more intuitive. However, in this case inhibition and electrical coupling between a cell and the rest of the network become so strong with increasing network size that they produce a damping of the amplitude of oscillations and their eventual suppression (as previously described[16]). Note also that this latter scaling regime implies that cells can sustain an arbitrarily large total conductance, implausible given their morpho-functional limits.

The switching rules are illustrated inFig. 10where they are summarized for 2- and 4-cell networks. Assuming stimulus delivery to 50% of the cell population, transitions from IP to AP are produced by a depolarizing stimulus if it is applied within a relatively wide time window located at mid-cycle (type X window) (upper panelFig. 10A). On the other hand, a hyperpolarizing stimulus can produce switching only by suppressing the spike of a cell and therefore this switching is very phase-specific (phases 0, 1, type Y window) (middle panelFig. 10A). If these two types of stimuli are applied simultaneously to different sub-populations of cells, the resulting time window is the sum of the two windows corresponding to depolarizing and hyperpolarizing stimuli (type X+Y window) (bottom panelFig. 10A).

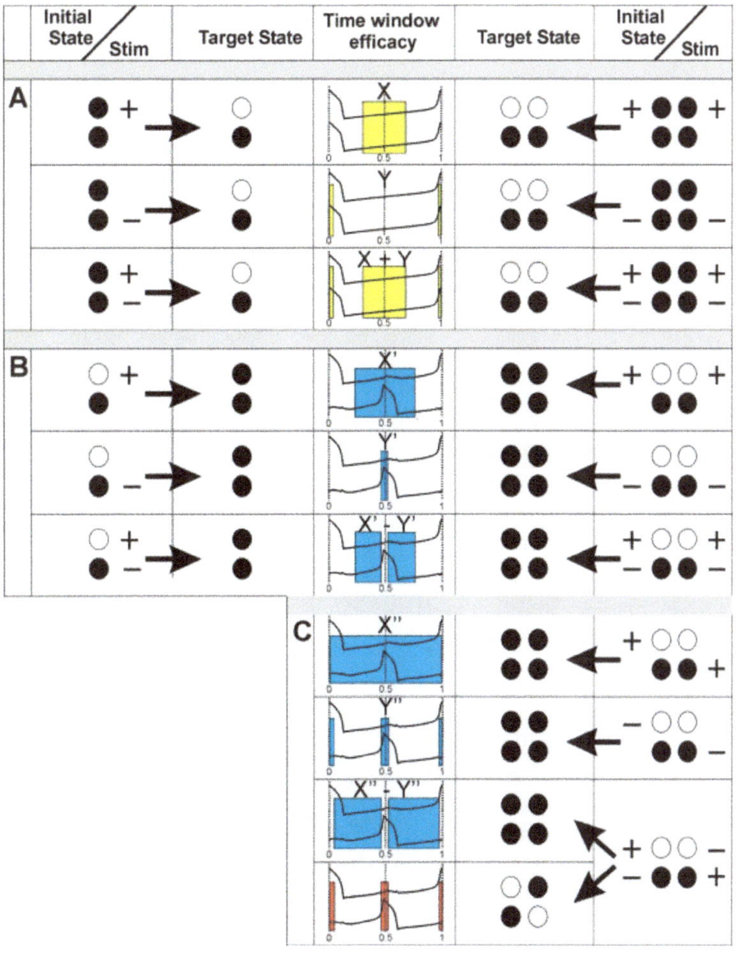

Figure 10: Rules of switching between multistable patterns depending on stimulus profile.

Reverse transitions are more complex. Indeed, the network expressing AP behavior is divided into two antagonistic groups of cells and therefore distribution of stimuli between these two groups becomes important. Consider two possibilities.

First, assuming that only cells belonging to one of these groups are stimulated, a transition from AP to IP occurs if a depolarizing signal arrives within a large mid-cycle window (type X′) (upper panelFig. 10B), or if a hyperpolarizing signal is applied in a very narrow window restricted to the cell firing phase (type Y′) (middle panelFig. 10B). When stimuli of both polarity are distributed among the network cells, the resulting window is now not a sum (see bottom panel,fig 10A) but a difference between the two window types (Type X′–Y′) (bottom panel,Fig. 10B).

Second, if stimuli of the same polarity are delivered to members of different groups, transitions to IP also occur. Here, depolarizing stimuli produce switching independently of the time of delivery (Type X″) (upper panel,Fig. 10C), the impact of hyperpolarizing stimuli is again restricted to the firing phases of neurons (Type Y″) (middle panel,Fig. 10C) and mixed stimuli provide switching if delivered anywhere in the cycle except during firing phases (Type X″–Y″) (upper line, bottom panelFig. 10C). Importantly however, during these firing phases the network switches from a given AP to a new AP pattern. The resulting AP pattern consists in a new division of the network into two new sub-populations of cells, corresponding to the distribution of hyperpolarizing and depolarizing stimuli among the network members (bottom line, bottom panelFig. 10C). Therefore the information carried by the transient stimulus is now encoded in a given persistent spatio-temporal oscillatory pattern expressed by the network.

These results indicate that, within networks consisting of oscillatory cells interconnected by fast inhibitory and electrical synapses, reconfiguration of activity patterns may be evoked by transient input and the new configuration encodes a profile of the stimulus.

The idea of storing the memory of a transient stimulus in the form of a given spatial distribution of active cells has been used in the bi-stable model network expressing switching between global OFF and multiple ON activity states which was proposed as a model of working memory[12]. There is no OFF state in an oscillatory network since activity is always expressed as synchronous, or one of the different patterns of asynchronous, firing of neurons. Instead of switching between OFF and one of the multiple ON states (depending on a given subpopulation of active cells) such a network expresses transitions between IP and one of the multiple AP states (depending on a given division of the network into two parts), that is a transition between two rhythmic outputs of different frequencies. Therefore in both network types the average frequency of neurons can be altered by a transient stimulus. Apart from this similariry the switching properties of oscillatory networks are quite different from non-oscillatory networks expressing bi-stability. Indeed, the impact of a transient input on the ongoing network activity is phase dependent. Therefore the same incoming information will have different effect on network behavior (or have no effect at all) if arriving in different phases of the oscillatory cycle. Moreover, stimuli of the same profile (i.e. same polarity and distribution among the cells) can produce switching back and forth between IP and AP patterns. By contrast, a specific stimulus is required to switch ON or OFF the activity in the non-oscillatory network.

Furthermore, in the oscillatory network direct switching between different AP states is possible, whereas in the non-oscillatory network in order to establish a new ON state the network activity must be first reset to the OFF state. Finally, switching between states can be very fast within oscillatory network.

Beside the possible function of storing information as proposed in models of working memory, the multi-stability of oscillatory networks may also play an important role in functional reconfiguration of dynamical systems. For example in motor control, during ongoing activity of the CPG network it has been shown that the sensory information from the periphery as well as feedback originating from special senses (vision, audition, vestibular) may shape the motor output in a phase dependant way (see review[24]). These inputs continuously adjust the output of the network during a given motor task. However, when a sudden change is needed, for example a transition from one gait to another, it can be executed by a transient signal which changes instantaneously and simultaneously the phase relationships between all the network elements involved in the task. Interestingly, in the area of bimanual finger tapping two coordination patterns of different stability have been found ([25],[26]). In the search for principles of pattern generation in complex biological systems, a theory of self-organization in non-equilibrium systems including order parameters dynamics, stability, fluctuations and times scales has been proposed[27]–[29]. From such a perspective, multi-stability of neural networks appears as a commonly occurring natural phenomenon. Indeed, in accordance with the theory, it has been demonstrated that a transition between bi-stable patterns of finger tapping can be elicited in the human brain by transient transcranial magnetic stimulation[30]. Unfortunately, in that study no attempt was made to determine time windows for susceptibility of switching between patterns. Relaxation oscillators used in this study are basically models of the slowly oscillating envelope of bursting neurons, but in a short duty cycle regime may be also applicable to spiking neurons[16]. Factors that may contribute to differences between our idealized cell model and a real spiking neuron include non-relaxation intrinsic cell dynamics and slow synapses. How they influence switching in bi-stable network should be tested in further modeling studies. Interestingly, our preliminary results indicate that 2- and 4-cell networks consisting of IF cell models express qualitative features of switching windows very similar to those described for a network composed of relaxation oscillators.

Our results are also applicable to networks consisting of oscillatory circuits, which express periodic changes of cells' mean firing rate (Fig. 9). It seems likely that switching rules found for a given topology of connections between relaxation oscillators, like those for full connectivity presented in this study, could be also applicable for such a "network of networks", independent of details of individual cells' or synapses' properties. This could further support a hypothesis that switching between multistable patterns can occur during gait control provided be GPGs networks which are known to consist of oscillatory units with a well-defined symmetry of connectivity[31],[32]. Our model requires, in addition to cross-inhibition, electrical coupling between oscillatory units to express AP pattern in the case of short duty cycle, as described previously[16]. Although such coupling has so far been described only in invertebrates' CPG, recent work suggests that it may also play an important role in mammalian CPG networks[33].

In summary, our data demonstrate that a given network operation can be altered without change of cellular or synaptic properties and with almost no activation time. A reconfiguration through neuromodulation has been shown to play an important role in shaping properties of a network's hardware elements in both developing and mature networks. However, as demonstrated by our data, in the multi-stable network, different stable rhythmic patterns can be selected by specific transient stimuli without any change of network topology, membrane or synaptic parameters.

MATERIALS AND METHODS

The Cell Model

Cells in the model network are modeled as a set of first order differential equations, each cell contributing two state variables to the set: the instantaneous membrane potential (V_i) and a slow recovery current (W_i) dependent on membrane potential. The variables have the (non-dimensionalised) dynamics defined by equation 1–2.

$$\tau_v \frac{dV_i}{dt} = -\left[V_i + W_i - \tanh\left(g^{fast} V_i\right) + I_i^{syn} + I_i^{el} + I_i^{in}(t)\right] \quad (1)$$

$$\tau_w(V_i) \frac{dW_i}{dt} = -\left[W_i - g^{slow} V_i\right] \quad (2)$$

In equations 1–2 g^{fast} determines the degree to which the instantaneous voltage-dependent current is N-shaped whereas g^{slow} models the voltage-dependent activation function of the slow current. Synaptic transmission is instantaneous, with a synaptic current given by

$$I_i^{syn} = \sum_{j=1}^{j=N} g^{syn} \sigma\left(\frac{V_j - \Theta^{syn}}{k^{syn}}\right)\left[V_j - E^{syn}\right] \quad (3)$$

where g^{syn} is the maximal synaptic conductance, V^i is the membrane potential of the the presynaptic cell j, E^{syn} is the synaptic reversal potential, Θ^{syn} represents the midpoint for synaptic activation and k^{syn} the steepness of the synaptic activation function. The function $\sigma(x)$ is defined as $\sigma(x)=1/(1+e^x)$.

Gap junction coupling is represented by

$$I_i^{el} = \sum_{j=1}^{j=N} g^{el}\left(V^j - V^i\right) \quad (4)$$

where g^{el} is electrical conductance. $I_i^{in}(t)$ is externally injected input current. τ_v and $\tau_{w(Vi)}$ are the membrane time constant and the time constant of slow current dynamics, the latter depending on the membrane potential V_i:

$$\tau_w(V_i) = \tau_2 + (\tau_1 - \tau_2)\sigma\left(\frac{V_i}{k^{tw}}\right) \quad (5)$$

with τ_1 and τ_2 specifying the minimum and maximum time constants and thereby determining the durations of the active and silent phases of the oscillator – and k^{tw} quantifying the rate of voltage dependence.

The complete model defined by equations 1–4 has, therefore, three time constants, two membrane and two junction conductances, synaptic threshold and reversal potentials and two rate constants (the k parameters). In principle, the junction parameters can vary per junction while the neuron parameters may vary per neuron; for tractability in the current work these parameters are identical for all junctions and neurons respectively, with the following values: $E^{syn}= -4, \Theta^{syn}=0, k^{syn}=0.02, g^{fast}=2, g^{slow}=2, \tau_1=5, \tau_2=50, k^{tw}=0.2, \tau_v=0.16$.

The parameters have been chosen to model neurons with relatively steep synaptic onset and short duty cycle (i.e. short fraction of the cycle when the cell is depolarised above threshold and may exert synaptic action). With this choice of parameters, equations 1–5 may be considered a model of spiking neurons. In the study presented here, the only parameters varied from the defaults are the conductances g^{el} and g^{syn} of the electrical and inhibitory synapses.

The model has been implemented as a set of Matlab functions which compute the quantities defined by the five equations above and integrate the set of ordinary differential equations using Matlab's standard ode45 solver with the default tolerance parameter settings. Note that the external timestep used (0.2 units) is long compared to the internal timesteps available to, and typically employed by, the ode45 integrator. The external input currents $I_i^{in}(t)$ are assumed to be piecewise constant, also over intervals long compared to the internal integration timestep. The implementation has been compared to an independent realisation using the xpp tool and found to give identical results.

Analysis Methods

The investigation of the oscillatory behaviours generated by networks of the type under study is time-consuming and has been automated. For a given choice of conductance parameters, the network dynamics are integrated from an initial state (see below). The first 30% of the simulation following the completion of any non-zero input signal is discarded to mitigate the effects of transients and the membrane potentials are computed at time points with an interval of 0.2 units. Given these values, an attempt (which may fails: typical causes of failure are chaotic network behaviour or very long period oscillation) is made to estimate a period of regular oscillation for the network by computing the positions of peaks in the autocorrelation of the signals and finding the highest common factor of inter-peak periods. If this calculation fails, the network is simulated further and the calculation repeated. If no period can be found with simulations up to 3000 units in duration, the signals are reported to be un-analysable. (The typical period of oscillation for the parameters used is 20–25 time units.) Once a period has been determined, the network signals are analysed. Samples for a single period are generated and the traces of the individual cells compared, to group cells into classes executing the same behaviour with possibly differing phases. In all cases reported here, cells execute the same behaviour, that is they all exhibit the same voltage trace to the resolution of the grouping test (measured normalised trace correlation exceeds 0.95) though their phases within that common trace may vary. Once the cell behaviours have been grouped, the classification of oscillatory modes is performed. The analysis distinguishes the behaviours illustrated inFigure 2.

For a given choice of parameters, the network exhibits a number of oscillatory behaviours. In this study, we vary the two principal conductance parametersg^{el}andg^{syn}, over the range in which interesting behaviours occur, for networks comprising 2, 4 and 6 cells. The reported results generated as follows. For each pair of parameter values investigated:

1. a set of 8 random initial states for the network are generated, using a zero mean Gaussian distribution with 0.025 standard deviation. Random current input of length 250 time units is then constructed using independent identically Gaussian distributed random values with zero mean and 0.005 standard deviation for each 0.2 time unit step. For each set of initial conditions the model is integrated with the input current for around 10 periods. After this, input is removed and the behaviour of the network that results is then analyzed and classified.
2. the model is integrated from a zero initial state, and the generation of IP behaviour is checked. If IP is generated, random input current as described above is applied to see whether the IP is stable in the presence of noise. The behaviour is then classified.
3. the model is integrated from the zero initial state as before, and if stable IP behaviour is generated an attempt is made to switch the network to AP: half the cells receive a 1 unit positive current injection and half a 1 unit negative current injection for 0.2 time units, applied in successive tests at each time point between phase Φ=0.4 and 0.6 in the cycle of oscillation. Again, random current inputs following the transient switching impulse are used to verify that the behaviour switched to is stable in the presence of noise. The behaviour is then classified.

The reported set of behaviours is the union of the results of the three steps above. This procedure, in our opinion, represents a reasonable compromise between computational effort and completeness of the results. Note, however, that it is not complete: the presence of any particular type of behaviour other than AP and IP is only detected if a suitable initial state is chosen (one that lies within the basin of attraction of that behaviour) and this, since only 8 initial states are generated at random, cannot be guaranteed.

Firing Rate Model Network

The mean field firing rate model of excitatory network activity with synaptic depression (formally equivalent to the relaxation oscillator model of a single cell described above) consists in the following equations (see[19]). $\tau_e e' = -e + f_e(wse - V)$ $\tau_s s' = -s + f_s(e)$Hereerepresents network firing rate and varies between 0 (no activity) and 1 (all cells fire at their maximal frequency),wrepresents network connectivity,sis the synaptic depression variable which indicates the fraction of synapses available andVis the average firing threshold in the population. The sigmoidal function$f_e(x)=1/(1+e^{-x/ka})$ represents the input-output function of the network. Here the effective input equal towse−Vdepends on activityebecause of recurrent excitation. Activity depresses synapses as indicated by sigmoidal function$f_{s(e)}=1/(1+e^{(e-\theta)/ka})$which decreases withe. Synaptic depression kinetics, determined by time constantτ_s, is assumed to be slow compared to the network recruitment time constantτ_e, so we are in a relaxation limit. The evolution of slow variablesproduces switches between low and high activity states, thus the firing rateeundergoes periodic changes.

We then consider a network consisting of two such oscillatory units which are interconnected by cross-inhibition and electrical coupling (network scheme,Fig. 9), described as follows:

$$\tau_e\, e_1' = -e_1 + f_e(ws_1e_1 - V - \beta(e_1+e_2)f_e(e_1+e_2-i\_tr) + g(e_2-e_1) + g_s e_1 + V_{app})$$

$$\tau_s\, s_1' = -s_1 + f_s(e_1)$$

$$\tau_e\, e_2' = -e_2 + f_e(ws_2e_2 - V - \beta(e_1+e_2)\; f_e(e_1+e_2-i\_tr) + g(e_1-e_2) + g_s e_2)$$

$$\tau_s\, s_2' = -s_2 + f_s(e_2)$$

Here the input resulting from cross-inhibition depends on a sume_1+e_2(since both excitatory units project to the same inhibitory population, on$f_e(e_1+e_2-i_tr)$which models a threshold-like activation of the inhibitory population with thresholdi_trand onβwhich represents the strength of cross-inhibitory connectivity. To model electrical coupling between oscillatory units we first notice that the average membrane potential of a cell belonging to a given population is proportional to its firing ratee. Indeed, if$d_s$is the duration and $a_s$is the voltage amplitude of a spike, whereas$d_{is}$and$a_{is}$are corresponding parameters characterized by inter-spike interval, then the mean voltage level⟨v⟩, averaged overNcycles expressed during timeT, is equal to$(N/T)(d_sa_s+d_{is}a_{is})$. Moreover, since$d_{is}=T/N-d_s$we obtain:$\langle v\rangle=(N/T)(d_s(a_s-a_{is})+T/N\,a_{is})$ and therefore$\langle v\rangle=(N/T)d_s(a_s-a_{is})+a_{is}$. Assuming$d_s$,$a_sanda_{is}$do not depend on the firing rate, we obtain⟨v⟩~e. Therefore the input resulting from electrical coupling between two different populations is equal to$g(e_2-e_1)$wheregrepresents connectivity strength and the average difference between the spike amplitude and inter-spike voltage level. Recurrent electrical input is described byg_se, where$g_s$represents the strength of recurrent connectivity.V_{app} represents a brief input.

REFERENCES

1. Llinas RR. The intrinsic electrophysiological properties of mammalian neurons: insights into central nervous system function.Science.1988;242:1654–1664.
2. Meyrand P, Simmers J, Moulins M. Construction of a pattern-generating circuit with neurons of different

networks.Nature.1991;351:60–63.

3. Marder E, Bucher D. Understanding circuit dynamics using the stomatogastric nervous system of lobsters and crabs.Annu Rev Physiol.2007;69:291–316.
4. Kristan WB, Jr, Calabrese RL, Friesen WO. Neuronal control of leech behavior.Prog Neurobiol.2005;76:279–327.
5. Hultborn H, Brownstone RB, Toth TI, Gossard JP. Key mechanisms for setting the input-output gain across the motoneuron pool.Prog Brain Res.2004;143:77–95.
6. Goldman-Rakic PS. Cellular basis of working memory. Neuron.1995;14:477–485.
7. Camperi M, Wang XJ. A model of visuospatial working memory in prefrontal cortex: recurrent network and cellular bistability.J Comput Neurosci.1998;5:383–405.
8. Zhang K. Representation of spatial orientation by the intrinsic dynamics of the head-direction cell ensemble: a theory.J Neurosci.1996;16:2112–2126.
9. Amit DJ, Brunel N. Model of global spontaneous activity and local structured activity during delay periods in the cerebral cortex.Cereb Cortex.1997;7:237–252.
10. RenartA, SongP, WangXJ. Robustspatialworkingmemory through homeostatic synaptic scaling in heterogeneous cortical networks.Neuron.2003;38:473–485.
11. Goldman MS, Levine JH, Major G, Tank DW, Seung HS. Robust persistent neural activity in a model integrator with multiple hysteretic dendrites per neuron.Cereb Cortex.2003;13:1185–1195.
12. Durstewitz D, Seamans JK. Beyond bistability: biophysics and temporal dynamics of working memory. Neuroscience.2006;139:119–133.
13. Van Vreeswijk C, Abbott LF, Ermentrout GB. When inhibition not excitation synchronizes neural firing.J Comput Neurosci.1994;1:313–321.
14. Lewis TJ, Rinzel J. Dynamics of spiking neurons connected by both inhibitory and electrical coupling.J Comput Neurosci.2003;14:283–309.
15. Bem T, Le Feuvre Y, Rinzel J, Meyrand P. Electrical coupling induces bistability of rhythms in networks of inhibitory spiking neurons.Eur J Neurosci.2005;22:2661–2668.
16. Bem T, Rinzel J. Short duty cycle destabilizes a half-center oscillator, but gap junctions can restabilize the anti-phase pattern.J Neurophysiol.2004;91:693–703.
17. Merriam EB, Netoff TI, Banks MI. Bistable network behavior of layer I interneurons in auditory cortex.J Neurosci.2005;25:6175–6186.
18. Rowat PF, Selverston AI. Modeling the gastric mill central pattern generator of the lobster with a relaxation-oscillator network.J Neurophysiol.1993;70:1030–1053.
19. Tabak J, O'Donovan MJ, Rinzel J. Differential control of active and silent phases in relaxation models of neuronal rhythms.J Comput Neurosci.2006;21:307–328.
20. Wilson HR. Computational evidence for a rivalry hierarchy in vision.Proc Natl Acad Sci U S A.2003;100:14499–14503.
21. Shpiro A, Curtu R, Rinzel J, Rubin N. Dynamical characteristics common to neuronal competition models.J Neurophysiol.2007;97:462–473.
22. Moreno-Bote R, Rinzel J, Rubin N. Noise-induced alternations in an attractor network model of perceptual bistability.J Neurophysiol.2007;98:1125–1139.
23. Wong KF, Wang XJ. A recurrent network mechanism of time integration in perceptual decisions.J Neurosci.2006;26:1314–1328.
24. Rossignol S, Dubuc R, Gossard JP. Dynamic sensorimotor interactions in locomotion.Physiol Rev.2006;86:89–154.
25. AramakiY, HondaM, OkadaT, SadatoN. Neuralcorrelates of the spontaneous phase transition during bimanual coordination.Cereb Cortex.2006;16:1338–1348.
26. Kelso JA. Phase transitions and critical behavior in human bimanual coordination.Am J Physiol.1984;246:R1000–1004.
27. Haken H, Kelso JA, Bunz H. A theoretical model of phase transitions in human hand movements.Biol Cybern.1985;51:347–356.
28. Jirsa VK, Fuchs A, Kelso JA. Connecting cortical and behavioral dynamics: bimanual coordination.Neural Comput.1998;10:2019–2045.
29. Schoner G, Kelso JA. Dynamic pattern generation in behavioral and neural systems. Science.1988;239:1513–1520.
30. Meyer-Lindenberg A, Ziemann U, Hajak G, Cohen L, Berman KF. Transitions between dynamical states of differing stability in the human brain.Proc Natl Acad Sci U S A.2002;99:10948–10953.
31. Golubitsky M, Stewart I, Buono PL, Collins JJ. Symmetry in locomotor central pattern generators and animal gaits.Nature.1999;401:693–695.
32. Grillner S, Deliagina T, Ekeberg O, el Manira A, Hill RH, et al. Neural networks that co-ordinate locomotion and body orientation in lamprey.Trends in Neurosciences.1995;18:270–279.
33. Tresch MC, Kiehn O. Motor coordination without action potentials in the mammalian spinal cord.Nat Neurosci.2000;3:593–599.

CHAPTER 10

CLUSTER ANALYSIS OF WEIGHTED BIPARTITE NETWORKS: A NEW COPULA-BASED APPROACH

Alessandro Chessa, Irene Crimaldi, Massimo Riccaboni and Luca Trapin

IMT Institute for Advanced Studies, Lucca, Italy

ABSTRACT

In this work we are interested in identifying clusters of "positional equivalent" actors, i.e. actors who play a similar role in a system. In particular, we analyze weighted bipartite networks that describes the relationships between actors on one side and features or traits on the other, together with the intensity level to which actors show their features. We develop a methodological approach that takes into account the underlying multivariate dependence among groups of actors. The idea is that positions in a network could be defined on the basis of the similar intensity levels that the actors exhibit in expressing some features, instead of just considering relationships that actors hold with each others. Moreover, we propose a new clustering procedure that exploits the potentiality of copula functions, a mathematical instrument for the modelization of the stochastic dependence structure. Our clustering algorithm can be applied both to binary and realvalued matrices. We validate it with simulations and applications to real-world data.

INTRODUCTION

In the last few years, network theory has attracted the interest of a widespread audience as a powerful tool to model and analyse complex relationship structures. In particular, the identification of network communities, known as cluster analysis, plays a central role and it represents an active field of research (e.g. [1], [2], [3] and [4]). *Community detection* allows us to extract sub-networks which exhibit different properties from the aggregate properties of the whole network and also to investigate information on groups of nodes with similar characteristics which are more likely to be connected to each other. Communities are usually defined as subsets of actors (nodes) that are densely connected, i.e., they are more connected among themselves than to the rest of the network. However, in many network applications, there is a meaningful group structure which does not coincide with the partition into dense communities: indeed, the groups may be characterized by similar patterns of interactions with other groups [5]. Within this context, *positional analysis* is particularly interesting since it deals with the identification of actors who occupy an equivalent position inside a system, i.e. play a similar role in the considered organization. Differently to the standard community detection where the clusters are represented by densely connected groups of actors, positional analysis aims at studying relational data in order to cluster

Citation: Chessa A, Crimaldi I, Riccaboni M, Trapin L. Cluster Analysis of Weighted Bipartite Networks: A New Copula-Based Approach. Tsoka S, ed. PLoS ONE. 2014;9(10):e109507. doi:10.1371/journal.pone.0109507.

the actors into some classes such that the elements of the same class occupy equivalent positions in the system. In order to illustrate the distinction between positional analysis and standard community detection, let us consider the following example of the e-mails sent among the employees of a company: it may be that we are able to identify different communities of individuals among which e-mails are more frequently exchanged. However, densely connected employees may occupy different positions in the organization and we need to run a positional analysis if we are interested in identifying groups of actors with equivalent positions.

In this work we aim at identifying clusters of "positional equivalent" actors in cases where the available data are the relationships defined among actors on one side and some features on the other one [6], [7], [8], instead of interpersonal relationships. Basically, the idea is that positions in a network structure can be defined according to the characteristics or behaviours that the actors exhibit, instead of the relationships that actors hold with other actors. Individual to attribute relations can be represented as a *weighted bipartite network* where the edge-weights represent the level to which actors show a particular feature. More precisely, a network is bipartite if its nodes can be divided into two sets in such a way that every edge connects a node in one set to a node in the other one [9]. Bipartite networks are thus very useful for representing data in which the elements under scrutiny belong to two categories (typically referred to as actors, or agents, and features, respectively), and we want to understand how the elements in one category are associated with those in the other one. Notable examples that have been analyzed include networks of company directors and the board of directors on which they sit [10], [11], scientific collaboration networks [12], [13], [4], networks of documents and words [14], as well as network of genes and genetic sequences [15]. Models generating bipartite networks can be found also in statistical mechanics (e.g. [16] and [17]).

The widespread approach to partition bipartite networks consists of applying standard community detection algorithms, such as the Girvan-Newman modularity [3], to the one-mode projection of the original network. Consider two types of nodes, say *a* and *b*, in a one-mode projection of the bipartite network, nodes of the same type, say *a*, are connected to each other if they share a common node of the other type, say *b*. For instance, in the CEO network, two CEOs are connected if they both sit in the same board. Although the one-mode projection procedure can give some insights on the topological properties of the network, at the same time it can imply the lost of relevant information. In fact, different bipartite networks may reduce to the same one-mode projection, and thus a clustering based on the latter may produce unreliable or incorrect results, as shown in [18] and [19]. Regardless of those critiques, in [20] the authors argue that under some circumstances, using multiple projections, the information extracted with this procedure is sound, and therefore the simplicity of this approach can be still exploited. However, several authors tried to solve this problem by defining measures and algorithms that could be directly applied to the original matrix associated to the bipartite network.

In the physics community, two different definitions of bipartite modularity have been proposed,[21], [22]. Both concepts extend the Girvan-Newman modularity, but pose different assumptions on the null model taken as the benchmark in the metric used for the module identification. They return good results compared to the one-mode projection, but their applicability is restricted to the case of binary bipartite networks.

Some applications of bipartite networks refer to affiliation networks [23], which capture social relationships, such as membership or event participation. Positional analysis is well established in social network literature, where the usual approach consists of applying the standard measures of structural or regular equivalence, and the related algorithms, to the one mode-projection of the affiliation network [24]. However, affiliation networks represent only a very special case of bipartite networks since the associated matrices are binary.

Other proposed methods for bipartite network clustering, that are mostly used by sociologists, are based on blockmodeling (e.g. [25], [26], [27] and [28]). The key idea of this approach is that the rows and the columns of the matrix associated to the bipartite network can be partitioned simultaneously by means of a criterion function, which measures the inconsistencies of the empirical blocks with the ideal ones. Therefore, blockmodeling works directly on the matrix by trying to permute rows and columns in order to fit, as closely as possible, idealized pictures. The differences between the various types of blockmodeling techniques concern the definition of the ideal blocks and the criterion functions. Blockmodeling is mostly applied to binary data, but it can also be exploited for weighted matrices (valued blockmodeling and homogeneity blockmodeling [28]). However, with the valued blockmodeling, information about the values above a pre-specified parameter is lost and a problem is to determine appropriately the value of this parameter. The homogeneity blockmodeling does not require any additional parameters to be set in advance and it uses all available information, but its main disadvantage is that it can consider only a few possible ideal blocks.

In [29], the authors proposed a bipartite stochastic block model where a parametric probabilistic structure is given, and the clusters are identified by solving the inference problem of finding the parameters that best fit the observed network. In particular, they model the generating process of the number of edges between two nodes of different types with a Poisson distribution with a certain intensity parameter. The authors show that their method outperforms the one-mode projection approach. Nevertheless, it does not deal with the case when we have weights on the edges. In [30], the authors try to go in this direction by proposing a stochastic block model for edge-weighted networks, but their method requires to choose the number of clusters (as in most stochastic block models).

The algorithm we propose realizes a partition of "positional equivalent" actors based on the entire information enclosed in the weighted bipartite network that describes their characteristics or behaviours. The main contribution of our work is twofold. First, we develop a methodological approach according to which actors are grouped with respect to their intrinsic multivariate stochastic dependence structure. In this framework, not only the magnitude of a single weight matters but the whole pattern of the values the actors show along all the features is relevant for the classification. Second, we propose a new clustering procedure that exploits the potentiality of copula functions, a mathematical instrument for the modelization of the multivariate stochastic dependence structure. In particular, copulas allow us to group actors according to their underlying dependence structure, without any assumption on their one-dimensional marginal distributions, and to take into account various kinds of stochastic dependence structures among actors. Moreover, there is no need to predefine the target number of clusters.

The paper is structured as follows. In Sections 1 and 2, we describe our approach, together with the mathematical tool we employ, and we illustrate an algorithm whose output is the exact solution of the optimization problem resulted by our clustering procedure. In Sections 3 and 4 we show the performance of our clustering algorithm applying it to simulated and real data. Finally, in Section 5 we conclude with a discussion on the potentiality of our method and give some heuristics that can be exploited to develop new versions of the algorithm that return "approximate" solutions but are computationally faster.

A COPULA-BASED APPROACH

As explained in the previous section, we consider the general setting where we have an $N\times M$real-valued matrix, that collects the information on the connections that go from a set of Nactors to a set of M items, representing some features or behaviours. The elements of such a matrix can be any real numbers, with zero representing the absence of a relationship and a non-zero value representing the presence of a relationships, together with its intensity. As an example, this framework can be used to analyse situations where we have actors on one side and personal qualities or interests on the other side, and the weighted-edges between the two sets can be used to represents the level to which an individual shows a certain quality or interest. Another example may be a set of individuals in a supermarket and the set of products they buy. In this case, an edge represent whether an individual bought a particular product or not, and its value gives the amount of product bought or its cost.

Against this background, we want to emphasize that actors may be classified into positions based on their patterns of characteristics, interests or behaviours that they exhibit and on the intensity wherewith the actors show them, instead of the kind of relationships that they keep with other actors. In other words, we move in the direction that the dependence (we mean positive dependence, i.e. similarity) in the expression levels of the considered features is related to the position that the actors occupy in the system. Hence, we say that some actors are *positional equivalent* if they show a significant dependence structure that join them. In this framework, the use of the traditional one-mode projection methods would be meaningless and misleading and also blockmodeling or modularity approaches adapted to bipartite networks could not give a clear answer to the problem because they are not well tailor made for the analysis of weighted bipartite networks.

Our purpose is to identify clusters of actors by means of the detection, from the original matrix, of some statistically significant dependencies among groups of actors. Basically, our assumption is that actors within a system have an underlying multivariate stochastic dependence structure which generates the data. In order to identify this intrinsic dependence structure, we propose to exploit the mathematical copula theory.

The concept of copula was introduced during the forties and the fifties with Hoeffding [31] and Sklar [32], but the evidence of a growing interest in this kind of functions in statistics started only in the nineties [33]. Copulas are functions that join or "couple" multivariate distribution functions to their one-dimensional marginal distributions. More precisely, we have the following definition and results.

Definition 1. *A d-dimensional copula* $C(\mathbf{u})=C(u_1,\ldots,u_d)$ *is a function defined on* $[0, 1]^{d}$ with values in $[0, 1]$, *which satisfies the following three properties:*

1. $C(1,\ldots,1,u_i,1,\ldots,1)=u_i$ *for every* $i\in\{1,\ldots,d\}$ *and* $u_i\in[0,1]$;

2. if $u_i=0$ *for at least one i, then* $C(u_1,\ldots,u_d)=0$;

3. for every $(a_1,\ldots,a_d),(b_1,\ldots,b_d)\in[0,1]^d$ *with* $a_i\le b_i$ *for all i*, $\sum_{j_1=1}^{2}\cdots\sum_{j_d=1}^{2}(-1)^{j_1+\cdots+j_d}C(u_{1,j_1},\ldots,u_{d,j_d})\ge 0$ *where, for each i,* $u_{i,1}=a_i$ and $u_{i,2}=b_i$.

The advantage of the copula functions and the reason why they are used in the dependence modeling is related to the Sklar's theorem [32]. It essentially states that every multivariate cumulative distribution function can be rewritten in terms of the margins, i.e. the marginal cumulative distribution functions, and a copula.

Theorem 1. *Let F be a multivariate cumulative distribution function with margins* $F_1,\ldots,F_d$.*Then there exists a copula* $C:[0,1]^d\to[0,1]$ *such that, for every* $x_1,\ldots,x_d\in\overline{\mathbb{R}}=[-\infty,+\infty]$ *, we have*

$$F(x_1,\ldots,x_d)=C(F_1(x_1),\ldots,F_d(x_d)) \tag{1}$$

If the margins $F_1,\ldots,F_d$ *are all continuous, then C is unique; otherwise C is uniquely determined on* $F_1(\overline{\mathbb{R}})\times\cdots\times F_d(\overline{\mathbb{R}})$.

Conversely, if C is a copula and $F_1,\ldots,Fd$ *are cumulative distribution functions, then F defined by (1) is a multivariate cumulative distribution function with margins* $F_1,\ldots,F_d$.

In the case when f and $f_1,\ldots,f_d$ are the marginal probability density functions associated to $F$and $F_1,\ldots,F_d$, respectively, the copula density c satisfies $f(x_1,\ldots,x_d)=c(F_1(x_1),\ldots,F_d(x_d))\prod_{i=1}^{d}f_i(x_i)$.

There are different families of copula functions that capture different aspects of the dependence structure: positive and negative dependence, symmetry, heaviness of tail dependence and so on. In our work, we limit ourselves to the principal copula functions of the Archimedean family (namely, Gumbel, Clayton and Frank copulas, see Text S1 for their definitions), which model, through a unique parameter , situations with different degrees of dependence. Nonetheless, it is worth to note that the application of our methodology is not restricted to those copula functions. For more details on copula theory, we refer to the various excellent monographs existing in literature, such as [34], [33] and [35].

METHODOLOGY

In this section we present a copula-based technique that realizes a partition of actors into clusters so that the actors belonging to the same cluster show a significant dependence structure that allows us to classify them as being "positional equivalent". Our approach is inspired by the work of Di Lascio and Giannerini [36], which introduced and studied a copula-based clustering algorithm, called CoClust, in the framework of microarray data in genetics. As they did, we use copula functions in order to model the multivariate stochastic dependence structure among groups of actors and we apply the maximized log-likelihood function criterion for the detection of the different clusters. Notwithstanding, our algorithm presents the following important differences with respect to the one proposed by Di Lascio and Giannerini:

- while they assume independence within clusters and dependence between clusters, we look for clusters of dependent actors;
- while they first find the optimal number K of clusters and then perform sequential extractions of K actors, where at each time one actor is added to each cluster in a certain way, we do not use a sequential extraction method but we directly look for the optimal partition of the actors into clusters;
- differently from them, we allow clusters to be of different sizes and we allocate all the actors into the clusters;
- whereas they assume identity in distribution for actors inside a certain cluster, i.e. each cluster identifies one margin, we do not make this assumption and we estimate for each actor his own cumulative distribution function.

Given N actors and M items, we can represent the data that describe the relationships between actors and items with a real-valued matrix X of dimension $N \times M$,

$$X = \begin{bmatrix} x_{11} & \cdots & x_{1m} & \cdots & x_{1M} \\ \vdots & \ddots & \vdots & \ddots & \vdots \\ x_{i1} & \cdots & x_{im} & \cdots & x_{iM} \\ \vdots & \ddots & \vdots & \ddots & \vdots \\ x_{N1} & \cdots & x_{Nm} & \cdots & x_{NM} \end{bmatrix} = \begin{bmatrix} x_{1\cdot} \\ \vdots \\ x_{i\cdot} \\ \vdots \\ x_{N\cdot} \end{bmatrix}$$

where x_{im} represents the value of the item m for the actor i and $x_{i\cdot}$ is the row-vector that contains all the item values of the actor i. With the language of network theory, this matrix can be seen as the matrix associated to a weighted bipartite network.

The procedure we propose takes as input this matrix and returns the optimal decomposition into clusters after the following four steps:

1. It derives the margin for each actor i by finding the empirical cumulative distribution function

$$\hat{F}_i(x) = \frac{1}{M}\sum_{m=1}^{M} I_{\{x_{im} \leq x\}}$$

based on the corresponding M-dimensional row $x_{i\cdot}$ of the items. For each actor i, we are taking the values $x_{i1}, \ldots, x_{iM}$ of the M items as i.i.d. realizations drawn from the same univariate distribution.

2. It considers each possible cluster $\mathcal{C}$ of actors, with $card(\mathcal{C}) \geq 2$, and it computes the maximum value of the copula log-likelihood associated to it. Formally, for each possible group, say $\mathcal{C} = \{i_1, \ldots, i_k\}$, with $2 \leq k \leq N$, of actors, it maximizes the copula log-likelihood function $\theta \mapsto \ell_{\mathcal{C}}(\theta) = \sum_{m=1}^{M} \ln c\left(\hat{F}_{i_1}(x_{i_1 m}), \ldots, \hat{F}_{i_k}(x_{i_k m}); \theta\right)$, defined as where $c(u_1, \ldots, u_k; \theta)$ denotes the parametric expression of the density for the chosen copula, and it records the value $\ell^*(\mathcal{C})$ such that $\ell^*(\mathcal{C}) = \max_{\theta \in \Theta} \ell_{\mathcal{C}}(\theta)$

Note that we are taking the vectors $\{(x_{i_1 m}, \ldots, x_{i_k m}) : m = 1, \ldots, M\}$ as M i.i.d. realizations drawn from the same k-variate distribution.

3. It considers the set $\mathcal{P}$ of all possible partitions of the N actors that do not contain clusters with a single actor. Hence, each $\pi \in \mathcal{P}$ is formed by a certain number of clusters $\mathcal{C}$ with $card(\mathcal{C}) \geq 2$. The set $\mathcal{P}$ represents the set of all possible decompositions into clusters that the procedure can return. For example, if we have 4 actors, numbered from 1 to 4, the set $\mathcal{P}$ is formed by the following partitions: $\pi_1 = \{\mathcal{C}_{1,1} = \{1,2\}, \mathcal{C}_{1,2} = \{3,4\}\}$, $\pi_2 = \{\mathcal{C}_{2,1} = \{1,3\}, \mathcal{C}_{2,2} = \{2,4\}\}$, $\pi_3 = \{\mathcal{C}_{3,1} = \{1,4\}, \mathcal{C}_{3,2} = \{2,3\}\}$ and $\pi_4 = \{\mathcal{C}_{4,1} = \{1,2,3,4\}\}$. For each $\pi \in \mathcal{P}$, it computes the value of the "global log-likelihood" of the partition ϖ as $\mathcal{L}(\pi) = \sum_{\mathcal{C} \in \pi} \ell^*(\mathcal{C})$.
4. Finally, the procedure returns ϖ^* with the highest "global log-likelihood" value among all $\pi \in \mathcal{P}$, that is $\pi^* \in \mathcal{P}$ such that $\mathcal{L}(\pi^*) = \max_{\pi \in \mathcal{P}} \mathcal{L}(\pi)$.

More precisely, it returns the clusters that form ϖ^* in a decreasing order with respect to the value $\ell^*(\mathcal{C})$ of each cluster $\mathcal{C}$ in ϖ^*.

The R code for this procedure is available at http://dx.doi.org/10.6084/m9.figshare.1162514.

Simulation Experiments

In order to verify the accuracy of the proposed algorithm, we conducted some simulation experiments by generating random weighted bipartite networks (i.e. their corresponding matrices X) by means of copula functions in order to create a clustering structure. In practice, when simulating from a copula of dimension d, we obtain d vectors $x_{i_1\cdot}, \ldots, x_{i_d\cdot}$ of M values that correspond to d rows of the matrix X associated to d actors forming a specific cluster.

An experiment foresees the generation of 50 random weighted bipartite networks of N=10 actors belonging to 3 different clusters. Table 1 reports the 9 scenarios under which we generated these networks. We repeated the simulations of these different scenarios for M=20, 50, 100, 250, thus developing a total of 36 experiments. These experiments were built with the purpose of pointing out different features of the algorithm: first, its performance under different number of items (this is the reason why we used several values of M); second, its ability to work with both continuous and discrete data (that explains the choice of the marginal distributions); third, its ability to detect clusters under similar dependence structures (hence we used the same copula type to generate different clusters).

Table 1: Description of the scenarios used in the simulation experiment

S	First cluster	Second cluster	Third cluster
1	$d=3$, Gu, N(0,1), $\theta=4$	$d=4$, Gu, N(0,1), $\theta=3$	$d=3$, Gu, N(0,1), $\theta=4$
2	$d=3$, Cl, N(0,1), $\theta=4$	$d=4$, Cl, N(0,1), $\theta=3$	$d=3$, Cl, N(0,1), $\theta=4$
3	$d=3$, Fr, N(0,1), $\theta=4$	$d=4$, Fr, N(0,1), $\theta=3$	$d=3$, Fr, N(0,1), $\theta=4$
4	$d=3$, Gu, Po(4), $\theta=4$	$d=4$, Gu, Po(4), $\theta=3$	$d=3$, Gu, Po(4), $\theta=4$
5	$d=3$, Cl, Po(4), $\theta=4$	$d=4$, Cl, Po(4), $\theta=3$	$d=3$, Cl, Po(4), $\theta=4$
6	$d=3$, Fr, Po(4), $\theta=4$	$d=4$, Fr, Po(4), $\theta=3$	$d=3$, Fr, Po(4), $\theta=4$
7	$d=3$, Gu, Pa(1,2), $\theta=4$	$d=4$, Gu, Exp(0.5), $\theta=3$	$d=3$, Gu, LogN(0,1), $\theta=4$
8	$d=3$, Cl, Pa(1,2), $\theta=4$	$d=4$, Cl, Exp(0.5), $\theta=3$	$d=3$, Cl, LogN(0,1), $\theta=4$
9	$d=3$, Fr, Pa(1,2), $\theta=4$	$d=4$, Fr, Exp(0.5), $\theta=3$	$d=3$, Fr, LogN(0,1), $\theta=4$

For each scenario (S) and each cluster, we report the number of actors in the cluster (d), the copula type (Gumbel (Gu), Clayton (Cl), Frank (Fr)), the margins (Normal (N), Poisson (Po), Pareto (Pa), Exponential (Exp), LogNormal (LogN)) and the dependence parameter θ, used to generate the data.

doi:10.1371/journal.pone.0109507.t001

As to the copula function employed in the clustering procedure, we first run the algorithm with the same copula used to generate the random network. After that, to test the performance of the algorithm under "misspecification", we generate again the first three scenarios for all the chosen values of M and run the algorithm with the two Archimedean copulas different from the one used in the simulation. For each of the described experiments, we checked the performance of the algorithm by counting the number of times it correctly recognizes the true clusters over the number of random networks generated. Summarizing the results, we observed that the choice of the copula in the algorithm has no great effect on its performance and the overall results seem quite good, especially in the case when M=100 or M=250. Some main remarks can be made:

- First of all, under all the possible scenarios, for M=100 or M=250, we always got a 100% percentage of successes in recognizing the clusters correctly.
- Second, when the observations are drawn from the Gumbel and the Clayton copulas, we got a percentage of successes equal to 100% already for M=50 and between 80% and 100% for M=20.
- Finally, when the observations are drawn from the Frank copula, we notice some problems for M=20. Indeed, for this copula type, 20 realizations are too few to generate an evident dependence structure and so the algorithm does not work well in recognized it. However, we observed a fast improvement for M getting larger and, starting from M=50, we can say that the percentage of successes are good (75–80%).

EMPIRICAL RESULTS

In this section, we describe two applications of our algorithm to real datasets. The first one deals with a benchmark real-valued bipartite network that we built on our own to test the algorithm. The second one refers to a widely studied social network that is described by a signed network.

Trade Data

The first application we show is based on the BACI-COMTRADE dataset, featuring the amounts of import-export trades among several countries in the world. We extracted a*weighted bipartite network* taking the export dollar values for the M=97 product categories of the HS2 classification, for selected N=12 countries, in the year 2011. More in details, we decided to select the countries according to their economies, in order to identify 3 hypothetical categories:

- a *First world* category composed by France, Germany, Canada and United states;
- a *Third world* category represented by Burundi, Zimbabwe, Liberia and Somalia;
- an *OPEC representative* category made by Kuwait, Saudi Arabia, Qatar and Iran.

We applied our procedure to the matrix, where the countries were in rows, the products in columns, and each cell contained the gross export value of a given country for a given product. Our aim was to create clusters of countries which are similar (i.e. positional equivalent in the International Trade Network) with respect to the products they export. Much of the literature that focuses on international trade looks for community detection, that is for communities of countries with a high number of connections among them, while being relatively less interconnected with countries outside the community they are part of [37], [38],[39], [40], [41]. Differently from the classical clustering analysis in international trade, we tried to define "positional equivalent" countries based on the products they trade and not on the basis of the countries wherewith they trade. Indeed, we were not interested in finding dense communities of countries for different commodities, but we wanted to identify countries that cover the same position in the trade network since they present a similarity in their exports. The result we obtained is reported in Table 2, together with the results provided by two other clustering methods:

Table 2: Trade data

Our approach			Modularity		K-means		
France	Iran	Burundi	Canada	France	Germany	Burundi	Sau. Ara.
Germany	Kuwait	Somalia	Liberia	USA	USA	France	
USA	Sau. Ara.	Zimbabwe	Sau. Ara.	Zimbabwe		Iran	
Canada	Qatar	Liberia	Iran	Germany		Kuwait	
			Kuwait	Somalia		Somalia	
			Qatar	Burundi		Zimbabwe	
						Qatar	
						Canada	
						Liberia	

doi:10.1371/journal.pone.0109507.t002

- *(Modularity optimization)* We derived a unipartite projection of the original weighted bipartite network using a cosine similarity measure between couples of countries and then we applied the modularity optimization approach with the well-known Louvain method [42].
- (*K-means*) with the number of clusters K chosen *a priori* equal to 3, see [43]. We use the K-means function of the stats R-package.

As we can see, our algorithm is able to perfectly recognize the above mentioned country groups; while the other two methods provide a different grouping. Since the hypothetical three groups were built according to a subjective judgement, we decided to analyze the data in order to provide a more robust explanation for the clusters we found. An overview of the differences between the three groups is provided by Figure 1, where we report for each country a coloured bar with the export shares for each of the 97 HS2 product categories over the total amount of export. In more detail, in Table 3 we report for each country, the percentage on the total amount of export for a selection of 21 HS2 categories out of the 97 available, in order to give some hints on the trade joint patterns that our algorithm recognize. Overall, we can agree on the fact that the result is coherent with the observed data. Regarding the *First world* category, we can see that at least a small amount of their total exports is allocated in each selected categories and about the 60% of their total export is concentrated in the nine categories, corresponding to the following commodities: **84** - Nuclear reactors, Boilers, Machinery and mechanicals appliances; **87** - Vehicles; **88** - Aircraft and Spacecraft; **85** - Electrical machinery, Telecommunications equipment, Sound and Television recorders; **30** - Pharmaceutical products; **90** - Optical, Photographic, Cinematographic, Measuring, Checking, Precision, Medical instruments. Conversely, for the *OPEC Representative* group, it is clear that the nature of the dependence arises from the fact that more than the 90% of the total export of these countries belongs to the following three categories: **27** - Mineral, Fuels, Oils; **29** - Organic chemicals; **39** - Plastic and Articles thereof. Nonetheless, we underline that our algorithm did not recognize this cluster just because of the large share of export these countries have in these few products, but it captured the whole dependence between these countries and so also the categories in which they do not trade, or trade a little, play an important role. This is clear by looking at the network structure for the *Third world* category in the last four columns of Table 3. As it can be seen, all these countries present a huge amount of the total export in a few specific commodities. For example, more than the 80% of the somalian export is in category **1** - Live animals, while the 78% of the burundian export is in category **9** - Coffee, Tea, Mate and Spices. Thus, we can affirm that these countries present a highly specific production and the dependence among them arise not as a consequence of the products in which they trade but rather from the products in which they do not trade. By looking carefully at Table 3, it is possible to notice that for most of the selected 21 HS2 categories, the share of export is almost zero in all these *Third World* countries. In this sense, they are similar to the *OPEC representative* countries but, as we already said, the latter present a specific dependence deriving from the common commodities they trade. Finally, *Canada*de serves some comments. It has an high value in category **27** as the countries in the *Opec representative* category, but its values for the other categories are more similar to those of the *First world* than the ones of the *Opec representative* group. Our algorithm is able to capture this aspect. An insight of all these distinguishing features between the clusters can also be grasped looking at Figure 2, where we depict the bipartite trade network between the countries and 15 macro-categories of the HS2 products classification.

Figure 1: Trade share plot.

In this figure we report for each country, classified in the relative cluster, a coloured bar representing the share of export for each of the 97 HS2 product categories over the total amount of export. Regarding *Cluster 1*, the high number of colours into the bar makes it clear that these countries use to trade in several product categories. Furthermore, an explicit dependence pattern arise from the proportion of the colours into the bars. In particular, the following product categories contributes to this strong relationship: **84, 87,88, 85, 30, 90**. Regarding *Cluster 2*, the dependence relationship mainly arises from these three categories: **27, 29, 39**. However, it is important to remark that our clustering approach takes in consideration also the fact that these countries trade in a very small number of products, as can be seen from the few colours in the respective bars. The same reasoning apply for *Cluster 3* where, although the countries are specialized in a unique product such as category **9** for Burundi or category **1** for Somalia, the common pattern that makes them similar is the fact that they do not trade in most of the 97 HS2 categories.

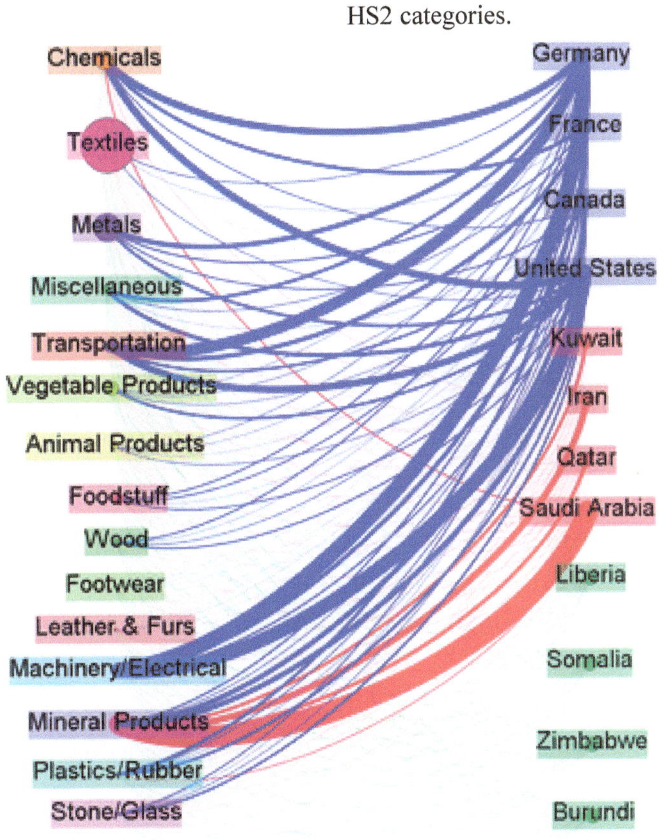

Figure 2: Trade network structure.

In this figure we show the weighted bipartite Trade network. On the right the three groups of countries, detected by our algorithm, and on the left the 97 products categories, grouped in 15 homogeneus macro categories in order to highlight the relevant connections among the two different type of nodes. The size of the macro categories are in proportion to the number of categories grouped in them. It is clear from the links partition how our metodology is able to disentangle different country categories according to the trade patterns, even for the third world countries (green background) for which the link weights are much smaller than the others.

Table 3: Selected sample of 21 HS2 products traded by each country

HS2	Countries											
	France	Germany	U.S.A	Canada	Iran	Kuwait	Saudi Arabia	Qatar	Somalia	Zimbabwe	Liberia	Burundi
84	11.14	17.83	15.20	7.05	0.41	0.09	0.29	0.11	0.04	0.57	0.54	0.86
87	9.74	17.86	8.22	12.07	0.21	0.06	0.17	0.01	0.00	0.15	0.06	0.69
88	8.86	2.41	3.63	2.34	0.02	0.04	0.08	0.00	0.00	0.12	0.00	0.00
85	7.60	9.85	10.38	3.34	0.22	0.05	0.21	0.03	0.02	0.36	2.27	0.21
30	6.06	4.62	4.01	1.44	0.10	0.03	0.05	0.01	0.00	0.13	0.04	0.02
90	2.97	4.34	5.96	1.29	0.05	0.01	0.03	0.01	0.00	0.02	0.04	0.10
27	4.64	3.08	9.02	26.22	85.69	93.33	87.79	92.33	0.00	1.87	17.29	0.00
39	3.70	4.84	4.36	2.82	2.02	1.19	3.84	2.09	0.52	0.20	0.09	0.03
29	2.65	2.47	3.38	1.32	2.53	3.38	4.19	1.50	0.00	0.02	0.10	0.00
31	0.09	0.27	0.39	1.96	0.50	0.43	0.45	1.03	0.00	0.21	0.00	0.00
1	0.43	0.12	0.08	0.33	0.03	0.01	0.03	0.01	80.23	0.04	0.00	0.05
9	0.06	0.19	0.07	0.11	0.14	0.00	0.01	0.00	0.00	0.58	0.15	78.11
71	1.38	1.56	3.68	5.31	0.34	0.03	0.20	0.15	0.01	19.09	2.10	0.29
40	1.66	1.31	1.14	0.93	0.05	0.09	0.01	0.00	0.00	0.23	46.07	0.04
97	0.45	0.07	0.36	0.05	0.01	0.00	0.00	0.02	0.00	0.11	0.07	0.00
96	0.24	0.17	0.10	0.02	0.01	0.00	0.00	0.00	0.00	0.03	0.00	0.02
95	0.26	0.39	0.34	0.23	0.00	0.00	0.00	0.00	0.00	0.03	0.00	0.00
93	0.07	0.06	0.22	0.05	0.00	0.00	0.00	0.00	0.00	0.00	0.20	0.00
92	0.04	0.05	0.05	0.02	0.00	0.00	0.00	0.00	0.00	0.00	0.00	0.02
91	0.28	0.11	0.06	0.01	0.00	0.01	0.00	0.02	0.00	0.00	0.22	0.00
86	0.20	0.36	0.23	0.10	0.00	0.00	0.00	0.00	0.00	0.02	0.01	0.00

The table contains the percentage on the total amount of export for some selected product categories; while we applied the algorithm directly on the export values for all the 97 categories.

Supreme Court Voting Data

The second application is based on the dataset used in [27] of the Supreme Court judges and their votes on a set of issues. We have a *signed bipartite network* [44] with N=9 justices, M=26 issues and the expressed votes.

In Table 4, we present both our result and the one in Doreian [27]. Although the number of clusters is different, we notice that the two approaches classify, exactly in the same way, the first two members of the first cluster and those ones of the second cluster. Contrarily, a remarkable difference stems from the fact that our algorithm groups together *Kennedy,O'Connor* and *Rehnquist* while Doreian [27] put them in three different clusters (two of which have a single element). Regarding this, we need to recall that our algorithm does not allow for the size of the cluster to be lower than two, thus the third cluster arises as a residual one.

Table 4: Justice Data

Our method			Doreian [27]			
Cluster 1	Cluster 2	Cluster 3	Cluster 1	Cluster 2	Cluster 3	Cluster 4
Scalia	Breyer	Kennedy	Scalia	Breyer	Kennedy	O'Connor
Thomas	Ginsburg	O'Connor	Thomas	Ginsburg		
	Souter	Rehnquist	Rehnquist	Souter		
	Stevens			Stevens		

Next to these first considerations, it is interesting to deepen the analysis by studying the data structure and try to give a more detailed explanation for the differences. To this end, we report in Table 5 a permuted version of the Supreme Court voting matrix, where the issues are blocked as in [25] and the judges are partitioned according to the results from our algorithm, whereas in Figure 3 we depict the bipartite network structure. Looking at the first cluster, containing *Scalia* and *Thomas*, and the second cluster, composed by *Breyer*, *Ginsburg,Souter*, and *Stevens*, we can easily recognize a voting pattern remarkably opposed one to each other and at the same time a coherent preference expression within the groups.

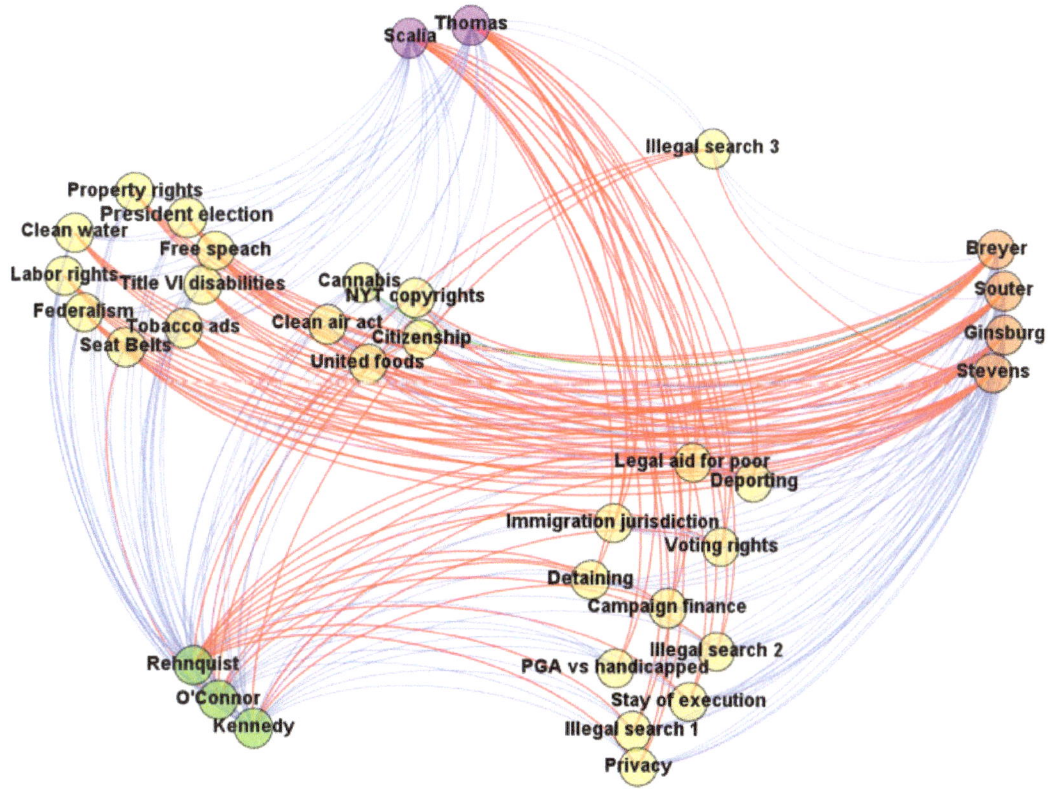

Figure 3: Justice sentences network.

This figure depicts the bipartite signed network of the US Supreme Court Justice votes upon 26 different issues. The blue edges correspond to votes in the majority (+1), the red edges correspond to votes in the minority (−1) and the unique green edge correspond to a case of abstention (0). Furthermore, the nodes are classified as follow: yellow for the 26 issues, violet for *Cluster 1*, orange for *Cluster 2* and green for *Cluster 3*. The network has been built so as to capture the sharpness of the clusters partitioning. In particular, an higher cohesiveness among the judges within the first and second clusters with respect to those ones in the third cluster can be ascertained by the fact that a more coherent coloured pattern can be glimpsed from the beam of edges that originate from the first two clusters with respect to the last one, i.e. two different stacks can be distinguished, a red one and a blue one.

Table 5: Supreme Court voting data

Issue ($M=26$)	Supreme Court justice ($N=9$)								
	Br	Gi	St	So	OC	Ke	Re	Sc	Th
President election	−1	−1	−1	−1	1	1	1	1	1
Federalism	−1	−1	−1	−1	1	1	1	1	1
Clean Water	−1	−1	−1	−1	1	1	1	1	1
Title VI Disabilities	−1	−1	−1	−1	1	1	1	1	1
Tobacco Ads	−1	−1	−1	−1	1	1	1	1	1
Labour rights	−1	−1	−1	−1	1	1	1	1	1
Property Rights	−1	−1	−1	−1	1	1	1	1	1
Citizenship	−1	−1	1	−1	−1	1	1	1	1
Free Speech	1	−1	−1	−1	1	1	1	1	1
Seat Belts	−1	−1	−1	1	−1	1	1	1	1
United Foods	−1	−1	1	1	−1	1	1	1	1
NYT Copyright	−1	1	−1	1	1	1	1	1	1
Cannabis for Health	0	1	1	1	1	1	1	1	1
Clean Air Act	1	1	1	1	1	1	1	1	1
PGA vs. Handicapped	1	1	1	1	1	1	1	−1	−1
Illegal Search 3	1	1	−1	1	−1	−1	−1	1	1
Illegal Search 1	1	1	1	1	1	1	−1	−1	−1
Illegal Search 2	1	1	1	1	1	1	−1	−1	−1
Stay of Execution	1	1	1	1	1	1	−1	−1	−1
Privacy	1	1	1	1	1	1	−1	−1	−1
Immigration Jurisdiction	1	1	1	1	−1	1	−1	−1	−1
Detaining Criminal Aliens	1	1	1	1	−1	1	−1	−1	−1
Legal Aid for the Poor	1	1	1	1	−1	1	−1	−1	−1
Voting Rights	1	1	1	1	1	−1	−1	−1	−1
Deporting Criminal Aliens	1	1	1	1	1	−1	−1	−1	−1
Campaign Finance	1	1	1	1	1	−1	−1	−1	−1

The data on the Supreme Court judges can be found in [27]. The blocks of the issues are based on [25]. The table is filled with +1 if the judge voted in the majority for that issue and with −1 if he was in the minority decision. In case a 0 is reported, it means that for that particular case the judge refrained to vote.

The unique puzzling doubt concerns the allocation of *Rehnquist* in the group of *Kennedy* and*O'Connor* rather than in the group of *Scalia* and *Thomas*. In order to further investigate this issue, we decided to check the global likelihood value in the case where we move *Rehnquist* in the first group. What we found is that the addition of him to the group of *Scalia* and *Thomas*considerably decreases the global likelihood. This effect is a consequence of the fact that our procedure recognizes the perfect dependence among these last two actors, and therefore it prefers to allocate *Scalia* and *Thomas* alone in one cluster in order to point out their "positional equality", and to group into the third cluster *O'Connor*, *Kennedy* and *Rehnquist*, which perfectly agree over half of the issues.

CONCLUSIONS AND FUTURE LINES OF RE-SEARCH

Clustering algorithms have increasingly assumed a central role for the identification of communities in complex networks. In this paper, we deal with a notion of community different from the classical one: while the network clustering analysis, namely the community detection, aims to identify clusters of densely connected actors, we try to determine groups of actors that play a similar role inside a certain organization basing on the characteristics or habits that they exhibit. In the social network literature, this is known as positional analysis.

To this end, we propose a new clustering algorithm that can be applied to situations which are suitably modelled through a *weighted bipartite network*. Starting from the associated real-valued matrix, with the actors on the rows, the features on the columns, and the weights as the elements, we try to capture possible similarities among groups of actors by analyzing the multivariate stochastic dependence among them.

The contribution of this paper has to be found in the methodological approach we propose for positional analysis that is based on the detection of the intrinsic multivariate stochastic dependence among groups of actors and in the development of a new related algorithm that uses copula functions in order to model these dependence structures. Furthermore, this algorithm directly operates on the matrix describing the actor-feature relationships, differently from many other algorithms that collapse the information of the bipartite network to a unipartite one and then apply the classical clustering procedure. In fact, this kind of operation can cause a lost of information and a consequent erroneous cluster identification. Another advantage of our technique is that it finds the optimal partition, without fixing *a priori* the number of clusters and the maximum number of elements per cluster (though we don't allow for cluster of single elements). Furthermore, our algorithm is able to work directly on any matrix, binary or weighted with real numbers.

This is the first time this methodology is applied to the network field, therefore it is not surprising that there are still some issues to be addressed, and that we leave for future research. The major drawback of our algorithm concerns the high computational burden it bears as a consequence of the fact that it explores all the possible combinations of groups of actors. Since our first purpose was to understand the potentiality of such a new approach, we have not tried to develop any optimized version of the algorithm yet. For the moment, we have provided an algorithm whose output is the exact solution of the optimization problem, as it explores all the possible combinations. However, we are convinced that a deeper study of its behaviour could give some criteria to reduce the number of combinations to explore and allow the development of a new version of the algorithm that provides an "approximate" solution but is computationally faster. For instance, on the left side of Figure 4 we report the maximum copula log-likelihood values of each couple of countries obtained from the trade example in Section 4. It can be noticed that from the log-likelihood values of the bivariate copulas, we already have some insights on the possible clusters. In fact, we can see that the bivariate copula log-likelihoods of those countries belonging to the same cluster tend to be higher than the others. Given this information, we could for example adopt an agglomerative approach, as it is common in the community detection literature [42], and group those actors that present a more significant bivariate dependence so as to avoid the calculation of all the possible combinations for the various dimensions.

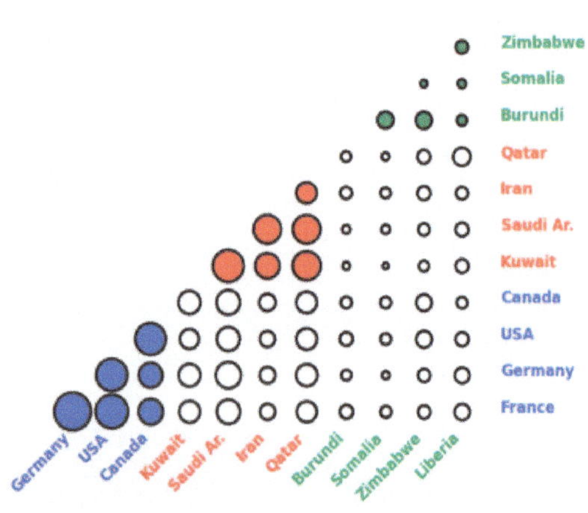

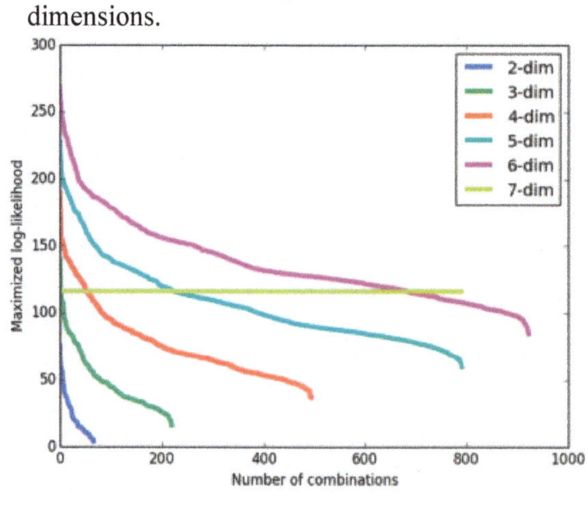

Figure 4: Log-likelihood plots.

(Left) For each couple of countries, the figure shows circles whose areas correspond to the maximum log-likelihood values of the bivariate copulas. The colours are used to identify the countries belonging to the same cluster. (Right) For different dimensions of the copula function, the figure shows the maximum log-likelihood values for each possible combination of countries, in decreasing order.

Another heuristic argument we could exploit to reduce the computational cost can be deduce from the right side of Figure 4, where we plot the maximum log-likelihood values of copulas with different dimensions for all the combination of countries used in the trade example in Section 4. We can see that, for this study case, the maximum log-likelihood value of the 7-dim copula is constant across the combinations so as to suggest that clusters larger than six countries are less plausible. Therefore, it seems that the algorithm recognizes some sort of upper bound for the cluster size, and we can exploit this information to avoid all those calculations over the sixth dimension.

A second issue concerning the proposed algorithm consists in that it does not allow for clusters with a single element, and in positional analysis it may be a limitation. We avoid to address this issue because it would cause an increase of computational cost, but it could be theoretically feasible to exploit the copula functions in such a way to consider also clusters of a single element. Regarding this point, we also point out that, since the present algorithm returns the clusters in decreasing order with respect to the maximum copula log-likelihood value, the eventual single elements are contained in the last (residual) cluster, see for instance Table 4.

In conclusion, though there are still some open issues to be solved in order to apply this new clustering algorithm to large networks, it seems to capture dependence patterns that other algorithms ignore. Therefore, we strongly believe it could have interesting implications on positional analysis in the future, and we foster future developments of this approach.

REFERENCES

1. Cerina F, Chessa A, Pammolli F, Riccaboni M (2014) Network communities within and across borders. Scientific Reports 4: 1–7.
2. Fortunato S (2010) Community detections in graphs. Physics Reports 486: 75–174.
3. Girvan M, Newman MEJ (2002) Community structure in social and biological networks. Proc Natl Acad Sci U S A 99(12): 7821–7826.
4. Newman MEJ (2001) Scientific collaboration networks. Network construction and fundamental results.Phys Rev E Stat Nonlin Soft Matter Phys 64: 016131.
5. Brandes U, Lerner J (2007) Role equivalent Actors in Networks. In: Obiedkov S, Roth C. ICFCA Satellite Workshop on Social Network Analysis and Conceptual Structures: Exploring Opportunities.
6. Borgatti SP, Everett MG (1997) Network analysis of 2-mode data. Social Networks 19: 243–269.
7. Borgatti SP (2008) 2-Mode Concepts in Social Network Analysis. In Meyers RA. Encyclopedia of Complexity and System Science. Springer.
8. Brusco M (2011) Analysis of two-mode network data using nonnegative matrix factorization. Social Networks 33: 201–210.
9. Asratian AS, Denley T, Häggkvist R (1998) Bipartite Graphs and their Applications. Cambridge University Press.
10. Davis GF, Greve HR (1997) Corporate elite networks and governance changes in the 1980. American journal of sociology 103(1): 1–37.
11. Mariolis P (1975) Interlocking directorates and control of corporations. Social Science Quarterly 56(3): 425–439.
12. Barabási AL, Jeong H, Néda Z, Ravasz E, Schubert A, Vicsek T (2002) Evolution of the social network of scientific collaboration. Physica A 311: 590–614.
13. Guimerà R, Uzzi B, Spiro J, Amaral LAN (2005) Team assembly mechanisms determine collaboration network structure and team performance. Science 308: 697–702.
14. Dhillon IS (2001) Co-clustering documents and works using bipartite spectral graph partitioning. Proceedings of the seventh international conference on knowledge discovery and data mining: 269–274.
15. Larremore DB, Clauset A, Buckee CO (2013) A Network Approach to Analyzing Highly Recombinant Malaria Parasite Genes. PLoS Comput Biol 9(10): e1003268 doi:10.1371/journal.pcbi.1003268
16. Agliari E, Barra A (2011) A Hebbian approach to complex network generation. Europhysics Letters94(1), 10002.
17. Agliari E, Barra A, Galluzzi A, Guerra F, Moauro F (2012) Multitasking associative networks. Physical review letters 109(26), 268101.
18. Good BH, de Montjoye YA, Clauset A (2010) The performance of modularity maximization in practical contexts. Phys Rev E Stat Nonlin Soft Matter Phys 81: 046106.
19. Zhou T, Ren J, Medo M, Zhang Y (2007) Bipartite network projection and personal recommendation.Phys Rev E Stat Nonlin Soft Matter Phys 76: 046115.
20. Everett MG, Borgatti SP (2013) The dual-projection approach for two-mode networks. Social Networks35: 204–210.
21. Barber MJ (2007) Modularity and community detection in bipartite networks. Phys Rev E Stat Nonlin Soft Matter Phys 76: 066102.
22. Guimerà R, Sales-Pardo M, Amaral LAN (2007) Module identification in bipartite and directed networks. Phys Rev E Stat Nonlin Soft Matter Phys 76: 036102.
23. Borgatti SP, Halgin D (2011) Analyzing Affiliation Network. In Carrington P, Scott J (eds). The Sage Handbook of Social Network Analysis.
24. Wasserman F, Faust K (1994) Social Network Analysis: Methods and Applications. Cambridge University Press.
25. Brusco M, Steinley D (2006) Inducing a blockmodel structure of two-mode binary data using seriation procedures. Journal of Mathematical Psychology 50: 468–477.
26. Brusco M, Steinley D (2007) A variable neighborhood search method for generalized blockmodeling of two-mode binary matrices. Journal of Mathematical Psychology 51: 325–338.
27. Doreian P, Batagelj V, Ferligoj A (2004) Generalized blockmodeling of two-mode network data. Social Networks 26: 29–53.
28. Ziberna A (2007) Generalized blockmodeling of valued networks. Social Networks 29: 105–126.

29. Larremore DB, Clauset A, Jacobs AZ (2014) Efficiently inferring community structure in bipartite networks. arXiv:1403.2933.

30. Aicher C, Jacobs AZ, Clauset A (2014) Learning Latent Block Structure in Weighted Networks. arXiv preprint arxiv:1404.0431v1.

31. Hoeffding W (1994) Scale invariant correlation theory. In Fisher NI, Sen PK (eds). The Collected Works of Wassily Hoeffding. Springer Series in Statistics. pp. 57–104.

32. Sklar A (1959) Fonctions de la repartition a n dimensions et leurs marges. Publications de l›Institute de Statistique de l›Universite de Paris 8: 229–231.

33. Nelsen RB (2006) An introduction to Copulas. Springer Series in Statistics.

34. Joe H (1997) Multivariate Models and Dependence Concepts. Chapman and Hall.

35. Trivedi PK, Zimmer DM (2005) Copula modeling: an introduction for practitioners. Foundations and trends in Econometrics 1(1): 1–111.

36. Di Lascio FM, Giannerini S (2012) A copula-based Algorithm for Discovering Patterns of Dependent Observations. Journal of Classification 29(1): 50–75.

37. Barigozzi M, Fagiolo G, Mangioni G (2011) Identifying the community structure of the international-trade multi-network. Physica A 390(11): 2051–2066.

38. Breiger RL (1982) Structures of Economic Interdependence Among Nations. In: Blau PM, Merton RK Continuities in Structural Inquiry: 353–80. Beverly Hills, CA: Sage.

39. Cerina F, Zhu Z, Chessa A, Riccaboni M (2014) World Input-Output Network. arXiv preprint.

40. Tzekina I, Danthi K, Rockmore DN (2008) Evolution of community structure in the world trade web.European Physics Journal B 63: 541–545.

41. Zhu Z, Cerina F, Chessa A, Caldarelli G, Riccaboni M (2014) The rise of China in the International Trade Network: A Community Core Detection Approach arXiv preprint arxiv:1404.6950. Plos One Forthcoming.

42. Blondel VD, Guillaume JL, Lambiotte R, Lefebvre E (2008) Fast unfolding of communities in large networks. J Stat Mech P10008.

43. Hartigan JA, Wong MA (1979) Algorithm AS 136: A K-Means Clustering Algorithm. J R Stat Soc Ser C Appl Sta 28: 100–108.

44. Mrvar A, Doreian P (2009) Partitioning Signed Two-Mode Networks. Journal of Mathematical Sociology 33: 196–221.

CHAPTER 11 IMPROVED ACTIVE HARMONIC CURRENT ELIMINATION BASED ON VOLTAGE DETECTION

Tianyuan Tan[1], Shuan Dong[2], Yingwei Huang[2] , Jian Liu[1] , Jian Le[1] , Kaipei Liu[1]

[1]School of Electrical Engineering, Wuhan University, Wuhan, Hubei, China,

[2]Department of Electrical and Computer Engineering, University of British Columbia, Vancouver, BC, Canada

ABSTRACT

With the increasing penetration of power electronic equipment in modern residential distribution systems, harmonics mitigation through the distributed generation (DG) interfacing converters has received significant attention. Among recently proposed methods, the socalled active resonance damper (ARD) and harmonic voltage compensator (HVC) based on voltage detection can effectively reduce the harmonic distortions in selected areas of distribution systems. However, it is found out that when traditional ARD algorithm is used to eliminate harmonic current injected by non-linear loads, its performance is constrained by stability problems and can at most eliminate half of the load harmonic currents. Thus, inspired by the duality between ARD and HVC, this paper presents a novel improved resistive active power filter (R-APF) algorithm based on integral-decoupling control. The design guideline for its parameters is then investigated through carefully analyzing the closed-loop poles' trajectory. Computer studies demonstrate that the proposed algorithm can effectively mitigate the load harmonic currents and its performance is much better than traditional ARD based on proportional control.

INTRODUCTION

With the rapid development of power electronics technology, energy efficient but harmonic producing power converters have been widely used in both commercial and residential installations, including motor-type loads fed through variable frequency drives (VFDs), personal computers (PCs), television sets (TVs), fluorescent lamps(FLs), etc. Despite the relative small capacity of each power electronic device, these non-linear loads combined are known to contribute considerable harmonics into the power systems, resulting in extra losses, adverse impact on system stability as well as other equipment [1–3].

At the same time, increasing number of distributed generation (DG) units such as photovoltaic panels, wind turbines, and energy storage devices are being connected to the grid [4], [5]. Most of these DG systems are connected to the grid through power electronic converters [6]. If designed and controlled improperly, the DG interfacing converters may also introduce harmonics into the power system and cause

Citation: Tan T, Dong S, Huang Y, Liu J, Le J, Liu K. Improved Active Harmonic Current Elimination Based on Voltage Detection. Hu X, ed. PLoS ONE. 2016;11(6):e0157057. doi:10.1371/journal.pone.0157057.

power quality concerns [7]. On the contrary, if designed and controlled properly, these DG interfacing converters can potentially provide many ancillary services to improve the system efficiency and power quality, including the power factor compensation and system harmonic compensation, etc. [8]

Although shunt active power filters (APF) have been researched and put into practice for decades, most of the research are focused on their use for a specific harmonic-producing customer. Typically, traditional shunt APF is controlled to inject harmonic currents with the same characteristics (amplitude and frequency) and opposite polarity of the harmonic currents drawn by the distorting load. The APFs must be installed in the vicinity of the non-linear loads. However, the locating place of DG interfacing converters are mainly decided by other considerations and are most often than not far away from the non-linear loads or the entrance of the feeder. So, traditional harmonic mitigating strategy based on current detection does not suit these converters anymore. Alternatively, two novel control schemes based on harmonic voltage detection have been proposed, namely the active resonance damper (ARD) or resistance-active power filter (R-APF) [9] and the harmonic voltage compensator (HVC) [10][11]. Instead of injecting harmonic currents to compensate those drawn by distorting loads, the R-APF acts as a small harmonic resistance installed at the end of a radial line to damp harmonic resonance between power factor correction capacitors and system inductances. The HVC directly generates the harmonic voltages to compensate those at the point of common coupling. Both methods can effectively mitigate harmonics caused by harmonic voltage source on the system side, without the need to detect harmonic currents of the load (or the total harmonic currents injected to the utility after compensation).

This paper considers the distribution system of a representative educational building (which has considerable non-linear loads), and investigates into the active harmonic mitigation algorithm which is based on voltage detection and suitable for DG interfacing converters. It is found out that although traditional proportional R-APF algorithm can extend to eliminate harmonic current injected by non-linear loads, its performance is constrained by stability problems and can at most eliminate half of the load harmonic currents. Thus, inspired by the iterative HVC algorithm, this paper proposes a novel improved R-APF algorithm, which is based on integral-decoupling control in the synchronous rotating reference frame at each harmonic frequency. The design of d-q axes decoupling control and the selection of integral coefficient are then analyzed in details. Finally, computer simulations are presented to validate the proposed methodology.

Configuration of the Subject System

For the purpose of this paper, the integrated ac-dc system of a representative educational Building is considered as depicted in Fig 1. Therein, the ac-dc system consists of two main parts, i.e., the ac distribution system connected to utility grid through step-down transformers, and the dc system comprising a large volume of battery storage system and a set of solar PV panels. In particular, the dc system can work as an islanding network, or connect to the ac system through the interfacing DC/AC converter. Additionally, a smart meter is installed at the outlet of the building's main transformer TX1, which monitors and records the total active power and reactive power consumed by the building, as well as the harmonic voltage at Bus 1 and the total harmonic currents injected into the grid.

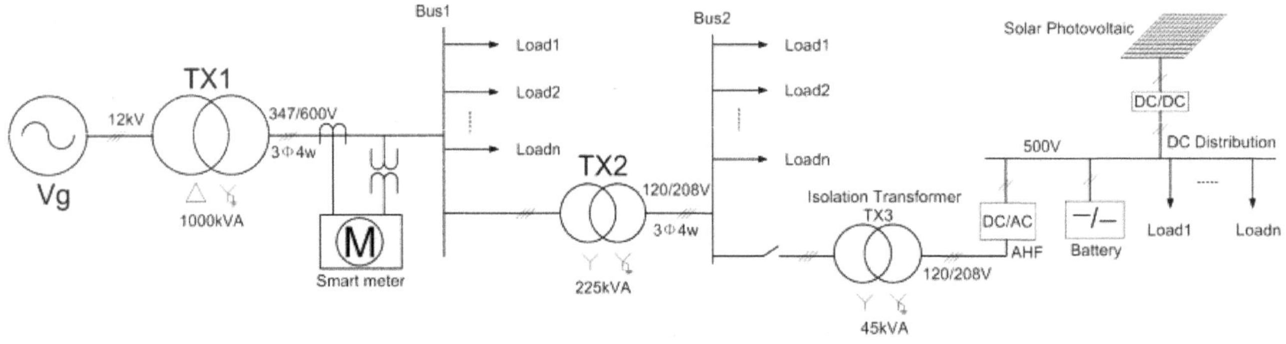

Figure 1: Configuration of the DG system in the representative educational Building.

The simplified equivalent circuit of this subject system is then modeled in PSCAD as shown inFig 2. Since the background harmonics from the ac grid are typically small, the harmonic currents are assumed to be generated by non-linear loads within the building. Therein, they can be approximated as two lumped equivalent harmonic current sources connected to Bus 1 and 2, respectively. Similarly, the linear loads are lumped into two equivalent R-L loads as shown in Fig 2. In order to mitigate harmonic currents, the DG interfacing converters is controlled as a three-phase controlled current source at the each harmonic frequency. The methods to control the voltage source converter as a controlled current source have been well studied in the literature, including algorithms such as hysteresis control, ramp comparison control, and deadbeat control [12]. Therefore, this paper will only focus on how to get the reference value of harmonic current for the inner control loop.

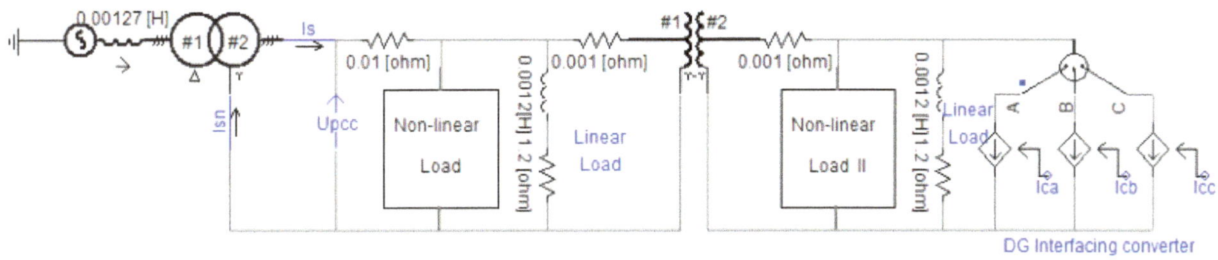

Figure 2: Simplified PSCAD simulation model of the DG system depicted in Fig 1.

HARMONIC ELIMINATION METHODS BASED ON VOLTAGE DETECTION

A.The Duality between R-APF and HVC

Originally designed to damp harmonic propagation caused by harmonic voltage source on the system side [9], the R-APF has been lately used as harmonic compensation methods to eliminate harmonic currents from non-linear loads on the customer side [13]. In contrast, the HVC [10], [11] was proposed as a voltage-control-method based harmonic control method suitable for DG units which are desired to provide direct voltage and frequency support for loads in micro grids. In fact, HVC and R-APF are duals, harmonic voltage compensation instructions for HVC can be easily converted into harmonic current compensation commands for R-APF by simply converting the HVC's Thevenin equivalent circuit into R-APF's Norton equivalent circuit, and vice versa. Therefore, here we will only focus on the R-APF algorithm.

B. Shortcomings of Traditional R-APF Algorithms

Traditional R-APF algorithm [13] controls the converter's output current and make it proportional to the PCC voltage at the harmonic frequencies, as shown in Fig 3. Wherein,

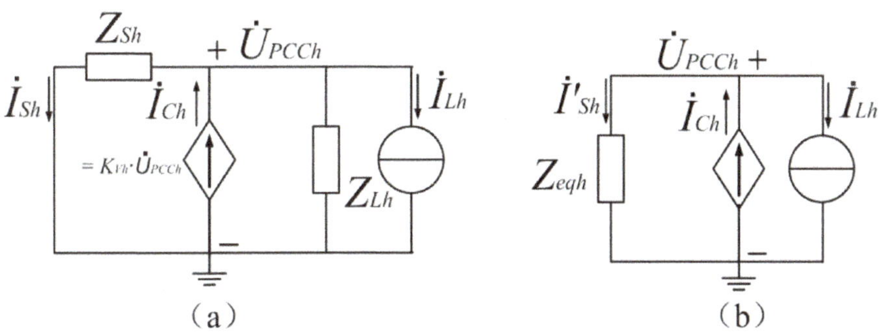

Figure 3: Principle circuit for R-APF: (a) per-phase equivalent circuit; (b) simplified.

Z_{sh} is the harmonic impedance of the supply network at order h

$\dot{I}_{Sh}$ is the harmonic current phasor inject into the supply network at order h

$\dot{I}_{Lh}$ is the current phasor for the equivalent harmonic current source of the nonlinear loads at order h

Z_{Lh} is the equivalent linear load impedance at order h

$\dot{I}_{Ch}$ is the injected compensation current phasor of R-APF at order h and its value is set to K_{vh}* $\dot{U}_{PCCh}$, where K_{vh} is a fix real number

$\dot{U}_{PCCh}$ is the harmonic voltage phasor of PCC at order h

Z_{eqh} is the parallel equivalent impedance of Z_{sh} and Z_{Lh}

$\dot{I}'_{Sh}$ is the current phasor injected to the equivalent parallel impedance, the relationship between $\dot{I}_{sh}$ and $\dot{I}'_{sh}$ is $\dot{I}_{sh} = \dot{I}'_{sh}\cdot Z_{Lh}/(Z_{Lh}+Z_{Lh})$

Applying KCL and KVL to the circuit in Fig 3(A) yields

$$\dot{I}_{Sh} = -\dot{I}_{Lh}\cdot\frac{1}{1+Z_{Sh}/Z_{Lh}-K_{Vh}\cdot Z_{Sh}}. \tag{1}$$

As shown in (1), I_{sh} (the amplitude of phasor $\dot{I}_{sh}$) decreases with a larger K_{Vh} for any fixed Z_{sh} and Z_{Lh}. If K_{Vh} tends to infinite, both I_{sh} and U_{PCCh} (the amplitude of phasor $\dot{U}_{PCCh}$) would tend to be zero. That's how the R-APF eliminates the non-linear load currents.

However, in practical systems the digital controller is used and the corresponding discrete-time compensation algorithm yields

$$i_{Ch}(k) = K_{Vh}\cdot u_{PCCh}(k-1). \tag{2}$$

Where, k is the discrete sample and control interval, i_{Ch} and u_{PCCh} are the instantaneous value of phasor $\dot{I}_{Ch}$ and $\dot{U}_{PCCh}$ respectively.

It means the R-APF can only adjust its present output according to the last sample value instead of the present value, because it needs time to sample, calculate, and generate outputs. I.e., there exists control delay. Unfortunately, the control delay, no matter how small it can be, will always lead to stability problems.

Applying KCL and KVL to the circuit in Fig 3(A), the mathematical model of discrete system can be obtained as

$$\dot{U}_{pcch}(k) = \dot{I}_{Sh}(k) \cdot Z_{Sh}, \tag{3}$$

$$\dot{I}_{Sh}(k) = [\dot{I}_{Ch}(k) - \dot{I}_{Lh}(k)] \cdot Z_{Lh}/(Z_{Sh} + Z_{Lh}). \tag{4}$$

Substitute Eqs (2) and (3) into Eq (4) yields

$$\dot{I}_{Sh}(k) = \dot{I}_{Lh}(k) \cdot \frac{Z_{Lh}}{Z_{Sh} + Z_{Lh}} - \dot{I}_{sh}(k-1) \cdot K_{Vh} \cdot \frac{Z_{Sh} \cdot Z_{Lh}}{Z_{Sh} + Z_{Lh}}. \tag{5}$$

It's obviously that the stable convergence condition for this discrete system described by Eq (5) is

$$|K_{Vh} \cdot Z_{eqh}| < 1 \tag{6}$$

As $|Z_{sh}| << |Z_{Lh}|$ holds most cases, and R-APF can be regarded as a resistor with the value of $1/K_{Vh}$, from Fig 3 we have

$$I_{Sh} = I_{Lh} \cdot \left| \frac{\frac{1}{Z_{Sh}}}{\frac{1}{Z_{Sh}} + K_{Vh} + \frac{1}{Z_{Lh}}} \right| > I_{Lh} \cdot \left| \frac{\frac{1}{Z_{Sh}}}{\frac{1}{Z_{Sh}} + \frac{1}{|Z_{eqh}|} + \frac{1}{Z_{Lh}}} \right| > 0.5 I_{Lh}. \tag{7}$$

Where, I_{sh} and I_{Lh} are the RMS amplitude of phasor $\dot{I}_{Sh}$ and $\dot{I}_{Lh}$ respectively.

It means that the optimal performance that traditional R-APF can achieve is eliminating about 50% of the load harmonic currents. Note that if K_{Vh} is too large, system will become unstable.

C. A novel improved integral control R-APF Algorithm

In order to improve R-APF algorithm's performance, this paper proposes an integral control by its duality to the iterative HVC method [11].

$$i_{Ch}(k) = i_{Ch}(k-1) + K_{Vh} \cdot u_{PCCh}(k-1) \tag{8}$$

As known to all, compared to the proportional control, the greatest advantage of integral control is that there is no need for a very large proportional K_{Vh} to realize zero static error control. If the system is stable, the controller can ideally track the dc reference signal within a finite time.

Thus, the integral controller is implemented in the synchronous rotating reference frame at harmonic frequency. As $U_{PCChd}(s)$ and $U_{PCChq}(s)$ are coupled together at the synchronous rotating reference frame, this paper adds an additional decoupling control loop following the integral controller to improve the controller's performance, as shown in Fig 4. Wherein,

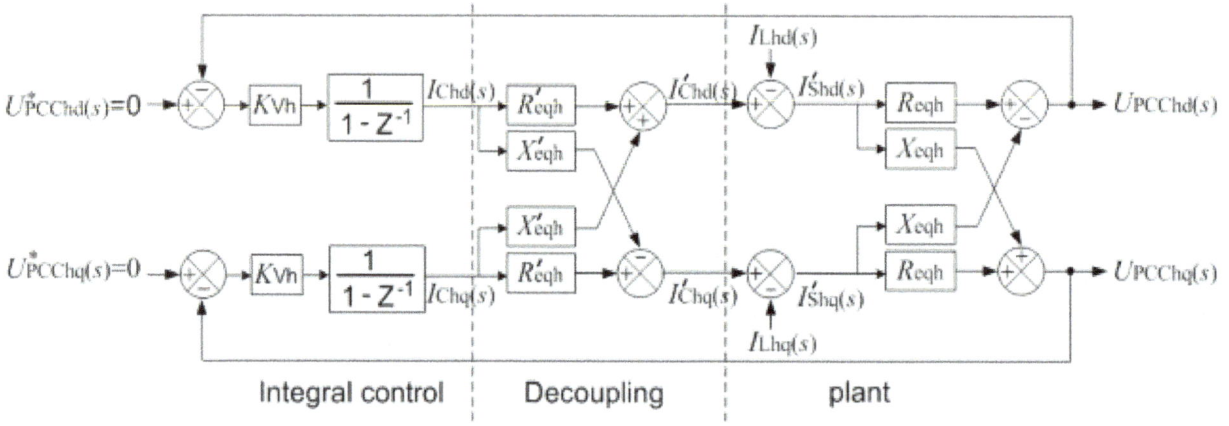

Figure 4: Integral-decoupling control in synchronously rotating reference frame.

http://dx.doi.org/10.1371/journal.pone.0157057.g004

R_{eqh} is the parallel equivalent resistance, real part of Z_{eqh};

X_{eqh} is the parallel equivalent reactance, imaginary part of Z_{eqh};

$\frac{1}{1-Z^{-1}}$ is the transfer function for the discrete integral controller.

D.Parameters design for impoved R-APF algorithm

The closed-loop transfer function of the system in Fig 4 is

$$U_{PCChd}(s) = U^{*}_{PCChd}(s)\frac{A^2 + B^2 - A}{A^2 + B^2} - U^{*}_{PCChq}(s)\frac{B}{A^2 + B^2} + I_{Lhd}(s)\frac{X_{eqh} \cdot B - R_{eqh} \cdot A}{A^2 + B^2} + I_{Lhq}(s)$$

$$\times \frac{R_{eqh} \cdot B - X_{eqh} \cdot A}{A^2 + B^2}, \tag{9}$$

$$U_{PCChq}(s) = U^*_{PCChq}(s)\frac{A^2 - B^2 - A}{A^2 + B^2} - U^*_{PCChd}(s)\frac{B}{A^2 + B^2} - I_{Lhd}(s)\frac{X_{eqh} \cdot A + R_{eqh} \cdot B}{A^2 + B^2} - I_{Lhq}(s)$$
$$\times \frac{R_{eqh} \cdot A - X_{eqh} \cdot B}{A^2 + B^2}. \tag{10}$$

Where,

$$A = 1 + \frac{K_{Vh}}{1 - Z^{-1}} \cdot (R_{eqh} \cdot R'_{eqh} + X_{eqh} \cdot X'_{eqh}),$$

$$B = \frac{K_{Vh}}{1 - Z^{-1}} \cdot \left(R_{eqh} \cdot X'_{eqh} - X_{eqh} \cdot R'_{eqh}\right).$$

The characteristic polynomial equation is

$$A^2 + B^2 = 0. \tag{11}$$

Solved Eq (11) gets the closed-loop poles of the system,

$$Z = 1 - K_{Vh} \cdot [(R_{eqh} \cdot R'_{eqh} + X_{eqh} \cdot X'_{eqh}) \pm j \cdot (R_{eqh} \cdot X'_{eqh} - X_{eqh} \cdot R'_{eqh})]. \tag{12}$$

Assume

$$K'_{Vh} = K_{Vh} \cdot \sqrt{R^2_{eqh} + X^2_{eqh}} \cdot \sqrt{R'^2_{eqh} + X'^2_{eqh}},\ \sin(\theta_1) = \frac{R'_{eqh}}{\sqrt{R'^2_{eqh} + X'^2_{eqh}}},\ \sin(\theta_2) = \frac{R'_{eqh}}{\sqrt{R^2_{eqh} + X^2_{eqh}}},$$

Eq (12) can be written as,

$$Z = 1 - K'_{Vh} \cdot e^{\pm j(\theta_1 - \theta_2)}. \tag{13}$$

According to Eq (13), the close-loop poles' trajectory can be shown as Fig 5. When K'_{Vh} is zero, the system has a pair of identical closed-loop poles at point of +1. If K'_{Vh} increases from zero, the closed-loop poles will move symmetrically towards left along the straight lines l_1 and l_2. And, the angle between the straight lines and the negative direction of real-axis is $\theta_1 - \theta_2$. Without decoupling control, this angle is determined by the equivalent impedance Z_{eqh}. With completely decoupled control, the angle becomes zero.

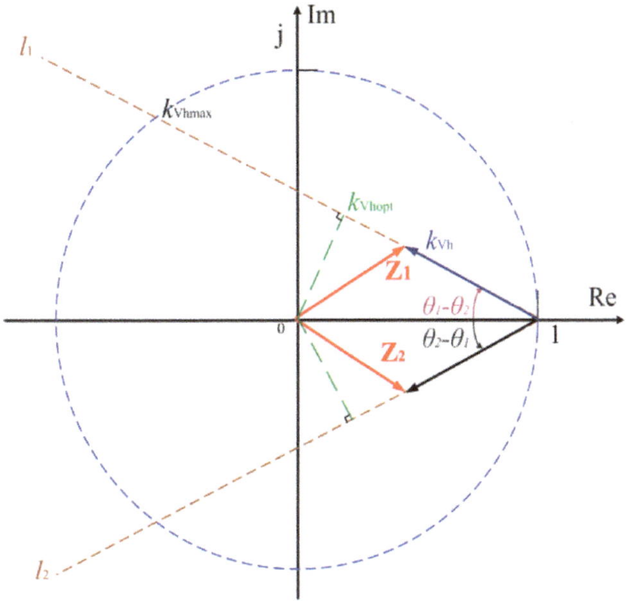

Figure 5: The poles of close-loop transfer function.

As is known to all, to ensure the discrete system's stability, all the poles at the Z plane should be placed within the unit circle. And the smaller the modulus of the closed-loop pole is, the faster state variables in the system converge. Based on these stability analysis guidelines, the added decoupling control can extend the system's stability range and accelerate the convergence. E.g. If Z_{eqh} is purely inductive and decoupling control is not added, the close-loop poles' trajectory will be perpendicular to the real axis at the point of +1. In this case, no matter what value K'_{Vh} takes, the system is always unstable. But if decoupled control is adopted, whatever the value of Z_{eqh} is, the system can always be stable and converge quickly as long as K'_{Vh} is set to approximately 1.

However, the equivalent impedance of loads and systems fluctuate all the time and their exact values are not available. Thus, only partial decoupling control with an estimated value of Z'eqhcan be used. With proper estimated parameters, the angle difference $\theta_1-\theta_2$ would be relatively small. And when K'_{Vh} increases from 0, the closed-loop poles will move symmetrically towards the left side along the straight line l_1 or l_2 and their moduli continuously decrease. The system becomes stable and its convergence speed will also continuously increase until K'_{Vh} reaches the optimal value $K'_{Vhopt} = \cos(\theta_1-\theta_2)$, which is slightly smaller than 1. When K'_{Vh} is set toK'_{Vhopt}, the closed-loop poles' moduli take the minimum value and the system achieves the optimal control performance. After that, if K'_{Vh} keeps increase, the closed-loop poles' moduli will increase rather than go down and the control performance begins deteriorating. Once $K'_{Vh}$is equal or greater than $K'_{Vhmax} = 2\cos(\theta_1-\theta_2)$, the closed-loop poles will be out of the unit circle and the system becomes unstable again. In conclusion, it is still practical to set $K'_{Vh}$to 1 as it is very close to the optimal value K'_{Vhopt}, and the system can be stable with a satisfying convergence speed.

COMPUTER STUDIES

A.Comparison of R-APF and Improved R-APF Algorithm

To simplify the comparison process, the circuit displayed in Fig 3A) is used as the simulation model. Assume all the impedance Z_{Sh} and Z_{Lh} are pure resistance, and the circuit has only h^{th}harmonic frequency components. In this case, there is no need to do harmonic detection and decoupling control, Eqs (2) and (8) can directly applied to the instantaneous value of i_C andu_{PCC}.

Fig 6 shows the instantaneous value of system harmonic current i_{Sh} before and after compensated by the traditional R-APF algorithm. It is obvious that traditional R-APF can only filter out half of the load harmonic currents at most, as shown in Fig 6(A). If $K_{Vh}\times Z_{eqh}$ keeps increasing and becomes larger than 1, the system harmonic current will diverge instead of decrease as shown in Fig 6(B). On the contrary, the improved R-APF can filter out almost all the load harmonic currents with a relative small K_{Vh}, as shown in Fig 7. In this paper, the characteristic harmonic of nonlinear load, i.e. h^{th}, is set to 5th, Z_{Sh} and Z_{Lh} are set to 1.2Ω and 6Ω respectively. But the conclusion is not confined to these particular set of simulation parameters, instead it can be extended to any other general parameters.

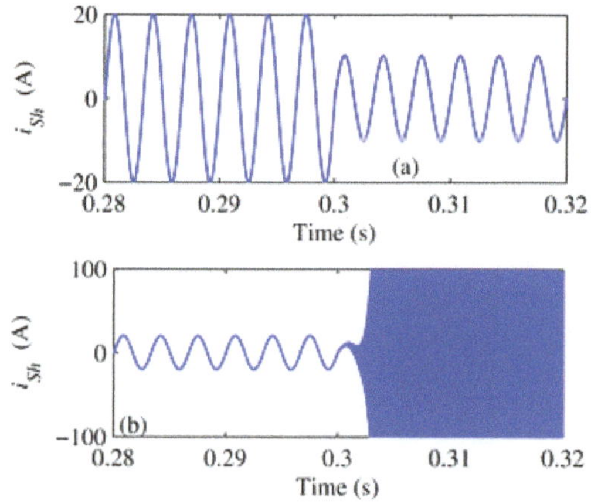

Figure 6: Performance of traditional R-APF algorithm: (a) With K_{Vh} set to $0.95/Z_{eqh}$; (b) With K_{Vh}set to $1.05/Z_{eqh}$.

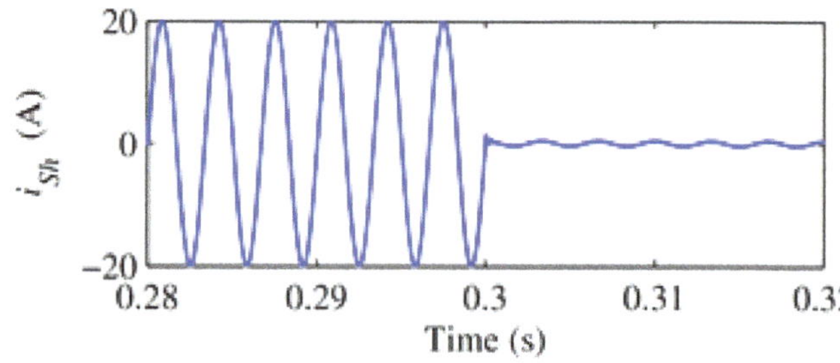

Figure 7: Performance of Improved R-APF algorithm With K_{Vh} set to $0.95/Z_{eqh}$.

B.Verify the effect of Decoupling Link

In order to verify the effect of decoupling link, let's assume all the impedance Z_{Sh} and Z_{Lh} are purely inductive. Here Z_{sh} and Z_{Lh} are set to j1.2Ω and j6Ω respectively, K_{Vh} is set to 0.95, and single-phase single-order harmonic detection algorithm (as shown in Fig 8 [14][15]) is adopted. Fig 9 shows improved R-APF's performance under this extreme test condition. It clearly shows that without decoupling loop (R'_{eqh} and X'_{eqh} are set to 1Ω and0Ωrespectively), the load harmonic currents cannot be filtered out at all. While by partial decoupling control (R'_{eqh} and X'_{eqh} are both set to 0.707Ω), system harmonic currents are reduced to nearly zero within less than 8 seconds. And finally with completely decoupling (R'_{eqh} and X'_{eqh} are set to 0Ω and 1Ωrespectively, the exactly true value of Z_{eqh}), the system harmonic currents are reduced to almost zero in less than 4 seconds, the fastest converge speed among the three algorithms. These simulation results confirmed that decoupling control can effectively improve the controller's convergence speed and extend its stability region.

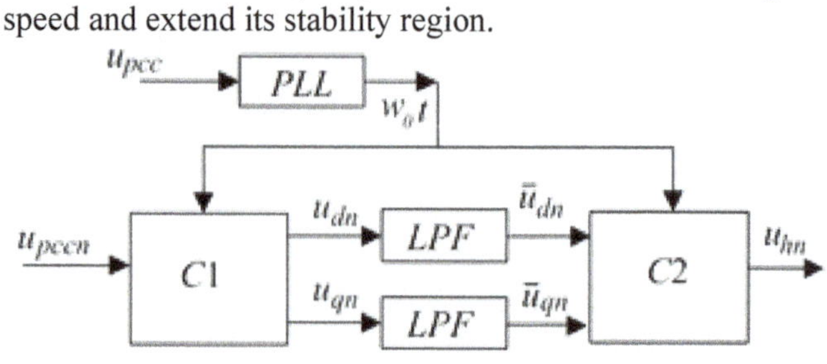

Figure 8: Sing-order Single-phase harmonic detection algorithm.

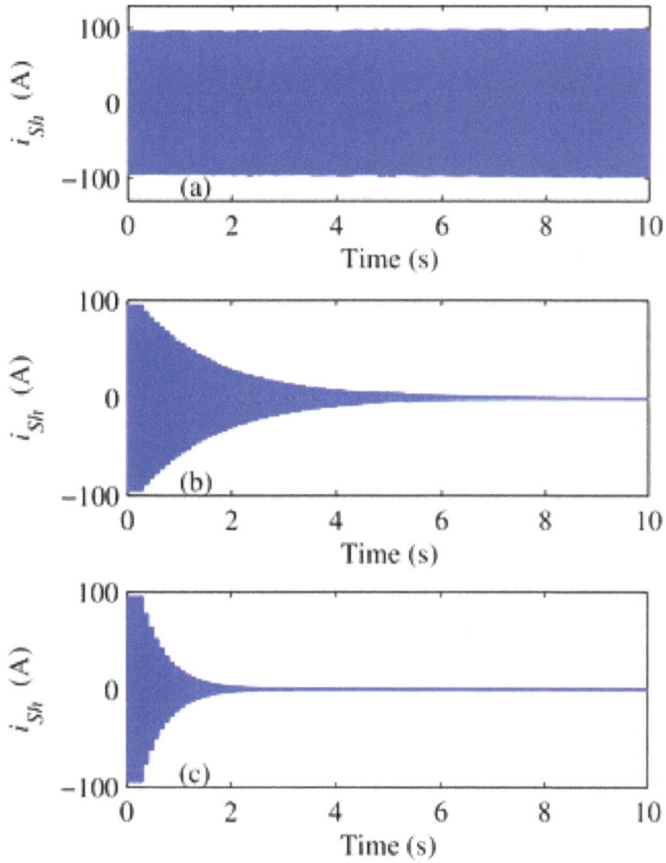

Figure 9: Purely inductive circuit compensate by improved R-APF: (a) Without decoupling by set θ_1 to 0°; (b) With partial decoupling by set θ_1 to 45°; (c) With completely decoupling by set θ_1 to 90°.

Where

$$C_1 = \begin{bmatrix} \cos(h\omega_0 t) \\ \sin(h\omega_0 t) \end{bmatrix};$$

$$C_2 = [2\cos(h\omega_0 t) \quad -2\sin(h\omega_0 t)];$$

n is a, b, c respectively;

h is the specific harmonic order for detection;

ω_0 is the fundamental frequency of the ac system.

C.Compensation Effects for the Example Building

Finally, we applied both traditional and improved R-APF algorithm to the simulation model shown in Fig 2. The dominant harmonics of non-linear load and non-linear load II are both set to third, fifth, and seventh orders, and the three dominant harmonic current values are all set equal to 10A according to the average weekday's recorded data from the smart meter [16]. As the system harmonic voltage is very small compared with the fundamental voltage (The total harmonic distortion of U_{PCC} is less than 1%), Butterworth low pass filter (with cut off frequency at 5 Hz) is connected in series to the slide cycle average filter to realize the LPF link for accurate harmonic detection. The simulation results are shown in Fig 10. It shows that improved R-APF can filter out much more non-linear load's harmonic current, but converges slower than the traditional R-APF due to the integral process. However, the required convergence time is less than 15 seconds which is still within the acceptable range for most harmonic elimination applications.

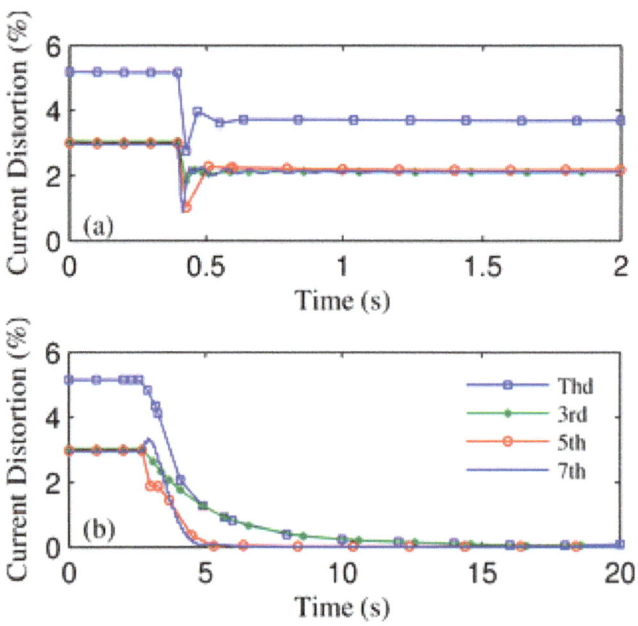

Figure 10: System current distortion dynamics during the compensation progress: (a) Compensated by traditional R-APF; (b) Compensated by improved R-APF.

CONCLUSION

This paper presented an investigation into the active harmonic elimination algorithm which is based on voltage detection and suitable for DG interfacing converters. It is found out that although traditional proportional R-APF algorithm can extend to eliminate harmonic current injected by non-linear loads, its performance is constrained by stability problems and can at most eliminate half of the load harmonic currents. Thus, inspired by the iterative HVC algorithm, this paper proposed a novel improved R-APF algorithm based on integral-decoupling control in the synchronous rotating reference frame at each harmonic frequency. By theoretically analyzing the trajectory of the discrete system's closed-loop poles, the benefits of decoupling control and the design guidelines for integral coefficient are both clearly demonstrated. Simulation results confirm that the proposed harmonic elimination algorithm can effectively mitigate all the load harmonic currents within 15 seconds.

ACKNOWLEDGMENTS

The authors would like to thanks NSFC (National Science Foundation of China) for their fund supporting to this research under Grant No. 51307127.

REFERENCES

1. Bagheri P., Xu W., "A technique to mitigate zero-sequence harmonics in power distribution systems,"IEEE Trans. on Power Del., vol. 29, no. 1, pp. 215–223, February 2014.
2. McBee K. D., Simoes M. G., "Evaluating the long-term impact of a continuously increasing harmonic demand on feeder-level voltage distortion," IEEE Trans. on Ind. Appl., vol.50, no.3, pp.2142–2149, May 2014.
3. J. Desmet, G. Vanalme, C. Debruyne, L. Vandevelde, "Influence of harmonic currents on cable losses for different grid configurations," in ICHQP2010, Bergamo, Italy, Sept., 2010.
4. Carrasco J., Franquelo L., Bialasiew J., et al. , "Power-electronic systems for the grid integration of renewable energy sources: A survey," IEEE Trans. on Power Electron., vol.53, no.4, pp. 1002–1016, August 2006.
5. Lasseter R., "Smart distribution: Coupled microgrids," Proc. of The IEEE, vol.99, no.6, pp. 1074–1082, June 2011.
6. Blaabjerg F., Chen Z., and Kjaer S. B., "Power electronics as efficient interface in dispersed power generation systems," IEEE Trans. Power Electron., vol. 19, no. 5, pp. 1184–1194, September 2004.
7. I. El-Samahy and E. El-Saadany, "The effect of DG on power quality in a deregulated environment,"IEEE Power Engineering Society General Meeting, 2005, vol.3, pp. 2969–2976, San Francisco, USA, 16 Jun. 2005.
8. He J., Li Y., and Munir S. A Flexible harmonic control approach through voltage-controlled DG-Grid Interfacing Converters. IEEE Trans. on Ind. Electron., vol.59, no.1, pp.444–455, January 2012.
9. Akagi H. "Control Strategy and Site Selection of a Shunt Active Filter for Damping of Harmonic Propagation in Power Distribution Systems," IEEE Trans. on Power Delivery, vol.12, no.1, pp.354–363, January 1997.
10. Jinwei He, Md. Shirajum Munir, Yun WeiLi. "Opportunities for power quality improvement through DG-Grid Interfacing Converters," IPEC2010, Sapporo, Japan, 21–24 Jun. 2010.
11. Menniti D., Burgio A., Sorrentino N., Pinnarelli A. "Implementation of the shunt harmonic voltages compensation approach," Electric Power Syst. Res., vol.81, no.3, pp. 798–804, January 2011.
12. Tianyuan Tan, Qirong Jiang, Gang Li, Yuxiang Lai. "Comparison of direct and indirect current control

strategy for DSTACTOM," POWERCON2006, Chongqing, China, 22–26 Oct. 2006.

13. Z.H. Yuan, Y. Du. "A shunt active harmonic filter based on a voltage detection method for harmonic voltage control," DRPT2004, vol. 2, pp. 763–768, Hong Kong, China, 5–8 April 2004.
14. Tan Tianyuan, Jiang Qirong, Ji Jianhui, Yue Jian. "Design of Security and Protection System for Shunt Active Power Filter," Automation of Electric Power Syst., vol.13, no.12, pp. 81–85, June 2007. (in Chinese)
15. Yi Fei Wang Yun WeiLi. "A Grid Fundamental and Harmonic Component Detection Method for Single-Phase Systems," IEEE Trans. on Power Electron., vol.28, No.5, pp.2204–2213, May 2013.
16. http://ion.energy.ubc.ca/ion/default.aspx?dgm=//bis-appionpme-p/ION-Ent/config/diagrams/ud/UBC_SUS/ sub_diagrams/Kaiser_313-device_template_elec.dgm&node=Buildings.Kaiser_313&logServerName=QUERYSERVER.BIS-APPIONPME-P&logServerHandle=327952

CHAPTER 12

PHOTOVOLTAIC GRID-CONNECTED MODELING AND CHARACTERIZATION BASED ON EXPERIMENTAL RESULTS

Ali M. Humada[1,2], Mojgan Hojabri[1] , Mohd Herwan Bin Sulaiman[1] , Hussein M. Hamada[3] , Mushtaq N. Ahmed[1]

[1] Faculty of Electrical & Electronics Engineering, University Malaysia Pahang, Pekan, Malaysia,

[2] Electricity Production Directorate of Salahaldeen, Ministry of Electricity, 34007, Baiji, Iraq,

[3] Faculty of Civil Engineering & Earth Resources, Universiti Malaysia Pahang, 26300, Gambang, Malaysia

ABSTRACT

A grid-connected photovoltaic (PV) system operates under fluctuated weather condition has been modeled and characterized based on specific test bed. A mathematical model of a small-scale PV system has been developed mainly for residential usage, and the potential results have been simulated. The proposed PV model based on three PV parameters, which are the photocurrent, I_L, the reverse diode saturation current, I_o, the ideality factor of diode, n. Accuracy of the proposed model and its parameters evaluated based on different benchmarks. The results showed that the proposed model fitting the experimental results with high accuracy compare to the other models, as well as the I-V characteristic curve. The results of this study can be considered valuable in terms of the installation of a grid-connected PV system in fluctuated climatic conditions.

INTRODUCTION

Solar energy is an important energy source that can be harvested from nature free of cost. The earth's surface receives hundreds of times more energy from the sun than the worldwide demand [1]. The collection of this energy and its conversion into a more useful source such as electrical power for daily usage is important; nevertheless, technologies have their own boundaries and difficulties that must be resolved before photovoltaic (PV) implementation on a large scale. Of these difficulties, PV system modeling and characterization and the performance compared to other conventional sources are the most important [2, 3].

Precise PV modeling has posed a challenge for researchers in order to achieve a model that strictly emulates the characteristics of a PV system within specified or non-specified climatic conditions. Unfortunately, PV modeling and characterization are location dependent, and every researcher developed a model on the basis of the available location and climate at a specific place [4]. In addition, the site of PV installation might affect the output power and eventually the PV performance in a positive or negative way.

Different previous studies have been reported for the power systems modeling. Some of the studies focused on comparative models [5–7], based on either equivalent circuit

Citation: Humada AM, Hojabri M, Sulaiman MHB, Hamada HM, Ahmed MN (2016) Photovoltaic Grid-Connected Modeling and Characterization Based on Experimental Results. PLoS ONE 11(4): e0152766. doi:10.1371/journal.pone.0152766

type [5, 7], or the system type [6]. The multi-swarm particle swarm optimization method, was employed by Hu et al., [5] to find the optimal model parameters, which used twelve equivalent circuit models for Li-ion batteries, selected from state-of-the-art lumped models stated in the previous works. Hu et al., [6], also examined three different system types from a Li-ion battery pack, a super capacitor pack, and a dual buffer, for a hybrid bus. In another study, three different types of equivalent circuit models for ultra-capacitors were tested comparatively [7]; the classic model, the multi-stage ladder model and the dynamic model, which support in improving the battery charging status [8]. Another study characterized the dynamic model by fitting the collected impedance data [9], to further verify the reliability of the model used. Meanwhile, an online model identification of lithium-ion battery for electric vehicles implemented [10]. The model presented a reasonable level of complexity, whereas the validation results showed that the on-line calibrated model can accurately predict the dynamic voltage behavior of the lithium-ion battery. However, in [11, 12] a prolonged Kalman Filter was used to recursively estimate the model parameters, where in [11] equivalent circuit model template composed of a bulk capacitor, a second-order capacitance-resistance network, and a series resistance. While an efficient model [12] structured from a second-order resistance-capacitance network and a simple analytical open circuit voltage, versus state of charge (SOC) map was applied to characterize the voltage performance of a lithium iron phosphate battery for electric vehicles.

In terms of PV modeling, many studies have been carried out with PV system modeling and characterization [13–19]. According to [13], an approach for finding the parameters of a single-diode model of a PV panel was proposed. The influence of both irradiation and temperature on these parameters was considered. However, methods for finding the model parameters in the case of instantaneous variations in the temperature and irradiance have not been considered. In [15], a PV model was built upon simple procedures to acquire the PV system parameters in an easy and fast manner. This model was used mainly to characterize these parameters by using MATLAB/Simulink. Nonetheless, the applicability of using this model is limited because the model did not consider fast climate change. In 2014, an improved four-parameter model was constructed [17]. Therefore, this study was conducted to build a model that is able to fit the variation in the current—voltage characteristics (I–V) under various operating conditions. However, the lack of a practical analysis in this study made the validation weak. The improved modeling technique in [17] is based on genetic-algorithm optimization with a number of PV panel parameters determined using this approach. Two models were developed: a single-diode model and double-diode model. On the basis of this study, the single-diode model is more efficient than the double-diode model. Nevertheless, it has computational steps in the computational process.

In this paper, we introduce a novel method presents a reliable and an accessible PV model distinct in accuracy of model parameters and its characteristics based on changing of both ambient temperature and irradiance level. Therefore, the current model differs from other compared models by accuracy and also flexibility of application under fluctuated weather, while the other models just based on specific weather conditions rather than another. Another contribution introduced in this study, the I-V and P-V characteristics measurements to ensure reliable results of the model parameters. Finally, this study provides valuable information for those who are interested in PV system modeling and installation in the fluctuated weather conditions.

PV SYSTEM MODELING AND CHARACTERIZATION

In this section, the methodology of PV system characterization is presented in detail. A five-parameter model is used to characterize the PV array. An accurate mathematical model for the PV system is derived on the basis of the realistic parameters derived from the mathematical calculations.

PV Array Modeling

In this study, a 5 kW PV system with 42 multicrystalline PV modules installed in Malaysia is consider as a case study, as shown in Fig 1. The system specifications are listed in Table 1.

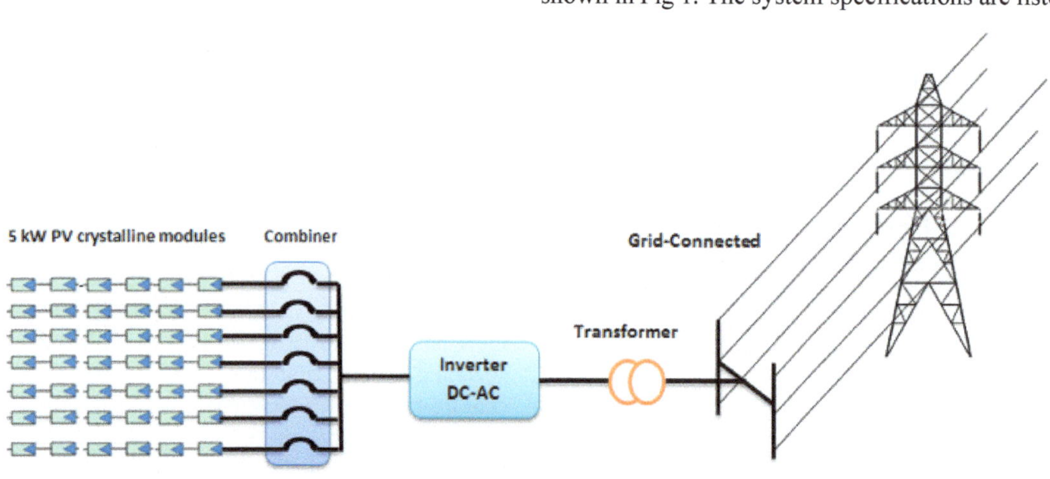

Figure 1: Schematic diagram of the PV system installed under Malaysia weather condition.

Table 1. Specifications of the proposed system.

Parameter	Value and Units
Number of PV modules	42
Maximum Power (P_{MP})	120 W
Maximum Voltage (V_{MP})	16.9 V
Maximum Current (I_{MP})	7.10 A
Open-Circuit Voltage (V_{OC})	21.5 V
Short-Circuit Current (I_{SC})	7.45 A

doi:10.1371/journal.pone.0152766.t001

In general, the PV system in this study is modeled on the basis of a single-diode model. Thus, a solar cell can be modeled by an equivalent circuit that consists of a current source, a reverse-biased diode, and a resistor connected in series, where each part of the model is associated with a specific parameter. The cell's photocurrent is represented by a current source, shown as the solar cell in the model. Moreover, the output voltage is represented by the reverse-biased diode. The diode's saturation current is represented by a shunt resistance. Finally, the cell's internal losses are indicated by a series resistance.

Under normal operation conditions or in the absence of sunlight, PV cell performance will be similar to a semiconductor diode in the dark. In such a case, this PV cell is represented by a normal diode, where its characteristics (current—voltage) can be expressed as

$$I_D = I_o\left(.\exp^{\frac{qV_D}{nkT}} - 1\right) \quad \textbf{(1)}$$

And

$$V_D = V + IR_S, \quad \textbf{(2)}$$

where I is the PV output current, I_o is the reverse saturation current of the diode, q is the electron charge equal to 1.602×10^{-19} C, k is the Boltzmann constant (1.381×10^{-23} J/K), T is the ambient temperature, V_D is the voltage across the diode terminals, V is the output voltage,R_S is the series resistance, and n is the ideality factor, also known as the quality factor or sometimes the emission coefficient.

On the other hand, an ideal cell is represented as a current generator connected in parallel with a diode when the solar cell is illuminated, and its I–V characteristics are described by Shockley [22] with the following equation:

$$I = I_L - I_D = I_L - I_o\left(\exp^{\frac{q(V+IR_S)}{nkT}} - 1\right) - \frac{V + IR_s}{R_{sh}}. \quad \textbf{(3)}$$

n usually takes values in the range 1–2 (although it might be larger in very few situations), which depends on the construction and semiconductor material.

Generally, the proposed PV system model is a five-parameter model, namely, I_L, I_o, a, R_s, andR_{sh}. This model can be used for an individual cell, a module consisting of several cells, or an array consisting of several modules.

Nonetheless, owing to the difficulty in finding an accurate value for n, we assume that

$$C_1 = \frac{q}{nk} \quad \textbf{(4)}$$

Then,

$$a = \frac{T_c}{C_1}. \quad \textbf{(5)}$$

As a result of this new relation as well as the expected higher shunt resistance, the shunt current becomes modest, and eventually, the new I–V characteristic equation can be simplified as

$$I = I_L - I_o\left(exp^{\frac{(V+IR_S)}{a}} - 1\right). \quad \textbf{(6)}$$

$$V = a.\ln\left(\frac{I_L - I}{I_o}\right) - IR_S. \quad \textbf{(7)}$$

Usually, the photocurrent (I_L) is proportional to the value of the solar irradiation, and it is supposed to be linearly dependent on the effective cell temperature (T_c). Consequently, this light-generation current could be expressed as

$$I_L = (C_2 + C_3.T - C_4)G_T. \quad \textbf{(8)}$$

where C_2–C_4 are coefficients, G_T is the solar irradiance, and T is the temperature of the cell. In the related literature [8], researchers demonstrated that T_c affects the diode saturation linearly as

$$I_o = C_5.T^3.\exp\left(-\frac{C_6}{T}\right), \quad \textbf{(9)}$$

where C_5 and C_6 are coefficients.

Solar Inverter Characterization

The performance of a PV system depends on more than one factor such as the inverter performance; this section is dedicated to a discussion of the inverter's characteristics. The inverter used in this study is Sunny Mini Central SMC 6000 inverter, which is the closest match to practical implementations.

In fact, a direct current/alternating current (DC/AC) inverter converts the DC current produced by the PV array into AC current. The efficiency of this energy conversion process can be expressed by

$$\eta(t) = (P_{in}(t) - P_{loss}(t))/P_{in}(t), \quad \textbf{(10)}$$

where P_{in} is the input power from the PV array, and P_{loss} is the conversion power loss.

In addition, a general relation between the inverter efficiency and the PV power is implemented in order to model and characterize the inverter as

$$\eta_{inv} = A\,P_{pv}^{n} + B \text{ for } 0 < P_{pv} < N, \quad \textbf{(11)}$$

$$\eta_{inv} = AP_{pv} + B \text{ for } P_{pv} \geq N, \quad \textbf{(12)}$$

where P_{pv} is the PV power, and A, B, and N are constants.

Therefore, the method used in this study models an inverter on the basis of a correlation method between the curve (characteristic curve) provided by the manufacturer and the experimental results. Thus, it may be an efficient model, which should be applicable for all inverter types in any climatic conditions.

Generally, Eqs (11) and (12) are applicable to this type of inverter (Sunny Mini Central inverter) in terms of the inverter efficiency. However, they can also be used and applied to other inverters of this kind. Therefore, the user needs to derive new equations for other types of inverters to obtain a more accurate inverter model.

MODEL EVALUATION CRITERIA

An efficient evaluation between the real curves of the photovoltaic panels and the proposed models has been done in this study. This evaluation is based on many benchmarks to ensure the accuracy of the proposed model with respect to the real data. All of these criteria show that the proposed model has a margin of error with respect to the real data from the PV panels. An evaluation based on the most famous factors such as the mean absolute percentage error (MAPE), the sum of the squares due to the error (SSE), the sum of squares due to regression (SSR), the sum of squares due to the total (SST), and the SSR divided by the SST (R-squared) is executed in this study. All of these factors are expressed as

$$MAPE = \left\{ \left| \frac{(R_v - P_m)}{Rv} \right| / n \right\} * 100\%, \quad (13)$$

$$SSE = \Sigma_{i=1}^{n} (Rv_i - Pm_i)^2, \quad (14)$$

$$SSR = \Sigma_{i=1}^{n} (Pm_i - Cel_i)^2, \quad (15)$$

$$SST = SSR + SSE, \quad (16)$$

$$R^2 = SSR/SST, \quad (17)$$

where Rv is the real value, Pm is the proposed model value, n is the number of tested points, and Cel is the central horizontal line drawn horizontally from the center of the theoretical curve.

RESULTS AND DISCUSSION

In this work, experimental data collected under Malaysian climatic conditions to obtain accurate values for the constants (C_1–C_6) of the global PV model. As mentioned in Table 1, the selected system consists of a 5 kW grid-connected PV system, which has been investigated by simulation for a month (from May 1, 2014 to May 31, 2014). Throughout this period, the irradiations ambient temperature, PV output power, and inverter efficiency are recorded every 0.1 s.

C_1–C_6 are accurately estimated on the basis of the experimental results in Table 2.

Table 2. Values of C_1–C_6.

Coefficient	Value
C_1	0.0062
C_2	0.0048
C_3	6.745×10^{-6}
C_4	3.237×10^{-8}
C_5	2.677×10^{-4}
C_6	6399

doi:10.1371/journal.pone.0152766.t002

This work has focused on a, I_L, and I_o. In other works such as [5], the characteristics are based on only a and I_L. Additionally, in other research works [6–8], the model only depends on the equations for I_L and I_o. Furthermore, the current work targets the new parameters within the tropical site (Malaysia as the case study), which might be applicable for all tropical areas for the first time. A set of new equations based on the extracted values are as follows:

$$a = \frac{T_c}{0.0062}, \quad (18)$$

$$I_L = (0.0048 + 6.745E - 6.T - 0.025)G_T, \quad (19)$$

$$I_o = 2.677E - 4.T^3.\exp\left(-\frac{6399}{T}\right). \quad (20)$$

Figs 2–4 show the results for parameters a, I_L, and I_o.

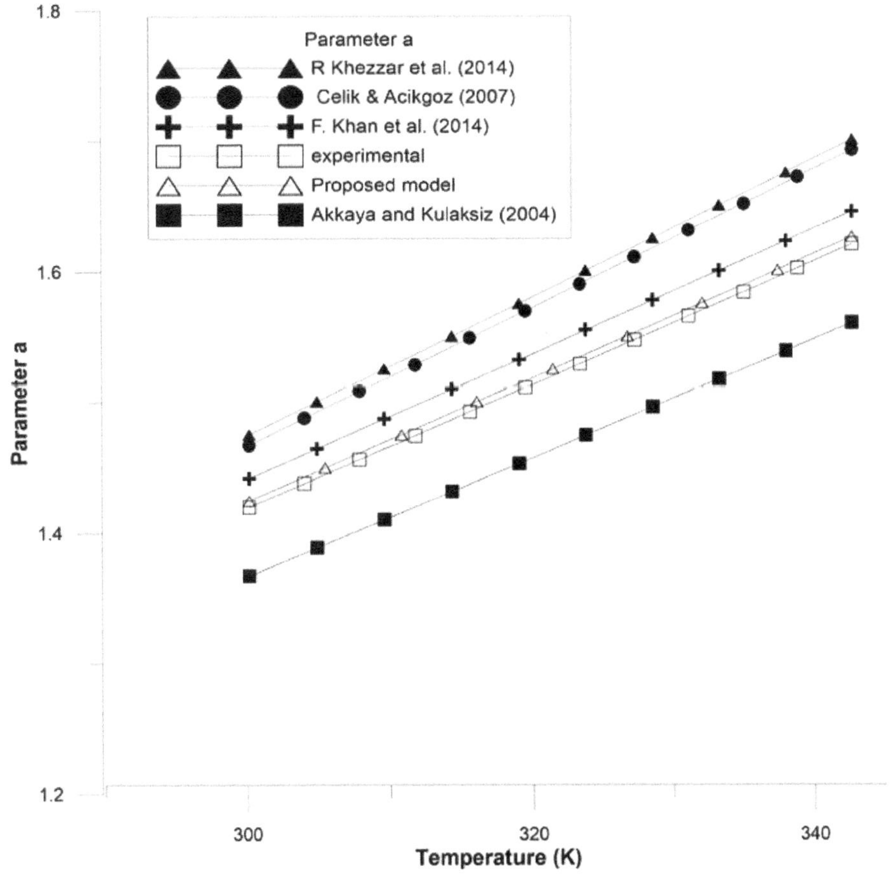

Figure 2. A comparison between the proposed equation for the parameter *a* **and** the experimental results with other models.

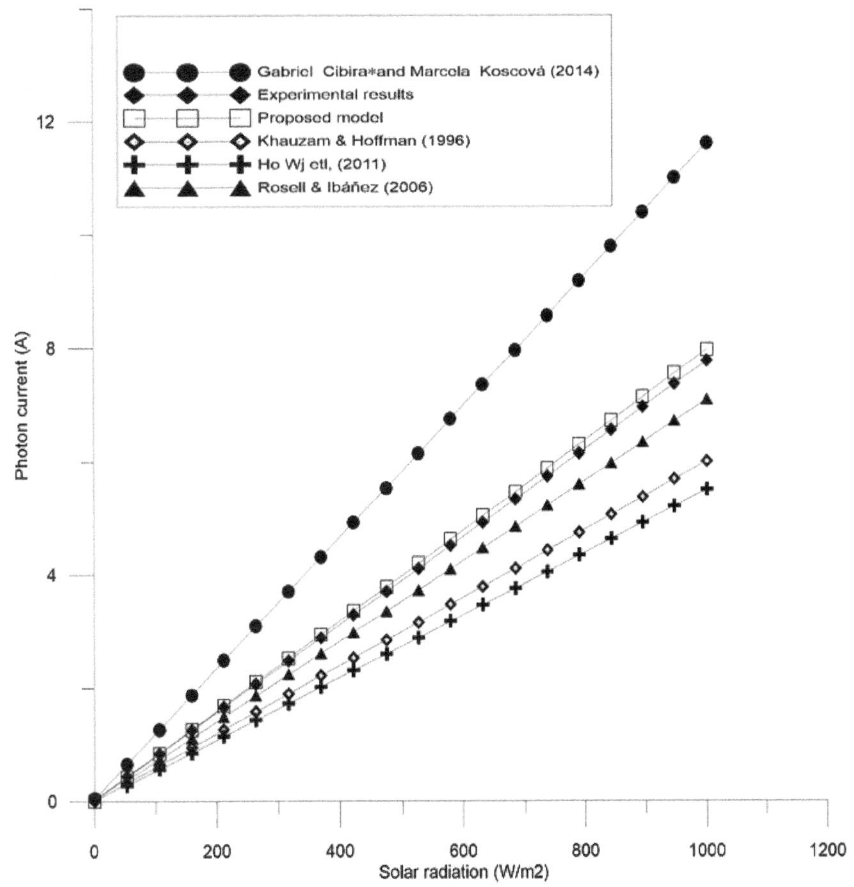

Figure 3. A comparison between the proposed equation for the photocurrent, I_L and the experimental results with other models.

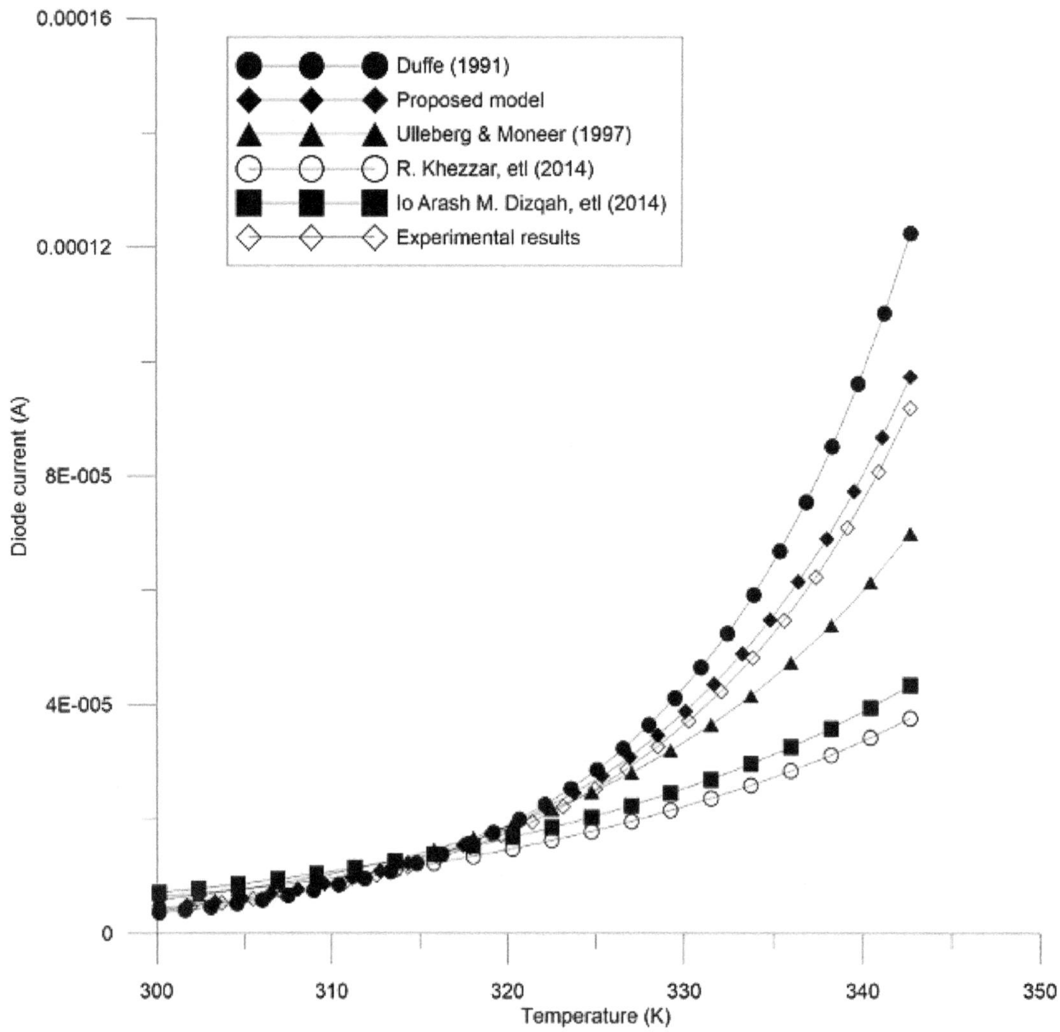

Figure 4. A comparison between the proposed equation for the reverse diode current, I_o and the experimental results with other models.

Generally, a validation of this study is utilized to confirm the accuracy of the proposed model, where it is based on several benchmarks such as the MAPE, R-squared, SSE, SSR, and SST, as stated before. The model evaluation criteria are presented in Table 3.

Table 3. Evaluation criteria of the proposed model.

Evaluation Criteria	Parameter *a*	Parameter I_o	Parameter I_L
MAPE	3.12%	6%	10.3%
SSE	2.198×10^{-16}	2.7281×10^{-15}	7.216×10^{-14}
R-squared	0.9998	0.998	0.997
SSR	1.09878×10^{-12}	1.36132×10^{-12}	2.39812×10^{-11}
SST	1.099×10^{-12}	1.364×10^{-12}	2.405×10^{-11}

doi:10.1371/journal.pone.0152766.t003

Although the PV model depends on five parameters (I_o, I_L, a, R_s, and R_{sh}), [20–23] some studies have focused on four parameters [24] or three parameters (R_s, R_{sh}, and a) [25]. However, in this research, R_{sh} is ignored because I_{sh} is too small. R_s is assumed to be fixed [3] and equal to 4.85 mΩ. Thus, the experimental data for the other three parameters (I_L, I_o, a) are used to estimate an accurate and exact value for C_1–C_6 by comparing them with the theoretical results. Nevertheless, owing to the rapid and continuous fluctuations in the weather conditions such as the radiance and temperature, continuous data for the current and voltage (every 0.5 s) have been logged.

In order to confirm the accuracy of the proposed model, a comparison is conducted between the real values (experimental results), the proposed theoretical values, and other models done before, for all of the parameter a, I_L, and I_o which are shown in Figs 5–7. Furthermore, these figures also present the performance of these parameters and its effect on the I-V and P-V characteristics.

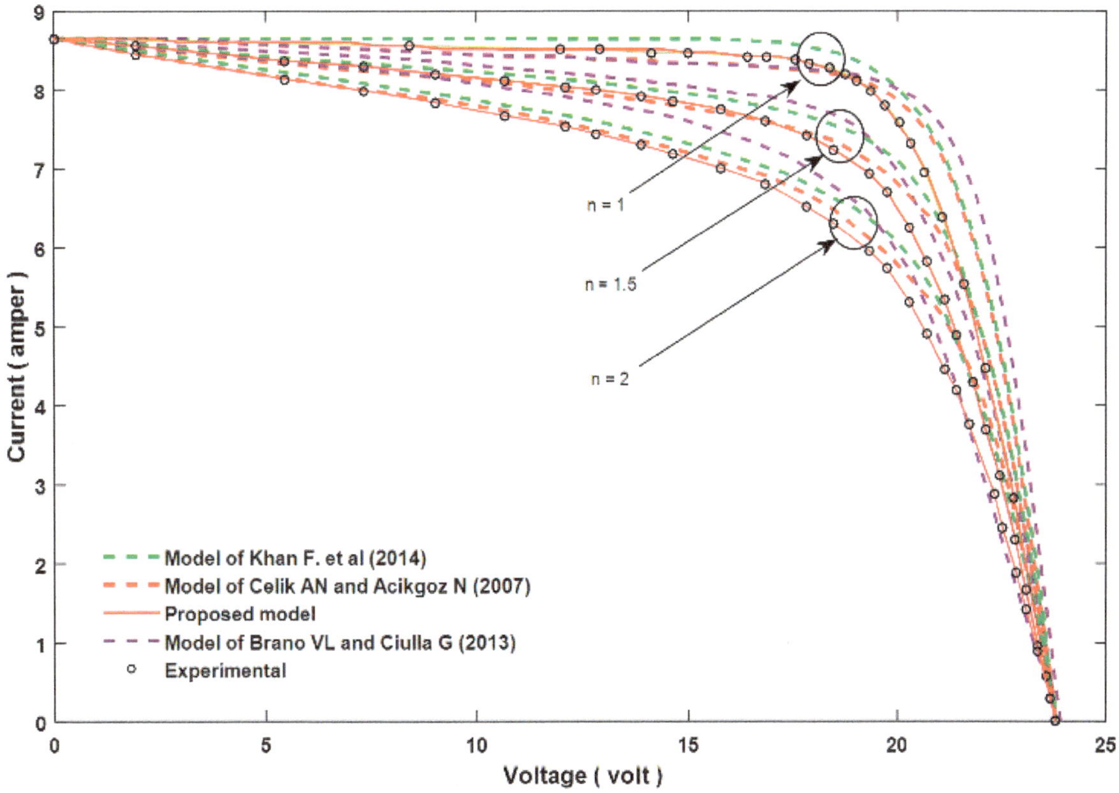

Figure 5. Influence of changing parameter "*a*" on the I–V characteristic curve, and comparing with experimental results and other models.

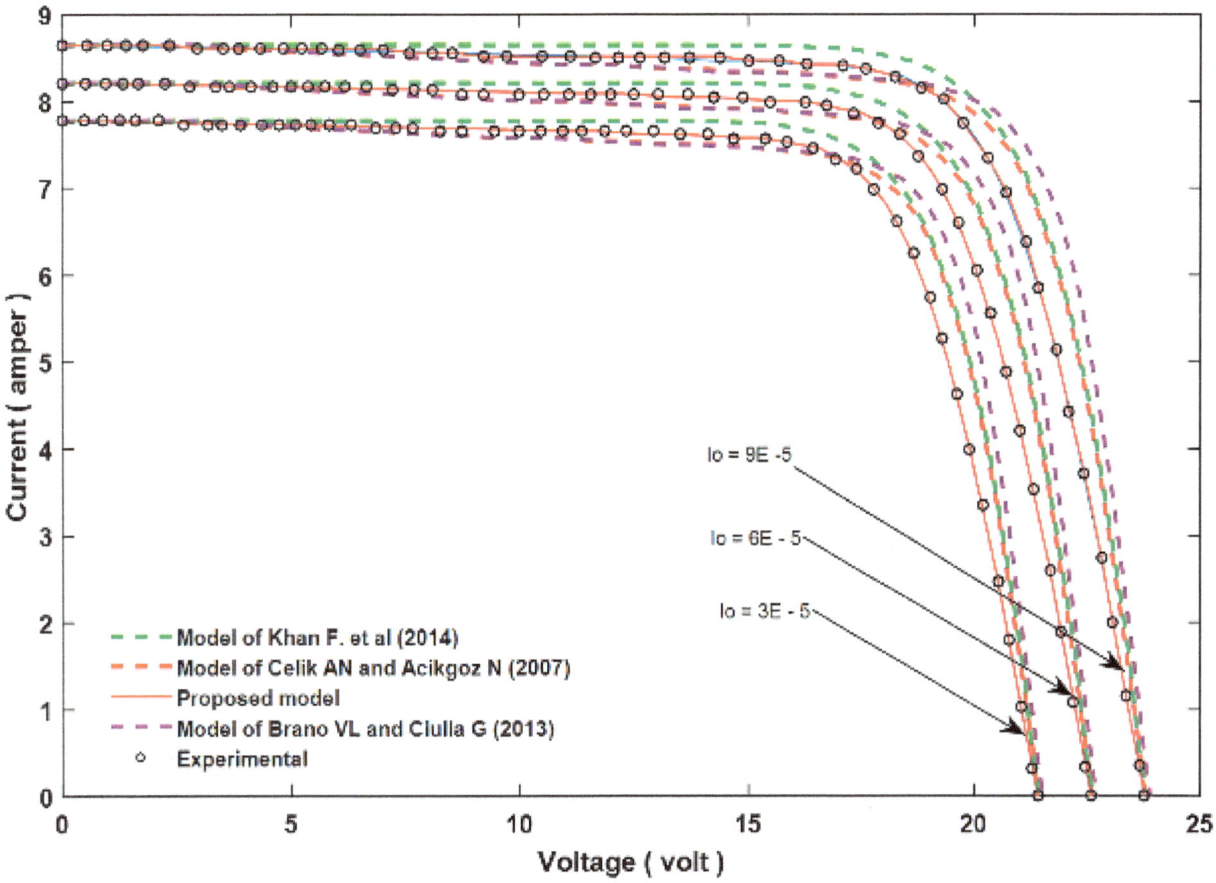

Figure 6. Influence of changing I_L on the I–V characteristic curve, and comparing with experimental results and other models.

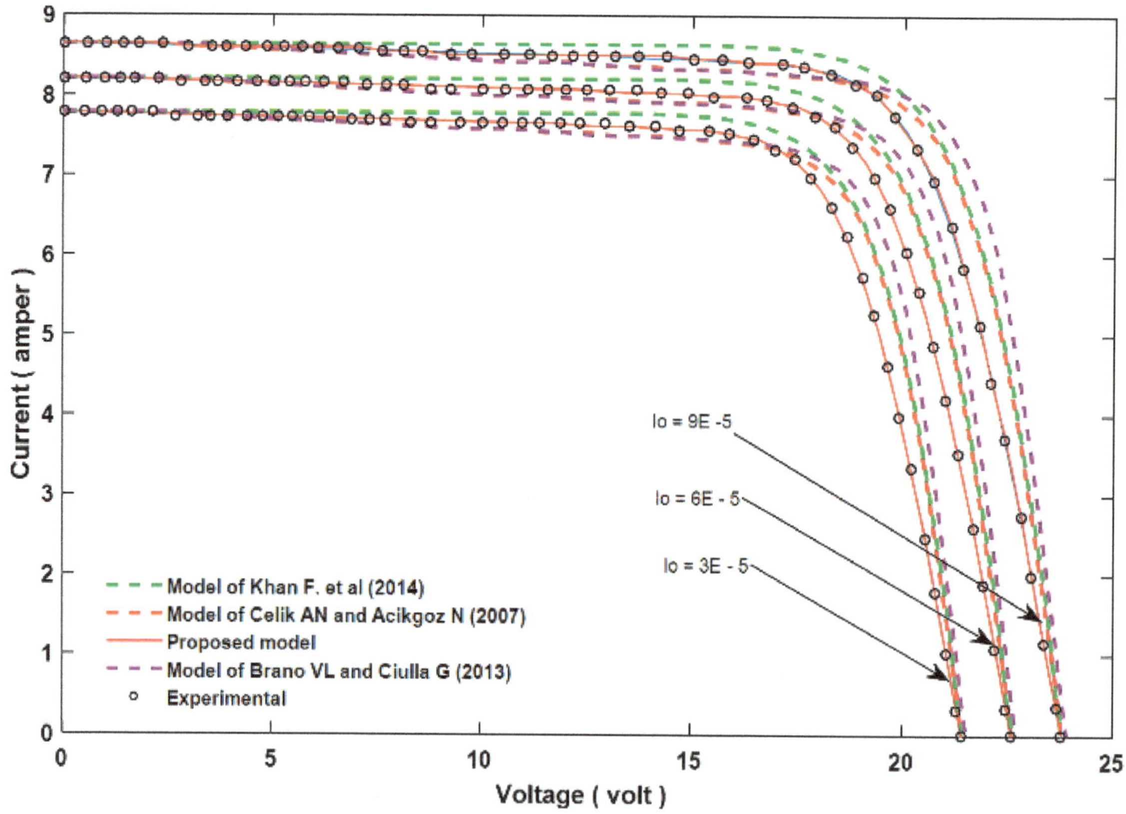

Figure 7. Influence of changing I_o on the I–V characteristic curve, and comparing with experimental results and other models.

The characterization results of number of meteorological datasets are collected on the basis of a month-long data, from sunrise to sunset. The MAPE, SSE, R-squared, SSR, and SST were employed to verify the accuracy of the model. The predicted values at each data point were compared with the measured values, providing the accuracy of the model. For instant, the least-squares error (SEE) for this study is close to zero, which indicates a good performance of the proposed mode. In addition, the R-squared values generally exhibited a good indication of the coefficient values used for this model, which are close to 1. Based on the above mentioned evaluation criteria, which used in the model parameters validation, the results of evaluation is listed in Table 3.

However, with respect to inverter characterization an innovative way is used in this study to derive an accurate relation between inverter efficiency and the PV power, which is based on a correlation method.

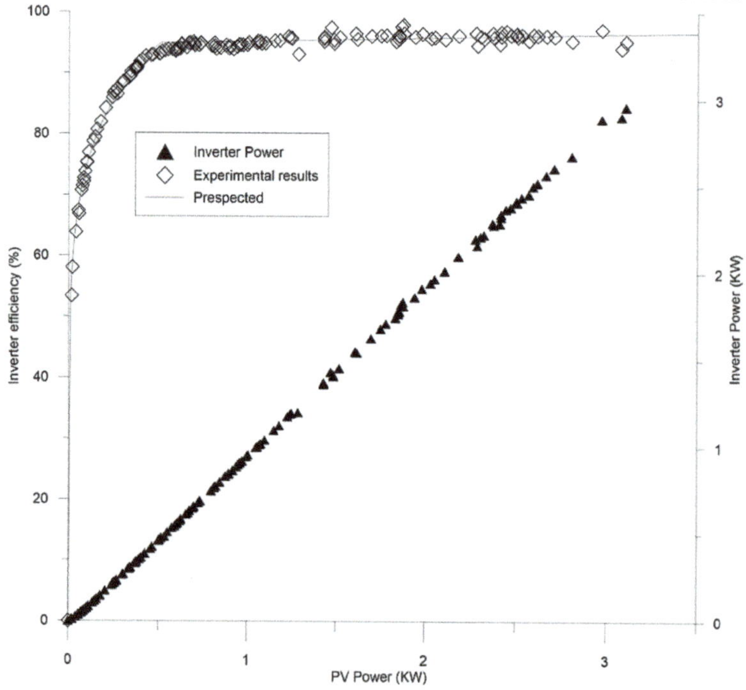

Figure 8. Inverter's power and efficiency with respect to PV power.

This method tries to correlate the real values of the curve with the curve provided by the manufacturer. Eventually, a new relation has been derived from this fitting as the standard for all inverter efficiency of this kind. The accuracy of this method was tested through finding MAPE to be only1.09%, and R-square to be 0.99998, proving its high degree of accuracy of this type of inverter. The evaluation for the inverter's efficiency which has been executed through the expected and real results is presented in Fig 8, and the relation is represented by equations below.

$$\eta_{inv} = 105.1\, P_{pv}^{0.1456} \text{ for } 0 < P_{pv} < 0.517 \quad (21)$$

$$\eta_{inv} = 0.6032 P_{pv} + 94.64 \text{ for } P_{pv} \geq 0.517 \quad (22)$$

CONCLUSION

Experimental and theoretical calculations have been performed to determine the PV model' parameters and I-V characteristic for a grid-connected photovoltaic system which is operated under fluctuated weather condition. In this purpose, an accurate mathematical PV model has been accomplished through theoretical and experimental evaluation of the PV parameters (the photocurrent, I_L, the reverse diode saturation current, I_o, the ideality factor of diode, n). Results of these parameters showed that the proposed model verified valued accuracy (based on different evaluation criteria) comparing with the other models. Moreover, the results of I-V characteristics based on changing all of the used model parameters also fitted the real results and recorded effect of each parameter on the I-V characteristics alone, which didn't deal before in the literature.

REFERENCES

1. Amin N, Lung CW, Sopian K. A practical field study of various solar cells on their performance in Malaysia. Renewable Energy. 2009;34(8):1939–46. doi: 10.1016/j.renene.2008.12.005
2. Humada AM, Samsuri FB, Hojabria M, Mohamed MB, Sulaiman MHB, Dakheel TH, editors. Modeling of photovoltaic solar array under different levels of partial shadow conditions. Power Electronics and Motion Control Conference and Exposition (PEMC), 2014 16th International; 2014: IEEE.
3. Humada AM, Hojabri M, Mohamed MB, Sulaiman B, Herwan M, Dakheel TH, editors. A Proposed Method of Photovoltaic Solar Array Configuration under Different Partial Shadow Conditions. Advanced Materials Research; 2014: Trans Tech Publ.
4. Micheli D, Alessandrini S, Radu R, Casula I. Analysis of the outdoor performance and efficiency of two grid connected photovoltaic systems in northern Italy. Energy conversion and management. 2014;80:436–45. doi: 10.1016/j.enconman.2014.01.053
5. Hu X, Li S, Peng H. A comparative study of equivalent circuit models for Li-ion batteries. Journal of Power Sources. 2012;198:359–67. doi: 10.1016/j.jpowsour.2011.10.013
6. Hu X, Murgovski N, Johannesson LM, Egardt B. Comparison of three electrochemical energy buffers applied to a hybrid bus powertrain with simultaneous optimal sizing and energy management. Intelligent Transportation Systems, IEEE Transactions on. 2014;15(3):1193–205. doi: 10.1109/tits.2013.2294675
7. Zhang L, Wang Z, Hu X, Sun F, Dorrell DG. A comparative study of equivalent circuit models of ultracapacitors for electric vehicles. Journal of Power Sources. 2015;274:899–906. doi: 10.1016/j.jpowsour.2014.10.170
8. Zhang L, Wang Z, Hu X, Dorrell D, editors. Residual Capacity Estimation for Ultracapacitors in Electric Vehicles Using Artificial Neural Network. World Congress; 2014.
9. Zhang L, Hu X, Wang Z, Sun F, Dorrell DG. Experimental impedance investigation of an ultracapacitor at different conditions for electric vehicle applications. Journal of Power Sources. 2015;287:129–38. doi: 10.1016/j.jpowsour.2015.04.043
10. Hu X-s, Sun F-c, Zou Y. Online model identification of lithium-ion battery for electric vehicles. Journal of Central South University of Technology. 2011;18:1525–31. doi: 10.1007/s11771-011-0869-1
11. Zhang L, Wang Z, Sun F, Dorrell DG. Online parameter identification of ultracapacitor models using the extended Kalman filter. Energies. 2014;7(5):3204–17. doi: 10.3390/en7053204
12. Hu X-s, Sun F-c, Cheng X-m. Recursive calibration for a lithium iron phosphate battery for electric vehicles using extended Kalman filtering. Journal of Zhejiang University SCIENCE A. 2011;12(11):818–25. doi: 10.1631/jzus.a1100141
13. Dizqah AM, Maheri A, Busawon K. An accurate method for the PV model identification based on a genetic algorithm and the interior-point method. Renewable Energy. 2014;72:212–22.
14. Akkaya R, Kulaksiz A. A microcontroller-based stand-alone photovoltaic power system for residential appliances. Applied Energy. 2004;78(4):419–31. doi: 10.1016/j.apenergy.2003.09.005
15. Cibira G, Koščová M. Photovoltaic module parameters acquisition model. Applied Surface Science. 2014. doi: 10.1016/j.apsusc.2014.05.080
16. Ismail M, Moghavvemi M, Mahlia T. Characterization of PV panel and global optimization of its model parameters using genetic algorithm. Energy Conversion and Management. 2013;73:10–25. doi: 10.1016/j.enconman.2013.03.033
17. Khezzar R, Zereg M, Khezzar A. Modeling improvement of the four parameter model for photovoltaic modules. Solar Energy. 2014;110:452–62. doi: 10.1016/j.solener.2014.09.039
18. Laudani A, Fulginei FR. Comments on "An efficient analytical approach for obtaining a five parameters model of photovoltaic modules using only reference data"(Appl. Energy 111 (2013) 894–903). Applied Energy. 2014. doi: 10.1016/j.apenergy.2014.04.107
19. Ishaque K, Salam Z. An improved modeling method to determine the model parameters of photovoltaic (PV) modules using differential evolution (DE). Solar Energy. 2011;85(9):2349–59. doi: 10.1016/j.solener.2011.06.025

20. Wolf P, Benda V. Identification of PV solar cells and modules parameters by combining statistical and analytical methods. Solar Energy. 2013;93:151–7. doi: 10.1016/j.solener.2013.03.018

21. Yuan X, Xiang Y, He Y. Parameter extraction of solar cell models using mutative-scale parallel chaos optimization algorithm. Solar Energy. 2014;108:238–51. doi: 10.1016/j.solener.2014.07.013

22. Dkhichi F, Oukarfi B, Fakkar A, Belbounaguia N. Parameter identification of solar cell model using Levenberg—Marquardt algorithm combined with simulated annealing. Solar Energy. 2014;110:781–8. doi: 10.1016/j.solener.2014.09.033

23. Humada AM, Hojabri M, Mekhilef S, Hamada HM. Solar cell parameters extraction based on single and double-diode models: A review. Renewable and Sustainable Energy Reviews. 2016;56:494–509. doi: 10.1016/j.rser.2015.11.051

24. Gong W, Cai Z. Parameter extraction of solar cell models using repaired adaptive differential evolution. Solar Energy. 2013;94:209–20. doi: 10.1016/j.solener.2013.05.007

25. Rajasekar N, Krishna Kumar N, Venugopalan R. Bacterial Foraging Algorithm based solar PV parameter estimation. Solar Energy. 2013;97:255–65. doi: 10.1016/j.solener.2013.08.019

CHAPTER 13

COMPLEX GENERALIZED SYNCHRONIZATION AND PARAMETER IDENTIFICATION OF NONIDENTICAL NONLINEAR COMPLEX SYSTEMS

Shibing Wang[1,2], Xingyuan Wang[1], Bo Han[2]

[1] Faculty of Electronic Information and Electrical Engineering, Dalian University of Technology, Dalian, 116024, China,

[2] School of Computer and Information Engineering, Fuyang Normal University, Fuyang, 236041, China

ABSTRACT

In this paper, generalized synchronization (GS) is extended from real space to complex space, resulting in a new synchronization scheme, complex generalized synchronization (CGS). Based on Lyapunov stability theory, an adaptive controller and parameter update laws are designed to realize CGS and parameter identification of two nonidentical chaotic (hyperchaotic) complex systems with respect to a given complex map vector. This scheme is applied to synchronize a memristor-based hyperchaotic complex Lü system and a memristor-based chaotic complex Lorenz system, a chaotic complex Chen system and a memristor-based chaotic complex Lorenz system, as well as a memristor-based hyperchaotic complex Lü system and a chaotic complex Lü system with fully unknown parameters. The corresponding numerical simulations illustrate the feasibility and effectiveness of the proposed scheme.

INTRODUCTION

Since Fowler et al. proposed a complex Lorenz system in 1982 [1], modeling, analyses and synchronization of complex systems have attracted more and more attention in nonlinear science and technology fields, the reasons of which can be roughly summed up in the following two aspects. On the one hand, some physical systems and phenomena should be accurately modeled by complex systems, such as rotating fluids, detuned lasers, disk dynamos, electronic circuits, and so on [1–4]; on the other, due to the existence of complex variables which can double the number of variables, complex systems can generate complicated dynamical behaviors with strong unpredictability, and synchronization of complex systems has widely potential applications to many fields of physics, ecological systems, signal and information processing, and system identification, especially to secure communication for achieving higher transmission efficiency and anti-attack ability [5–7].

As we well know, chaos synchronization is the precondition of chaotic secure communication, digital cryptography, chaotic image encryption, etc. Since the pioneering work by Pecora and Carrol in 1990 [8], chaos synchronization of real systems has been extensively investigated theoretically and experimentally, while the synchronization of complex systems has been explored for less than a decade. In the

Citation: Wang S, Wang X, Han B (2016) Complex Generalized Synchronization and Parameter Identification of Nonidentical Nonlinear Complex Systems. PLoS ONE 11(3): e0152099. doi:10.1371/journal.pone.0152099

beginning stages, some synchronization schemes were directly used to synchronize complex systems, such as complete synchronization (CS) [9–10], lag synchronization (LS) [7, 11], projective synchronization (PS) [12–13], phase synchronization (PhS) [14], combination synchronization [15], etc. Recently, some complex synchronization methods were presented based on their real versions. Liu et al. proposed a complex modified hybrid projective synchronization (CMHPS) scheme to synchronize complex Dadras systems, with different dimensions and complex parameters, up to a desired complex transformation matrix [16]. Wang et al. investigated a hybrid synchronization method containing complex modified projective synchronization and module-phase synchronization [17]. Sun et al. realized complex combination synchronization of three identical chaotic complex systems with complex scaling matrices [18]. Jiang et al. designed a general controller to achieve combination complex synchronization for fractional-order chaotic complex systems [19]. It is worth noting that Refs [20–21] have explored the synchronization issues of complex systems with unknown parameters which are likely to exist in practice. Zhang et al. investigated the complex modified projective synchronization (CMPS) and parameter identification of uncertain real chaotic systems and complex chaotic systems [20]. Liu et al. used an adaptive complex modified projective synchronization (ACMPS) method to synchronize two chaotic (hyperchaotic) complex systems up to a complex scaling matrix, and to estimate the unknown complex parameters successfully [21].

Based on the above-mentioned complex synchronization methods, the response complex systems can be synchronized with the drive complex systems up to the desired complex scaling matrices. Shall we further generalize these synchronization schemes and synchronize the complex systems with respect to a given complex functional relationship? That is, can generalized synchronization (GS) be extended to synchronize complex systems? Rulkov et al. firstly proposed the generalized synchronization, where two chaotic systems are said to be synchronized if a given functional relation can be realized between the variables of drive and response systems [22]. With different given functions, GS can degenerate to various PSs, antisynchronization (AS) and CS. Furthermore, the given functions are almost impossible to be predicted, which can enhance secure performance when GS is applied to chaotic secure communication. In the recent two decades, GS of chaotic or hyperchaotic real systems has been widely investigated. For instance, Refs [23–25] realized GS of different chaotic and hyperchaotic systems, while Refs [26–28] achieved adaptive generalized synchronization (AGS) and parameter identification of different chaotic systems with unknown parameters. However, to our best knowledge, up to now, there are few published achievements on CGS of nonidentical nonlinear complex systems. So, it is meaningful and challenging to extend GS from real systems to complex systems, and to realize CGS and parameter identification of chaotic and hyperchaotic complex systems with unknown parameters.

Motivated by the above discussions, this paper investigates CGS and parameter identification of different chaotic and hyperchaotic complex systems with unknown parameters. In practice, the parameters of some nonlinear systems cannot be exactly known, so we choose uncertain nonlinear complex systems as the research objects, and use adaptive control and Lyapunov stability theory to design CGS and parameter estimation scheme for them. In our proposed scheme, CGS is defined by extending GS from real space to complex space, and designed with consideration of error feedback control gains which are introduced to adjust converging velocity. Furthermore, according to the orders of the drive and response nonlinear complex systems (i.e., same-order, increased-order, and reduced-order), three different examples are presented to verify the correctness, feasibility, and efficiency of the proposed scheme.

The rest of this paper is organized as follows. The definition and design of CGS of nonidentical complex systems are given in Section 2. CGS and parameter identification of a memristor-based hyperchaotic complex Lü system and a memristor-based chaotic complex Lorenz system with the same orders, a chaotic complex Chen system and a memristor-based chaotic complex Lorenz system via increased order, as well as a memristor-based hyperchaotic complex Lü system and a chaotic complex Lü system via reduced order, are investigated theoretically and illustrated numerically in Section 3–5, respectively. Finally, some conclusions are drawn in Section 6.

DESIGN OF CGS

Definition of CGS

Consider the following nonidentical drive and response complex systems with fully unknown parameters

$$\dot{x} = F(x)\theta + f(x) \quad (1)$$

$$\dot{y} = G(y)\delta + g(y) + u(x,y) \quad (2)$$

where $x = (x_1, x_2, \cdots x_n)^T$ and $y = (y_1, y_2, \cdots x_m)^T$ are complex state vectors of the drive system (1) and response system (2) respectively, $x_k = x_{k,r} + jx_{k,i}(k = 1, \cdots, n)$, $y_k = y_{k,r} + jy_{k,i}(k = 1, \cdots, m)$, $j = \sqrt{-1}$, the subscripts r and i denote the real and image parts of the complex variables, vectors and matrices throughout this paper. $\theta \in R^p$ and $\delta \in R^q$ are real vectors of unknown parameters. $F(x) \in C^{n\times p}$ and $G(y) \in C^{m\times q}$ are complex matrices, $F(x) = F_r(x) + jF_i(x)$, $G(y) = G_r(y) + jG_i(y)$. $f(x) \in C^n$ and $g(y) \in C^m$ are vectors of nonlinear complex functions, and $f(x) = f_r(x) + jf_i(x)$, $g(y) = g_r(y) + jg_i(y)$. $u(x, y) \in C^m$ is the complex control vector, and $u(x, y) = u_r(x, y) + ju_i(x, y)$.

Remark 1 Some nonlinear complex systems can be formed as system (1), such as complex Lorenz system, complex Chen system, complex Lü system, memristor-based complex Lorenz system, memristor-based complex Lü system, and so on. For synchronizing such complex systems, the complex variables and functions could be divided into the real parts and imaginary parts.

Definition 1 For the drive system (1) and response system (2), CGS is achieved if there exist a complex controller $u(x, y)$ and a given complex map $\phi(x)$:$C^n \rightarrow C^m$ such that

$$\lim_{t\to\infty} \|y - \phi(x)\| = 0 \quad (3)$$

where $\phi(x) = [\phi_1(x), \phi_1(x), \cdots \phi_m(x)]^T$ is a nonzero complex map vector whose elements are continuously differentiable complex functions of x, and $\phi(x) = \phi_r(x) + j\phi_i(x)$.

Remark 2 If $\phi(x) = \Theta x$, some types of synchronization are special cases of CGS, such as complex modified hybrid projective synchronization (CMHPS) as $\Theta \in \mathbf{C}^{m\times n}$, complex modified projective synchronization (CMPS) as $\Theta = \mathrm{diag}(\vartheta_1, \vartheta_2, \cdots \vartheta_n) \in \mathbf{C}^{m\times n}$, complex projective synchronization (CPS) as $\Theta = \mathrm{diag}(\vartheta, \vartheta, \cdots \vartheta) \in \mathbf{C}^{n\times n}$, modified hybrid projective synchronization (MHPS) as $\Theta \in \mathbf{R}^{m\times n}$, modified projective synchronization (MPS) as $\Theta = \mathrm{diag}(\vartheta_1, \vartheta_2, \cdots \vartheta_n) \in \mathbf{R}^{n\times n}$, projective synchronization (PS) as $\Theta = \mathrm{diag}(\vartheta, \vartheta, \cdots \vartheta) \in \mathbf{R}^{n\times n}$, antisynchronization (AS) as $\Theta = \mathrm{diag}(-1, -1, \cdots -1)$, and complete synchronization (CS) as $\Theta = \mathrm{diag}(1, 1, \cdots 1)$.

General scheme of CGS and parameter identification

Define the complex CGS error vector as

$$\begin{aligned} e &= y - \phi(x) = e_r + je_i \\ &= (y_r - \phi_r(x)) + j(y_i - \phi_i(x)) \end{aligned} \quad (4)$$

where $e = (e_1, e_2, \cdots e_m)^T \in \mathbf{C}^m$, $e_r = (e_{1,r}, e_{2,r}, \cdots e_{m,r})^T \in \mathbf{R}^m$, $e_i = (e_{1,i}, e_{2,i}, \cdots e_{m,i})^T \in \mathbf{R}^m$. By taking the derivative of Eq 4 with respect time, the CGS error dynamical system is obtained as

$$\dot{e} = \dot{y} - J(\phi)\dot{x} \quad (5)$$

where $J(\phi) \in \mathbf{C}^{m\times n}$ is the Jacobian matrix of $\phi(x)$, and $J(\phi) = J_r(\phi) + jJ_i(\phi)$. By substituting Eqs 1and 2 into Eq 5, Eq 5 can be represented by

$$\begin{aligned} \dot{e} &= \dot{e}_r + j\dot{e}_i \\ &= \{g_r(y) - J_r(\phi)f_r(x) + J_i(\phi)f_i(x) - [J_r(\phi)F_r(x) - J_i(\phi)F_i(x)]\theta + G_r(y)\delta + u_r(x,y)\} \\ &+j\{g_i(y) - J_r(\phi)f_i(x) - J_i(\phi)f_r(x) - [J_r(\phi)F_i(x) + J_i(\phi)F_r(x)]\theta + G_i(y)\delta + u_i(x,y)\} \end{aligned} \quad (6)$$

Therefore, the problem of CGS for two nonidentical complex systems (1) and (2) is transformed to the stability analysis of zero solution of the error dynamical system (6). Adaptive CGS scheme is given in Theorem 1 and is proved based on Lyapunov stability theory.

Theorem 1 For a given complex map vector $\phi(x)$, CGS and parameter identification of the response system (2) and the drive system (1) can be achieved if the complex adaptive controller and the parameter update laws are designed

as

$$\begin{aligned} u(x,y) &= u_r(x,y) + ju_i(x,y) \\ &= \{-g_r(y) + J_r(\phi)f_r(x) - J_i(\phi)f_i(x) + [J_r(\phi)F_r(x) - J_i(\phi)F_i(x)]\hat{\theta} - G_r(y)\hat{\delta} - Ke_r\} \\ &+j\{-g_i(y) + J_r(\phi)f_i(x) + J_i(\phi)f_r(x) + [J_r(\phi)F_i(x) + J_i(\phi)F_r(x)]\hat{\theta} - G_i(y)\hat{\delta} - Ke_i\} \end{aligned} \quad (7)$$

$$\begin{cases} \dot{\hat{\theta}} = \dot{\tilde{\theta}} &= -[J_r(\phi)F_r(x) - J_i(\phi)F_i(x)]^T e_r - [J_r(\phi)F_i(x) + J_i(\phi)F_r(x)]^T e_i - K_\theta\tilde{\theta} \\ \dot{\hat{\delta}} = \dot{\tilde{\delta}} &= [G_r(y)]^T e_r + [G_i(y)]^T e_i - K_\delta\tilde{\delta} \end{cases} \quad (8)$$

where $\hat{\theta}$ and $\hat{\delta}$ denote the estimated parameter vectors of θ and δ, $\tilde{\theta} = \hat{\theta} - \theta$ and $\tilde{\delta} = \hat{\delta} - \delta$ denote the parameter error vectors. $K = \mathrm{diag}(k_1, k_2 \cdots k_m)$, $K_\theta = \mathrm{diag}(k_{\theta,1}, k_{\theta,2} \cdots k_{\theta,p})$ and $K_\delta = \mathrm{diag}(k_{\delta,1}, k_{\delta,2} \cdots k_{\delta,q})$ are error feedback control strength whose elements are all positive constants, which can adjust converging velocity.

Proof We introduce a positive Lyapunov function as

$$V(t) = \frac{1}{2}[(e_r)^T e_r + (e_i)^T e_i + \tilde{\theta}^T\tilde{\theta} + \tilde{\delta}^T\tilde{\delta}] \quad (9)$$

The time derivative of $V(t)$ along the trajectories of the error dynamical system (6) is calculated as

$$\begin{aligned} \dot{V}(t) &= (\dot{e}_r)^T e_r + (\dot{e}_i)^T e_i + \tilde{\theta}^T\dot{\tilde{\theta}} + \tilde{\delta}^T\dot{\tilde{\delta}} \\ &= \{g_r(y) - J_r(\phi)f_r(x) + J_i(\phi)f_i(x) - [J_r(\phi)F_r(x) - J_i(\phi)F_i(x)]\theta + G_r(y)\delta + u_r(x,y)\}^T e_r \\ &+\{g_i(y) - J_r(\phi)f_i(x) - J_i(\phi)f_r(x) - [J_r(\phi)F_i(x) + J_i(\phi)F_r(x)]\theta + G_i(y)\delta + u_i(x,y)\}^T e_i \\ &+\tilde{\theta}^T\dot{\tilde{\theta}} + \tilde{\delta}^T\dot{\tilde{\delta}} \end{aligned} \quad (10)$$

Substituting Eqs 7 and 8 into Eq 10, then

$$\begin{aligned} \dot{V}(t) &= \{[J_r(\phi)F_r(x) - J_i(\phi)F_i(x)]\tilde{\theta} - G_r(y)\tilde{\delta} - Ke_r\}^T e_r \\ &+\{[J_r(\phi)F_i(x) + J_i(\phi)F_r(x)]\tilde{\theta} - G_i(y)\tilde{\delta} - Ke_i\}^T e_i \\ &-\tilde{\theta}^T\{[J_r(\phi)F_r(x) - J_i(\phi)F_i(x)]^T e_r + [J_r(\phi)F_i(x) + J_i(\phi)F_r(x)]^T e_i - K_\theta\tilde{\theta}\} \\ &+\tilde{\delta}^T\{[G_r(y)]^T e_r + [G_i(y)]^T e_i - K_\delta\tilde{\delta}\} \\ &= -(e_r)^T Ke_r - (e_i)^T Ke_i - \tilde{\theta}^T K_\theta\tilde{\theta} - \tilde{\delta}^T K_\delta\tilde{\delta} \\ &< 0 \end{aligned} \quad (11)$$

Based on Lyapunov stability theory, since $V(t)$ and $\dot{V}(t)$ are positive and negative respectively, the CGS errors and the parameter errors asymptotically converge to zero as the time tends to infinity, i.e., $\lim_{t\to\infty} e_r(t) = 0$, $\lim_{t\to\infty} e_i(t) = 0$, $\lim_{t\to\infty} \tilde{\theta}(t) = 0$ and $\lim_{t\to\infty} \tilde{\delta}(t) = 0$, which indicate that CGS and parameter identification are realized. The proof is completed.

CGS of a Memristor-Based Hyperchaotic Complex Lü System and a Memristor-Based Chaotic Complex Lorenz System (n =m)

In this section, we investigate CGS of two nonidentical complex systems with the same orders. On the basis of a memristor-based hyperchaotic Lü system proposed in [29], a memristor-based hyperchaotic complex Lü system is introduced as the drive system, which is described as

$$\begin{cases} \dot{x}_1 = a_1(x_2 - x_1) \\ \dot{x}_2 = -x_1x_3 + a_2x_2 - a_3(\alpha_1 + 3\beta_1x_4^2)x_1 \\ \dot{x}_3 = \frac{1}{2}(\bar{x}_1x_2 + x_1\bar{x}_2) - a_4x_3 \\ \dot{x}_4 = \frac{1}{2}(\bar{x}_1 + x_1) \end{cases} \quad (12)$$

where $x_1, x_2 \in C$, $x_3, x_4 \in R$, $\bar{x}_1, \bar{x}_2 \in C$ denote the complex conjugate variables of x_1, x_2. a_1, a_2, a_3 and a_4 are unknown real parameters, α_1 and β_1 are considered as known positive constants. When $\alpha_1 = 4$, $\beta_1 = 0.01$, $a_1 = 36$, $a_2 = 20$, $a_3 = 3.2$, $a_4 = 3$ and $x(0) = [-1 + 2j, 1 + j, 2, -1]^T$, the Lyapunov exponents of system (12) are calculated as (0.262, 0.103, 0, 0, -15.764, -17.553), and a hyperchaotic attractor is plotted in Fig 1.

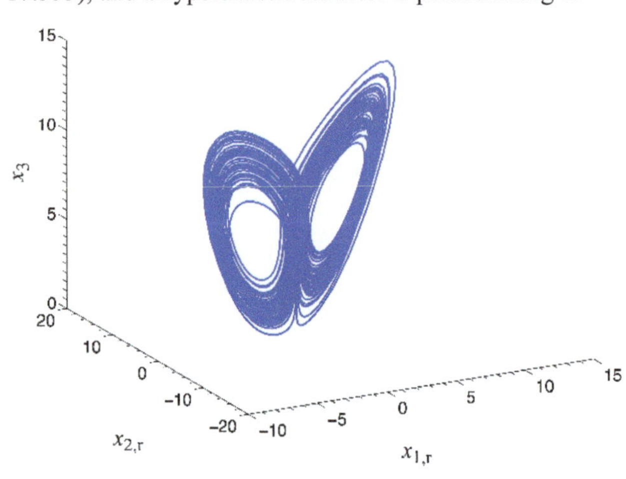

Figure 1. Hyperchaotic attractor of the memristor-based complex Lü system.

A memristor-based chaotic complex Lorenz system, proposed in [30], is introduced as the response system

$$\begin{cases} \dot{y}_1 = -b_1y_1 - (\alpha_2 + 3\beta_2y_4^2)y_1 + b_2y_2 + u_1 \\ \dot{y}_2 = b_3y_1 - y_2 - y_1y_3 + u_2 \\ \dot{y}_3 = \frac{1}{2}(\bar{y}_1y_2 + y_1\bar{y}_2) - b_4y_3 + u_3 \\ \dot{y}_4 = -\frac{1}{2}(\bar{y}_1 + y_1) + u_4 \end{cases} \quad (13)$$

where $y_1, y_2 \in C$, $y_3, y_4 \in R$, b_1, b_2, b_3 and b_4 are unknown real parameters, α_2 and β_2 are considered as known positive constants. u_1, u_2, u_3 and u_4 are controllers. When $\alpha_2 = 0.67 \times 10^{-3}$, $\beta_2 = 0.02 \times 10^{-3}$, $b_1 = 8$, $b_2 = 11$, $b_3 = 50$, $b_4 = 8/3$ and $y(0) = [2, 1 + 4j, 0.1, 0]^T$, the system (13) operates in chaotic orbits without control, as shown in Fig 2.

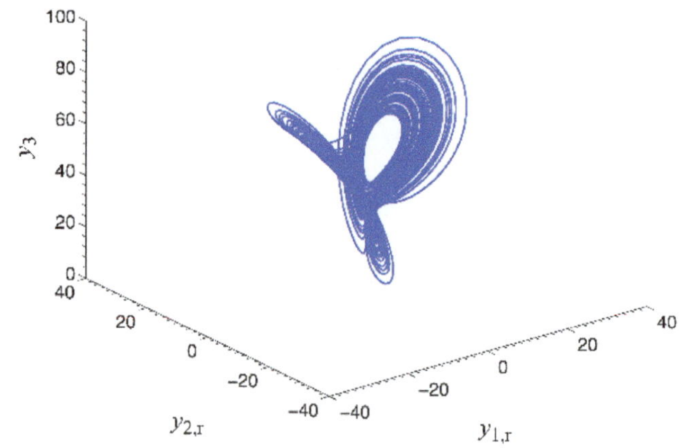

Figure 2. Chaotic attractor of the memristor-based complex Lorenz system.

The drive system (12) and response system (13) can be rewritten with the form of Eqs 1 and 2, where $\boldsymbol{\theta} = [a_1, a_2, a_3, a_4]^T$, $\boldsymbol{\delta} = [b_1, b_2, b_3, b_4]^T$, $\boldsymbol{u} = [u_1, u_2, u_3, u_4]^T$, and

$$F(x) = \begin{bmatrix} x_2 - x_1 & 0 & 0 & 0 \\ 0 & x_2 & -(\alpha_1 + 3\beta_1x_4^2)x_1 & 0 \\ 0 & 0 & 0 & -x_3 \\ 0 & 0 & 0 & 0 \end{bmatrix}, \quad f(x) = \begin{bmatrix} 0 \\ -x_1x_3 \\ (x_1\bar{x}_2 + \bar{x}_1x_2)/2 \\ (x_1 + \bar{x}_1)/2 \end{bmatrix}$$

$$G(y) = \begin{bmatrix} -y_1 & y_2 & 0 & 0 \\ 0 & 0 & y_1 & 0 \\ 0 & 0 & 0 & -y_3 \\ 0 & 0 & 0 & 0 \end{bmatrix}, \quad g(y) = \begin{bmatrix} -(\alpha_2 + 3\beta_2y_4^2)y_1 \\ -y_2 - y_1y_3 \\ (y_1\bar{y}_2 + \bar{y}_1y_2)/2 \\ -(y_1 + \bar{y}_1)/2 \end{bmatrix}$$

The complex map vector is given by

$$\phi(x) = [x_1 + jx_2, (2 - j)x_2, x_3 + x_4, x_4^2]^T \quad (14)$$

The Jacobian matrix of the complex map vector is calculated as

$$\boldsymbol{J}(\phi) = \begin{bmatrix} 1 & j & 0 & 0 \\ 0 & 2-j & 0 & 0 \\ 0 & 0 & 1 & 1 \\ 0 & 0 & 0 & 2x_4 \end{bmatrix} \quad (15)$$

According to Eqs 7 and 8, the complex adaptive controller and parameter estimator can be obtained as

$$
\begin{aligned}
u_1 &= [(\alpha_2 + 3\beta_2 y_4^2)y_{1,r} + x_{1,i}x_3 + (x_{2,r} - x_{1,r})\hat{a}_1 - x_{2,i}\hat{a}_2 + (\alpha_1 + 3\beta_1 x_4^2)x_{1,i}\hat{a}_3 + y_{1,r}\hat{b}_1 - y_{2,r}\hat{b}_2 - k_1 e_{1,r}] \\
&\quad + \mathrm{j}\,[(\alpha_2 + 3\beta_2 y_4^2)y_{1,i} - x_{1,r}x_3 + (x_{2,i} - x_{1,i})\hat{a}_1 + x_{2,r}\hat{a}_2 - (\alpha_1 + 3\beta_1 x_4^2)x_{1,r}\hat{a}_3 + y_{1,i}\hat{b}_1 - y_{2,i}\hat{b}_2 - k_1 e_{1,i}] \\
u_2 &= [y_{2,r} + y_{1,r}y_3 - (2x_{1,r} + x_{1,i})x_3 + (2x_{2,r} + x_{2,i})\hat{a}_2 - (2x_{1,r} + x_{1,i})(\alpha_1 + 3\beta_1 x_4^2)\hat{a}_3 - y_{1,r}\hat{b}_3 - k_2 e_{2,r}] \\
&\quad + \mathrm{j}\,[y_{2,i} + y_{1,i}y_3 - (2x_{1,i} - x_{1,r})x_3 + (2x_{2,i} - x_{2,r})\hat{a}_2 - (2x_{1,i} - x_{1,r})(\alpha_1 + 3\beta_1 x_4^2)\hat{a}_3 - y_{1,i}\hat{b}_3 - k_2 e_{2,i}] \\
u_3 &= -y_{1,r}y_{2,r} - y_{1,i}y_{2,i} + x_{1,r}x_{2,r} + x_{1,i}x_{2,i} + x_{1,r} - x_3\hat{a}_4 + y_3\hat{b}_4 - k_3 e_3 \\
u_4 &= y_{1,r} + 2x_{1,r}x_4 - k_4 e_4
\end{aligned} \tag{16}
$$

$$
\begin{aligned}
\dot{\hat{a}}_1 &= -(x_{2,r} - x_{1,r})e_{1,r} - (x_{2,i} - x_{1,i})e_{1,i} - k_{\theta,1}(\hat{a}_1 - a_1) \\
\dot{\hat{a}}_2 &- x_{2,i}e_{1,r} - x_{2,r}e_{1,i} - (2x_{2,r} + x_{2,i})e_{2,r} - (2x_{2,i} - x_{2,r})e_{2,i} - k_{\theta,2}(\hat{a}_2 - a_2) \\
\dot{\hat{a}}_3 &= [-x_{1,i}e_{1,r} + x_{1,r}e_{1,i} + (2x_{1,r} + x_{1,i})e_{2,r} + (2x_{1,i} - x_{1,r})e_{2,i}](\alpha_1 + 3\beta_1 x_4^2) - k_{\theta,3}(\hat{a}_3 - a_3) \\
\dot{\hat{a}}_4 &= x_3 e_3 - k_{\theta,4}(\hat{a}_4 - a_4)
\end{aligned} \tag{17}
$$

$$
\begin{aligned}
\dot{\hat{b}}_1 &= -y_{1,r}e_{1,r} - y_{1,i}e_{1,i} - k_{\delta,1}(\hat{b}_1 - b_1) \\
\dot{\hat{b}}_2 &= y_{2,r}e_{1,r} + y_{2,i}e_{1,i} - k_{\delta,2}(\hat{b}_2 - b_2) \\
\dot{\hat{b}}_3 &= y_{1,r}e_{2,r} + y_{1,i}e_{2,i} - k_{\delta,3}(\hat{b}_3 - b_3) \\
\dot{\hat{b}}_4 &= -y_3 e_3 - k_{\delta,4}(\hat{b}_4 - b_4)
\end{aligned} \tag{18}
$$

where $e_{1,r} = y_{1,r} - x_{1,r} + x_{2,i}$, $e_{1,i} = y_{1,i} - x_{1,i} - x_{2,r}$, $e_{2,r} = y_{2,r} - 2x_{2,r} - x_{2,i}$, $e_{2,i} = y_{2,i} - 2x_{2,i} + x_{2,r}$, $e_3 = y_3 - x_3 - x_4$, $e_4 = y_4 - x_4^2$.

In order to verify the validity and effectiveness of CGS between system (12) and (13) with respect to the complex vector (14), ODE45 algorithm is used to solve the systems based on Matlab 2013a. The values of known parameters are $\alpha_1 = 4$, $\beta_1 = 0.01$, $\alpha_2 = 0.67 \times 10^{-3}$, $\beta_2 = 0.02 \times 10^{-3}$, the true values of unknown parameters are $\theta = [36, 20, 3.2, 3]^T$, $\delta = [8, 11, 50, 8/3]^T$. The initial conditions of system (12) and (13) are randomly selected as $\boldsymbol{x}(0) = [-1 + 2\mathrm{j}, 1 + \mathrm{j}, 2, -1]^T$, $\boldsymbol{y}(0) = [10 - 8\mathrm{j}, 4 - 3\mathrm{j}, 6, -5]^T$. The initial values of all unknown parameters are randomly chosen as zero, and the control strength is set as $\boldsymbol{K} = \mathrm{diag}(20, 20, 20, 20)$, $\boldsymbol{K}_\theta = \mathrm{diag}(10, 10, 10, 10)$, $\boldsymbol{K}_\delta = \mathrm{diag}(10, 10, 10, 10)$. The corresponding simulation results are shown in Figs 3, 4 and 5. The CGS process is plotted in Fig 3, which indicate that the response system (13) is synchronized with the drive system (12) with respect to the given complex map vector (14). The synchronization errors, as shown in Fig 4, converge to zero in a short time.Fig 5 shows the identifying processes of unknown parameters, which indicates that the estimated values tend to be their true values adaptively, i.e., $\hat{\theta} \to [36,\ 20,\ 3.2,\ 3]^T$ and $\hat{\delta} \to [8,\ 11,\ 50,\ 2.667]^T$.

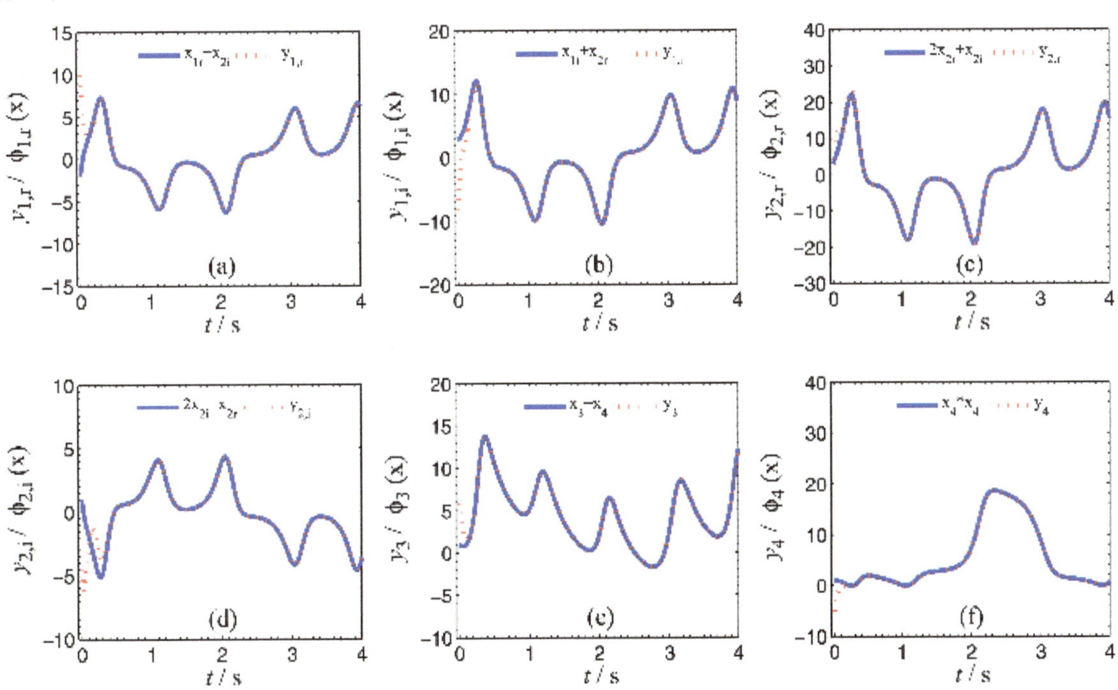

Figure 3. CGS process of systems (12) and (13) with respect to the given complex map vector.

$\phi(x) = [x_1 + j\, x_2,\ (2 - j)x_2,\ x_3 + x_4,\ x_4^2]^T$. (a) $x_{1,r} - x_{2,i}$, $y_{1,r}$; (b) $x_{1r} - x_{2,r}$, $y_{1,i}$; (c) $2x_{2,r}+x_{2,i}$, $y_{2,r}$; (d) $2x_{2,i} - x_{2,r}$, $y_{2,i}$; (e) x_3+x_4, y_3; (f) x_4^2, y_4

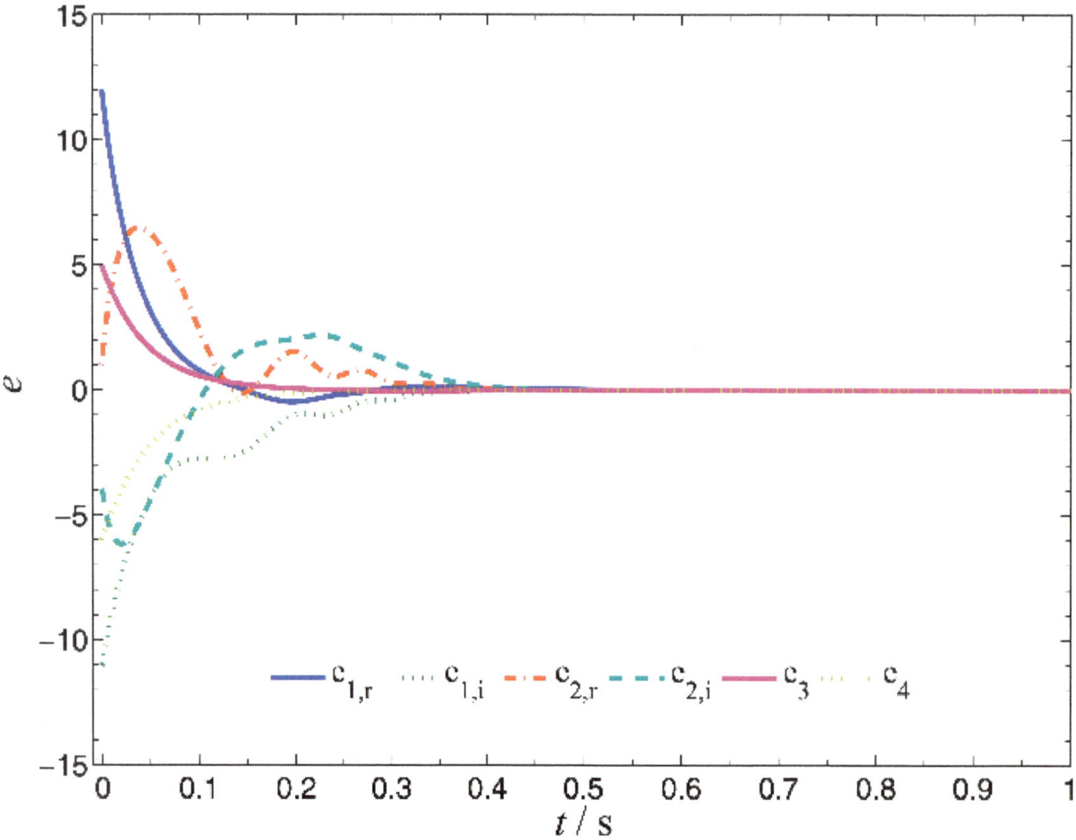

Figure 4. CGS errors of systems (12) and (13).

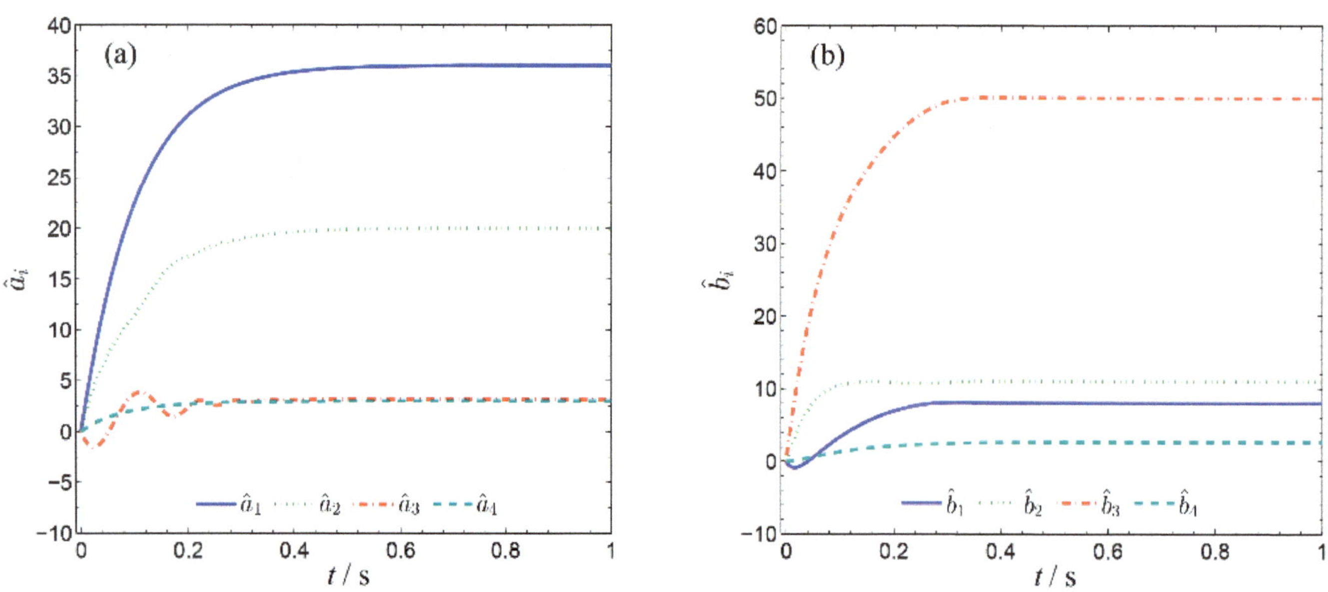

Figure 5. Identification of unknown parameters of systems (12) and (13).

(a) $\hat{a}_1$, $\hat{a}_2$, $\hat{a}_3$, $\hat{a}_4$; (b) $\hat{b}_1$, $\hat{b}_2$, $\hat{b}_3$, $\hat{b}_4$.

CGS of a Chaotic Complex Chen System and a Memristor-Based Chaotic Complex Lorenz System (n<m)

In this section, we investigate CGS of two nonidentical complex systems via increased order. A chaotic complex Chen system, investigated in [9], is introduced as the complex drive system, which is described as

$$\begin{cases} \dot{x}_1 = c_1(x_2 - x_1) \\ \dot{x}_2 = (c_2 - c_1)x_1 - x_1x_3 + c_2x_2 \\ \dot{x}_3 = \dfrac{1}{2}(\bar{x}_1x_2 + x_1\bar{x}_2) - c_3x_3 \end{cases} \tag{19}$$

where $x_1, x_2 \in C$, $x_3 \in R$, c_1, c_2 and c_3 are unknown real parameters. When $c_1 = 27$, $c_2 = 23$, $c_3 = 1$, and $x(0) = [-3 - 2j, -1 - 5j, -4]^T$, the complex Chen system (19) operates in chaotic orbits, as shown in Fig 6. The memristor-based chaotic complex Lorenz system, i.e., system (13), is also served as the complex response system.

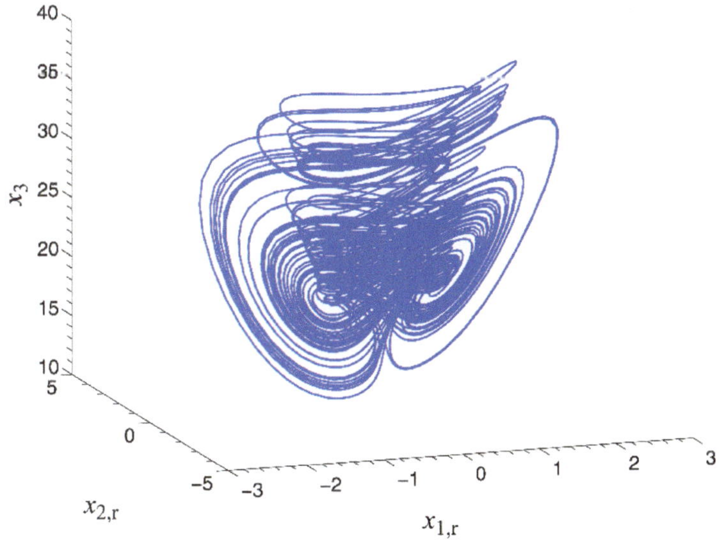

Figure 6. Chaotic attractor of the complex Chen system.

The drive system (19) and response system (13) can be rewritten with the form of Eqs 1 and 2, where $\boldsymbol{\theta} = [c_1, c_2, c_3]^T$, $\boldsymbol{\delta} = [b_1, b_2, b_3, b_4]^T$, $\boldsymbol{u} = [u_1, u_2, u_3, u_4]^T$, and

$$F(x) = \begin{bmatrix} x_2 - x_1 & 0 & 0 \\ -x_1 & x_2 - x_1 & 0 \\ 0 & 0 & -x_3 \end{bmatrix}, f(x) = \begin{bmatrix} 0 \\ -x_1x_3 \\ (x_1\bar{x}_2 + \bar{x}_1x_2)/2 \end{bmatrix}$$

$$G(y) = \begin{bmatrix} -y_1 & y_2 & 0 & 0 \\ 0 & 0 & y_1 & 0 \\ 0 & 0 & 0 & -y_3 \\ 0 & 0 & 0 & 0 \end{bmatrix}, g(y) = \begin{bmatrix} -(\alpha_2 + 3\beta_2 y_4^2)y_1 \\ -y_2 - y_1y_3 \\ (y_1\bar{y}_2 + \bar{y}_1y_2)/2 \\ -(y_1 + \bar{y}_1)/2 \end{bmatrix}$$

The complex map vector is given by $\phi(x) = [-jx_1, -jx_2, -x_3, x_3]^T$ **(20)**

The Jacobian matrix of the complex map vector is calculated as

$$\boldsymbol{J}(\phi) = \begin{bmatrix} -j & 0 & 0 \\ 0 & -j & 0 \\ 0 & 0 & -1 \\ 0 & 0 & 1 \end{bmatrix} \tag{21}$$

According to Eqs 7 and 8, the complex adaptive controller and parameter estimator can be obtained as

$$\begin{aligned} u_1 &= [(\alpha_2 + 3\beta_2 y_4^2)y_{1,r} + (x_{2,i} - x_{1,i})\hat{c}_1 + y_{1,r}\hat{b}_1 - y_{2,r}\hat{b}_2 - k_1e_{1,r}] \\ &\quad + j\,[(\alpha_2 + 3\beta_2 y_4^2)y_{1,i} - (x_{2,r} - x_{1,r})\hat{c}_1 + y_{1,i}\hat{b}_1 - y_{2,i}\hat{b}_2 - k_1e_{1,i}] \\ u_2 &= [y_{2,r} + y_{1,r}y_3 - x_{1,i}x_3 - x_{1,i}\hat{c}_1 + (x_{2,i} + x_{1,i})\hat{c}_2 - y_{1,r}\hat{b}_3 - k_2e_{2,r}] \\ &\quad + j\,[y_{2,i} + y_{1,i}y_3 + x_{1,r}x_3 + x_{1,r}\hat{c}_1 - (x_{2,r} + x_{1,r})\hat{c}_2 - y_{1,i}\hat{b}_3 - k_2e_{2,i}] \\ u_3 &= -y_{1,r}y_{2,r} - y_{1,i}y_{2,i} - x_{1,r}x_{2,r} - x_{1,i}x_{2,i} + x_3\hat{c}_3 + y_3\hat{b}_4 - k_3e_3 \\ u_4 &= y_{1,r} + x_{1,r}x_{2,r} + x_{1,i}x_{2,i} - x_3\hat{c}_3 - k_4e_4 \end{aligned} \tag{22}$$

$$\dot{\hat{c}}_1 = -(x_{2,i} - x_{1,i})e_{1,r} + (x_{2,r} - x_{1,r})e_{1,i} + x_{1,i}e_{2,r} - x_{1,r}e_{2,i} - k_{\theta 1}(\hat{c}_1 - c_1)$$
$$\dot{\hat{c}}_2 = -(x_{2,i} + x_{1,i})e_{2,r} + (x_{2,r} + x_{1,r})e_{2,i} - k_{\theta 2}(\hat{c}_2 - c_2)$$
$$\dot{\hat{c}}_3 = -x_3e_3 + x_3e_4 - k_{\theta 3}(\hat{c}_3 - c_3) \quad (23)$$
$$\dot{\hat{b}}_1 = -y_{1,r}e_{1,r} - y_{1,i}e_{1,i} - k_{\delta 1}(\hat{b}_1 - b_1)$$
$$\dot{\hat{b}}_2 = y_{2,r}e_{1,r} + y_{2,i}e_{1,i} - k_{\delta 2}(\hat{b}_2 - b_2)$$
$$\dot{\hat{b}}_3 = y_{1,r}e_{2,r} + y_{1,i}e_{2,i} - k_{\delta 3}(\hat{b}_3 - b_3)$$
$$\dot{\hat{b}}_4 = -y_3e_3 - k_{\delta 4}(\hat{b}_4 - b_4) \quad (24)$$

where $e_{1,r} = y_{1,r} - x_{1,i}$, $e_{1,i} = y_{1,i}+x_{1,r}$, $e_{2,r} = y_{2,r} - x_{2,i}$, $e_{2,i} = y_{2,i}+x_{2,r}$, $e_3 = y_3+x_3$, $e_3 = y_4 - x_3$.

Numerical simulations are presented to verify the validity and effectiveness of CGS between systems (19) and (13) with respect to the complex vector (20), under the following parameter configurations and initial conditions: the known parameters $\alpha_2 = 0.67 \times 10^{-3}$, $\beta_2 = 0.02 \times 10^{-3}$, the true values of unknown parameters $\theta = [27,23,1]^T$, $\delta = [8, 11, 50, 8/3]^T$, the initial conditions of system (19) and (13) $x(o) = [-3 - 2j, -1 - 5j, -4]^T$, $y(0) = [2 - 2j, 1 - j, 6, 1]^T$, the initial values of unknown parameters $\hat{\theta}(0) = [10,\ 10,\ 10,\ 10]^T$, $\hat{\delta}(0) = [10,\ 10,\ 10]^T$, and the control strength $K = \mathrm{diag}(20, 20, 20, 20)$, $K_\theta = \mathrm{diag}(10, 10, 10, 10)$, $K_\delta = \mathrm{diag}(10, 10, 10, 10)$. The corresponding simulation results are shown in Figs 7, 8 and 9. The CGS process is plotted in Fig 7, from which one can see that $y_{1,r}$, $y_{2,r}$, y_4 are synchronized with $x_{1,i}$, $x_{2,i}$, x_3, and $y_{1,i}$, $y_{2,i}$, y_3 are antisynchronized with $x_{1,r}$, $x_{2,r}$, x_3. The synchronization errors, as shown in Fig 8, converge to zero in a short time. Fig 9 shows the identifying processes of unknown parameters, which indicates that the estimated values tend to be their true values adaptively, i.e., $\hat{\theta} \to [27,\ 23,\ 1]^T$ and $\hat{\delta} \to [8,\ 11,\ 50,\ 2.667]^T$.

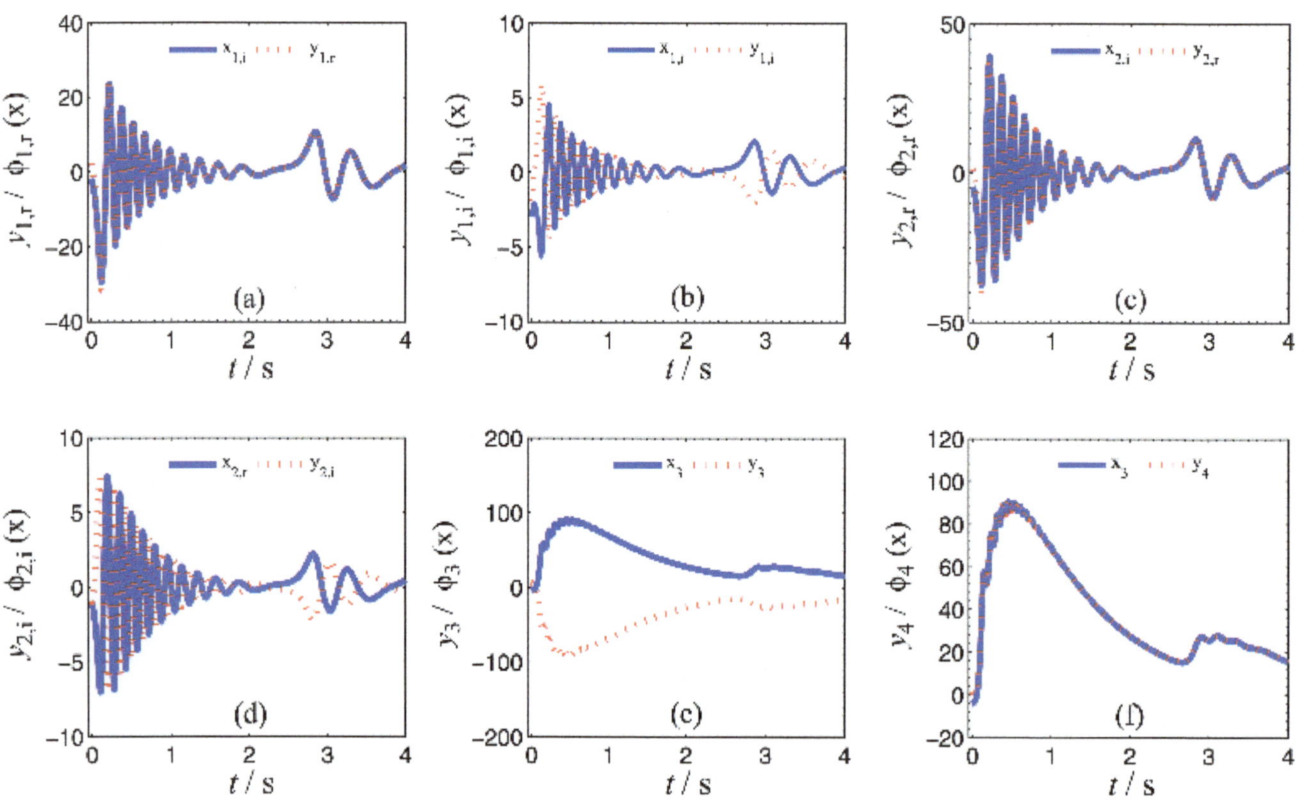

Figure 7. CGS process of systems (19) and (13) with respect to the given complex map vector $\phi(x) = [-jx_1, -jx_2, -x_3, x_3]^T$.

(a) $x_{1,i}$, $y_{1,r}$; (b) x_{1r}, $y_{1,i}$; (c) $x_{2,i}$, $y_{2,r}$; (d) $x_{2,r}$, $y_{2,i}$; (e) x_3, y_3; (f) x_3, y_4.

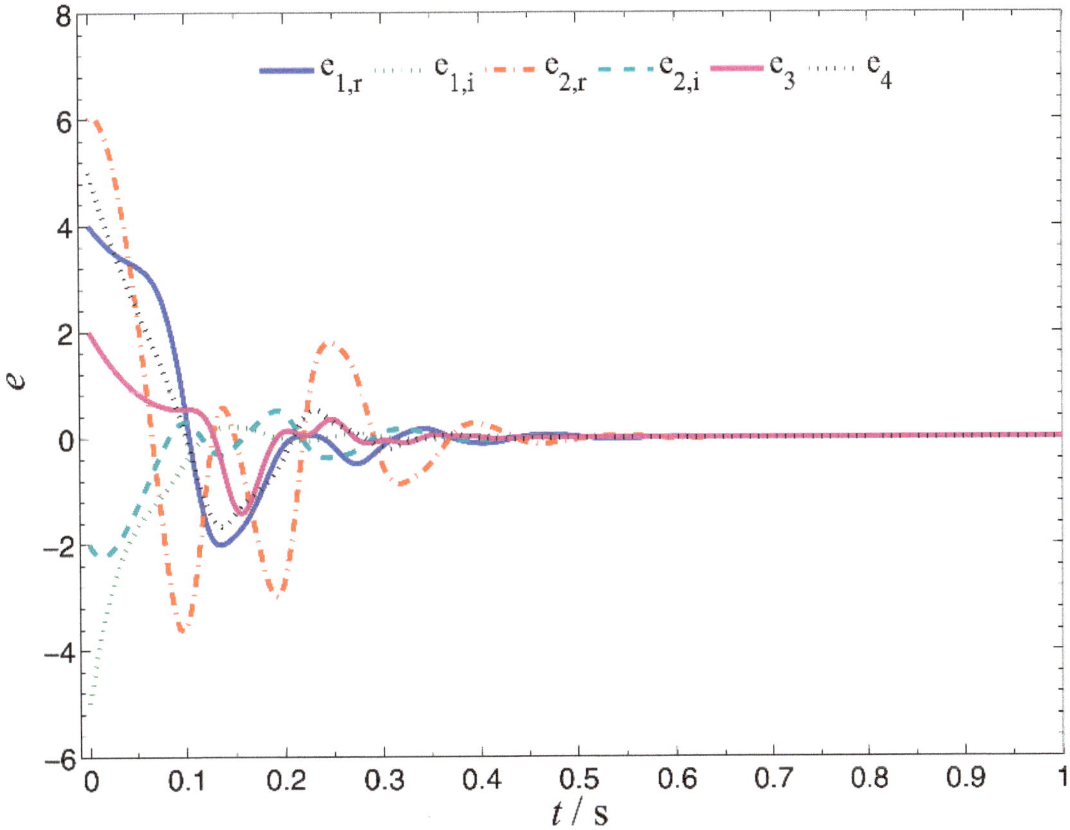

Figure 8. CGS errors of systems (19) and (13).

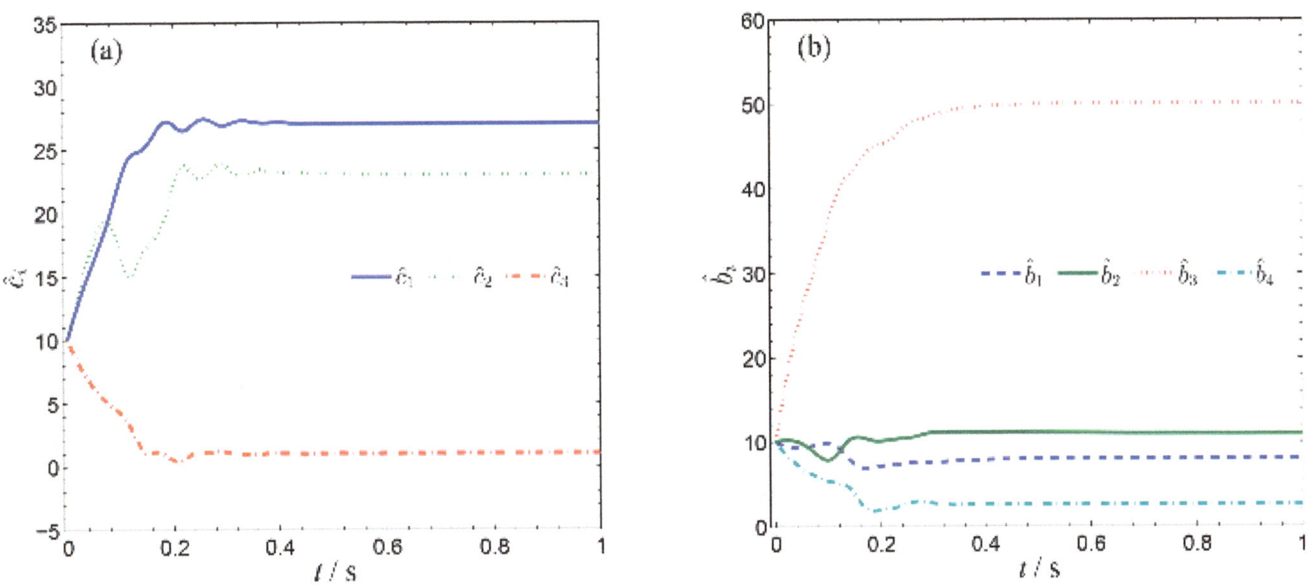

Figure 9. Identification of unknown parameters of systems (19) and (13).

(a) $\hat{c}_1$, $\hat{c}_2$, $\hat{c}_3$; (b) $\hat{b}_1$, $\hat{b}_2$, $\hat{b}_3$, $\hat{b}_4$.

CGS of a Memristor-Based Hyperchaotic Complex Lü System and a Chaotic Complex Lü System (n>m)

In this section, we investigate CGS of two nonidentical complex systems via reduced order. The memristor-based hyperchaotic complex Lü system, i.e., system (12), is acted as the drive complex system. And a chaotic complex Lü system, investigated in [9], is introduced as the response complex system, which is described as

$$\begin{cases} \dot{y}_1 = d_1(y_2 - y_1) + u_1 \\ \dot{y}_2 = -y_1 y_3 + d_2 y_2 + u_2 \\ \dot{y}_3 = \frac{1}{2}(\bar{y}_1 y_2 + y_1 \bar{y}_2) - d_3 y_3 + u_3 \end{cases} \quad (25)$$

where y_1, $y_2 \in C$, $y_3 \in R$, d_1, d_2 and d_3 are unknown real parameters, u_1, u_2 and u_3 are controllers. When $d_1 = 29$, $d_2 = 21$, $d_3 = 2$, and $y(0) = [4 + 10j, 6 + 10j, 12]^T$, the complex Lü system (25) operates chaotically without control, as shown in Fig 10.

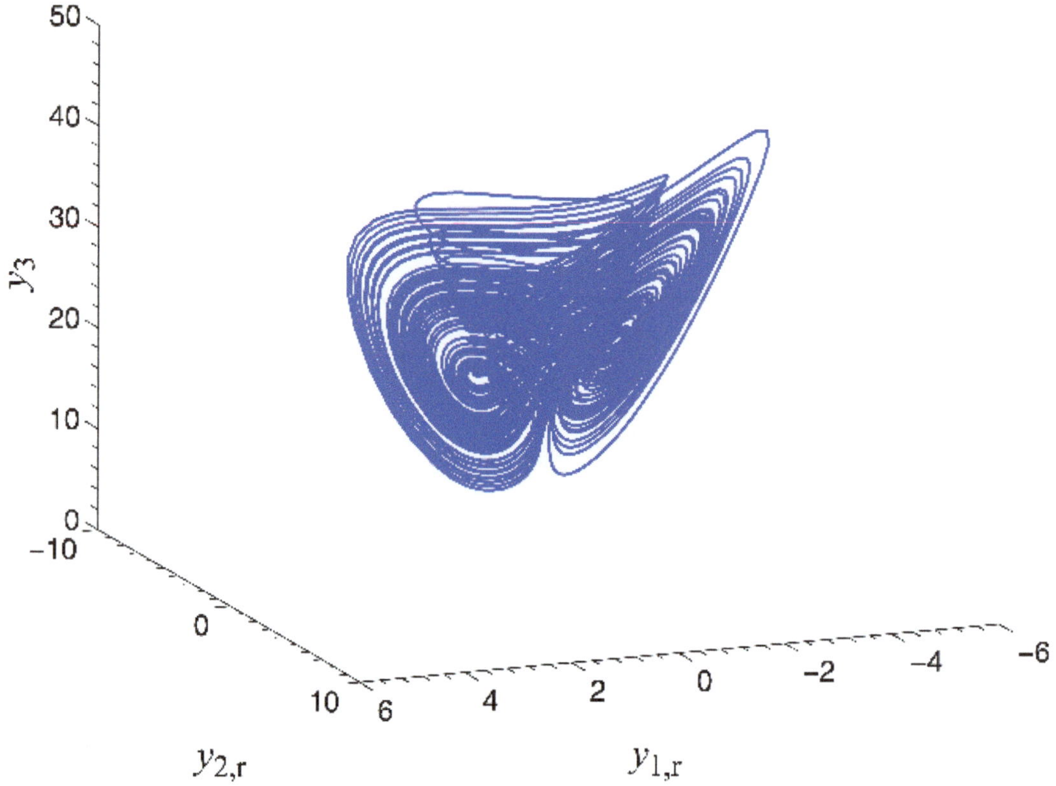

Figure 10. Chaotic attractor of the complex Lü system.

The drive system (12) and response system (25) can be rewritten with the form of Eqs 1 and 2, where $\boldsymbol{\theta} = [a_1, a_2, a_3, a_4]^T$, $\boldsymbol{\delta} = [d_1, d_2, d_3]^T$, $\boldsymbol{u} = [u_1, u_2, u_3]^T$, and

$$F(x) = \begin{bmatrix} x_2 - x_1 & 0 & 0 & 0 \\ 0 & x_2 & -(\alpha_1 + 3\beta_1 x_4^2)x_1 & 0 \\ 0 & 0 & 0 & -x_3 \\ 0 & 0 & 0 & 0 \end{bmatrix}, f(x) = \begin{bmatrix} 0 \\ -x_1 x_3 \\ (x_1 \bar{x}_2 + \bar{x}_1 x_2)/2 \\ (x_1 + \bar{x}_1)/2 \end{bmatrix}$$

$$G(y) = \begin{bmatrix} y_2 - y_1 & 0 & 0 \\ 0 & y_2 & 0 \\ 0 & 0 & -y_3 \end{bmatrix}, g(y) = \begin{bmatrix} 0 \\ -y_1 y_3 \\ (y_1 \bar{y}_2 + \bar{y}_1 y_2)/2 \end{bmatrix}$$

The complex map vector is given by

$$\phi(x) = [jx_2, jx_1, x_3 - x_4^2]^T \quad (26)$$

The Jacobian matrix of the complex map vector is calculated as

$$J(\phi) = \begin{bmatrix} 0 & j & 0 & 0 \\ j & 0 & 0 & 0 \\ 0 & 0 & 1 & -2x_4 \end{bmatrix} \quad (27)$$

According to Eqs 7 and 8, the complex adaptive controller and parameter estimator can be obtained as

$$\begin{aligned}
u_1 &= [x_{1,i}x_3 - x_{2,i}\hat{a}_2 + (\alpha_1 + 3\beta_1 x_1^2)x_{1,i}\hat{a}_3 - (y_{2,r} - y_{1,r})\hat{d}_1 - k_1 e_{1,r}] \\
&\quad + \mathrm{j}\,[-x_{1,r}x_3 + x_{2,r}\hat{a}_2 - (\alpha_1 + 3\beta_1 x_1^2)x_{1,r}\hat{a}_3 - (y_{2,i} - y_{1,i})\hat{d}_1 - k_1 e_{1,i}] \\
u_2 &= [y_{1,r}y_3 - (x_{2,i} - x_{1,i})\hat{a}_1 - y_{2,r}\hat{d}_2 - k_2 e_{2,r}] \\
&\quad + \mathrm{j}\,[y_{1,i}y_3 + (x_{2,r} - x_{1,r})\hat{a}_1 - y_{2,i}\hat{d}_2 - k_2 e_{2,i}] \\
u_3 &= -y_{1,r}y_{2,r} - y_{1,i}y_{2,i} + x_{1,r}x_{2,r} + x_{1,i}x_{2,i} - 2x_{1,r}x_4 - x_3\hat{a}_4 + y_3\hat{d}_3 - k_3 e_3
\end{aligned} \quad (28)$$

$$\begin{aligned}
\dot{\hat{a}}_1 &= (x_{2,i} - x_{1,i})e_{2,r} - (x_{2,r} - x_{1,r})e_{2,i} - k_{\theta 1}(\hat{a}_1 - a_1) \\
\dot{\hat{a}}_2 &= x_{2,i}e_{1,r} - x_{2,r}e_{1,i} - k_{\theta 2}(\hat{a}_2 - a_2) \\
\dot{\hat{a}}_3 &= (-x_{1,i}e_{1,r} + x_{1,r}e_{1,i})(\alpha_1 + 3\beta_1 x_1^2) - k_{\theta 3}(\hat{a}_3 - a_3) \\
\dot{\hat{a}}_4 &= x_3 e_3 - k_{\theta 4}(\hat{a}_4 - a_4)
\end{aligned} \quad (29)$$

$$\begin{aligned}
\dot{\hat{d}}_1 &= (y_{2,r} - y_{1,r})e_{1,r} + (y_{2,i} - y_{1,i})e_{1,i} - k_{\delta 1}(\hat{d}_1 - d_1) \\
\dot{\hat{d}}_2 &= y_{2,r}e_{2,r} + y_{2,i}e_{2,i} - k_{\delta 2}(\hat{d}_2 - d_2) \\
\dot{\hat{d}}_3 &= -y_3 e_3 - k_{\delta 3}(\hat{d}_3 - d_3)
\end{aligned} \quad (30)$$

where

$e_{1,r} = y_{1,r} + x_{2,i}, e_{1,i} = y_{1,i} - x_{2,r}, e_{2,r} = y_{2,r} + x_{1,i}, e_{2,i} = y_{2,i} - x_{1,r}, e_3 = y_3 - x_3 + x_1^2$.

In order to verify the validity and effectiveness of CGS between Systems (12) and (25) with respect to the complex vector (26), simulation results are presented in Figs 11, 12 and 13, with the following parameters and initial conditions: $\alpha_1 = 4$, $\beta_1 = 0.01$, $\theta = [36, 20, 3.2, 3]^T$, $\delta = [29,21,2]^T$, $x(0) = [-1 + 2j, 1 + j, 2, -1]^T$, $y(0) = (4 + 10j, 6 + 10j, 12)$, $\hat{\theta}(0) = [10,\ 10,\ 10,\ 10]^T$, $\hat{\delta}(0) = [0,\ 0,\ 0]^T$, $\boldsymbol{K} = \mathrm{diag}(20, 20, 20, 20)$, $\boldsymbol{K}_\theta = \mathrm{diag}(10, 10, 10, 10)$, $\boldsymbol{K}_\delta = \mathrm{diag}(10, 10, 10, 10)$. The CGS process is plotted in Fig 11, from which one can see that $y_{1,r}$, $y_{2,r}$ are antisynchronized with $x_{2,i}$, $x_{1,i}$, $y_{1,i}$, $y_{2,i}$ are synchronized with $x_{2,r}$, $x_{1,r}$, and y_3 is synchronized with $x_3 - x_1^2$, respectively. The synchronization errors converge to zero quickly, as shown in Fig 12. Fig 13 shows that the estimated values of the unknown parameters tend to be their true values adaptively, i.e., $\hat{\theta} \to [36,\ 20,\ 3.2,\ 3]^T$ and $\hat{\delta} \to [29,\ 21,\ 2]^T$

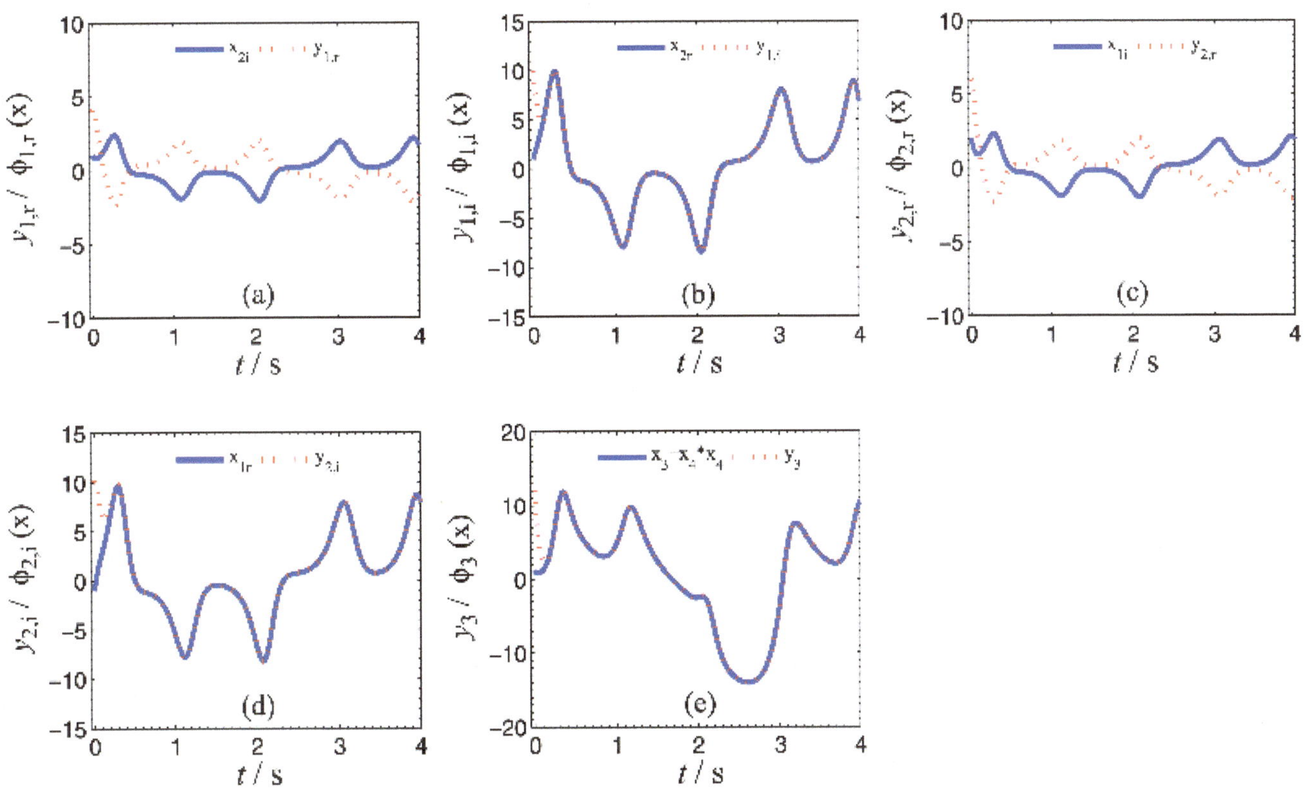

Figure 11. CGS process of systems (12) and (25) with respect to the given complex map vector $\phi(x) = [\mathrm{j}\,x_2,\ \mathrm{j}\,x_1,\ x_3 - x_1^2]^T$.

(a) $x_{2,i}$, $y_{1,r}$; (b) x_{2r}, $y_{1,i}$; (c) $x_{1,i}$, $y_{2,r}$; (d) $x_{1,r}$, $y_{2,i}$; (e) $x_3 - x_1^2$, y_3.

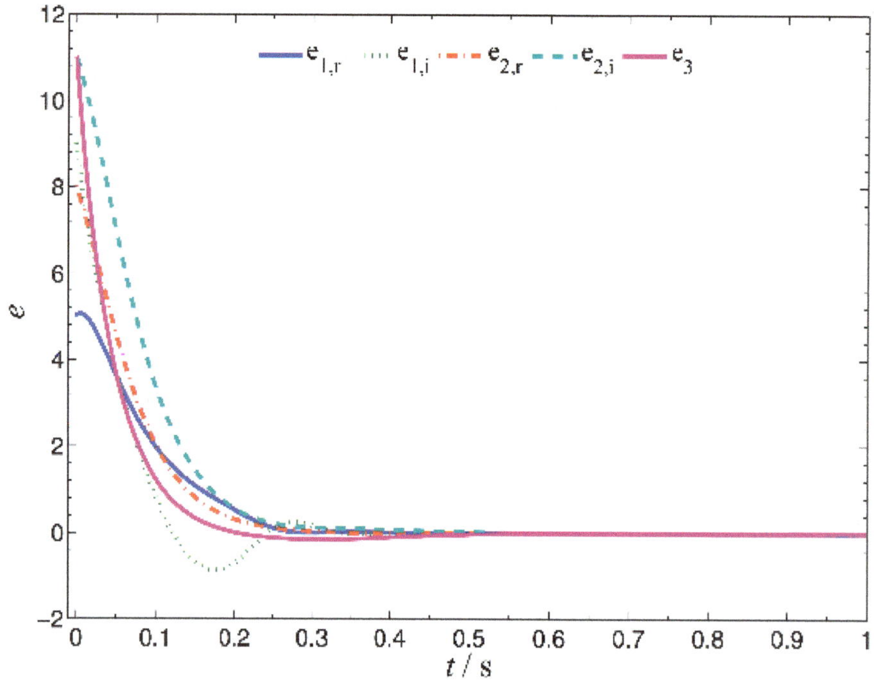

Figure 12. CGS errors of systems (12) and (25).

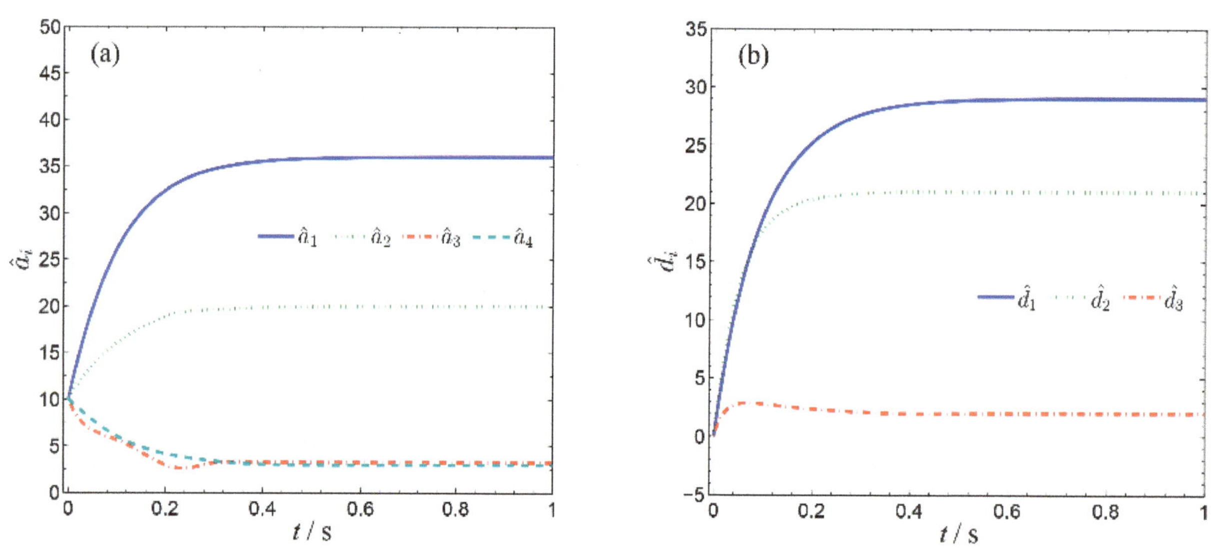

Figure 13. Identification of unknown parameters of systems (12) and (25).

(a) $\hat{a}_1$, $\hat{a}_2$, $\hat{a}_3$, $\hat{a}_4$; (b) $\hat{d}_1$, $\hat{d}_2$, $\hat{d}_3$, $\hat{d}_4$.

CONCLUSIONS

This paper investigates a novel synchronization scheme named complex generalized synchronization, and its application to synchronization and parameter identification of two nonidentical complex nonlinear systems with fully unknown parameters. An adaptive controller and a parameter estimator are proposed and proved theoretically based on Lyapunov stability theory. Three illustrative examples are presented to verify the correctness and effectiveness of the proposed scheme, namely, CGS of a memristor-based hyperchaotic complex Lü system and a memristor-based chaotic complex Lorenz system, CGS of a chaotic complex Chen system and a memristor-based chaotic complex Lorenz system, as well as CGS of a memristor-based hyperchaotic complex Lü system and a chaotic complex Lü system. The proposed CGS scheme has some advantages, for instance, it can be applied to synchronize complex systems with different orders (generalizability), can be transformed to other types of synchronization with different given complex map vectors (feasibility), can be achieved in a short time with the appropriate control strength (timelines), and can be almost impossibly predicted with the complex map vector (security). So, CGS has extensively potential applications to secure communication, digital cryptography, and so on, which will be involved in our future works.

AUTHOR CONTRIBUTIONS

Conceived and designed the experiments: XW SW. Performed the experiments: SW BH. Analyzed the data: SW XW BH. Contributed reagents/materials/analysis tools: SW BH. Wrote the paper: SW.

REFERENCES

1. Fowler AC, Gibbon JD. The complex Lorenz equations. Physica D. 1982; 4(2): 139–163. doi: 10.1016/0167-2789(82)90057-4
2. Gibbon JD, Mcguinness MJ. The real and complex Lorenz equations in rotating fluids and lasers. Physica D. 1982; 5(1): 108–122. doi: 10.1016/0167-2789(82)90053-7
3. Ning C, Haken H. Detuned laser and the complex Lorenz equations: subcritical and supercritical Hopf bifurcations. Phys Rev A. 1990; 41(7): 3826–3837. pmid:9903557 doi: 10.1103/physreva.41.3826
4. Cveticanin L. Resonant vibrations of nonlinear rotors. Mech Mach Theory. 1995; 30(4): 581–588. doi: 10.1016/0094-114x(94)00059-t
5. Luo C, Wang X. Chaos generated from the fractional-order complex Chen system and its application to digital secure communication. Int J Mod Phys C. 2013; 24(4): 72–77. doi: 10.1142/s0129183113500253
6. Zhang F, Liu S. Self-time-delay synchronization of time-delay coupled complex chaotic system and its applications to communication. Int J Mod Phys C. 2014; 25(3): 559–583. doi: 10.1142/s0129183113501027
7. Zhang F. Lag synchronization of complex Lorenz system with applications to communication. Entropy. 2015; 17(7): 4974–4985. doi: 10.3390/e17074974
8. Pecora LM, Carroll TL. Synchronization in chaotic systems. Phys Rev Lett. 1990; 64(8): 821–824. pmid:10042089 doi: 10.1103/physrevlett.64.821
9. Mahmoud GM, Bountis T, Abdel-Latif GM, Mahmoud EE. Chaos synchronization of two different chaotic complex Chen and Lü systems. Nonlinear Dyn. 2008; 55(1): 43–53. doi: 10.1007/s11071-008-9343-5
10. Luo C, Wang X. Chaos in the fractional-order complex Lorenz system and its synchronization. Nonlinear Dyn. 2013; 71(1–2): 241–257. doi: 10.1007/s11071-012-0656-z
11. Mahmoud GM, Ahmed ME. Modified projective synchronization and control of complex Chen and Lü systems. J Vib Control. 2011; 17(17): 1184–1194. doi: 10.1177/1077546310378871
12. Nian F, Wan X, Zheng P. Projective synchronization in chaotic complex system with time delay. Int J Mod Phys B. 2013; 27(19): 2252–2279. doi: 10.1142/s0217979213501117
13. Mahmoud GM, Mahmoud EE. Phase and antiphase synchronization of two identical hyperchaotic complex nonlinear systems. Nonlinear Dyn. 2010; 61(1–2): 141–152. doi: 10.1007/s11071-009-9637-2
14. Wang X, Zhang H. Backstepping-based lag synchronization of a complex permanent magnet synchronous motor system. Chin Phys B. 2013; 22(4): 558–562. doi: 10.1088/1674-1056/22/4/048902
15. Zhou X, Jiang M, Huang Y. Combination synchronization of three identical or different nonlinear complex hyperchaotic systems. Entropy. 2013; 15(9): 3746–3761. doi: 10.3390/e15093746
16. Liu J, Liu S, Zhang F. A novel four-wing hyperchaotic complex system and its complex modified hybrid projective synchronization with different dimensions. Abstr Appl Anal. 2014; 2014(1): 1–16. doi: 10.1155/2014/257327
17. Wang X, Zhang H, Lin X. Module-phase synchronization in hyperchaotic complex Lorenz system after modified complex projection. Appl Math Comput.2014; 232(3): 91–96. doi: 10.1016/j.amc.2013.12.191
18. Sun J, Cu G, Wang Y, Shen Y. Combination complex synchronization of three chaotic complex systems. Nonlinear Dyn. 2015; 79(2): 953–965. doi: 10.1007/s11071-014-1714-5
19. Jiang C, Liu S, Wang D. Generalized Combination Complex Synchronization for Fractional-Order Chaotic Complex Systems. Entropy. 2015; 17(8):5199–5217. doi: 10.3390/e17085199
20. Zhang F, Liu S, Yu W. Modified projective synchronization with complex scaling factors of uncertain real chaos and complex chaos. Chin Phys B. 2013; 22(12): 141–151. doi: 10.1088/1674-1056/22/12/120505
21. Liu J, Liu S, Yuan C. Adaptive complex modified projective synchronization of complex chaotic (hyperchaotic) systems with uncertain complex parameters. Nonlinear Dyna. 2015; 79(2): 1035–1047. doi: 10.1007/s11071-014-1721-6
22. Rulkov NF, Sushchik MM, Tsimring LS, Abarbanel HD. Generalized synchronization of chaos in directionally coupled chaotic systems. Phys Rev E. 1995; 51(2): 980–994. doi: 10.1103/physreve.51.980
23. Wang YW, Guan ZH. Generalized synchronization of continuous chaotic system. Chaos Soliton Fract. 2006; 27(1): 97–101. doi: 10.1016/j.chaos.2004.12.038
24. Cai N, Li W, Jing Y. Finite-time generalized synchronization of chaotic systems with different order. Nonlinear Dyna. 2011; 64(4): 385–393. doi: 10.1007/s11071-010-9869-1
25. Martínez-Guerra R, Mata-Machuca JL. Fractional generalized synchronization in a class of nonlinear fractional order systems. Nonlinear Dyna. 2014; 77(4): 1237–1244. doi: 10.1007/s11071-014-1373-6
26. Chen L, Shi Y, Wang D. Adaptive generalized synchronization between Chen system and a multi-scroll chaotic system. Chin Phys B. 2010; 19(10): 145–147. doi: 10.1088/1674-1056/19/10/100503
27. Wang X, Wang Y. Adaptive generalized synchronization of hyperchaotic systems. Int J Mod Phys B. 2011; 25(32): 4563–4571. doi: 10.1142/s0217979211059449
28. Zhao J, Wu Y, Wang Y. Generalized finite-time synchronization between coupled chaotic systems of different orders with unknown parameters. Nonlinear Dyn. 2013; 74(3): 479–485. doi: 10.1007/s11071-013-0970-0

29. Li Q, Zeng H, Li J. Hyperchaos in a 4D memristive circuit with infinitely many stable equilibria. Nonlinear Dyn. 2015; 79(4): 2295–2308. doi: 10.1007/s11071-014-1812-4

30. Wang S, Wang X, Zhou Y. A memristor-based complex Lorenz system and its modified projective synchronization. Entropy. 2015; 17(11): 7628–7644. doi: 10.3390/e17117628

CHAPTER 14

A NOVEL PICOSECOND PULSE GENERATION CIRCUIT BASED ON SRD AND NLTL

Jianming Zhou[1], Qiuyuan Lu[1], Fan Liu[1], Yinqiao Li[2]

[1] School of Information and Electronics, Beijing Institute of Technology, Beijing, 100081, China,
[2] Institute of Telecommunication Satellite, CAST, Beijing, 100094, China

ABSTRACT

Because of the importance of ultra-wideband (UWB) radar in various applications, short pulse generation in UWB systems has attracted a lot of attention in recent years. In order to shorten the pulse, nonlinear transmission line (NLTL) is imported, which expands the application of step recovery diode (SRD) for pulse generation. Detailed analysis and equations for this SRD and NLTL-based pulse generation are provided and verified by simulation and experimental results. Factors that could cause pulse waveform distortions are also analyzed. The generator circuit presented in this paper generates 130ps and 3.3V pulse, which can be used in UWB radar systems that require sub-nanosecond pulses.

INTRODUCTION

Nowadays, UWB radars are finding many applications in the areas of medical imaging, non-destructive testing, subsurface identifying, distance measuring, automobile traffic control and security systems [1–6], by transmitting high-intensity pulses and analyzing the reflection signals. Initially, the frequency spectrum of the UWB radar signals can be extended from low frequency to ultra-high frequency, so that it is highly penetrating and has great resolution. Furthermore, the UWB radar has low spectral density and is quite interference-proof, which is very helpful in short-range transmission. Therefore, this radar technology has attracted a lot of researchers and concerned industries across the globe to use it in any and every way for academic, business, and research purposes since the Federal Communications Commission (FCC) made the use of UWB license-free in 2002 [7].

To achieve a reliable sensing performance, however, it is necessary to develop a pulse generator with sufficient peak power and the shortest possible rise-time. Various approaches have been proposed for the design of a pulse generator for radar sensor application. CMOS integrated circuits-based pulse generators are developed to attain flexibility in controlling the pulse shape [8, 9]. However, this method has a long development time and high design cost because some of the components are customized. Other off-the-shelf designs include avalanche transistors [10], tunnel diodes [11], nonlinear transmission lines (NLTLs) [12], photoconductive switches [13], bipolar transistors [14], field effect transistors (FETs) [15], and SRDs [16–24].

Citation: Zhou J, Lu Q, Liu F, Li Y (2016) A Novel Picosecond Pulse Generation Circuit Based on SRD and NLTL. PLoS ONE 11(2): e0149645. doi:10.1371/journal.pone.0149645

Wang *et al.* [10] reported that an ultra-wideband nanosecond pulse was designed based on the avalanche effect of the avalanche transistor, where the pulse full width is 890ps and pulse amplitude is -11.2V. However, the maximum pulse repetition frequency by this method is limited, and the transistor lifetime is short. In Ruai and Konishi's study [11], a resonant tunnel diode was utilized to produce very short pulses for switching and harmonic generation applications, but the output pulse amplitude was limited, generally speaking, not greater than 1V. Among the off-the-shelf designs, the SRD has been used as a key device because it can be easy to fabricate, cost-effective and capable of generating pulses with sharp transition edge. With the progress in electronics, the width of the narrow pulses generated via SRD is limited and cannot meet further requirements on bandwidth due to the constraints on transit time and the carrier's lifetime. Later on, NLTL was introduced to the narrow pulse circuit.

This paper proposes a method which can generate picosecond pulses by using both SRD and NLTL. SRD is the key narrow pulse-generating component used to generate 220ps narrow bands and then NLTL is used to further narrow the width to 130ps, with the amplitude being 3.3V.

The rest of the paper is organized as follows: Section II presents the pulse generator circuit design, which consists of SRD structure, circuit generating and simulation. Section III discusses the principle of NLTL. In Section IV, we discuss our experimentation/evaluation procedure and analyze the results achieved. Section V finally concludes the paper.

CIRCUIT DESIGN

SRD Structure

SRD is a PN junction diode whose impurity is distributed unusually, as shown in Fig 1. Between the high doping P^+ layer and the high doping N^+ layer is a low doping N-type layer. It is a typical slowly varying junction structure. When SRD converts from forward exciting voltage to negative exciting voltage, a strong backward current flows continuously until it terminates at a time instant, forming a steep step voltage. The narrow pulse can be generated in this way.

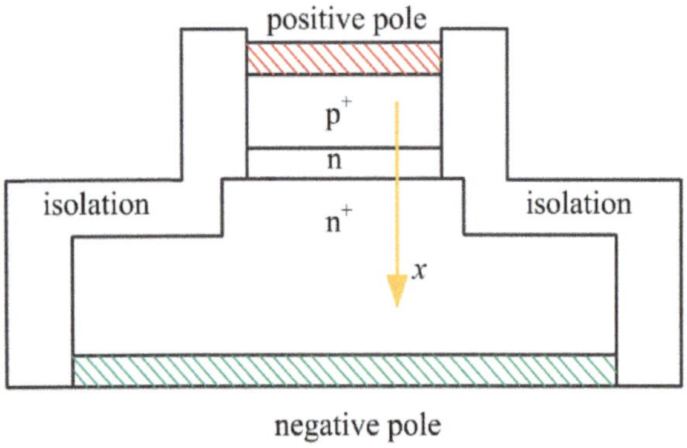

Figure 1. Impurity profile of general SRD.

The principles for this phenomenon are as follows:

- When SRD is in the positive bias, both sides of the PN junction are infused with many minority carriers. The special impurity distribution in SRD facilitates the increase in the injected minority carriers, and creates the retarding fields at both sides of the junction which can impede the proliferation of minority carriers, thus concentrating a large number of minority carriers in the narrow regions near the junction. Furthermore, the lifetime of the minority carriers is so long that they cannot be recombinant during the period of positive bias.
- When the positive bias converts to the negative bias, these stored minority stored will flow in the direction opposite to the injection, forming a strong backward current. When all minority carriers are extracted, the backward current will be reduced to an extremely low level suddenly, cutting off the diode and forming the step voltage.

Pulse-generating Circuit

The SRD pulse-generating circuit is shown in Fig 2(A). SRD can be treated equivalently as a small resistance and a large capacitance when the forward direction is conducting and its on-state voltage is about 0.5V. The on-state equivalent circuit is shown in Fig 2(B). In the case of the SRD conversion from the forward to the backward bias, SRD is still on at a voltage of about 0.3V and the current is in the reverse direction before the SRD junction charge is depleted. Furthermore, SRD can be equivalently seen as a variable capacitance at reverse cut-off, and the equivalent circuit is shown in Fig 2(C).

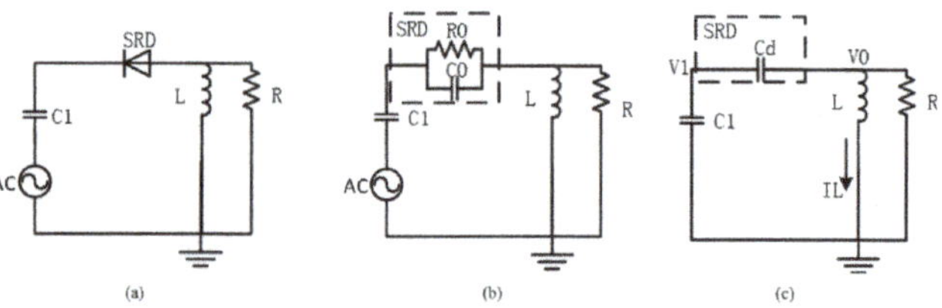

Figure 2. Pulse producing circuit based on SRD and equivalent circuit.

(a) Principle chart (b) Equivalent circuit during conduction (c) Equivalent circuit during cut-off.

The time domain response of the circuit since the instance of the SRD cut-off will be analyzed as follows. To facilitate analysis, consider that the capacitance value C_d is constant. The voltages at both sides of SRD are the on-state voltages, when SRD is on and stable. In Fig 2(C), according to the Kirchhoff theorem, we have:

$$C_1\frac{dV_1}{dt}+I_L+\frac{V_0}{R}=0 \quad (1)$$

$$L\frac{dI_L}{dt}=V_0 \quad (2)$$

$$C_1\frac{dV_1}{dt}=C_d\frac{d(V_0-V_1)}{dt} \quad (3)$$

Eliminating V_1 and I_L in the above equation yields the third-order differential equation of the voltage V_0 at both sides of SRD:

$$\frac{C_1C_d}{C_1+C_d}\frac{d^2V_0}{dt^2}+\frac{dV_0}{Rdt}+\frac{V_0}{L}=0 \quad (4)$$

Consider that the values of V_0, V_1 and I_L at the time instance of zero are equal to $V_{0(0)}$, $V_{1(0)}$, and $I_{L(0)}$, respectively, then the boundary condition in Eq 4 is:

$$\begin{cases} V_0(0) = V_0(0) \\ \dfrac{dV_0(0)}{dt} = -\dfrac{C_1 + C_d}{C_1 C_d}\left(I_L(0) + \dfrac{V_0(0)}{R}\right) \end{cases} \tag{5}$$

According to the infinitesimal analysis principles, V_0 can be computed using Eq 4 and Eq 5when the values of C_d, L, C_1 and R are known as Eq 6:

$$V_0(t) = \frac{-\dfrac{C_1 + C_d}{C_1 C_d}\left(I_L(0) + \dfrac{V_0(0)}{R}\right) - V_0(0)x_2}{x_1 - x_2} e^{x_1 t} + \frac{-\dfrac{C_1 + C_d}{C_1 C_d}\left(I_L(0) + \dfrac{V_0(0)}{R}\right) - V_0(0)x_1}{x_2 - x_1} e^{x_2 t} \tag{6}$$

Where

$$x_1 = \frac{-\frac{C_1 + C_d}{C_1 C_d R} + \sqrt{\frac{(C_1 + C_d)^2}{(C_1 C_d R)^2} - \frac{4(C_1 + C_d)}{C_1 C_d L}}}{2}, \quad x_2 = \frac{-\frac{C_1 + C_d}{C_1 C_d R} - \sqrt{\frac{(C_1 + C_d)^2}{(C_1 C_d R)^2} - \frac{4(C_1 + C_d)}{C_1 C_d L}}}{2}$$

Circuit simulation

In order to analyze the influence of C_d, L, C_1 and R on the V_0, we design simulations in Matlab, as shown in Fig 3.

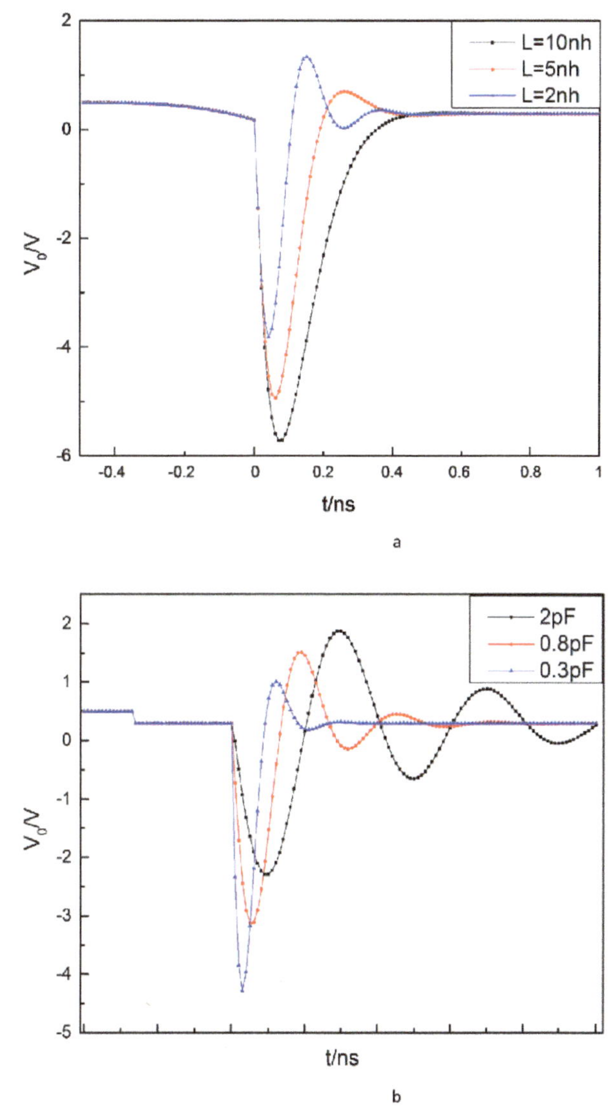

Figure 3. Simulation curves of pulse production circuit.

(a) $C_d = 0.8pF$, $C_1 = 1\mu F$, $R = 50\Omega$ (b) $L = 0.2nH$, $C_1 = 1\mu F$, $R = 50\Omega$.

Fig 3(A) shows the amplitudes of V_0 when L is 2nH, 5nH, and 10nH, respectively, for given values of $C_d = 0.8pF$, $C_1 = 1\mu F$, and $R = 50\Omega$. Fig 3(B) presents the amplitudes of V_0 when C_d is 0.3pF, 0.8pF, and 2pF, respectively, for given values of L = 2nH, $C_1 = 1\mu F$, and $R = 50\Omega$. From Fig 3(A) and Fig 3(B), it can be concluded that the width, amplitude and shape of the generated pulse is largely dependent on the exciting inductance L and C_d. When other parameters are given, a small value of L means that the pulse width is narrow, the amplitude is small, and the pulse ringing is serious. When other parameters are given, a small value of C_d means that the pulse width is narrow, the amplitude is large, and the pulse ringing is slight. This conclusion indicates that the SRD with small junction capacitance (C_d) is recommended for the circuit design, and the value of L should be chosen taking into account pulse width and amplitude.

NLTL CIRCUIT

Nonlinear transmission line (NLTL) is in a high impedance TEM uniform load on a transmission line consisting of varactor ladder network, which encompasses several micro-strip transmission lines with an interval of d [25]. Between the micro-strip transmission lines are the reverse bias Schottky diode, whose junction capacitance varies with the value of reverse bias. The structure of NLTL is shown in Fig 4(A). According to the micro-strip line principle, each section of the lossless micro-strip transmission line can be equivalently seen as a combination of distributed inductance and distributed capacitance. Fig 4(B) shows the equivalent circuit of NLTL, where L_0 and C_0 denote the distributed inductance and distributed capacitance of the lossless micro-strip transmission line, respectively, $C_m(V)$ and R_m denote the junction capacitance and the parasitic series resistance of the Schottky diode, respectively.

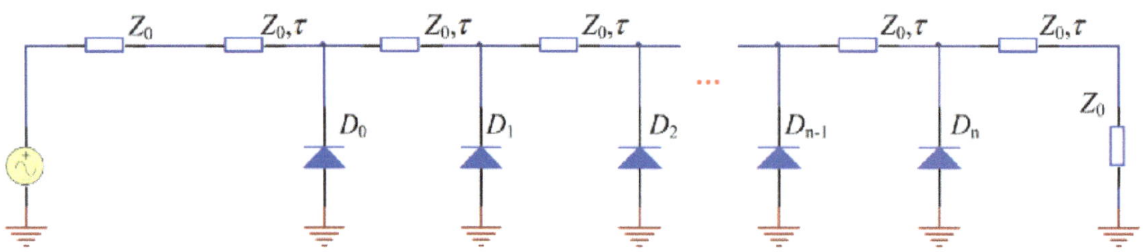

a

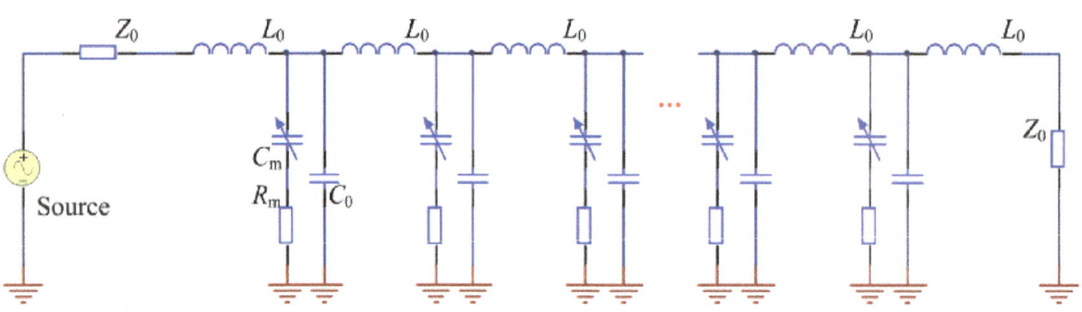

b

Figure 4. Structure and equivalent circuit of NLTL.

(a) Principle diagram (b) Equivalent circuit.

The network in Fig 4(B) can be seen as a low-pass filter, and the cutoff frequency is:

$$\omega_{per} = \frac{2}{L_0[C_0 + C_m(V)]} \tag{7}$$

The operating frequency of NLTL is upper bounded by the cutoff frequency of the Schottky diode. Consider that $R_m = 0$, namely, the micro-strip line is lossless, and the voltage of the next node is:

$$V_o(t) = V_{in}[t - T(V)] \tag{8}$$

Where

$$T(V) = \sqrt{L_0[C_0 + C_m(V)]}$$

This equation demonstrates that NLTL's delay is related to the junction capacitance of the Schottky diode, which can be expressed as:

$$C_m(V) = \frac{C_{j0}}{\left(1 + \frac{V}{\Phi}\right)^k} \tag{9}$$

Where $\approx 0.4V$ (for HSMS-2820 Schottky diode), k denotes the coefficient of the diode and is usually in the range 1–3.

From Eq 1 and Eq 2, it can be known that the larger the value of reverse bias applied to the Schottky diode, the smaller the delay. For different voltages V_h and V_l ($V_h > V_l$), the delay difference of NLTL for these two voltages is:

$$\Delta T = T(V_l) - T(V_h) = \sqrt{L_0[C_0 + C_m(V_l)]} - \sqrt{L_0[C_0 + C_m(V_h)]} \quad \textbf{(10)}$$

Therefore, when a forward narrow pulse passes through NLTL, the pulse rise time will be shortened, and the fall time will be lengthened. To shorten the falling edge time, a grounded resistance is added to each Schottky diode in NLTL, which can steepen the falling edge.

MEASUREMENT RESULTS AND DISCUSSION

According to the above analysis, the narrow pulse circuit consists of the SRD pulse-generating circuit and the NLTL circuit. As shown in Fig 5, at the left is the SRD pulse generating circuit, where SRD is of the type mp4023, with junction capacitance being C_d(-6V) = 0.5pF(max), transit time t_t = 50ps, carrier lifetime t_r = 12ns, C_1 = 1μF, L = 5nH, and R = 50Ω. On the right is the NLTL module used to further narrow the width of the pulse generated by SRD, whereD_1... D_4 denote the Schottky diode, R_1...R_4 = 50Ω, the micro-strip transmission line length is 3mm, and the characteristic impedance of the transmission line is 80Ω. According to the actual test, the waveform of V_{out} is shown as in Fig 6. The circuit of the pulse generator is made utilizing Teflon boards. Fig 6(A) shows the prototype of designed pulse generator, the circuit structure of which is very compact. Furthermore, the waveform is monitored by Lecroy Wave Master 8600A 6GHz DSO oscilloscope as shown in Fig 6(B). The narrow pulse amplitude is 3.3 V and the pulse width is 130ps.

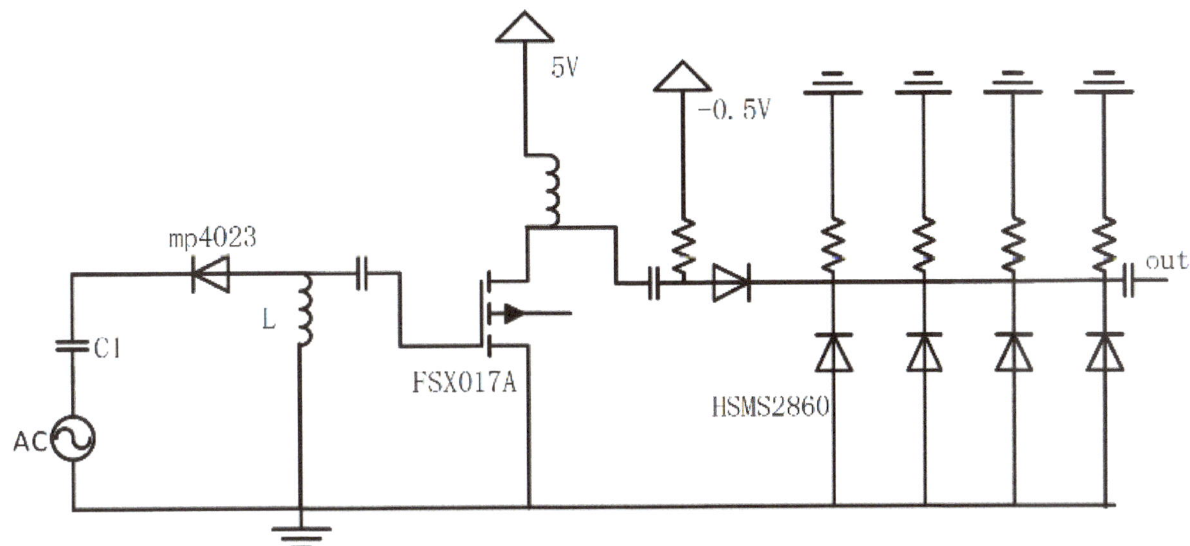

Figure 5. Principle diagram of pulse production circuit.

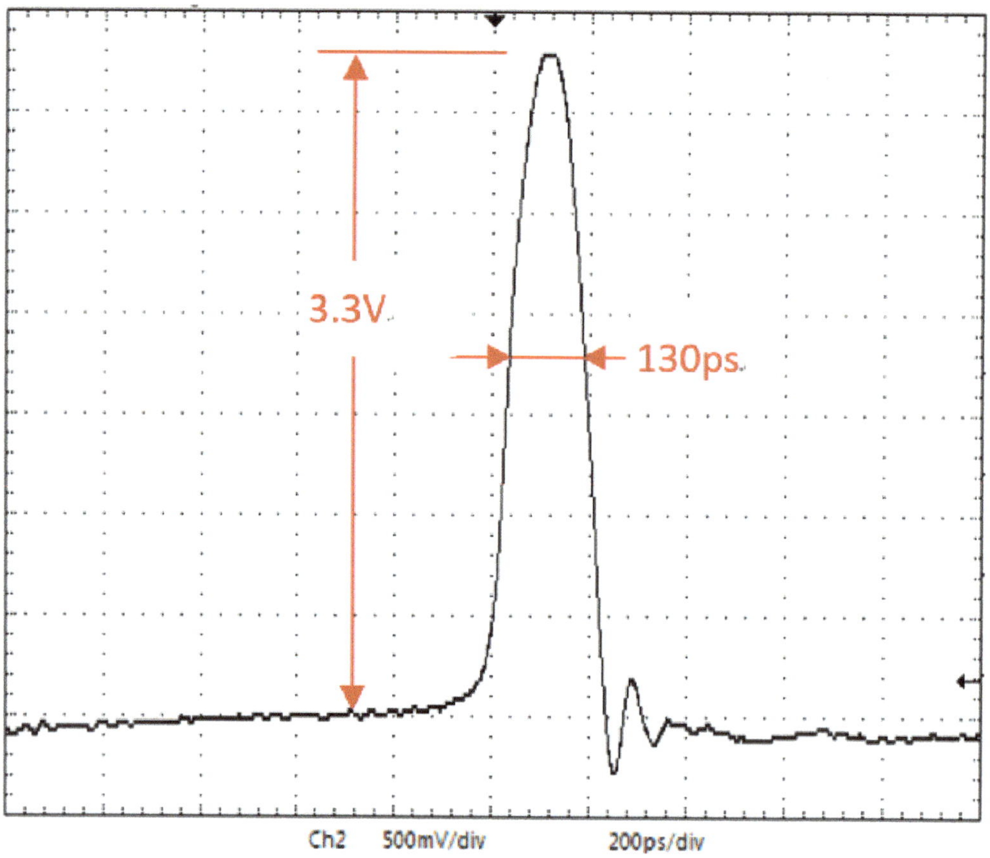

b

Figure 6. Prototype and measured waveform of designed pulse generator.

(a) Prototype of designed pulse generator (b) Measured output pulse of the generator.

CONCLUSION

A narrow pulse-generating circuit is proposed based on SRD and NLTL. The influence factors in the pulse width and amplitude are discussed. Simulation results indicate that a small exciting inductance means that the amplitude of the generated pulse is small and the pulse width is narrow. The SRD with small junction capacitance will yield pulses with narrow width and high amplitude. Therefore, proper inductance and SRD with the smallest possible junction capacitance are recommended for UWB pulse-generated circuit design. To further reduce the width of the narrow pulse, the NLTL circuit is used, which can generate a narrow pulse with a half-amplitude width of 130ps and amplitude of 3.3V.

ACKNOWLEDGMENTS

This project is supported by the Chinese Defense Advance Research Program of Science and Technology, China (Grant No. 40404110203).

AUTHOR CONTRIBUTIONS

Conceived and designed the experiments: JZ QL. Performed the experiments: JZ FL. Analyzed the data: JZ FL YL. Contributed reagents/materials/analysis tools: YL QL FL. Wrote the paper: JZ QL.

REFERENCES

1. Immoreev I, Samkov SV (2004) Ultrawideband radar for remote detection and measurement of parameters of the moving objects on small range. Ultrawideband and Ultrashort Impulse Signals, Second International Workshop: 214–216. doi: 10.1109/UWBUS.2004.1388105.
2. Benedetto A, Benedetto F, De Blasiis M R, Giunta G, (2005) Reliability of signal processing technique for pavement damages detection and classification using ground penetrating radar. Sensors Journal, IEEE. 5:471–480. doi: 10.1109/JSEN.2005.846176.
3. Immoreev Y I, (2006) Practical Application of Ultra-Wideband Radars. Ultrawideband and Ultrashort Impulse Signals, The Third International Conference, Sevastopol:44–49. doi: 10.1109/UWBUS.2006.307156.
4. Salvador S, Vecchi G, (2007) On some experiments with UWB microwave imaging for breast cancer detection. Antennas and Propagation Society International Symposium, Honolulu, 253–256. doi: 10.1109/APS.2007.4395478.
5. De Angelis A, Dionigi M, Moschitta A, Carbone P, (2009) A Low-Cost Ultra-Wideband Indoor Ranging System. Instrumentation and Measurement, IEEE Transactions on. 58:3935–3942. doi: 10.1109/TIM.2009.2020834.
6. Hirsch O, Janson M, Wiesbeck W, Thoma R S, (2010) Indirect Localization and Imaging of Objects in an UWB

Sensor Network. Instrumentation and Measurement, IEEE Transactions on. 59:2949–2957. doi: 10.1109/TIM.2010.2046359.

7. Kamal A, Bhattacharya A, Tamrakar M, Roy C, (2014) Low-ringing and reduced-cost step recovery diode based UWB pulse generators for GPR applications. Microwave and Optical Technology Letters. 56:2289–2294. doi: 10.1002/mop.28581.

8. Zito F, Pepe D, Zito D. (2010) UWB CMOS Monocycle Pulse Generator.Circuits and Systems I: Regular Papers, IEEE Transactions on. 57:2654–2664. doi: 10.1109/TCSI.2010.2047751.

9. Lemaire O, Tian X, (2009) Design of a monolithic width programmable Gaussian Monocycle Pulse generator for Ultra WideBand radar in CMOS technology.Circuits and Systems and TAISA Conference. NEWCAS-TAISA '09. Joint IEEE North-East Workshop on, Toulouse: 1–4. doi: 10.1109/NEWCAS.2009.5290490.

10. Wang Q, Tian X, Liu Y, Bo l, (2008) Design of an ultra-wideband pulse generator based on avalanche transistor. Dalian, China: Inst. of Elec. and Elec. Eng. Computer Society: 1–4. doi: 10.1109/WiCom.2008.263.

11. Ruai Y Y, Konishi Y, Allen S T, Reddy M, Rodwell J W, (1994) A traveling-wave resonant tunnel diode pulse generator. Microwave and Guided Wave Letters, IEEE. (NLTL) harmonic and pulse generators. Microwave Theory and Techniques, IEEE Transactions on.47:1118–1122. doi: 10.1109/22.775445.

12. Salameh D, Linton D, (1999) Microstrip GaAs nonlinear transmission-line (NLTL) harmonic and pulse generators. Microwave Theory and Techniques, IEEE Transactions on. 47:1118–1122. doi: 10.1109/22.775445.

13. Holzman J F, Vermeulen F E, Elezzabi A Y, (2000) Recombination-independent photogeneration of ultrashort electrical pulses. Applied Physics Letters. 76:134–136. doi: 10.1063/1.125679.

14. Gerding M, Musch T, Schiek B, (2004) Generation of short electrical pulses based on bipolar transistors.Advances in Radio Science. 2:7–12. doi: 10.5194/2.7.2004.

15. Ouslimani A, Vernet G, Hafdallah H, Adde R, (1990) Large amplitude picosecond step generation with FETs, Electronics Letters, 26:1563–1564. doi: 10.1049/el:19901003.

16. Jeong S L, Cam N, Scullion T, (2001) New uniplanar subnanosecond monocycle pulse generator and transformer for time-domain microwave applications. Microwave Theory and Techniques, IEEE Transactions on. 49:1126–1129. doi: 10.1109/22.925501.

17. .Jeong S L, Cam N, (2001) Novel low-cost ultra-wideband, ultra-short-pulse transmitter with MESFET impulse-shaping circuitry for reduced distortion and improved pulse repetition rate. Microwave and Wireless Components Letters, IEEE. 11:208–210. doi: 10.1109/7260.923030.

18. Jeongwoo H, Cam N, (2002) A new ultra-wideband, ultra-short monocycle pulse generator with reduced ringing. Microwave and Wireless Components Letters, IEEE. 12:206–208. doi: 10.1109/LMWC.2002.1009996.

19. Jeongwoo H, Cam N, (2005) Coupled-slotline-hybrid sampling mixer integrated with step-recovery-diode pulse generator for UWB applications.Microwave Theory and Techniques, IEEE Transactions on 53:1875–1882. doi: 10.1109/TMTT.2005.848091.

20. Jianming Z, Xiaowei G, Yuanchun F, (2006) A new CAD model of step recovery diode and generation of UWB signals. IEICE Electronics Express, 3:534–539. doi: 10.1587/elex.3.534.

21. Cemin Z, Fathy A E, (2006) Reconfigurable Pico-Pulse Generator for UWB Applications. Microwave Symposium Digest. IEEE MTT-S International, San Francisco, CA:407–410. doi: 10.1109/MWSYM.2006.249557.

22. Chan K K M, Rambabu K, Tan A E C, Chia M Y, (2010) Efficient passive low-rate pulse generator for ultra-wideband radar. Microwaves, Antennas & Propagation, IET.4:2196–2199. doi: 10.1049/iet-map.2010.0030.

23. .Wong Choi G, Joo Choi J, Hoon Han S, (2011) Note: Picosecond impulse generator driven by cascaded step recovery diode pulse shaping circuit.Review of Scientific Instruments. 82:16106. doi: 10.1063/1.3523342.

24. Tian X, Venkatachalam A S, Huston D, (2012) A High-Performance Low-Ringing Ultrawideband Monocycle Pulse Generator. Instrumentation and Measurement, IEEE Transactions on. 61: 261–266. doi: 10.1109/TIM.2011.2161022.

25. Chow W H, Steenson D P, Piotrowski T T, Piotrowska, A, (2003) A fully integrated distributed frequency tripler for broadband harmonic generation in submillimeter wave applications. Asia-Pacific Conference on Applied Electromagnetics: 21–25. doi: 10.1109/APACE.2003.1234459.

CHAPTER 15 DYNAMICS OF COMPLEX SYSTEMS BUILT AS COUPLED PHYSICAL, COMMUNICATION AND DECISION LAYERS

Kühnlenz F[1], Nardelli PHJ[1].

[1]University of Oulu, Department of Communications Engineering, Oulu, FI-90014, Finland.

ABSTRACT

This paper proposes a simple model to capture the complexity of multilayer systems where their constituent layers affect, and are affected by, each other. The physical layer is a circuit composed by a power source and resistors in parallel. Every individual agent aims at maximizing its own delivered power by adding, removing or keeping the resistors it has; the delivered power is in turn a non-linear function that depends on the other agents' behavior, its own internal state, its global state perception, the information received from its neighbors via the communication network and a randomized selfishness. We develop an agent-based simulation to analyze the effects of number of agents (system size), communication network topology, communication errors and the minimum power gain that triggers a behavioral change on the system dynamic. Our results show that a wave-like behavior at macro-level (caused by individual changes in the decision layer) can only emerge for a specific system size. The ratio between cooperators and defectors depends on the minimum gain assumed—lower minimal gains lead to less cooperation, and vice-versa. Different communication network topologies imply different levels of power utilization and fairness at the physical layer, and a certain level of error in the communication layer induces more cooperation.

INTRODUCTION

The modernization of large-scale engineering infrastructures introduces new challenges into their already complicated design [1–3]. For example, electric power grids are large-scale engineering systems built to generate, transmit and distribute electricity from generators to end-users [4–6]. Although their technological development has never stopped, a strong political demand for a structural change is taking place. Such change basically consists in decentralizing generating units (e.g. from nuclear to solar panels and wind turbines), spreading of electric vehicles (which are mobile batteries and loads) and controlling demand based on information technologies; all in all, the traditional consumer is predicted to become a prosumer: a consumer who participate more actively in the grid management either by supplying electricity or decreasing their consumption. Modern power grids will become more dynamic and distributed. This will bring new complexities to their already complex dynamic together with new research challenges to cope with them [7].

Citation: Kühnlenz F, Nardelli PHJ (2016) Dynamics of Complex Systems Built as Coupled Physical, Communication and Decision Layers. PLoS ONE 11(1): e0145135. doi:10.1371/journal.pone.0145135

The same trends—although considered in their own context—can be seen when analysing the modernization of other large-scales systems, from smart cities [8, 9] to factories of the future [10] or the 5-th generation of cellular systems [11]. As in power grids, new complexities in those systems will emerge followed by a need for a new body of knowledge. Notwithstanding the unquestionable technical evolution, there is still a limited number of simple analytic models that are able to capture the dynamics of these modern systems, where the physical infrastructure, the information network and regulations affect, and are affected, by each other dynamics. In this context the present article proposes a discrete-time agent-based model assuming these three layers as constitutive parts of a multilayer system composed by an electric circuit as the physical infrastructure, a communication network where agents exchange local information and a set of regulations that define the agents' behavior.

The electric circuit is composed by one constant voltage source including its inner resistance and resistors (loads) in parallel [12]. The resistors in parallel are grouped by their controlling agent, as shown in Fig 1. Every agent may add or remove one of the resistors under its control at every time step. One can expect that, the greater the number of active resistors a given agent has, the more power is delivered to it. The actual delivered power is, however, a non-linear, concave, function of the electric current flowing in the circuit; there exists then a saturation point where adding more resistors will decrease the delivered power for the whole system. This behavior is somehow comparable to what happens in real power systems, where overuse leads to a drop in frequency and voltage, reducing the delivered power for all users.

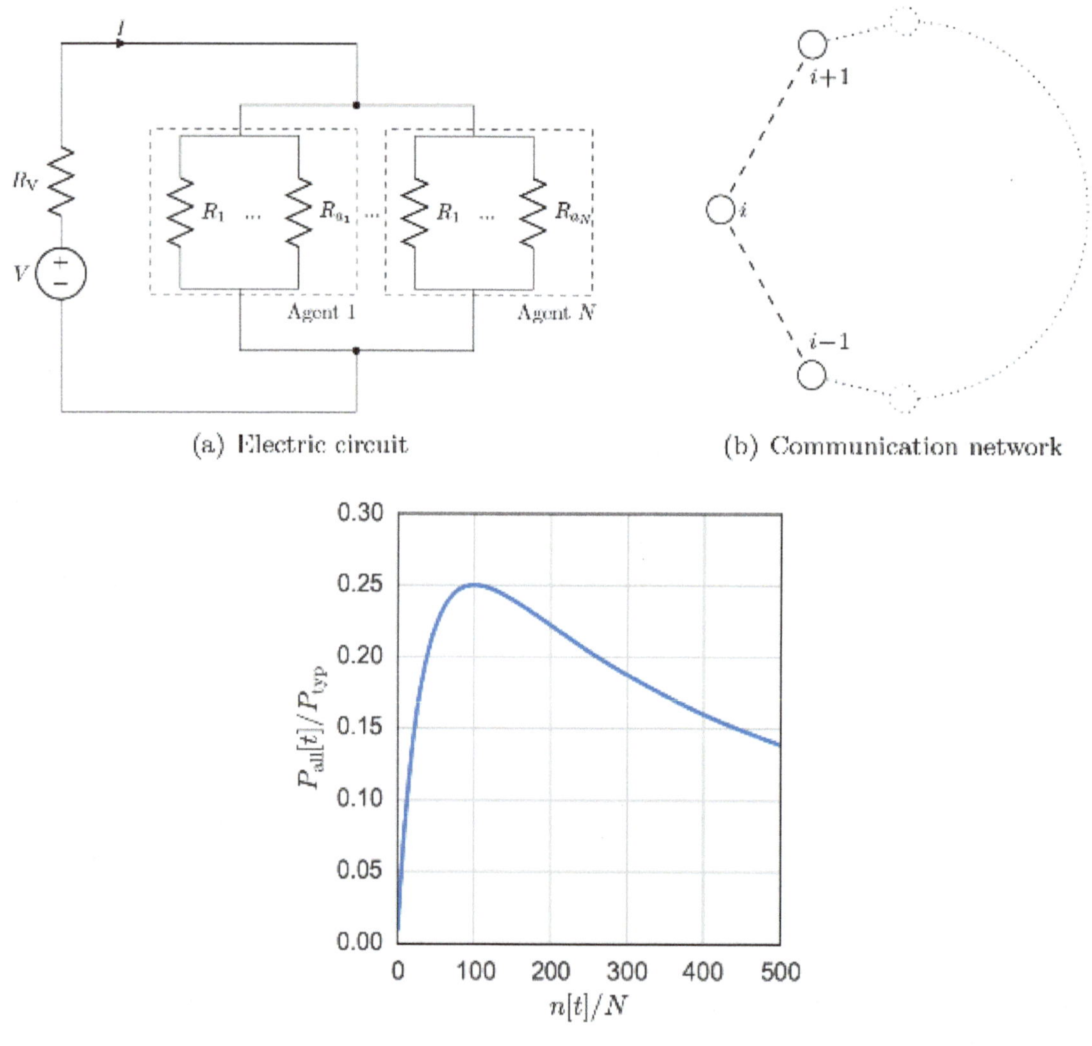

(c) Normalized power

Fig 1. (a) Electrical circuit representing the physical layer of the system. The circuit is composed by a power source V and R_V, and resistors of R in parallel, generating a current I. These resistors are related to N agents that can add, remove or keep the resistors under their control in the circuit. The minimum number of resistors an agent can have is one and there is no maximum. We also consider N as the size of the system. (b) The agents are connected in a communication network so that a given agent has access to the information related to the previous action of their first-order neighbours. In the ring topology illustrated here, every agent is connected with two other agents. In this case agent i is connected with agents i − 1 and i+1 with i = 1, 2, …, N. In the ring topology, agents 1 and N are neighbours. (c) At time step t, the normalized power delivered $P_{all}[t]/P_{typ}$ to the agents with rising number of resistors n[t] in the system, where $P_{typ} = \frac{V^2}{R_V}$ and $P_{all}[t] = \sum_{i \in \mathcal{A}} P_i[t]$ with $P_i[t]$ given by Eq (1).

Looking at the whole system, a "tragedy of the commons" kind of problem arises [13], where adding a resistor is individually beneficial, while socially harmful. However, in our case, the resource recovers very quickly. The agent's decision regarding the resistors (adding, subtracting or maintaining) is built upon the following criteria: the behavior of the agent's neighbors at the last time step, the previous state of the whole system and its own selfishness gene. As we will discuss later, this interactive decision procedure resembles the prisoners dilemma [14–16]. In this case, the agents' neighborhood is defined by the communication network (where links can be in error), while the selfishness genes of the agents are independent and identically distributed random variables.

Complexity Sciences

Before we start presenting our contribution in more detail, it is worth indicating the theoretical ground that supports our findings: complexity sciences. Complexity is a term used in several diverse research fields [17–19], from theoretic physics to social sciences and biology, to characterize a state that is neither completely deterministic nor random. The so-called complex behavior emerges in systems whose elements interact; they may be heterogeneous and may also adapt their relation rules in accordance to internal and/or external factors.

In his extensive work [20, 21], Wolfram has shown that simple interaction rules applied in one-dimensional cellular automata may lead to unexpected intricate patterns—defined therein as complex—over time. This work tells us that, when looked at a higher level, the spatial-temporal dynamics of a fairly simple deterministic system composed by homogeneous agents that follow fixed interrelation rules may generate complexity. This fact suggests that decentralized systems, based only in local information, might be functional without any controlling entity. In Wolfram's case the spatial-temporal pattern is determined by the interaction rule. Following his classification, four kind of behaviors can emerge in the one-dimensional automata, namely homogeneous, periodic, chaotic and complex [18, 20].

For some researchers, this fact indicates the system is able to self-organize without any explicit centralized controller. We can cite here few illustrative examples regarded as self-organized [17]: ants working in colonies [22], neurons building a capable brain [17, 23] and birds flying in groups [24] or criticality in plasma turbulence [25]. As an interesting counter point to this perspective, one may argue that the interaction rule that the agents follow is per se a kind of central control or a strict regulative force [26]. By using this view, many questions may be posed: Where do the interaction rules come from? Are they evolving? Are they changing in a much slower time-scale that can be considered as given? These questions in fact still cause hot philosophical debates among biologists, economists, social scientists and other theorists concerning who controls the "invisible hand" of the system [27].

When dealing with large-scale engineering systems, these questions seem to have clear answers as far as it is designed and follows predefined requirements. This is true for some systems, but it is far from being a universal feature, mainly when the infrastructure is heavily dependent on human actions and interactions. Road networks provide an educative example when one tries to understand the formation of traffic jams [28, 29]. Without going into further details, the key for solving the traffic puzzle is not found by looking at what happens in individual cars or in the design of the whole transportation infrastructure. While these aspects are necessary conditions to the formation of the jam, they are not sufficient to explain the phenomenon. The most accepted theory is built upon the interactions between cars and reactions to the individual behaviors within a specific region of the road network: one car slowing down in highly dense highway causes other nearby cars to slow down as well to avoid collisions, which may trigger a traffic jam that will fade away after some time.

This simple example identifies few important characteristics of complex phenomena: they are spatial and temporal, they never reach stable equilibrium states, the context where the individuals interact and their perception are important to individual decisions, and one individual action might cause a local change that might also trigger changes in the global state of the system. The so-called complexity sciences tries to deal with phenomena that present such characteristics [30].

It is also worth pointing out that simplified models for the power grid (like the "DC Power Flow" [31]) have a long-standing tradition in the literature [32, 33]. While they were initially constructed to cope with available computational power limitation, their use is still widespread nowadays with much more powerful computers [34]. For instance, simplified models for the synchronization in the grid as in [35] are an active focus of the research community (e.g. [36–38]). Such models are able to predict the stability of the network against perturbations, showing ways to optimize its underlying topology [39]. The study of cascade effects [40, 41] to understand the propagation of blackouts and to find the critical links in the grid can be seen as another, more recent, development based on simplified power system models [42, 43]. An agent-based approach (as in the present work) can be also employed to model a wide range of aspects in the power grid, going from electricity market simulations [44] to very specific appliance usage behavior [45] or even the smart grid system as a whole [46].

We follow here the idea of using simplified models to understand the complex behavior that arises in the power grid. However, in contrast to the engineering-focused models as in [47–50], we concentrate more on the higher level interactions across the different layers of the system. Consequently, we have chosen a model that keeps essential features of the system without having a detailed specification of its entities. For this reason, the nature of our work can be seen as "exploratory", rather than "performance-optimizer" (in the engineering sense) [51].

Contributions

Motivated by a growing literature in complexity sciences in general and their application in engineering systems in specific, this articles presents a new perspective to analyze multilayered, strongly coupled, systems. We construct a simple, while illustrative, multilayer model composed by agents that control a set of resistors in an electrical circuit. These agents play an evolutionary "prisoners' dilemma" style of game to decide if they should collaborate or not, based on the local information gathered from their communication network, the estimated state of the whole system and their own random selfishness.

Our results indicate that: (i) a wave-like behavior at macro-level spatial-temporal dynamics, which is caused by changes in individual behaviors at the decision layer, can only emerge for a specific system size, (ii) the ratio between cooperators and defectors depends on the minimum gain assumed—lower minimal gains lead to less cooperation and vice-versa, (iii) different communication network topologies—ring, Watt-Strogatz-Graph and Barabasi-Albert-Graph [52]—imply different levels of power utilization and fairness at the physical layer, and (iv) a certain level of error in the communication layer induces more cooperative behavior at the decision layer, affecting the physical layer dynamics in terms of power utilization and fairness accordingly.

RESULTS

Before starting, we think it is worth describing the key aspects of the proposed model that will help to understand our results. We also systematized some useful notation in Table 1. More details about the multilayer system proposed here can be found in the Methods section. The implementation of our model can be found under [53].

Table 1. Notations.

Notation	Meaning
$t \in \mathbb{Z}$	discrete time
$\mathcal{A} = \{1, 2, ..., N\}$	set of all agents, where N is the size of the system
$\mathcal{A} \backslash \{i\}$	set of all agents without agent i
$i \in \mathcal{A}$	agent i
$\mathcal{N}_i \subset \mathcal{A}$	neighborhood set of agent i
$n[t] \in \{N, N+1, \ldots\}$	active number of resistors in the system at time t
$a_i[t] \in \mathbb{N}^+$	active resistors of agent i
$r_i[t] = n[t] - a_i[t]$	active resistors excluding agent i
$P_i[t] > 0$	consumed power of agent i [in units of power]
$\lambda_i[t] \in \mathbb{R}$	gain in power of agent i
$\lambda_{min} \in \mathbb{R}$	system-wide predefined minimum gain
$S_i[t] \in \{-1, 0, +1\}$	state of agent i: +1 (defect), 0 (ignore), or −1 (cooperate)
$s_i \in [0, 1]$	selfishness gene of agent i
$p_{err} \in [0, 1]$	error probability in a communication link

doi:10.1371/journal.pone.0145135.t001

Agents' Decision Process

We assume a discrete-time system such that the changes in the agent behavior occur in time-steps, denoted by $t \in \mathbb{Z}$. At every time-step t, each agent wants to maximize its own power, so their interactions can be then viewed as a round-based game [15]. To achieve that goal, the agent has three options: add a resistor (defecting), remove it (cooperating), or do nothing (ignoring).

To make a decision at time t, every agent i looks at its gain from the previous strategy $S_i[t-1]$ in order to decide its new state $S_i[t]$. The decision process for the agent i is the following. If the gain $\lambda_i[t-1]$ is greater than or equal to a system-wide pre-defined minimum λ_{min}, the agent sticks to its (successful) strategy at time t, i.e. $S_i[t] = S_i[t-1]$. If $\lambda_i[t] < \lambda_{min}$, then agent icompares its strategy with its neighborhood $\mathcal{N}_i$, which will be defined later in this section. If the majority is cooperative, then $\sum_{j \in \mathcal{N}_i} S_j[t-1] < 0$ and the agent under analysis will also cooperate, leading to $S_i[t] = -1$. Otherwise, the agent draws a random number between 0 and 1 to be compared to its own selfishness gene s_i (which is also randomly generated as discussed later) in order to decide whether it will start cooperating. If it does not cooperate, it again draws a random number to be compared to the selfishness gene s_i, but now to decide if stays inactive (i.e. $S_i[t] = 0$) or adds another load in the circuit (i.e. $S_i[t] = +1$). The agent decision procedure is shown in Fig 2.

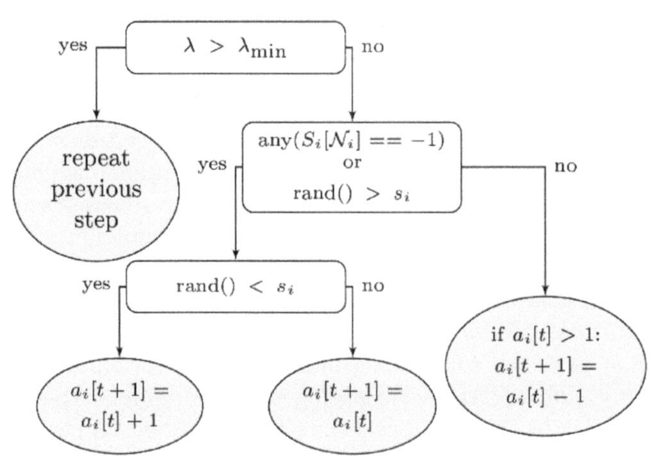

Fig 2. Schematic of agent *i*'s decision procedure.

Communication network

In the multilayer system proposed here, agent i knows the state $S_j[t-1]$ of the agents $j \in \mathcal{N}_i$ through a communication network. We assume that agent j always transmits its actual state $S_j[t]$ to agent i. The neighborhood $\mathcal{N}_i$ of agent i is defined as the agents $j \in \mathcal{A} \backslash \{i\}$ that are directly linked with it. In the case of ring topology, the cardinality of $\mathcal{N}_i$ is 2 for all agents $i \in \mathcal{A}$. For more complex network topologies, $\mathcal{N}_i$ will be characterized differently [52], as discussed later.

The communication links can also experience errors. An error event means the received message by agent i contains a different information than agent j has sent. Let $S_{j\to i}[t-1] = S_j[t-1]$ be the state information transmitted from j to i at time-step t and $\hat{S}_{j\to i}[t-1]$ be the information received by i. We consider that error events are independent and identically distributed such that the probability of the event: $\Pr[\hat{S}_{j\to i}[t-1] \neq S_{j\to i}[t-1]] = p_{\text{err}}$ for all $t \in \mathbb{Z}$, $i \in \mathcal{A}$ and $j \in \mathcal{N}_i$, where $\Pr[\cdot]$ refers to the probability that a given event occurs. It is worth mentioning that the network is a bidirectional graph so that an error event at i → j does not imply an error event at j → i, and vice-versa.

If an error event happens, the received information $\hat{S}_{j\to i}[t-1]$ will be uniformly and identically distributed between the other possible states. For example, if $S_{j\to i}[t-1] = -1$ and error happens, then $\hat{S}_{j\to i}[t-1] = 0$ or $\hat{S}_{j\to i}[t-1] = +1$ will happen with 50% chance each.

Physical system

For the physical systems presented in Fig 1, there exists a certain number of resistors that leads to the maximum power gain in the system. If the delivered power is below the maximum on the right, then there will be a gain by removing a resistor until the system has reached such point. Conversely, if it is below on the left, then there will be a gain by adding a resistor.

In this case, one may ask the following question: Is it possible for the agents to reach the optimal point while fairly delivering power among them (i.e. they indiviadually consume about the same amount of power)? In the presence of a central control unit this would be a fairly easy problem. First, we need to find the number of resistors that lead to optimal power to then fairly allocate them among the agents by some kind of centralized coordination mechanism. This kind of solution resembles time division schemes in computer networks or cellular systems [54]. For example, if there are ten agents and the optimal number of resistors is twenty, then the central control coordinates the behavior such that all ten agents have two active resistors, summing up to twenty. However, as discussed before, our model does not consider the presence of a central control and the agents have a limited knowledge about other agents.

At time-step t, the power each agent consumes $P_i[t]$ with $i \in \mathcal{A} = \{1, \ldots, N\}$ and is given by:

$$P_i[t] = P_{\text{typ}} \frac{a_i[t]\mu}{(a_{\text{avg}}[t] + \mu)^2}, \quad (1)$$

where $P_{\text{typ}} = \frac{V^2}{R_V}$, $\mu = \frac{R}{R_V}$, $a_i[t]$ is the number of active resistors the agent i possesses, $r_i[t]$ is the number of active resistors in the system excluding the source resistor R_V and the ones controlled by agent i, and $a_{\text{avg}}[t] = (a_i[t]+r_i[t])/N$.

The physical system is then described by its size N, the ratio μ of the resistance values and the power source V. The resistors are scaled so that the optimal average number of resistors (a^*_{avg}) is independent of N while the voltage might be scaled with $\sqrt{N}$ to have a constant ratio of power per agent, as explained later on. The gain that agent i experiences at time-step t is then defined as:

$$\lambda_i[t] = \frac{P_i[t] - P_i[t-1]}{P_i[t-1]} = \frac{\Delta P_i}{P_i[t-1]}. \quad (2)$$

This implies that the agents only use the information about the previous time-step t − 1. If we expand Eq (2) using Eq (1), the resulting equation that determines $\lambda_i[t]$ becomes more complicated. To make the analysis clearer, we choose to apply the following approximation (more details in the Methods section):

$$\lambda_i[t] \approx \frac{dP_i}{P_i[t]} \approx \frac{\Delta a_i[t]}{a_i[t]} - \frac{2}{N}\frac{1}{a_{\text{avg}}[t] + \mu}(\Delta r_i[t] + \Delta a_i[t]), \quad (3)$$

such that the gain $\lambda_i[t]$ is now a function of the variations in agent i's own number of resistors$\Delta a_i[t] = a_i[t] - a_i[t-1]$ and in the number of resistors controlled by other agents $\Delta r_i[t] = r_i[t] - r_i[t-1]$, as well as the average number of resistors $a_{\text{avg}}[t]$ and the system parameters N andμ.

Numerical results

Let $\mathcal{C}_t \subseteq \mathcal{A}$ be the cooperative agents at time-slot t. In this case, $\#(\mathcal{C}_t) \leq \#(\mathcal{A}) = N$ where $\#(\cdot)$ is the cardinality of the set. The spatial-temporal average number of cooperators in the system (c_{avg}) is then:

$$c_{\text{avg}} = \frac{1}{N} \lim_{T\to\infty} \frac{1}{T} \sum_{t=0}^{T-1} \#(\mathcal{C}_t). \quad (4)$$

Fig 3 shows the change of the system behavior with varying size N. The left side shows the changes in the spatial-temporal average number of cooperators in the system c_{avg} as a function of the system size N, while the right side shows a representation of a typical spatial-temporal system behavior for three different sizes N. In the latter, each line of vertical pixels represents the state of the system for one time-step: white means cooperation, red means defection and black means doing nothing.

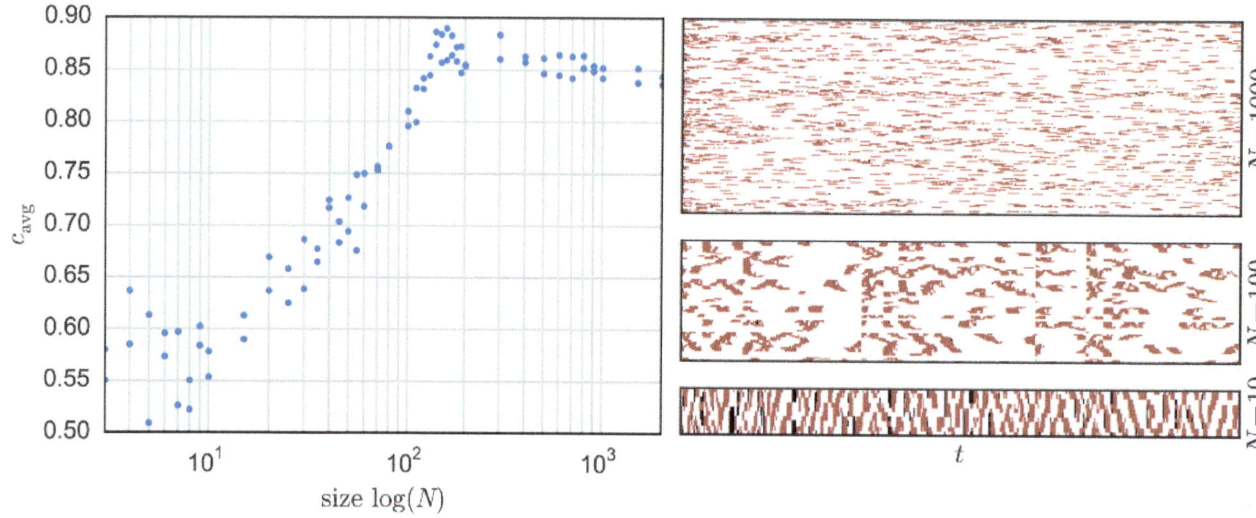

Fig 3. On the left: change in the average cooperation c_{avg} depending on the system size N. On the right: examples of a typical system behavior as a function of time t where the points (pixels) represent the agent state $S_i[t]$ such that red means defection, white cooperation, and black doing nothing for N = 1000 (top), N = 100 (middle) and N = 10 (bottom). The system parameters are: $\lambda_{min} = 0.0005$, $R_V = 2\Omega$, $R_0 = R/N = 200\Omega$, $p_{err} = 0.01$ and V = 1 V. The communication network is configured as a ring.

For small sizes (as when N = 10), one can see a kind of checkerboard pattern where cooperators and defectors alternate on time and space axes. For middle-sized systems (as when N = 100), the most striking feature is that there exist certain points in time when sudden changes in the behavior happen. The system seems to move closer and closer to a global cooperation state until suddenly it falls back to a state with much less cooperation. Such pattern becomes even more pronounced for a meshed communication network built as a Watts-Strogatz graph [52], as seen in Fig 4. For larger systems (as when N = 1000), one can see that a pattern where cooperation is dominant and only few stripes of defecting appear. As we will see next, this behavior is not due to simple scaling effects in the system variables, but rather it results from inherent scaling effects within the physical layer. In other words, certain behaviors can be only observed for certain system sizes N. therefore, for a given N, one cannot pre-set the system variables expecting a certain kind of behavior. Rather, the size of the system is itself a variable that influences its own macro-level behavior.

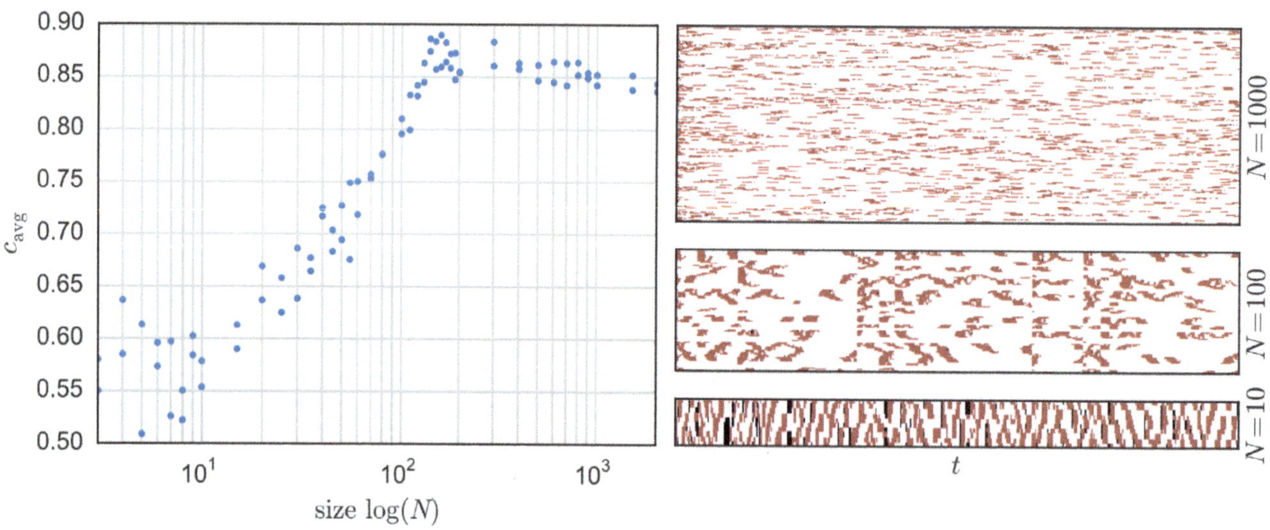

Fig 4. On the left: change in the average cooperation c_{avg} depending on the system size N. On the right: examples of a typical system behavior as a function of time t where the points (pixels) represent the agent state $S_i[t]$ such that red means defection, white cooperation, and black = doing nothing for N = 1000 (top), N = 100 (middle) and N = 10 (bottom). The system parameters are: $\lambda_{min} = 0.0005$, $R_V = 2\Omega$, $R_0 = R/N = 200\Omega$, $p_{err} = 0.01$ and V = 1 V. The communication network is configured as Watts-Strogatz graph.

Fig 5 shows how the minimal gain λ_{min} affects the agents' behavior quantified by average number of cooperators in the system c_{avg} for two different system size N. One can see that bigger values of λ_{min} lead to more cooperation in the system and different behavior patterns. But only in mid-sized systems (as when N = 100) one can see wave-like patterns for certain ranges. We can then infer that the system is dominated by the agent behaviors for high and low thresholds of λ_{min}, while complex behavior only emerges in few cases where a proper interplay between the layers occurs.

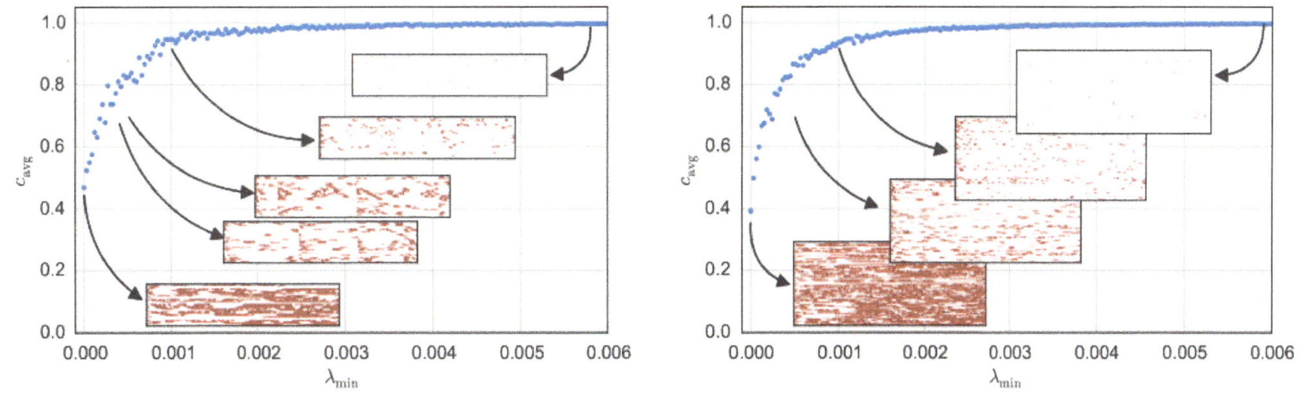

(a) $N = 100$ (b) $N = 500$

Fig 5. Influence of minimal gain λ_{min} on system behavior for (a) $N = 100$ and (b) $N = 500$.

Bigger minimum gains leads to more cooperation while smaller ones lead to defection. More complex behavior can be observed for values close to $\lambda_{min} = 0.0001$ in mid sized systems. The systems parameters are $R_V = 2\Omega$, $R_0 = R/N = 200\Omega$, $p_{err} = 0.01$ and $V = 1$ V. The communication network is configured as a ring.

To have a better understanding on how the minimal gain influences the behavior, we need to analyze Eq (3). We find that the upper limit for the tipping point is given by $\frac{1}{\lambda_{min}}$ (more details in Methods section), meaning that after such a point the gain of adding another resistor for a single agent becomes too small. This stands in contrast to the global optimum, which represents the tipping point after which another resistor added to the system as a whole will result in reduced power delivered to the agents. Only in the case that all agents behave equally at every point in time, i.e. $a_i[t] = a_{avg}[t] \ \forall \ i \in \mathcal{A}$, the tipping point for each agent also becomes the global optimum of $a_{avg}[t] = \mu$.

As the system grows, the feedback that each agent can infer is then reduced, so is its influence on the system as a whole. For large systems the deviation of a single agent from the average of the rest of the system has little influence on the average of the whole system. This reduced feedback leads to a situation where agents will become trapped in a state of what we call cooperative solidarity. Agents in this trapped state have reduced their number of resistors to minimum (i.e. only one active resistor), while having still not seen a positive gain. Consequently, they remain cooperative as do their neighbours.

In this scenario, all resources of the system will be used by the agents that are not yet trapped, leading to high inequality levels. For large systems the feedback about individual behaviors are so small that the only way to skip from this solidarity trap is, surprisingly, through communication errors. In this case, the trapped agents (wrongly) believe that some neighbours stopped cooperating.

For middle-sized systems, however, the gain may become large enough if a sufficient number of agents synchronize in reducing their number of resistors. This results in a positive gain to all the trapped agents since the system recovers from a state of overusing. This positive gain then leads to agents that no longer seek cooperation as they are already in the lowest state possible and the system has recovered. This in turn explains the wave-like behavior in mid-size systems.

Fig 6 shows the system from a different perspective. Let us first define the power utilization P_{util} as the fraction of power that is utilized by the system and the available power:

$$P_{util} = \frac{4}{P_{typ}} \sum_{i \in \mathcal{A}} P_{i,avg}, \quad (5)$$

where $P_{i,avg}$ is the time average power of agent i computed as:

$$P_{i,avg} = \lim_{T \to \infty} \frac{1}{T} \sum_{t=0}^{T-1} P_i[t]. \quad (6)$$

By looking at the power utilization P_{util} and the average number of resistors a_{avg}, one can see that both are related to each other. Note that all systems in this example are stable in the sense that number of resistors varies within a certain range and does not diverge. This is not necessarily true. Depending on the choices of μ and λ_{min} the system can behave differently, e.g. all agents remain with only one resistor, or end up collecting more and more resistors. How close the system can operates to the optimum wildly varies between the different system sizes. The only system that can operate very close to the optimum is the very small system with a size of only five agents ($N = 5$). We also see the sudden jumps in behavior for mid-size systems, while large ones appear to be the most stable.

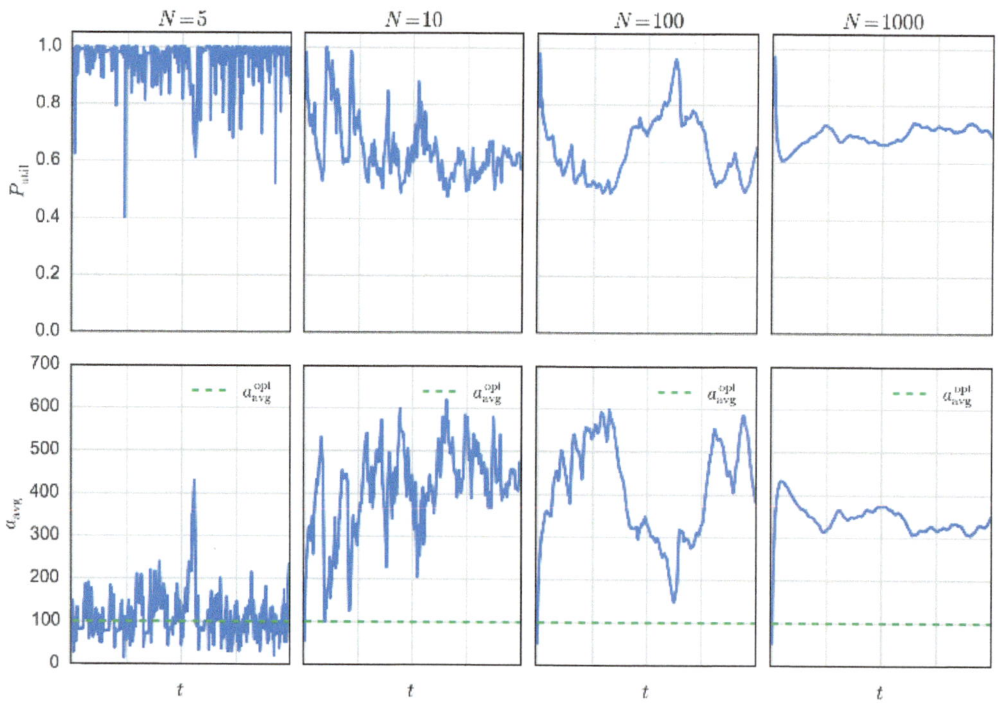

Fig 6. Typical behavior of very small (*N* = 5), small (*N* = 10), medium (*N* = 100) and large systems (*N* = 1000).

The small systems can operate much closer to the optimum, while mid-size systems show big jumps after stable periods. The system parameters are $\lambda_{min} = 0.005$, $R_V = 2\Omega$, $R_0 = R/N = 200\Omega$, $p_{err} = 0.01$ and V = 1 V. The communication network is configured as a ring.

To better understand what happens in large systems, we analyze Fig 7, which illustrates the changes in power utilization and inequality (fairness) in power usage between the agents depending on the size of the system N and different topologies of communication network. The inequality (fairness) is measured here by the Gini index [55]:

$$G = \frac{2}{n}\left(\frac{\sum_{i\in A} iP_{i,avg}}{\sum_{i\in A} P_{i,avg}}\right) - \frac{n+1}{n}, \tag{7}$$

where $P_{i,avg} \leq P_{i+1,avg}$ such that full equality is G = 0 and the highest level of inequality is G = 1.

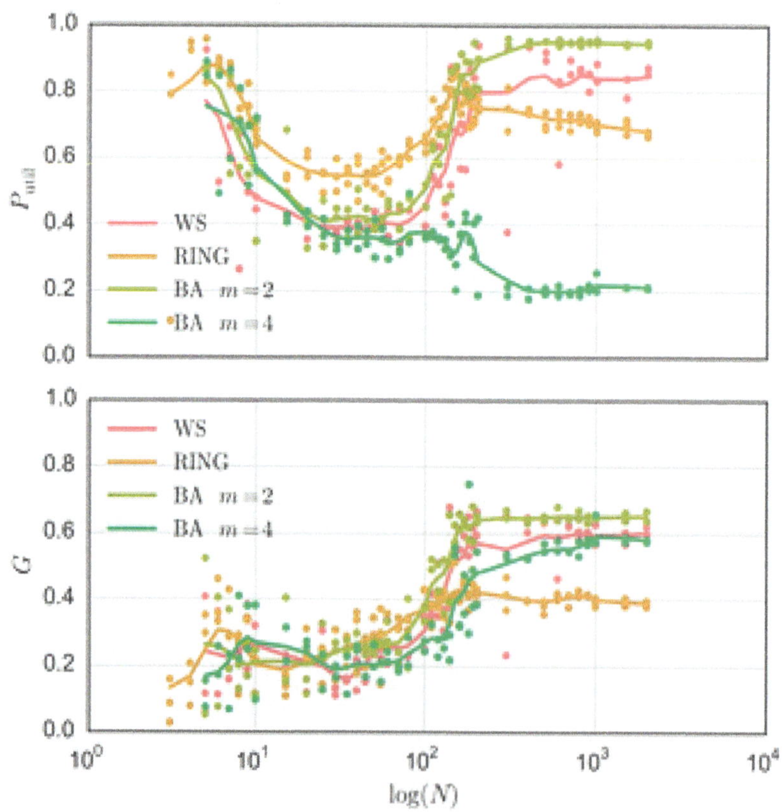

Fig 7. Power utilization P_{util} (top) and Gini index G (bottom) as a measure of inequality of power distribution, where $G = 1$ representing the biggest inequality.

The Watt-Strogatz-Graph (WS) setting is: mean degree K = 4, rewiring probability $\beta = 0.5$. Barabasi-Albert-Graph (BA) setting is: number of nodes to attach to m = 2,4. The system parameters are: $\lambda_{min} = 0.005$, $R_V = 2\Omega$, $R_0 = R/N = 200\Omega$, $p_{err} = 0.01$ and V = 1 V.

We see that, for small systems, the results are very close together specially for the complex network Watt-Strogatz and Barabasi-Albert [52]. When the system size increases, on the other hand, one can see a growing difference between the results of different topologies, suggesting that the communication layer plays a big role in the system dynamics.

One can also see a drastic change for the Barabasi-Albert network with m = 4 that shows a much lower power utilization than all other networks. This is due to the fact that the probability that a node with a degree lower than four exists is very low. This means that, for a given agent breaking free from the solidarity trap, at least four communication errors must happen, instead of two in the ring topology or only one in Watt-Strogatz (for the nodes with a degree of one). therefore, the power is underutilized for the Barabasi-Albert network.

The Gini index analysis indicates, that when the system size grows, few agents receive most of the power, which from a global perspective makes the system very stable. We also see how the outcome is dominated by the structure of the communication network when large systems are considered.

Fig 8 presents more evidence on how the communication system starts dominating the system dynamics when the system size N grows. For small systems, one can only see a small reaction with a lot of scattering when rising the communication error probability. Surprisingly we can see global maxima appearing for mid-size and large systems. This fact may indicate that the communication error probability has a similar effect on our systems as temperature on the susceptibility of physical systems [56]. When $p_{err} = 0$, the system can become trapped in a state of solidarity with 100% cooperation (minimal power consumption). With increasing the error probability, the system has a random aspect that allows for agents to defect. However, if the error probability becomes too high, the state information exchange becomes worthless and the system is dominated by the randomness.

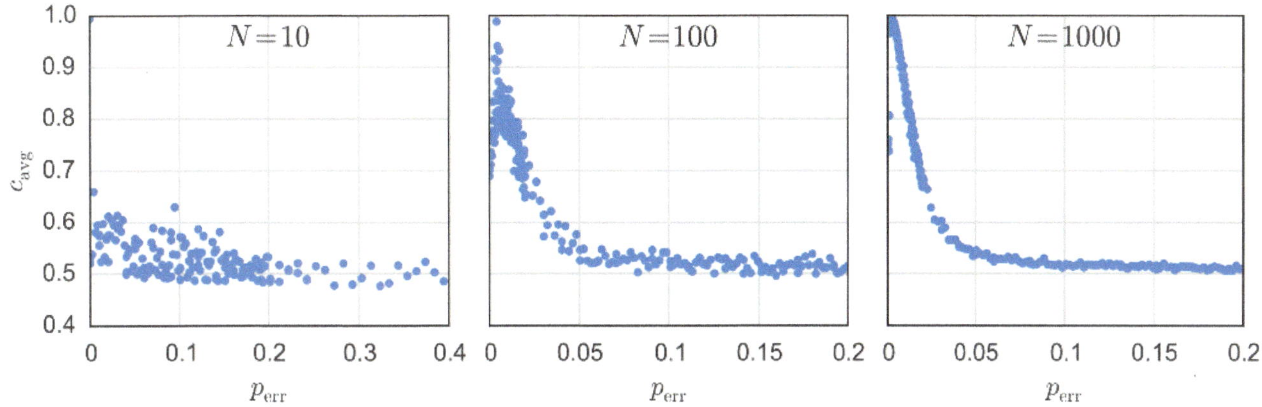

Fig 8. Influence of communication error probability p_{err} on systems with different sizes *N*.

The parameters are $\lambda_{min} = 0.005$, $R_V = 2\Omega$, $R_0 = R/N = 200\Omega$ and V = 1 V. The communication network is configured as a ring.

DISCUSSIONS

We believe that our proposed multilayer system can indeed emulate features of real-world systems with coupled physical, communication and decision layers. Nonetheless, our framework has not been developed to model any specific infra-structure. Our idea is to construct a toy-model where the components are rather simple and easy to understand, but where unpredictable behavior can emerge in certain circumstances, resembling real-world phenomena as modern power grids [5] or cities [9]. As previously mentioned, large-scale systems built upon those layers are getting more and more usual. In any case, we believe that it is also worth discussing the design of the components employed herein. Let us first deal with the rules the agents follow. One might compare the agents to humans or machines acting in behalf of humans. In either case, the possible variety of behaviors may be as large as infinite. The same can be said for the interactions that occur between the agents. In this work, the decision procedure and the communication network connections have been arbitrarily chosen to be understandable and justifiable. Although our simulation assumes the network topology and the decision rules (including the selfishness gene and the minimal power gain) as given, both of them could be evolved as part of the simulation. We could argue that our model allows for complete explanations in the sense that we need not to find explanations that are external to the system; everything can be constructed within the system domain. This, however, might mask the results by, for example, slowing down changes in behavior [26].

For the basic agent principle of maximizing power, it is important to remember that usually power consumption is just a by-product of making life more comfortable and less manual labour intensive by using more loads in the electricity power grid. Similarly to humans, the agents assumed here are most of the time reluctant to remove a resistor once it is installed. They only consider to do so when they did not had a large enough gain from adding a resistor (which means that the system might be overused) or when the social pressure is too much (by being non-cooperative in a cooperative neighbourhood).

To further justify the concept of cooperative solidarity, one has to understand the prisoners-dilemma-type of situations [16]. It is also worth noting that is has been shown that cooperation arises in the evolution of social systems [57, 58]. If the system is close to the optimal point, the agents see a very low gain so that they would have to change their strategy. If most of them reduce their number of resistors, they might receive a little less power (in the case of the system being on the left side of the optimum) or they receive a little more by getting closer to the optimum. However, if only a certain percentage of them reduces their number of resistors while others raise their numbers, the latter gain more power even if the system is very overused. If most of them add resistors, however everyone is worse off than before, which resembles the tragedy of the commons [13].

One of the core findings of this report is that, not only is it possible to create systems with complex behavior through a combination of a few simple parts [20], but indeed every layer influences the systems behavior in nontrivial ways. And in some cases, one layer can even dominate the global system behavior. A special note should be taken in the strong size-dependency of the model, since as far as real-world engineering systems are always subject to changes in the number of users after the initial deployment, leading to unforeseen situations (e.g. power grids [5], cities [9] or highways [28]).

Another interesting aspect can be found in the system behavior in response to communication errors. As was shown in Fig 8, a sharp peak exists for the number of cooperators in the system for a communication error probability of about 1%. From an engineering standpoint, one might prefer a system without errors, which (ideally) leads to a stable and a more predictable behavior. However, the existence of even a small amount of errors leads to a significant change in the behavior and sometimes it might even be desired (e.g. to unfreeze the system from solidarity trap).

Let us assume that the system should work on a state of very high cooperation. Our results indicate that an external attacker trying to disturb the system does not have to shut down the whole communication network to break the dominant cooperative state of the whole system. Rather, it would suffice to generate a small amount of randomly-generated erroneous messages as this will unfreeze the system, which might create a new system dynamic. For an attacker, this would then mean that he does not have to capture the whole communication network to disturb the desired behavior, due to the coupled nature of the system as a whole. Consequently, security precautions should be designed accordingly.

All in all, the present research shall open several options for future work. For example, the inclusion of multiple power sources would be used to simulate a more decentralized power grid topology. The power source could be added as an active agent in the system, having a role of similar to a central controller. It would be also possible to model additional layers like a market where the price for the demanded power (consumed energy) would be set.

METHODS

Physical layer

The physical layer used in this paper is depict in Fig 1. The value of the resistors R that are under the control of the agents $i \in \mathcal{A}$ should be scaled with the number of agents in the system so that

$$R = NR_0, \tag{8}$$

where R_0 is a constant value, arbitrarily chosen, independent from the system size.

If all agents have in total k appliances, the equivalent resistance of the system is $R_{eq} = \frac{R}{k}$, i.e. k resistors of R in parallel [12]. The system starts with the different agents having a random number of resistors so that the equivalent resistance is above the system-wide optimal point $R^*_{eq} = R_V$, computed in terms of power consumed by the agents.

Let us now describe the system from the point of view of a single agent $i \in \mathcal{A}$. For agent i, all the other individual agents can be combined at time-slot t into

$$R_{sys,i}[t] = \frac{R}{r_i[t]}, \tag{9}$$

where $r_i[t]$ stands for the number of resistors in the system that do not belong to agent i. The agent itself is then described by

$$R_i[t] = \frac{R}{a_i[t]}. \tag{10}$$

We can then derive the power $P_i[t]$ that agent i consumes at time-slot t by

$$P_i[t] = \frac{(V\sqrt{N} - IR_V)^2}{R_i[t]} = P_{typ}\frac{a_i[t]\mu N^2}{(a_i[t] + r_i[t] + N\mu)^2}, \tag{11}$$

where V is the voltage source, I is the electric current passing through the source resistor R_V, $P_{typ} = \frac{V^2}{R_V}$ and $\mu = \frac{R}{R_V}$.

Note that we scale the voltage with the square-root of the system size so that the power available for the agents stays constant. We could then write P_i as

$$P_i[t] = P_{typ}\frac{a_i[t]\mu}{(a_{avg}[t] + \mu)^2}, \tag{12}$$

where $a_{avg}[t] = (a_i[t]+r_i[t])/N$.

Communication Layer

The communication layer allows for exchange of information between the agents, which is a necessary condition to coordinate their actions in the system. In this case, we need to describe what kind of information is sent by the agents and how they build links creating then their neighbourhood set.

Every agent $i \in \mathcal{A}$ sends to their neighbours (to be defined next) a message containing its own state in that time step t such that $S_i[t] \in \{-1,0,+1\}$. The transmitted message may be in error with a given error probability $p_{err} \in [0, 1]$, which is independent from anything else and uniformly distributed. If an error event happens, the receiving agent sees one of the two other possible states (instead of the transmitted one) with the same probability. The error probabilityp_{err} is the only parameter we control. It is worth mentioning that, although we assume p_{err} as given, it in fact is a result of the communication strategy used [54]. Nevertheless, we believe that this more realistic approach goes beyond the focus of this work.

The topology of the communication network defines the neighbourhood set of the agents. In this report we focused on three classes of graphs: ring, Watts-Strogatzs (WS) and Barabasi-Albert (BA) [52]. The ring network is defined in a way that agent i is connected with to the agents i − 1 and i+1 (refer to Fig 1). In this case, agent 1 is connected to agent N and vice-versa, so the graph topology resembles a ring

To define more complex neighbourhoods, we employ the Watts-Strogatzs (WS) and the Barabasi-Albert (BA) graphs for social networks. The WS graph is constructed as follows. The graph starts with a regular lattice where each node has exactly K neighbours. The links are then rewired with probability β resulting in a more random structure.

The BA graph is formed by adding the desired number of nodes step-by-step, starting with a small initial set. Each new node is then preferably connected to nodes with an already high degree (k), with probability p_i such that

$$p_i = \frac{k_i}{\sum_j k_j}, \quad (13)$$

generating then a network whose degree distribution is given by a power law.

Agent behavior

We explain here the behavior of the agents and its relation to the physical and communication layers previously defined. Let us start in the scenario where none of the neighbours of agent i, defined by the neighbourhood set $\mathcal{N}_i$, is cooperative. This is the default state in the beginning. Agent i will then behave randomly according to its selfishness gene s_i. The selfishness gene is a random number with uniform distribution assigned to every agent $i \in \mathcal{A}$ before start the system simulation itself.

The decision procedure is the following: a random number ξ is drawn. If $\xi > s_i$, agent i will switch to the cooperative mode and remove one resistor. Otherwise, it will switch to one of the non-cooperative modes. This means that, when s_i is big, agent i is more selfish. Conversely, agent i is more cooperative when s_i is small

For the non-cooperative modes, the agent will again draw a random number do decide if it will add a resistor if $\xi < s_i$ or do nothing otherwise. The decision process is consistent, but depends on random variables. therefore the higher the selfishness, the higher the probability that an agent starts accumulating resistors.

The agent behavior also depends on the minimal gain λ_{min} that the agents needs to stick to their strategy. We assume that λ_{min} is fixed and pre-defined before the simulation. The gain $\lambda_i[t]$ that agent i has at time-slot t is computed as

$$\lambda_i[t] = \frac{P_i[t] - P_i[t-1]}{P_i[t-1]} = \frac{\Delta P_i[t]}{P_i[t-1]}. \quad (14)$$

Let us now assume that the functions of t are continuous so that we can use the total derivative rule as follows:

$$dP_i = P_{typ}\left[\frac{\mu}{(a_{avg}[t]+\mu)^2}da_i - \frac{2}{N}\frac{a_i\mu}{(a_{avg}[t]+\mu)^3}da_i - \frac{2}{N}\frac{a_i\mu}{(a_{avg}[t]+\mu)^3}dr_i\right]. \quad (15)$$

Now returning to the discrete domain, we consider $\Delta P_i[t] \approx dP_i$, $\Delta a_i[t] \approx da_i$, $\Delta r_i[t] \approx dr_i$ and $P_i[t] \approx P_i[t-1]$. Then, the gain $\lambda_i[t]$ can be evaluated as

$$\lambda_i[t] \approx \frac{dP_i}{P_i[t]} \approx \frac{\Delta a_i[t]}{a_i[t]} - \frac{2}{N}\frac{1}{a_{avg}[t]+\mu}(\Delta r_i[t] + \Delta a_i[t]) = \frac{\Delta a_i[t]}{a_i[t]} - \frac{2}{a_{avg}[t]+\mu}\Delta a_{avg}[t]. \quad (16)$$

The advantage of proceeding in this way is that one can see that the that the gain not only depends on the amount of resistors agent i possesses and the behavior of the system, but also on the system size N. The higher the number of resistors agent i has, the smaller the first term is since $\Delta a_i[t]$ can only be −1, 0, or +1. For a very large system ($N \to \infty$) and agent i non-cooperative (i.e. $\Delta a_i[t] = 1$), agent i reaches the minimum gain when it reaches

$$a_{max} = \frac{1}{\lambda_{min}}. \quad (17)$$

For example, the minimal gain $\lambda_{min} = 0.0005$ used for most of the simulation scenarios leads to $a_{max} = 2000$, which is far above the optimal point $a^*_{avg} = \mu = 100$.

The second term, which has a negative leading sign, provides feedback. We can then split the term in the feedback from individual actions $\Delta a_i[t]$ and external actions $\Delta r_i[t]$. The negative leading sign means that this term will reduce the gain in case of rising amount of resistors ($\Delta a_i[t] = 1$) or will deliver a positive gain in case of cooperation $\Delta a_i[t] = -1$ or keep its state by doing nothing $\Delta a_i[t] = 0$. In any case, the effect of such feedback will diminish with rising system size N.

ACKNOWLEDGMENTS

We would like to acknowledge the computing facilities of CSC—IT Center for Science Ltd. (Finland) that was used to run the simulation scenarios.

AUTHOR CONTRIBUTIONS

Conceived and designed the experiments: FK PHJN. Performed the experiments: FK. Analyzed the data: FK. Contributed reagents/materials/analysis tools: FK PHJN. Wrote the paper: PHJN FK.

REFERENCES

1. Helbing D. Globally networked risks and how to respond. Nature. 2013;497(7447):51–59. doi: 10.1038/nature12047.
2. Nikolic I. Co-evolutionary method for modelling large scale socio-technical systems evolution. TU Delft, Delft University of Technology; 2009.
3. Dam V, et al. Agent-based modelling of socio-technical systems. vol. 9. Springer Science & Business Media; 2012.
4. Kremers EA. Modelling and simulation of electrical energy systems through a complex systems approach using agent-based models. KIT Scientific Publishing; 2013.
5. Nardelli PHJ, et al. Models for the modern power grid. The European Physical Journal Special Topics. 2014;223(12):2423–2437. doi: 10.1140/epjst/e2014-02219-6.
6. Bush SF. Smart Grid: Communication-enabled Intelligence for the Electric Power Grid. John wiley & sons; 2014.

7. Bale CS, Varga L, Foxon TJ. Energy and complexity: New ways forward. Applied Energy. 2015;138:150–159. doi: 10.1016/j.apenergy.2014.10.057.
8. Batty M. Cities and complexity: understanding cities with cellular automata, agent-based models, and fractals. The MIT press; 2007.
9. Batty M. The new science of cities. The MIT press; 2013.
10. Herrmann C, et al. Sustainability in Manufacturing and Factories of the Future. International Journal of Precision Engineering and Manufacturing-Green Technology. 2014;1(4):283–292. doi: 10.1007/s40684-014-0034-z.
11. Hossain E, et al. Evolution toward 5G multi-tier cellular wireless networks: An interference management perspective. IEEE Wireless Commun. 2014;21(3):118–127. doi: 10.1109/MWC.2014.6845056.
12. Dorf RC, Svoboda JA. Introduction to electric circuits. John Wiley & Sons; 2010.
13. Hardin G. The tragedy of the commons. Science. 1968 Dec;162(3859):1243–8. doi: 10.1126/science.162.3859.1243.
14. Szabó G, Fath G. Evolutionary games on graphs. Physics Reports. 2007;446(4):97–216. doi: 10.1016/j.physrep.2007.04.004
15. Archetti M, Scheuring I. Review: Game theory of public goods in one-shot social dilemmas without assortment. Journal of Theoretical Biology. 2012;299:9–20. doi: 10.1016/j.jtbi.2011.06.018. pmid:21723299
16. Gianetto DA, Heydari B. Network Modularity is essential for evolution of cooperation under uncertainty. Scientific Report. 2015;5. doi: 10.1038/srep09340
17. Mitchell M. Complexity: A Guided Tour. Oxford University Press; 2009.
18. Furtado BA, Sakowski PAM. Complexity: A review of the classics. Policy and Complex Systems. Fall 2014;1(2):3–18. doi: 10.18278/jpcs.1.2.1
19. Ott E. Chaos in dynamical systems. Cambridge university press; 2002.
20. Wolfram S. A New Kind of Science. Wolfram Media; 2002.
21. Wolfram S. Universality and complexity in cellular automata. Physica D: Nonlinear Phenomena. 1984;10(1):1–35. doi: 10.1016/0167-2789(84)90245-8.
22. Wang DQ, Gong QG, Shen XF. An Improved Personnel Evacuation Cellular Automata Model Based on the Ant Colony Optimization Algorithm. In: Applied Mechanics and Materials. vol. 513. Trans Tech Publ; 2014. p. 3287–3291.
23. Iarosz K, et al. The influence of connectivity on the firing rate in a neuronal network with electrical and chemical synapses. Physica A: Statistical Mechanics and its Applications. 2012;391(3):819–827. doi: 10.1016/j.physa.2011.09.014.
24. Vicsek T, Czirók A, Ben-Jacob E, Cohen I, Shochet O. Novel type of phase transition in a system of self-driven particles. Physical review letters. 1995;75(6):1226. doi: 10.1103/PhysRevLett.75.1226.
25. dos Santos Lima G, et al. Self-organized criticality in MHD driven plasma edge turbulence. Physics Letters A. 2012;376(5):753–757. doi: 10.1016/j.physleta.2011.12.026.
26. Hodgson GM. From pleasure machines to moral communities: An evolutionary economics without homo economicus. University of Chicago Press; 2012.
27. Hodgson GM. Economics and evolution: Bringing life back into economics. University of Michigan Press; 1997.
28. Helbing D. Traffic and related self-driven many-particle systems. Reviews of Modern Physics. 2001;73(4):1067. doi: 10.1103/RevModPhys.73.1067.
29. Abramson G, Semeshenko V, Iglesias JR. Cooperation and Defection at the Crossroads. PLoS ONE. 2013 04;8(4):e61876. Available from:http://dx.doi.org/10.1371%2Fjournal.pone.0061876. doi: 10.1371/journal.pone.0061876.
30. Arthur WB. Complexity and the economy. Oxford University Press; 2014.
31. Stott B, Jardim J, Alsac O. DC Power Flow Revisited. IEEE Transactions on Power Systems. 2009;24(3):1290–1300. doi: 10.1109/TPWRS.2009.2021235.
32. Hahn W. Load studies on the DC calculating table. General Electric Review. 1931;34:444.
33. Casazza J, Ku W. The co-ordinated use of AC and DC network analyzers. In: Proceedings of American Power Conference. vol. 16; 1954.
34. Purchala K, et al. Usefulness of DC Power Flow for Active Power Flow Analysis
35. Filatrella G, Nielsen AH, Pedersen NF. Analysis of a power grid using a Kuramoto-like model. The European Physical Journal B. 2008;61(4):485–491. Available from:http://www.springerlink.com/index/10.1140/epjb/e2008-00098-8. doi: 10.1140/epjb/e2008-00098-8.
36. Rohden M, Sorge A, Witthaut D, Timme M. Impact of network topology on synchrony of oscillatory power grids. Chaos: An Interdisciplinary Journal of Nonlinear Science. 2014;24(1):013123. Available from:http://arxiv.org/abs/1305.1634$\delimiter"026E30F$nhttp://scitation.aip.org/content/aip/journal/chaos/24/1/10.1063/1.4865895. doi: 10.1063/1.4865895.
37. Florian D, Bullo F. Synchronization and Transient Stability in Power Networks and Non-Uniform Kuramoto Oscillators. 2010;p. 930–937.
38. Nishikawa T, Motter AE. Comparative analysis of existing models for power-grid synchronization. New Journal of Physics. 2015 Jan;17(1):015012. Available from:http://stacks.iop.org/1367-2630/17/i=1/a=015012?key=crossref.64c23e9d1bbe3eaad717d9306453ddf9. doi: 10.1088/1367-2630/17/1/015012.
39. Menck PJ, et al. How dead ends undermine power grid stability. Nature Communications. 2014 Jun;5. Available from:http://www.nature.com/doifinder/10.1038/ncomms4969. doi: 10.1038/ncomms4969.
40. Bak P, Tang C, Wiesenfeld K. Self-organized criticality: An explanation of the 1/f noise. Physical review letters. 1987;59(4):381. doi: 10.1103/PhysRevLett.59.381.

41. Carreras BA, et al. Evidence for Self-Organized Criticality in a Time Series of Electric Power System Blackouts. IEEE Transactions on Circuits and Systems I: Regular Papers. 2004;51(9):1733–1740. Available from:http://ieeexplore.ieee.org/lpdocs/epic03/wrapper.htm?arnumber=1333223. doi: 10.1109/TCSI.2004.834513.

42. Holmgren AJ. Using graph models to analyze the vulnerability of electric power networks. Risk analysis: an official publication of the Society for Risk Analysis. 2006;26(4):955–969. Available from: http://www.ncbi.nlm.nih.gov/pubmed/16948688. doi: 10.1111/j.1539-6924.2006.00791.x.

43. Huang Z, et al. Modeling cascading failures in smart power grid using interdependent complex networks and percolation theory. 2013 IEEE 8th Conference on Industrial Electronics and Applications (ICIEA). 2013;p. 1023–1028. Available from:http://ieeexplore.ieee.org/lpdocs/epic03/wrapper.htm?arnumber=6566517.

44. Krause SM, Boerries S, Bornholdt S. Econophysics of adaptive power markets: When a market does not dampen fluctuations but amplifies them. 2013;012815:5. Available from: http://arxiv.org/abs/1303.2110.

45. Kremers E, et al. Emergent synchronisation properties of a refrigerator demand side management system. Applied Energy. 2013;101:709–717. doi: 10.1016/j.apenergy.2012.07.021.

46. Kremers E, Gonzalez De Durana J, Barambones O. Multi-agent modeling for the simulation of a simple smart microgrid. Energy Conversion and Management. 2013;75:643–650. doi: 10.1016/j.enconman.2013.07.050.

47. Pipattanasomporn M, et al. Multi-Agent Systems in a Distributed Smart Grid: Design and Implementation. Control. 2009;p. 1–8. doi: 10.1109/psce.2009.4840087

48. Hernandez L, et al. A multi-agent system architecture for smart grid management and forecasting of energy demand in virtual power plants. IEEE Communications Magazine. 2013;51(1):106–113. doi: 10.1109/MCOM.2013.6400446.

49. Ramchurn SD, et al. Agent-Based Control for Decentralised Demand Side Management in the Smart Grid. 2011;p. 5–12.

50. Divenyi D, Dan AM. Agent-based modeling of distributed generation in power system control. IEEE Transactions on Sustainable Energy. 2013;4(4):886–893. doi: 10.1109/TSTE.2013.2253811.

51. Schuster P. Models: From exploration to prediction: Bad reputation of modeling in some disciplines results from nebulous goals. Complexity. 2015 Sep;21(1):6–9. Available from: http://arxiv.org/abs/1103.4838 http://dx.doi.org/10.1002/cplx.20234http://doi.wiley.com/10.1002/cplx.21729. doi: 10.1002/cplx.21729.

52. Newman M, Barabási AL, Watts DJ. The Structure and Dynamics of Networks. Princeton University Press; 2006.

53. Python implementation available at: https://github.com/tharwan/CoopCPS

54. Marsic I. Computer networks: Performance and quality of service. Rutgers University; 2010.

55. Gini C. Variabilità e mutabilità. Memorie di metodologica statistica. 1912;p. 156.

56. Wolf WP. The Ising Model and Real Magnetic Materials. Brazilian Journal of Physics. 2000;30(4):794–810. doi: 10.1590/S0103-97332000000400030.

57. Miranda L, et al. Complex Transition to Cooperative Behavior in a Structured Population Model. PLoS ONE. 2012 06;7(6):e39188. Available from:http://dx.doi.org/10.1371%2Fjournal.pone.0039188. doi: 10.1371/journal.pone.0039188. pmid:22761736

58. Traag VA, Van Dooren P, De Leenheer P. Dynamical Models Explaining Social Balance and Evolution of Cooperation. PLoS ONE. 2013 04;8(4):e60063. Available from:http://dx.doi.org/10.1371%2Fjournal.pone.0060063. doi: 10.1371/journal.pone.0060063.

CHAPTER 16

DSTAT: A VERSATILE, OPEN-SOURCE POTENTIOSTAT FOR ELECTROANALYSIS AND INTEGRATION

Dryden MD[1], Wheeler AR[2].

[1]Department of Chemistry, University of Toronto, Toronto, ON, Canada.

[2]Department of Chemistry, University of Toronto, Toronto, ON, Canada; Institute for Biomaterials and Biomedical Engineering, University of Toronto, Toronto, ON, Canada; Donnelly Centre for Cellular and Biomolecular Research, 160 College Street, Toronto, ON, Canada.

ABSTRACT

Most electroanalytical techniques require the precise control of the potentials in an electrochemical cell using a potentiostat. Commercial potentiostats function as "black boxes," giving limited information about their circuitry and behaviour which can make development of new measurement techniques and integration with other instruments challenging. Recently, a number of lab-built potentiostats have emerged with various design goals including low manufacturing cost and field-portability, but notably lacking is an accessible potentiostat designed for general lab use, focusing on measurement quality combined with ease of use and versatility. To fill this gap, we introduce DStat (http://microfluidics.utoronto.ca/dstat), an open-source, general-purpose potentiostat for use alone or integrated with other instruments. DStat offers picoampere current measurement capabilities, a compact USB-powered design, and user-friendly cross-platform software. DStat is easy and inexpensive to build, may be modified freely, and achieves good performance at low current levels not accessible to other lab-built instruments. In head-to-head tests, DStat's voltammetric measurements are much more sensitive than those of "CheapStat" (a popular open-source potentiostat described previously), and are comparable to those of a compact commercial "black box" potentiostat. Likewise, in head-to-head tests, DStat's potentiometric precision is similar to that of a commercial pH meter. Most importantly, the versatility of DStat was demonstrated through integration with the open-source DropBot digital microfluidics platform. In sum, we propose that DStat is a valuable contribution to the "open source" movement in analytical science, which is allowing users to adapt their tools to their experiments rather than alter their experiments to be compatible with their tools.

INTRODUCTION

Electrochemistry is an important topic of modern chemical research, spanning analytical, inorganic, organic, physical chemistry, and beyond. An abundance of electroanalytical techniques have been developed and most require the precise control of potentials in an electrochemical cell. Naïvely, one might suggest controlling the applied potential with a simple circuit such as a voltage divider in series with a battery. This strategy fails, however, as current passing through the cell causes a potential drop across the source's impedance (and there are practical limits to how small the source's output impedance

Citation: Dryden MDM, Wheeler AR (2015) DStat: A Versatile, Open-Source Potentiostat for Electroanalysis and Integration. PLoS ONE 10(10): e0140349. doi:10.1371/journal.pone.0140349

can be made), resulting in considerable error even for low current flow. Further, in many electrochemical experiments, the cell current varies significantly with time, causing drastic changes in the apparent potential. These challenges led to the development of the potentiostat in the 1940s. [1]

Modern potentiostats provide a reliable means of controlling the potential of a working electrode in an electrochemical cell, relying on feedback to accurately maintain the cell potential regardless of changes in cell impedance during the measurement. Potentiostats can be purchased as rack-mount units for corrosion and energy research, bench-top instruments for analytical use, and even pocket-sized devices for blood glucose measurement. Unfortunately, most commercial potentiostats operate as "black boxes" with limited information available to users about their circuitry and behaviour. As noted by Bard and Faulkner, [2] this imposes significant constraints on researchers who are developing new measurement techniques and applications.

The "black box" potentiostat conundrum has recently spawned a cottage industry of home-made potentiostats that can be modified as needed for varying applications. These circuits largely fall into four classes: (1) tiny instruments intended for implantation or wearable use, [3–7] (2) inexpensive instruments designed to feature extreme cost savings or field-portability [8–12] (at the expense of performance), (3) multiplexed instruments designed for specialized applications involving arrays of electrodes, [13–15] or (4) bench-scale instruments constructed around "virtual instrument" frameworks [15–17] (which are useful for prototyping, but are expensive and lack robustness and portability). We applaud the "open-source" philosophy that has driven the development of lab-built potentiostats, which is part of a broader movement in analytical science that is allowing users to adapt their tools to suit their experiments rather than altering their experiments to suit their tools. [18] But none of the previously reported circuits [3–17] are a perfect match for general experimental use—that is, there are no lab-built potentiostats that match all of the characteristics that are associated with commercial potentiostats (high precision, low noise, compatibility with low current measurements, robustness, ease of use, and portability). Further, while considerable detail has been reported for many of the homemade potentiostats described previously [4, 10, 12], only two of them are truly open source [8, 9]—with explicit rights granted and encouragement given to any user who wishes to construct and modify the original design. There is thus great need for an open-source potentiostat intended for use in research, featuring picoampere-level measurement capabilities, compact and robust form-factor, and intuitive cross-platform software.

In recognition of the need described above, we introduce DStat, an open-source potentiostat designed for high-performance laboratory experimentation. All salient details about DStat, including schematics, parts lists, control software, and assembly instructions, are available athttp://microfluidics.utoronto.ca/dstat. The open nature of DStat makes it attractive when compared to commercial instruments; all aspects of DStat's operation are disclosed and fully modifiable, facilitating adaptation to experiments for which it was not initially designed as well as integration with other instruments. Here we describe the design of DStat, and compare its performance with that of (a) a "black box" commercial potentiostat (EmStat 1, PalmSens BV, Utrecht, NL), (b) a popular open-source potentiostat reported previously, the "CheapStat," [8] and (c) a commercial benchtop pH meter (Accumet AR50 benchtop meter, Thermo Fisher Scientific, Waltham MA, USA).

MATERIALS AND METHODS

Design

The capabilities of potentiostats vary greatly in terms of current capacity, potential range, resolution, etc., depending on their intended use. The hardware design goals for DStat were to allow amperometric and voltammetric measurements for conditions commonly found in research laboratories—modest currents at small electrodes, voltages typical of aqueous electrochemistry, and an emphasis on accurate low current measurements for sensing applications. Further, DStat was designed to be controlled and powered with a USB connection (providing both power and data), allowing portability for field use when combined with a battery-powered computer. Finally, considerations were made for ease of assembly and reduced cost (where possible) without compromising performance. DStat's major components are shown inFig 1 and an examination of each component follows. Additional details are found in S1 Supporting Information.

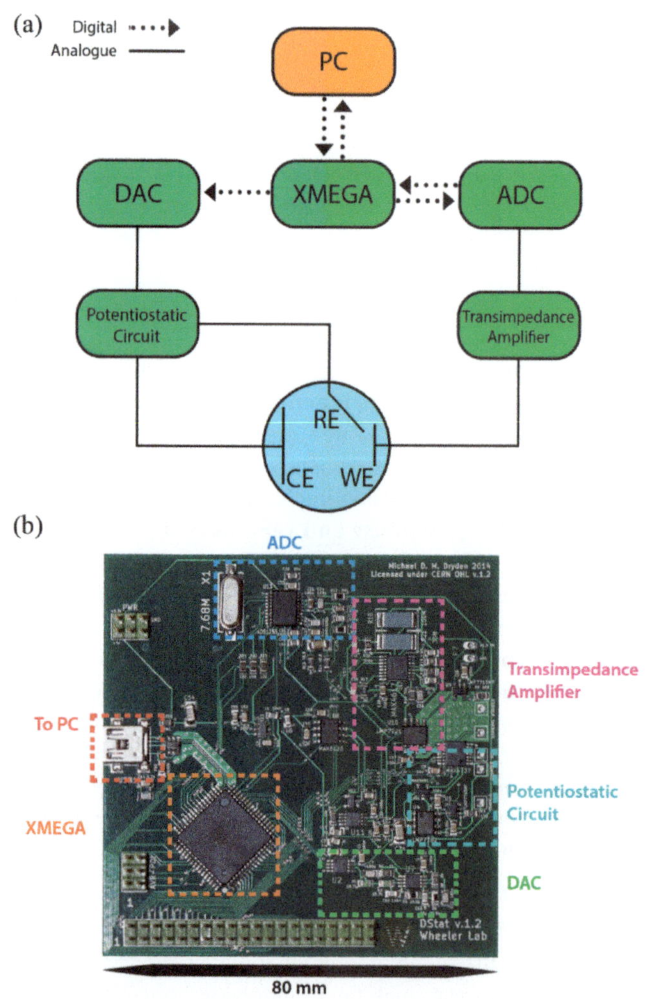

Fig 1. The DStat. (a) Schematic overview of key DStat components, including the computer (PC), the microcontroller (XMEGA), the analogue-to-digital converter (ADC), the digital-to-analogue converter (DAC), the potentiostatic circuit, and transimpedance amplifier. The DStat is interfaced to a three-electrode electrochemical cell, including

a working electrode (WE), a counter electrode (CE), and a reference electrode (RE). Modules integral to DStat are coloured in green. Solid lines represent analogue connections. Dotted arrows represent digital connections. (b) Top-view picture of the DStat circuit board with labels corresponding to schematic components.

http://dx.doi.org/10.1371/journal.pone.0140349.g001

Potential control circuit.

The most important function of a potentiostat is to control the interfacial potential at a working electrode (WE) in an electrochemical cell to allow for current to be measured at constant potential. This is typically achieved using a three-electrode cell in which a voltage is applied to a counter electrode (CE), which provides enough current to compensate for redox reactions occurring at the WE. This voltage is set by feedback from a reference electrode (RE). The use of a three-electrode cell provides two main advantages: (1) the RE is not susceptible to polarization error (where current flow results in a change in potential) and (2) the RE can be small enough to be placed very near the working electrode surface, minimizing potential error caused by solution resistance. As shown in Fig 2(a), a three-electrode cell can be modelled as two resistances in series, between CE and RE (R_c) and between RE and WE (R_u). A simple potentiostatic circuit relying on one op-amp (U1) is shown in Fig 2(b). As indicated, the RE is positioned in a negative feedback loop, and the op-amp output is applied to CE. This allows the op-amp to supply the current required to compensate for the IR drop across R_c (the compensated cell resistance). A working potential between RE-WE can be programmed by biasing the circuit with a control signal (described below) through the summing resistors (R). Thus, the only unwanted resistance in the circuit is R_u (the uncompensated cell resistance), which is kept as low as possible by positioning the RE close to the WE.

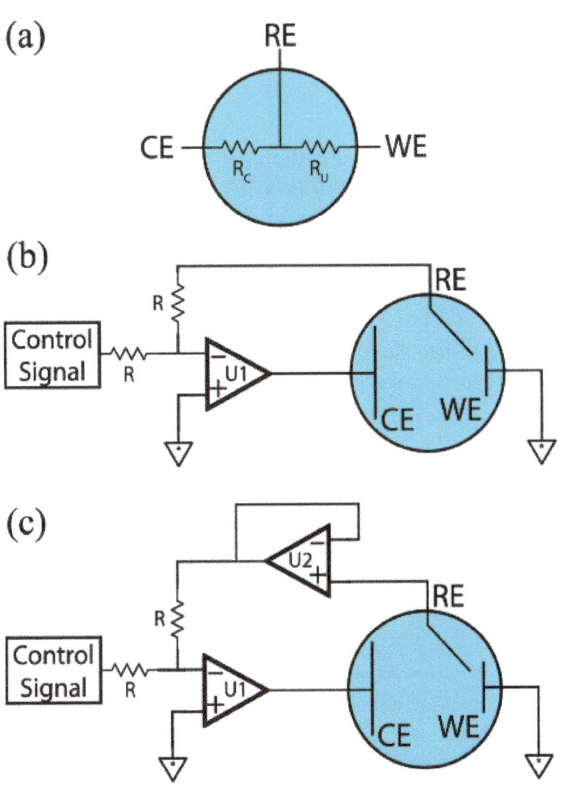

Fig 2. Electrochemical cells and potentiostatic circuits.

RE: Reference Electrode, CE: Counter Electrode, WE: Working Electrode, R: Summing resistors, U1: Control amplifier, U2: Reference buffer amplifier, R_c: Compensated cell resistance, R_u: Uncompensated cell resistance. (a) Simplified three electrode cell model. (b) Basic potentiostatic circuit. (c) DStat potentiostatic circuit.

The circuit in Fig 2(b) is functional, but most modern potentiostats, including DStat, rely on a modified circuit, depicted in Fig 2(c). The main difference between Fig 2(b) and 2(c) is the addition of a second op-amp (U2), which serves as a unity gain buffer to limit any current that might otherwise flow through RE. This is particularly important given that the summing resistors typically have low resistance to minimize thermal noise (e.g., in DStat, R = 15 kΩ), meaning that significant current would pass through the reference electrode if not for U2. When potential control is not required U2 is also useful in (a) measuring a cell's open circuit potential, and (b) buffering electrodes for potentiometric measurements, by bypassing U1 and measuring the output directly. The selection of op-amps U1 and U2 is critically important to the performance of the potentiostatic circuit and is detailed in S1 Supporting Information.

CONTROL SIGNAL.

Most potentiostats are designed such that the working electrode potential can be modulated as a function of time in a pattern dependent on the type of experiment, e.g., a linear change for linear sweep voltammetry. (Note that some lab-built potentiostats [7, 13] do not include this capacity, and thus require external control signals.) This control signal, which is applied to the negative feedback loop of the circuit, was historically produced using analogue circuits, a practice that is still in place in some lab-built potentiostats described in the recent literature. [9] But most modern potentiostats use a digital to analogue converter (DAC) to provide arbitrary control signals without needing electronic reconfiguration to change experiments.

A DAC can output only quantized voltage steps and therefore cannot represent every possible voltage within its output range. The difference between the intended output and the nearest DAC step is known as quantization error and varies with the intended output, reaching a maximum halfway between steps. The output range of a DAC is divided into 2^n steps where $n$is its resolution in bits. Quantization error was an important consideration in the design for DStat—for example, it would have been straightforward to use the 12-bit DAC that is included (by default) in the microcontroller (see Fig 1) used to control DStat. This practice was not adopted, however, as for the 0–3 V range targeted for DStat, a 12-bit DAC step in this configuration would be approximately 0.73 mV, resulting in a maximum quantization error of 0.37 mV. This magnitude of error can be problematic in applications that have small waveform amplitudes (e.g., see the square wave voltammetry data in the following sections). For this reason, we elected to use an external DAC with a resolution of 16 bits in DStat, resulting in a step size of 46 μV, an order of magnitude improvement over the 12-bit resolution of the microcontroller's DAC. The quantization error for the 16-bit DAC-driven control signal in DStat is much lower than that of the DAC-controlled lab-built potentiostat circuits described previously (that rely on 4- [11],

8- [4], 10- [10], and 12-bit [3, 5, 8] DACs, respectively). The DAC's sample rate and reconstruction filter are also important for producing accurate waveforms and are discussed in detail in S1 Supporting Information.

CURRENT MEASUREMENT.

The potentiostatic circuit and control signal are sufficient to maintain a desired working electrode potential, but for almost all experiments involving a potentiostat, measurement of the current passing through the working electrode is required. Because the majority of analogue to digital converters (ADC) cannot measure a current directly, the current must first be converted to voltage to obtain a digital signal suitable for recording by a computer. The simplest technique to accomplish this (used in some of the home-made potentiostats described in the literature [14, 17]) is the current shunt, shown in Fig 3(a), where the voltage drop is measured across a measurement resistor R_M placed in series between the counter electrode and the control amplifier output. In practice, because ADCs cannot measure an infinitely large range of voltages, it is necessary to switch between different R_Ms to cover the several orders of magnitude of currents of interest in electrochemical experiments.

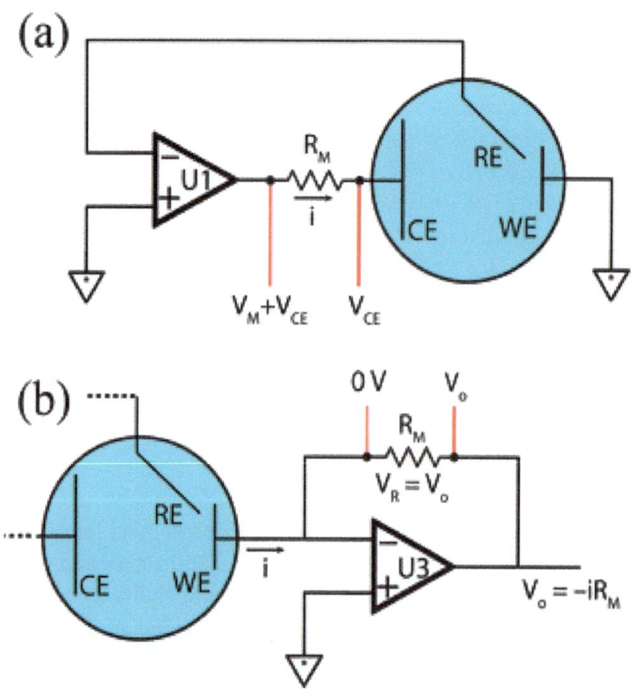

Fig 3. Cell current conversion to voltage for ADC.

(a) Current measurement by shunt resistor. The measurement resistor R_M causes a voltage drop proportional to the cell current i by Ohm's Law. The voltage drop is measured across the resistor but the counter electrode voltage V_{CE} (present on both sides of the resistor) complicates measurement. (b) Current measurement using a transimpedance amplifier. The measurement resistor R_M is placed in a negative feedback loop of an op amp (U3) whose inverting input is connected to the working electrode. U3's non-inverting input is tied to ground, producing a virtual ground at the inverting input. When current i flows through the working electrode, it induces a voltage drop V_R across R_M, which is balanced by U3 output V_O to maintain the virtual ground at its inverting input.

The current shunt approach has a number of disadvantages that make it undesirable for use in DStat: the output voltage is not referenced to ground (requiring the capability to make a differential measurement using an ADC that is tolerant of the counter-electrode voltage V_{CE} that is applied to both inputs); the measurement resistor forms part of the negative feedback loop, thus limiting the compliance voltage (i.e., the maximum voltage that op-amp U1 can produce to set the working electrode potential); and the measurement circuit must be designed to draw very little current to avoid influencing the measurement. To circumvent these limitations, DStat employs a transimpedance amplifier in series with the working electrode (Fig 3(b)). This type of circuit is commonly used for low current measurements, as the output voltage is provided by an op-amp and thus does not require high input impedance in the voltage measurement circuit. The conversion mechanism is similar to that of the current shunt, but R_M is in the negative feedback loop of a third op-amp (U3), to which the WE is connected via the inverting input. In this configuration, the measurement voltage is referenced to ground, allowing straightforward (non-differential) ADC measurement which does not affect the compliance of the potentiostatic amplifier (U1); and, if the transimpedance amplifier is set to have a maximum output that is the same as the maximum input of the ADC, no additional circuitry is required for protection.

Once the working electrode current has been converted to a voltage, it is passed to an ADC for measurement. Similar to DACs (described above), ADCs generate quantized measurements at discrete time intervals. The ADC's voltage-resolution determines the size of the voltage increments between successive digital values. The ADC's sample rate limits the highest frequency signal which may be measured; aliasing will occur if the analogue signal is not band-limited to below the Nyquist frequency. Resolution and sample rate also control the volume of data produced, an important consideration as data must be collected from the ADC, transmitted to a computer, and stored.

To aid in selection of an ADC for the DStat, the current measurement circuit was simulated (as described in the Experimental section) and the input-referred current noises calculated for each of 7 R_Ms from 100 Ω–100 MΩ. It was found that for any ADC resolution up to 16-bits (the maximum resolution reported for any lab-built potentiostat with integrated ADC reported previously [3–6, 8–11, 16, 17]) and all values of R_M, the size of an ADC step is the limiting factor in overall resolution, rather than analogue noise. Therefore, to utilize the current to voltage conversion circuitry most efficiently, a 24-bit ADC (the highest commonly available resolution) was chosen for DStat. The particular ADC that was selected is of the sigma-delta type, which has several advantages for DStat: sampling occurs at a much higher frequency than the output rate so the requirements for the anti-aliasing filter are relaxed, and a digital filter is a part of the conversion process which can be adjusted to give either higher data rates or reduced noise measurements, depending on the needs of the experiment being performed. The digital filter can also be used to reduce environmental noise pickup (especially 50/60 Hz mains noise) by matching the output sample rate to the noise frequency as the filter has zeros in its frequency response at multiples of the output sample rate.

MICROCONTROLLER

The analogue components of a potentiostat may place absolute limits on performance, but to make full use of the instrument's capabilities, it must be possible to update the DAC at the necessary rate, acquire ADC data as it is collected, and send it to a computer for recording. The requirements of these tasks vary with the type of experiment being performed, but it is often necessary to run all three tasks nearly simultaneously; e.g. for a cyclic voltammetry measurement, the voltage must be swept continuously by the DAC, ADC measurements must be collected as they are produced, and data must be sent to a computer for storage and processing as it is impractical to store the data from many cycles on the instrument. One method for performing these functions is to use a "virtual instrument" in which a computer commands and receives data from a so-called "data acquisition" device containing integrated DACs, ADSs, and switches (e.g., the CompactDAQ system—National Instruments, Austin, TX). These kinds of devices are useful for prototyping and rapid instrument-assembly, and have been used in some lab-built systems described in the literature. [15–17] But systems relying on these kinds of devices are limited in that the electronics must be connected externally (limiting the robustness and portability of the assembled system), computer requirements are more stringent because of proprietary software and the necessity for direct control over peripherals, and flexibility is lost in (a) the selection of components tailored to the intended use of the instrument, and (b) the difficulty of separating the computer software from the instrument hardware (which can hinder integration with other instruments). Another option for controlling the potentiostat hardware is an integrated microcontroller. [19] A microcontroller is essentially a low-power computer processor (CPU) coupled with memory and other peripherals such as data converters and communications modules, intended for embedded use—performing specific tasks as part of a larger device, rather than being suited for general use. To accomplish these tasks, DStat makes use of an ATxmega256A3U microcontroller (Atmel Corporation, San Jose CA, USA), chosen to balance performance with cost.

In DStat, the microcontroller manages the digital components of the instrument—the DAC, ADC, and switches for connecting the electrochemical cell and setting the R_M. Additionally, the microcontroller features integrated USB support, obviating the need for a separate module to communicate with a computer. Because DStat is not intended to operate without a computer connection, any data manipulation such as conversion of ADC and DAC units to amperes and volts or digital processing are done on the much more powerful computer. Details of the software implementation of electrochemical experiments and strategies to limit processor loading are discussed in S1 Supporting Information.

Some previously reported lab-built potentiostats also made use of microcontrollers. [3–6, 8–10] Notably, the Cheapstat [8] uses a different model of Atmel microcontroller; DStat's model has more memory (and allows for more complex firmware), and in addition allows for convenient, internal USB connection (not requiring an external chip).

REAGENTS AND MATERIALS

Analytical purity reagents were purchased from Sigma-Aldrich Canada Co. (Oakville, CA). Fresh solutions were prepared as needed using 5.6 μS/m deionized water. Measurements of potassium hexacyanoferrate (III) were performed on DRP-223AT disposable screen printed electrode sets with gold working and counter electrodes and a silver pseudoreference electrode purchased from DropSens (Llanera, Spain). 4-aminophenol solutions were measured using microfabricated electrode devices on silicon substrates. These devices feature an array of 20 gold nanostructured microelectrode working electrodes formed as described previously [20] and two rectangular gold electrodes that serve as counter and pseudoreference electrodes for the array of working electrodes. The working electrodes were measured separately, rather than as an ensemble, to highlight instrument performance at low current levels.

Electrochemical Control Systems

DStat was built as described per the parts lists and assembly instructions in S1 File, operated by running the custom software on a laptop via USB connector. The most recent version can be retrieved from http://microfluidics.utoronto.ca/dstat. A CheapStat was built and operated as described previously [8], and an EmStat 1 and an Accumet AR50 were used as received from PalmSens BV (Utrecht, NL) and Thermo Fisher Scientific (Waltham, MA, USA), respectively.

TINA-TI simulations

TINA-TI version 9 (Texas Instruments and DesignSoft Inc.) was used to simulate DStat's current measurement circuit. The DC absolute current error was set to 50 fA and the DC absolute voltage error was set to 1 nV, while other analysis parameters were left at default levels. The software's noise analysis function was used to calculate the total noise between 16 mHz and 60 Hz (corresponding to the open circuit noise measurements described below), for each value of R_M.

Open Circuit Noise Measurements

To quantify the noise of the current measurement circuit, the working electrode input was left open and a 60 s current measurement was acquired for each R_M at a sample rate of 60 Hz (to reflect typical measurement conditions and reduce AC mains noise, as described above). The noise value was taken as the standard deviation of the data. The measurements were performed in a typical laboratory setting without special precautions to reduce environmental noise (e.g., enclosure in a Faraday cage).

Potassium hexacyanoferrate (III) measurements

A 10 mM solution of potassium hexacyanoferrate (III) in pH 7 McIlvaine buffer [21] was prepared and used for measurements on the screen printed electrodes. The electrode substrate was clamped horizontally and a drop of measurement solution (~ 100 μL) was pipetted onto the electrode cell. A new electrode cell was used for each potentiostat as repeated measurements were observed to alter electrode response. A fresh droplet of solution was used for each measurement after washing the electrode cell with deionized water three times, removing the previous droplet with a paper wipe.

Cyclic voltammograms were recorded from -250 to 520 mV at a scan rate of 100 mV/s. DStat's sample rate was set to 60 Hz and the gain fixed to 30 kV/A. The EmStat's sample rate was set to 1 mV/sample (100 Hz) and was allowed to switch range settings between 1 and 100 μA full scale. The CheapStat's gain was set to 27.5 kV/A and (because of its limited storage capacity) samples were only acquired every 6 mV. Five sequential scans were acquired by each potentiostat and the ultimate scans used for the comparison.

Square wave voltammograms (SWVs) were recorded from -150 to 500 mV with a step height of 2 mV, an amplitude of 25 mV, and a frequency of 70 Hz. DStat's sample rate was set to 500 Hz and neither the EmStat nor the Cheapstat have provisions for controlling sampling time during SWV experiments. All three potentiostats' gain settings were the same as for the cyclic voltammetry experiments (above). Only a single scan was acquired for each electrode cell as repeated SWV of the measurement solution was observed to affect the electrode response.

4-aminophenol measurements

Four solutions of 4-aminophenol (100, 50, 25, and 10 μM) were prepared in 50 mM pH 9 Tris-HCl buffer for measurement with the microfabricated electrode devices. The devices were clamped horizontally and 30 μL of a measurement solution was pipetted to cover the electrode surfaces. Four working electrodes were used for each potentiostat with a single droplet of measurement solution. The working electrodes were measured in sequence before replacement of the droplet, with rinsing as described for the potassium hexacyanoferrate(III) measurements.

Differential pulse voltammograms were acquired from -300 to 250 mV with a step size of 5 mV, a pulse height of 50 mV, a pulse period of 100 ms, and a pulse width of 50 ms. DStat performs differential pulse voltammetry similarly to SWV and the sample rate was set to 500 Hz as above, with a gain setting of 300 kV/A. The EmStat was allowed to switch gains between 1 nA and 10 μA full scale. The CheapStat was not able to produce a recognizable peak at any available setting and was thus excluded from the experiment. Data was normalized by subtracting the current of each measurement at -150 mV from each sample to correct for changes in background current between measurements.

RESULTS AND DISCUSSION

Noise measurements

One of the most important performance specifications of a potentiostat, particularly for one that is intended for use in analytical measurements, is the ability to precisely measure small currents. With the advent of nano- and micro-scale electrodes, this is particularly important as the current response of a single electrode may be in the pA—nA range. To establish a performance level for the current measurement system, DStat's open-circuit noise level (without a connected electrochemical cell) was measured. The measured standard deviations (blue diamonds) are plotted in Fig 4 as the equivalent current at the working electrode input (representing the analogue noise in the system) as a function of gain (set by the values of R_M). For comparison, the currents associated with a single voltage step in a 12-, 16-, and 24-bit ADC are also plotted as dashed red lines. As shown, higher resolution ADCs have smaller steps (and thus can measure lower currents), and the size of each step decreases with increasing gain (as it takes a smaller current at the working electrode to produce a given output voltage at the transimpedance amplifier). Thus, for a specified gain and ADC resolution, the smallest current that can be measured is limited by either the size of the ADC's steps or the analogue noise of the measurement circuit. Lower resolution ADCs, such as the 16- and 12-bit circuits represented in the figure, limit the precision of the current measurement at all gain settings and thus cannot achieve the resolution of which the analogue circuitry is capable. That is, the dashed lines for the 12- and 16-bit ADCs are far above the level of the analogue noise for all levels of gain. The utility of the DStat's 24-bit ADC is clearly demonstrated in the figure as this circuit enables sufficient resolution at all gain settings to avoid truncating data above the analogue noise of the measurement circuit—that is, the dashed line for the 24-bit ADC is below the level of the analogue noise at all values of R_M.

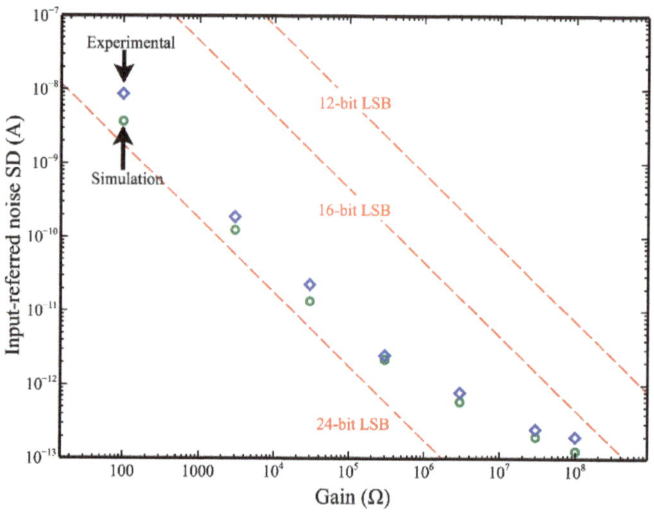

Fig 4. Open circuit DStat input-referred measurement noise standard deviations (SD) as a function of gain (set by the different DStat R_Ms) at a sample rate of 60 Hz measured over 60 s.

Blue diamonds are experimental measurements and green circles are TINA-TI simulation results. The equivalent input currents of a least significant bit (LSB) for three different ADC resolutions are shown as dashed red lines.

As shown in Fig 4, DStat's measured analogue noise (blue diamonds) decreases with increasing gain before levelling off at approximately 200 fA (approaching the largest value of R_M), placing the instrumental limit of detection at approximately 600 fA. (The experimentally observed noise is closely mirrored by the TINA-TI simulated values shown in green circles; see S2 Supporting Information for additional discussion of the trend in noise.) A lower current measurement limit in the hundreds of femtoamperes is sufficient for the currents of most experiments and DStat's noise performance is unlikely to be limiting except in extremely low current measurements in well-shielded measurement cells. Note that this value (600 fA) is approximately five orders of magnitude lower than the only one of the lab-built potentiostats described previously that reported a comparable value (i.e., Cumyn et al. [14] reported a noise limit of 10 nA).

Electrochemical Performance

DStat's voltammetric performance was compared to that of two peer-systems: an EmStat purchased from PalmSens BV (Utrecht, NL), and a CheapStat constructed following the instructions provided by Rowe et al. [8] Each of these systems is inexpensive (DStat ~ $120 CAD/materials, EmStat ~ 1000 EUR/unit, CheapStat ~ $60 CAD/materials), portable (DStat 92×84×31 mm plus laptop, EmStat 61×43×16 mm plus laptop, CheapStat 140×66×28 mm), and is designed to enable multimodal electroanalytical analysis in the lab or in the field. DStat and CheapStat are open source; EmStat operates as a black box. Fig 5(a) shows representative cyclic voltammograms and square wave voltammograms of 10 mM potassium hexacyanoferrate(III), an analyte exhibiting a chemically reversible reduction under most conditions. While all three potentiostats produced the classic double peak-shaped cyclic voltammograms (left) and the single well-defined peak on the square wave voltammograms (right) expected of a reversible redox couple, some differences were observed between instruments. The DStat and EmStat displayed almost identical voltammograms, characterized by smooth responses which were free of noise; the slight differences between them likely caused by variations in individual electrodes. In contrast, the voltammograms of the CheapStat are significantly different: the CheapStat's cyclic voltammogram has unusually wide peak separation and reduced peak heights, and its square wave voltammogram peak is asymmetric, with significant background current. Further, both of the CheapStat's voltammograms are visibly noisy.

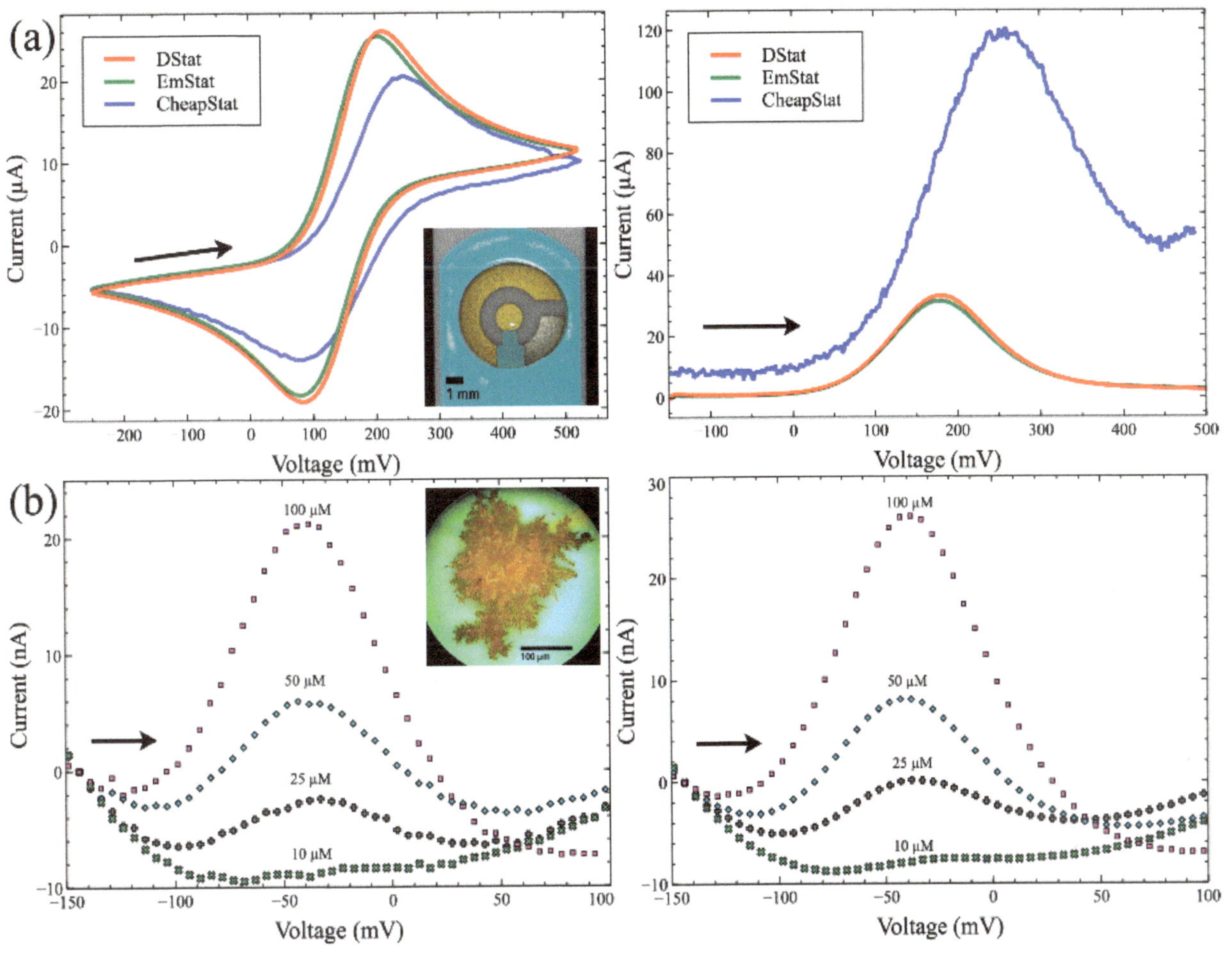

Fig 5. Comparison of voltammetric measurements between instruments.

Arrows indicate scan directions. (a) Cyclic voltammetry (left) and square wave voltammetry (right) of 10 mM potassium hexacyanoferrate (III) collected using (commercial) screen printed electrodes. DStat (red traces), EmStat (green traces), and CheapStat (blue traces). Inset: picture of a screen printed electrode. (b) Differential Pulse Voltammetry of 4-aminophenol (10–100 μM) with DStat (left) and EmStat (right) collected using nanostructured microelectrodes. Curves were shifted vertically to align the current at -150 mV to 0 A to correct for changes in background current. Inset: picture of a nanostructured microelectrode.

http://dx.doi.org/10.1371/journal.pone.0140349.g005

The distortions in the CheapStat peak shapes may be caused by the limited compliance voltage of the control amplifier (~ ±1 V) or the bandwidth of its transimpedance amplifier—at the square wave frequency selected, 70 Hz, TINA-TI simulation indicates that the CheapStat's amplifier's frequency response rolls off above 90 Hz, severely distorting signals with higher frequency components. The observed noise in the CheapStat's voltammograms may be caused by the use of the microcontroller's on-board 12-bit DAC as a reference for the ADC: the DAC is itself referenced to the system's 3.3 V power line which may be subject to more noise than DStat's precision reference voltage source. In addition, the increased noise in the CheapStat's voltammograms could be related to the aliasing effects observed in this system (See S1 Supporting Information). Regardless, it is apparent in the case of the relatively large currents of the screen printed electrodes that DStat exceeds the capabilities of the expense-oriented CheapStat and is indistinguishable from the commercial EmStat instrument.

To examine low-current applications, differential pulse voltammetry measurements of 4-aminophenol were performed using a custom sensor bearing integrated gold nanostructured microelectrodes (NMEs). [20] As shown in the inset to Fig 5(b), the large surface areas of these specialized features allows for high-density attachment of antibodies and other probe molecules, which has attracted significant attention in the biosensor community. [22–24] But the improvement in sensitivity for NMEs comes at a cost—the small overall dimensions of NMEs are associated with small redox currents, requiring more sensitive instrumentation than what is needed for (more standard) experiments using screen printed electrodes. NMEs were used here as unmodified WEs to evaluate the conversion of 4-aminophenol to 4-quinoneimine at four concentrations from 10 to 100 μM. As shown in Fig 5(b), DStat and EmStat produced very similar voltammograms with peaks located at identical voltages within the resolution of the experiment. Note that the DStat traces appear to have slightly higher levels of noise; however, it seems that the "black box" software of the EmStat performs an uninterruptible data-smoothing routine after the experiment is complete, making comparison of unfiltered signals impossible. Access to unfiltered data is useful for scientists who wish to apply (and report) their own processing routines prior to sharing or publication. Nevertheless, both the EmStat and DStat are clearly compatible with low-current measurements using NMEs, while the CheapStat did not produce recognizable oxidation peaks at these current levels.

Neither of the analytes probed in the voltammetry experiments described here (Fig 5) were measured in conditions with high cell capacitance or RE resistance, but DStat's performance under such conditions (which favour instability of the potentiostatic circuit) is discussed in S3 Supporting Information.

Finally, DStat was designed to be compatible with current-measuring applications such as voltammetry (as per Fig 5), but also with voltage-measurement applications such as potentiometry. While most commercial potentiostat systems (including EmStat) are compatible with potentiometry, only one of the lab-built systems described previously [3] has this capability. To evaluate DStat's capabilities for potentiometry, measurements of pH calibration standards were collected and compared with those generated using an Accument AR50 benchtop pH meter. As shown in S4 Supporting Information, the two instruments' performances are virtually indistinguishable—both demonstrated the expected Nernstian response with root mean square errors from a linear least squares fit of 1.9 mV and 2.3 mV for the AR50 and DStat, respectively, which lies within the normal variation of a glass pH electrode. Further, because DStat samples at up to 30 kHz (compared to the 1 Hz sampling of the AR50), we propose that DStat may also be useful in applications that can take advantage of fine temporal resolution such as flow potentiometry [25] and carbon nanotube based sensors [26].

Extensibility

A great advantage that open-source instruments often have over commercial instruments is complete access to both the electronic hardware and the software used to operate it, giving exceptional flexibility in extending the instruments to new uses. [18] While the EmStat offers a software development kit to allow access to built-in features from third party software, the hardware design and firmware (software that runs within the instrument) of the instrument are not disclosed. Conversely, for DStat, the full hardware schematics and source code for the computer software and instrument firmware are freely available (http://microfluidics.utoronto.ca/dstat) for modification or integration into other projects. This means, for example, that it is trivial to adapt the existing DStat program for square wave voltammetry into a custom routine for cyclic square wave voltammetry, with the addition of less than 5 lines of code to the firmware. Similarly, programs for small amplitude and large amplitude pulse voltammetry, specialized techniques that are used for voltammetric electronic tongues [27], can be implemented by simple modifications to the existing firmware.

Perhaps most importantly, DStat software can be connected to third-party software, permitting the use of the standard DStat user interface, triggered by signals from another program. This functionality uses the open-source ZeroMQ distributed messaging system (http://zeromq.org) to provide simple connectivity between the DStat software and other programs running on the same computer or across a network. The hardware can also be controlled directly by means of a simple emulated serial interface over USB.

To demonstrate the flexibility of DStat, a simple plug-in for the open-source Dropbot digital microfluidics control system [28] was created, providing automated electrochemical analysis including programmable microscale fluid manipulation. Fig 6 illustrates the operation of the plugin: μDrop, the control software for Dropbot operates by iterating through a list of pre-programmed steps of droplet manipulations. The new plug-in (which can be found athttp://microfluidics.utoronto.ca/dstat) allows the creation of special steps in which droplet manipulation is paused and a request for an electrochemical measurement is sent to the DStat software using ZeroMQ, which then initiates an experiment on DStat (Fig 6(a)). When the DStat experiment is complete and the DStat software has recorded the data, a signal reporting a finished measurement is sent back to μDrop via ZeroMQ, allowing μDrop to resume droplet manipulation (Fig 6(b)). A video demonstration of combined droplet manipulation and electrochemical measurement can be found in S1 Video with experimental details in S5 Supporting Information. Thus, the extensibility of DStat makes it an attractive tool for the burgeoning area of digital microfluidic electrochemistry [29–33].

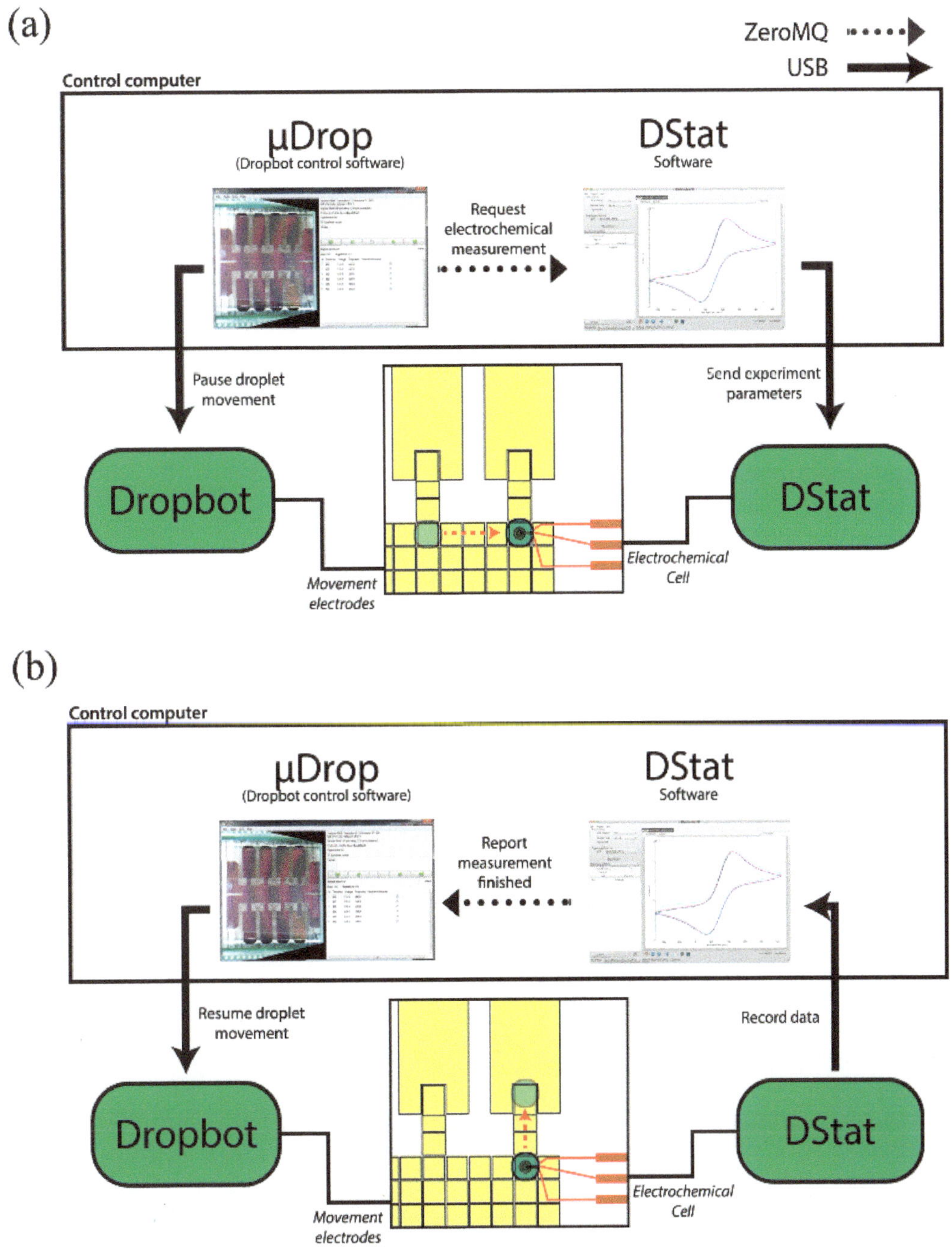

Fig 6. DStat/Dropbot integration.

Solid arrows represent communication between the control computer and instruments over USB and dotted arrows represent communication between programs within the control computer over ZeroMQ. (a) When Dropbot's control software µDrop reaches a programmed electrochemical measurement step, it pauses droplet actuation (in the figure, represented by a droplet parked at a circular electrochemical cell similar to the one described by Dryden et al. [31]) and requests an electrochemical measurement from the DStat software. The DStat software processes the request by initiating an experiment on the DStat hardware. (b) As the DStat hardware performs the experiment, the DStat software records the data. When the experiment is complete, the DStat software reports to µDrop that the measurement is complete and µDrop resumes its programmed droplet movement. A movie depicting the full process can be found in S1 Video.

The DStat joins the growing ranks of inexpensive, freely-modifiable open-source analytical instruments that both complement and compete with commercial instruments. We propose that DStat will prove compatible with a wide range of customized lab-built systems, such as the PublicLab spectrometer (http://publiclab.org/wiki/spectrometer) and miniature SPR systems [34], as well as commercial devices including microfluidic flow controllers, autosamplers, and chromatography instruments. DStat is also applicable beyond electrochemical cells, for use with photodiodes, photomultiplier tubes, Faraday cups, and other devices requiring measurement of minuscule currents.

CONCLUSIONS

The DStat joins the growing ranks of inexpensive, freely-modifiable open-source analytical instruments that both complement and compete with commercial instruments. We demonstrated its capabilities for low-current voltammetry in laboratory settings and found its performance to be comparable to that of a compact commercial potentiostat as well as being superior to that of a previously reported open-source instrument. DStat was also demonstrated to be useful for potentiometry (mostly unique among lab-built potentiostats) with performance comparable to that of a commercial pH meter. Finally, DStat provides robust integration with other instruments by allowing either direct communication with the hardware or using the DStat software as intermediary, which was demonstrated by connecting the DStat software with the Dropbot digital microfluidics platform. With this contribution to the toolkit of open-source analytical instruments, we hope to foster free modification and allow researchers to adapt their tools to suit experiments rather than alter experiments to suit tools.

REFERENCES

1. Bewick A, Fleischmann M. The design and performance of potentiostats. Biochem Biophys Res Commun. 1963 Mar;8(3):89–106. doi: 10.1016/0013-4686(63)80009-2
2. Bard AJ, Faulkner LR. Electrochemical Methods: Fundamentals and Applications. 2nd ed. Fundamentals and Applications. Wiley; 2000.
3. Bembnowicz P, Yang GZ, Anastasova S, Spehar-Deleze AM, Vadgama P. Wearable electronic sensor for potentiometric and amperometric measurements. In: 2013 IEEE International Conference on Body Sensor Networks (BSN). IEEE; 2013. p. 1–5.
4. Kwakye S, Baeumner A. An embedded system for portable electrochemical detection. Sens Actuators, B. 2007 Apr;123(1):336–343. doi: 10.1016/j.snb.2006.08.032.
5. Huang CY, Syu MJ, Chang YS, Chang CH, Chou TC, Liu BD. A portable potentiostat for the bilirubin-specific sensor prepared from molecular imprinting. Biosens Bioelectron. 2007 Mar;22(8):1694–1699. doi: 10.1016/j.bios.2006.07.036. pmid:16962762
6. Beach RD, Conlan RW, Godwin MC, Moussy F. Towards a Miniature Implantable In Vivo Telemetry Monitoring System Dynamically Configurable as a Potentiostat or Galvanostat for Two- and Three-Electrode Biosensors. IEEE Trans Instrum Meas. 2005 Feb;54(1):61–72. doi: 10.1109/TIM.2004.839757.
7. Gore A, Chakrabartty S, Pal S, Alocilja EC. A Multichannel Femtoampere-Sensitivity Potentiostat Array for Biosensing Applications. IEEE Trans Circuits Syst I. 2006 Nov;53(11):2357–2363. doi: 10.1109/TCSI.2006.884432.
8. Rowe AA, Bonham AJ, White RJ, Zimmer MP, Yadgar RJ, Hobza TM, et al. CheapStat: An Open-Source, "Do-It-Yourself" Potentiostat for Analytical and Educational Applications. PLoS ONE. 2011 Sep;6(9):e23783. doi: 10.1371/journal.pone.0023783. pmid:21931613
9. Friedman ES, Rosenbaum MA, Lee AW, Lipson DA, Land BR, Angenent LT. A cost-effective and field-ready potentiostat that poises subsurface electrodes to monitor bacterial respiration. Biosens Bioelectron. 2012 Feb;32(1):309–313. doi: 10.1016/j.bios.2011.12.013. pmid:22209069
10. Gopinath AV, Russell D. An inexpensive field-portable programmable potentiostat. Chem Educ. 2005;.
11. Cruz AFD, Norena N, Kaushik A, Bhansali S. A low-cost miniaturized potentiostat for point-of-care diagnosis. Biosens Bioelectron. 2014 Dec;62:249–254. doi: 10.1016/j.bios.2014.06.053. pmid:25016332
12. Steinberg MD, Lowe CR. A micropower amperometric potentiostat. Sens Actuators, B. 2004 Feb;97(2–3):284–289. doi: 10.1016/j.snb.2003.09.002.
13. Stanacevic M, Murari K, Rege A, Cauwenberghs G, Thakor NV. VLSI Potentiostat Array With Oversampling Gain Modulation for Wide-Range Neurotransmitter Sensing. IEEE Trans Biomed Circuits Syst. 2007 Mar;1(1):63–72. doi: 10.1109/TBCAS.2007.893176. pmid:23851522
14. Cumyn VK, Fleischauer MD, Hatchard TD, Dahn JR. Design and testing of a low-cost multichannel pseudopotentiostat for quantitative combinatorial electrochemical measurements on large electrode arrays. Electrochem Solid-State Lett. 2003;6(6):E15–E18. doi: 10.1149/1.1570031.
15. Li H, Luo X, Liu C, Jiang L, Cui D, Cai X, et al. Multi-channel electrochemical detection system based on LabVIEW. In: Proceedings of the 2004 International Conference on Information Acquisition, ICIA 2004; 2004. p. 224–227.
16. Gostowski R. Teaching Analytical Instrument Design with LabVIEW. J Chem Educ. 1996 Dec;73(12):1103. doi: 10.1021/ed073p1103.
17. Stević Z, Andjelković Z, Antić D. A New PC and LabVIEW Package Based System for Electrochemical Investigations. Sensors 2008, Vol 8, Pages 1819–1831. 2008 Mar;8(3):1819–1831. doi: 10.3390/s8031819
18. Pearce JM. Chapter 1—Introduction to Open-Source Hardware for Science. In: Pearce JM, editor. Open-Source Lab. Boston: Elsevier; 2014. p. 1–11.
19. Urban PL. Universal electronics for miniature and automated chemical assays. Analyst. 2015;140(4):963–975. doi: 10.1039/C4AN02013H. pmid:25535820
20. Soleymani L, Fang Z, Sun X, Yang H, Taft BJ, Sargent EH, et al. Nanostructuring of Patterned Microelectrodes To Enhance the Sensitivity of Electrochemical Nucleic Acids Detection. Angew Chem Int Ed. 2009 Oct;48(45):8457–8460. doi: 10.1002/anie.200902439.
21. McIlvaine TC. A BUFFER SOLUTION FOR COLORIMETRIC COMPARISON. J Biol Chem. 1921;p. 183–186.
22. Soleymani L, Fang Z, Sargent EH, Kelley SO. Programming the detection limits of biosensors through controlled nanostructuring. Nature Nanotech. 2009 Sep;4(12):844–848. doi: 10.1038/nnano.2009.276.
23. Soleymani L, Fang Z, Lam B, Bin X, Vasilyeva E, Ross

AJ, et al. Hierarchical Nanotextured Microelectrodes Overcome the Molecular Transport Barrier To Achieve Rapid, Direct Bacterial Detection. ACS Nano. 2011 Apr;5(4):3360–3366. doi: 10.1021/nn200586s. pmid:21410241

24. Lam B, Fang Z, Sargent EH, Kelley SO. Polymerase Chain Reaction-Free, Sample-to-Answer Bacterial Detection in 30 Minutes with Integrated Cell Lysis. Anal Chem. 2012 Jan;84(1):21–25. doi: 10.1021/ac202599b. pmid:22142422

25. Montenegro MCBSM, Araújo AN. Flow Potentiometry. In: Advances in Flow Analysis. Wiley-VCH Verlag GmbH & Co. KGaA; 2008. p. 425–454.

26. Zelada-Guillén GA, Bhosale SV, Riu J, Rius FX. Real-Time Potentiometric Detection of Bacteria in Complex Samples. Anal Chem. 2010 Nov;82(22):9254–9260. doi: 10.1021/ac101739b. pmid:20961052

27. Winquist F, Krantz-Rülcker C, Lundström I. Electronic Tongues and Combinations of Artificial Senses. Sens Update. 2002 Dec;11(1):279–306. doi: 10.1002/seup.200211107.

28. .Fobel R, Fobel C, Wheeler AR. DropBot: An open-source digital microfluidic control system with precise control of electrostatic driving force and instantaneous drop velocity measurement. Appl Phys Lett. 2013;102(19):193513–193518. doi: 10.1063/1.4807118.

29. Shamsi MH, Choi K, Ng AHC, Wheeler AR. A digital microfluidic electrochemical immunoassay. Lab Chip. 2014;14(3):547–554. doi: 10.1039/C3LC51063H. pmid:24292705

30. Yu Y, Chen J, Li J, Yang S, Fan SK, Zhou J. Microfabrication of a digital microfluidic platform integrated with an on-chip electrochemical cell. J Micromech Microeng. 2013 Aug;23(9):095025. doi: 10.1088/0960-1317/23/9/095025.

31. Dryden MDM, Rackus DDG, Shamsi MH, Wheeler AR. Integrated Digital Microfluidic Platform for Voltammetric Analysis. Anal Chem. 2013;85(18):8809–8816. doi: 10.1021/ac402003v. pmid:24001207

32. Karuwan C, Sukthang K, Wisitsoraat A, Phokharatkul D, Patthanasettakul V, Wechsatol W, et al. Electrochemical detection on electrowetting-on-dielectric digital microfluidic chip. Talanta. 2011 Jun;84(5):1384–1389. doi: 10.1016/j.talanta.2011.03.073. pmid:21641456

33. Rackus DG, Dryden MDM, Lamanna J, Zaragoza A, Lam B, Kelley SO, et al. A digital microfluidic device with integrated nanostructured microelectrodes for electrochemical immunoassays. Lab Chip. 2015; 15(18):3776–3784. doi: 10.1039/C5LC00660K. pmid:26247922

34. Zhao SS, Bukar N, Toulouse JL, Pelechacz D, Robitaille R, Pelletier JN, et al. Miniature multi-channel SPR instrument for methotrexate monitoring in clinical samples. Biosens Bioelectron. 2015 Feb;64:664–670. doi: 10.1016/j.bios.2014.09.082. pmid:25441416

CHAPTER 17

A NOVEL BYTE-SUBSTITUTION ARCHITECTURE FOR THE AES CRYPTOSYSTEM

Fakir Sharif Hossain[1,] and Md. Liakot Ali[2]

[1]Department of Electrical and Electronic Engineering, International Islamic University Chittagong, Chittagong, Bangladesh

[2]Institute of Information and Communication Technology, Bangladesh University of Engineering and technology, Dhaka, Bangladesh

ABSTRACT

The performance of Advanced Encryption Standard (AES) mainly depends on speed, area and power. The S-box represents an important factor that affects the performance of AES on each of these factors. A number of techniques have been presented in the literature, which have attempted to improve the performance of the S-box byte-substitution. This paper proposes a new S-box architecture, defining it as ultra low power, robustly parallel and highly efficient in terms of area. The architecture is discussed for both CMOS and FPGA platforms, and the pipelined architecture of the proposed S-box is presented for further time savings and higher throughput along with higher hardware resources utilization. A performance analysis and comparison of the proposed architecture is also conducted with those achieved by the existing techniques. The results of the comparison verify the outperformance of the proposed architecture in terms of power, delay and size.

INTRODUCTION

Encryption algorithms are broadly classified as symmetric and asymmetric algorithms based on the type of keys used. Due to the complexity of asymmetric algorithms, symmetric ciphers are always preferred for their speed and simplicity. AES (the Rijndael algorithm) is one such symmetric algorithm for encryption which replaced triple-DES and eventually became the number one choice for security algorithms all over the world by 2001. Therefore, NIST declared AES to be the standard for privacy and security of information [1]. Since then, it has been used for countless different applications ranging in size and scale such as military, e-banking and different data communication purposes.

There have been many novel design techniques for AES that focus on obtaining high throughput or low area usage. The demand for fast and area-efficient AES implementations is rapidly growing and is becoming more crucial than the demand for a smaller active device on the chip. The traditional basic lookup table implementations are relatively fast and can achieve better performance with some modifications. The use of smaller look up tables (LUTs) of different sizes ranging from 16 to 128 bytes has become more reliable for getting higher speed. This paper proposes the LUT of small size, which reduces the indexing and provides satisfactory results in terms

Citation: Hossain FS, Ali ML (2015) A Novel Byte-Substitution Architecture for the AES Cryptosystem. PLoS ONE 10(10): e0138457. doi:10.1371/journal.pone.0138457

of power, area and speed. A significant portion of the overall silicon area for implementing AES architectures is occupied by the S-box. The size of SubBytes is, in turn, determined by the number of S-boxes and their concrete implementation. Various implementation options for the AES S-box have been investigated in the recent past [2–12]. One of our previous work [13], we show that the speed of the AES processor can be maximized by optimizing the S-box and MixColumn stages. That work reports the high performance in terms of throughput and latency. In recent years, hardware implementations in CMOS technology received a lot of preference due to their good performance. An initial attempt of optimizing AES S-box is introducing the composite field decomposition technique of S-box, in which a multi-stage positive polarity Reed-Muller architecture has been introduced [14]. In this S-box, the hazard-transparent XOR gates are located after the other gates which may block the hazards.

Moreover, there are a lot of applications coming out at present, such as contactless smart card, wireless sensor network, small computing devices etc., where low power is important. This is the reason why a number of research works have been proposed and further research works are still continuing focusing on low power [15]. The use of embedded functional blocks instead of general purpose logic elements is a good idea to reduce the dynamic power consumption of the designs [16]. It is seen that internal routing of embedded system block is more power efficient than the routing used for general purpose logic. It has been also commented that a large amount of power consumption in an AES processor is due to its S-box and that it is responsible for consuming 75% of its total power. Clock gating is another commonly used technique for dynamic power reduction [17]. Studies show that basic pipelining technique can reduce 31% dynamic power consumption, while it can increase up to 82% due to heavy pipelining. Wong [18] aims to have achieved a high throughput compact AES S-box with minimal power consumption. They have proposed a novel pipelining arrangement over the compact composite field S-box such that both high throughput and low power are optimized.

Some literatures provided good results for FPGA implementations too. The optimized implementation on composite field arithmetic has introduced to reduce both static and dynamic power consumption of S-box along with pipelining and dynamic voltage scaling [19]. Besides, minimizing the supply voltage apparently reduces the power dissipation in designs. The T-box AES design is intended to have high throughput and low power usage [20]. The T-box method has its potential in embedded system to have power and energy efficient design since it relies on embedded RAM blocks rather than general purpose logic. Another technique is to use low data path width for AES design in order to reduce the power consumption [21].

Now-a-days there are a lot of applications coming in the market where an increasing number of battery-powered embedded systems like PDAs, cell phones, networked sensors, smart cards, RFID etc. are used to store, access, manipulate, or communicate sensitive data. Eventually, this makes security a very important concern. Since these devices are resource constrained and battery powered, low power and small area are some of the primary requirements. This paper focuses on the solution of this particular problem and has presented a novel technique in designing a low power, least delay and area efficient S-box for an AES processor. In the process of proving the claim, a fair comparison among area, delay and power estimation is presented based on target delay. The graphical representation of (i) GE versus target value for critical path delay, (ii) Total Power versus target value for critical path delay and (iii) Power area product versus target value for critical path delay are performed which shows the novelty of the work.

The remainder of this paper is organized as follows. In Section 2 The AES S-box and its different implementation techniques along with the realization are discussed. In Section 3, the S-box algorithm is proposed and followed by the implementation of SubByte in both CMOS and FPGA is discussed in Section 4. Furthermore, Section 5 presents the results and performance analysis of proposed S-box architecture followed by comparison to other recent related works in the Section 6. We conclude in Section 7.

AES S-BOX AND RELATED IMPLEMENTATION STRATEGIES

It is well known that the S-box is the most weighted transformation among the four rounds of the AES algorithm. The substitution byte (S-box) serves the purpose of bringing confusion to the data that is to be encrypted. The S-box is a 16 by 16 matrix box containing a total of 256 byte hexadecimal and indexed in a row and column pattern. The S-boxes used in the SubBytes function are created in such a way that they are invertible for using as inverse S-boxes in the InvSubBytes function. The S-box computation involves basically two steps, the multiplicative inverse and the affine transformation. The multiplicative inverse is complex to perform in GF (2^8), so in order to simplify, composite field arithmetic is used by some researchers. This sort of implementation has good response in terms of area, but due to the large signal activities, consumes more power. In order to achieve high throughput and low power, many literatures present the hardware look-up table implementation of S-box. This paper presents an optimized look-up table implementation of S-box.

Logically, the SubBytes transformation substitutes all of the 16 bytes of the state independently using the S-box. In software, the S-box is typically realized in the form of a look-up table since inversion in the Galios Field (GF) cannot be calculated efficiently on general-purpose processors. In case of hardware, on the other hand, the implementation of the S-box is directed to the desired trade-off among area, delay, and power consumption. The most obvious implementation approach of S-box takes the form of hardware look-up tables. Our proposed design will explain how the hardware look-up table works efficiently in the next couple of sections. More sophisticated approaches include the calculation of S-box function in hardware using its algebraic properties [22]. Composite field based design is a good example of calculating S-box. The main drawback of composite field approach is greater power consumption, but delay is much less compared to other architectures. The minimal power consumption for implementing the AES S-box is approached by Bertoni et al [23]. He used an intermediate one-hot encoding of the input and arbitrary logic functions (including cryptographic S-boxes) to realize minimal power consumption. Relatively large silicon area is the main drawback of this approach. Tiltech [24] describes a total of eight different implementations of the AES

S-box in which he grouped them into three basic categories: look-up implementations, calculating implementations, and low-power implementations. In order to validate our approach, a fair comparison with Tiltech's work will be established, as he covers all the implementations aspects of S-box.

On the other hand, Implementations which calculate the S-box transformation in hardware were first proposed by Wolkerstorfer et al. [25] and Satoh et al. [26]. The former approach decomposes the elements of finite field into polynomials over the subfield and performs inversion there. Canright [27] improved the calculation of the S-box by switching the representation to a normal basis. The low-power approach of Bertoni et al. use a decode stage to convert the eight bits of the input byte and the control bit which selects encryption or decryption into a one-hot representation consisting of 29 ¼ 512 bits. Due to the decoder-permute-encoder structure, there is only very little signal activity within the circuit when the input changes, resulting in low power consumption. It should be noted that the structure of Bertoni's approach makes it easily possible to introduce pipeline stages. However, it may be necessary to add a large number of additional flip-flops when the pipeline stage is placed between the decoder and encoder. It results large power consumption. This proposed algorithm substitutes a byte through small table look-up without inserting any flip flop when pipelined. Therefore, a change of a few input bits affects the evaluation of all output bits separately. As normally some output bits will remain unchanged, the signal activity within this particular path is low. Thus it limits the overall power consumption of the S-box. The second implementation of Bertoni uses a two stages decoder structure so as to reduce the critical path delay of the circuit. This paper approaches a single stage decoder function which performs better compared to Bertoni.

Elazm [28] shows a composite Galois Field design of S-box to reduce the size and the delay of the circuit. Transmission gate is employed to reduce power consumption of the mentioned circuit. This design suffers long critical path delay due to switching and glitch. The proposed work ignores the algebraic properties of the substitution and simply implements the Boolean equations of the input/output relation. Therefore, less switching activities ensure lower power consumption. Due to simple Boolean implementations, the synthesizer has a much higher degree of freedom for optimizing the proposed circuit, which allows for a shorter critical path at a little expense of the silicon area.

In a recent paper, Shanthini [29] presents an optimized composite field arithmetic S-box implementation in a four stage pipeline. Here the S-box operation is divided into the Galios Field multiplication and its inverse operation and later illustrated in a step-by-step manner. The main constrain is appeared when considered the critical path versus the area-power product. Comparatively, the implementation of our proposed work on FPGA had a very good result in terms of area, power and product. Another work by Ahmed [30] presents a full custom CMOS design of S-box/Inversion S-box (Inv S-box) mapped in low power GF (2^8) inversion. He used polynomial basis using composite field arithmetic and got a fascinating result in both silicon area and power consumption. But the main drawback is its critical path delay, which is five to six times than that of the proposed design. The next Section shows the proposed S-box architecture in detail.

Proposed S-box Architecture

In the previous Section, the three general techniques for realizing the S-box has already been discussed, of which, the proposed architecture uses the combination of both the Hardware and the Software technique. In one case the multiplicative inverse in GF (2^8) is realized as look-up table, while the affine transformation is computed as in hardware techniques [24]. This approach has the benefits of avoiding the complexity of inversion and reducing LUT space requirements to half that of the LUT used for the whole S-box. The basic idea of this approach is that the original S-box is broken down into a set of smaller size multiplexer-switched truth-table of say n-variable functions using the Shannon expression. The smaller tables are then mapped into n-LUT of Altera FPGA. The mapping of LUTs is provided by the following pseudo code:

```
INITIALIZING, i, j, GR
GR ← 3 (Binary value)
CASE GR OF
CASE(00): for i ← 0 TO 3 for j ← 0 TO 7
DO (i,j) ← (i,j) AND DO (i+1, j) ← (i, j+8)
ENDFOR
CASE(01): for i ← 4 To 7 for j ← 0 To 7
DO (i,j) ← (i,j) AND DO (i+1, j) ← (i, j+8)
ENDFOR
CASE(10): for i ← 8 TO B for j ← 0 TO 7
DO (i,j) ← (i,j) AND DO (i+1, j) ← (i, j+8)
ENDFOR
CASE(11): for i ← C TO F for j ← 0 TO 7
DO (i,j) ← (i,j) AND DO (i+1, j) ← (i, j+8)
ENDFOR
ENDCASE
```

Initially, the single S-box is decomposed into 4 tables of 64 bytes, which are called as groups. Within a group, there are 16 separate tables of 2×2 bytes. The decomposition of these tables is similar to the group formation itself. In case of a single S-box of 16×16 bytes hexadecimal values, the substitution of a single byte of AES state from the S-box requires a 16×16 table look up. Therefore, large number of iterations are initiated which results longer delay and larger power consumption. On the contrary, the proposed design constructs an effectively small look-up table of only 2×2 bytes.

To illustrate the look-up process, consider a state of 16 bytes (Fig 1). Supposedly, the byte to be substituted has the hexadecimal value of {b9}. Here binary representation of {b9} is {10111001} and is a binary string, where the most significant bit is regarded as a_7 and the least significant bit is a_0. The first step is group selection which is based on the a_7 and a_6 of the processed byte, which corresponds to Group 3 in this case. The row and column values of the corresponding group are specified by the bits a_5-a_2. Finally, bits a_0 and a_1 select the substitution value. Thus, in case of the above mentioned example, the substitution value is obtained as {56}. The steps required in the proposed substitution method are summarized in the algorithm (Fig 2).

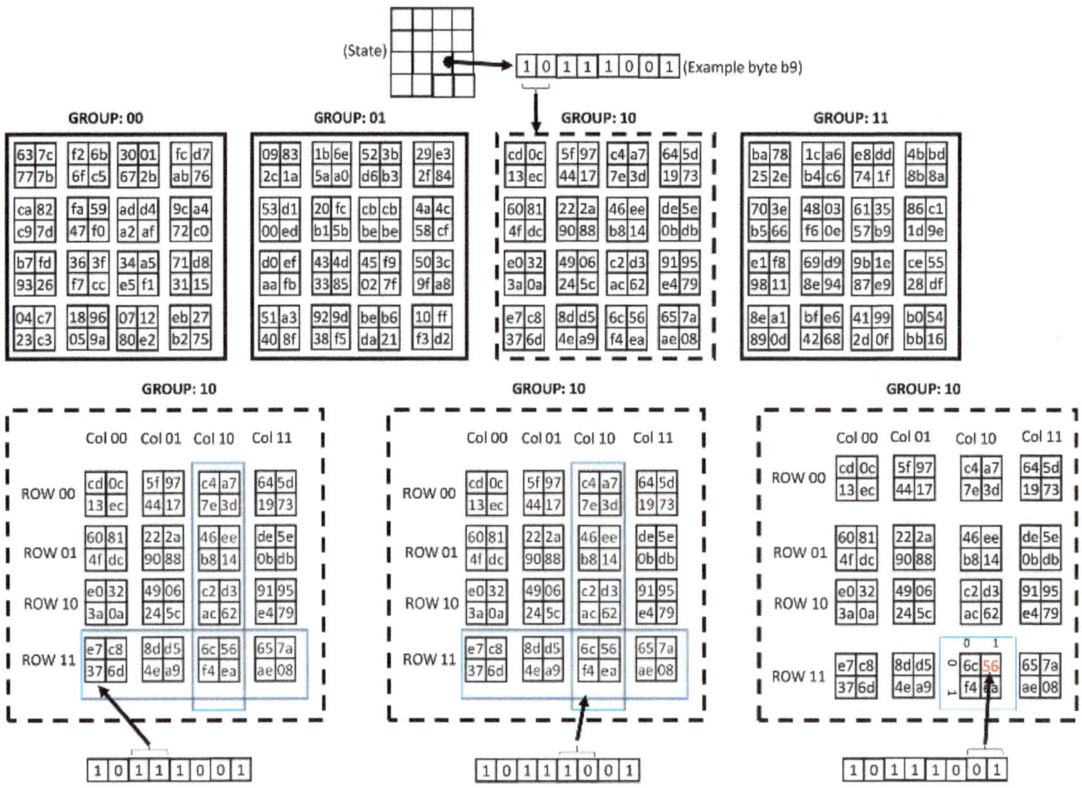

Figure 1. An illustrative example of the proposed S-box architecture.

```
FOR i: 1 n DO                    // n is the number of iterations required to substitute a 16-byte AES state
        FOR all bytes processed simultaneously DO
        Stage 1 (GRP) → Left-most 2 bits to select a group out of four groups
        Stage 2 (RW) → Next left-most 2 bits to select a row within the selected group
        Stage 3 (CL) → Next left-most 2 bits to select a column within the group
        Stage 4 (LUT) → Right-most 2 bits as an index to identify 2X2 lookup table to obtain substitute value
        END FOR
END FOR
END ALGORITHM
```

Figure 2. The proposed substitution byte algorithm.

The S-box is optimized by breaking down the large matrix into groups to eliminate the delay producing algebraic and matrix operation. Therefore, this optimization technique reduces the number of iteration to substitute a single byte which increases speed and decreases latency. As composite field design of S-box requires more arithmetic operations, it simply consumes more power compared to look up table. This proposed algorithm uses groups of small tables which is further beneficial as it simplifies table indexing and results in the reduction of delay and power consumption.

PROPOSED S-BOX IMPLEMENTATION

This Section introduces the hardware implementation of the proposed S-box algorithm in both CMOS and FPGA. The S-box has been designed and synthesis using the 0.35 µm CMOS standard cell library with the Synopsys Design Analyzer. First, we consider the CMOS design. For each step in the algorithm (Fig 2) the requirement of the hardware components is discussed. The selection of groups, rows, and columns is implemented using decoders. On the other hand, S-box LUT is implemented using multiplexers (Fig 3).

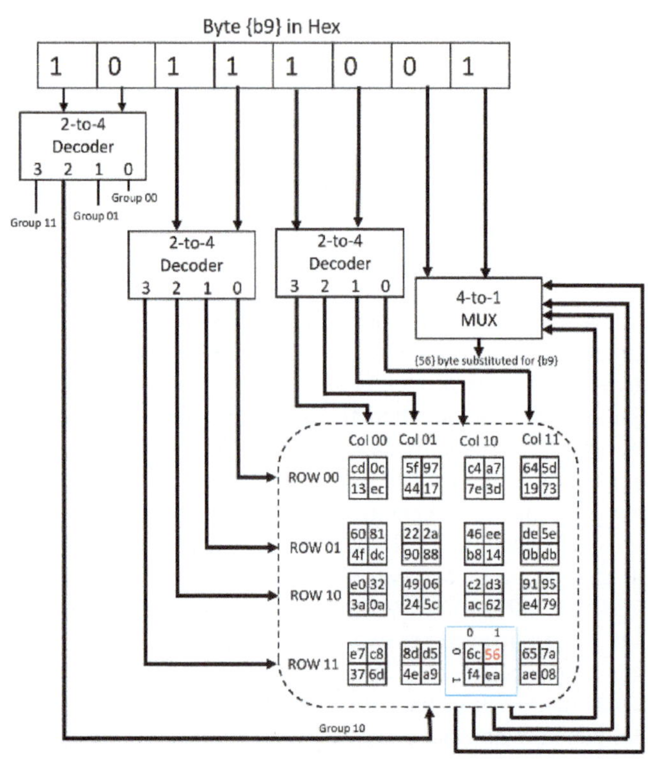

Figure 3. Block diagram for a single byte substitution.

In order to choose one group out of four, a 2-to–4 decoder is used. Two more 2-to–4 decoders are required to choose the row and column within the selected group. We select to use two input NAND (NAND2) decoders to comply with the standard CMOS technology. The NAND2 and the 2-to–4 decoder circuits are shown in Fig 4(A), and Fig 4(B) respectively. Once decoding on the group, row, and column levels are done, the LUT to be used is known. The two right most bits of the byte processed are used as an index to the 2×2 LUT. These two bits are connected to the select lines of a 4-to–1 multiplexer having the table data as inputs and the S-box substitution value as the output. All the 4-to–1 multiplexers implemented are constructed using three 2-to–1 multiplexers for simplicity (Fig 4(C)). The following is an explanation of three possible designs to implement 2-to–1 multiplexers:

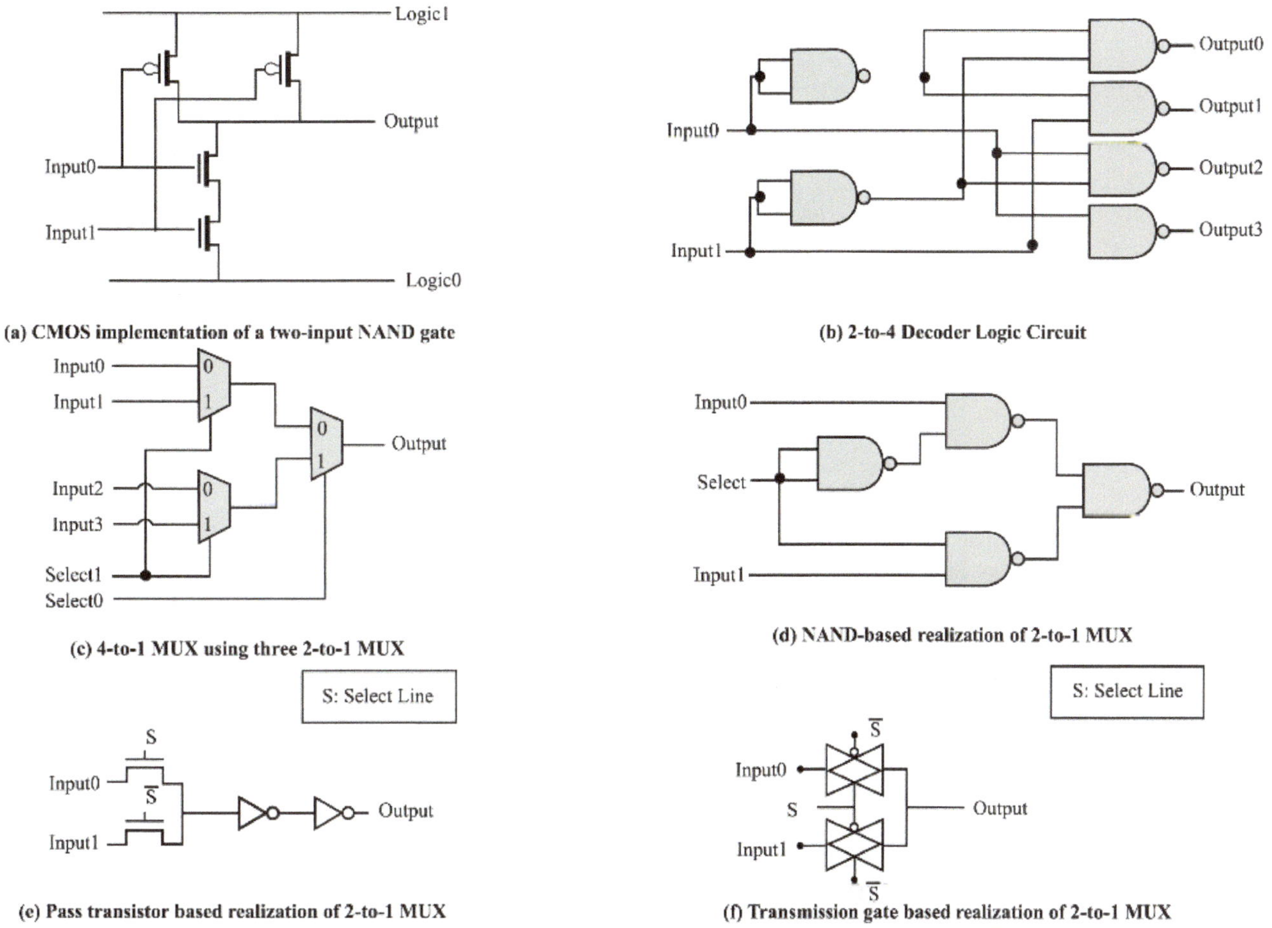

Figure 4. The CMOS realization circuits.

First Design (Gate-Level (NAND-NAND) CMOS Implementation)

Each CMOS NAND2 gate consists of four transistors. Four NAND2 gates and an inverter can be used as shown in Fig 4(D) to perform the operation of a 2-to1 MUX. For our 2×2 LUT we need a 4-to–1 MUX which is constructed using three 2-to–1 MUX as shown in Fig 4(C).

Second Design (Pass Transistors Implementation)

Pass transistor logic can be used as shown in Fig 4(E) to implement a 2-to–1 multiplexer. The two inverters added at the output are used to retain the logic level. The 4-to–1 multiplexer needed for S-box LUT is constructed using three 2-to–1 multiplexers.

Third Design (Transmission Gates Implementation)

Transmission gates are simply switches which can act as two-to-one multiplexer as shown inFig 4(F). In this case the number of transistors required is less than the former implementations discussed above. Similarly, 4-to–1 multiplexers are constructed out of 2-to–1 ones.

Second, the proposed S-box is implemented in FPGA device of family Altera, Cyclone II, EP2C35F672C6 device. The simulation is performed in Quartus-II simulation software with Verilog HDL code. In this work, 128 bit data block is given input to the S-box sub module as 'boxin'. After getting the clock 'clk' the output is generated at 'boxout'. This sub module is named as aes_sub_byte (Fig 5). The resources that have been utilized are provided in Table 1.

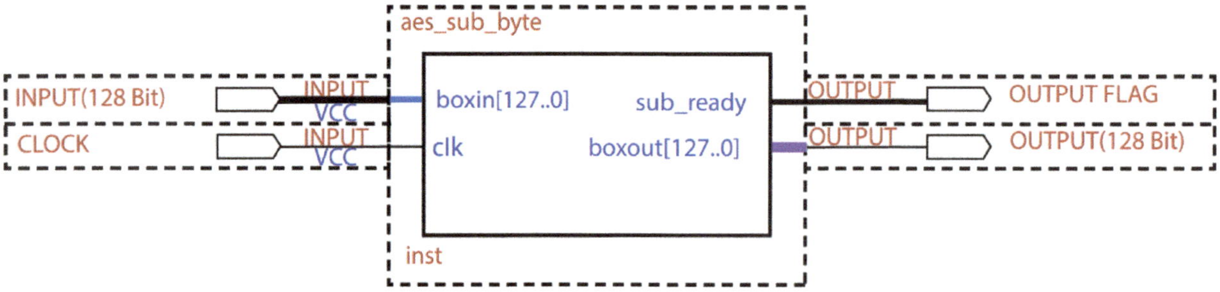

Figure 5. Block Diagram of S-BOX Sub module.

Table 1. Resource utilization in percentage for proposed s-box.

Specification	Actual quantity	Used resource	% of Utilization
Total Logic Elements	33216	57	0.11
Total Registers	3124	16	0.51
Input Output (I/O) Registers	33216	n/ a	
Total Combinational Functions	33216	57	<1
Dedicated Logic Registers	33216	16	<0.5
Total Memory bits	483840	32768	6.7
Total PLL	4	0	0

doi:10.1371/journal.pone.0138457.t001

The algorithm steps shown in Fig 2 can be optimized through pipelining. Each step can represent a stage in the pipeline architecture. Further speedup can be achieved by merging the second and the third steps of the algorithm since they are totally independent in terms of data and hardware resources required (Fig 6). The pipeline performance can be measured by identifying the number of stages required to complete the processing of one state substitution denoted by ‘n’, the number of iterations (m) needed to complete the processing of one state substitution, and the time (t) of the slowest stage in the pipeline.

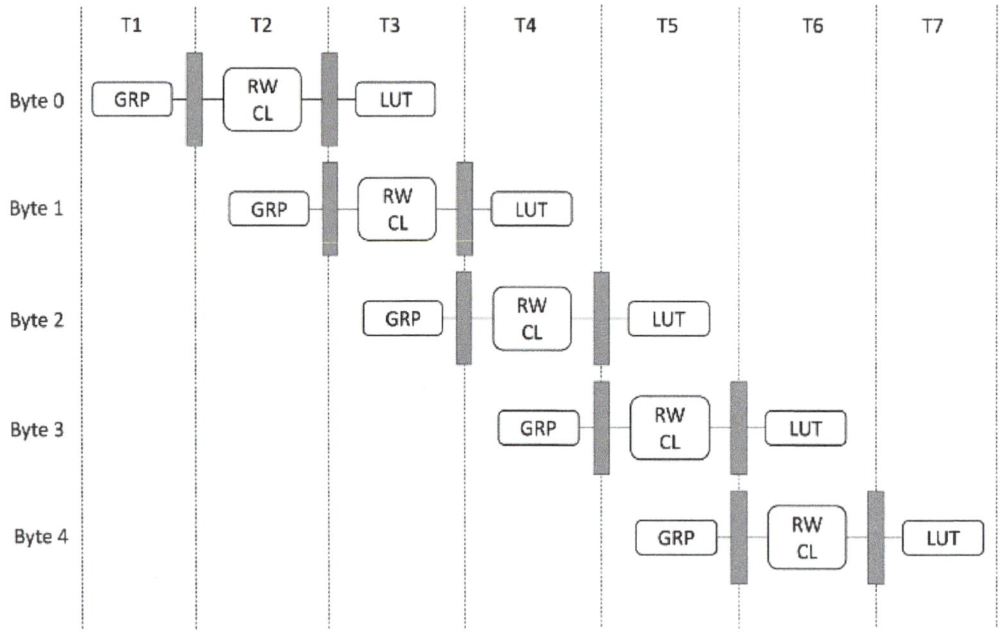

Figure 6. Optimized pipelined architecture for byte substitution.

Pipelining speed, throughput, and efficiency can be computed as discussed in [31] using Eqs1, 2, and 3. The benefits of pipelining byte substitution can be clearly noticed as the number of bytes processed per iteration decreases. As there are no additional gates are needed when pipelined, therefore, no hardware complexities and glitches. Therefore, our proposed algorithm has low power, higher throughput and higher efficiency compare to Bertoni [23] as he used additional one-hot encoder to substitute bytes.

Speed, $$S(n) = \frac{m \times n}{n + m - 1} \quad (1)$$

Throughput, $$U(n) = \frac{m}{(n + m - 1) \times t} \quad (2)$$

$$\text{Efficiency,} \quad E(n) = \frac{m}{n+m-1} \tag{3}$$

RESULTS AND PERFORMANCE ANALYSIS

The performance analysis of the proposed and simulated design is on the 0.35 μm CMOS technology of AMS Corporation [32]. The proposed architecture consists of two parts: the decoder unit which performs the selection among the groups and the row as well as column selection; the multiplexer unit which substitutes the value of the AES state with the S-box one. All of the three proposed designs are same for the first unit (decoder) as it is implemented with 2-input NAND gates. Therefore, the power dissipation, associated delay and area are consequently identical for the decoder part. On the other hand, all three proposed techniques share the same idea of creating a 4-to–1 multiplexer by using only 2-to–1 multiplexers. Thus, four bytes of a state require twelve 2-to–1 (Fig 4(B)), critical path delay for 4-to–1 multiplexer is twice the delay of a 2-to–1 multiplexer. Given that every four bytes of a state are processed simultaneously, the total delay is eight times that of a 2-to–1 multiplexer. With a 16-byte state, the architecture flexibility allows varying the bytes processed from a single byte at a time to 16 bytes in parallel with power of twos increments, i.e., 1, 2, 4, 8, and 16. The delay and area estimation for 1, 4 and 16 combinations are shown in Table 2. It can be observed that the more bytes processed in parallel, the more area and power are needed and the less delay is required. To clarify the results obtained, the case of processing four bytes in parallel is considered here (without pipelining).

Table 2. Delay, Power and Area Estimation of the Proposed Designs

Architectural Realization	Design–1			Design–2			Design–3		
	1-byte	4-byte	16-byte	1-byte	4-byte	16-byte	1-byte	4-byte	16-byte
Decoders Delay (ns)	6.4	1.6	0.4	6.4	1.6	0.4	6.4	1.6	0.4
Multiplexers Delay (ns)	9.6	2.4	0.6	8	2	0.5	3.2	0.8	0.2
Total Delay (ns)	**16**	**4**	**1**	**14.4**	**3.6**	**0.9**	**9.6**	**2.4**	**0.6**
Total Power (mW)	**0.12**	**0.5**	**2**	**0.14**	**0.55**	**2.22**	**0.21**	**0.83**	**3.33**
Decoders Area (GE)	18	72	288	18	72	288	18	72	288
Multiplexers Area (GE)	96	384	1536	84	336	1344	48	192	768
Total Area (GE)	**114**	**456**	**1824**	**102**	**408**	**1632**	**66**	**264**	**1056**

doi:10.1371/journal.pone.0138457.t002

In the FPGA analysis, the S-box simulation is performed by Quartus-II simulator. Fig 7(A)shows the result for S-box operation. Among all the three proposed architectures the simulation result that is provided here is the third one. Here the boxin takes input as the positive edge clk getting signal and generate the 128 bit output to the boxout. All the 16-byte (128 bits) of AES state is replaced by the S-box values. The Throughput = 128 bits/ (cycle per substitution * time period) and the Latency = Clock cycles/Fclk. The timing analysis provides the maximum frequency 99.79MHz and the speed performance is determined on the basis of this clock cycle. After 4 clock cycles the input flag is one. So the latency is 4. The time periods of 99.79 MHz signal = $1/99.79\times10^6$ = 10 ns. Again a cycle processes a data sample of 128 bits and it requires 4 cycles to provide output. So the throughput of the proposed processor is = 128/4*10ns = 3.2 Gbps. The Power Play Power Analyzer tool of Quartus-II simulator estimates the total power consumption of the proposed design, which is shown in Fig 7(B). Total dynamic power dissipation for S-box is obtained 1.57 mW.

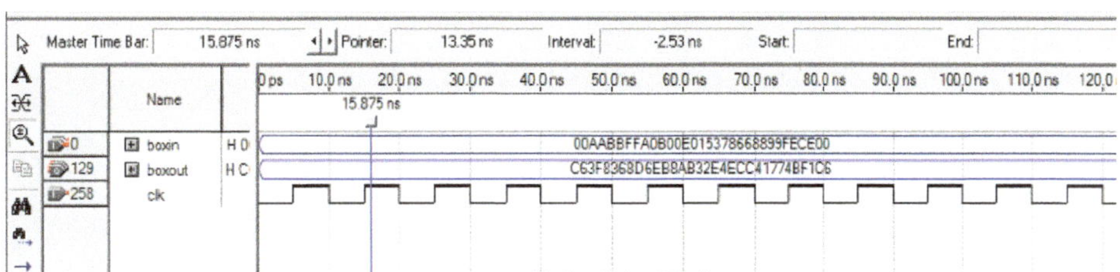

(a) Simulation Window

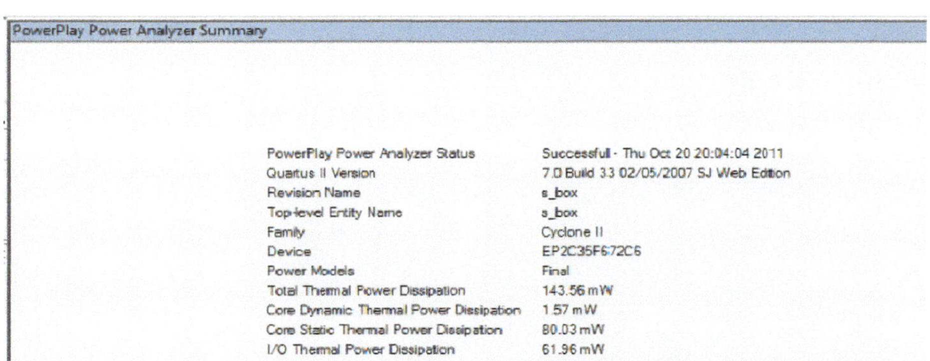

(b) Power Estimation by PPP Analyzer

Figure 7. Quartus-II simulator output for power analysis of the S-box.

Furthermore, the pipelined structure (Fig 6) that has been described by the Eqs 1, 2, and 3 is iterated in Table 3. The benefits of pipelining byte substitution can be clearly noticed, as the number of bytes processed per iteration decreases. The optimal speed and hence higher efficiency is achieved when the state is taken single byte at a time. In this particular case, the pipelined solution is $8/3 \approx 2.67$ times faster than the non-pipelined one. This is significantly fast, for one state completes its byte substitution in 6 ns rather than 16 ns for the 1-byte case. Regardless of the design selected, the intermediate cases (i.e., when 2-bytes, 4-bytes, or 8-bytes are processed per pipeline stage) represent a compromise between delay and area. Those intermediate cases take advantage of both pipelining and parallelism to reduce delay, while consuming reasonable hardware resources.

Table 3. Pipeline architecture evaluation.

Comparison Criterion	Design–1			Design–2			Design–3		
	1-byte	4-byte	16-byte	1-byte	4-byte	16-byte	1-byte	4-byte	16-byte
Number of Iterations, m	16	4	1	16	4	1	16	4	1
Stage 1: Group decoding delay(ns)	3.2	0.8	0.2	3.2	0.8	0.2	3.2	0.8	0.2
Stage 2: Row/Col decoding delay(ns)	3.2	0.8	0.2	3.2	0.8	0.2	3.3	0.8	0.2
Stage 3: Multiplexers delay(ns)	9.6	2.4	0.6	8	2	0.5	3.2	0.8	0.2
Maximum stage delay normalized, t	48	12	3	40	10	2.5	16	4	1
Speed, S(n)	2.67	2	1	2.67	2	1	2.67	2	1
Throughput, T(n)	0.02	0.07	0.3	0.02	0.09	0.36	0.06	0.22	0.89
Efficiency, E(n)	0.89	0.67	0.33	0.89	0.67	0.33	0.89	0.67	0.33
Total delay (ns)	**16**	**4**	**1**	**14.4**	**3.6**	**0.9**	**9.6**	**2.4**	**0.6**
Total delay with pipelining (ns)	**5.99**	**2**	**1**	**5.39**	**1.8**	**0.9**	**3.6**	**1.2**	**0.6**

doi:10.1371/journal.pone.0138457.t003

The performance of all the three designs, with and without pipelined, are explained in this Sections and the results are listed in Table 4 in the next Section. In this table we compare our work with other recent related works in terms of power, area, area-power product and area-delay squared product with respect to target critical path delay. The next Section will show these comparisons in graphs.

Comparison

In this Section, we list all the proposed designs including pipelined design alongside other related works (Table 4). A comparison of the proposed designs with the state of the art substitution box implementations have been shown graphically. Delay and area values for the existing techniques are obtained from the survey done by Tillich et al [24]. As stated earlier our design is implemented as a combination of hardware look-up table and calculation of S-box, we simply compare our architecture with other recent literatures.

Table 4. Delay, Power and Area Comparisons.

Implementation		Area, A (GE)	Critical Path Delay, τ (ns)	Area Delay Squared Product Normalized, $A\tau^2$	Power Consumption (mW)	Area, Power Product Normalized
	Wolkerstorfer [5]	382.5	8	0.800	1.1	420.75
	Wong [18]	95	2.5	0.02	34.98	3323.1
	Bertoni [23]	1608.75	3	0.473	1.86	2992.3
	hw_lut [24]	1203.75	3	0.354	2.5	3009.4
	Tillich [24]	1912.5	4	1.000	1.57	3002.6
	Satoh [26]	360	9	0.953	30.55	10998
	Canright [27]	281.25	8	0.588	28.44	7999
	Elazm [28]	415.3	6	0.49	18.62	7732.8
	Shanthini [29]	99	6.275	0.127	503.9	49886.1
	Li [33]	1920	2.8	0.492	n/a	n/a
	Nabihah[34]	147	3.235	0.05	7.98	1173
	Hongge[36] (FPGA)	28BRAM + 544 LE	97	n/a	0.575	328.9
	Our Design (FPGA)	**57 Reg+16 LE**	**40**	**n/a**	**1.57**	**114.6**
First	1-byte	114	5.99	0.954	0.12	14
Proposed	4-byt e	456	2	0.238	0.5	228
Solution	16-byte	1824	1	0.060	2	3648
Second	1-byte	102	5.39	0.691	0.14	14
Proposed	4-byte	408	1.8	0.173	0.55	224.4
Solution	16-byte	1632	0.9	0.043	2.22	3624
Third	1-byte	66	3.6	0.199	0.21	14
Proposed	4-byte	264	1.2	0.050	0.83	219.12
Solution	16-byte	1056	0.6	0.012	3.33	3516

Note: normalization constant, X is found by the equation such as; $X \times V^2 \times f = P$, where p is the given power. Our delay data is pipelined.

doi:10.1371/journal.pone.0138457.t004

The work of Bertoni [23], Tillich [24] and Li [33] presents the hardware LUT implementations and reports a significant improvement in critical path delay along with low power at the expense of silicon area. Amongst three designs, Li's delay is minimum (Table 4) but large in size. As he decomposes the S-box with 32 small tables, his design requires a flag bit in each table. If the flag bit is 'on' the controller is kept waiting which results in delay and requires more area for this extra flag bit. This proposed architecture selects a group without checking any flag bit, thus reducing the delay. The area delay squared product graph (Fig 8) shows that our design performs much better compare to Li, Tillich and Bertoni' work.

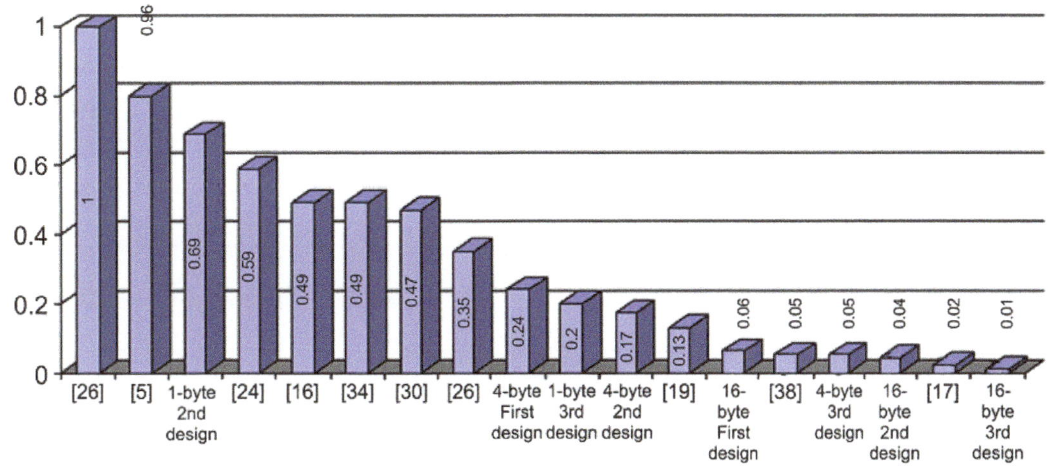

Figure 8. Area, delay squared product of different works.

The area-delay graph shows the better performance of our design when synthesized for a specific critical path delay (Fig 9). Each legend cites the functions in the same top–down order as they are contained in the respective Fig. The area is given in gate equivalents (GE) and calculated as total area divided by the size of a two-input NAND with the lowest drive strength (Table 2). Amongst the three implementations (at the bottom of the Fig 9), our proposed Design–3 is clearly the best. It has the smallest size out of all ten S-boxes. Though Wong's implementation has almost same silicon area, it suffers from a longer critical path. The other four designs including Nabihah [34] and Choi [35] are the calculating implementations and show smaller area than the other three works [24, 28, 33]. This is because they make use of the algebraic structure of the S-box to implement the substitution. On the other hand, these structures have a relatively long critical path. The shortest critical path can be achieved by hw_lut [24] and Li [33], but their size is about three to four times higher in magnitude than that of Proposed Design–3. That is because the synthesizer of proposed work has a much higher degree of freedom for optimizing the circuit, which allows for a shorter critical path.

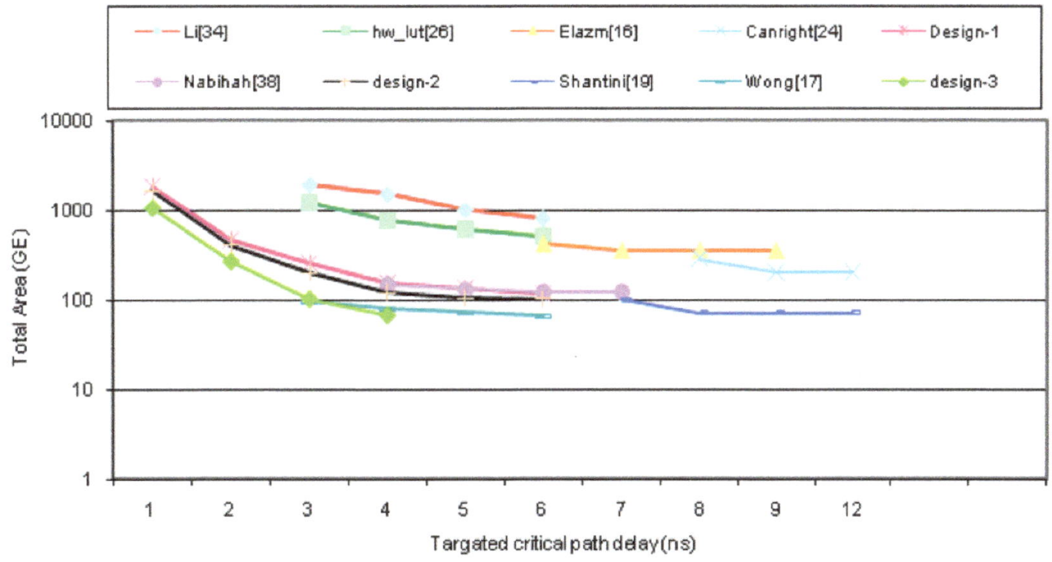

Figure 9. Area (GE) versus target value for critical path delay (ns).

There are seven designs including the proposed works have been plotted (Fig 10). The proposed design of FPGA implementation is also plotted against most recent FPGA implemented design of Hongge [36]. The FPGA implementation results much higher delay compare to CMOS implementation. Therefore, the delay is normalized by a factor of twenty. It is clearly shown that the power consumption of Hongge's design consumes much less power than the proposed design. This is because the reconfigurable architectures in cell array reduce the glitches in the routing paths. However, the critical path delay is more than twice that obtained in the proposed design. The reconfiguration cell array processing elements are connected to each other through the interconnect routing and switchbox in Hongge's design. The operation of SubBytes and XOR is implemented with internal cell of array. Due to the interconnected routing and more switching it has long delay and large area.

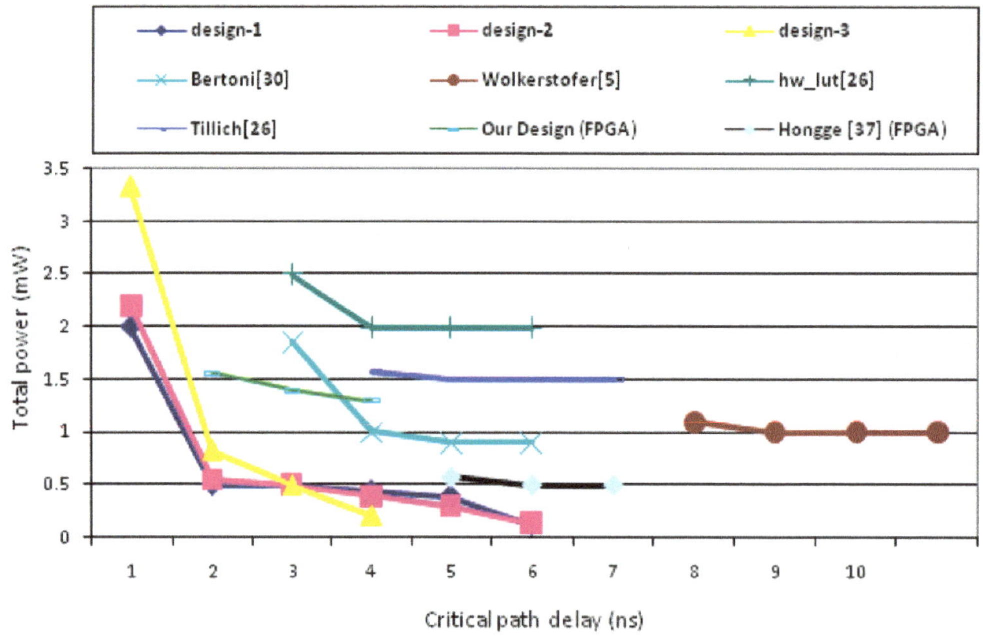

Figure 10. Total power vs. target critical path delay.

Moreover, all the proposed design outperformed the literatures [5, 23, 24]. A very close outcome is seen in Bertoni's design with an optimum critical path delay, but, the power consumption is around twice. Wilkertofer's s-box achieves similar results but the long critical path is a disadvantage. The other two approaches consume three times as much power as the proposed design, while hw-lut [24] consumes about four times more power.

Fig 11 shows the area-power consumption graph plotted against the target critical path delay. All the literatures are not shown in the graph because the normalized outcome of some literatures is too large compared to the proposed designs. It is clearly shown that the proposed design–3 has minimum area-power product compared to the designs [5, 18, 23, 24, 27, 28, 30,34]. The proposed design have less iteration or indexing as it has been broken down small tables. Furthermore, these ensure no extra internal flip flops in between transitions which in turn reduces the signal activities. Therefore, the signal activity within that particular path is low, which limits the overall power consumption. Amongst the eight, Wolkerster [5] shows less area power product compare to others, but suffering large critical path delay. The second better performance comes from Nabihah [34] with very good critical path delay. The area power product is slightly higher than Wolkerster's because the power consumption of [34] is seven times higher in magnitude due to calculation of S-box in combinational basis (polynomial basis).

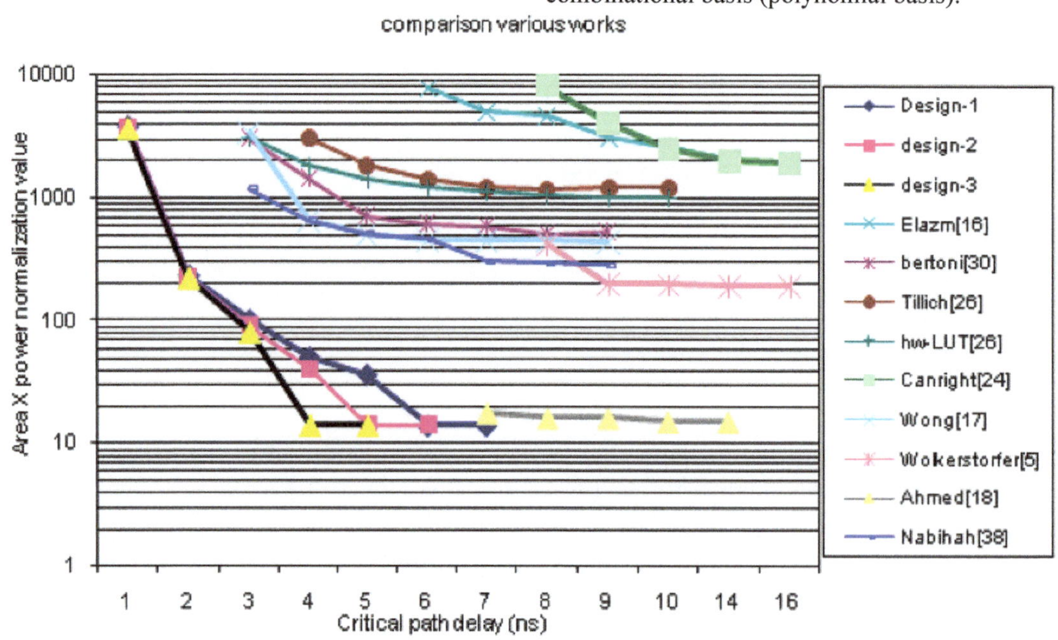

Figure 11. Area, power product vs. target critical path delay.

CONCLUSION

This paper discusses the design and simulation of a new AES byte substitution technique. It is initiated and implemented in three different hardware combinations in 0.35 μm CMOS technology. The design is also simulated in the Quartus-II simulator for an FPGA platform to determine its power, delay and area. The proposed pipeline architecture of S-box shows that the throughput can be maximized by reducing the delay of the critical path. Compared to other well-known previously reported techniques, the analysis of the results indicates that the proposed design is capable of significantly outperforming the existing solutions in terms of power, delay and area as measured by simulation.

ACKNOWLEDGMENTS

This material is based upon work supported by the Institute of Information and Communication Technology under Bangladesh University of Engineering and Technology. This contribution is acknowledged.

AUTHOR CONTRIBUTIONS

Conceived and designed the experiments: FSH. Performed the experiments: FSH. Analyzed the data: FSH MLA. Contributed reagents/materials/analysis tools: FSH MLA. Wrote the paper: FSH.

REFERENCES

1. Advanced encryption standard (AES). (2001) Federal Information Processing Standards Publication (FIPS PUB) 197, National Institute of Standards and Technology (NIST), Available: http://csrc.nist.gov/publication/drafts/dfips-AES.pdf.
2. Hodjat A, Verbauwhede I, (2005) A 21.54 Gbits/s Fully Pipelined AES Processor on FPGA. 12th IEEE Symposium on Field-Programmable Custom Computing Machines, pp-308-309.
3. Zhang X, Parhi KK. (2004) High-Speed VLSI Architectures for the AES Algorithm. IEEE Transaction on Very Large Scale Integration (VLSI) System, pp-45–52.
4. Hossain FS, Ali L, Roy N. (2010) Design and analysis of a high performance AES processor. International Conference on Topic(s): Bioengineering; Communication, Networking & Broadcasting; Computing & Processing (Hardware/Software), IEEE, pp. 562–565.
5. Wolkerstorfer J, Oswald E, Lamberger M. (2002) An ASIC Implementation of the AES SBoxes. Proceedings of the Cryptographer's Track at the RSA Conference on Topics in Cryptology, pp–67–78.
6. Rouvroy G, Standaert F, Quisquater J, Legat J. (2004) Compact and efficient encryption/decryption module for FPGA implementation of the AES Rijndael very well suited for small embedded applications. Information Technology: Coding and Computing, ITCC 2, pp- 583–587.
7. Good T, Benaissa M. (2006) Very small FPGA application-specific instruction processor for AES. IEEE Trans. Circuits System, pp- 1477–1486. doi: 10.1109/tcsi.2006.875179
8. .Granado-Criado J, Miguel A, Rodriguez V, Juan M, Perz S, Gomez-Pulido AJ. (2010) A new methodology to implement the AES algorithm using partial and dynamic reconfiguration, Integration. VLSI journal, Elsevier, pp-72–80. doi: 10.1016/j.vlsi.2009.05.003
9. Iko S, Men I, Schl F. (2008) Using Normal Bases for Compact Hardware Implementations of the AES S-box. Security and Cryptography for Networks, Springer Verlag, A lecture Notes in Computer Science, pp. 236–245.
10. Ahmad N, Hasan R, Jubadi WM. (2010) Design of AES S-box using combinational logic optimization, Symposium on Industrial Electronics & Applications (ISIEA), IEEE.
11. .Ming WM, Ling DWM. (2013) A new lightweight and high performance AES S-box using modular design. Int. Conf. on Circuits and Systems (ICCAS), IEEE.
12. Natale DG, Doulcier M, Flottes ML, Rouzeyre B. (2009) A Reliable Architecture for Parallel Implementations of the Advanced Encryption Standard. J Electron Test 25:269–278 doi: 10.1007/s10836-009-5106-6.
13. Hossain FS, Ali L, Roy N. (2010) Design and analysis of a high performance AES processor. International Conference on Electrical and Computer Engineering (ICECE), pp. 562–565.
14. Morioka S, Akashi A. (2003) An optimized S-box circuit architecture for low power AES design, Cryptographic Hardware and Embedded Systems-CHES, Springer Berlin Heidelberg, pp-172–186.
15. Wilton SJE, Ang S, Luk W. (2004) The Impact of Pipelining on Energy per Operation in Field-Programmable Gate Arrays. Conference on Field Programmable Logic and Application, pp- 719–728.
16. Zhang J, Zuo Q, Zhang T. (2007) Reducing the power consumption of the AES S-box by SSC. International Conference on Wireless Communications, Networking and Mobile Computing, WiCOM, pp- 2226–2229.
17. Zhang Y, Roivainen J, Mammela A. (2006) Clock-Gating in FPGAs: A Novel and Comparative Evaluation, Digital System Design: Architectures, Methods and Tools, EUROMICRO Conference, pp-584-590.
18. Wong M, Wong D. (2010) A high throughput low power compact AES S-box implementation using composite field arithmetic and Algebraic Normal Form representation. 2nd Asia Symposium on Quality Electronic Design (ASQED), pp-318-323.
19. Chow CT, Tsui LSM, Leong PS, Luk W, Wilton JSE. (2005) Dynamic voltage scaling for commercial FPGAs. Proceedings, IEEE International Confe-rence, pp-173-180.
20. Rejeb J, Lee T, Kaginele S. (2006) Compact and power conscious private-key cryptosystem for wireless devices. International Conference on Wireless and Mobile Communications, ICWMC, pp-88-91.

21. Maslennikow O, Rajewska M, Berezowski R. (2007) Hardware Realization of the AES Algorithm S-Block Functions in the Current-Mode Gate Technology. Proc. of the 9th Int. Experience of Designing and Application of CAD Systems in Microelectronics, IEEE Catalog Number 07EX1594, pp.211-217.

22. Rijmen V. (2002) Efficient Implementation of the Rijndael S-box [online]. Available:http://www.esat.kuleuven.ac.be/rijmen/rijndael/sbox.pdf.

23. Bertoni G, Macchetti M, Negri L, Frangneto P. (2004) Power-efficient ASIC Synthesis of Cryptographic Sboxes. Proc. of the 14th ACM Creat Lakes symposium on VLSI, GLSVLSI, ACM Press, pp. 277–281.

24. Tillich S, Feldhofer M, Popp T, Großschädl J. (2008) Area, delay, and power characteristics of standard-cell implementations of the AES S-box. Journal Sign Process System doi: 10.1007/s11265-007-0158-2, pp. 251–261.

25. Kamel D, Standaert F. (2009) Scaling trends of the AES S-box low power consumption in 130 and 65 nm CMOS technology nodes. IEEE international symposium on circuits and system, pp- 1385–1388.

26. Satoh A, Morioka S, Takano K, Munetoh S. (2001) A compact Rijndael hardware architecture with S-box optimization. Advances in Cryptology, ASIACRYPT, LNCS, pp. 239–254.

27. Canright D. (2005) A very compact S-box for AES. Cryptographic Hardware and Embedded Systems, CHES, Springer Verlag, 3659 of Lecture Notes in Computer Science, pp. 441–455.

28. Elazm LA, El-Moursy MA, Elsimary H, Dessouky IM, Shawki F. (2010) High speed low power composite field SBOX. 5th International conference on Design and Test Workshop (IDT), PP-24-27.

29. Shanthini M, Rajasekar P, Mangalam H. (2014) Design of low power S-box in Architecture Level using GF. International journal of engineering research and general science (IJERG), pp-1–9.

30. Hossain FS, Ali L, Abedin Syed MA. (2011) Design of a very low power and High Throughput AES Processor. IEEE conference on Computer and Information Technology (ICCIT), doi: 10.1109/ICCITechn.2011.6164810 pp. 339–343.

31. Abd-El-Barr M, El-Rewini H. (2005) Fundamentals of computer organization and architecture. Wiley, Hoboken, N.J.

32. AMS Corp., Specialty Process 0.35µm CMOS Application Notes, Austria, [Online]. Available: http://www.ams.com/eng/Products/Full-Service-Foundry/Process-Technology/CMOS/0.35-m-CMOS-Application-Notes.

33. Li H. (2004) A parallel S-box architecture for AES byte substitution. Int. Conf. on Communications, Circuits and Systems, ICCCAS, pp. 1–3.

34. Nabihah A, Rezaul Hasan SM. (2014) Low-power compact composite field AESS-box/InvS-box design in 65 nm CMOS using Novel XOR Gate INTEGRATION, the VLSI journal 46. doi: 10.1016/j.vlsi.2012.06.002

35. .Choi H, Choi JH, Kim J. (2008) Low power AES design using parallel architecture. International conf. on Convergence and hybrid information technology, pp-413–416.

36. Hongge L, Jinpeng D, Yongjun P. (2012) Cell array reconfigurable architecture for high-efficiency AES system, Microelectronics Reliability 52, pp–2829–2836. doi: 10.1016/j.microrel.2012.04.020

CHAPTER 18

SIGNIFICANCE OF POLARIZATION CHARGES AND ISOMAGNETIC SURFACE IN MAGNETOHYDRO-DYNAMICS

Zhu-Xing Liang[1] and Yi Liang[2]

[1]18-4-102 Shuixiehuadu, Zhufengdajie, Shijiazhuang, Hebei, 050035, China
[2]University of California San Diego, UNITED STATES

ABSTRACT

From the frozen-in field lines concept, a highly conducting fluid can move freely along, but not traverse to, magnetic field lines. We discuss this topic and find that in the study of the frozen-in field lines concept, the effects of inductive and capacitive reactance have been omitted. When admitted, the relationships among the motional electromotive field, the induced electric field, the eddy electric current, and the magnetic field becomes clearer. We emphasize the importance of isomagnetic surfaces and polarization charges, and show analytically that whether a conducting fluid can freely traverse magnetic field lines or not depends solely on the magnetic gradient along the path of the fluid. If a fluid does not change its density distribution and shape (can be regarded as a quasi-rigid body) and moves along isomagnetic surface, it can freely traverse magnetic field lines without any magnetic drag, no matter how strong the magnetic field is. Besides theoretical analysis, we also present experimental results to support our analysis. The main purpose of this work is to correct a fallacy among some astrophysicists.

INTRODUCTION

The concept of frozen-in magnetic field originated from Alfvén [1] is often used in plasma physics and magnetohydrodynamics (MHD). This concept and the concept of conservation of magnetic flux are often referred to collectively as Alfvén's Theorem. The concept of frozen-in field lines has been presented in various forms. A common interpretation is that a highly conducting fluid can move freely along, but cannot freely traverse, magnetic field lines. Because the frozen-in concept is of prime importance in MHD theory, it is widely mentioned in the literature [2, 3], and presented in many books of MHD and plasma physics [4–8]. Although the applicability of this concept has long been contested [3, 9], and Alfvén, the concept's founder, also criticized its use and stated that it is often misleading [10, 11], it still plays an important role, specially in astrophysics. Here we present experimental and analytical evidence to support a conclusion that the concept of frozen-in field lines should not be used in MHD.

It has been established by Bellan that under certain conditions, a highly conducting fluid can freely cross magnetic field lines [12]. Here we develop and extend Bellan's viewpoint.

Citation: Liang Z-X, Liang Y (2015) Significance of Polarization Charges and Isomagnetic Surface in Magnetohydrodynamics. PLoS ONE 10(8): e0136936. doi:10.1371/journal.pone.0136936

ANALYSIS ON THE INTERACTION BETWEEN CONDUCTING FLUID AND MAGNETIC FIELD LINES

For convenience, the term "fluid" used in the following means an ideal conducting fluid.

Although the concept of frozen-in field lines is often used by some authors, it currently lacks a specific definition. The following two definitions are familiar to many readers.

1. The magnetic flux through a fluid is conserved (we designate this definition "conservation theorem").
2. Any motion of the fluid perpendicular to the field lines carries the field lines with the fluid (we designate this definition "frozen theorem"). This frozen theorem is often presented in another form: "a fluid cannot freely traverse magnetic field lines."

Magnetic flux can be conserved in both scenarios:

1. All field lines within a fluid move along with the fluid.
2. The number of field lines entering a given fluid equals that leaving it at any instant.

Hence the two theorems are actually not equivalent. We accept the conservation theorem but question the frozen theorem.

There is a corollary to the frozen theorem: At low beta where the magnetic field is strong and produced by external coils, one pictures the fluid being pushed around by the magnetic field (so if the field is stationary, so is the fluid), while at high beta where the magnetic field is weak, one pictures the fluid pushing the magnetic field around. In either case, the magnetic field and the fluid move together. Note that this corollary and the frozen theorem include two notions:

1. Under the conditions that the external magnetic body and its magnetic field are stationary, if a fluid moves perpendicularly to the field lines, the field lines must bend and exert a resistive force on the fluid.
2. The magnitude of the resistive force exerted on the fluid depends on the magnetic field strength. The stronger the magnetic field, the greater the resistive force.

It is indisputable that in most cases when a fluid traverses a magnetic field, a resistive force will be exerted on the fluid. However, this does not mean that the traverse motion must result in the appearance of magnetic drag. In this paper, we seek those special conditions under which a fluid can freely traverse magnetic field without any magnetic drag, no matter how strong the magnetic field is.

Condition for Fluid's Freely Traversing Magnetic Field Lines

The frozen theorem follows from the evolution equation of the magnetic field (also referred to as frozen-in field equation)

$$\frac{\partial \mathbf{B}}{\partial t} = \nabla \times (\mathbf{u} \times \mathbf{B}), \quad \textbf{(1)}$$

where $\mathbf{u}$ is the relative velocity of the fluid element moving through the magnetic field $\mathbf{B}$, and $\mathbf{u}\times \mathbf{B}$ is the motional electromotive field. Eq (1) describes the evolution (namely turbulence) of the magnetic field with fluid motion traversing the magnetic field.

From Eq (1), we realize that

1. For any spatial position passed by a fluid, the magnetic evolution depends on the crossing motion of the fluid. Without crossing motion, there must be no magnetic evolution; and
2. Even a fluid crosses a magnetic field, namely $\mathbf{u} \times \mathbf{B} \neq 0$, as long as $\nabla \times (\mathbf{u} \times \mathbf{B}) = 0$, there must be no magnetic evolution.

This indicates that field-line crossing is a necessary, but not sufficient, condition for magnetic evolution. The magnetic evolution arising from the motion of the fluid always co-exists with magnetic drag and neither phenomenon can appear alone, because both arise from one and the same eddy current. Therefore, field-line crossing is also a necessary but not sufficient condition for magnetic drag. In other words, even if fluid crosses a magnetic field, i.e. $\mathbf{u} \times \mathbf{B} \neq 0$, the magnetic evolution and magnetic drag can be absent as long as the condition $\nabla \times (\mathbf{u} \times \mathbf{B}) = 0$ is satisfied.

It is known that the essential condition for a force acting between the fluid and the magnetic field is the presence of an eddy current within the fluid, whereas the essential condition for the presence of eddy current is the presence of an eddy motional electromotive field $\mathbf{u} \times \mathbf{B}$. When both sides of Eq (1) are zero, the motional electromotive field within the fluid is irrotational. In this case, neither an eddy motional electromotive field nor an eddy current exists in the fluid. Consequently, no magnetic force is exerted on the fluid when it crosses a magnetic field with velocity $\mathbf{u}$.

Now, the purpose to determine the condition under which a fluid can freely traverse magnetic field without magnetic drag turns into another one to determine the condition under which both sides of Eq (1) are equal to zero. To solve the latter problem, we expand Eq (1) as

$$\frac{\partial \mathbf{B}}{\partial t} = \mathbf{u}(\nabla \cdot \mathbf{B}) - \mathbf{B}(\nabla \cdot \mathbf{u}) - (\mathbf{u} \cdot \nabla)\mathbf{B} + (\mathbf{B} \cdot \nabla)\mathbf{u}. \quad \textbf{(2)}$$

The first term on the right-hand side involves the divergence of the magnetic field $\nabla \cdot \mathbf{B}$, which, according to Maxwell's equation, is always zero.

The factor $\nabla \cdot \mathbf{u}$ in the second term is the divergence of the velocity field. If the density distribution of the fluid remains constant, this term also equals zero.

When each fluid element moves along an isomagnetic surface, the third term $(\mathbf{u} \cdot \nabla)\mathbf{B}$vanishes.

If the fluid elements that synchronously cross the same magnetic field line have the same velocity (i.e., do not exhibit differential movement), the fourth term $(\mathbf{B} \cdot \nabla)\mathbf{u}$ vanishes too. In general, the differential movement is related to a change in shape of the fluid.

Eq (2) incorporates three essential factors that control the interaction between fluid and magnetic field:

1. The expansion or compression of the fluid, i.e., the change in density;
2. The differential movement of the fluid, i.e., the change in shape of the fluid; and

3. The change in magnetic field along the path of fluid's movement.

These essential factors indicate that the so-called frozen-in phenomenon in reality relates to some changes. Without these changes, the frozen-in phenomenon cannot appear.

If a fluid does not change its density distribution and shape, it can be regarded as a quasi-rigid body. The following simple law applies: When crossing a magnetic field along isomagnetic surface, a rigid or quasi-rigid body will not be subject to any magnetic force, no matter how strong the magnetic field is and how fast the fluid moves. This law fits the scenarios shown in Figs 1, 2 and 3. The three scenarios share two characteristics:

1. All of the fluid elements cross the magnetic field along isomagnetic surfaces.
2. The motional electromotive field **u** × **B** inside the fluid is everywhere nonzero but curl-free.

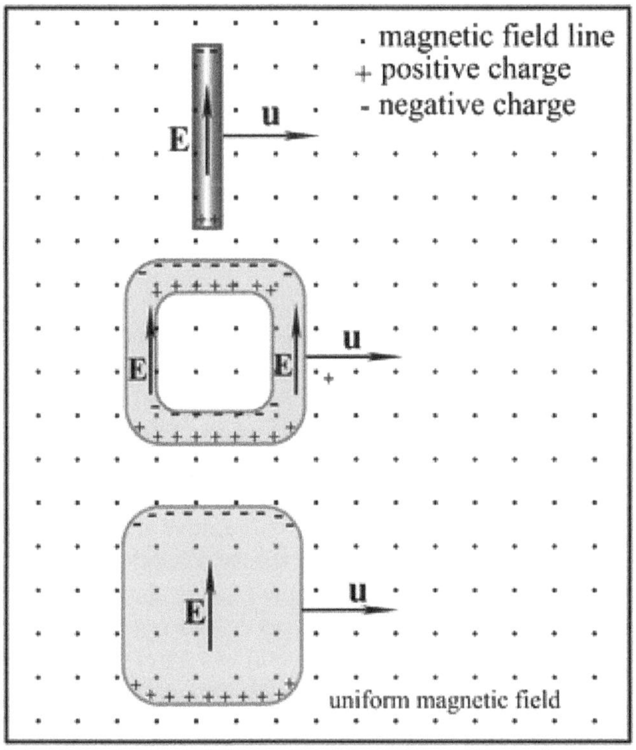

Figure 1. First non-frozen scenario.

Moving across a uniform magnetic field, a fluid experiences no magnetic drag. Here, the distributions of the charges and electric fields have been simplified.

In a cylindrically symmetric magnetic field, the fluid rotation around the magnetic axis would not result in frozen-in drag, even if the outer and inner fluids rotate at different angular speeds. This scenario mirrors the situation near the equatorial plane of aligned pulsar or the Sun.

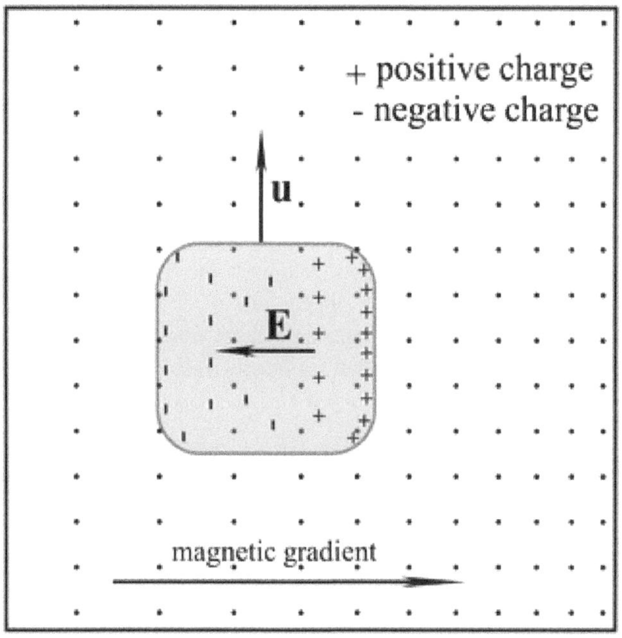

Figure 2. Second non-frozen scenario.

When a fluid moves across non-uniform magnetic field, there is no frozen-in effect provided the fluid elements move along isomagnetic surfaces.

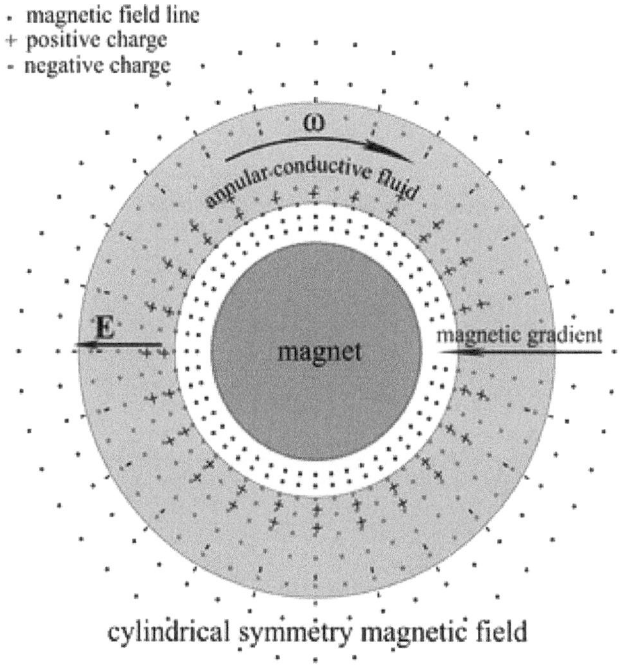

Figure 3. Third non-frozen scenario.

For the case shown in Fig 3, even if the outer and inner fluids rotate at different angular speeds, i.e. $\omega = f(r)$, no magnetic force acts on the fluid. However, if the differential rotation can be described as $\omega = f(z)$ (z is the axial coordinate), a magnetic force will act on the fluid. This distinction arises from the fourth term of the right-hand side of Eq (2). If $\omega = f(r)$, then $(\mathbf{B} \cdot \nabla)\mathbf{u} = 0$ and no magnetic force appears; if $\omega = f(z)$, then $(\mathbf{B} \cdot \nabla)\mathbf{u} \neq 0$ and a magnetic drag will appear. This result is consistent with the law of iso-rotation (Ferraro's theorem) which states that in the steady state, angular velocity is constant along magnetic lines [13]. If $\omega = f(r)$, the angular velocity varies only along the direction perpendicular to the field lines. In this situation, although the fluid is no longer quasi-rigid because of the appearance of differential rotation, it can still traverse magnetic field lines freely. This indicates that the constraint condition of "quasi-rigid" can be softened to a certain extent.

Alfvén & Fälthammar has described an example similar to that in Fig 1, for which the fluid can cross a uniform magnetic field under certain conditions [13]. Our work extends this idea by softening the constraint conditions for other cases of non-uniform magnetic field and/or differential rotation of the fluids.

Because the case shown in Fig 3 illustrates the situation in the vicinity of the equatorial plane of an aligned pulsar, we come to an important conclusion: the plasma near the equatorial plane of an aligned pulsar can cross the magnetic field and cannot be frozen with the magnetic field lines. In other words, the plasma can neither drive the magnetic field lines, nor be driven by the magnetic field lines. This conclusion is supported by the results of our magnetohydrodynamic experiments (see the section: Experiments on the isomagnetic surface).

Figs 1, 2 and 3 do not include all of the scenarios in which fluid can freely cross magnetic field lines. The conditions in the three scenarios merely ensure that all terms of the right-hand side of Eq (2) are zero. More generally, even if some terms are non-zero, so long as the terms sum to zero, the fluid can freely cross the magnetic field lines. For example, if a fluid element undergoes an apropos expansion rate, it can cross magnetic field lines against the direction of magnetic gradient.

Fig 4 shows a scenario in which the fluid experiences magnetic drag and results in magnetic evolution. When compare Fig 2 with Fig 4, the significance of isomagnetic surface can be seen clearly.

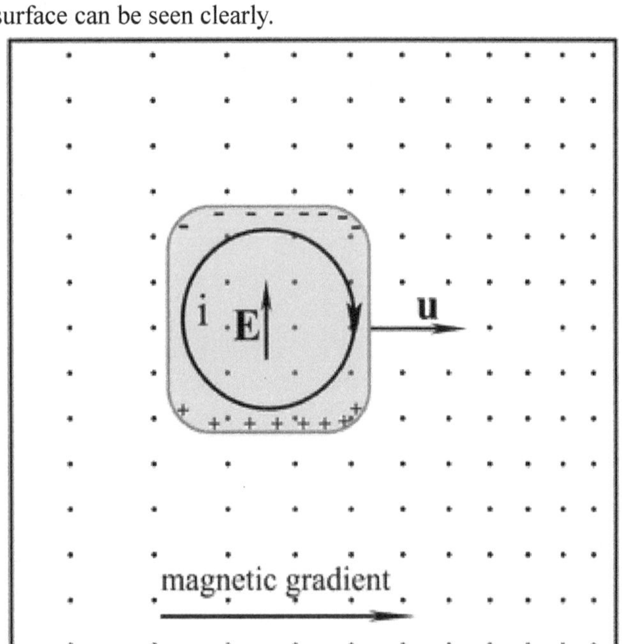

Figure 4. Magnetically frozen scenario.

If the fluid velocity has a component in the direction of the magnetic field gradient, the fluid movement will result in a magnetic evolution and magnetic drag. The field lines caused by the eddy current were not illustrated.

If a magnetic field changes in the direction of fluid movement, the fluid will generally experience drag. In particular, if the length of fluid along the direction of its motion is greater than the extent of the magnetic field, magnetic drag is inevitable at the magnetic boundary because the magnetic field changes sharply and the magnetic gradient is very high there.

Now, it has been clear that when a quasi-rigid fluid crosses a uniform magnetic field, the system is always force-free, no matter what velocity the fluid is moving with and how strong the magnetic field is. On the other hand, every steady magnetic field can be regarded as a superposition of uniform and non-uniform components and only the non-uniform component may, not must, result in magnetic drag. From this perspective, we can clearly understand the interaction between fluid and magnetic field and avoid to be misled by the frozen theorem.

Effects of the Polarization Charges and Polarization Electrostatic Field

The following equation describes the distribution of polarization charges inside the fluid:

$$\frac{q}{\epsilon_0} = -\nabla \cdot (\mathbf{u} \times \mathbf{B}). \quad (3)$$

In MHD literature, it seems that this equation is often belittled [14] even discarded from the MHD equations [15]. This might arise from the concept that conducting fluid is always electrically neutral anywhere inside a conducting fluid. In fact, the interaction between the fluid and the magnetic field can destroy the electrical neutrality and result in the appearance of surplus positive or negative charges inside the fluid. Especially, under the special conditions (such as Figs 1, 2 and 3), the fluid's moving along the isomagnetic surface can result in neither magnetic disturbance nor magnetic force, but can result in electric field and surplus charges to appear in the systems. In these special cases, only the effects of the electric field and charges are noteworthy. Their importance can be shown by two examples. First, in the magnetosphere of pulsars, the density distribution of charges has been studied by Goldreich & Julian [16] and known by pulsar scientists as Goldreich-Julian density [17]. Second,the output voltage of magnetohydrodynamic generator is just caused by the induced electric field.

This demonstrates that in some cases, the electrical neutrality approximation must be abandoned and the effects of the electric field and charges must be considered.

According to conventional physics, a straight wire, closed wire or conducting plate (see Fig 1) moving perpendicularly in a uniform magnetic field can neither produce electric current nor experience drag from the magnetic field. Thus, the magnetic field lines were not considered to be frozen within the conductors. Because this phenomenon is independent of the type or conductivity of the materials, even if the objects shown in Fig 1 comprise fluid such as mercury or plasma, the frozen-in effect does not apply. However, in the MHD theory, the fluids in Fig 1 will be considered to be frozen in the magnetic field and cannot cross freely through the field lines.

This presents an apparent contradiction between conventional physics and MHD theory.

In previous studies on the frozen-in effect, the effects of the polarization charges and electrostatic field **E** (all the electric field mentioned in this paper is the lab frame electric field) shown in Figs 1, 2 and 3 have been disregarded. In fact, it is the electric field **E** that produces a fluid drift and "thaws" the magnetic-frozen states. A simple calculation using the drift theory of charged particles [5] verifies that the drift velocity of both the ions and electrons produced by **E** and **B** is always equal to the macroscopic moving velocity of the fluid, i.e., $\mathbf{v}_{drift} = (\mathbf{E} \times \mathbf{B})/B^2 \equiv \mathbf{u}$ [18, 19].

Bellan [12] has demonstrated that a plasma immersed in a static magnetic field **B** and a static electric field **E**, with **E** perpendicular to **B**, will freely drift across the magnetic field lines. Based on Bellan's viewpoint, we claim that the static electric field **E**, which is established by polarization charges, can naturally appear under certain conditions. The process by which this can occur is summarized below:

- A fluid moving across the magnetic field lines induces an irrotational motional electromotive field $\mathbf{u} \times \mathbf{B}$ inside the fluid;
- As a result of this irrotational motional electromotive field, polarization charges appear inside the fluid or its boundaries;
- The polarization charges result in a static polarization electric field, and the motional electromotive field is balanced by the polarization electric field, $\mathbf{E} = -\mathbf{u} \times \mathbf{B}$;
- **E** combines with **B** to "force" all the particles (ions and electrons) to drift with velocity$\mathbf{v}_{drift}$ equal to **u**. Namely, the velocity of the guiding-center drift equal to the motion velocity of the fluid.

Finally, the system is force-free and the fluid can move freely as the magnetic field is absent.

When an individual charged particle travels through a magnetic field, it is subject to Lorentz forces which compel it to gyrate around the magnetic field lines. However, within a fluid, the presence of both polarization charges and electric field create a very different situation. Under some special conditions, such as those illustrated in Figs 1, 2 and 3, the static electric field produced by the polarization charges can counteract the Lorentz force and the fluid elements will drift across the magnetic field lines without any drag.

In the situations shown in Figs 1, 2 and 3, the relative velocity between the fluids and the field lines cannot be determined by magnetism method, because the magnetic fields have no evolution. However, it is incorrect to think the relative velocity is arbitrary, even zero (frozen-in), because the relative velocity can be determined by electrical method. For example, by measuring the output voltage of a magneto hydrodynamic generator, the relative velocity can be determined.

Infinite Conductivity vs. Finite Current

There is an opinion in some books [5–7] whose typical description is following [8]:

Because the conductivity of ideal conducting fluid is infinite, if the induced electric field appears inside the fluid, the induced current must be infinite. Hence the induced electric field cannot appear inside the ideal conducting fluid.

Their opinion is incorrect and the root of this mistake is that the Ohm's law ($I = V/R$ or $\mathbf{J} = \sigma \mathbf{E}$) was incorrectly used to the non-steady or open circuit system.

From electrical engineering we know that in a non-steady circuit system, beside resistance, inductive and capacitive reactance can also restrain the current growth. In other words, it is the complex impedance (not only the resistance) that controls the current growth. This law is also valid in MHD field because the electric field, current, and magnetic field are generally time-variant. It is similar that in the DC circuit, only resistance is considered, but for the AC circuit, the reactance must be considered. Below, we show how the inductive reactance and capacitive reactance restrain the current growth and why the fluid can traverse magnetic field lines.

When a fluid traverses magnetic field lines, a motional electromotive field $\mathbf{u} \times \mathbf{B}$ must appear to drive a current to grow. At the same time, an induced electric field **E** immediately appears to restrain the current growth and makes the current always finite. The relation between them is $\mathbf{E} = -\mathbf{u} \times \mathbf{B}$. Since the motional electromotive field $\mathbf{u} \times \mathbf{B}$ has two components, rotational and irrotational components, the induced electric field **E** has two components too.

The rotational component of the motional electromotive field is $\nabla \times (\mathbf{u} \times \mathbf{B})$. The opposite component of the induced electric field is $\nabla \times \mathbf{E} = -\partial \mathbf{B}/\partial t$. This induced electric field component is caused by the time-variant magnetic field. The time-variant magnetic field is caused by the time-variant eddy current and this eddy current is caused by the rotational motional electromotive field. As long as the direction of $\nabla \times (\mathbf{u} \times \mathbf{B})$ does not reverse, the eddy current will grow continually. But the rate of growth depends on the inductive reactance. In a real system, the magnetic field caused by the eddy current only offsets the change of the external magnetic field along the motion path and conserves the magnetic flux; so the eddy current must be finite unless the external magnetic field can become infinitely strong. From that, it is the inductive reactance that restrain the eddy current to be always finite inside the ideal conducting fluid.

When a rotational electric field appears inside an ideal conducting fluid, the system must be evolutive. The Ohm's law cannot be used in such non-steady system.

The irrotational component of the motional electromotive field is $\nabla \cdot (\mathbf{u} \times \mathbf{B})$ and the opposite component of induced electric field is $\nabla \cdot \mathbf{E} = q/\epsilon_0$. This induced electric field component is caused by the polarization charges and the polarization is driven by the irrotational motional electromotive field. As long as a fluid traverses a magnetic field, this irrotational component of the induced electric field is always non-zero as shown in Figs 1–4. Because relating usually to slow variation the capacitive reactance is very high, so that the capacitive current can usually be ignored. Namely, it is the capacitive reactance that restrain the irrotational current. For the isolated fluids as shown in Figs 1, 2 and 3, we can regard them as batteries (but the chemical electromotive force is replaced by the motional electromotive force) without external circuit. The Ohm's law cannot be used in such open circuits.

However, the boundary conditions can affect the irrotational current. In the cases shown in Figs 1, 2 and 3, there are irrotational electric fields but no current. Now we assume to add an external wire connected to the two boundaries where the electrons accumulated. Will an electric current appear? There are two cases: First, if the external wire moves or rotates with the fluid and cuts the field lines, the induced electric field inside the fluid will counteract the one inside the wire and no current will appear; Second, if the external wire is stationary, induced current and magnetic drag will appear—this is just the principle of magnetohydrodynamic generator and homopolar generator. Significantly, even if in the second case, the induced electric field **E** and the motional electromotive field (**u** × **B**) are still nonzero.

Inside the conducting fluid (shaded area in Figs 1–4), it is correct to think always **E**+(**u** × **B**) = 0; but it is wrong to think always **E** = 0 and **u** × **B** = 0. When taking the inductive and capacitive reactances into account, we can understand why $\mathbf{E} \neq 0$ and $\mathbf{u} \times \mathbf{B} \neq 0$ would not result in an infinite current inside ideal conducting fluid.

From the above analyses, we can get following logical relation: If a fluid cannot traverse magnetic field lines, the motional electromotive field **u** × **B** must be equal to zero. If $\mathbf{u} \times \mathbf{B} \equiv 0$, the induced electric field **E** must be equal to zero. If $\mathbf{E} \equiv 0$, then $\partial \mathbf{B}/\partial t \equiv 0$ and $q \equiv 0$. In this manner, the evolution equations $\partial \mathbf{B}/\partial t = -\nabla \times (\mathbf{u} \times \mathbf{B})$ and $q = \epsilon_0 \nabla \cdot (\mathbf{u} \times \mathbf{B})$ will be meaningless.

All in all, the non-zero motional electromotive field caused by the fluid's traversing motion is the root of the system evolution and would not result in an infinite current. Supposing that the fluid freezes with the field lines and deny the field-line crossing, we will actually deny the system evolution. Therefore we have to accept the concept that a conducting fluid can traverse magnetic field lines. The field-line crossing is not only acceptable but also indispensable.

Problems arising from the Frozen Theorem

We have discussed that the fluid elements can freely cross magnetic field lines in the cases of the uniform magnetic field and quasi-rigid fluids. Other researchers [20], however, demonstrated that if the fluid elements are fixed on the magnetic field lines and move always together, Eq (1) is equally satisfied. Some researchers thus advocated that both choices are valid [21]: 1) the fluid moves across magnetic field lines; and 2) the fluid and the magnetic field lines move together (i.e. frozen theorem). However, following careful analysis, some problems will arise from the frozen theorem.

In previous discussions on the frozen theorem, attention has usually been devoted to only the fluid and the magnetic field lines inside the fluid. However, as long as the system studied is extended to also include the external magnet and the magnetic field lines outside the fluid (seeFig 5), we will see that contradictions are unavoidable.

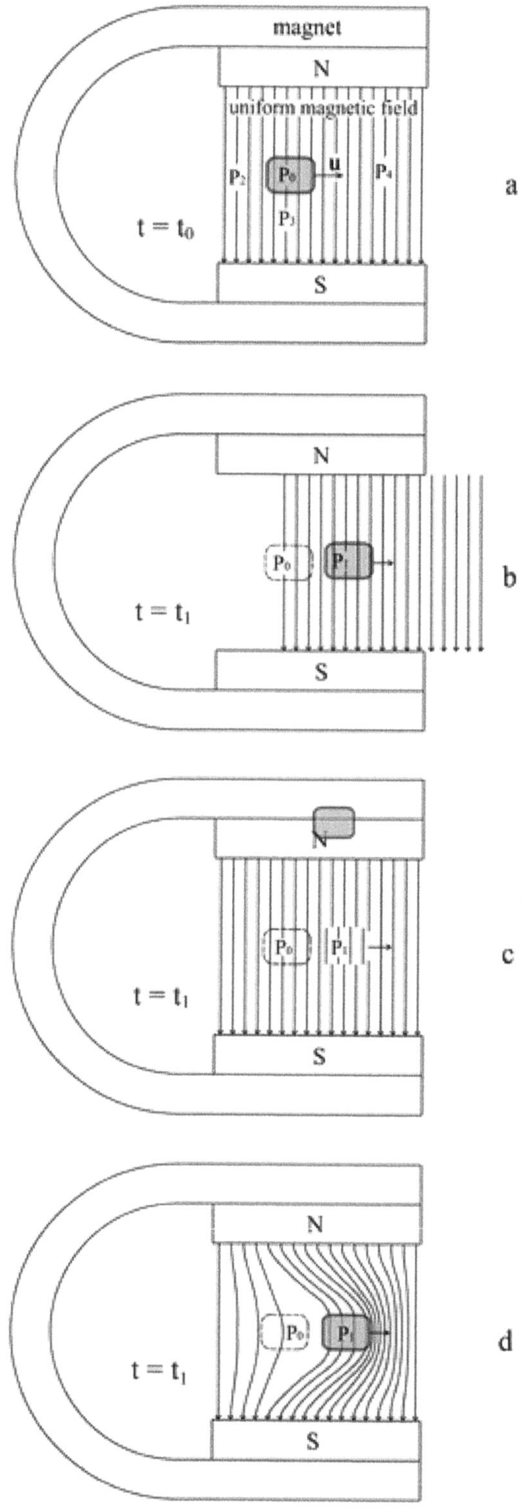

Figure 5. Different scenarios for the magnetic evolution outside a fluid.

(a) The fluid will move across the uniform magnetic field. (b) If the fluid can carry the field lines inside and outside the fluid with the same velocity, the field lines will translate and retain their shape. (c) If the fluid can carry only the field lines inside the fluid, the field lines will be repeatedly cut off and reconnected at the fluid boundary. (d) If the fluid can carry the field lines inside the fluid and all field lines remain continuous, the field will become non-uniform.

First, we assume that the magnetic field is uniform, the magnet is immobile and the quasi-rigid fluid moves with velocity **u** relative to the magnet, as shown in Fig 5a. Then we consider the changes of the magnetic field lines outside the fluid.

If the field lines outside the fluid respond to the fluid motion, only three possible solutions can be considered, as illustrated in Fig 5b, 5c and 5d.

1. In Fig 5b, all magnetic field lines outside the fluid translate with the fluid. As the velocities are identical everywhere, the configuration of the field lines cannot change and the field lines must be cut off at the boundary of the magnet. Apparently, this solution is unacceptable.

2. In Fig 5c, all the magnetic field lines outside the fluid are stationary relative to the magnet. In this scenario, the field lines must be cut off by the fluid boundary and must repeatedly reconnect. However, this result contradicts the alternative representation of the frozen theorem: "Any fluid element that is at one instant on a magnetic field line will be on the original magnetic field line at any other instant". Because a reconnected magnetic field line is not the original one, then the fluid cannot remain attached to the original magnetic field lines. If we accept that the magnetic field lines can be cut off, we have actually changed the frozen theorem to that any field-lines passing through fluid will be cut off by fluid's crossing motion. Apparently, this solution is also unacceptable.

3. In Fig 5d, the magnetic field lines outside the fluid are dragged by the fluid and change the magnetic field configuration. However, this configuration induces a magnetic evolution and magnetic drag, and is inconsistent with the analysis above. Therefore, it should be abandoned, too.

Some problems arisen from the misuse of the concept of moving field lines have been discussed by other researchers [18, 22]. With the help of our new visual angle and the analyses above, we conclude that, as long as the system studied is extended and the magnet and its field lines outside the fluid are also included, the frozen theorem always leads to contradictions.

Better Interpretation than the Frozen Theorem

We suggest using a better method to describe the relationship between moving fluid and magnetic field lines. When a fluid crosses a magnetic field along the isomagnetic surface, we can consider that the field lines are stationary with the magnet and the fluid crosses them freely. If a fluid crosses a non-uniform magnetic field along the direction of magnetic gradient, as shown in Fig 6a, we can still consider that the field lines caused by the external magnet are stationary, but the magnetic gradient creates an eddy current inside the fluid and the fluid has become a fluidic magnet. The field lines associated with this fluidic magnet are shown with dashed lines in Fig 6b.

When moving from P_0 to P_1, the fluid becomes a magnet, as shown in panel b. When the two magnetic fields in panel b are combined, the magnetic configuration can be illustrated as panel c.

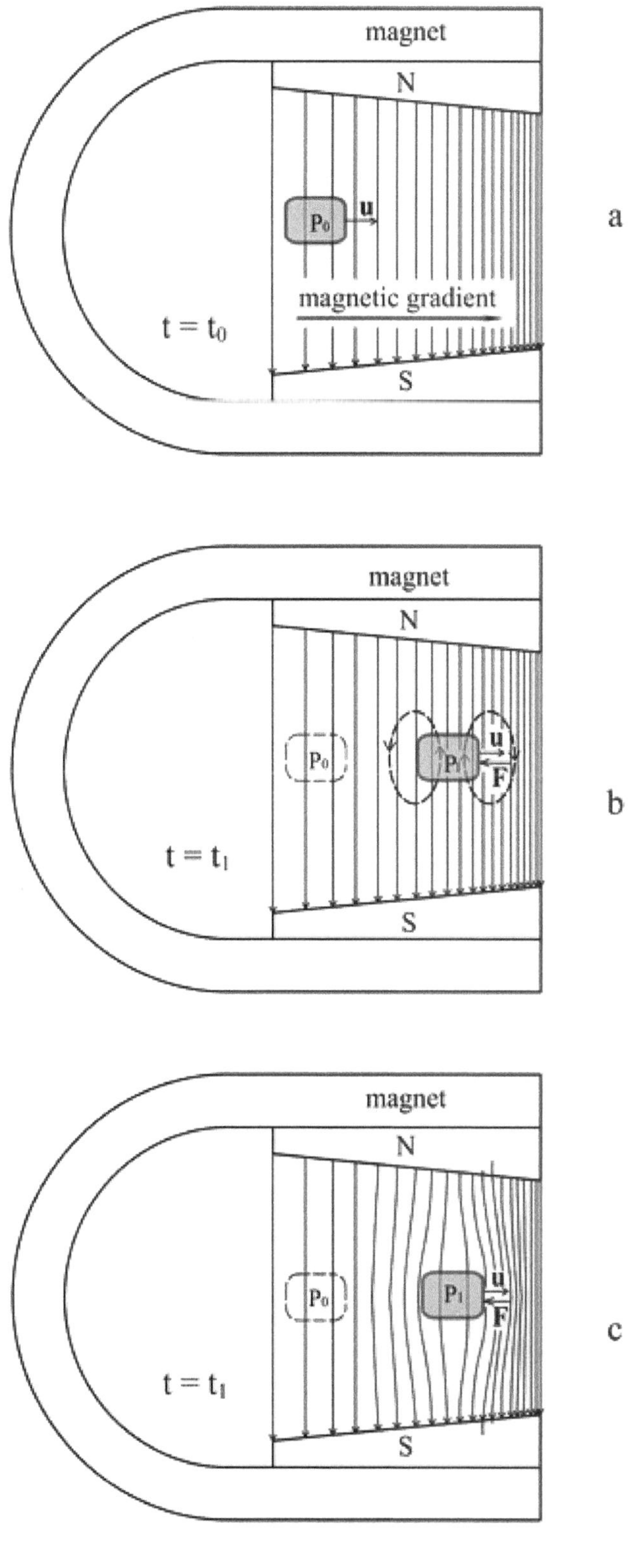

Figure 6. Two-magnet interpretation for the interaction between fluid and magnetic field lines.

The magnetic drag is, in fact, the force acting between the external magnet and the fluidic magnet. Although the forces acting on the front and rear sides of the fluid are always opposite, the magnetic gradient makes their magnitudes different. No matter what direction the fluid is moving, parallel or opposite to the magnetic gradient, the result of the forces is always opposite to the motion direction.

When the two magnetic fields are combined to form one field, Fig 6b becomes Fig 6c. The magnetic flux in the fluid remains constant but the magnetic configuration outside the fluid has changed compared with Fig 6a.

A notable point is that the dashed field lines at P_1 in Fig 6b are produced in P_1 instead of pulled from P_0, because these dashed magnetic field lines had not appeared when the fluid was at P_0. Therefore, this two-magnet interpretation needs neither frozen-in field lines nor moving field lines.

Under the condition that the fluid is a quasi-rigid body, this two-magnet interpretation infers the following:

1. When a fluid crosses magnetic field lines, eddy current can appear inside the fluid.
2. The eddy current turns the fluid into a fluidic magnet and causes an additional magnetic field to appear.
3. Because the two-magnets interact with each other, the magnetic drag appears.
4. The additional magnetic field always counteracts changes in magnetic flux caused by the external magnet and conserves the total flux inside the fluid.
5. The additional magnetic field will change the magnetic configuration outside the fluid.
6. Because the eddy current depends on the magnetic gradient, the effects above disappear outright if the fluid moves along the isomagnetic surface.

Compared with the frozen theorem, this two-magnet interpretation has the following strengths:

1. Using the two-magnet interpretation, we can clearly understand not only the magnetic conservation inside the fluid but also the magnetic variation outside the fluid.
2. The concept of magnetic reconnection has no longer been needed, even on the fluid boundary.
3. The problems shown in Fig 5b–5d can be avoided altogether.
4. Since this two-magnet interpretation emphasizes that the eddy current depends on the magnetic gradient, the importance of the isomagnetic surface become easier to understand.
5. Since this two-magnet interpretation emphasizes the field-lines crossing, it comes clear that the fluid motion causes the volume density distribution of the polarization charges.

Note that this interpretation is very different with the frozen theorem. As shown in Fig 6c, when the fluid moves from P_0 to P_1, the field lines to the left of P_1 grow denser instead of sparser. If the frozen theorem holds and field lines have been carried by the fluid from P_0 to P_1, the field lines there must become sparser and are similar to Fig 5d. Similarly, when the fluid moves left, ahead of the fluid, the field lines do not become denser; quite the reverse, they become sparser. This indicates that this two-magnet interpretation is not compatible with the frozen theorem. In other words, from the two concepts, we cannot derive identical evolution results for the magnetic field lines outside the fluid. Therefore, it is impossible maintain the two concepts concurrently and one must be abandoned.

Summary contrasts in tables

In Table 1, we contrast two cases and clarify the relationship between the electromagnetic phenomena and Eq (1).

Table 1. Contrast between two cases of Eq (1).

	case A	case B
both sides of Eq (1)	$=0$	$\neq 0$
property of magnetic field	steady magnetic field	time-varying magnetic field
eddy current in fluid	absence	presence
magnetic drag	absence	presence
illustration	Figs 1, 2 and 3	Fig 4

doi:10.1371/journal.pone.0136936.t001

For clarity, the analysis results of Eqs (1) and (3) are summarized in Table 2. Previous studies have mainly focused on those properties listed in column A and have overlooked all of the aspects listed in column B; that is, the frozen-in effect has been emphasized whereas the drift effect has been largely ignored.

Table 2. Summary of the analysis results of Eqs (1) and (3).

	magnetic freezing (column A)	magnetic "thaw"(column B)
correlative equations	$\partial \mathbf{B}/\partial t = \nabla \times (\mathbf{u} \times \mathbf{B})$	$q/\epsilon_0 = -\nabla \cdot (\mathbf{u} \times \mathbf{B})$
motional electromotive field parameter	curl	divergence
induction phenomena	inductive eddy current	polarization charges and electric field
correlative magnetic field parameter	magnetic field gradient	magnetic field strength
direction of fluid movement	parallel to magnetic gradient	perpendicular to magnetic gradient
effect of magnetic force	resisting the traversing motion	inducing field-line traversing
illustration	Fig 4	Figs 1, 2 and 3

doi:10.1371/journal.pone.0136936.t002

The frozen theorem was expressed in several forms, which are summarized in Table 3. All of the expressions listed in the right-hand column are derived from the frozen theorem, and hence are incorrect or incomplete.

Table 3. Summary of the expressions of the frozen theorem.

correct expressions	incorrect or incomplete expressions
The magnetic flux in any fluid element is conserved.	Any motion of fluid, perpendicular to the field lines, carries the field lines with the fluid.
Any two elements of the same fluid that are at one instant on a common magnetic field line will be on a common magnetic field line at any other instant [14, 23].	Any fluid element that is at one instant on a magnetic field line will be on the original magnetic field line at any other instant.
Quasi-rigid fluid can freely traverse magnetic field lines only along the isomagnetic surface.	A fluid cannot freely traverse magnetic field lines.

doi:10.1371/journal.pone.0136936.t003

EXPERIMENTS ON THE ISOMAGNETIC SURFACE

To verify the special significance of isomagnetic surface, we conducted a series of magnetohydrodynamic experiments. The configuration of the device is the same as that of Fig 3. For simplicity and clarity, the experiments were recorded and the videos can be viewed on YouTube or Tudou (for Chinese). Figs 7 and 8 depict the device configurations and the sizes of the main components. Apart from the magnet, all components are made of non-magnetic material (plastic or copper). The mercury was placed in a cylindrical trough surrounding a rotating platform. At the magnet surface, the magnetic field intensity is about 0.6 T. The rotational rates are shown in the relevant videos.

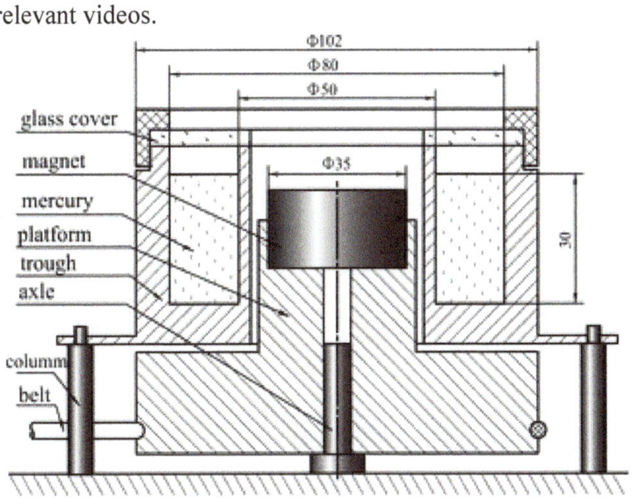

Figure 7. Schematic figure of drive experimental device.

The unit of length is millimeter. The belt drives the rotation of the platform and magnet; the other components are stationary.

The axis, support block, and the magnet are stationary. The belt drives the rotation of other parts.

The experiments were divided into two groups. The first group comprised three pairs of experiments to determine the conditions under which the magnet can drive rotation of the mercury. In each experiment the basis of comparison is an aligned magnetic rotator, a cylindrically symmetric magnet whose magnetic axis aligns with its rotation axis. The three experiments are as follows:

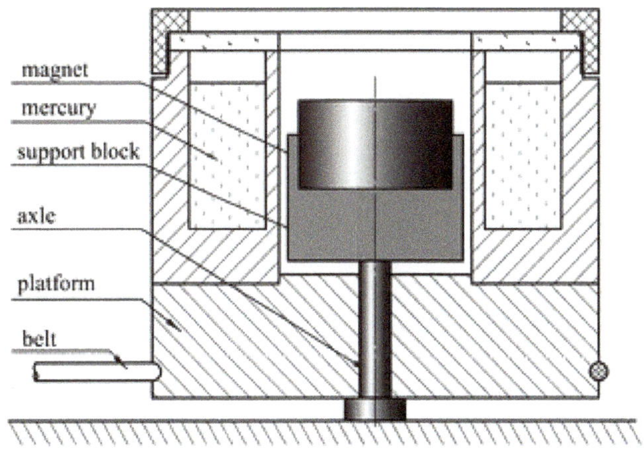

Figure 8. Schematic figure of braking experimental device.

1. Drive experiment A [24]. Revealed the contrast between the aligned rotator and a rotator with magnetic axis orthogonal to the rotation axis. This contrast test indicates that the transverse magnetic field can drive the mercury to rotate, but the aligned magnetic field cannot do that.
2. Drive experiment B [25]. Revealed the contrast between the aligned rotator and a magnet with magnetic axis parallel to, but displaced from the rotation axis. This contrast test indicates that the eccentricity magnetic field can drive the mercury, but the coaxial magnetic field cannot do that.
3. Drive experiment C [26]. Revealed the contrast between the aligned rotator and a magnet that is not cylindrically symmetric. This contrast test indicates that the cylindrically asymmetric magnetic field can drive the mercury, but the cylindrically symmetric magnetic field cannot do that.

The first group of experiments demonstrated that an aligned magnetic rotator cannot drive the mercury to rotate. However, this result has not proved the absence of the magnetic frozen effect in such cases, since this result can be attributed to another cause: the magnetic field lines don't co-rotate with the aligned magnetic rotator. When a magnet rotates around its own magnetic axis, whether the magnetic field corotates with the magnet has been a controversial issue. This issue is also named as Faraday paradox. Although most of astrophysicists think the magnetic field corotates with the magnet, we take the opposite point of view because it is accepted by the most of general physical scientists and supported by more experiments for Faraday paradox.

Fälthammar once pointed that field lines are not tangible objects that move in the normal sense. One cannot distinguish the axisymmetric field of a cylindrical magnet rotating about its axis from the field of a non-rotating magnet and so one cannot assign a rotation to the magnetic field lines [18]. Backus also pointed that no effect appears outside an aligned magnetic rotator [27]. Hence, the result cannot prove the absence of the magnetic frozen effect in the experiments above.

The value of these experiments is to answer the question: Can an aligned pulsar drive its plasma and achieve the co-rotation state? The answer is NO.

In the second group of experiments, the conditions under which rotating mercury can be slowed by a stationary magnet were determined. The mercury trough (rather than the central magnet) was spun until the mercury revolution reached a steady state. In each experiment the basis of comparison was an aligned magnet, a cylindrically symmetric magnet whose magnetic axis matched that of the mercury rotation axis. In this case, the mercury eventually revolved at the same rate as the trough. For the three comparison cases, braking forces reduced the rotation of the mercury. We used the same magnets in every pair of braking experiments, designated A, B and C and described below.

1. Braking experiment A [28]. Revealed the contrast between the aligned magnet and the orthogonal magnet. This contrast test indicates that the orthogonal magnetic field can slow down the mercury, but the aligned magnetic field cannot do that.
2. Braking experiment B [29]. Revealed the contrast between the aligned magnet and the off-axis magnet. This contrast test indicates that the eccentricity magnetic field can slow down the mercury, but the aligned magnetic field cannot do that.
3. Braking experiment C [30]. Revealed the contrast between the aligned magnet and the cylindrically asymmetric magnet. This contrast test indicates that the cylindrically asymmetric magnetic field can slow down the mercury, but the cylindrically symmetric magnetic field cannot do that.

The braking experiments demonstrated that even if the magnetic field is non-uniform, fluid can experience no frozen-in effect, as long as all of the fluid elements move along isomagnetic surface. Thereby, the analyses for Fig 3 have been corroborated by our experimental results.

These experimental results have verified the special significance of isomagnetic surface: Along isomagnetic surface, a magnetic field can neither drive nor brake conducting fluid.

DISCUSSION

Our ideas are embodied in the following quote from Feynman et al. [31]: "It makes no sense to say something like: When I move a magnet, it takes its field with it, so the lines of **B** are also moved. There is no way to make sense, in general, out of the idea of 'the speed of a moving field line.'"

In fact, a magnetic field essentially cannot be ascribed a movement. Time-varying magnetic fields exist, whereas moving ones do not. While it can be intuitive and useful to regard magnetic field lines as moving, this approach is often unsafe as discussed by Fälthammar & Mozer [18].

In conventional physics, certain electromagnetic problems have been correctly solved by assuming moving field lines. But in those situations, the magnetic poles always move with the field lines. By contrast, typical discourses on the frozen theorem did not clarify whether the magnetic source body is in motion or at rest. If the external magnet is at rest (generally the default condition), the assumption that the field lines are movable always makes the physics more complex and even leads to wrong results. Herein lies the root of the problem caused by the frozen theorem.

For some astrophysical objects, the magnetic field may be very strong, but the magnetic gradient in the direction of the plasma movement is usually very small, especially for the cases similar to that shown in Fig 3. Consequently, the effect of magnetic drag should be much weaker than that expected and the plasma can in fact freely cross the magnetic field lines. In other words, in some astrophysical objects, the magnetic frozen-in effect can be ignored provided that the magnetic gradient along the path of plasma movement can be ignored.

Magnetic confinement technology has been widely applied in nuclear fusion engineering. In those devices, plasma is restrained in the magnetic beam and cannot move laterally. One interpretation for this phenomenon is that the very strong magnetic field restrains the plasma. Actually, it is the transverse magnetic gradient that does the restraining, especially near the boundary surface of the magnetic beam. Any uniform magnetic field, regardless of strength, cannot restrain a conductive substance. But some people think that at low beta where the magnetic field is strong, the fluid will be pushed around by the magnetic field lines and if the field is stationary, so is the fluid. The reason why some people think so may be that they were misled by the frozen theorem.

When the magnetic evolution and magnetic drag are the study objects, the electrical neutrality is indeed an excellent approximation. However, when the drift of fluid particles and fluid's crossing motion are concerned, we must pay more attention to the electric field and the charges distribution. In the latter case the electrical neutrality approximation is unacceptable.

Whether a quasi-rigid conducting fluid can freely traverse magnetic field lines or not depends solely on the magnetic gradient along the fluid path. No matter how strong the magnetic field is or how fast the fluid speed is, a fluid can freely traverse the magnetic field lines as long as it moves along the isomagnetic surface. Especially, no matter how strong the magnetic field is, a uniform magnetic field cannot push around conducting fluid.

The literal meaning of "frozen-in" is liable to promote an erroneous association between fluid traversing motion and magnetic drag. Therefore, we suggest that the use of this term should be avoided whenever possible. In particular, the frozen theorem should not be used to study MHD problems.

AUTHOR CONTRIBUTIONS

Conceived and designed the experiments: ZXL. Performed the experiments: ZXL. Analyzed the data: ZXL YL. Contributed reagents/materials/analysis tools: ZXL. Wrote the paper: ZXL YL.

REFERENCES

1. Alfvén H (1942) Existence of electromagnetic-hydrodynamic waves. Nature 150: 405–406. doi: 10.1038/150405d0.
2. Ivonin IA, Pavlenko VP, Persson H (1998) An influence of frozen-in law violation effects on the turbulent equipartition in tokamaks. Physics of Plasmas 5: 2893–2901. doi: 10.1063/1.873011.
3. .Lundin R, Yamauchi M, Sauvaud JA, Balogh A (2005) Magnetospheric plasma boundaries: a test of the frozen-in magnetic field theorem. Annales Geophysicae 23: 2565–2578. doi: 10.5194/angeo-23-2565-2005.
4. Boyd TJM, Sanderson JJ (2003) The physics of plasmas. Cambridge University Press. P. 79.
5. Bittencourt JA (2004) Fundamentals of plasma physics. Springer, third edition. P. 312, 51, 315.
6. Li D, Chen YH, Ma JX, Yang WH (2006) Plasma Physics. Higher Education Press. P. 69, Chinese.
7. Ma JC, Hu XW, Chen YH (2012) Fundamentals of plasma physics. University of Science and Technology of China Press, second edition. P. 188, Chinese.
8. Zheng CK (2009) Plasma Physics. Peking University Press. P. 79, Chinese.
9. Akasofu SI (1978) The interaction between a magnetized plasma flow and a magnetized celestial body—a review of magnetospheric studies. Space Science Reviews 21: 489–526. doi: 10.1007/BF00240906.
10. Alfvén H (1958) On the theory of magnetic storms and aurorae. Tellus 10: 104–116. doi: 10.1111/j.2153-3490.1958.tb01991.x.
11. Alfven 76 (1976) On frozen-in field lines and field-line reconnection. J Geophys Res 81(22): 4019–4021. doi: 10.1029/JA081i022p04019.
12. Bellan PM (2006) Fundamentals of plasma physics. Cambridge University Press. P. 100.
13. Alfvén H, Fälthammar CG (1963) Cosmical electrodynamics: fundamental principles. Clarendon Press, second edition. P. 110, 190, Fig 5.10.
14. Goldston RJ, Rutherford PH (1995) Introduction to plasma physics. Institute of Physics Publishing. P. 118, P. 124.
15. Bateman G (1978) MHD Instabilities. Cambridge University Press. P. 30.
16. Goldreich P, Julian WH (1969) Pulsar electrodynamics. The Astrophysical Journal 157: 869–880. doi: 10.1086/150119.
17. Lyne AG, Graham-Smith F (2005) Pulsar Astronomy. Cambridge University Press, third edition. P. 23.
18. Fälthammar CG, Mozer FS (2007) On the concept of moving magnetic field lines. EOSTr 88: 169. doi: 10.1029/2007eo150002
19. Newcomb WA (1958) Motion of magnetic lines of force. Annals of Physics 3: 347. doi: 10.1016/0003-4916(58)90024-1.
20. Stern DP (1966) The motion of magnetic field lines. Space Science Reviews 6: 147–173. doi: 10.1007/BF00222592.
21. Northrop TG (1963) Adiabatic charged-particle motion. Rev Geophys 1: 283–304. doi: 10.1029/RG001i003p00283.
22. Vasyliunas VM (1972) Nonuniqueness of magnetic field line motion. J Geophys Res 77: 6271. doi: 10.1029/JA077i031p06271.
23. Fälthammar CG (2006) Comments on the motion of magnetic field lines. Am J Phys 74: 454–455. doi: 10.1119/1.2180285.
24. Liang ZX, Liang Y (2009). http://www.youtube.com/watch?v=YCc4ybfKiY0, YouTube, or http://www.tudou.com/programs/view/ht-ul8dQTtE, Tudou.
25. Liang ZX, Liang Y (2009). http://www.youtube.com/watch?v=ZiVNxVAqUKc, YouTube, or http://www.tudou.com/programs/view/3j2xWprd3Tw, Tudou.
26. Liang ZX, Liang Y (2009). http://www.youtube.com/watch?v=SBAzUBzc2xM, YoTube, or http://www.tudou.com/programs/view/iJPoWvxCDAQ, Tudou.
27. Backus G (1956) The external electric field of a rotating magnet. ApJ 123: 508. doi: 10.1086/146187.
28. Liang ZX, Liang Y (2009). http://www.youtube.com/watch?v=C7DxRoVdtxw, YoTudou, or http://www.tudou.com/programs/view/NMJX9YamFqA/.
29. Liang ZX, Liang Y (2009). http://www.youtube.com/watch?v=p9UzfT6UHcE, YoTudou, or http://www.tudou.com/listplay/bEwfXoxQnO4/g9ZBnvKqF5c.html.
30. Liang ZX, Liang Y (2009). http://www.youtube.com/watch?v=Eq0B5XR_o8U, YouTube, or http://www.tudou.com/listplay/bEwfXoxQnO4/ZXyBWp4V3LI.html, Tudou.
31. Feynman RP, Leighton RB, Sands M (1964) The Feynman Lectures on Physics, volume 2. Addison wesley. P. 13–10.

CHAPTER 19

A NOVEL LOW-RINGING MONOCYCLE PICOSECOND PULSE GENERATOR BASED ON STEP RECOVERY DIODE

Jianming Zhou, Xiao Yang, Qiuyuan Lu, and Fan Liu

School of Information and Electronics, Beijing Institute of Technology, Beijing, 100081, China.

INTRODUCTION

Ultra-wideband narrow pulse is an important aspect of any study relating to ultra-wideband (UWB) radar and the UWB wireless communication system [1–3] owing to its high-resolution applications and simple system architecture. Numerous impulse radars have been developed for the purposes of detection, identification and scanning by analysis of transmitted and received signals [4–5]. The UWB narrow pulse can be further segregated into the classifications of step pulse, Gaussian pulse and the single-cycle pulse. All these pulses have wide frequency spectrums [6]. Step pulse and Gaussian pulse are suitable to be adopted to the receivers, because their high DC components are difficult to be emitted by the antenna. On the other hand, the single-cycle pulse can be used in the senders, owing to its lack of DC components and its minimal amount of low-frequency components.

In recent years, several studies have reported methods of generating UWB pulse, including the tunnel diode based generator [7], oscillator-based generator [8], transistor-based generator [9] and step recovery diode (SRD) based generators [1–2, 10–13]. Components should be carefully selected according to each system's unique requirements and depending on its output pulse power and width. The SRD-based is the most popular design method for all kinds of pulse generating solution, due to its effective ability to sharpen pulse transition edge [12] and its advantage of being easy to fabricate. However many researchers have encountered the same problem, namely, a high ringing level of the pulse, which has an undesirable effect on the resolution power of sensing radars. In former research [14], we introduced a subnanosecond-wide Gaussian pulse using the shunt-connected SRD model, resulting in a ringing level of about -15dB. Through experimentation, [15] better results were attained, with a ringing level of -22dB, by using resistive stubs for suppressing the ringing tail. Nevertheless, the only shortcoming is that, the peak-to-peak pulse amplitude is very small (550mV) compared with other methods.

In this paper, our intention is to design a low-ringing monocycle picosecond pulse and to advance our former work [14, 16], with the aim of generating a signal which possesses both lower ringing and an acceptable amplitude. The remainder of this paper is structured as follows. Section II introduces the SRD model in brief. Section III describes the design circuit of the pulse generator. The test results achieved in the simulation and experiment are provided in Section IV, with conclusions provided in Section V.

Citation: Zhou J, Yang X, Lu Q, Liu F (2015) A Novel Low-Ringing Monocycle Picosecond Pulse Generator Based on Step Recovery Diode. PLoS ONE 10(8): e0136287. doi:10.1371/journal.pone.0136287

SRD MODEL

SRD Structure and Characteristics

SRD is a PN junction diode, whose impurity exhibits an unusual distribution, as shown in Fig 1. Between the high doping P^+ layer and the high doping N^+ layer is a low doping N-type layer. This has a typical slowly varying junction structure. The characteristics of forward conduction and reverse cut-off, produced by the excitement of a sine wave, will be presented to an ordinary diode. In the case of the SRD, the waveforms of current and voltage are different and are shown in Fig 2. When SRD converts from forward exciting voltage to negative exciting voltage, a strong backward current flows continuously until terminating at a time instant, thus forming a steep step voltage. The narrow pulse can be generated in this way.

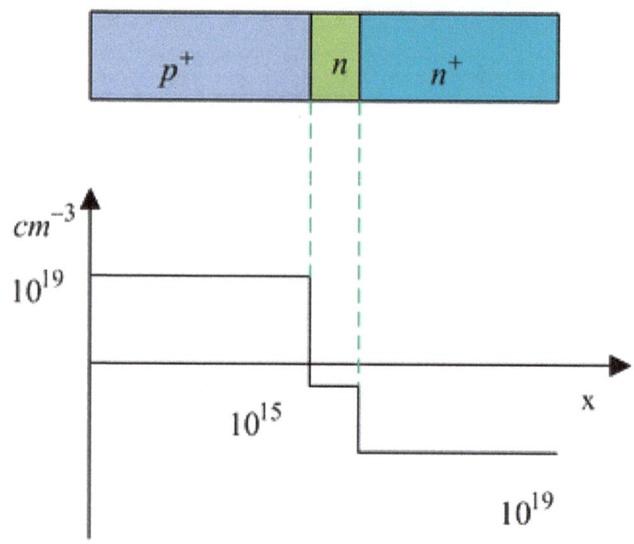

Figure 1. Impurity profile of SRD.

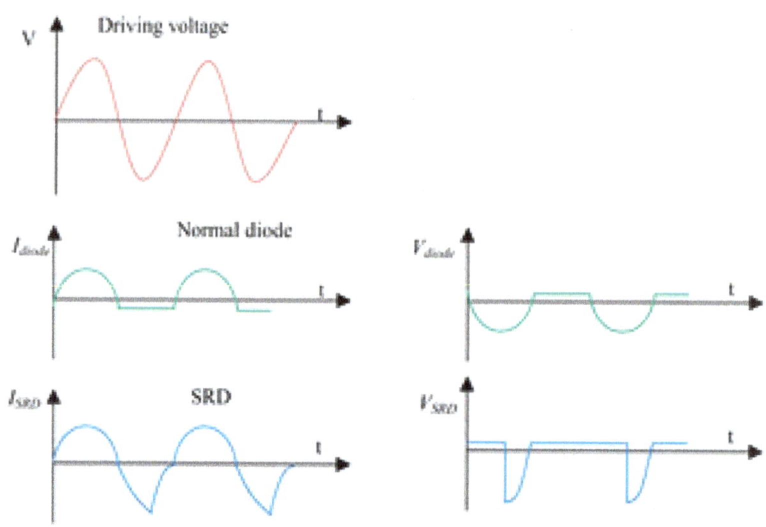

Figure 2. Voltage and current characteristics curves of common diode and SRD.

The principles for this phenomenon are as follows:

- When SRD is in a positive bias, both sides of the PN junction become infused with many minority carriers. The special impurity distribution in SRD facilitates the increase in these injected minority carriers, and creating retarding fields on both sides of the junction eliciting impedance in the minority carriers' proliferation, thus forming a concentration of minority carriers in the narrow regions near the junction. Furthermore, the increased longevity of the minority carriers is such that they are prevented from rejoining during a period of positive bias.
- When the positive bias converts to a negative bias, minority carriers stored will flow in the opposite direction to the injection, thus forming a strong backward current. When extraction of all the minority carriers has taken place, the backward current is suddenly reduced to an extremely low level, cutting off the diode and forming the step voltage.

SRD Equivalent Circuit Analysis

The SRD equivalent circuit is depicted in Fig 3, where C_f represents the forward-bias diffusion capacitance, C_r denotes the backward-bias depletion layer capacitance, R_f represents the junction resistance of the diode, R_s denotes the series resistance of the diode, and V_0, the barrier potential of the junction. The equivalent circuit shows two types of working status in the forward and backward biases. Under the forward-bias voltage, the equivalent circuit consists of the large C_f and R_f, whereas the equivalent circuit consists of the small C_r under the backward-bias voltage.

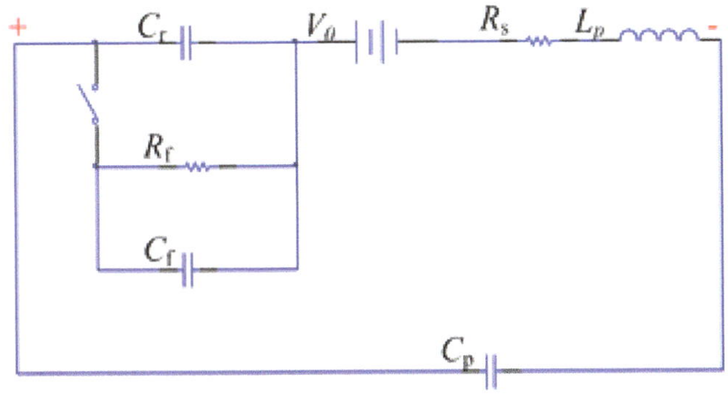

Figure 3. Equivalent circuit of the SRD.

Generally, the SRD parameters encompass γ, C_0, V_0 and τ. According to Kotzebue's derivation: $\tau = R_f C_f$ **(1)** Where, τ is the lifetime of the minority carrier, and C_f can be computed with τ and the forward on-resistance R_f. The forward resistance R_f can be computed by measuring SRD's I-Vcharacteristics. Typical I-V characteristics and forward resistance curves are shown in Fig 4. From the figure, it can be seen that the SRD's forward resistance R_f is computed by measuring SRD's I-V characteristics, so the forward capacitance C_f can be computed as well. With γ, C_0, V_0 and other diode parameters, the diode's model can be represented both easily and effectively. As the model is more accurate, consequent improvements to the hardware design are possible, along with speedier production rates in the design.

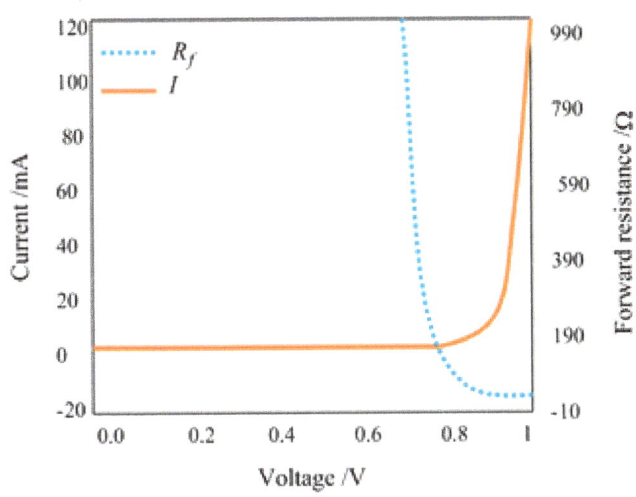

Figure 4. I-V characteristic and forward resistance changing curves.

M-Pulse Microwave MP4023 is used as SRD in this paper. The parameters of τ is 15ns, t_t (the transition time) is 50ps, C_r is within 0.2~0.5pF, and R_s is 0.8Ω. The value of C_f can be calculated by the existing parameters and the I-V curve, as show in Fig 4. When the values of all components in the SRD equivalent circuit are known, the Spice Model can be constructed according to the relationship between SRD quantity of electricity and voltage, as shown in Eq (2) [13].

$$Q(V) = \begin{cases} C_r V & V \le 0 \\ \dfrac{C_f - C_r}{2V_0}\left(V + \dfrac{C_r V_0}{C_f - C_r}\right)^2 - \dfrac{C_r^2}{2(C_f - C_r)} V_0 & 0 < V < V_0 \\ C_f V - \dfrac{C_f - C_r}{2} V_0 & V \ge V_0 \end{cases} \quad \textbf{(2)}$$

Fig 5 presents the simulation diagram in ADS, where SDD denotes the relationship between current, voltage and their differentials of different ports in the N-port component. The component's properties can be expressed by defining the relationship between ports with their algebraic expressions. By representing the voltage-current relation in Eq (1) with SDD and defining the SRD parameters of C_f and C_r that have been acquired above as the input, we can obtain the simulation model.

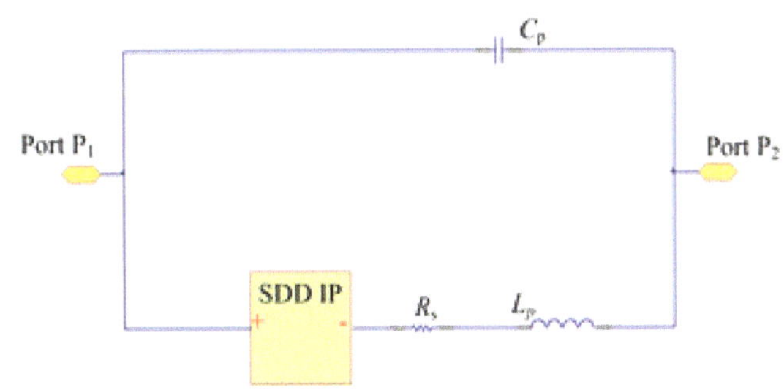

Figure 5. Spice model of the SRD.

PULSE GENERATOR CIRCUIT DESIGN

Overall design

To generate the required Gaussian narrow pulse, the circuit of the pulse generator is designed based on the prototype in [2], in which the small amplitude of output signal highlights an inevitable shortcoming. In order to overcome this issue, we add a FET module to amplify the output pulse signal. In addition, another function of the FET module is to act as a buffer between the signal generating module and the signal shaping module. Fig 6 shows the overall circuit design of the pulse generator, which consists of a pulse generating circuit, isolating and amplifying circuit, as well as the shaping circuit. The pulse generating circuit comprises a coupled circuit, match circuit, step recovery diode (SRD), and a micro-strip short-circuit line. The isolating and amplifying circuit consists of FET module, with the shaping circuit being made up of Schottky diode. A summary of parameters of main component in Fig 6 appears inTable 1, and other values for resistances and capacitances are marked in the figure.

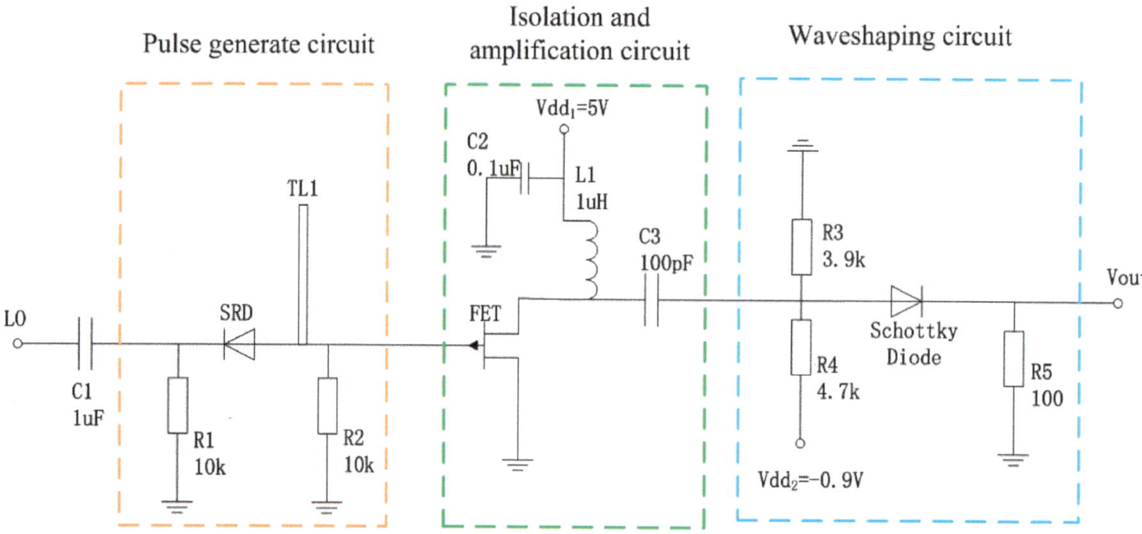

Figure 6. Circuit of the picosecond pulse generator.

Table 1. Parameters of main components of circuit.

Function	Type	Key parameter
Signal input	Square wave	10MHz
Substrate	FR-4	$\varepsilon_r = 9.6$
SRD	MP4023	$\tau = 15ns$, $t_t = 50ps$, $C_r = 0.2\text{~}0.5$ pF
Transmission line	TL1	400 mil
Schottky diode	HSMS2820	Turn-On Voltage 0.34 V at 1 mA
FET	FSX017LG	$I_{DSS} = 55mA$, $C_{GS} = 0.55pF$

doi:10.1371/journal.pone.0136287.t001

Pulse Generating Circuit

The input periodic square wave signal excites SRD via the coupled circuit and the match circuit. The SRD self-bias circuit, consisting of the coupled circuit and R_L, eliminates the need for the extra DC biasing circuit, thereby reducing the overall size of the circuit, exercises good control over charge storage and ensures an optimum output of the pulse at high amplitude. The match circuit is used to achieve maximum transmission of power, owing to the input impedance of SRD being within the range 10–20Ω, while the input impedance of the entire system is 50Ω. Furthermore, an extremely fast step pulse can be generated after the signal passes through SRD. In addition, it will yield a narrow pulse with a long tail and width by subtracting the forward-propagation step pulse from the reflected step pulse after passing through the micro-strip short-circuit line. Therefore the process needs to be carried out by the subsequent circuits.

The following matter requires special consideration during the design process. The length of the micro-strip short-circuit line is determined by the pulse width, as shown in Eq (3). $t_A = \frac{2l}{v}$ **(3)**Where, t_A denotes the pulse width, l represents the length of the micro-strip short-circuit line, and $v = \frac{c}{\sqrt{\varepsilon_{re}}}$ (c is the speed of light), ε_{re} is effective dielectric constant. According to Eq (3), the length of the short-circuit line can be acquired after the pulse width t_A is achieved.

Isolating and Amplifying Circuit

The function of FET module has two aspects, the first and more important role is to amplify the pulse signal, and the other is to isolate the pulse generating circuit from the pulse shaping circuit, which can be seen in the Fig 6. The working principle of the amplifier circuit is as follows: the positive DC bias voltage is applied to the drain electrode of FET by V_{dd1}, and the pulse signal generated by MP4023 is connect to the grid electrode. Before the narrow pulse coming, FET is functioning in a saturation zone and fails to work. However, when the negative pulse arriving, FET works in the linear amplification zone due to the negative bias voltage, and amplifies the narrow pulse signal. After being amplified by FET, the narrow pulse will be of larger amplitude and convert from a negative pulse to a positive pulse.

Function of Schottky Diode

The ringing level of pulse signal is further reduced by the Schottky diode in the shaping circuit, serving as a high-speed switch, which only allows a pulse greater than a certain threshold to pass. This threshold is determined by the DC bias voltage V_d. The negative bias voltage can lower the pulse form overall and theoretically eliminate any positive and negative ringing. Despite this, it is impossible as the switch time of the Schottky diode could not be equal to zero. So the phenomenon of ringing still exists in the output and the value of V_d is determined by the value of the ringing. In this design, the V_d is set by -0.9V, as shown in Fig 6.

SIMULATION AND EXPERIMENTAL RESULTS

According to the SRD model and designed circuit as shown in Fig 6, we simulate the pulse generator in ADS software. Fig 7 shows the waveform of the output pulse in simulation. In the figure, the SRD model has been applied to the pulse generator. One can see that the pulse width is about 300ps and the pulse amplitude is about 1.96 V. The waveform in the simulation is satisfactory because nearly all tails and ringing have been eliminated.

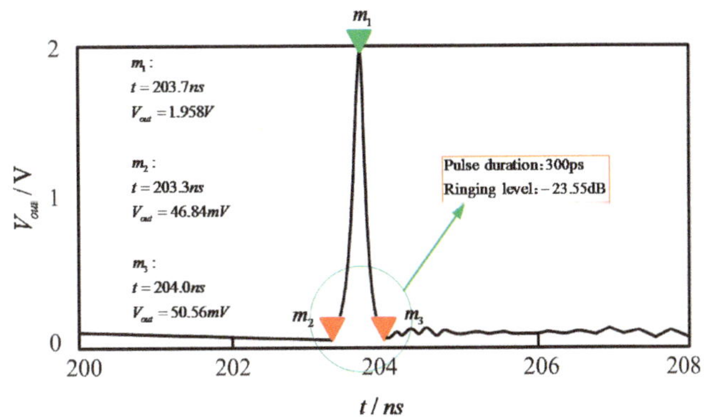

Figure 7. Simulation of the output pulse.

The detailed ringing level R_l, can be calculated by Eq (4), which was reduced to -23.55dB, with the peak-to-peak amplitude of ringing at about 130mV.

$$R_l = 20\log\frac{Amplitude\ of\ ringing_{peak-to-peak}}{Amplitude\ of\ pulse_{peak-to-peak}} \quad (4)$$

The circuit of the pulse generator is made utilizing Teflon boards. Its permittivity is 9.6, its density 0.8mm, and the micro-strip line is 50Ω. The design of the circuit structure is compact, as shown in Fig 8. The input signal is 10 MHz rectangular wave, and the waveform is monitored by Lecroy Wave Master 8600A 6GHz DSO oscilloscope as shown in Fig 9. The pulse amplitude is 1.88 V and the pulse width is 307ps. A comparison between the experimental result and the simulation result demonstrates that the pulse amplitude in the test is smaller than that in the simulation, and the pulse ringing in the test is greater than that in the simulation. The ringing level of pulse is -22.5dB, with the peak-to-peak amplitude of ringing being 135mV. Overall the two basic results are consistent. Moreover, the generated narrow pulse is highly symmetric and without huge tails and ringing.

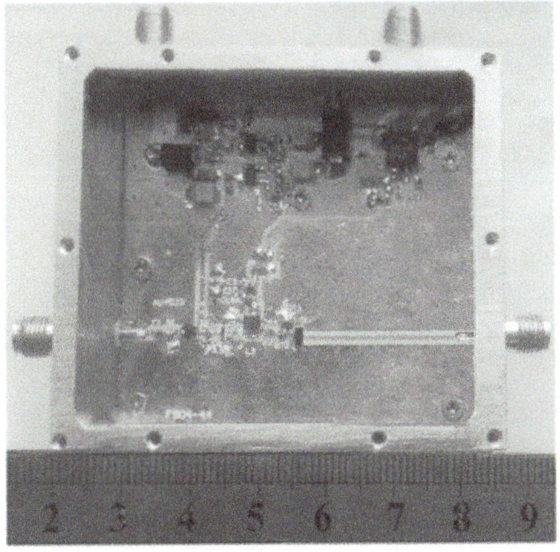

Figure 8. Prototype of designed pulse generator.

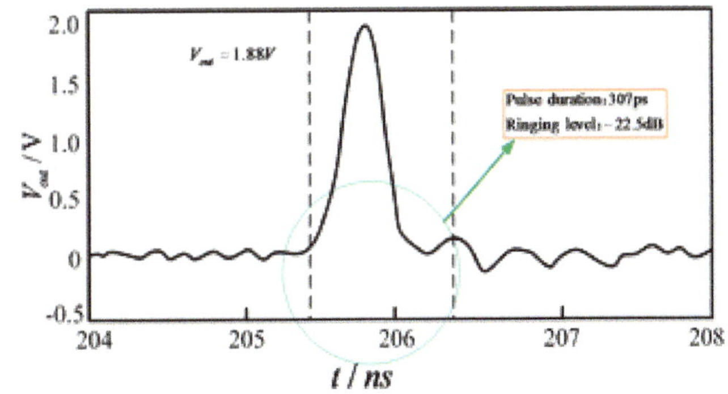

Figure 9. Measured output pulse of the generator.

Furthermore, in order to evaluate the performance of the proposed pulse generator, a comparison of various UWB pulse generators constructed from discrete components which have been used in recent research has been given as shown in Table 2. It can be inferred that our design has a very low ringing level [2, 10, 12, 13] and narrow pulse [10, 12, 13]. In [2], the circuit was more complicated and exhibited an increase in power consumption owing to the second DC bias Schottky Diode. It can be said however, compared to the literature noted in [12, 14], which also possess relatively low ringing results, that our designed pulse achieves an acceptable amplitude.

Table 2. Comparisons with pulse generations in literatures.

Reference	Pulse amplitude /V	Pulse duration /ps	R_l /dB
[1]	0.7	350	-20.9
[2]	0.4	300	-17
[10]	0.2	600~780	-20
[12]	0.87	170	-22
[13]	1.8~1.85	1000	-17.15
[14]	15	400	-15.56
[15]	0.55	320	-22
This work-S	1.96	300	-23.55
This work-E	1.88	307	-22.5

doi:10.1371/journal.pone.0136287.t002

CONCLUSION

A SRD model is constructed by using ADS simulation software in this paper. The researchers also design, simulate, construct and test a UWB picosecond pulse generator. The proposed generator proves to be structurally compact, cheap to build and easy to implement. The width and amplitude of the tested pulse are 307ps and 1.88V respectively. The test results are consistent with the simulation results. The proposed generator can therefore be adapted to practical applications and be introduced to either UWB pulse emitting components or down-conversion sampling receivers. We conclude that this model has great potential to be widely used.

AUTHOR CONTRIBUTIONS

Conceived and designed the experiments: JZ XY FL. Performed the experiments: QL FL. Analyzed the data: JZ XY QL. Contributed reagents/materials/analysis tools: JZ. Wrote the paper: JZ XY.

REFERENCES

1. Lee JS, Nguyen C, Scullion T (2001) New uniplanar subnanosecond monocycle pulse generator and transformer for time-domain microwave applications. IEEE Transactions on Microwave Theory and Techniques 49: 1126–1129. doi: 10.1109/22.925501.
2. Han J, Nguyen C (2002) A new ultra-wideband, ultrashort monocycle pulse generator with reduced ringing. IEEE Microwave Wireless Components Letters 2: 206–208. doi: 10.1109/LMWC.2002.1009996.
3. Han J, Nguyen C (2006) on the development of a compact sub-nanosecond tunable monocycle pulse transmitter for UWB applications. IEEE Transactions on Microwave Theory and Techniques 54: 285–293. doi: 10.1109/TMTT.2005.860299.
4. Benedetto F, Benedetto MR, De Blasiis MR, Giunta G, (2005) Reliability of signal processing technique for pavement damages detection and classification using ground penetrating radar. IEEE Sensors Journal, 5: 471–480. doi: 10.1109/JSEN.2005.846176.
5. De Angelis A, Dionigi M, Moscitta A, Carbone P, (2009) A low-cost ultra-wideband indoor ranging system, IEEE Transactions on Instrumentation and Measurement. 58: 3935–3942. doi: 10.1109/TIM.2009.2020834.
6. Andrews JR, (2003) UWB signal sources, antennas and propagation, IEEE Topical Conference on Wireless Communication Technology. 15–17: 439–440. doi: 10.1109/WCT.2003.1321594.
7. Ruai YY, Konishi Y, Allen ST, Reddy M, Mark JW, (1994) A traveling-wave resonant tunnel diode pulse generator, IEEE Microwave and Guided Wave Letters. 4: 220–222. doi: 10.1109/75.298246.
8. Teshirogi T, Saito S, Uchino M, Ejima M, Hamaguchi K, Ogawa H, Kohno R, (2005) Residual-carrier-free burst oscillator for automotive UWB radar applications, Electronics Letters. 41: 535–536. doi: 10.1049/el:20050604.
9. Gerding M, Musch T, Schiek B, (2004) Generation of short electrical pulses based on bipolar transistors, Advances in Radio Science. 2: 7–12. doi: 10.5194/ars-2-7-2004.
10. Han J, Nguyen C, (2005) Coupled-slotline-hybrid sampling mixer integrated with step-recovery-diode pulse generator for UWB applications, IEEE Transactions on Microwave Theory and Techniques. 53: 1875–1882. doi: 10.1109/TMTT.2005.848091.
11. Protiva P, Mrkvica J, Machac J, (2010) A Compact Step Recovery Diode Subnanosecond Pulse Gnerator, Microwave and Optical Technology Letters. 52: 438–440. doi: 10.1002/mop.24945.
12. Kamall A, Bhattacharya A, Tamrakar M, Roy C, (2014) Low-ringing and reduced-cost step recovery diode based UWB pulse generators for GPR applications, Microwave and Optical Technology Letters. 56:2289–2294. doi: 10.1002/mop.28581.

13. Xia T, Venkatachalam AS, Dryver H, (2012) A high-performance low-ringing ultrawideband monocycle pulse generator, IEEE Transactions on Instrumentation and Measurement. 61: 261–266. doi: 10.1109/TIM.2011.2161022.
14. Zhou JM, Gao XW, Fei YC, (2006) A new CAD model of step recovery diode and generation of UWB signals, IEICE Electronics Express. 3: 534–539.doi.org/10.1587/elex.3.534
15. Ma TG, Wu CJ, Cheng PK, Chou CF, (2007) Ultrawideband monocycle pulse generator with dual resistive loaded shunt stubs, Microwave and Optical Technology Letters. 49: 459–462. doi: 10.1002/mop.22145.
16. Liu BS, Zhou JM, Zhou J, (2012) An improved ultra-wideband, ultra-short monocycle pulse generator, Advanced Materials Research. 588–589: 781–784. doi: 10.4028/www.scientific.net/AMR.588-589.781.

CHAPTER 20

EFFECTS OF ELECTRODE MATERIAL ON THE VOLTAGE OF A TREE-BASED ENERGY GENERATOR

Hao Z, Wang G, Li W, Zhang J, Kan J.

School of Technology, Beijing Forestry University, Beijing, China.

ABSTRACT

The voltage between a standing tree and its surrounding soil is regarded as an innovative renewable energy source. This source is expected to provide a new power generation system for the low-power electrical equipment used in forestry. However, the voltage is weak, which has caused great difficulty in application. Consequently, the development of a method to increase the voltage is a key issue that must be addressed in this area of applied research. As the front-end component for energy harvesting, a metal electrode has a material effect on the level and stability of the voltage obtained. This study aimed to preliminarily ascertain the rules and mechanisms that underlie the effects of electrode material on voltage. Electrodes of different materials were used to measure the tree-source voltage, and the data were employed in a comparative analysis. The results indicate that the conductivity of the metal electrode significantly affects the contact resistance of the electrode-soil and electrode-trunk contact surfaces, thereby influencing the voltage level. The metal reactivity of the electrode has no significant effect on the voltage. However, passivation of the electrode materials markedly reduces the voltage. Suitable electrode materials are demonstrated and recommended.

INTRODUCTION

When two metal electrodes are installed in a tree and the adjacent soil, a voltage develops between the electrodes [1]. This voltage has been regarded as an innovative renewable energy generator. Compared with other natural energy sources, such as solar energy and wind energy, this type of energy has certain advantages, including eco-friendliness, a long lifetime, and no restrictions with respect to the hermetic environment in the forest. Hence, scholars have forecasted practical applications of the tree-voltage that include a wide variety of trickle chargers for niche environmental sensors and mesh-networked devices, drastically decreasing the need for in-the-field battery changes [2]. Sensors and networks used in forestry have extremely low energy consumption as a result of their low-power design and sleep function. The tree-based voltage has the ability to provide uninterruptible energy when charging a low-voltage battery to meet the demands of discontinuous power consumption. Therefore, the tree-based voltage is a promising energy source. This source is expected to provide a brand-new power generation system for the low-power electrical equipment used in forestry. However, studies

Citation: Hao Z, Wang G, Li W, Zhang J, Kan J (2015) Effects of Electrode Material on the Voltage of a Tree-Based Energy Generator. PLoS ONE 10(8): e0136639. doi:10.1371/journal.pone.0136639

have shown that this type of energy is weak, i.e., the voltages obtained are typically in the tens to hundreds of millivolts range, while the short circuit currents are in the microampere range [2]. A low electrical power in the microwatt range (approximately 20 μW) was measured in a previous study. These features are insufficient for directly driving the low-power electronic equipment currently used in forests.

The technology for harvesting and utilizing micro-energy, which includes piezoelectric energy, photovoltaic energy, and thermoelectric energy, is relatively well-developed [3–8]. To acquire the suitable voltage level necessary to charge a storage circuit and subsequently to power electronic devices, a boosting operation with a direct current-to-direct current (DC-DC) converter is generally required [9, 10]. However, the voltage between a standing tree and its surrounding soil is quite low and cannot reliably drive the present DC-DC circuit modules. That is, the existing challenge in this regard is to increase the voltage. To solve this problem, relevant studies have focused on two major topics: 1) ascertaining the mechanism behind this voltage [2], thereby determining whether the voltage may be artificially increased, and 2) finding novel boosting methods while designing innovative low-voltage electronics [11, 12].

Research on the mechanism of tree-based energy is an important task. It is well-known that electric potential differences exist in plant bodies. However, this type of voltage is typically caused by the physiological activities of plants [13–16]. This phenomenon can be explained at a microscopic level, in particular at the cellular level. The electric potential difference caused by physiological activities is extremely weak (at most tens of millivolts) and sometimes transient (generated in response to external stimuli) [17]. This is negligible in studies of the tree-soil voltage, which is typically in the tens to hundreds of millivolts range. Studies of the voltage that arises between a standing tree and its surrounding soil belong to a new field of research. Early observations of tree trunk electrical activity were confirmed by an experiment on a spruce tree [18], which further reported a non-linear relationship between the electric potential variation and the intensity of the solar radiation. Some scholars have claimed that sap flow is the dominating mechanism for voltage generation [19]. Moreover, other scholars have proposed a mechanism based on charge diffusion from the conductive sap flow channels into the resistive xylem walls [18]. However, electrical signals with more erratic time variations were still observed in the experiments, indicating that other mechanisms, possibly unrelated to sap flow, may also contribute. Atmospheric electricity was claimed to contribute to temporal voltage variations. However, inherent voltages were also observed in those studies [20–22]. In addition, it was found that the pH difference between the interior of the tree and its surrounding soil significantly affects the voltage [2]. Therefore, the mechanism behind the tree-based energy generator remains controversial, leading to significant unknown factors that continue to affect its application.

The invention of innovative electronics is another objective that must be met to utilize tree-based energy. A DC-DC converter can boost the input voltage and generate constant output, but such a circuit requires a minimum threshold voltage as the input, which a standing tree cannot reliably generate. In response to this problem, some researchers have designed a boost-circuit that has low power consumption and a low input voltage, as well as a low-power clock circuit. Both circuits have been driven by a standing tree with relatively good performance [11].

However, to utilize this type of electricity more reliably, various factors, such as the harvesting, conversion, and storage of electricity, must be considered. During the process of utilizing standing-tree electricity, electrodes should be arranged in the standing tree and in the surrounding soil, as the front-end equipment for energy harvesting. However, the electrode material may affect the magnitude and stability of the electricity obtained. Because the mechanism behind the tree-based voltage remains unclear, no universal standard has been established for electrode selection during the process of measuring and utilizing tree electricity [2, 11, 12, 18–22]. However, metal electrodes remain the preferred material of scientists, based on the relevant literature. Most previous studies have used steel electrodes [11, 12,18–22]. Moreover, platinum (Pt) electrodes have also been used in some studies [2]. Regardless, to take advantage of such a weak energy source with high efficiency, the choice of a suitable electrode is a central issue.

The stability (metal reactivity) of the electrode material is an important factor for consideration because the trunk and soil can cause electrode corrosion. Steel and Pt electrodes offer good corrosion resistance, which yields a stable electrical signal when measured over time. However, it has not yet been shown whether the stability of the materials significantly affects the voltage during collection and utilization. Moreover, the process requires the highest possible voltage during power collection and utilization. Therefore, conductivity is also an important factor. In a previous study, a higher voltage was measured using electrodes with a lower resistivity, i.e., better conductivity [23]. However, the power source formed by a standing tree and its surrounding soil has a high internal resistance. Internal resistances of tens of thousands of ohms have been observed, according to the relevant literature [11, 12, 24]. The metal electrodes act as a series resistor with a low resistance between the anode and cathode of the tree-source. In this case, the conductivity of the electrode material exerts little effect on the output voltage, which is inconsistent with the previous study. Therefore, the mechanism by which the electrode material affects the voltage requires further study. This work aimed to preliminarily ascertain the rules and mechanisms that underlie the effect of the electrode material on the voltage between a standing tree and its surrounding soil, as well as to provide guidance for choosing suitable electrode materials in relevant studies, thereby promoting the utilization of this innovative energy generator. Both the conductivity and the stability of the metal electrodes studied here were considered.

MATERIALS AND METHODS

Experimental Electrodes

Based on the objective of this study, three different materials with different conductivities and stabilities, including copper (Cu), aluminum (Al), and iron (Fe), were selected. The conductivities of Cu, Al, and Fe are different, varying in the order of Cu to Al and Fe for strong to weak conductivity. The resistivities of the three materials are approximately 1.75 × 10^-8 Ωm (Cu), 2.83 × 10^-8 Ωm (Al), and 9.78 × 10^-8 Ωm (Fe).

The reactivities are also different, varying in the order of Cu to Fe and Al for low to high reactivity. Significantly different values for both resistivity and metal reactivity exist among the three metals. All electrodes were of the same size, with a diameter of 0.6 cm and a length of 8 cm. For the convenience of comparison, two additional electrodes (Al and Fe) of the same size were chosen. However, these two electrodes were treated with a 10-μm-thick Cu plating, which caused a negligible effect on the electrode size. Moreover, artificial damage (a minor scratch) was applied to the Cu plating of the Cu-plated Al electrode, which was employed as a control in the experiment. The purpose in this case was to ascertain the effect of the Cu plating.

Electrode Arrangement

A naturally grown, healthy poplar (*Populus X canadensis Moench*) with a diameter of 46 cm (at the height of 0.5 m where the electrodes were arranged) was chosen, and five electrodes (trunk electrodes) were inserted into its trunk at even spacing in the order of Cu-plated Al, Al, Cu, Fe, and Cu-plated Fe (the electrode position has no effect on the voltage [2]), as shown in Fig 1. The internal end of the electrode was implanted to a depth of up to 5 cm into the trunk, and the external end was attached to a wire. Another five electrodes (ground electrodes) were evenly arranged in the soil surrounding the standing tree in the same order. The ground electrodes were inserted to a depth of 80 cm [18]. Lines connecting any two adjacent electrodes to the center of the trunk had an angle of 72°. The ground surrounding the tree was flat, and the nearby soil composition was uniform.

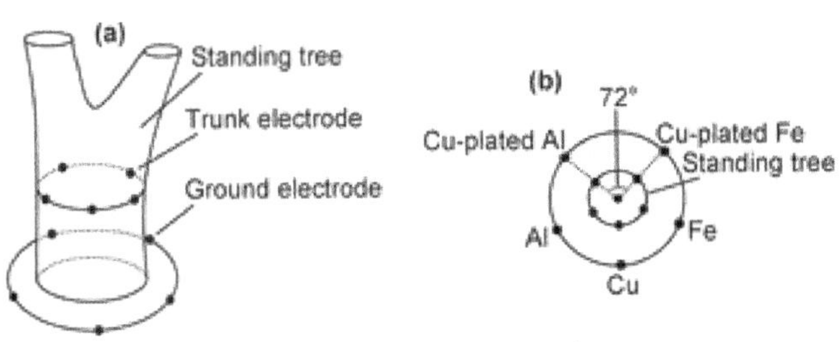

Figure 1. Electrode arrangement.

(a) Five different electrodes were inserted into the trunk. Another five electrodes were arranged in the soil surrounding the standing tree. (b) In both sets, the electrodes were in the order of Cu-plated Al, Al, Cu, Fe, and Cu-plated Fe. Lines connecting any two adjacent electrodes to the center of the trunk had an angle of 72°.

Measurements

A wire was introduced from each trunk electrode and its corresponding ground electrode. A load resistor was connected to the wires between the trunk electrode and the ground electrode in series so that a current circuit was formed through the load resistor [11]. The voltage across the resistor was measured using a high-input impedance voltmeter (Keithley 2000).

It has been previously observed that the electrical activity of trees strongly depends on the season, with more stable and coherent voltage variations measured during spring and summer [18]. Therefore, the tree-based energy generator is expected to operate during spring and summer. The present study was conducted during summer (June-August 2014). Every measurement was conducted at noon.

The experimental site located in an experimental forest in Beijing Forestry University for which specific permission was not required. The field studies did not involve endangered or protected species.

The electrode-soil contact Resistance

To ascertain the effect of the electrode-soil resistance on the internal resistance of the power source formed by a standing tree and its surrounding soil, an additional experiment (the first additional experiment) was performed. This experiment was undertaken to help explain the effect of the electrode conductivity on the voltage. As shown in Fig 2, two additional Cu electrodes were arranged in the trunk with a separation of 30 cm, while two additional Cu electrodes were arranged in the soil with a separation of 30 cm.

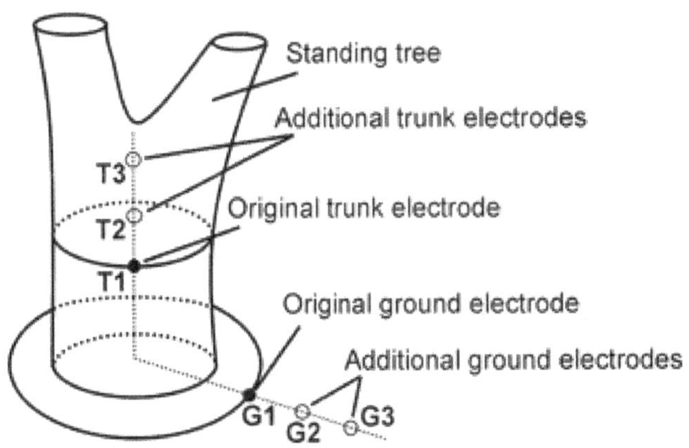

Figure 2. The first additional experiment.

T1 and G1 denote the original Cu electrode in the trunk and the original Cu electrode in the soil, respectively. T2 and T3 are the additional Cu electrodes in the trunk. G2 and G3 are the additional Cu electrodes in the soil.

T1 and G1 denote, respectively, the original Cu electrode in the standing tree and the original Cu electrode in the soil. T2 and T3 are the additional Cu electrodes in the trunk. G2 and G3 are the additional Cu electrodes in the soil. Each measurement of the voltage between the trunk electrodes and the ground electrodes, as captured using the load resistor, was recorded as $V_{T1\text{-}G1}$, $V_{T1\text{-}G2}$, $V_{T1\text{-}G3}$, $V_{T2\text{-}G1}$, $V_{T2\text{-}G2}$, $V_{T2\text{-}G3}$, $V_{T3\text{-}G1}$, $V_{T3\text{-}G2}$, and $V_{T3\text{-}G3}$. After tamping the surface soil at G1, G2, and G3, the voltages were recorded again.

The Electrode-Trunk Contact Resistance

To ascertain the effect of the contact resistance between the electrode and the trunk on the internal resistance of the tree-source, a second additional experiment was conducted. As shown in Fig 3, five cylindrical Cu electrodes (trunk electrodes) with different diameters (0.5 cm, 1.0 cm, 1.5 cm, 2.0 cm, and 2.5 cm) were inserted into the tree trunk. These electrodes were all implanted at the same depth (5 cm) in the trunk. As a result, the electrodes had different contact areas with the trunk. Another Cu electrode (ground electrode) was arranged in the soil. The voltages between each trunk electrode and the ground electrode were measured.

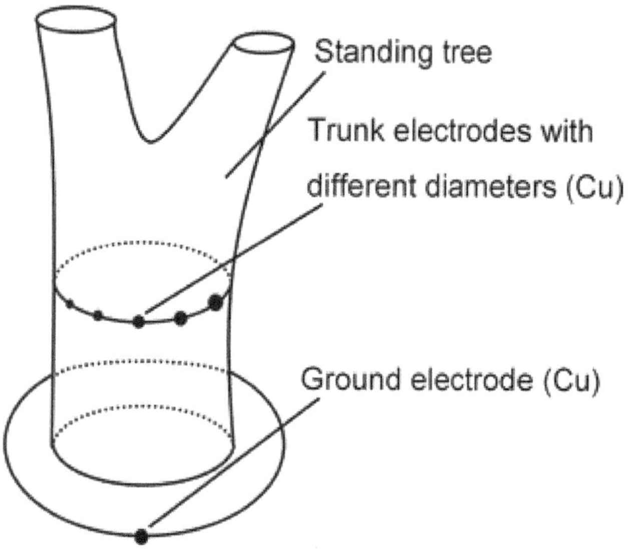

Figure 3. The second additional experiment.

Five cylindrical Cu electrodes with different diameters were inserted into the tree trunk. Another Cu electrode was arranged in the soil.

Electrodes with Nonmetallic Inclusions

A supplementary experiment was conducted to test the performance of electrodes with nonmetallic inclusions. This supplementary experiment was similar to the primary experiment. However, four nonmetallic materials were used as the inclusions in the supplementary experiment (Fig 4). Moreover, the thickness of the coating was 25 μm, which was thicker than that in the primary experiment.

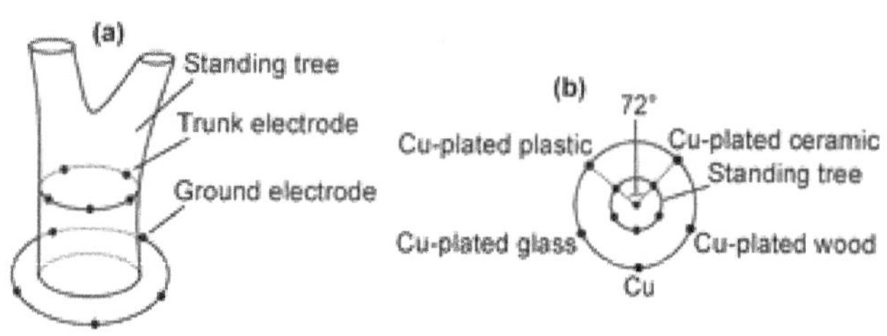

Figure 4. Supplementary experiment.

(a) Five different electrodes were inserted into the trunk. Another five different electrodes were arranged in the soil surrounding the standing tree. (b) The electrodes were in the order of Cu-plated plastic, Cu-plated glass, Cu, Cu-plated wood, and Cu-plated ceramic.

RESULTS

Primary Experiment

Thirty-three sets of effective data were acquired from the primary experiment. The voltage variations are shown in Fig 5. The y-axis displays the voltages measured, and the x-axis shows the serial number of each data set, which varies with time. The voltage measured by the three metal electrodes (Cu, Al, and Fe) did not show any specificity except for differences in the magnitude and amplitude of variation. The Al electrode demonstrated a slightly different voltage trend relative to the other two metals. Among the three metals (Cu, Al, and Fe), the Cu electrode yielded the highest measured voltage, followed by Al and Fe. The curves for the three metal electrodes, i.e., Cu, Al and Fe, all fluctuated but showed an overall decreasing trend, and the final recorded point in each case was the lowest. For the Cu electrode, the last data point was 848 mV, representing a decrease of 39 mV from the first recorded point (887 mV). For the Al electrode, the voltage decreased by 132 mV. For the Fe electrode, the voltage decreased by 43 mV. The voltage measured by the Cu electrode decreased the least, followed by the Fe electrode, whereas the Al electrode registered the largest decrease in voltage. The voltage curve acquired from the Cu-plated Fe electrode was closest to that of the Cu electrode. These two curves were nearly identical, especially at the data sets prior to group 22. Likewise, the Cu-plated Al electrode also demonstrated properties similar to the Cu electrode at the first data point. However, its voltage curve then approached the curve of the Al electrode.

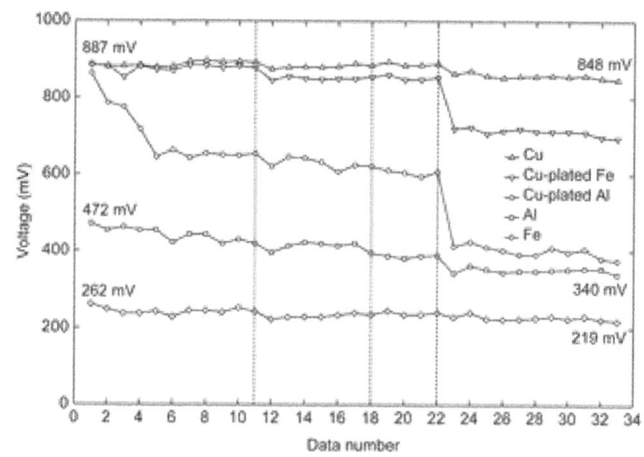

Figure 5. Voltage variations in the primary experiment.

Five curves display the voltage variations measured with the five different electrodes. All curves show an overall decreasing trend. The Cu electrode yields the highest measured voltage, followed by Al and Fe. The curve acquired from the Cu-plated Fe electrode is closest to that of the Cu electrode. The curve of the Cu-plated Al electrode declines sharply.

The Electrode-Soil Contact Resistance

The results from the first additional experiment are presented in Fig 6. Fig 6A shows the voltages before the soil was tamped. The voltages after tamping are presented in Fig 6B. There are no common differences among the voltages in Fig 6A. The voltage change did not correlate with the position shift of the electrodes. In Fig 6B, every voltage is greater than the voltages shown in Fig 6A.

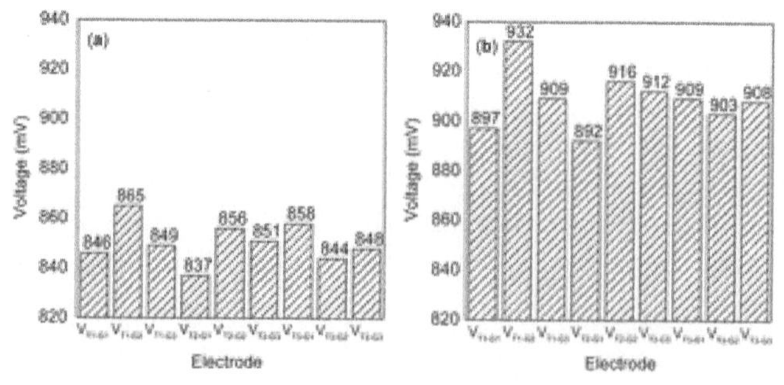

Figure 6. Voltages recorded in the first additional experiment.

Each measurement of the voltage between the electrodes in the tree trunk and the surrounding soil using the load resistor was recorded as $V_{T1\text{-}G1}$, $V_{T1\text{-}G2}$, $V_{T1\text{-}G3}$, $V_{T2\text{-}G1}$, $V_{T2\text{-}G2}$, $V_{T2\text{-}G3}$, $V_{T3\text{-}G1}$, $V_{T3\text{-}G2}$, and $V_{T3\text{-}G3}$. (a) The voltage had no correlation with the position shift of the electrodes. (b) All voltages increased after the soil was tamped.

The Electrode-Trunk Contact Resistance

The result of the second additional experiment is presented in Fig 7. This figure shows the voltages measured by the trunk electrodes of different diameters, which varied from 0.5 cm to 2.5 cm in 0.5 cm intervals. The voltage rose discernably with increasing electrode diameter. That is, the measured voltage increased with electrode diameter (increasing contact area with the tree trunk).

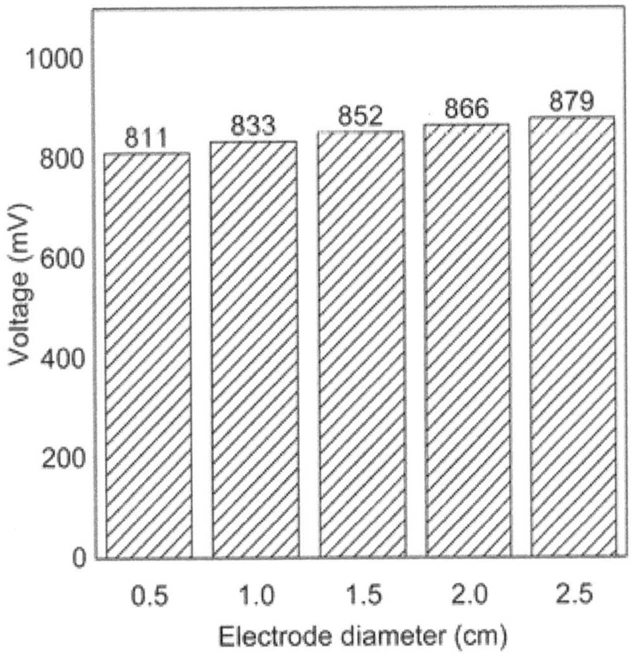

Figure 7. Voltages recorded in the second additional experiment.

THE ELECTRODE WITH THE LARGEST DIAMETER OBTAINED THE HIGHEST VOLTAGE.

Electrodes with nonmetallic inclusions

The result of the supplementary experiment is shown in Fig 8. The y-axis displays the voltages and the x-axis shows the serial number of each data set, which varies with time. The curves inFig 8 all follow the same trend. The voltage drops of the Cu-plated electrodes were smaller than those recorded in the primary experiment (Fig 5). There is no obvious difference in amplitude between the Cu electrode and the Cu-plated electrodes. However, the voltages measured by the Cu-plated electrodes were slightly higher than those of the Cu electrode.

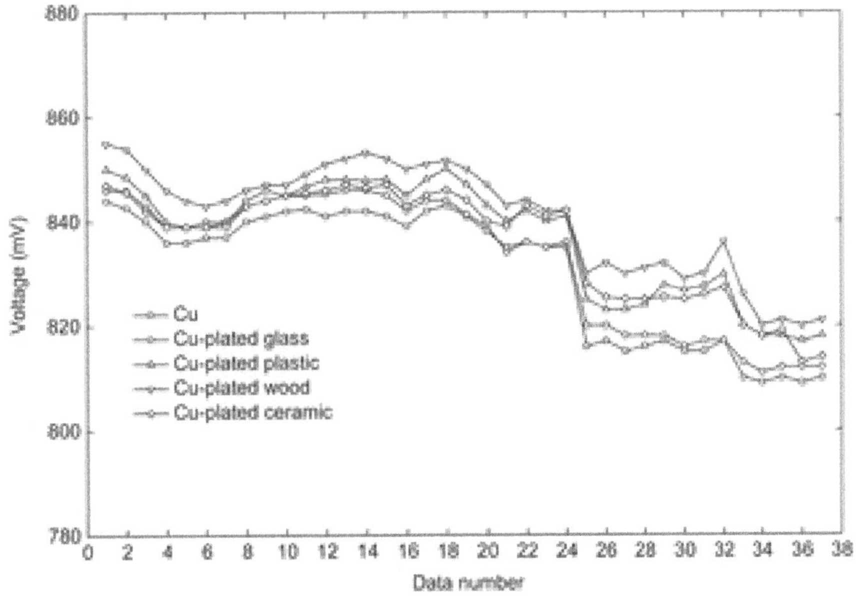

Figure 8. Voltage variations in the supplementary experiment.

Five curves display the voltage variations measured with the five different electrodes. All curves follow the same trend. There is no obvious difference in amplitude among the curves.

DISCUSSION

Conductivity

The magnitudes of the voltages measured with the three different electrodes (Cu, Al, and Fe) in the primary experiment, from large to small, were in the order of Cu to Al and Fe, which is consistent with the conductivities of the three metals (Fig 5). However, the internal resistance of the power source formed by the standing tree and the soil is large (at least 17.9 kΩ in the present study). The electrodes act as a part of the source. However, because each electrode has a small resistance, it should not affect the size of the internal resistance and the measured voltage. Therefore, the difference in the resistance of the three electrodes was not the immediate cause of the different voltages. To uncover the actual phenomenon, two additional experiments were conducted (Figs 2 and 3).

In the first additional experiment (Fig 2), the distance between the electrodes was increased from position T1 to position T3 in the standing tree and from G1 to G3 in the soil (Fig 2). The corresponding data (Fig 6A) revealed that the voltage change did not correlate with the shift in position, indicating that the position of an electrode does not strongly affect the internal resistance of the tree-source. Therefore, the contributions from the standing tree and the soil to the internal resistance are negligible. However, when the surface soil at G1, G2, and G3 was tamped, all corresponding voltages increased by at least 50 mV (Fig 6B). Likewise, tamping the surface soil of the Al, Fe, Cu-plated Al, and Cu-plated Fe electrodes also produced a similar effect on the voltage. This finding suggests that the contact resistance between an electrode and the soil is a major component of the internal resistance of the tree-based power source. In the second additional experiment (Fig 3), higher voltages were obtained from electrodes with larger diameters (Fig 7). That is, increasing the contact area between the electrode and the trunk also increased the measured voltage. This finding suggests that the contact resistance between an electrode and tree trunk is also an important part of the internal resistance of the tree-source. The value of this contact resistance may be thousands of ohms, in consideration of the high level of internal resistance present in the tree-source (in the range of 15.9 kΩ to 21.1 kΩ in the second additional experiment). Therefore, the reason for the different voltages among the three electrodes (Cu, Al, and Fe, Fig 5) is the difference in the contact resistance of electrode-soil and electrode-trunk contact surfaces and not the difference in the electrode resistance alone. That is, smaller contact resistances between the electrode and the soil (or trunk) caused higher voltages. Moreover, under the same soil and trunk environment, the metal with the higher conductivity also achieved a smaller contact resistance with the soil and the trunk. Therefore, the Cu electrode (which has the highest conductivity) achieved a smaller contact resistance with the soil and the trunk than Al electrode and Fe electrode, resulting in the highest voltage obtained in the primary experiment (Fig 5). The internal resistance of the tree-source was also measured by all three metal electrodes (Cu, Al, and Fe). The measured resistances were 17.9 kΩ (Cu), 105.7 kΩ (Al), and 188.9 kΩ (Fe). The magnitudes of the resistances measured with the three different electrodes (Cu, Al, and Fe), from small to large, were Cu, Al, and Fe, which was consistent with the resistivities of the three metals. Moreover, the metal with the highest conductivity (Cu) decreased the internal resistance (and the contact resistance) by tens of thousands of ohms. This result indicated that the metal with the higher conductivity achieved a smaller contact resistance and smaller internal resistance of the tree-source. In this case, the effects of metal conductivity on voltage are primarily determined by the surface metal materials in direct contact with the soil and the trunk. The primary experiment also demonstrated that cheap metals, such as Fe and Al, can be selected for inclusion by coating a more conductive metal, such as Cu. As an extension of this concept, a supplementary experiment was conducted to test the performance of electrodes with nonmetallic inclusions (Fig 4).

In the supplementary experiment (Fig 4), the magnitudes of the voltages measured by the electrodes with nonmetallic inclusions (plastic, glass, wood, and ceramic) were similar to that of the Cu electrode (Fig 8). These results indicate that nonmetallic materials, such as plastic, glass, wood, and ceramic, can also be good choices for electrode construction. In addition, when Cu is plated on the surface of a nonmetallic material, the resulting surface is slightly rougher than when Cu is plated on a metal. This surface roughness can increase the contact area between the electrode and the soil. Therefore, higher voltages were measured by the Cu-plated electrodes in the supplementary experiment.

Stability

The resistivity of Al is closer to that of Cu than Fe, but the voltage curve measured with the Al electrode was closer to that of the Fe electrode (Fig 5). This result was obtained because Al oxidizes more readily, forming a high-resistance oxide layer [25], which increases the contact resistance between the electrode and the soil (and the trunk). As a result, the voltage curve measured with the Al electrode was closer to that of the Fe electrode. In addition, the Al electrode exhibited significant instability throughout the entire experiment, also yielding the most rapidly decreasing voltage curve. In addition to oxidation, Al also undergoes a process of self-passivation, in which a compact oxide coating forms on its surface [26]. This phenomenon likely occurred in the experiment, reducing the contact area between the Al metal and the soil (and the trunk). In contrast, the metals Cu and Fe are resistant to passivation in natural or mildly acidic soil and tree trunk conditions, hence these electrodes resulted in relatively flat corresponding curves. Fe can oxidize rapidly in wet environments; however, in this experiment, the corresponding voltage decrease was slightly larger than that of Cu, but not as significant as that of Al. The reason for this is that no passivation occurred on the surface of the Fe electrode. That is, although a large oxidized area developed on the Fe surface, the oxide did not form a coherent oxide layer. Therefore, the contact area between the Fe electrode and the soil (and the trunk) or the moisture in the soil (and the trunk) did not significantly decrease. Furthermore, due to the specific nature of the Al electrode, as discussed, its corresponding voltage curve differed from those of the Fe and Cu electrodes. For example, data sets 17 to 19 (Fig 5) for the Cu and the Fe electrodes display slowly increasing voltages, whereas the corresponding curve for the Al electrode decreases continuously. These results suggest that during such a period, factors associated with either the environment or the trunk of the standing tree caused the voltage to increase, while the passivation of the Al electrode severely affected the voltage ultimately obtained. Thus, the stability of the electrode material has no significant effect on the voltage. However, passivation of the electrode material can significantly reduce the voltage obtained.

Cu plating

Higher voltages were measured for the Cu-plated Al and Fe electrodes compared with the non-plated Al and Fe electrodes. When the first measurement was recorded (Fig 5), each electrode was in its initial state such that the difference in the measured voltage was determined by the conductivity of each electrode. The measured voltages recorded with Cu, Cu-plated Al, and Cu-plated Fe were almost identical, indicating that the Cu plating on the Al and Fe electrodes provided these complex electrodes with nearly the same characteristics as the Cu electrode. It is easy to comprehend that after plating with Cu, the Al and Fe electrodes acquired surface and contact resistances with the soil and trunk that were similar to those of the Cu electrode. However, as revealed by the first data set, the Cu-plated Al electrode had a smaller voltage because the plating was artificially damaged before the experiment. Because the degree of damage was limited, this electrode's voltage was not markedly different from that of either the Cu electrode or the Cu-plated Fe electrode. However, after time had passed, the voltage curve of the Cu-plated Al electrode decreased significantly and eventually merged with the corresponding curve of the Al electrode. In contrast, the Cu-plated Fe electrode showed little decrease in voltage before data set 11. These results suggest that in these wet soil and trunk environments, the minor damage to the Cu coating of the Cu-plated Al electrode before the experiment resulted in the rapid degradation of the plating quality. After data sets 11 and 22 were recorded, the voltage curve of the Cu electrode significantly decreased, suggesting that the Cu had oxidized. Evidence of oxidation also occurred on the Cu coatings of the Cu-plated Al and the Cu-plated Fe electrodes. Moreover, destruction of the Cu coatings on the Cu-plated Al and the Cu-plated Fe electrodes altered the material exposed at the electrode surface. Therefore, the voltage curves of the Cu-plated Al electrodes and the Cu-plated Fe electrodes displayed more significant decreases, especially the Cu-plated Al electrode that had been artificially damaged prior to the experiment. Unsurprisingly, the voltage increased when using the Al and Fe electrodes with the Cu plating. However, the 10-μm-thick layer of Cu plating could not maintain the performance of the electrode for an extended period. Based on these results, one option would be to increase the thickness of the plating treatment, which is demonstrated in the supplementary experiment.

CONCLUSIONS

The metal reactivity of an electrode has no significant effect on the voltage between a standing tree and its surrounding soil. However, passivation of the electrode materials markedly reduces the voltage. The conductivity of the metal electrode has an effect on the contact resistance of the electrode-soil and electrode-trunk contact surfaces, which significantly influences the voltage level. The metal with the higher conductivity leads to a smaller contact resistance, as well as to a higher voltage level. Therefore, the effects of metal conductivity on voltage are primarily determined by the surface metal materials in direct contact with the soil and the trunk. It is suggested that cheap metals, such as Fe and Al, can be selected for inclusion within a metal coating (with better conductivity), which would most likely achieve good efficiency, stability, and economy. Moreover, it is demonstrated that cheap nonmetallic materials, such as plastic, glass, wood, and ceramic, are also good choices for the inclusion. In addition, the thickness of the coating must be increased to obtain higher stability and reliability.

ACKNOWLEDGMENTS

We thank Chao Feng and Chongxin Chen for their help with fieldwork.

AUTHOR CONTRIBUTIONS

Conceived and designed the experiments: ZH GW WL JZ JK. Performed the experiments: ZH GW WL JZ JK. Analyzed the data: ZH GW WL JZ JK. Contributed reagents/materials/analysis tools: ZH GW WL JZ JK. Wrote the paper: ZH GW WL JZ JK.

REFERENCES

1. Yamaguchi T, Hashimoto S. A green battery by pot-plant power. IEEJ T Electr Electr. 2012;7: 441–442. doi: 10.1002/tee.21754
2. Love CJ, Zhang SG, Mershin A. Source of sustained voltage difference between the xylem of a potted ficus benjamina tree and its soil. PLOS ONE. 2008;3: e2963. doi: 10.1371/journal.pone.0002963. pmid:18698415
3. Paradiso JA, Starner T. Energy scavenging for mobile and wireless electronics. IEEE Pervas Comput. 2005;4: 18–27. doi: 10.1109/mprv.2005.9
4. Saadon S, Sidek O. A review of vibration-based MEMS piezoelectric energy harvesters. Energ Convers Manage. 2011;52: 500–504. doi: 10.1016/j.enconman.2010.07.024
5. Suzuki K, Fukuda T, Liao YJ. Electrosprayed molybdenum trioxide aqueous solution and its application in organic photovoltaic cells. PLOS ONE. 2014;9: e106012. doi: 10.1371/journal.pone.0106012. pmid:25148047
6. Rodriguez-Barreiro R, Abendroth C, Vilanova C, Moya A, Porcar M. Towards a microbial thermoelectric cell. PLOS ONE. 2013;8: e56358. doi: 10.1371/journal.pone.0056358. pmid:23468862
7. Dincer I, Acar C. A review on clean energy solutions for better sustainability. Int J Energ Res. 2015;39: 585–606. doi: 10.1002/er.3329
8. Remeli MF, Tan L, Date A, Singh B, Akbarzadeh A. Simultaneous power generation and heat recovery using a heat pipe assisted thermoelectric generator system. Energ Convers Manage. 2015;91: 110–119. doi: 10.1016/j.enconman.2014.12.001

9. Arutchelvi M, Daniel SA. Composite controller for a hybrid power plant based on PV array fed wind-driven induction generator with battery storage. Int J Energ Res. 2007;31: 515–524. doi: 10.1002/er.1262

10. Ghosh S, Wang HT, Leon-Salas WD. A circuit for energy harvesting using On-Chip solar cells. IEEE T Power Electr. 2014;29: 4658–4671. doi: 10.1109/tpel.2013.2273674

11. Himes C, Carlson E, Ricchiuti RJ, Otis BP, Parviz BA. Ultralow voltage nanoelectronics powered directly, and solely, from a tree. IEEE T Nanotechnol. 2010;9: 2–5. doi: 10.1109/tnano.2009.2032293

12. Himes C, Carlson E, Ricchiuti RJ, Taylor DW, Otis B, Parviz BA. Using plants for directly powering nanoelectronic circuits. Nanotechnology Perceptions. 2010;6: 29–40. doi: 10.4024/n01hi10a.ntp.06.01

13. Labady A, Thomas D, Shvetsova T, Volkov AG. Plant bioelectrochemistry: effects of CCCP on electrical signaling in soybean. Bioelectrochemistry. 2002;57: 47–53. pmid:12049756 doi: 10.1016/s1567-5394(01)00175-x

14. Lautner S, Grams TEE, Matyssek R, Fromm J. Characteristics of electrical signals in poplar and responses in photosynthesis. Plant Physiol. 2005;138: 2200–2209. pmid:16040648 doi: 10.1104/pp.105.064196

15. Fromm J, Lautner S. Electrical signals and their physiological significance in plants. Plant Cell Environ. 2006;30: 249–257. doi: 10.1111/j.1365-3040.2006.01614.x

16. Gurovich LA, Hermosilla P. Electric signalling in fruit trees in response to water applications and light-darkness conditions. J Plant Physiol. 2009;166: 290–300. doi: 10.1016/j.jplph.2008.06.004. pmid:18760501

17. Volkov AG, Vilfranc CL, Murphy VA, Mitchell CM, Volkova MI, O'Neal L, et al. Electrotonic and action potentials in the Venus flytrap. J Plant Physiol 2013;170: 838–846. doi: 10.1016/j.jplph.2013.01.009. pmid:23422156

18. Gibert D, Le Mouël JL, Lambs L, Nicollin F, Perrier F. Sap flow and daily electric potential variations in a tree trunk. Plant Sci. 2006;171: 572–584. doi: 10.1016/j.plantsci.2006.06.012

19. Morat P, Le Mouël JL, Granier A. Electrical potential on a tree. CR Acad Sci. 1994;317: 98–101.

20. Koppán A, Szarka L, Wesztergom V. Temporal variation of electric signal recorded in a standing tree. Acta Geod Geophy Hu. 1999;34: 169–180.

21. Koppán A, Szarka L, Wesztergom V. Annual fluctuation in amplitudes of daily variations of electrical signals measured in the trunk of a standing tree. CR Acad Sci. 2000;323: 559–563. doi: 10.1016/s0764-4469(00)00179-7

22. Koppán A, Fenyvesi A, Szarka L, Wesztergom V. Measurement of electric potential difference on trees. Acta Biologica Szegediensis. 2002;46: 37–38.

23. Hao ZB, Li WB, Kan JM, Jiang LY, Feng C. Bioelectricity in standing Trees—a potential energy for wireless sensor networks. Telkomnik. 2013;11: 4841–4846. doi: 10.11591/telkomnika.v11i8.3148

24. Li XW, Gao L, Li WB, Yu WY. Exploration on trans-root potential of living trees. Journal of Information and Computational Science. 2013;10: 6131–6138. doi: 10.12733/jics20102993

25. Bartzsch H, Glöß D, Böcher B, Frach P, Goedicke K. Properties of SiO2 and Al2O3 films for electrical insulation applications deposited by reactive pulse magnetron sputtering. Surface and Coatings Technology. 2003;174: 774–778. doi: 10.1016/s0257-8972(03)00384-0

26. Sheffer M, Groysman A, Mandler D. Electrodeposition of sol-gel films on Al for corrosion protection. Corros Sci. 2003;45: 2893–2904. doi: 10.1016/s0010-938x(03)00106-9

CHAPTER 21

EFFECTS OF EDGE DIRECTIONS ON THE STRUCTURAL CONTROLLABILITY OF COMPLEX NETWORKS

Yandong Xiao,[1,*] Songyang Lao,[1] Lvlin Hou,[1,2] Michael Small,[2] and Liang Bai[1]

[1]Science and Technology on Information Systems Engineering Laboratory, National University of Defense Technology, Changsha, Hunan, China

[2]School of Mathematics and Statistics, The University of Western Australia, Crawley, WA, Australia

ABSTRACT

Recent advances indicate that assigning or reversing edge direction can significantly improve the structural controllability of complex networks. For directed networks, approaching the optimal structural controllability can be achieved by detecting and reversing certain "inappropriate" edge directions. However, the existence of multiple sets of "inappropriate" edge directions suggests that different edges have different effects on optimal controllability—that is, different combinations of edges can be reversed to achieve the same structural controllability. Therefore, we classify edges into three categories based on their direction: critical, redundant and intermittent. We then investigate the effects of changing these edge directions on network controllability, and demonstrate that the existence of more critical edge directions implies not only a lower cost of modifying inappropriate edges but also better controllability. Motivated by this finding, we present a simple edge orientation method aimed at producing more critical edge directions—utilizing only local information—which achieves near optimal controllability. Furthermore, we explore the effects of edge direction on the controllability of several real networks.

INTRODUCTION

One of the most fundamental challenges in network science is to understand the impact of structural properties on network functionality. In part, this is because understanding the network structure is prerequisite to answering the challenging questions related to the system's dynamics [1–3]. Structure and dynamics are always coupled and ultimately led to many remarkable advances in the past decade in such areas as epidemic spreading [4, 5], random walks [6, 7], cascade failure [8, 9], and synchronization [10, 11]. Questions concerning the management and control of complex networks are important in engineering [12], finance [13], biology [14] and other fields because the ultimate proof of our understanding of such complex systems and their basic principles is reflected in our ability to control [15–19] and ultimately observe them [20]. The framework for computing the controllability of complex networks proposed by Liu and Barabási [19] offers a general, rigorous, and well-understood means of investigating how we can control complex networks with the fewest input signals. Recent advances in the application of control theory to complex networks have shed new light on this problem [21–30]. The

Citation: Xiao Y, Lao S, Hou L, Small M, Bai L (2015) Effects of Edge Directions on the Structural Controllability of Complex Networks. PLoS ONE 10(8): e0135282. doi:10.1371/journal.pone.0135282

main finding has been that the application of external signals to some subset of nodes can cause a system to approach a desired state within finite time.

Obviously, controllability in general can be achieved through the control of only the subset of nodes termed driver nodes. The minimum driver node set can be efficiently identified using the Minimum Inputs Theorem of Ref. [19]. Based on this approach to the minimization of the driver node set, several advances in the optimization of network controllability have already been made, the most representative methods of which rely on adding edges [25, 31], rewiring edges [32] and assigning edge directions [33, 34]. Compared with the first two methods (which stem from the modification of the network structure), assigning edge directions to optimize network controllability appears to be the most effective from the perspective of designing a network with improved or even optimal controllability because it neither changes the original structure of the network nor incurs the external cost of adding links. By *edge orientation*, we refer to the process of assigning edge directions to undirected edges in an undirected network or (equivalently) reversing the directions of directed edges in a directed network. This method aims to approach optimal controllability without requiring any modification of the network structure, by which we mean that the presence or absence of a link between each pair of nodes remains unchanged. To this end, Xiao et al. [34] have systematically proposed the definition and solution for the edge orientation of optimal controllability (EOOC). Solving the EOOC problem requires constructing a corresponding network and transforming the problem into one of finding a maximum independent set (MIS) of this corresponding network.

For directed networks, there are certain "inappropriate" edge directions that may weaken the controllability of a network, i.e., so-called dilations and inaccessibility. First, we must identify all these "inappropriate" edge directions in a network and then reverse them. However, there are several different "inappropriate" direction sets for a given network, and the existence of multiple "inappropriate" direction sets suggests that different edges play different roles in optimal controllability. Previous work has focused on how to detect these "inappropriate" edge directions while ignoring the effects of edge direction on the optimal network controllability. In this work, we briefly review the definition of the EOOC and the framework in which to solve this problem. The remainder of this paper is organized as follows. We first classify all edge directions into three categories: critical edge directions, which always appear in the optimal direction set during the optimization process and are also called the skeleton of optimal controllability; redundant edge directions, which have no effect on optimization; and intermittent edge directions, which participate in some optimal direction sets but not others. In Ref. [29], Jia et al. also propose the similar definition of node classification to explore the role of individual nodes in acting as a driver node in all, some or none of the control configurations. However, though the definitions of node classification and edge classification are similar ideas, the research points do not have directed relations. It is because that we study the roles of edge direction when we assign them to approach the optimal controllability for a given network skeleton. Next, we study the correlation between critical edge directions and driver nodes and demonstrate that the existence of more critical edge directions in a network implies not only a lower cost of modifying inappropriate edges but also better controllability. Motivated by this finding, we analyze the structural properties of the three categories of edge directions and develop a simple edge orientation method based on the generation of more critical edge directions. The results of numerical experiments suggest that this method achieves a near-optimal optimization effect while requiring only local structural information. Finally, we apply the developed tool to a series of real networks and successfully explain why the structures of electronic circuit networks take advantage of controllability.

EDGE ORIENTATION FOR OPTIMAL CONTROLLABILITY

Ref. [34] provides a general solution to the problem of finding an edge direction set for optimal controllability, summarized as follows. First, construct a corresponding network and transform the EOOC problem into a problem of finding a maximum independent set of vertices in the corresponding network. A directed network G (Fig 1(a)) and its corresponding symmetric directed network G' (Fig 1(b)) are a pair (V, E) and (V, E') that consisted of a set of nodes V and edges E, E'. If each directed edge (v_i, v_j) in G' corresponds to a node a_{ij}, then we can construct a corresponding network $H = (A, B)$ that consisted of a set of nodes A and edges B. The construction of links in H follows three simple principles.

- Rule I: two nodes in H that correspond to a pair of symmetric directed edges of G' must be connected (green edges in Fig 1(c)).
- Rule II: two or more nodes in H that correspond to the edges pointing to a tail node must be connected (purple edges in Fig 1(c)).
- Rule III: two or more nodes in H that correspond to the edges pointing from a head node must be connected (orange edges in Fig 1(c)).

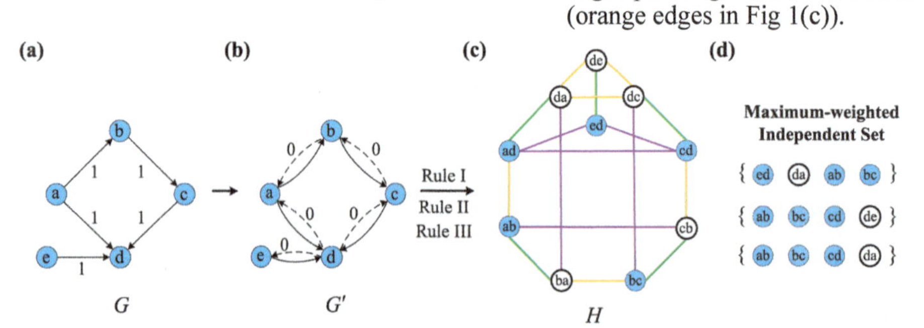

Figure 1. Illustration of Edge Orientation for Optimal Controllability.

(a) A directed network $G = (V, E)$ with 5 nodes and 5 directed edges. For directed networks, some edges with "inappropriate" direction affect the controllability of networks, such as e_{ed}. If we change its direction, we can improve the controllability. (b) G' is the symmetric directed network. Here we assume that the weight of real edge is 1 otherwise it is 0. Thus it results in the nodes of H with different weight. (c) The corresponding network H. The maximum-weighted independent set means not only the optimal edge orientation but also the least number of edges required to have their direction changed, because the node with weight 0 (the white nodes) in the maximum-weighted independent set implies the "inappropriate" edge of G. (d) The different maximum-weighted independent sets result in the different control configurations. The light blue nodes represent the real edges of G.

The next step is to calculate the maximum independent vertex set of H. Ref. [34] has shown that through the assignment of edge directions based on the MIS of H, the optimal controllability can be approached for a given undirected network. The detailed proof of this assertion can be found in Ref. [34]. In fact, the EOOC effectively mitigates the negative effects of inaccessibility and dilations, which are the two main factors that weaken network controllability.

In directed networks, the EOOC can allow for the detection of several "inappropriate" edges and the reversal of their directions to approach optimal controllability. For example, in Fig 1(a), the edge e_{ed} weakens the controllability because this directed edge results in the inaccessibility of node e. If we reverse the original direction of e_{ed}, the number of required driver nodes decreases from 2 to 1. The extent of the directed network for the EOOC only considers the edge weights of the original network. We assume a directed graph $G = (V, E, W)$ and its symmetric directed graph $G' = (V, E', W')$, both of which are edge-weighted (W, W' represent the edge weight set). The weight of any real edge is 1 if it exists in G'; otherwise, it is 0 (Fig 1(b)). Thus, every node of $H = (A, B, W')$ corresponds to weight 0 or 1. The maximum-weighted independent set (MWIS) of vertices in H corresponds to the orientation set for optimal controllability of the directed network G. The basic theory follows from the analysis of the EOOC for an undirected network. The principle of maximum weight guarantees that the independent set contains the most nodes of weight 1 and the fewest nodes of weight 0, meaning that the number of edges that need to be modified is minimal. For example, Fig 1(d) shows the MWIS of H. The white nodes represent the reversal of "inappropriate" edge directions in Fig 1(a). It has been proven that the calculation of the MWIS is a typical NP-hard problem in computational complexity theory [35–37]; thus, a polynomial-time algorithm to find MWIS solutions for arbitrary graphs is not feasible. In the following, we will proceed using an integer linear programming (ILP) formulation for MWIS computation, in which the optimal solution was calculated using the IBM ILOG CPLEX v.12.6. From $H = (A, B, W')$, the ILP instance is constructed as following:

$$\begin{aligned} \max \quad & Z = \sum w'_i x_i \\ \text{s.t.} \quad & x_i + x_j \leq 1, \forall (v_i, v_j) \in B \\ & x_i = \{0, 1\}, v_i \in A \end{aligned} \tag{1}$$

The set $\{v | x_v = 1\}$ then clearly corresponds to a maximum-weighted independent set.

CATEGORIES OF EDGE DIRECTIONS FOR OPTIMAL STRUCTURAL CONTROLLABILITY

A directed network possesses several sets of "inappropriate" edges because there are multiple MWIS configurations by which the network can approach optimal controllability. This phenomenon suggests that different edge directions have different effects on the optimal structural controllability. Therefore, the existence of these multiple configurations leads to the classification of edge directions into three categories: *critical edge directions*, corresponding to edges that are always present in the MWIS configurations; *redundant edge directions*, describing those edges that are never a part of an MWIS; and *intermittent edge directions*, corresponding to edges that participate in some MWISs but not in others. According to these definitions, edges that belong to the critical direction set play a significant role in the optimal controllability because they must appear in any optimal orientation set. Thus, the critical direction set can be regarded as the skeleton of optimal controllability. Conversely, the redundant direction set has no effect on the optimal controllability. The role of intermittent edge directions lies somewhere between these two extremes, as some cases require the directions of these edges to be reversed to approach optimal controllability. Fig 2 shows all optimal control configurations identified using the MWIS approach for Fig 1(a). The red edges in Fig 2(a), 2(b) and 2(c) and the red nodes in Fig 2(d) indicate the critical edge directions of the initial directed network G. The blue nodes in Fig 2(d) correspond to the intermittent edge directions. The blue dashed edge in Fig 2(a), 2(b) and 2(c) becomes an "appropriate" edge after the reversal of the original directions.

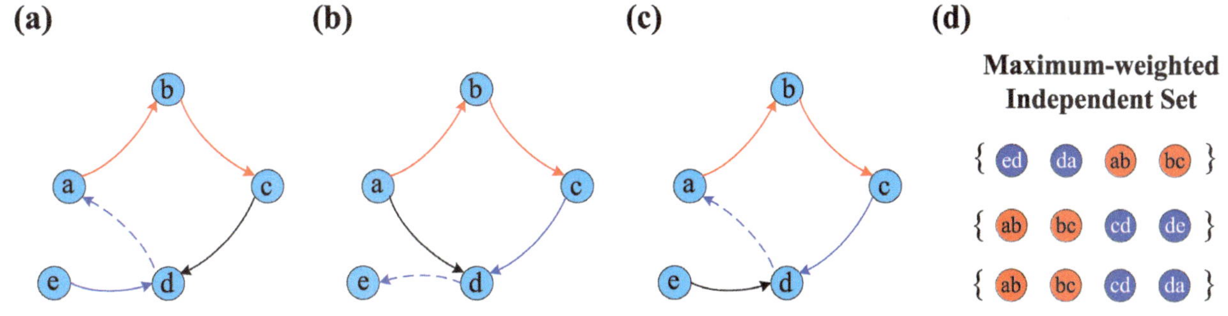

Figure 2. Illustration of classification of edge direction for EOOC in a directed network.

(a, b, c) The networks are modified by maximum-weighted independent sets showing optimal controllability. (d) The different maximum-weighted independent sets show the different control configurations. The red nodes, e_{ab} and e_{bc}, always appear on the MWIS, called the critical edge direction. The blue nodes, defined as intermittent edge directions, participate in some MWISs but not every MWIS.

The detailed procedures *Critical*MWIS (Algorithm 1 in S1 File) and *Redundant*MWIS (Algorithm 2 in S1 File) for the classification of edge directions are included in S1 File. Fig 3 shows the fractions of critical, redundant and intermittent edge directions in two basic network models of different average degree ⟨*k*⟩, the Erdös-Rényi (ER) model [38], and scale-free (SF) model [39]. SF networks are generated from the static model in Ref. [40]. Note that in the case of $\rightarrow \infty$, this model is equivalent to the classical ER random network model. The green columns represent edges with weight 0, i.e., the non-real edges in the original directed networks. According to the definition of critical edge directions, the directions of edges with weight 0 (green columns) in the critical set must be modified during the optimization process. However, as ⟨*k*⟩ increases, the proportion of the critical set consisting of edges with weight 0 decreases and may even vanish. In the redundant edge direction set, non-real edges constitute the larger proportion, and as ⟨*k*⟩ increases, the redundant set tends to consist entirely of non-real edges. Compared with the redundant set, the intermittent edge direction set exhibits the opposite tendency of variation, as real edges constitute the larger proportion of this set. In particular, for an ER network with high ⟨*k*⟩, the intermittent set tends to consist entirely of real edges.

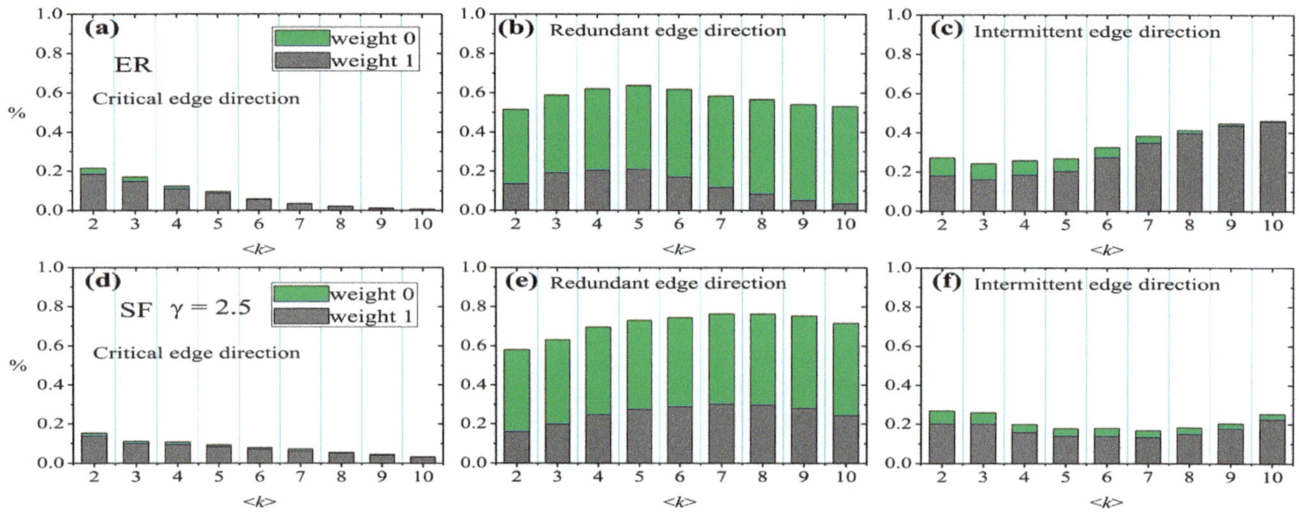

Figure 3. Characteristics of the fraction of three different edge direction sets in the directed networks.

(a-c) ER network under different average degree ⟨*k*⟩. (d-f) SF network with $= 2.5$ under different average degree ⟨*k*⟩. The grey columns represent the real edges in the original directed networks *G* or nodes with weight 1 in the corresponding network *H*, while the green columns imply the non-real edges in *G* or nodes with weight 0 in *H*. The number of nodes is 10^3.

In fact, the critical edge direction set can be regarded as the skeleton of optimal controllability because these directions can never be modified. In other words, these directions are always appropriate for a given network. If a network contains a larger number of critical edge directions, it implies not only a lower cost for modifying "inappropriate" edge directions but also better controllability. Therefore, we analyze the relationship between driver nodes and critical edge directions. Here, the fraction of driver nodes is a measure of the network controllability because the existence of fewer driver nodes implies better controllability. For a network with a fixed average degree, as shown in Fig 4, we consider various fractions of critical edge directions and their corresponding driver nodes in the ER and SF models. Here, a different fraction of critical edge directions in a given network is produced by edge swapping while keeping the degree of each node unchanged. Hence, in the original network, we swap the connections of two randomly chosen edges; that is, the edges e_{ij} and e_{kl} become edges e_{il} ande_{kj}, respectively. At each step, we calculate and compare the fractions of critical edge directions before and after the edge swap. If the fraction of critical edge directions decreases, we consider the swap to be successful. If it is unsuccessful, the swap is reversed, and another swapping step is tested. As seen in Fig 4, for both ER and SF model, the number of driver nodes decreases with an increasing fraction of critical edge directions. The numerical results confirm the above analysis.

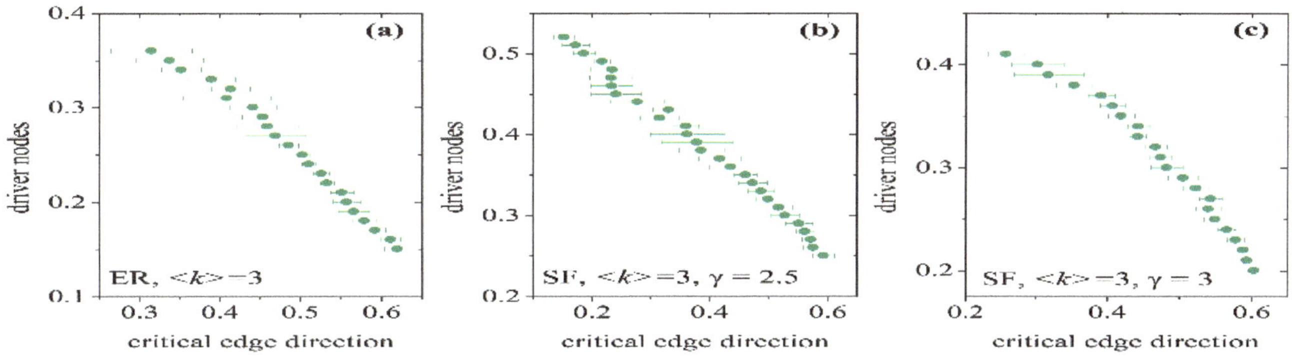

Figure 4. Scatterplot of the faction of critical edge directions the corresponding driver nodes.

The number of nodes is 10^3. We repeat this procedure until the total number of swapping reaches 10^6. The results are 10 independent realizations.

Structural Analysis of Critical Edge Directions

To more deeply understand the properties of the three different edge direction sets, we analyze the corresponding degrees of edges with critical, redundant and intermittent edge directions. Here, the corresponding degree of an edge means its number of neighboring nodes in the corresponding network H, as every directed edge corresponds to a node in H. Fig 5(a) and 5(b)reproduce portions of Fig 1(c) and 1(b), respectively, to illustrate the meaning of the corresponding degree of an edge. The four nodes in Fig 5(a) correspond to the four edges inFig 5(b), according to the rules of EOOC. In fact, these four edges in Fig 5(b) represent three "inappropriate" control conditions: two edges pointing toward the common tail (red and purple edges), two edges pointing from the head node (red and orange edges) and two edges constituting a 2-cycle (red and green edges). The first two "inappropriate" control conditions, called inaccessibility and dilation, respectively, can weaken controllability and should appear in a network as rarely as possible. The last condition, edges constituting a 2-cycle, is meaningless with regard to edge orientation because EOOC only assigns a single direction for an undirected link. According to the rules of link construction in H, the node in Fig 5(a) is connected with other nodes which produces the above three "inappropriate" conditions. Therefore, the corresponding degree of an edge reflects its associated number of "inappropriate" control conditions. Ref. [34] has deduced the node degree of the corresponding network H, i.e., $k_{a(i,j)} = k_{a(j,i)} = k_i + k_j - 1$. **(2)**Here, $a_{(i,j)}$ and $a_{(j,i)}$ are the symmetric directed edges and correspond to two nodes in H, and$k_{a(i,j)}$ is the corresponding degree of a directed edge.

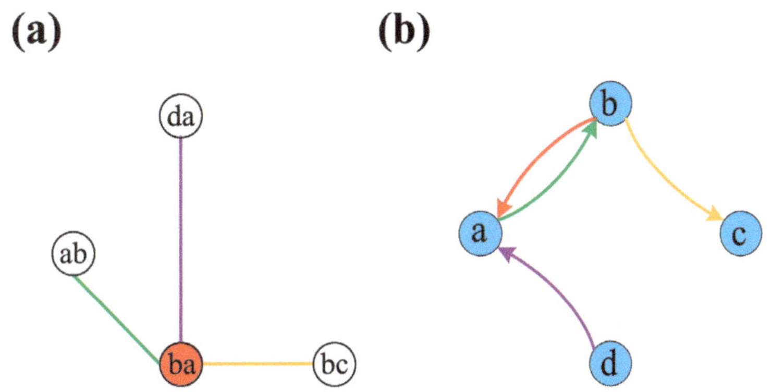

Figure 5. Illustration of three "inappropriate" control conditions.

The red and green edges of (b) constitute a 2-cycle—which is meaningless for EOOC. The red and orange edges of (b) point from the common head node which produces dilation in the network. The red and purple edges of (b) point to the common tail node which increases an inaccessible node in the network. Actually, the corresponding degree of directed edge v_{ba} means the number of "inappropriate" control conditions.

Fig 6 shows the average corresponding degrees of the critical, redundant and intermittent edge direction sets under various values of $\langle k \rangle$ for the ER and SF networks. The average corresponding degrees of the three direction categories represent the average numbers of associated "inappropriate" control conditions. In Fig 6(a) and 6(b), as $\langle k \rangle$ increases, the average corresponding degrees of all three categories also increase. However, compared with the other two direction sets, the critical direction set has the smallest average corresponding degree. Meanwhile, the redundant edge set has the largest average corresponding degree. The corresponding degree of the intermittent edge set is between those of the critical and redundant direction sets. Fig 6(c) and 6(d) display the corresponding degrees of edges with a weight of 1 (real edges) or 0 (non-real edges). For all three direction categories, the average corresponding degrees of real edges are larger than those of non-real edges. Moreover, the corresponding degree of critical edge directions associated with non-real edges initially increases and then decreases with increasing $\langle k \rangle$. It is because that, with the increase of $\langle k \rangle$, the fraction of critical edge directions corresponding to non-real edges become smaller and even disappeared, which could be approved by Fig 3(a) and 3(d). So these non-monotonic results are caused by the decrease in the number of critical edge directions associated with non-real edges. Therefore, an edge direction associated with fewer "inappropriate" control conditions is more likely to be a critical edge direction.

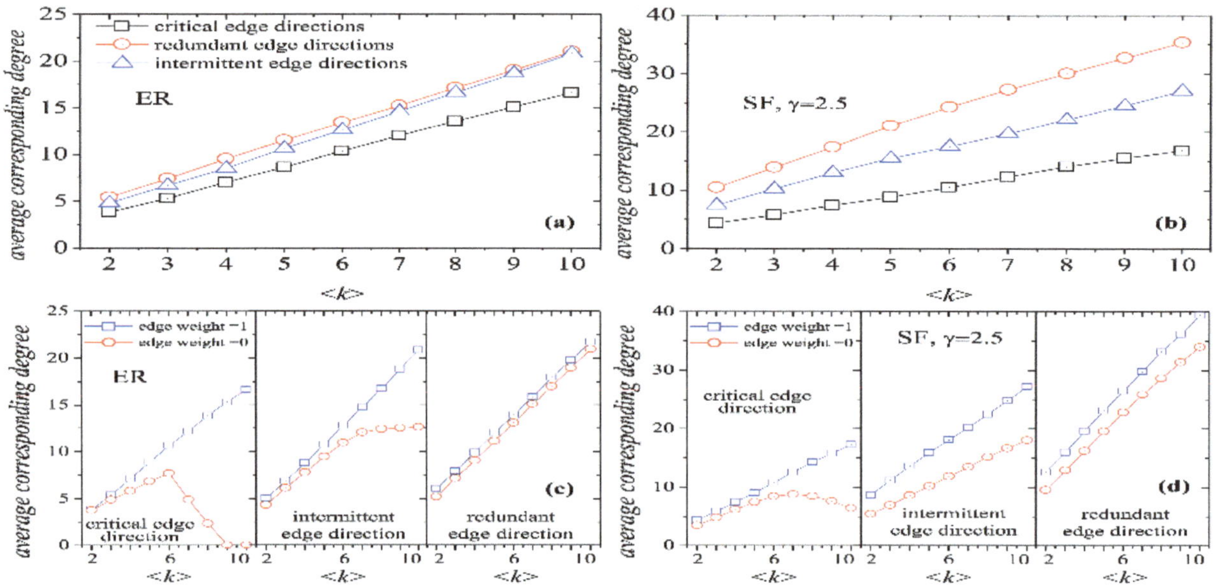

Figure 6. Characteristics of the corresponding degree of critical, redundant and intermittent edge direction set under different ⟨k⟩ for ER and SF networks.

The corresponding degree of edge direction means the number of "inappropriate" control conditions. The subplots (c, d) display the degree of edge with weight 1 (real edges) and 0 (non-real edges) respectively. The number of nodes is 10^3.

In Fig 7, we classify the real edges into three categories and rank the nodes in ascending order of corresponding degree. In accordance with the symmetric property of the corresponding network, we also display the category of each non-real edge. Thus, the *x* axis of Fig 7 refers to pairs of symmetric directed edges (real and non-real edges). Notably, the degrees of the symmetric non-real edges are also ranked in ascending order, and the two symmetric non-real edges have same degree. As seen from Fig 7, all symmetric non-real edges corresponding to edges in the critical edge direction set appear in the redundant edge direction set. This is because the critical edge directions appear in every MWIS and, therefore, their symmetric edges can never appear in any MWIS. With regard to the real edges associated with intermittent edge directions, their symmetric non-real edges of low degree also tend to belong to the category of intermittent edge directions, whereas most of their symmetric non-real edges of high degree are likely to appear in the redundant edge direction set. With regard to the real edges associated with redundant edge directions, their symmetric non-real edges of low degree tend to appear in the intermittent edge direction set or even the critical edge direction set, but their symmetric non-real edges of high corresponding degree are still likely to have redundant edge directions. These results indicate that nodes of low degree may have either significant (due to their critical edge directions) or partial (due to their intermittent edge directions) effects on optimal controllability.

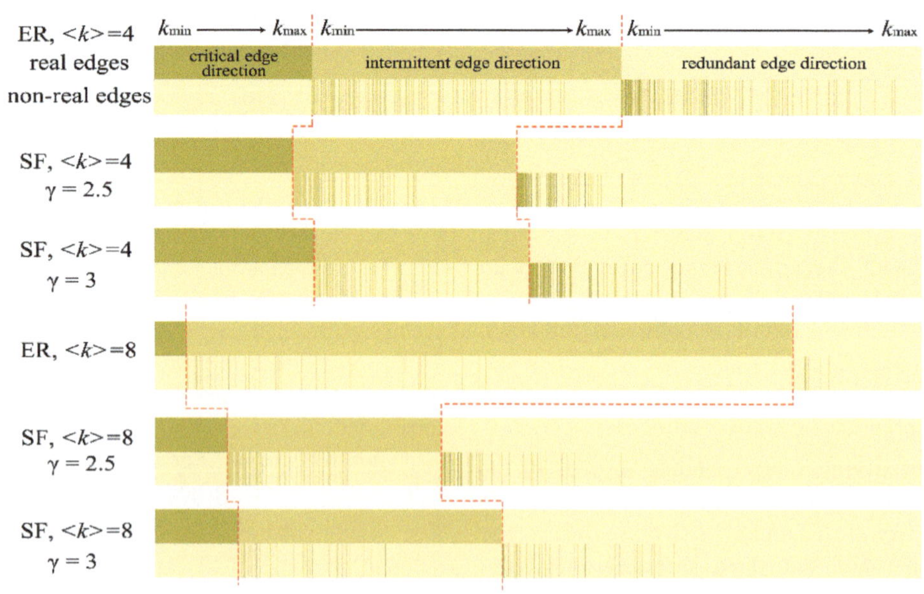

Figure 7. Characteristics of the category of symmetric real and non-real edges for ER and SF models.

The x-axis displays every two symmetric directed edges. The real edges are divided into three categories and are ranked in ascending order of node degree. Due to the symmetric real and non-real edges having the same degree, the non-real edges are also ranked in the ascending order of degree. The number of nodes is 10^3.

Edge Orientation by Critical Directions

In this section, we present a method for generating more critical edge directions, which we call*edge orientation by critical directions* (EOCD). The different categories of edge directions play different roles in the optimal controllability of a network. Based on the above analysis, we can draw two conclusions: (i) more critical edge directions are beneficial for enhancing controllability and decreasing the cost of improvements because there are fewer driver nodes and fewer "inappropriate" directions to be reversed, and (ii) an edge direction associated with fewer "inappropriate" control conditions is more likely to be a critical edge direction, that is, low-degree nodes have positive effects on optimal controllability. Moreover, previous studies of network controllability have indicated that the number of driver nodes is correlated with the control path [33] and the density of low in- and out-degree nodes [31]. In fact, the EOOC [34] approach attempts to produce the longest disjoint control path after the orientation of edge directions. Thus, we propose an edge orientation algorithm to produce the longest possible disjoint control path and as many critical edge directions as possible, starting from a node of the lowest degree. Consider an undirected network $G(V, E)$. The EOCD method can be described as follows. The residual degree k' of a node represents the number of undirected links of that node; k' is initially equal to k, where k is the degree of the node. Note that if there are multiple such nodes matching the conditions, we randomly select one of them.

1. Compute $k'(i) + k'(j)$ for two nodes i and j connected by a link e_{ij}. Select the two nodes with the smallest sum of their residual degree. The selected node with the smaller degree is denoted as V_1, and the selected node with big degree is labelled as V_2. Note that we do not consider the isolated nodes.
2. Assign the edge direction to be from V_1 to V_2. Consequently, the residual degree of the selected nodes is reduced, i.e., $k'(V_1) = k'(V_1) - 1$, $k'(V_2) = k'(V_2) - 1$.
3. Select the node with the smallest degree among the neighbors of V_2, and confirm that the newly selected node is not yet labelled. The newly selected node is denoted by V_2, and the node formerly labeled V_2 is now re-labelled as V_1. Note that V_1 and V_2 are different.
4. Repeat step (ii) until all neighbors of V_2 are labeled.
5. If k' is equal to 0 for all nodes, proceed to step (vi). Otherwise, clear the labels all nodes, delete the assigned edges, and repeat step (i).
6. Orient all edge directions assigned at step (ii).

For comparative experiments, we consider the method of random direction assignment (RAD), a method based on the node residual degree (NRD) [33] and the method of edge orientation for optimal controllability (EOOC) [34]. Assigning directions based on the node residual degree (NRD) is an effective method of enhancing network controllability that is superior to random direction assignment (RAD). However, the NRD method cannot consider the effects of critical edge directions. The EOCD method is similar to the NRD method except for the manner in which the starting node is selected for each orientation step. Fig 8 (a), 8(b) and 8(c) present the optimization results of EOCD, which are close to the optimal EOOC solutions and superior to the NRD results. Fig 8 (d), 8(e) and 8(f) indicate that EOCD can generate more critical edge directions than the NRD method but, naturally, fewer than the EOOC. Moreover, the EOCD method is advantageous in terms of time complexity because it neither constructs a corresponding graph nor calculates the maximum independent set. In other words, EOCD requires only local structural information but achieves a near-optimal result.

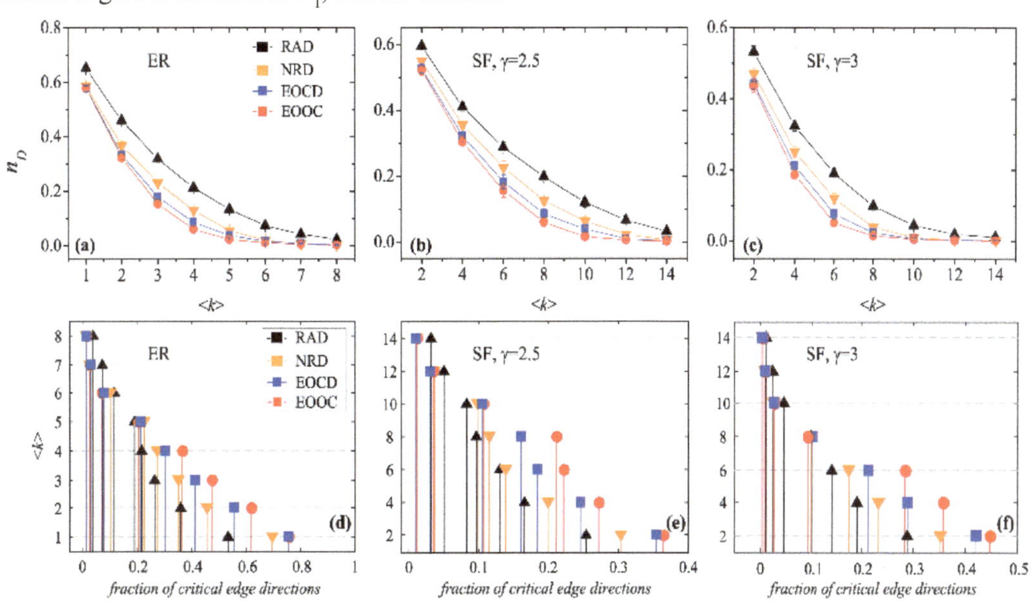

Figure 8. Characteristics of fraction of driver nodes (n_D) and critical edge directions as a function of ⟨k⟩ for the method of random direction assignment (RAD), the method based on node residual degree (NRD), the method of edge orientation for optimal controllability (EOOC) and the method of edge orientation by critical directions (EOCD) on (a, d) ER networks, (b, e) SF networks with $\gamma = 2.5$, (c, f) SF networks with $\gamma = 3$.

The number of nodes is 10^3.

Analysis of Real Networks

We now use the tools developed above to explore the controllability of several real networks, presented in Table 1. Previous work [19] has shown that there is no correlation between the N_D of an original network and the N_D of its randomized counterpart because a system's controllability is, to a great extent, encoded by the underlying network's degree distribution. To identify the topological features that affect the optimization of network controllability, we randomize each real network using a full randomization procedure (rand-ER) that transforms the network into a directed random ER network with N and L unchanged. We also apply a degree-preserving randomization procedure (rand-Degree), which leaves the in-degree and out-degree of each node unchanged but randomly selects which nodes are linked to each other. From the results presented in Fig 9(b), we find that the optimization is also affected by the network structure because $n_D^{real}(opt)$ is similar to $n_D^{rand-Degree}(opt)$. In fact, it can be said that the EOOC optimizes the controllability without changing the network skeleton. Moreover, we find that the networks of electronic circuits possess features distinct from those of other real networks. Generally, $n_D^{rand-ER} < n_D^{rand-Degree} \approx n_D^{real}$, because random networks are more easily controlled. However, the $n_D^{rand-Degree}$ of an electronic circuit network is smaller than $n_D^{rand-ER}$, and its $n_D^{rand-Degree}(opt)$ is also smaller than $n_D^{rand-ER}(opt)$. These results imply that the structure of an electronic circuit network is highly controllable. Meanwhile, compared with the other networks shown in Fig 9(c), the three electronic circuit networks possess a high number of critical edge directions, which can be regarded that the main skeleton of optimal controllability in these network is higher than other real networks. We also present the degree distributions of the electronic circuit networks in Table 2. Nodes of low degree (k_{in} or k_{out} = 1 or 2) account for a large proportion of the degree distribution. The number of driver nodes is determined be the density of low in- and out-degree [31]. Obviously, according to this conclusion, the electronic circuit networks should exhibit poor controllability. However, the true situation is precisely the opposite. The results indicate that the structures of the three electronic circuit networks is beneficial for structural controllability, and in the case of same average degree they require the fewer number of driver nodes.

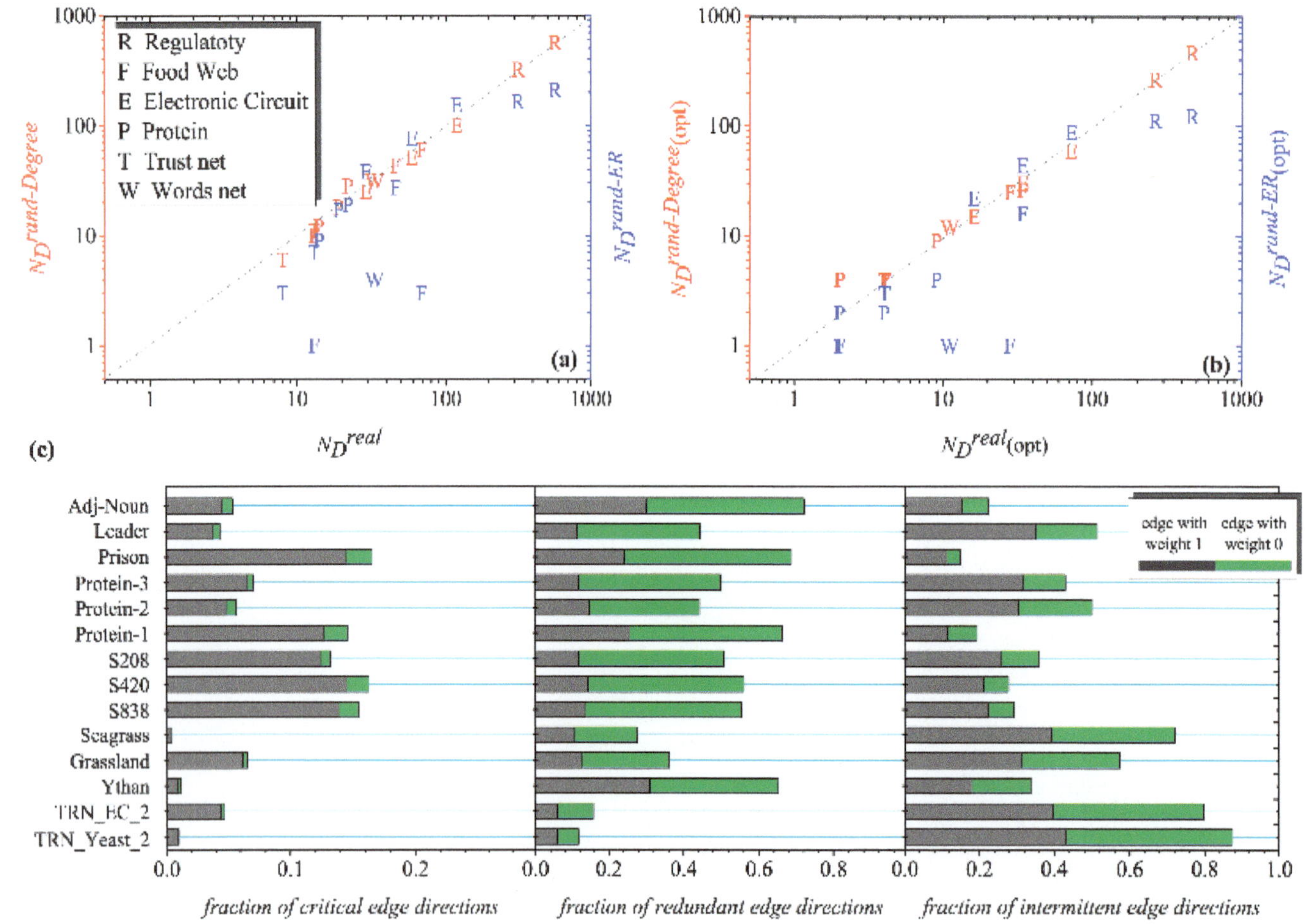

Figure 9. Plot of drive nodes of real, rand-Degree and rand-ER network (a) before (n_D^{real}, $n_D^{rand-Degree}$, $n_D^{rand-ER}$) and (b) after optimization by EOOC ($n_D^{real}(opt)$, $n_D^{rand-Degree}(opt)$, $n_D^{rand-ER}(opt)$), and (c) the faction of critical, redundant and intermittent edge direction of 14 real networks.

Table 1. The characteristics of the real networks analyzed in the paper.

Type	#	Name	N	L	n_D^{real}	$n_D^{real}(opt)$	$n_D^{rand-Degree}$	$n_D^{rand-Degree}(opt)$	$n_D^{rand-ER}$	$n_D^{rand-ER}(opt)$
Regulatory	1	TRN_YEST_2	688	1069	0.821	0.670	0.811	0.669	0.303	0.177
	2	TRN_EC_2	423	519	0.754	0.620	0.755	0.623	0.388	0.264
Food Web	3	Ythan	135	601	0.511	0.207	0.438	0.185	0.017	0.003
	4	Grassland	89	137	0.523	0.375	0.479	0.285	0.297	0.176
	5	Seagrass	49	226	0.265	0.041	0.201	0.009	0.016	0.001
Electronic Circuits	6	S838	512	819	0.232	0.139	0.195	0.114	0.298	0.173
	7	S420	252	399	0.234	0.135	0.199	0.116	0.304	0.174
	8	S208	122	189	0.238	0.131	0.203	0.120	0.306	0.180
Protein	9	Protein_1	95	213	0.190	0.032	0.181	0.032	0.171	0.075
	10	Protein_2	53	123	0.245	0.038	0.224	0.059	0.161	0.064
	11	Protein_3	99	212	0.222	0.091	0.275	0.000	0.190	0.090
Trust	12	Prison	67	182	0.194	0.060	0.156	0.053	0.103	0.038
	13	Leader	32	96	0.219	0.031	0.180	0.005	0.072	0.023
Words	14	Adj_Noun	112	425	0.295	0.098	0.274	0.105	0.034	0.009

doi:10.1371/journal.pone.0135282.t001

For each network, we show its type, name; number of nodes (N) and links (L); driver nodes of real network n_D^{real}; driver nodes of real network after optimization $n_D^{real}(opt)$; driver nodes of rand-Degree network $n_D^{rand-Degree}$; driver nodes of rand-Degree network after optimization $n_D^{rand-Degree}(opt)$; driver nodes of rand-ER network $n_D^{rand-ER}$; driver nodes of rand-ER network after optimization $n_D^{rand-ER}(opt)$ respectively. All the data used are publicly available in the network databases from Ref. [42].

Table 2. The degree distribution of Electronic Circuits networks.

Name	$\langle k \rangle$	in-degree		out-degree
		$P(k_{in} = 1)$	$P(k_{in} = 2)$	$P(k_{out} = 1)$
S838	3.199	0.371	0.473	0.768
S420	3.167	0.373	0.468	0.766
S208	3.098	0.377	0.459	0.762

doi:10.1371/journal.pone.0135282.t002

However, of the real networks considered in this paper, the Prison and Protein-1 networks also have high fractions of critical edge directions; why are these two networks unable to demonstrate such excellent controllability? This can be explained in terms of $P(k_{in} = 0)$. Nodes with $k_{in} = 0$ are called source nodes [41] because they must be controlled by input signals, that is, these nodes are driver nodes. In Table 3, it is seen that the $P_{rand-ER}(k_{in} = 0)$ values of S838, S420 and S208 are much larger than $P_{real}(k_{in} = 0)$, whereas the $P_{rand-ER}(k_{in} = 0)$ values of the Prison and Protein-1 networks are nearly equal to $P_{real}(k_{in} = 0)$. Here, $P_{rand-ER}(k_{in} = 0)$ is calculated using $P(k_{in}) = P(k_{out}) = e^{-z_0} z_0^k / k!$ with $z_0 = z/2 = \langle k_{out} \rangle = \langle k_{in} \rangle$. In the three real electronic circuit networks, the low $P_{real}(k_{in} = 0)$ values contribute to the fewer driver nodes. By contrast, in rand-ER networks with fixed average degree, the high $P_{rand-ER}(k_{in} = 0)$ values give rise to more driver nodes. Therefore, from the perspective of $P(k_{in} = 0)$ and critical edge directions, we can fully explain why the structures of electronic circuit networks are more advantageous with regard to controllability than those of any other real networks.

Table 3. The $P(k_{in} = 0)$ of five real networks.

	S838	S420	S208	Prison	Protein-1
$\langle k \rangle$	3.199	3.167	3.098	5.433	4.484
$P_{real}(k_{in} = 0)$	0.066	0.071	0.082	0.060	0.116
$P_{rand-ER}(k_{in} = 0)$	0.202	0.205	0.213	0.066	0.106

doi:10.1371/journal.pone.0135282.t003

DISCUSSION

In a directed network, the edge directions are the most significant properties that represent the ubiquitous dynamics of real networks. The edge directions and their correlations influence the driver nodes and are therefore especially relevant to the controllability of complex networks. Previous work has focused on developing edge orientation solutions to achieve the optimal controllability without changing the network structure, and this approach is more economical and practical than other optimization methods, such as adding or rewiring edges. However, it still lacks the ability to reveal the effects of different edge directions on optimal controllability, which could aid in understanding how the network structure affects controllability. For example, the structures of electronic circuit networks are advantageous for controllability despite the vast majority of nodes in these real networks having k_{in} and k_{out} values of 1 or 2. Based on the conclusion of previous work, controllability is determined by the density of low in- and out-degree nodes [31]. It is obvious that the electronic circuit networks should exhibit poor controllability. However, the true situation is precisely the opposite. Moreover, through degree-preserving randomization, the controllability of electronic circuit networks decreases noticeably. These behaviors can be explained by observing that these networks contain high concentrations of critical edge directions for optimal controllability. In summary, this work reveals the effects of the different classes of edge directions on optimal controllability and presents a simple edge orientation method based on the properties of the different direction sets. This simple method requires only local information but achieves a near-optimal optimization effect. All results demonstrate that the effects of edge directions can be recognized as a complement to previous measures in understanding network control.

REFERENCES

1. Barabási AL, Albert R (1999) Emergence of scaling in random networks. Science 286: 509–512. doi: 10.1126/science.286.5439.509. pmid:10521342
2. Newman M (2003) The structure and function of complex networks. SIAM Review 45: 167–256. doi: 10.1137/S003614450342480.
3. Boccaletti S, Latora V, Moreno Y, Chavez M, Hwang DU (2006) Complex networks: Structure and dynamics. Physics Reports 424: 175–308. doi: 10.1016/j.physrep.2005.10.009.
4. Moreno Y, Nekovee M, Pacheco AF (2004) Dynamics of rumor spreading in complex networks. Phys Rev E 69: 066130. doi: 10.1103/PhysRevE.69.066130.
5. Brockmann D, Helbing D (2013) The hidden geometry of complex, network-driven contagion phenomena. Science 342: 1337–1342. doi: 10.1126/science.1245200. pmid:24337289
6. Noh JD, Rieger H (2004) Random walks on complex networks. Phys Rev Lett 92: 118701. doi: 10.1103/PhysRevLett.92.118701. pmid:15089179
7. Rosvall M, Bergstrom CT (2008) Maps of random walks on complex networks reveal community structure. Proc Natl Acad Sci USA 105: 1118–1123. doi: 10.1073/pnas.0706851105. pmid:18216267
8. Motter AE (2004) Cascade control and defense in complex networks. Phys Rev Lett 93: 098701. doi: 10.1103/PhysRevLett.93.098701. pmid:15447153
9. Buldyrev S V, Parshani R, Paul G, Stanley HE, Havlin S (2010) Catastrophic cascade of failures in interdependent networks. Nature 464: 1025–1028. doi: 10.1038/nature08932. pmid:20393559
10. Donetti L, Hurtado PI, Munoz MA (2005) Entangled networks, synchronization, and optimal network topology. Phys Rev Lett 95: 188701. doi: 10.1103/PhysRevLett.95.188701. pmid:16383953
11. Arenas A, Díaz-Guilera A, Kurths J, Moreno Y, Zhou C (2008) Synchronization in complex networks. Physics Reports 469: 93–153. doi: 10.1016/j.physrep.2008.09.002.
12. Sorrentino F, Bernardo M, Garofalo F, Chen G (2007) Controllability of complex networks via pinning. Phys Rev E 75: 046103. doi: 10.1103/PhysRevE.75.046103.
13. Delpini D. et al (2013) Evolution of controllability in interbank networks. Scientific Reports 3: 1626. doi: 10.1038/srep01626. pmid:23568033
14. Wuchty S (2014) Controllability in protein interaction networks. Proc Natl Acad Sci USA 111: 7156–7160. doi: 10.1073/pnas.1311231111. pmid:24778220
15. Kalman RE (1963) Mathematical description of linear dynamical systems. Journal of the Society for Industrial & Applied Mathematics, Series A: Control 1: 152–192. doi: 10.1137/0301010.
16. Lin CT (1974) Structural controllability. IEEE Transactions on Automatic Control 19: 201–208. doi: 10.1109/TAC.1974.1100557.
17. Rugh WJ (1996) Linear System Theory (Prentice-Hall, Englewood Cliffs, NJ) 2nd ed.
18. Lombardi A, Hörnquist M (2007) Controllability analysis of networks. Physical Review E 75: 056110. doi: 10.1103/PhysRevE.75.056110.
19. Liu YY, Slotine JJ, Barabási AL (2011) Controllability of complex networks. Nature 473: 167–173. doi: 10.1038/nature10011. pmid:21562557
20. Liu YY, Slotine JJ, Barabási AL (2013) Observability of complex systems. Proc Natl Acad Sci USA 110: 2460–2465. doi: 10.1073/pnas.1215508110. pmid:23359701
21. Gao J, Liu YY, D'Souza RM, Barabási AL (2014) Target control of complex networks. Nature Communication 5: 5415. doi: 10.1038/ncomms6415.
22. Yuan ZZ, Zhao C, Di ZR, Wang WX, Lai YC (2013) Exact controllability of complex networks. Nature Communication 4: 2447. doi: 10.1038/ncomms3447.
23. Nepusz T, Vicsek T (2012) Controlling edge dynamics in complex networks. Nature Physics 8: 568–573. doi: 10.1038/nphys2327.
24. Liu YY, Slotine JJ, Barabási AL (2012) Control centrality and hierarchical structure in complex networks. PLoS ONE 7: e44459. doi: 10.1371/journal.pone.0044459. pmid:23028542
25. Wang WX, Ni X, Lai YC, Grebogi C (2012) Optimizing controllability of complex networks by minimum structural perturbations. Phys Rev E 85: 026115. doi: 10.1103/PhysRevE.85.026115.
26. Hou LL, Small M, Lao SY (2014) Maximum entropy networks are more controllable than preferential attachment networks. Phys Lett A 378: 3426–3430. doi: 10.1016/j.physleta.2014.09.057.
27. Pósfai M, Liu YY, Slotine JJ, Barabási AL (2013) Effect of correlations on network controllability. Scientific Reports 3: 1067. doi: 10.1038/srep01067. pmid:23323210
28. Hou LL, Lao SY, Small M, Xiao YD (2015) Enhancing complex network controllability by minimum link direction reversal. Physics Letters A 379: 1321–1325. doi: 10.1016/j.physleta.2015.03.018.
29. Jia T. et al (2013) Emergence of bimodality in controlling

complex networks. Nature Communication 4: 2002. doi: 10.1038/ncomms3002.

30. Jia T, Barabási AL (2013) Control capacity and a random sampling method in exploring controllability of complex networks. Scientific Reports 3: 2354. doi: 10.1038/srep02354. pmid:23912679

31. Menichetti G, Dall'Asta L, Bianconi G (2014) Network controllability is determined by the density of low in-degree and out-degree nodes. Phys Rev Lett 113: 078701. doi: 10.1103/PhysRevLett.113.078701. pmid:25170736

32. Hou LL, Lao SY, Bu J, Bai L (2013) Enhancing Complex Network Controllability by Rewiring Links. IEEE Inter. Conf. on Intelligent System Design and Engineering Applications 709–711. doi: 10.1109/isdea.2012.168

33. .Hou LL, Lao SY, Liu G, Bai L (2012) Controllability and Directionality in Complex Networks. Chin Phys Lett 29: 108901. doi: 10.1088/0256-307X/29/10/108901.

34. Xiao YD, Lao SY, Hou LL, Bai L (2014) Edge orientation for optimizing controllability of complex networks. Phys Rev E 90: 042804. doi: 10.1103/PhysRevE.90.042804.

35. Gazmuri PG. Independent sets in random sparse graphs. Networks 14: 367–377. doi: 10.1002/net.3230140302.

36. Balaji S, Swaminathan V, Kannan K (2010) A simple algorithm to optimize maximum independent set. Adv Model Optim 12: 107–118.

37. Robson J M (1986) Algorithms for maximum independent sets. J Algorithms 7: 425–440. doi: 10.1016/0196-6774(86)90032-5.

38. Erdős P, Rényi A (1960) On the evolution of random graphs. Publ Math Inst Hungar Acad Sci 5 17–61.

39. .Barabási AL, Albert R (1999) Emergence of scaling in random networks. Science 286: 509–512. doi: 10.1126/science.286.5439.509. pmid:10521342

40. Goh KI, Kahng B, Kim D (2001) Universal behavior of load distribution in scale-free networks. Phys Rev Lett 87: 278701. doi: 10.1103/PhysRevLett.87.278701. pmid:11800921

41. Ruths J, Ruths D (2014) Control profiles of complex networks. Science 343: 1373–1376. doi: 10.1126/science.1242063. pmid:24653036

INDEX

H

I

K

L

M

N

O

P

Q

R

S

T

U

V

W